Strengthening

Our

Families

STRENGTHENING OUR FAMILIES

AN IN-DEPTH LOOK AT THE PROCLAMATION ON THE FAMILY

EDITED BY
DAVID C. DOLLAHITE

SCHOOL OF FAMILY LIFE
BRIGHAM YOUNG UNIVERSITY

Library of Congress Cataloging-in-Publication Data

Strengthening our families : an in-depth look at the proclamation on the family . edited by David C. Dollahite.
    p.   cm.
  Includes bibliographical references and index.
  ISBN 1-57345-824-4 (HB)
  1. Family—Religious life.   I. Dollahite, David C. (David Curtis)
BV4526.2.S755   2000
248.4'89332—dc21

00-037933

Printed in the United States of America

72082-6719

10 9 8 7 6 5 4 3

CONTENTS

Acknowledgments

A great many people have put an enormous amount of effort into this book, and I am grateful to them and wish to acknowledge their many and important contributions:

Professor Alan Hawkins, Director of the Family Studies Center in the School of Family Life at BYU, who had the vision to initiate this project and the commitment to provide continual substantive support and encouragement for this project at all stages; Clayne Pope of the College of Family, Home, and Social Sciences and Jim Harper, Director of the School of Family Life at BYU for their financial support and for their helpful feedback on the manuscript.

The authors who labored diligently and faithfully to write the chapters and essays and consecrated their time and talents to this work. These friends and colleagues were always open to feedback from both editors and students and were a joy to work with.

The members of the Proclamation Book Editorial Board, who have worked together wonderfully in conceptualizing the book, working with the authors at various stages of writing, and assisting in editing the manuscripts:

Linda Hunter Adams, Ph.D. English, BYU

Howard M. Bahr, Ph.D., Department of Sociology, BYU

Mae Blanch, Ph.D., Professor of English (ret.), BYU

Alan J. Hawkins, Ph.D., Marriage, Family, and Human Development, BYU

Daniel K Judd, Ph.D., Department of Ancient Scripture, BYU

Elaine S. Marshall, R.N., Ph.D., School of Nursing, BYU

Kyle L. Pehrson, Ph.D., School of Social Work, BYU

Gawain M. Wells, Ph.D., Department of Psychology, BYU

Mark Butler, Dan Judd, Shirley Klein, Lloyd Newell, Richard Swan, and Laura Gilpin, members of the School of Family Life 100 Course Development Committee, who gave helpful feedback on chapters as we developed the Proclamation course at BYU.

Lisa Bolin Hawkins, J.D., for her wonderful work in final editing of the manuscript, Linda Hunter Adams for her great help in copyediting and managing the source-checking, and Kent Minson for yeoman's work formatting all the endnotes.

The members of the Bookcraft team who worked to bring the book to press including Sheri Dew, Emily Watts, Richard Peterson, Richard Erickson, Tonya Facemyer, and Jack Lyon. They were always professional and cordial, even when I didn't meet agreed-upon deadlines.

Cathy Weber and Jo Scofield, secretaries in the Family Studies Center, who assisted in many ways including managing the project budget. Cathy spent countless hours coordinating others' work on word processing and helping with innumerable details.

Victor Sorensen, Richard Wilson, Shelly Wilson, Susan M. Hawkins, T. Brent Hawkins, Robin Zenger Baker, Sam Ray, and other members of the Church, who read drafts in various stages and gave helpful feedback and encouragement.

Laura Gilpin, Richelle Hobbs, Ashlee Howes, and Heather White, who served as my editorial assistants and helped me stay on top of the innumerable details entailed in managing this large project and assisted with source-checking. Laura Gilpin—especially—spent countless hours working on various aspects of the project.

The many secretaries and receptionists who helped with word processing: Emma Hernandez, Mellani Howes, Emily Fuller, Nicole Norris, LaRita Johnson, Lani Owen, Vicky Utley, Ashlee Nemrow, Marianne Snyder, and Lori Olsen. Kenneth Lund for many trips back and forth between the Kimball Tower and the Humanities Publication Center.

The hundreds of BYU students who participated by reading the book at various stages and giving helpful feedback to authors and editors, including the students in the Winter 1999 Proclamation Seminar, who read chapter outlines (and some early drafts) of the chapters and gave invaluable guidance to the authors as they began their work: Jack Andrews, Joy Bethards, Matt Bethards, Bethany Clawson, Troy Faddis, Nancy Griffin, Richelle Hobbs, Heidi Knight, Gary Little, Elizabeth Merritt, Jennifer Parks, Heather Peterson, Heather Price, Melica Stevens, Micki Taylor, Michelle Vander Veur, Heather White, and Andrea Williams.

The following students in the Spring 1999 Proclamation Seminar read early drafts of the chapters and gave excellent written and oral feedback to authors in the revision process and also began the process of developing the application activities that are included at the end of the book: Karla Bergevin, Ruth Black, Hillary Blankenship, Elizabeth Brinton, Natalie Broekman, Rebecca Bulloch, Peggy Burt, Kori Christiansen, Melissa Clark, Amy Devocht, Kristen Dinsmore, Diana Fenn, Brita Fletcher, Rebecca Fletcher, Kimberly Gardner, James Gordon, Clinton Gudmunson, Sheree Harper, Carol Higbee, Bryce Jorgensen, Jill Judkins, Melinda Kehl, Alicia Ormsby, Janelle Peck, Kristina Potter, Damon Roberts, Melissa Ruggles, Cicely Salatino, Jennifer Schoenwald, Mary Seaquist, Katherine Shipley, Emily Smith, Josh Smith, and Sharlene Snyder.

The students in the Fall 1999 Proclamation Seminar who read the "final drafts" of chapters, gave the editors excellent feedback, wrote term papers about chapters, and also helped finalize the application activities: Aleisha Anderson, Julia Bedke, Allison Bird, Kerry Black, Michelle Bowman, Shauna Brown, Sabrina Burdette, Melissa Chalk, Susan Chamberlain, Laura Cote, Kristine Daly, Jedediah Darrington, Rachel Denning, Deneal Farr, Jennifer Flinders, Lindsey Green, Heather Harper, Robin Heath, Rachel Hickman, Dallas Jensen, Heather Jensen, Jenni Jergensen, Leslie Jones, Melissa Judson, Alicia Knighton, Jenneka Lindorf, Sarah Long, Elisabeth Malmgren, Charisse Mask, Cindy McArthur, Magaret McFarland, Kelli Medaris, Kerri Melchin, Marea Mowry, Erin O'Bryant, Nicole Perry, Carrie Petersen, Megan Royall, Lisa Sherwood, Julianna Smally, Shareen Smith, Amanda Sorenson, Melissa Stowers, Heather Tanner, Sarah Taylor, Kendyl Thomas, Heidi Vogeler, Paul Warner, Angela West, Robin West, Stacy Whitman, Kelli Williams, Martha Yorgason.

The students in Linda Adams's editing class at BYU who spent hundreds of hours in meticulous source-checking of the thousands of references cited in this book: These students, ably supervised by Melinda Hale, Rebeka Vranes, and Ashlee Howes, included Anna Maria Anderson, Adria Bennett, Rozalyn Bird, Johanna Buchert, Edith Amanda Campbell, Eric Ryan Carlson, Erick Carlson, Peter Carr, Dana Carver, Seth Christensen, Trent Christensen, Nathan Cox, Karen Jean Cromar, Chris Dennis, Amanda Dillon, Kristen Eldredge, Cristy Fathers, Amy Felix, Kristine Fielding, Gerald Galbraith, Alissa Galyean, Hilary Hendricks, Kimberly Hicken, Coral Hicks, Jennifer Hodge, Amber Lee Hoeger, Martha Ann Holloman, Peter Jasinski, Jennifer Kruse, Rachael Lauritzen, Leslie Marchant, Richard McClellan, Tara McKinney, Kimberley Meyer, Scarlett Miller, Melissa Moreton, Cynthia Munk, Jennifer Phipps, Sarah Pierce, Jennifer Ann Rieck, Daniel Smith, Katherine Smith, Erica Theobald, Melody Warnick, Quinn Warnick, Emily Wegener, Daniel Wells, and Matthew Willden.

All of these wonderful BYU students went the extra mile on behalf of their fellow students, for whom this book will serve as a textbook for a class on the Proclamation we have developed, and have helped us produce a more readable and relevant volume for the Church.

My deepest thanks to my eternal companion, Mary, for her continual support and encouragement during this challenging project. Mary typifies everything good about Latter-day Saint family life, and our children and I are forever blessed to be part of her family.

Finally, we who have worked on this project acknowledge that we have experienced the guiding, sustaining, and comforting influence of the Lord in various and marvelous ways in our work. We are all deeply grateful for those blessings, and we gladly acknowledge the good and merciful hand of God in all things.

We dedicate this book to all the families of the earth—especially to our friends in the rising generation—in the hope that they will establish and maintain joyful eternal marriages and rear their children in the nurture and admonition of the Lord.

David C. Dollahite, Provo, Utah

THE PROCLAMATION AS PROPHETIC GUIDANCE FOR STRENGTHENING THE FAMILY

DAVID C. DOLLAHITE, EDITOR

We, the First Presidency and the Council of the Twelve Apostles of
The Church of Jesus Christ of Latter-day Saints, solemnly proclaim that . . .
the family is central to the Creator's plan for the eternal destiny of His children.
(The Family: A Proclamation to the World, ¶ 1).

President Gordon B. Hinckley introduced and read *The Family: A Proclamation to the World*[1] on September 23, 1995, in the General Meeting of the Relief Society. It was only the fifth proclamation issued by the First Presidency and the Quorum of the Twelve Apostles of The Church of Jesus Christ of Latter-day Saints during its 170-year history.

In the Proclamation, Church leaders "solemnly proclaim that marriage between a man and a woman is ordained of God and that the family is central to the Creator's plan for the eternal destiny of His children" (¶ 1). The Proclamation sets forth fundamental gospel doctrine about marriage, family, gender, Heavenly Father's plan of happiness, the sacred responsibilities of spouses and parents, and principles of successful marriage and family life. The Proclamation also provides a solemn warning that those who violate the law of chastity or who neglect or abuse spouse or children will be accountable to God. It further warns that calamities will result from the rejection of eternal truths about family life and calls upon individuals and governments to "promote those measures designed to maintain and strengthen the family as the fundamental unit of society" (¶ 9). As Elder Merrill J. Bateman said about the Proclamation, "The statement is an extraordinary document outlining Church doctrine concerning the family and the relationships between husband and wife, parents and children."[2]

President Hinckley explained why such emphasis on the importance of the family was needed:

> Why do we have this proclamation on the family now? Because the family is under attack. All across the world families are falling apart. The place to begin to improve society is in the home. Children do, for the most part, what they are taught. We are trying to make the world better by making the family stronger.[3]

Indeed, many forces negatively influence contemporary marriage and family relationships and threaten the institutions of marriage and family in society. At a time when radical individualism, hedonism, materialism, and secularism are increasing throughout the world, the Lord's living prophets have proclaimed that marriage and family relationships transcend all earthly ties and that family happiness transcends all earthly joys. Thus, like all inspiration, the Proclamation contains eternal truth and timeless wisdom suited to the circumstances and needs of the people to whom it is given.

THE PURPOSE OF THIS VOLUME

The purpose of this volume is to teach and support the principles of happy and successful family life as revealed in *The Family: A Proclamation to the World*. The book was written to assist Latter-day Saints both to prepare for and strengthen their own marriages and families and to help Church members more confidently articulate and defend Proclamation doctrines and principles using both sacred and scholarly sources.

In keeping with the Prophet Joseph Smith's well-known statement about teaching the Saints "correct principles," this book (a) more fully articulates the principles found in the Proclamation using the words of ancient and modern prophets, (b) provides a reasoned critique of those philosophies in opposition to Proclamation principles, and (c) suggests various ways to successfully apply these principles in order to strengthen both marriages and families and the institutions of marriage and family in society. In addition, the volume presents abundant scholarship that supports these principles. The volume is extensively documented from both sacred and scholarly sources. The nearly 2,000 sources cited include almost 800 scriptures, 450 quotes from the prophets and apostles, and over 700 citations from secular scholarship. Thus, 64% of the citations are from sacred sources and 36% are from scholarly.

THE PROCLAMATION AS A SIGN OF INCREASING PROPHETIC EMPHASIS ON FAMILY

The Proclamation on the family is a clear manifestation of an increasing emphasis by Church leaders on family in recent decades. Of course, from the time the Prophet Joseph Smith received revelations regarding the eternal nature of marriage and family in God's plan, The Church of Jesus Christ of Latter-day Saints has expended vast resources to emphasize the importance of marriage and family relationships, to assist couples and families in strengthening their commitments and relationships, and to provide temples so that couples and families may receive those "sacred ordinances and covenants" that make it possible for "families to be united eternally" (Proclamation, ¶ 3).

This emphasis has increased even more in the latter part of the twentieth century. In addition to the issuance of the Proclamation, in recent decades this emphasis on family is manifest in: (a) the recent increase in the number of talks in general conference devoted to family, and training concerning family principles given in various meetings of the Church, (b) the various changes in Church policies and curricula designed to support families (e.g., the consolidated Sunday schedule and new manuals for priesthood and Relief Society), (c) the acceleration of

temple building, (d) the change of name from "LDS Social Services" to "LDS Family Services" and the attendant change of emphasis toward strengthening the family, (e) the change of name and emphasis from "genealogy" to "family history," and (f) the recent First Presidency letters emphasizing the family.[4] It seems fair to conclude that in recent years the Lord's prophets have emphasized the eternal importance of marriage and family and taken steps to strengthen the Saints in their family responsibilities more than at any other time in sacred history.

In an address focusing on *The Family: A Proclamation to the World,* Elder Henry B. Eyring stated:

> Three things about the title are worth our careful reflection. First the subject: the family. Second, the audience, which is the whole world. And third, those proclaiming it are those we sustain as prophets, seers, and revelators. All this means that the family must be of tremendous importance to us, that whatever the proclamation says could help anyone in the world, and that the proclamation fits the Lord's promise when he said, "Whether by mine own voice or by the voice of my servants, it is the same." (D&C 1:38)[5]

Indicative of the importance of the Proclamation to the Church, since 1995, the Proclamation has been used extensively both within the Church and as an important missionary tool. Within the Church, the Proclamation has been the subject of or impetus for training given by General Authorities to Church leaders, as well as in training given by stake and ward leaders. Attractive copies of the Proclamation were distributed to all Church members. It is now prominently displayed in Church buildings and in the homes of many members. As a missionary tool, the Proclamation has been translated into dozens of languages and has been presented to numerous world leaders, used to articulate the Church's doctrine on family on the Church's Internet site (www.ldschurch.org), and given to countless individuals to explain the doctrine of the Church on family.

In the years President Hinckley has presided over the Church, he has emphasized several important issues, including such things as taking the Church out of obscurity through the media, encouraging the Saints to maintain an optimistic outlook for the future of the Church, and strengthening new converts. However, in my view, two things stand out in his ministry and administration: the Proclamation and unprecedented worldwide temple building.

Since the Proclamation is to "the world," and

since temples are being built throughout the earth to provide the ordinances and covenants that bless and bind couples and families eternally, President Hinckley is leading the Church and its members in fulfilling two Old Testament prophecies. In the first prophecy, the Lord promises Abraham that ". . . in thee and in thy seed shall all the families of the earth be blessed" (Gen. 28:14). The second prophecy promises, "Behold, I will send you Elijah the Prophet . . . and he will turn the heart of the fathers to the children and the heart of the children to their fathers . . ." (Mal. 3:4–5). The Church's temples and teachings, priesthood and programs, ordinances and covenants are all centered on blessing and exalting all the families that have ever lived on the earth by turning the hearts of family members to God and to one another and turning the hearts of living family members to their deceased kin.

Origins of This Volume on the Proclamation

In 1997, the Family Studies Center in the School of Family Life at BYU initiated a project to create a one-volume book on strengthening marriage and family, based on the Proclamation and written by Latter-day Saint family scholars and other authors. School of Family Life director James Harper and Family Studies Center director Alan Hawkins appointed me as editor and we selected a distinguished interdisciplinary editorial board. Together, we decided the book should benefit Latter-day Saint students and general readers.

Thus, this book is intended to be helpful to two groups of people: first, students at Brigham Young University as well as students at other Church colleges and universities. This volume attempts to respond faithfully to a call made by President Boyd K. Packer in his address at the creation of the School of Family Life at BYU. President Packer called for BYU faculty to produce textbooks on family that would be worthy of a great university, that would be filled with moral and spiritual truths in full harmony with the restored gospel, and that would help students be good spouses and parents.

In an effort to produce this kind of volume for students, the editorial board provided extensive peer review of manuscripts at every stage of development. We also sought and received significant feedback from more than one hundred students at BYU in three successive "Proclamation Seminars." Students read

---

MISSION OF THE SCHOOL OF FAMILY LIFE BRIGHAM YOUNG UNIVERSITY

In response to the increasing need to strengthen families, the Brigham Young University Board of Trustees created a new School of Family Life. At the inauguration of the School on September 10, 1998, Elder Boyd K. Packer, Acting President of the Quorum of the Twelve Apostles of The Church of Jesus Christ of Latter-day Saints, stated that the charter for the school was to be *The Family: A Proclamation to the World* and the principles it contains. In announcing the school, President Packer gave the charge to make the Proclamation central to all of the school's activities. He declared, "I know of no greater service that this, the Lord's university, can give to His church than through this School of Family Life to turn the hearts of young fathers and young mothers to their children."

The School is fulfilling President Packer's charge with the Proclamation to guide teaching, discover new knowledge, and reach out to the public and decision-makers who affect policy. Specifically, it is doing so by:

Educating the minds and spirits of university students about successful principles of marriage, parenting, optimal human development and home life in an environment that is spiritually strengthening and then extending these educational blessings by using new technologies to learners across the globe.

Discovering and advancing truth and knowledge about successful marriage and family life and optimal human development to strengthen families and thereby to help resolve societal and world problems.

Becoming a repository of this knowledge so it can be shared with the public; and by extending the blessings of this knowledge to members of the Church and others in all parts of the world to increase their happiness and improve their quality of living.

Box 1.1

---

chapter outlines and first and second drafts and provided extensive feedback to authors and the editorial board. Students were thrilled to assist us in our effort to create a faithful, scholarly sound, and helpful book.

Our second target audience is the general Latter-day Saint reader interested in greater depth and detail in understanding, appreciating, and applying the Proclamation. Some who read the Proclamation may wonder how a volume of hundreds of pages could be generated in response to that 607–word, straightforward statement of doctrine and principle. The Proclamation, like other inspired documents such as the Articles of Faith or the U.S. Constitution, packs a great amount of truth with a large number of implications into a few inspired words. While this volume is by no means exhaustive in its treatment of either the Proclamation or marriage and family relations, it does provide much information on many issues mentioned in or implied by the Proclamation. We hope the volume will be a valuable resource for and will strengthen testimonies of Latter-day Saints. Much of the feedback provided by students was helpful here, but we also received input from numerous Latter-day Saints who are not affiliated with BYU.

THE AUTHORS

Brigham Young University has the largest community of family scholars of any university in the world. Many of the authors of this volume are leading experts in their fields of scholarship. The book is authored by 53 men and 48 women from more than 30 academic disciplines and a wide variety of professional and personal backgrounds who are all committed to the gospel of Jesus Christ and to strengthening families.

All authors have been associated with BYU in one way or another—most as faculty, many as students. Eighty of the authors are current or retired BYU professors or instructors and several others are former BYU graduate students who are now professors or graduate students at other universities. There are also homemakers, attorneys, physicians, and other professionals. Collectively, the authors have spent thousands of years involved in professional activities related to strengthening families, such as research, writing, educating, counseling, and consulting. Indeed, I am not aware of any volume available that brings so many people together who are so professionally qualified and personally committed to strengthening family life.

Almost all the authors are married and have children and collectively have thousands of years of experience in family relationships. Some have personal experience with being unable to marry, or the loss of a spouse through death or divorce, or other serious challenges. For more information about each author, please see the list of contributors at the end of the volume.

Not only are these authors professionally and personally prepared to strengthen families, but they have been willing to submit their work to rigorous peer and student review. I know of no other volume

written by leading scholars that has had such extensive involvement by students. Because of the unique nature of this volume, the writing and editorial process has been most challenging. However, authors have enthusiastically supported student input and have responded wonderfully to student suggestions and concerns.

This project has also been a labor of love and consecration by these authors. No one involved in writing or editing this book will receive any income from it. All royalties will be donated to a Proclamation Scholarship Fund to be administered by the School of Family Life at BYU.

WHAT THE BOOK CONTAINS

There are many kinds of books about marriage and family life, including advice-giving, secular scholarship, and religious treatises. This book draws from both sacred and scholarly sources and attempts to provide both principle-based and practical information on marriage and family life. While the emphasis of this book is on sound principles for strengthening marriage and family life, it also contains hundreds of great practical ideas that can strengthen marriage and family life. One of the features of this volume is the diversity of information and the various ways it is presented. It was decided that a variety of information would best meet the diverse needs, situations, and learning styles of contemporary Latter-day Saint students and Church members. However, probably the most unique and important contribution of this volume is the presentation of an abundance of scholarly support for Proclamation principles.

The Proclamation can serve Latter-day Saint families as a modern-day Liahona (I Ne. 17:2–3) to guide them in the challenges of contemporary family life.[6] The Proclamation sets out a divinely inspired pattern for ideal marriage and family living. Any person, couple, or family who prayerfully seeks to strengthen their understanding and testimony of the principles in the Proclamation and who moves forward with faith in applying those principles will be blessed and strengthened as family members. Since the volume is filled with sound scholarship supporting the Proclamation, a person who makes a careful study of this book will also be able to articulate and defend fundamental principles of strong families with confidence in a variety of settings.

A reasonable question may be asked, "Why include scholarship in addition to scripture and prophetic teachings since this mixes human wisdom with eternal truth?" We as authors and editors were concerned about this issue. Thus, we worked hard in our attempt to create a volume that would consist of the teachings of God's prophets—supported and supplemented by reason and sound scholarship.[7] We were encouraged by the fact that from the beginning, leaders of The Church of Jesus Christ of Latter-day Saints have had expansive views of truth and the duty of the Saints in regard to it. The Church has always been open to correct principles and praiseworthy ideas from sources beyond the Church. President Brigham Young spoke extensively on these matters:

> "Mormonism," so called, embraces every principle pertaining to life and salvation, for time and eternity. No matter who has it. . . . All that is good, lovely, and praiseworthy belongs to this Church and Kingdom. "Mormonism" includes all truth. There is no truth but what belongs to the Gospel. . . .
>
> It is the business of the Elders of the Church . . . to gather up all the truths in the world pertaining to life and salvation, to the Gospel we preach, . . . to the sciences, and to philosophy, wherever it may be found in every nation, kindred, tongue, and people and bring it to Zion.[8]

Indeed, Brigham Young University, at least in part, exists to facilitate this process. Thus, one of the purposes of this book is to "gather to Zion" some of the best ideas or correct principles that have emerged from the best scholarship. Many important things about marriage and family life have been learned by scholars—including Latter-day Saint scholars—who study couples and families. An understanding of these ideas, in concert with Proclamation principles, can be of great value in strengthening marriage and families in a contemporary culture that often undervalues marriage and family.

In this volume, Latter-day Saint scholars have labored to bring forth from dozens of disciplines good ideas that are consistent with gospel perspectives. They also have used the skills they have developed to critique carefully those ideas that are not consistent with a gospel perspective. This is not to suggest that every idea expressed herein is the doctrine of the Church. Rather, we believe that the ideas herein are in harmony with gospel doctrine as we understand it.

SUMMARY OF THE VOLUME

The volume has 27 chapters and 20 essays with numerous application-oriented boxes and tables throughout.

Section I includes this introductory essay and a chapter that briefly articulates the centrality of marriage and family in Latter-day Saint doctrine on our Heavenly Father's plan of happiness.

Section II discusses marriage as the foundation of family life and includes a summary of the research demonstrating the benefits of marriage, a thorough treatment of the teachings of prophets and the best scholarship on preparing for marriage, and a chapter and essay on chastity, fidelity, and personal purity as fundamental to marriage and family life.

Section III provides extensive information about the sacred responsibilities of parents and extended family members. Included here are careful discussions of the principles of equal partnership and the sacred responsibilities of mothers and fathers as well as the ways in which home is a sacred center of family life. Emphasis is also given here to scriptural and prophetic counsel on parenting and grandparenting along with a review of the significant empirical support for that counsel.

Section IV addresses principles for successful marriages and families mentioned in the seventh paragraph of the Proclamation, including faith, prayer, repentance, forgiveness, respect, love, compassion, work, and wholesome recreational activities. In the spirit of focusing on principles and encouraging the Saints to "govern themselves," these chapters do not provide a great many practical suggestions. Of course, there is really nothing quite so practical as a true principle.

Section V focuses on the sanctity of each human life and the divine nature and eternal worth of each person. The section also discusses the family relationships of single adults, including never-married and divorced or widowed individuals and single parents. Every marriage and family is made up of individuals who are each "a beloved spirit son or daughter of heavenly parents" (Proclamation, ¶ 2).

Section VI is inspired by the statements in the Proclamation that "Disability, death, or other circumstances may necessitate individual adaptation" (¶ 7) and the warnings about spouse and child abuse (¶ 8). It addresses how to reconcile the divine ideals of family life found in the Proclamation with the adversity of children who choose other paths or make serious mistakes. Chapters also focus on awareness of abuse, abuse prevention and healing, as well as how to meet the challenge of a variety of serious adversities in family life.

Section VII responds to the Proclamation statement calling for the promotion of "those measures designed to maintain and strengthen the family as the fundamental unit of society" (¶ 9) and includes chapters on government resources and policies and defending the family through national and international law and policy. Additional chapters focus on practical activities that strengthen marriages and families, and how to preserve and pass along meaningful family traditions across the generations.

Section VIII compares and contrasts Proclamation principles with ideas on marriage and family, based on several philosophies that are prominent and influential in the contemporary world and compares Proclamation principles with the beliefs of many world faiths about the importance of marriage and family and highlights the different ways world faiths try to strengthen marriage and family.

Though there are hundreds of activities and applied suggestions throughout the book, a section of additional helps is provided at the end of this volume. Over seventy activities are provided, which will assist individuals, couples, and families apply the principles found in the Proclamation.

CONCLUSION

It has been a tremendous personal and professional privilege to work with so many faithful and dedicated scholars and students in the creation of this book. We have labored diligently for three years to bring forth a volume that would be a blessing to its readers. In so doing, we have been richly blessed ourselves. I have heard many stories from authors about the personal and spiritual insights they have received. As we have had the privilege to study, ponder, pray,

and write about the inspired principles contained in the Proclamation, we realize that we have only begun to plumb its depths. We encourage Latter-day Saints and our friends of other faiths to make a careful and prayerful study of these doctrines and principles and to seek the aid of heaven in applying these true principles in your homes and communities. You will thereby be doing your part to turn the hearts of family members to one another and bless the families of the earth.

NOTES

1. The Family: A Proclamation to the World (1995, November) *Ensign, 25,* 102.

2. Merrill J. Bateman (1998), The eternal family, *Brigham Young Magazine, 52(4),* 26.

3. Sheri L. Dew (1997), *Teachings of Gordon B. Hinckley,* (Salt Lake City: Deseret Book), 209

4. The February 11, 1999 letter called on parents and Church leaders to give the "highest priority" to family. The October 4, 1999 letter reiterated the high priority of family and stressed the importance of family home evening in families and the Church.

5. Henry B. Eyring (1998, February). The family, *Ensign, 26* (2), 10–17.

6. A. J. Hawkins (1998), Some of BYU's Responses to *The Family: A Proclamation to the World, Brigham Young University 1997–1998 Speeches* (Provo, UT: Brigham Young University Publications & Graphics).

7. This book was written mainly with the Latter-day Saint reader in mind. Therefore, some familiarity with the teachings and practices of The Church of Jesus Christ of Latter-day Saints is assumed. Thus, there are places where someone not acquainted with Latter-day Saint doctrine and life may not fully understand the issues. The best source of detailed, accurate information on The Church of Jesus Christ of Latter-day Saints is the four-volume *Encyclopedia of Mormonism,* which is available at most major libraries. In addition, basic Church doctrine is available on the Internet site of The Church of Jesus Christ of Latter-day Saints (ldschurch.org). The Proclamation contains nine paragraphs. Throughout this volume, the symbol for paragraph (¶) is used to refer to cited passages.

8. *Teachings of the Presidents of the Church: Brigham Young* (1997). Salt Lake City: The Church of Jesus Christ of Latter-day Saints, 16–17.

CHAPTER 1

FAMILIES AND THE GREAT PLAN OF HAPPINESS

DANIEL K JUDD, GUY L. DORIUS, AND DAVID C. DOLLAHITE

We, the First Presidency and the Council of the Twelve Apostles of The Church of Jesus
Christ of Latter-day Saints, solemnly proclaim that marriage between a man and
a woman is ordained of God and that the family is central to the
Creator's plan for the eternal destiny of His children.
(The Family: A Proclamation to the World, ¶ 1)

INTRODUCTION

The Proclamation teaches that marriage and family relationships are fundamental to the Lord's plan for our eternal destiny.[1] Even though we are personally responsible to work out our own salvation, eternal life—life in the presence of God—is impossible without an eternal companion at our side. The Apostle Paul taught that "neither is the man without the woman, neither the woman without the man, in the Lord" (1 Cor. 11:11). President Joseph F. Smith stated:

> God instituted marriage in the beginning. He made man in his own image and likeness, male and female, and in their creation it was designed that they should be united together in sacred bonds of marriage, and one is not perfect without the other.[2]

Prophets have taught that if we are able to fully accept the Lord's plan, especially the "merits, and mercy, and grace of the Holy Messiah" (2 Ne. 2:8), we will one day be blessed to have eternal associations with other family members. The prophet Mormon recorded:

> And the day soon cometh that your mortal must put on immortality . . . and then ye must stand before the judgment-seat of Christ, to be judged according to your works; and if it so be that ye are righteous, *then are ye blessed with your fathers who have gone before you.* (Morm. 6:21, emphasis added)

The eternal nature of the marriage covenant and the promise of everlasting family association are among the most beautiful and essential doctrines of the restored gospel. In fact, the purpose of the gospel and the Church is to exalt the family. Elder Hugh B. Brown stated:

> The family concept is one of the major and most important of the whole theological doctrine. In fact, our very concept of heaven itself is the projection of the home into eternity. Salvation, then, is essentially a family affair, and full participation in the plan of salvation can be had only in family units.[3]

The purpose of this chapter is to help the reader to comprehend the doctrinal foundation of the Proclamation on the Family. Also, we intend this overview of the "plan of salvation" (Jarom 1:2) to provide a framework for the chapters that follow (see Alma 12:32). We begin by discussing the premortal origin of the plan of salvation and then follow with applications of marriage and family relationships to the doctrines of the Creation, the fall of man, and the Atonement of Jesus Christ.

THE PLAN OF REDEMPTION

Prior to mortal birth we lived as spirit sons and daughters of heavenly parents (Proclamation, ¶ 2; see also Jer. 1:5; Eccl. 12:7; John 1:1–8; and Alma 13:3). During this premortal period a great council was held where Father in Heaven presented "the great plan of the Eternal God" (Alma 34:9) to all of His children (see Abr. 3:21–28 and Moses 4:1–4).[4] While the plan presented by our Heavenly Father included many glorious doctrines, at the center was the Atonement of Jesus Christ. In this council we learned that "the plan of redemption" (Alma 12:25) required a savior to take upon himself "the sins of the world" (1 Ne. 10:10), thus allowing the obedient and repentant to return and dwell in the presence of God. Satan made a selfish and vain attempt to usurp the role of savior, but it was Jesus Christ, the "Firstborn" (see Col. 1:15; D&C 93:21) of the Father's spirit children, who was chosen.

At some point, all of God's children who supported Heavenly Father's plan will have the opportunity and responsibility to live in and create families. Understanding our missions as sons and daughters, sisters and brothers, husbands and wives, and mothers and fathers is fundamental to fulfilling our divine destinies. President Joseph F. Smith reminded us: "to do well those things which God ordained to be the common lot of all man-kind, is the truest greatness. To be a successful father or a successful mother is greater than to be a successful general or a successful statesman. One is universal and eternal greatness, the other is ephemeral."[5]

CREATION, FALL, AND ATONEMENT

"The great plan of happiness" (Alma 42:8) presented by our Heavenly Father in the premortal council is designed "to bring to pass the immortality and eternal life of man" (Moses 1:39) and is founded upon three basic doctrines—the Creation of the earth; the Fall of Adam, Eve, and all humankind; and the Atonement of Jesus Christ. Elder Bruce R. McConkie described these doctrines as the "three pillars of eternity."[6]

The Creation, Fall, and Atonement are historic events. They have direct application to our physical creation, separation from God, mortal experience, death, and resurrection. They have a metaphoric or interpretive application to many of the significant events in our lives, characterized by periods of creation followed by the fall or opposition and eventual achievement of reconciliation. They apply directly to our personal and family lives.[7]

The Creation

The scriptures teach that all human beings are created in the image of God. As stated in the Proclamation, "each is a beloved spirit son or daughter of heavenly parents, and as such, each has a divine nature and destiny" (¶ 2). From this brief statement we learn several profound truths:

- We were created by God.
- We were created in the image of God.
- We have heavenly parents—a Father and a Mother.
- We are literally the spirit offspring of God.
- Our nature or essential identity is of divine origin.
- Our spirit creation includes identity as male or female.
- We have a divine destiny.

While there is much we do not know about the specifics of the Creation, latter-day prophets have taught that we have both divine origin and divine potential. The First Presidency issued a statement in 1909:

> Man is the child of God, formed in the divine image and endowed with divine attributes, and even as the infant son of an earthly father and mother is capable in due time of becoming a man, so the undeveloped offspring of celestial parentage is capable, by experience through ages and aeons, of evolving into a God.[8]

Understanding that we are literally children of heavenly parents in whose image we are created is necessary if we are to know our true identity and potential. The Prophet Joseph Smith said, "If men do not comprehend the character of God, they do not comprehend themselves."[9]

Marriage, Families, and the Fall

The doctrine of the Fall provides an additional key to understanding our earthly existence. The Proclamation teaches we came to earth to "obtain a physical body and gain earthly experience to progress toward perfection" (¶ 3). Birth into a family was the way God chose to send His spirit children to earth. Marriage and family relationships are the central means He has prepared to achieve His purposes. We learn the lessons of life, not in an Edenic garden, but in a context where we face challenge, opposition, hardship, and temptation (see 2 Ne. 2:11). Unlike traditional Christianity, Latter-day Saints believe the Fall was a necessary part of the Lord's plan for us: "Adam fell that men might be; and men are, that they might have joy" (2 Ne. 2:25).

After creating the earth and all things upon it, God created Adam and Eve. He taught them the sanctity of marriage and the importance of families. They were instructed, "Therefore shall a man leave his father and his mother, and shall cleave unto his wife: and they shall be one flesh" (Gen. 2:24). In our time, many people deny the sanctity of marriage, treating it merely as a contract between two parties, but the Latter-day Saints have been taught its true significance. The Lord told the Prophet Joseph Smith, "Wherefore, it is lawful that he [man] should have one wife, and they twain shall be one flesh, and all this that the earth might answer the end of its creation; And that it might be filled with the measure of man, according to his creation before the world was made" (D&C 49:16–17). He was also instructed that "whoso forbiddeth to marry is not ordained of God, for marriage is ordained of God unto man" (D&C 49:15).

The eternal nature of marriage and the possibility of continued family relationships beyond the grave are essential features of the restored gospel. Priesthood ordinances and covenants make this continuity possible. The prophet Elias appeared to Joseph Smith and Sidney Rigdon, restoring the doctrine of celestial marriage, and the prophet Elijah restored the necessary keys to make these marriages and all other ordinances binding for eternity. Elder Bruce R. McConkie explained the significance of these events:

> Elias appeared, and "committed the dispensation of the gospel of Abraham," meaning the great commission given to Abraham that he and his seed had a right to the priesthood, the gospel, and eternal life. Accordingly, Elias promised those upon whom these ancient promises were then renewed that in them and in their seed all generations should be blessed. (D&C 110:12–16.) Thus, through the joint ministry of Elijah, who brought the sealing power, and Elias, who restored the marriage discipline of Abraham, the way was prepared for the planting in the hearts of the children of the promises made to the fathers. (D&C 2:2.) These are the promises of eternal life through the priesthood and the gospel and celestial marriage.[10]

Through those keys and authority, Joseph Smith was able to officiate in all ordinances necessary for the salvation and exaltation of men and women. President Ezra Taft Benson taught:

Elijah brought the keys of sealing powers—that power which *seals* a man to a woman and *seals* their posterity to them endlessly, that which *seals* their forefathers to them all the way back to Adam. This is the power and order that Elijah revealed—that *same order* of priesthood which God gave to Adam and to all the ancient patriarchs which followed after him.[11]

Therefore the Proclamation states: "The divine plan of happiness enables family relationships to be perpetuated beyond the grave. Sacred ordinances and covenants available in holy temples make it possible for individuals to return to the presence of God and for families to be united eternally" (¶ 3).

Ordinances and covenants have important ramifications for the present and eternal nature of the family. As we enter into the new and everlasting covenant of marriage, the Lord explains our relationship with Him: "This is eternal lives—to know the only wise and true God, and Jesus Christ, whom he hath sent. I am he. Receive ye, therefore, my law" (D&C 132:24).

Not only does the covenant of marriage bring with it the promises of eternity, it allows us to know God and better emulate His example in this life. The fact that the Lord provides this opportunity within the context of family is of vital importance. It seems that our relationship with God has always been in a family context, and so it is in mortality. Within the family comes the fulness of the gospel and its covenants.

Once a family unit is started by the marriage of a man and woman, the plan continues to unfold by the addition of children to this family. The Proclamation states:

> The first commandment that God gave to Adam and Eve pertained to their potential for parenthood as husband and wife. We declare that God's commandment for His children to multiply and replenish the earth remains in force. We further declare that God has commanded that the sacred powers of procreation are to be employed only between man and woman, lawfully wedded as husband and wife. We declare the means by which mortal life is created to be divinely appointed. We affirm the sanctity of life and of its importance in God's eternal plan. (¶ 4)

Adam and Eve in the Garden of Eden were unable to fulfill this commandment to multiply and replenish the earth. The Fall was necessary for the creation of families. Lehi taught:

> And now, behold, if Adam had not transgressed he would not have fallen, but he would have remained in

the garden of Eden. And all things which were created must have remained in the same state in which they were after they were created; and they must have remained forever, and had no end.

And they would have had no children; wherefore they would have remained in a state of innocence, having no joy, for they knew no misery; doing no good, for they knew no sin. (2 Ne. 2:22–23)

By partaking of the fruit of the tree of knowledge of good and evil and thereby becoming mortal, Adam and Eve were able to obey the first commandment given to them as husband and wife: they could become parents.

By obtaining the ability to bring children into the world and receiving the ordinances necessary to be sealed as families through eternity, Adam and Eve and all parents to follow became responsible to "rear their children in love and righteousness, to provide for their physical and spiritual needs, to teach them to love and serve one another, and to observe the commandments of God" (Proclamation, ¶ 6). Thus, parents have the important responsibility to rear their children in the light of the gospel. The Lord has said: "And again, inasmuch as parents have children in Zion, or in any of her stakes which are organized, that teach them not to understand the doctrine of repentance, faith in Christ the Son of the living God, and of baptism and the gift of the Holy Ghost by the laying on of the hands, when eight years old, the sin be upon the heads of the parents" (D&C 68:25–27).

President Ezra Taft Benson observed that the "overarching message" of righteous Book of Mormon fathers was "the great plan of the Eternal God—the Fall, rebirth, Atonement, Resurrection, Judgment (and) eternal life."[12] The "great plan" is a family plan which not only provides children with the covenants and ordinances necessary for exaltation, but it creates a nurturing environment where children learn the important ways of life.

The Atonement of Christ and Eternal Families

The doctrines of the Creation and the Fall are essential if we are to understand who we are and how life is to be lived, but they are not enough. The Proclamation teaches us that "happiness in family life is most likely to be achieved when founded upon the teachings of the Lord Jesus Christ" (¶ 7). In other words, "it is upon the rock of our Redeemer, who is Christ, the Son of God, that ye must build your foundation" (Hel. 5:12). At the heart of the Savior's teachings is the doctrine of His atoning sacrifice. The Prophet Joseph Smith taught "all other things which pertain to our religion are only appendages to it."[13] The Atonement of Jesus Christ makes possible "eternal lives" (D&C 132:24), or life with our families in the presence of God. God's work and glory is to unite couples and families together, and only through the Atonement of Christ is this possible.

According to the Proclamation, "family is central to the Creator's plan for the eternal destiny of His children" (¶ 1). Thus, not only are family relationships of utmost importance and a source of joy and growth in this life, but as it is stated in the Proclamation: "The divine plan of happiness enables family relationships to be perpetuated beyond the grave. . . . Sacred ordinances and covenants available in holy temples make it possible for individuals to return to the presence of God and for families to be united eternally" (¶ 3).

Jesus Christ took upon Himself the sins of the world and it is only through faith in Him and obedience to the laws and ordinances of His gospel that salvation and exaltation are possible (Alma 34:8). Because of the redeeming sacrifice of the Son of God, eternal families are possible. Without the Atonement, no one could live in God's presence or inherit all He has, or be sealed for eternity. The Atonement allows God's children to be reconciled to Him (Eph. 2:16); to be cleansed from all sin (D&C 76:52); to be sealed by the Holy Spirit of promise (D&C 76:53); to become gods (D&C 76:58) and receive all that God has (D&C 76:59); to be made perfect (D&C 76:69); and to dwell forever in the presence of God and Christ in the celestial kingdom as husbands and wives in eternal families.

Eternal Life Is Familial

Elder Henry B. Eyring stated that "Eternal life means to become like the Father and to live in families in happiness and joy forever."[14]

Elder Bruce R. McConkie said:

From the moment of birth into mortality to the time we are married in the temple, everything we have in the whole gospel system is to prepare and qualify us to enter that holy order of matrimony which makes us husband and wife in this life and in the world to come. . . . There is nothing in this world as important as the creation and perfection of family units.[15]

In fact, the ecclesiastical structure of the Lord's Church is designed to bring the benefits of the eternal sealing powers of the temple to marriage and family relationships, so those relationships can endure throughout eternity. Elder M. Russell Ballard said, "The family is where the foundation of personal, spiritual growth is built and nurtured; the Church, then is the scaffolding that helps support and strengthen the family."[16]

The doctrine that eternal life is familial is one of the unique teachings of the restored gospel. These teachings have brought joy and consolation to millions of souls. Many people from all faiths, even though their religion does not teach this principle, personally hope their lifelong and deeply cherished relationships with spouse and family members will continue beyond the grave. Only the teachings and temple ordinances of The Church of Jesus Christ of Latter-day Saints can provide the realization of these blessings for all of Heavenly Father's children.

Truths of Eternity Restored to the Prophet Joseph Smith

During the ministry of the Prophet Joseph Smith he received numerous revelations pertaining to the doctrine of eternal families. For example:

> And as pertaining to the new and everlasting covenant, it was instituted for the fulness of my glory; and he that receiveth a fulness thereof must and shall abide the law, or he shall be damned, saith the Lord God.
>
> And verily I say unto you, that the conditions of this law are these: All covenants, contracts, bonds, obligations, oaths, vows, performances, connections, associations, or expectations, that are not made and entered into and sealed by the Holy Spirit of promise, of him who is anointed, both as well for time and for all eternity . . . are of no efficacy, virtue, or force in and after the resurrection from the dead. (D&C 132:6–7)

In the same revelation, the Lord told the Prophet that if a couple is married in the new and everlasting covenant and this union is "sealed unto them by the Holy Spirit of promise" (D&C 132:19) then will they

> inherit thrones, kingdoms, principalities, and powers, dominions, all heights and depths . . . and they shall pass by the angels, and the gods, which are set there, to their exaltations and glory in all things, as hath been sealed upon their heads, which glory shall be a fulness and a continuation of the seeds forever and ever. (D&C 132:19)

Following the revelation of these profound truths,

the Lord further explained about the "sealing power" given by Elijah and of the power and authority to seal a husband and a wife to one another and to bind their children to them:

> And verily, verily, I say unto you, that whatsoever you seal on earth shall be sealed in heaven; and whatsoever you bind on earth, in my name and by my word, saith the Lord, it shall be eternally bound in the heavens. (D&C 132:46)

This same power was given by the Savior to Peter (Matt. 16:19) and is held by all Presidents of the Church, who in turn have bestowed this authority on others who then perform these sacred ordinances in the holy temples. Pertaining to these ordinances, Elder A. Theodore Tuttle of the Seventy taught:

> Frequently we perform marriages in the temple. These marriages are properly called celestial marriages, temple sealings, or eternal marriages. The thing that we really do is to organize the most basic unit in the Church—the family. The family is the most important relationship in this life. In reality, the bride and groom are called to assignments in the family from which they are never released, except by transgression. This is the one eternal unit which can exist in the presence of God.[17]

In speaking of the importance of keeping marriage covenants, President Spencer W. Kimball said, "Marriage according to the law of the Church is the most holy and sacred ordinance. It will bring to the husband and the wife, if they abide in their covenants, the fullness of exaltation in the kingdom of God."[18]

Eternal Families

Not only can marriage last beyond the grave, but so can sibling and family relationships endure across generations. In the Doctrine and Covenants we read, "And that same sociality which exists among us here will exist among us there, only it will be coupled with eternal glory, which glory we do not now enjoy" (D&C 130:2). The Prophet Joseph Smith saw a vision of the celestial kingdom as it would one day exist and said, "I saw Father Adam and Abraham; and my father and my mother; my brother Alvin, that has long since slept" (D&C 137:5). It is significant that of all the great and noble people Joseph could have named, he mentions his own parents, who were still living at the time of the vision, and his beloved elder brother Alvin. Adam, one of our "first parents" (Alma

42:2), and Abraham, the "Father of the Faithful" (Abr. 2:10) have a familial relationship with those who will live with God in the celestial kingdom.

Elder Robert D. Hales taught that "the plan of the Father is that family love and companionship will continue into the eternities. . . . The family relationships we have here on this earth are important, but they are much more important for their effect on our families for generations in mortality and throughout all eternity."[19] Elder Merrill J. Bateman stated the following in summarizing the family nature of the Father's plan:

> The creation of the earth, the fall of Adam, and the atonement of Christ are essential elements or pillars in the Father's plan for the progression and development of his children—both as individuals and as families. . . . These three doctrinal pillars of the plan of salvation are intimately involved in the creation of new eternal families and their extension into the eternities.[20]

It follows that more of our time and attention should focus on the creation of "eternal families" and perhaps less on simply enjoying the fun and entertainment the world offers (see 1 Cor. 10:7). The truth that the binding of humanity into eternal families is the whole purpose of the creation is demonstrated by the prophecy of Malachi (see Mal. 4:5–6). President Joseph F. Smith's vision of the redemption of the dead states:

> The Prophet Elijah was to plant in the hearts of the children the promises made to their fathers, foreshadowing the great work to be done in the temples of the Lord in the dispensation of the fulness of times, for the redemption of the dead, and the sealing of the children to their parents, lest the whole earth be smitten with a curse and utterly wasted at his coming. (D&C 138:47–48).

The sealing powers restored by Elijah make possible the joy of being sealed to one's immediate family and beyond in a great chain from Adam and Eve to the last woman and man (see D&C 128:18).

The misery of living through eternity alone is suggested by the Lord: "And upon them that hearken not to the voice of the Lord shall be fulfilled that which was written by the prophet Moses, that they should be cut off from among the people . . . and the day that cometh shall burn them up, saith the Lord of hosts, that it shall leave them neither root nor branch" (D&C 133:62–64; see also 3 Ne. 25:1 and Mal. 4:1).

Thus, part of the penalty for wickedness is being "cut off from the people" and being left with neither roots (ancestors) nor branches (descendants) throughout eternity.

All who will dwell in the celestial kingdom are spirit children of Heavenly Father and thus are brothers and sisters. And all the Saints from every dispensation will be sealed to one another in what the Prophet Joseph Smith called a "whole and complete and perfect union" (D&C 128:18).

Although the exact nature of family relationships after this life has not been fully revealed and we do not fully comprehend what God has prepared for the righteous (see 1 Cor. 2:9), the Lord has revealed that marriage is essential for exaltation in the celestial kingdom (see D&C 132:15–16). Each exalted couple will, like God, be involved in the creative process of bringing forth spirit children who will have the opportunity to experience mortality for themselves (see D&C 131:4).

Conclusion

God and His plan are eternal. God instituted marriage and family in the beginning. God created the earth, the garden, and our first parents in order to create families for all of His children to be born into and experience mortal life—especially mortal family life. The Fall occurred because Adam and Eve chose to obey God's commandment to multiply and replenish the earth and thus create the first family. The Lord Jesus Christ—the Son of God—completed the Atonement in order to reconcile God's children with God and with one another. Thus, the great plan of happiness is a plan that centers on family in time and eternity.

God commands his children to marry and become one, and the Savior taught that "what therefore God hath joined together, let not man put asunder" (Matt. 19:6). Marriage and family are eternal and priesthood keys have been given to prophets to seal on earth and in heaven. The Lord told Moses, "Behold this is my work and my glory, to bring to pass the immortality and eternal life of man" (Moses 1:39), and He told the Prophet Joseph Smith that the new and everlasting covenant of marriage "was instituted for the fulness of my glory" (D&C 132:6). The work and glory of God is to assist His children to make and keep sacred covenants designed to allow them to be sealed together eternally to one another and to Him and thereby enjoy all God enjoys. It should be the work and glory of all of God's children—but especially all Latter-day Saints—to make and keep these sacred covenants, to teach these transcendent truths to those who do not yet know of them, and to work in God's holy temples to make these covenants and ordinances available to all the children of God who desire to form eternal families.

NOTES

1. The family: A proclamation to the world (1995, November), *Ensign, 25,* 102.

2. Joseph F. Smith (1986), *Gospel doctrine* (Salt Lake City: Deseret Book), 272; see also Conference report (1913, April), 118–119.

3. Hugh B. Brown (1966, October), in Conference report, 103; or *Improvement Era* (1966, December), 1095.

4. See M. Russell Ballard (Nov. 1993), *Ensign, 23,* 76; see also Abr. 3.

5. Joseph F. Smith (1986), *Gospel doctrine* (Salt Lake City: Deseret Book), 285–86.

6. Bruce R. McConkie (1985), *A new witness for the Articles of Faith* (Salt Lake City: Deseret Book), 84.

7. See Daniel K Judd (1999), *The simpleness of the way.* Salt Lake City: Bookcraft.

8. Joseph F. Smith, John R. Winder, and Anthon H. Lund (1909, November), The origin of man, *Improvement Era, 13,* 61.

9. Joseph Smith (1938), *Teachings of the Prophet Joseph Smith,* comp. Joseph Fielding Smith (Salt Lake City: Deseret Book), 343.

10. Bruce R. McConkie, 322.

11. Ezra Taft Benson (1985, Aug.), What I hope you will teach your children about the temple, *Ensign, 8,* 10.

12. Ezra Taft Benson (1985, November), Worthy fathers, worthy sons, *Ensign, 15,* 36.

13. Joseph Smith, *Teachings,* 121.

14. Henry B. Eyring (1998, February), The family, *Ensign, 28*(2), 10–18.

15. Bruce R. McConkie (1970, June), *Improvement Era,* 43–44.

16. M. Russell Ballard (1996, May), *Ensign, 26,* 81.

17. A. Theodore Tuttle (1969, December), *Improvement Era,* 107.

18. Spencer W. Kimball (1962, October), The importance of keeping marriage covenants, in Conference report, 57–59.

19. Robert D. Hales (1996, November), The eternal family, *Ensign, 26,* 65.

20. Merrill J. Bateman (1998), The eternal family, *Brigham Young Magazine, 52*(4), 26.

DRAWING SPECIFIC INSPIRATION FROM THE PROCLAMATION

E. JEFFREY HILL

The first time I heard *The Family: A Proclamation to the World* is indelibly engraved in my mind and heart. I had just completed a Ph.D. in family and human development at Utah State University and was serving on the Logan Utah Central Stake high council. As part of my calling, I was asked to attend the broadcast of the General Relief Society meeting on September 23, 1995.

I sat comfortably in the chapel. It had been a long week and the lights were low, so, even though the talks were inspiring and interesting, I found myself drifting into sleep on occasion. Then President Gordon B. Hinckley got up to speak and so I rallied my energy to listen to the prophet. He spoke a few words and then announced he would read *The Family: A Proclamation to the World.*

Immediately I felt something like a brilliant light inside me. I sat up straight and tuned in my hearing. I resonated to every word President Hinckley spoke. Here was the prophet, illuminating in clear, understandable words, the undefiled principles upon which to build a successful family. Almost audibly, I cheered every pronouncement. Here was gospel truth unfettered by the world. As he concluded, I reflected that I had learned more truth in six minutes of listening to the Proclamation than I had learned in four years of graduate study in family life.

In the weeks that followed I couldn't stop thinking about the Proclamation. When the *Ensign* came I

pondered and prayed about its words. I wanted the Proclamation to become a part of me and my family. I felt impressed to memorize the Proclamation. I was 42 years old at the time, and since my Ph.D. it had become much more difficult for me to memorize things, especially long passages. But the impression came again, "Memorize the Proclamation!" I made several copies of the Proclamation and took it with me wherever I went. As I jogged, I memorized. As I drifted off to sleep in the evening, the words of the Proclamation were flowing through my mind. As I waited for my luggage in airports around the country, I held a tattered copy of the Proclamation, trying to memorize. Though difficult, in about a month I could say the complete Proclamation almost word for word.

Then came the process of truly digesting and drawing specific inspiration from the Proclamation. I am a devout jogger and often have impressions, which I believe are from the Spirit, as I jog. I felt that while jogging I should be open to letting the Spirit use the Proclamation as a means to provide inspiration about my family.

Each morning, as I jogged, the Spirit would bring to mind a different paragraph or a different sentence. One morning I was concerned about my teenage daughter and the friends she associated with. As I ran through the Proclamation in my mind, the Spirit highlighted in my thoughts the sentence that says "extended families should lend support when needed." I paused and the picture of my sister, struggling with trials and soon expecting her seventh child in a distant state, came to mind. I thought that we, as extended family, should lend her support because she definitely needed it. When I got home from jogging I bought inexpensive plane tickets for my oldest daughter and oldest son to enable them to spend a week serving in my sister's home. As part of that trip my daughter and my sister had many long talks. They were able to talk about things in a way that I, as a father, had been unable to do. My daughter returned from the trip with a clearer perspective and made wise decisions that blessed her life. My sister, her family, and my children were all greatly blessed by this experience inspired by the Proclamation.

Another time my responsibility to provide for my family seemed heavy. My job seemed to be draining the life energy right out of me. I had difficulty sleeping. On my morning jog the Spirit highlighted, "By divine design, fathers . . . are responsible to provide the necessities of life and protection for their families. Mothers are primarily responsible for the nurture of their children. In these sacred responsibilities, fathers and mothers are obligated to help one another as equal partners." I recognized that in the frazzle to provide, I had been neglecting the nurture of my children, and that, as the Proclamation said, I had an obligation to help my wife Juanita in this regard as an equal partner. I asked her what I could do and she said putting the kids to bed would be the most helpful. So I became more consistent in reading to the children, helping them brush their teeth, kneeling with them for their prayers, and putting them to bed with a song. These activities, right before I retired for the night, were calming and peaceful. They provided a prelude to joyful rest. With peaceful rest at night, I had more energy to put things in perspective.

Then I wondered how Juanita might help me, as an equal partner, in my responsibility to provide. I felt certain the Lord did not want this mother of nine to go out and get a job to help out financially. The answer came on another morning jog during another internal recitation of the Proclamation. As I went through the "provider" paragraph, the picture of Juanita and I walking and talking came to my mind. Then I realized she could help me by being a sounding board and helping me talk through my work problems and come to solutions. I asked Juanita if she would get up and walk with me in the mornings. She agreed and we started strolling around the neighborhood to talk about my work problems. Juanita is a good listener, and I found that just talking through my work problems with her enabled me to generate solutions that I had never thought of before. My work life got easier and easier. When something frustrating happened during the day I could just think, "Tomorrow morning, Juanita and I will talk about it, and we'll figure this out." So then I could go on without the feelings of frustration.

These are just two examples. Most inspiration has not been this grand. The Proclamation has more often been the conduit for simple ideas. But the hundreds of little ideas have combined to be a powerful force for good in our family. I know by the Spirit that *The Family: A Proclamation to the World* is an inspired document for families today and, if seriously studied and pondered, can open the way for divine assistance in our own families.

The Enduring, Happy Marriage: Findings and Implications from Research

Elizabeth VanDenBerghe

Marriage between a man and a woman is ordained of God.
(The Family: A Proclamation to the World, ¶ 1)

Preface: Why Study the Secular?

The Family: A Proclamation to the World states that "marriage between a man and a woman is ordained of God" and goes on to declare that "husband and wife have a solemn responsibility to love and care for each other" through fidelity, faith, respect, and "happiness in family life" (¶¶ 1, 6, 7). Such happiness, particularly happiness in married life, seems illusory to modern skeptics, whose own proclamations cite the demise of conventional marriage and declare it an impossible ideal. Yet if marriage is truly a deep source of happiness, the experience should speak for itself, and there should be evidence showing it to be a positive, healthy, and realistic way of life.

This chapter examines some of the evidence, drawing upon studies by social scientists and the insights of novelists. Sociological studies alone can't enable the reader to "see much of other people's thought processes or know much of their experience. . . . But the entire impulse of novels is to provide just such information, as 'thickly' as possible."[1] The surveys may provide the statistics, but they rarely talk to the heart, as good fiction may. Taken together, they offer substantial support for the Proclamation's stance on marriage. While most other chapters in this volume contain extensive references to both prophetic and scholarly sources of support, this chapter—given the voluminous scholarship available—focuses mainly on empirical support for the value of marriage.

Introduction: Austen vs. the Moderns

At the close of the twentieth century, amid high divorce rates and the alleged collapse of traditional marriage, an ironic cultural phenomenon took place in the United States. People flocked to movies based on novels by nineteenth-century novelist Jane Austen. Promoting the "universally acknowledged" truth, according to Miss Austen, that single men and women could find true happiness only in marriage, the films entertained modern audiences in a divorce-saturated culture by promoting the ideals of fidelity, commitment, and sacred vows uttered before a church-attending public. In Austen's world, unions based on sheer romance or, even worse, illicit passion, often met their demise before the engagement news could be posted at the village parsonage. Sometimes, though, two self-indulgent types did marry, their regard for each other stemming more from outward appearances or family politics than from loyalty, self-sacrifice, and a disposition toward family life. In the 1800s the bad matches stayed together. "I have a high respect for your nerves," says Mr. Bennet to Mrs. Bennet in *Pride and Prejudice*. "They are my old friends. I have heard you mention them with consideration these twenty years at least."[2]

A century later, Mr. and Mrs. Bennet would have divorced. In fact, married couples now divorce so often that marriage seems a demoralized institution, and there is "widespread belief that American marriages are weak and troubled."[3] Half of the public believe that married people aren't any happier than the unmarried.[4] The media flout alternatives to marriage, from one-night stands to cohabitation, as preferable to the challenges of legal union. Feminists deride matrimony as oppressive to women. Even family studies textbooks display a surprising ignorance of the statistical evidence about marriage, "almost without exception," writes one academic reviewer, "downplay[ing] the value of marriage."[5]

Thus, the texts that train clergy, counselors, and impressionable college students employ warm platitudes to describe nontraditional unions, but emphasize the problems of conventional marriage—a depiction one respected social scientist labeled as tantamount to "educational malpractice."[6] Even such purveyors of human well-being as psychologists and psychiatrists sometimes tend toward what another family scientist labels "therapist-assisted marital suicide," becoming "cheerleader[s] for divorce" by wrongly assuming that what's good for the family can't be good for the individual.[7]

Offered such an unflattering portrait of marriage, not only by the culture at large, but also by the parents who doubled the divorce rate in this country, post-baby-boom young adults feel understandably wary about tying the knot. A majority of the younger generation yearns for a return to stable family life, and they are much less likely than their elders to consider divorce a good option.[8] Even so, opines an academic psychologist, "they don't have a clue how to make their relationships work."[9] A recent national survey finds that, strong desires for successful marriages aside, young people today remain increasingly anxious and pessimistic about marriage and display a remarkable increase in acceptance of out-of-wedlock childbearing, single parenting, and living together before marriage. No wonder the marriage rate has dropped to a 40-year low.[10]

Anxiety. Pessimism. Wariness. Does the institution of marriage truly merit such unenthusiastic feelings? Loaded with an abundance of objective, long-term, well-designed studies analyzing data from various countries, races, and economic classes, a growing number of family scientists are trying to get the word out: No! Marriage, it turns out, is good for you. A lasting marriage proves to be more beneficial physically, mentally, economically, even sexually than exercise programs, medical treatments, financial investments, or therapy sessions. The research even shows why marriage contributes to so many facets of adult well-being and, perhaps most helpful, pinpoints qualities common to couples whose marriages have lasted—qualities even fallible humans are capable of achieving.

The skeptic at this point may claim he's seen too many unhappy marriages to believe otherwise. He would do well to note that academic research deals in objective statistics and trends, not exceptions. Couples in some families, neighborhoods, or tabloids may be unsuccessful in marriage, but that doesn't negate the fact that the vast majority of couples who remain married end up happier and healthier than those who stay single, divorce, or live together. By the same token, while the research puts the happily married at a statistical advantage, that doesn't mean that a loyal husband or wife won't face problems common to all human beings, like illness, financial strain, or the blues. Data are not destiny. Exceptions can, do, and will always exist. Despite the possible exceptions, the patterns and trends revealed in the research may enlighten and instruct us. In this chapter, they offer the what, why, and how of successful marriages. They even reveal that Jane Austen and her ilk were right. For most people, an enduring, happy marriage means a happy life.

PART ONE: THE BENEFITS OF MARRIAGE

Charlotte Bronte's Jane Eyre endures 500 pages of grief and emotional trauma before finally, at book's end, marrying Mr. Rochester. The wedding is worth the wait. After ten years of marriage, she confides, "I hold myself supremely blest—blest beyond what language can express; because I am my husband's life as fully as he is mine. . . . I know no weariness of my Edward's society: he knows none of mine, any more than we each do of the pulsation of the heart that beats in our separate bosoms; consequently, we are ever together."[11] After marriage, it seems, Jane's emotional and economic dilemmas disappear. As for Edward, even his blindness is cured. Jane reiterates for the reader in her epilogue, "My Edward and I, then, are happy."[12] Their marriage brings with it multiple benefits.

Unhappy marriages run a complex gamut from

the dissatisfied couples for whom the present marriage, though flawed, is better than the alternatives, to couples whose complete breakdown as a union inflicts psychological or bodily harm to both. "In other words," explains marriage researcher John Gottman, "they feel physically stressed and usually emotionally stressed as well . . . [resulting] in any number of physical ailments, including high blood pressure and heart disease, and in a host of psychological ones, including anxiety, depression, suicide, violence, psychosis, homicide, and substance abuse."[13] The following recital of the benefits of marriage apply mainly to *happy* marriages, which continue to constitute the majority of marriages.

Physical Health Benefits

Married people live longer, a statistical reality that's true across different cultures, societies, and demographic groups.[14] They suffer less from illness and disease and are better off than their never-married or divorced counterparts when they do fall ill.[15] In fact, recovery rates are so much higher for married individuals that scientists writing in the *Journal of the American Medical Association* argue that "the decreases in survival associated with being unmarried are not trivial and apply to a large population at risk."[16] The married also exhibit fewer risk-taking behaviors such as drunk driving, smoking, drug abuse, and have much lower rates of suicide and alcoholism.[17]

To counter this impressive list of benefits to body and health associated with marriage, some analysts proffer a selectivity theory which argues that already physically healthy individuals are selected into marriage, leaving a disproportionate number of frail singles behind who get sick more often and die sooner. Thus it has been argued that marriage itself does little to cause all of the benefits; it just reflects the kind of already healthy, happy people who get married. However, current research more often leans to a causal than a selection theory, for the data often show positive changes taking place after marriage, as well as negative changes resulting when a marriage dissolves.[18] One marriage scholar aptly summarizes the research by admonishing couples, "Remember, working briefly on your marriage every day will do more for your health and longevity than working out at a health club."[19]

Mental Health Benefits

Unlike the pre-twentieth-century sages of literature, modern comedians get laughs by portraying marriage as neurosis-inducing and bad for the brain. One in particular starred in 1970s-era movies featuring complaints to psychiatrists about the various mental ills inflicted by numerous former wives. Long-term male–female relationships, he quipped, were doomed from the start: he'd never want to belong to a club that would have him for a member, so all the women who wanted him in their "club" must be losers in the first place.

Fortunately, the research invalidates this comedian's point of view. Marriage is as good for the mind as it is for the body. Married people have lower rates of depression and suffer significantly less from any psychiatric disorder than their divorced, never-married, or cohabiting counterparts.[20] Interestingly, these findings are consistent across black and white populations, with researchers from Yale University and UCLA concluding that "one of the most consistent findings in psychiatric epidemiology is that married persons enjoy better mental health than the unmarried."[21]

This robust mental health, however, can't be attributed simply to lack of depression or mental illness. Married people are happier in all facets of life and enjoy higher general well-being than any unmarried segment of the population.[22] The findings are summarized this way: "no part of the unmarried population—separated, divorced, widowed, or never married—describes itself as being so happy and contented with life as the married."[23] Again, the advantages of marriage for personal well-being extend across races, various countries, and socio-economic classes. Like the physical health benefits, the mental health findings cannot be explained away by selectivity. According to one prominent researcher, "The positive effect of marriage on well-being is strong and consistent, and selection of the psychologically healthy into marriage or the psychologically unhealthy out of marriage cannot explain the effect."[24]

Economic Benefits

Never-married Jane Austen showed a keen appreciation of economic security in her novels. In *Sense and Sensibility,* for example, Marianne Dashwood, always prone to idealistic romanticism, cries out, "What have wealth or grandeur to do with happiness?" To which her very sensible sister Elinor replies, "Grandeur has but little, . . . but wealth has much to do with it." While neither extravagant nor greedy, Elinor nevertheless realizes that the basic comforts of life come with a price. When she and her beau Edward decide to marry, "their intimate knowledge of each other seemed to make their happiness certain," except for one problem: finances. Neither of them, writes Austen, were "quite enough in love to think that three hundred and fifty pounds-a-year would supply them with the comforts of life."[25]

In the end, things work out happily for Elinor and Edward, just as they always do for worthy matches in Austen's world. But in the real world? According to statistics, Elinor and Edward would still be wise to tie the knot. Getting and staying married, it turns out, is a wise economic move. Married couples are wealthier and spend less than divorced, never married, and widowed households. Married couples also save more by living, as one researcher put it, "as cheaply as one—or maybe one and a half." They tend to delay gratification more readily than the unmarried in order to invest in such family-oriented goals as homes, college educations, and retirement.[26]

Obviously, not all married couples are frugal; some charge cruises and cars to their over-extended VISA cards. But the economic security a stable marriage offers doesn't simply mean being able to remodel the kitchen every five years. It means access to health care, to food and clothing, to education, and especially to a secure family life far from crime-infested streets. In fact, says the Progressive Policy Institute, "It is no exaggeration to say that a stable, two-parent family is an American child's best protection against poverty."[27] The studies unequivocally show that current levels of poverty result more from family structure than from economic factors. The presence of one parent, typically a single mother, usually means poverty for a family. The presence of two married parents usually means that children "will never be poor during childhood."[28]

Sexual Benefits

Perhaps research offers its most counterintuitive findings in evaluating sexuality in marriage, for there it defies common assumptions about the connection between marriage and sex, or lack thereof. Movies, television, and print media have long depicted marriage as the water hose guaranteed to douse the flames of passion, perhaps within months of the ceremony. The novelists have chimed in: the philandering husband looking for excitement outside his affectionless marriage remains a staple tale. Even women in books can't seem to satisfy their physical desires within

marriage. In Kate Chopin's *The Awakening,* Edna Pontellier feels so burdened by the sexual repression of her marriage she walks suicidally into the sea and drowns.[29]

Someone needs to get the message across that "the public image of sex," according to a landmark study on the subject, "bears virtually no relationship to the truth."[30] Research from such venues as *The National Health and Social Life Survey* and the *Journal of the American Medical Association* consistently find that faithfully married people report being well-satisfied with their sex lives, more so than any other category of sexually active people. Morever, married men and women are least likely to lack interest in sex or to consider it unpleasurable and are also least likely to associate sex with feelings of fear, anxiety, or guilt.[31] Considering the current epidemic of sexually transmitted diseases, with 12 million new infections per year in the United States, the finding on lack of marital anxiety about sex can hardly be a surprise. As one writer explained, "Sex cannot be successful when it has to be approached with the same caution exhibited in handling toxic waste."[32] A marriage marked by fidelity, obviously, circumvents the need for such caution and offers a secure, rewarding, and emotionally safe context for displaying physical affection.

Where Do the Benefits Go?

The surveys show undeniably that satisfaction levels of people in good marriages are high. But these data hardly guarantee perfect physical health, constant happiness, complete financial security, or blissful intimate relations. What they do reveal are general trends. And just as the married, generally, are well off, those that end up in alternatives to marriage generally are not. Marriage's benefits, say the researchers, do not extend to its copycats.

In *The Age of Innocence,* Edith Wharton depicts a jaded, worldly Countess Olenska whose experiences have made her wise to the hazards of alternatives to marriage. When her naive suitor Newland Archer asks her to run away with him, she bluntly asks him, "Is it your idea, then, that I should live with you as your mistress—since I can't be your wife?" To which he confesses that he wants only to take her to a place "where words like that—categories like that—won't exist." But Countess Olenska sagely replies, "Oh, my dear—where is that country? Have you ever been there? . . . I know so many who've tried to find it; and, believe me, they all got out by mistake at wayside stations: at places like Boulogne, or Pisa, or Monte Carlo—and it wasn't at all different from the old world they'd left, but only rather smaller and dingier and more promiscuous."[33]

Throughout history, couples have tried to find a "country" other than marriage in which to cohabit. In the last quarter of the twentieth century there has been a huge proliferation in the number of men and women living together without a marriage license.[34] "We take marriage so seriously," they say, "that we want to practice for it." Or they say they don't believe pure and unencumbered love needs validity from that "piece of paper," the marriage license. Yet the research continues to show that, despite the best, most idealistic intentions of the couples who expatriate from marriage, countries outside a legal union truly are dingier, more promiscuous, and even more dangerous for families living in them.

Cohabiting couples experience greater conflict, lower quality of relationships, lower stability, and lower equality for the women involved. Domestic violence is far more common among couples living together than those who are married, leading one analyst to note that the phrase "wife beating" is a misnomer. A more precise term would be "girlfriend beating."[35] Women who live with a man also experience much higher levels of depression and economic insecurity and are more likely than other women to be forced into sexual relations against their will. And both men and women involved in a cohabiting relationship report lower levels of sexual satisfaction, with infidelity a prime problem area.[36]

"It is difficult to argue," concludes one study, "that cohabitors resemble married people."[37] Apparently theirs *is* an entirely different country, and a much more impoverished one at that. Children living with their mother's boyfriend experience much higher levels of abuse than those living with their fathers. Young adults are more likely to revert to dependence on their parents after a cohabiting relationship than after marriage. And when cohabiting couples do marry, they manifest very high divorce rates. A common pattern is divorce followed by another episode of cohabitation. Cohabiting couples who marry have higher rates of adultery, alcohol and drug abuse, and their cohabiting phase is characterized by more separateness in handling finances, spending free time, and envisioning the future. Conversely, couples who abstain from premarital sex are less likely to hold nontraditional attitudes about marriage, attitudes that

---

THE BENEFITS OF MARRIAGE

1. Married people live longer, suffer less from illness, and recover quicker. They also exhibit fewer risk-taking behaviors and have the lowest rates of suicide and alcoholism.

2. Married people are happier and enjoy higher well-being in all facets of life. They suffer significantly less from depression and other psychiatric disorders.

3. Married people are better off economically, spend less, and save more. Two-parent families are a powerful barrier against poverty.

4. Married people are more fulfilled in their sexual relations than other sexually active people. They are less likely to be disinterested in or to feel anxiety over sex.

5. These benefits do not extend to cohabiting relationships and apply in lesser degree to remarriages.

Box 2.1

---

contribute to adultery, separating, divorce, and lower sexual satisfaction with a marital partner.[38]

Judging from the statistics, another alternative to conventional marriage, remarriage, while manifesting fewer liabilities than cohabitation, does not generate all the benefits of a first marriage. Remarriages after divorce are marked by higher instability, lower quality, and higher divorce rates than first-time marriages. However, remarriage after death of a spouse tends to avoid these hazards, and the stepfamily challenge following widowhood is not as daunting as that faced by post-divorce stepparents.[39] Of course, the statistics merely reflect general tendencies, and there are many exceptions. To say that remarriages are more difficult than first marriages does not mean that they are not preferable to remaining single or to other alternatives to marriage. But persons confronting the challenges of remaining in first-time marriage should consider the odds before bailing out, thinking it might be easier to start over. Apparently, it's not easy, and it's not like starting over.

WHY IS MARRIAGE GOOD FOR PEOPLE?

Researchers often attribute the benefits of marriage to rather predictable—some might call them mundane—reasons. Marriage provides someone to raise the kids with, to scrimp and to save with, a partner to share work and worship, the good times and the challenges. The sharing of ordinary life seems to promote the well-being of married people, but at the same time is rarely the stuff of high drama or romantic adventure as portrayed in the media. Yet to persons deprived of the small pleasures of ordinary family life, the true benefits and long-term advantages inherent in them appear painfully obvious. Countess Olenska's sudden exposure to traditional family life in *The Age of Innocence* causes her to realize that "under the dullness there are things so fine and sensitive and delicate that even those I most cared for in my other life look cheap in comparison. . . . It seems as if I'd never before understood with how much that is hard and shabby and base the most exquisite pleasures may be paid."[40] Indeed, the "dullness" of a lifelong marriage often masks things fine and sensitive—the simple reasons behind the benefits of marriage:

Marriage offers couples a spiritual connection to their deepest values. In most cultures, marriage is not just a legal tie to another person, but also represents a sacred vow before God and a religious community. Many religions define marriage as a sacramental union, thus offering the couple a deep connection to the spiritual values they cherish.[41] Thus the union between man and wife "isn't just about raising kids, splitting chores, and making love. It can also have a spiritual dimension that has to do with creating an inner life together."[42] In fact, there is evidence that the deeper a couple shares this inner life, the better their marriage relationship will be.

Marriage satisfies the deep, human need for emotional and physical closeness. Marriage is a "personal safety net" in times of distress, and an anchor of stability in a frenetic and rapidly changing world.[43] This safety net not only rescues husbands and wives emotionally in times of stress by offering constant human companionship, but it also encourages healthy behaviors in times of normalcy: spouses remind each other to eat well, to establish regular sleep patterns, and to see the doctor periodically. The companionship between husband and wife also creates a "tranquilizing effect," as one psychology professor put it, which lessens the chances of disease, aids in the recovery process, and offers motivation to stay alive and well.[44]

Marriage offers the couple an extended social network to turn to for assistance, advice, and support. Partners in marriage not only have their own spouse and children on which to lean, but also the resources of two extended families, effectively doubling their support system. Further benefits come through other social institutions to which married couples belong, such as churches, community organizations, and neighborhoods.[45]

Marriage offers legal rights and privileges. Shared health and work benefits, joint tax returns, government and medicare benefits, legal inheritances, and the right to make medical decisions for one another are all benefits of marriage.[46]

Marriage enables couples to "specialize" in their labors. Researchers point out that the long-term horizon for marriage encourages each partner to develop skills that complement those of the other partner. Thus, a husband with poor financial management skills may rely on a well-organized wife to compensate for that weakness, just as he may compensate for her inexperience in household repair or auto mechanics. A cooperating pair may draw upon at least twice the specialties either could muster alone. Thus, couples find that, over time, marriage enables them to accomplish a great deal through a solid partnership.[47]

Marriage offers the ultimate meaningful role in society. In preindustrial society, one's role as a farmer, blacksmith, or seamstress was closely allied with his or her roles in the family and community. Often, people worked from their houses or on their land, and their responsibilities at home and at work were intertwined. In contrast, careers today are highly specialized and tend to be centered away from home and family. Thus, one's job as a factory worker, a computer programer, or a financial bond analyst seems worlds removed from one's role as a parent or community member. Moreover, the specialized work role involves only part of the self and may even be, in the Marxian sense, "alienating" to the self in that work is not intrinsically meaningful. In contrast, marriage and family still involve the unspecialized, holistic self, providing a context in which people bring together their many specialized roles, and are able to complain about work, discuss their children's problems, and strategize about the future of family and career within a union that provides value and continuity, a meaningful "backstage."[48]

Male and female differences. Some of the benefits differ by sex. For example, while both men and women live longer if they are married, women benefit more than men from what researchers call the "increased financial resources" of marriage. Married women are much better off economically, with all of the associated health and lifestyle benefits, than their single counterparts. Marriage and children tend to reduce a woman's earning power, and much of a married woman's financial advantage stems from the combination of her earnings with those of her husband, whose income tends not to be reduced by marriage and children. When a marriage dissolves, so does a married woman's economic advantage, often with devastating results.[49]

Married people live longer. Another benefit of marriage that differs by sex is the mortality rate. Married women have slightly lower death rates than single women, but men experience a sharp decrease in mortality rates almost immediately upon marrying. The reason, say researchers, lies in a markedly improved lifestyle for men, one that effectively counteracts the lifestyle that single men are prone to: risky behaviors, lack of social integration, and irregular meal and sleep habits.[50] In addition, "the institution of marriage, at least in its most traditional form, is a socially approved mechanism for the expression of masculinity."[51] That is, marriage allows healthy expression of masculinity by enabling a man to father children, provide for a family, and protect that family in respectable and healthy ways. Consequently, married men work more, earn more, achieve more, enjoy greater occupational prestige, and participate more in church and community groups than do single men. But like women, they lose these benefits when a marriage dissolves; divorce often reduces a man's occupational prestige and earning power, and under some circumstances so does remarriage.[52]

With so much to offer, why don't marriages last nowadays? Despite the demonstrated benefits of marriage, high divorce rates and even higher rates of cohabitation have marked the last few decades. It is not clear why the apparently rational personal and societal benefits of marriage have no longer been sufficient to counter the individualistic tendencies that now seem so powerful. Perhaps people no longer give marriage the long-term time horizon it requires. Also, the nurturing "backstage" of spouse and children has been systematically eroded by the competitive outside attributes of the world. People begin marriage expecting magazine-cover looks, power careers, and sexual prowess to rival cable TV scenes. Couples are victimized by a pervasive outlook that one writer describes as hostile to family love, one that "regards ordinary marriage as uninteresting and great passion as real

---

THE REASONS MARRIAGE IS BENEFICIAL

1. Marriage offers couples a spiritual connection to their values and to each other.

2. Marriage fosters emotional and physical closeness, which contribute to mental and physical well-being and also encourage healthy behavior.

3. Marriage brings an extended social network of family, church, and community associations.

4. Marriage comes with legal rights, protection, and privileges.

5. Marriage encourages each spouse to develop skills that the other is weak in, creating a profitable "specialization" of labor.

6. Marriage offers respite from the complex, often artificial demands of an external economy, offering a "backstage" where the holistic self is valued.

7. Marriage provides women with substantial economic benefits.

8. Marriage dramatically improves men's lifestyles and facilitates their achievement in the workplace and community.

9. The benefits of marriage are being undermined by a growing public contempt for traditional values, contempt evidenced by rampant individualism and a tendency to separate and divorce quickly rather than devote the time necessary to work on marital problems.

Box 2.2

---

life."[53] Perhaps most insidious, too many couples no longer sacrifice for each other, instead displaying individualistic, narcissistic attitudes that some social scientists say are a leading cause of divorce. After all, it's hard to share sorrows and joys, scrimp and save together, and find lasting emotional closeness when one or both partners is primarily interested in him- or herself. Narcissism, worldly value systems, and contempt for traditional norms are not the qualities associated with successful marriage.

HOW DO LASTING, HAPPY MARRIAGES BECOME THAT WAY?

Novelists sometimes grapple with the question of what makes a marriage by showing what marriage is not. Tolstoy's *Anna Karenina* is a vivid example of the married woman whose pursuit of passion ultimately dooms her relationships. Anna disregards the small, practical things that create a loving partnership and becomes a tragic symbol of misplaced desire.[54] Jane Austen takes a more humorous approach, poking fun at such romantic ideals as a woman's search for the one and only "right" person, the knight in shining armor who will transport her from ordinary life to the romantic ideal. In *Sense and Sensibility,* the idealistic Marianne is rescued from a sprained ankle by a passing gentleman, Mr. Willoughby. He sweeps her into his arms and carries her back home, where his "youth, beauty, and elegance" compel her to fall madly in love. The problem is, "uncommonly handsome" looks aside, Willoughby is a rogue. Fortunately, by the end of the book, Marianne has matured and now appreciates the many worthy attributes of close family friend Colonel Brandon. Contrite and repentant, she ends up with a suitable match after all.[55]

Actually, in the times of Tolstoy and Austen, romance played less a part in engagement and marriage than did the approval of parents. Mature fathers and mothers oversaw, or at least heavily influenced, their children's mate selection. Through the marriages of their children, parents brought family names or estates together, created economic security, and observed political or social alliances. Carefully chaperoned and supervised "courtship" ensured parental control up until the 1920s, when "dating" took over and the couples themselves assumed the power of choice in mate selection. Consequently, romance and passion gained and have kept the upper hand in modern courtship.[56]

Few would argue for a return to chaperoned courting, arranged marriages, or engagements based purely on objective criteria. But if passion is dangerous and arranged marriage is out, how, then, do happy marriages come to be? "The difficulty is to find a suitable person," advises Everard Bone in Barbara Pym's *Excellent Women.* The unmarried Mildred Lathbury responds, "Perhaps one shouldn't try to find people deliberately like that. . . . I mean, not set out to look for somebody to marry as if you were going to buy a saucepan or a casserole."[57] In fact, research suggests that at least part of the search should lean toward the practical, casserole side: most successful marriages have crucial elements in common. Knowing what these qualities are, and cultivating them both before and after marriage, may help to assure happiness in marriage. We now consider several of these qualities. Many of them are more utilitarian than romantic, yet they make possible the long-term cohesion and support necessary to the continuance of marital romance and commitment.

Religion: A "prime mover" for happily married couples. Although family scientists haven't prioritized the common denominators of successful marriages, one particular quality—marriage commitment—seems to underlie and sustain many others. Studies dating back to the 1930s have found that religious couples are more likely than others to have successful marriages, marriages marked by a stated willingness to wed the same person again, an absence of discord, and a low probability of divorce. For a long time, researchers tried to explain away these findings through notions of "conventionalization." It was argued that religious couples were only responding the way they thought they should and not telling the whole truth about their marriages. But important studies in the 1980s provided evidence that conventionalization did not account for all of the positive response effects of religious commitment on marriage. Indeed, after appropriate controls, religiosity remained a strong predictor of marital happiness, even stronger than socioeconomic status or familial conditions.[58]

Given that religious commitment has beneficial effects on marriage, it is still not clear just how a couple's religiosity sustains their marriage. Some studies suggest that shared religious commitment by itself does not ensure high-quality marriages. Some have theorized that, "instead of being the number one or two factor, religion serves as a 'prime mover' influencing all other variables in the model."[59] In other words, the faith of deeply religious people may strengthen them, and at the same time encourage the development of qualities like selflessness and commitment that are crucial to a successful union.[60] Spiritual faith also enhances marital intimacy and helps couples communicate by promoting interpersonal skills such as patience, forgiveness, respect, and conflict resolution.[61] And certainly a crucial component of the "religion effect" is the spiritual strength couples draw on in times of crisis, decision-making, or even simply day-to-day living.[62]

Most successful couples, the studies conclude, share the same religion. Religiously unaffiliated couples have exceptionally high divorce rates, and potential bad matches and high divorce rates also occur when members of different religions wed.[63] Also, certain types of religious expression seem healthier for a marriage than others. Dividing religion into two categories, the dogmatic and the caring, the former represents religiosity in its superficial or extrinsic form—lots of talk, perhaps, but an ultimate emphasis on gaining social status or endorsement for one's own way of life. By contrast, the caring approach is intrinsic. It values faith and love and "floods the whole life with motivation and meaning."[64] Obviously, the latter tends to promote marital satisfaction more than the former does. Thus, the effects of one's religiosity in a marriage depend on its nature as well as its presence or absence. Quiet, unspoken faith may be more resilient and lasting than highly vocal commitment.

Happily married couples maintain a selfless, realistic, and committed vision of marriage. Expectations have much to do with marital success. Ironically, "if happiness becomes the primary goal of a marriage, it is likely to lead to an unhappy marriage and unhappy individuals."[65] In other words, husbands and wives shouldn't expect automatically to receive all of the benefits marriage can bestow. Instead, good health, happiness, prosperity, and fulfilling sexual relations seem to be byproducts of unions between people who are prepared to face hard times and who are willing to sacrifice their own desires for the good of spouse and children. Successful couples realize that family life may be difficult and burdensome,[66] but despite the burdens of marriage, divorce is not an option for them. Instead, their commitment is for better or for worse, and the longer a couple remains married, the less likely they are to divorce.[67] A realistic perspective refrains from imagining, when problems arise, that "Oh no! I haven't married the right person after all!" or "If only we could manage to just stay in love!" Couples in love have problems and the list of crucial characteristics of successful marriages does not include having found the perfect spouse or sustaining the honeymoon.[68]

Happily married couples create an intimate friendship, reflecting shared experiences, fondness, and admiration. Studies of couples who have remained together for many years find intimacy to be the central quality of their marriage, a closeness marked by "shared interests, activities, thoughts, feelings, values, joys, and pains."[69] When each spouse focuses on the admirable qualities of the other, a positive "overflow" of good feelings is created that enables the resolution of disagreements during the strains common to family life. Marriages also become closer when each spouse makes "cognitive room" for the other. Becoming intimately familiar with the other's world—her favorite movies, his deep-seated fears, her colleagues and enemies at work—helps "protect" a couple when stressful events arise, such as the birth of a baby or

---

QUALITIES COMMON TO SUCCESSFUL MARRIAGES

1. Religious commitment is a strong predictor of marital happiness and seems to encourage and promote other qualities associated with marital success.

2. Happily married couples understand that family life is sometimes difficult and are willing to sacrifice their own desires and maintain their commitment when problems arise.

3. Successful couples form a deep friendship marked by positive, nurturing feelings toward each other. They acquire an intimate understanding of one another, defend each other, and respect each other's opinions and choices.

4. Marriages succeed despite chronic conflicts (things that never really get resolved) through forgiveness, compromise, mutual tolerance, and acceptance.

5. Successful couples solve many problems by resolution techniques that are nondestructive and do not distance the partners from each other.

6. Happily married couples tend to agree on their marriages' strengths and weaknesses.

7. Successful couples tend to have married later, in their early twenties or beyond, rather than in their teens.

BOX 2.3

---

the loss of a job, events that otherwise might throw a marriage off course. Finally, close-friendship couples defend each other against the world and value each other's opinions.[70]

Happily married couples manage to deal with perpetual and unresolvable conflicts without hurting each other. There are two kinds of marital conflict, the unsolvable and the solvable. The majority of marital conflicts are unsolvable.[71] He isn't neat enough and she nags. She wants more children but he doesn't. He needs physical intimacy more often than she does. Couples needn't resolve all their conflicts for their marriage to thrive. But they do need to make the problems less painful through forgiveness, patience, compromise, and the communication of basic acceptance and love. Positive thoughts and feelings about each other, as well as an understanding of the other's deep-seated needs and goals, help to diminish the intensity of perpetual problems, problems that might otherwise destroy an unstable marriage. Successful marriages deal with problems in nondestructive ways and treat the unsolvable conflicts in ways that allow the marriage to continue its positive functions without distancing each spouse from the other.

Solvable problems also require compromise and tolerance, as well as some healthy communication techniques. Typical solvable problems, as well as helpful ways to solve them, usually arise in the following areas of domestic life: work (couples need to take time to de-stress); in-laws (couples must put their own solidarity first); money (couples should establish a budget and work toward financial goals together); sex (couples can learn to talk about it in ways that feel safe); housework (marriages in which men contribute to the housework are much more satisfying); and new parenthood (the husband must follow the wife into the realm of parenthood). For both solvable and unsolvable problems, communication skills are *not* the vital priority. It is the underlying friendship and a deep sense of meaning that are the salient features of the lasting marriage.[72]

Happily married couples display a high degree of "congruence." Both partners perceive the strengths and weaknesses in their marriage similarly. In other words, one partner doesn't view the marriage as terrific and the other see it as mediocre or terrible. Both hold similar opinions on how well they communicate, how intimate they are, or how religiously devoted they are. Even when identifying their weaknesses, successful couples experience a sense of attunement.[73]

Happily married couples avoid marrying at young, immature ages. According to the 1999 report of the National Marriage Project, "age at marriage is one of the strongest and most consistent predictors of marital stability ever found by social science research."[74] The marriages of teenagers are less stable and have much higher divorce than the marriages of people in their twenties or older.[75] Had Shakespeare allowed Romeo and Juliet to survive at the play's conclusion, the chances of survival for their youthful marriage remains questionable. Research suggests that major benefits come with delaying marriage until the early twenties, but that delays to the late twenties or beyond do not produce additional benefits.[76] It seems that the younger the age at marriage, the less prepared the couple is in two key areas: maturity and readiness to marry. Teenagers especially have less time to search for a compatible spouse and have a weak understanding of what they want in a lifetime mate.[77]

Perhaps most interesting in this list of characteristics of successful marriages are the elements that do not appear. No studies show that a man needs to be athletic, handsome, drive an expensive car, or make a six-figure salary in order to be a suitable husband. Nor is there evidence that a woman must be beautiful, wear a size six dress, or cook well in order to be a good wife.

CONCLUSION

At the end of *Mansfield Park,* as in every Jane Austen novel, the single man and the single woman have undergone a rocky courtship marked by misjudgment, misunderstanding, and many self-revelations. One or the other realizes by now how he or she was previously duped into love with a beautiful, superficial woman or a handsome scoundrel. He or she previously overlooked remarkable qualities in a spurned suitor, qualities like loyalty, selflessness, honesty, and financial stability. And now, the heroine or hero is fortunate enough to discover that, after all, the neglected neighbor or cousin or family friend is the best marriage prospect around. In Fanny and Edmund's case, "with so much true merit and true love, and no want of fortune or friends, the happiness of the [couple] must appear as secure as earthly happiness can be—Equally formed for domestic life, and attached to country pleasures, their home was the home of affection and comfort."[78]

The marital ideal involves affection, comfort, and a long life with health and happiness. Not all marriages reach or even approach it. And not all marriages can or should be preserved (see Box 2.4 for a perspective on divorce). But couples who abandon the marital ideal altogether pay high costs, such as increased physical, mental, and emotional problems for themselves, and higher rates of delinquency, crime, substance abuse, depression, teen pregnancy, poverty, and poor academic achievement for the children.[79] Society suffers, too, from the loss of the ideal. Not only is marriage good for the adults and children involved, but it is also good for the economy, for married spouses work harder, save more, and buy more homes. Marriage is good for neighborhoods—it is the "seedbed of civic virtue and moral character" that drives out crime and violence.[80] And traditional marriage is good for taxpayers, who must subsidize the single-parent families who form the core of poverty and welfare dependency.[81] Finally, the institution of marriage encourages responsible sexual union and ensures the security of the offspring it produces.[82]

A Perspective on Divorce

Alan J. Hawkins

God intends for marriage to be eternal. Jesus told the Pharisees who were arguing about divorce: "What therefore God hath joined together, let not man put asunder" (Matt. 19:7). Unfortunately, almost all of us these days are touched by the sadness of divorce, whether we lived through it as a child, experienced it directly as an adult, or had a close friend or family member go through divorce. How should Latter-day Saints think about divorce? A perspective I find helpful involves three points:

First, our most important personal responsibility is to do all we can to establish and maintain happy marriages. This includes proper preparation, both spiritually and temporally. Fortunately, research documents that good preparation for marriage can reduce the risk of serious problems leading to divorce.[83] In addition, we are obligated to follow those principles that sustain happy marriages day to day. The Proclamation specifies many important spiritual principles that keep marriages strong and vital. Many of these spiritual principles find a parallel in secular principles that are known to keep marriages strong and prevent divorce,[84] including a complete commitment to a spouse and to the institution of marriage.[85] Without a full commitment to the marriage, the conflicts that result from imperfect people living together in challenging circumstances cannot be resolved. Moreover, if relationship problems become serious enough to threaten the stability of the marriage, I believe we are obligated to seek help. Because of the spiritual basis of marriage, we should counsel with a bishop who is entitled to special inspiration to guide us. He may also recommend professional counseling, which research shows can help resolve serious marital problems.[86]

A second point is to understand what the living prophets, who understand clearly the challenges of our day, teach us about when divorce is justified. I have found the following statement by President James E. Faust to be one of the most succinct, helpful, and sensitive statements on the subject:

> Those marriages performed in our temples, meant to be eternal relationships, then, become the most sacred covenants we can make. . . . What, then, might be "just cause" for breaking the covenants of marriage? Over a lifetime of dealing with human problems, I have struggled to understand what might be considered "just cause" for breaking of covenants. I confess I do not claim the wisdom nor authority to definitively state what is "just cause." Only the parties to the marriage can determine this. They must bear the responsibility for the train of consequences which inevitably follow if these covenants are not honored. In my opinion, "just cause" should be nothing less serious than a prolonged and apparently irredeemable relationship which is destructive of a person's dignity as a human being.
>
> At the same time, I have strong feelings about what is not provocation for breaking the sacred covenants of marriage. Surely it is not simply "mental distress," nor "personality differences," nor "having grown apart," nor having "fallen out of love." This is especially so where there are children.[87]

Finally, it is important that we not judge others who have gone through a divorce. Seldom are we in a position to know enough about others' intimate circumstances to fully understand why a divorce occurred. But even if we are, our responsibility is still to love and support each other (Mosiah 18: 8–9) through such difficulties.

Box 2.4

For these and many other reasons, marriage continues to be good for men, women, and children everywhere.

NOTES

1. G. Morson (1998, Autumn), Prosaics: An approach to the humanities, *The American Scholar,* 57(4), 526.

2. J. Austen (1990a), *Pride and prejudice* (New York: Oxford University Press), 3.

3. S. Nock (1998), *Marriage in men's lives* (New York: Oxford University Press), 5.

4. General social surveys (1994).

5. N. D. Glenn (1997a), A textbook assault on marriage, *The Responsive Community,* 7(4), 58.

6. N. D. Glenn (1997a), N. D. Glenn (1997b), A critique of twenty family and marriage and family textbooks, *Family Relations, 46,* 197–208.

7. W. J. Doherty (1997), How therapists threaten marriages, *The Responsive Community,* 7(3).

8. K. Hamilton and P. Wingert (1998, July 20), Down the aisle, *Newsweek,* 54–57; D. Popenoe and B. D. Whitehead (1999, June), *The state of our union: Social health of marriage in America* (New Brunswick, NJ: National Marriage Project, Rutgers), 21–22.

9. Hamilton and Wingert (1998, July 20), 56.

10. Popenoe and Whitehead (1999, June).

11. C. Bronte (1961), *Jane Eyre* (New York: Dell), 509.

12. Bronte (1961), 510.

13. J. Gottman (1999), *The seven principles for making marriage work* (New York: Crown), 5.

14. L. A. Lillard and L. J. Waite (1995). 'Til death do us part: Marital disruption and mortality, *American Journal of Sociology, 100,* 1131.

15. R. H. Coombs (1991), Marital status and personal well-being: A literature review, *Family Relations, 40,* 97–102; G. T. Stanton (1997), *Why marriage matters: Reasons to believe in marriage in postmodern society* (Colorado Springs: Pinon Press); J. J. Waite (1995), Does marriage matter? *Demography, 32,* 483–507; W. R. Gove (1973), Sex, marital status, and mortality, *American Journal of Sociology, 79,* 45–67.

16. J. S. Goodwin, W .C. Hunt, C. R. Key, and J. M. Samet (1987), The effect of marital status on stage, treatment, and survival of cancer patients, *Journal of the American Medical Association, 258,* 3129.

17. Lillard and Waite (1995); Stanton (1997); J. A. Burr, P. L. McCall, and E. Powell-Griner (1994), Catholic religion and suicide: The mediating effect of divorce, *Social Science Quarterly, 75,* 300–318; Coombs (1991); L. N. Robins and D. A. Regier, (1991). *Psychiatric disorders in America: The epidemiologic catchment area study* (New York: Free Press).

18. Stanton (1997); W .R. Gove, C. B. Style and M. Hughes, The effect of marriage on the well-being of adults: A theoretical analysis, *Journal of Family Issues, 11,* 4–35; S. Nock (1998); S. Stack and J. R. Eshleman (1998), Marital status and happiness: A 17-nation study, *Journal of Marriage and the Family, 60,* 527–536.

19. Gottman (1999), 261.

20. Robins and Regier (1991); Stanton (1997).

21. D. R. Williams, D. T. Takeuchi, and R. K. Adair (1992), Marital status and psychiatric disorders among blacks and whites, *Journal of Health and Social Behavior, 33,* 141.

22. Stanton (1997); see also Gove, Style, and Hughes (1990); K. A. Loscocco and G. Spitze (1990), Working conditions, social support, and the well-being of female and male factory workers, *Journal of Health and Social Behavior, 31,* 313–327; Stack and Eshleman (1998); Waite (1995); W. Wood, N. Rhodes, and M. Whelan (1989), Sex differences in positive well-being: A consideration of emotional style and marital status, *Psychological Bulletin, 2,* 249–264.

23. Coombs (1991), 100.

24. C. E. Ross (1995), Reconceptualizing marital status as a continuum of social attachment, *Journal of Marriage and the Family, 57,* 129.

25. J. Austen (1990b), *Sense and sensibility* (New York: Oxford University Press), 78, 324.

26. Waite (1995), 493; R. R. Rindfuss and A. VandenHeuvel (1990), Cohabitation: Precursor to marriage or an alternative to being single? *Population and Development Review, 16,* 703–726.

27. R. J. Shapiro (1990, September 27), The family under economic stress, in E. C. Karmack and W. A. Galston (Eds.), *Putting children first: A progressive family policy for the 1990s,* Whitepaper from the *Progressive Policy Institute, 12.*

28. D. T. Ellwood (1988), *Poor support: Poverty in the American family* (New York: Basic Books), 46.

29. K. Chopin (1984), *The awakening and selected stories by Kate Chopin,* ed. S. M. Gilbert (New York: Viking Penguin).

30. R. T. Michael, J. H. Gagnon, E. O. Laumann, and G. Kolata (1994). *Sex in America: A definitive survey* (Boston: Little, Brown, and Company), 1.

31. Michael et al. (1994); E. O. Laumann, A. Paik, and R. C. Rosen (1999), Sexual dysfunction in the United States: Prevalence and predictors, *Journal of the American Medical Association, 281,* 537–544.

32. Stanton (1997), 44.

33. E. Wharton (1998), *The age of innocence* (New York: Tom Doherty Associates), 254.

34. Stanton (1997).

35. D. Blankenhorn (1995), *Fatherless America: Confronting our most urgent social problem* (New York Basic Books), 330; see also Stanton (1997).

36. Stanton (1997).

37. F. Goldscheider, A. Thornton, and L. Young-DeMarco (1993), A portrait of the nest-leaving process in early adulthood, *Demography, 30,* 695.

38. Stanton (1997); Nock (1998); Waite (1995).

39. J. H. Bray (1988), Children's development during early remarriage, in E. M. Hetherington and J. D. Arasteh (Eds.), *Impact of divorce, single-parenting, and step-parenting on children* (Hillsdale, NJ: Lawrence Erlbaum Associates), 279–298; Stanton (1997).

40. Wharton (1998), 211–212.

41. T. Ooms (1998), *Toward more perfect unions: Putting marriage on the public agenda* (Washington, DC: Family Impact Seminar).

42. Gottman (1999), 243.

43. Ooms (1998), 15.

44. Stanton (1997); J. J. Lynch (1979), *The broken heart: The medical consequences of loneliness* (New York: Basic Books).

45. Nock (1998); Waite (1995).

46. Ooms (1998).

47. Waite (1995).

48. P. Berger and H. Kellner (1964, Summer), Marriage and the construction of reality, *Diogenes, 1–25.*

49. Lillard and Waite (1995); Waite (1995).

50. Lillard and Waite (1995).

51. Nock (1998), 59.

52. Nock (1998).

53. Morson (1998, Autumn), 523.

54. L. N. Tolstoy (1996), *Anna Karenina* (New York: W. W. Norton & Co).

55. Austen (1990b), 36.

56. Nock (1999).

57. B. Pym (1978). *Excellent women* (New York: Penguin Books), 188.

58. E. E. Filsinger and M. R. Wilson (1984), Religiosity, socioeconomic rewards, and family development: Predictors of marital satisfaction, *Journal of Marriage and the Family, 46,* 663, 670; M. R. Wilson and E. E. Filsinger (1986), Religiosity and marital adjustment: Multidimensional interrelationships, *Journal of Marriage and the Family, 48,* 147–151; N. D. Glenn and C. N. Weaver (1978), A multivariate, multisurvey study of marital happiness, *Journal of Marriage and the Family, 40,* 269–282; S. F. Hartley (1978), Marital satisfaction among clergy wives, *Review of Religious Research, 19,* 178–191; R. A. Hunt and M. B. King (1978), Religiosity and marriage, *Journal for the Scientific Study of Religion, 17,* 399–406; Religion plays key role in marriage stability (1989), *Emerging Trends, 11*(6), 4; W. R. Schumm,

S. R. Bollman, and A. P. Jurich (1982), The "marital convention-alization" argument: Implications for the study of religiosity and marital satisfaction, *Journal of Psychology and Theology, 10,* 236–241; D. L. Thomas and C. Carver (1990), Religion and adolescent social competence, in T. Gullota, (Ed.), *Advances in adolescent development: Vol. III, Developing social competency in adolescence* (Beverly Hills, CA: Sage); D. L. Thomas and M. Cornwall (1990), Religion and family in the 1980s: Discovery and development, *Journal of Marriage and the Family, 52,* 983–992.

59. L. C. Robinson and P. W. Blanton (1993), Marital strengths in enduring marriages, *Family Relations, 42,* 38.

60. L. C. Robinson (1994), Religious orientation in enduring marriage: An exploratory study, *Review of Religious Research, 35,* 207–218; see also L. E. Larson and J. W. Goltz (1989). Religious participation and marital commitment, *Review of Religious Research, 30,* 387–400; A. Thornton (1985), Reciprocal influences of family and religion in a changing world, *Journal of Marriage and the Family, 47,* 381–394.

61. W. Brueggermann (1977), The covenanted family: A zone for humanness, *Journal of Current Social Issues, 14,* 18–23; Robinson (1994); Robinson and Blanton (1993).

62. Robinson and Blanton (1993).

63. H. Bahr (1981), Religious intermarriage and divorce in Utah and the Mountain States, *Journal for the Scientific Study of Religion, 20,* 251–261; E. L. Lehrer (1996), The role of the husband's religious affiliation in the economic and demographic behavior of families, *Journal for the Scientific Study of Religion, 35,* 145–155.

64. G. W. Allport (1966), Religious context of prejudice, *Journal for the Scientific Study of Religion, 5,* 455; see also M. G. Dudley and F. A. Kosinski Jr. (1990), Religiosity and marital satisfaction: A research note, *Review of Religious Research, 32* (1), 78–86.

65. Gove, Style, and Hughes (1990), 27.

66. Gove, Style, and Hughes (1990), 27.

67. Z. Wu and M. J. Penning (1997), Marital instability after midlife, *Journal of Family Issues, 18,* 459–478.

68. Ooms (1998).

69. Robinson and Blanton (1993).

70. Gottman (1999).

71. Gottman (1999).

72. Gottman (1999).

73. Robinson and Blanton (1993).

74. Popenoe and Whitehead (1999), 19.

75. Popenoe and Whitehead (1999), 19.

76. T. B. Heaton (1998, October), *Factors contributing to increasing marital stability in the United States.* Presented at the National Conference on the National Survey of Family Growth. Washington, DC.

77. Wu and Penning (1997); Popenoe and Whitehead (1999).

78. J. Austen (1990c), *Mansfield Park* (New York: Oxford University Press), 432.

79. Stanton (1997).

80. Council on Families in America (1996), Marriage in America: A report to the nation, in D. Popenoe, J. B. Elshtain, and D. Blankenhorn (Eds.), *Promises to keep: Decline and renewal of marriage in America* (Lanham, MD: Rowman & Littlefield Publishers).

81. Ooms (1998).

82. D. Popenoe (1994, Spring), A world without fathers, *Wilson Quarterly, 20*(2), 12–14.

83. J. H. Larson and T. B. Holman (1994, April), Premarital predictors of marital quality and stability, *Family Relations, 43,* 228–237; S. M. Stanley, H. J. Markman, M. St. Peters, and B. D. Leber (1995, October), Strengthening marriages and preventing divorce: New directions in prevention research, *Family Relations, 44,* 392–401.

84. Gottman (1999).

85. S. Stanley (1998). *The heart of commitment* (Nashville, TN: Thomas Nelson).

86. J. H. Bray and E. N. Jouriles (1995, October). Treatment of marital conflict and prevention of divorce, *Journal of Marital and Family Therapy, 21,* 461–473.

87. James E. Faust (1993, May), Father, come home, *Ensign, 23*(5), 36–37.

THE MARRIAGE MOVEMENT IN AMERICA

BRENT A. BARLOW

We . . . solemnly proclaim that marriage between a man and a woman is ordained of God. . . .
Marriage between man and woman is essential to His eternal plan.
(The Family: A Proclamation to the World, ¶¶ 1, 7)

A few years ago, President Gordon B. Hinckley spoke at a BYU Devotional of the most challenging aspect of his duties as President of The Church of Jesus Christ of Latter-day Saints:

> I deal much with cases of divorce and requests for cancellation of temple sealings. It is the most difficult of all the things with which I have to do. Almost without exception, each case involves deception, dishonesty, broken promises, violated covenants, heartbreak, and tragedy. Begin with your own home to preserve the sanctity of your marriage, the eternity of your covenants, and the happiness that comes where there is love and security and trust in the family. Put the comfort and happiness of your companion and your children ahead of your own and reach out with a helping hand to those whose marriages have become troubled.[1]

The last sentence struck me hard: "Reach out with a helping hand to those whose marriages have become troubled." Since that time, I have devoted a great deal of professional thought and time to how I can help strengthen marriages. I'm certainly not alone. Perhaps sensing a call from the same Source, many influential leaders in the United States now are reaching out to help couples have good marriages.

It's not difficult to see why many are concerned about the institution of marriage. A series of recent reports have chronicled the challenge. In 1995, the same year *The Family: A Proclamation to the World* was published, a diverse group of excellent family scholars concluded:

> The divorce revolution—the steady displacement of a marriage culture by a culture of divorce and unwed parenthood—has failed. It has created terrible hardships for children, incurred unsupportable social costs, and failed to deliver on its promise of greater adult happiness. The time has come to shift the focus of national attention from divorce to marriage. . . . To reverse the current deterioration of child and societal well-being in the United States, we must strengthen the institution of marriage. . . . Strengthening marriage. . . . must become our most important goal. For unless we reverse the decline of marriage, no other achievements—no tax cut, no new government program, no new idea—will be powerful enough to reverse the trend of declining child well-being. . . . We call for the nation to commit itself to this overriding goal: To increase the proportion of children who grow up with their two married parents and decrease the proportion of children who do not . . . Who, today, is still promoting marriage? Who is even talking about it? In place of a national debate about what has happened to marriage there has been silence—stone-cold silence.[2]

Well, that silence has now been broken; there are many now talking boldly about the need to strengthen marriage. Other influential reports followed that documented the decline in the institution of marriage and raised serious questions.[3] During the same time period, a number of influential books and articles were published documenting the benefits to individuals, couples, families, communities, and nations of strong marriages and the consequences of failed marriages.[4] Also, many valuable books have been published now, based on good research, that help couples understand what is needed to establish and maintain a stable and happy marriage.[5]

In addition, the silence of public policy leaders has been broken at community, state, and national levels. For instance, in more than one hundred communities across the United States, religious leaders have joined together to make sure engaged couples receive a good education about how to make a happy, lasting marriage before they can be married in their religious community. Also, many of these faith communities are providing "marriage mentors" to young couples to help guide them through some of the challenges of establishing a successful marriage.

States, which have the legal responsibility to regulate marriage and divorce in the United States, and which bear a heavy financial burden for the costs of failed marriages, seem to be especially active in exploring ways to support the institution of marriage better. For instance, two states, Louisiana and Arizona, have passed legislation giving couples the choice to choose a more committed form of marriage (usually called "covenant marriage") that requires couples, among other things, to receive some form of premarital counseling and to receive marital counseling if serious problems arise in the marriage, and specifies limited grounds for divorce (e.g., abuse, infidelity, drug or alcohol abuse, felony crime). Many other states are considering similar legislation. Governor Keating of Oklahoma in his inaugural address announced a goal to reduce the divorce rate in his state—the second highest in the nation—by one-third by 2010. Similarly, Governor Huckabee of Arkansas declared a "state of marital emergency" and called for a 50 percent reduction in divorce by 2010. Wisconsin was the first state in the union to hire a "marriage czar" to work in government with civic and religious leaders to strengthen marriage. Governor and First Lady Mrs. Leavitt of Utah formed the first state commission specifically on marriage—not families—to explore ways of strengthening marriage in their state. Several governors have issued proclamations on marriage similar to the one signed in 1999 by Utah Governor Leavitt:

Whereas, marriage in every known human society creates new families, binds men and women together in a network of affection, mutual aid, and mutual obligation, commits fathers and mothers to their children and connects children to a wider network of welcoming kin; and

Whereas, a healthy, loving marriage deserves our special respect because it provides irreplaceable personal happiness and creates the safest place for children to flourish and to enjoy the full emotional, moral, educational and financial benefits of both parents; and

Whereas, research indicates that men and women who marry and stay married in mutually supportive relationships generally live longer, experience better health, and enjoy more satisfying lives; and

Whereas, marriage breakdown takes a toll on the emotional, physical, and financial well-being of all family members and communities and also increases the cost to taxpayers of many public service programs; and

Whereas, Utahns are committed to promoting enrichment opportunities and resources that strengthen marital relationships and enhance personal growth, mutual fulfillment, and family well-being; and

Whereas, I wish to applaud and encourage efforts by Utah citizens, faith communities, businesses, organizations, and local government and community leaders to strengthen marriages in a variety of ways, including marriage education programs, conferences, enrichment seminars and public policies that support marriage;

Now, Therefore, I , Michael O. Leavitt, Governor of the State of Utah, declare a Marriage Awareness Week, and urge each husband and wife to reflect upon their marriage and to commit to building and maintaining a healthy, loving marriage and family.

At the national level, anticipating the legal challenge of those who desire to make marriage available to same-sex couples, the U.S. Congress passed the Defense of Marriage Act in 1996, defining marriage as a relationship between a man and a woman. Also, the U.S. House of Representatives recently passed the "Fathers Count" Act, which specifically links the promotion of good fathering to strengthening marriage by providing more funding to organizations working to strengthen marriage.

The last fifty years have seen an unprecedented increase in divorce, nonmarital births, nonmarital cohabitations, sexual relations outside of marriage, spouse abuse, and other trends harmful to the institution of marriage and the participants. It's not surprising, then, that young people today are more cautious about marriage and even more doubtful that they can attain a lasting and happy marriage.[6]

Thankfully, however, there is also a burgeoning marriage movement in the United States and elsewhere that seeks to reverse these trends by establishing public policies that support marriage and educating couples on how to achieve lasting and happy marriages. One of the great blessings in my life has been the professional opportunity to be a small part of this movement and to help train students to participate in it, as well, to be "anxiously engaged in [this] good cause, and do many things of their own free will, and bring to pass much righteousness" (D&C 58:27).

NOTES

1. Gordon B. Hinckley, *BYU speeches of the year 1996–1997* (Provo, UT: Brigham Young University), 24.

2. Council on Families in America (1995), *Marriage in America: A report to the nation* (New York: Institute for American Values), 1, 4.

3. The National Marriage Project (1999, June), *The state of our unions 1999* (New Brunswick, NJ: Rugters, the State University of New Jersey, The National Marriage Project).

4. D. Blankenhorn (1995), *Fatherless America: Confronting our most urgent social problem* (New York: Basic Books); M. Gallagher (1996), *The abolition of marriage: How we destroy lasting love* (Washington, DC: Regnery); D. B. Larson, J. P. Swyers, and S. S. Larson (1995), *The costly consequences of divorce: Assessing the clinical, economic and public health impact of marital disruption in the United States* (Rockville, MD: National Institute for Healthcare Research); S. L. Nock (1998), *Marriage in men's lives* (New York: Oxford University); G. T. Stanton (1997), *Why marriage matters: Reasons to believe in marriage in postmodern society* (Colorado Springs, Co: Pinon); L. J. Waite (1995), Does marriage matter? *Demography, 32.*

5. J. M. Gottman and N. Silver (1999), *The seven principles for making marriage work* (New York: Crown); M.J. McMannus (1993), *Marriage savers: Helping your friends and family stay married* (Grand Rapids, MI: Zondervan); S. Stanley (1998), *The heart of commitment* (Nashville: Thomas Nelson); J. Wallerstein and S. Blakeslee (1995), *The good marriage: How and why love lasts* (Boston: Houghton Mifflin); M. Weiner-Davis (1992), *Divorce busting: A revolutionary and rapid program for staying together* (New York: Simon & Schuster).

6. D. Popenoe and B. D. Whitehead (1999, January). *Should we live together: What young adults need to know about cohabitation before marriage* (New Brunswick, NJ: Rutgers, The State University of New Jersey, The National Marriage Project).

CHAPTER 3

PREPARING FOR AN ETERNAL MARRIAGE

THOMAS B. HOLMAN, JEFFRY H. LARSON, AND ROBERT F. STAHMANN

. . . marriage between a man and a woman is ordained of God. . . .
Marriage between man and woman is essential to His eternal plan.
(The Family: A Proclamation to the World, ¶¶ 1, 7)

President Gordon B. Hinckley said of marriage: "This will be the most important decision of your life, the individual whom you marry. . . . Marry the right person in the right place at the right time."[1] Similarly, Elder Bruce R. McConkie stated: "The most important things that any member of The Church of Jesus Christ of Latter-day Saints ever does in this world are: 1. To marry the right person, in the right place, by the right authority; and 2. To keep the covenant made in connection with this holy and perfect order of matrimony."[2]

Why is this such an important decision? Where is the "right place" and what is the "right authority"? Who is the "right person"? When is the "right time"? "How does one become and find a person who will "keep the covenant" associated with temple marriage?

In this chapter we address these and other questions about the process of selecting an eternal companion. We begin with the words of Apostles and prophets on the importance of the marriage decision and the present prophetic counsel on where to marry and by what authority. We then turn to a discussion of both being and finding a "right person" to marry. Since a right person is not fashioned or found in a vacuum, we turn next to a discussion of establishing a "right relationship" before marriage and of recognizing how things from past and present environments influence relationships and the people in them. Timing is also important, and we consider the "right time" in life for

marriage as well as how to move through the process called courtship and engagement. Since all serious relationships, and even engagements, do not and should not result in marriage, we also deal with breaking up. Lastly we briefly examine the engagement period, the wedding, and the honeymoon.

THE MOST IMPORTANT DECISION

The Proclamation states that marriage between a man and a woman is essential to God's plan for us, His children. It follows that the decision to marry is therefore of utmost importance. Numerous prophets have commented on why the marriage decision is so momentous. President Spencer W. Kimball put it this way: "Marriage is perhaps the most vital of all the decisions and has the most far-reaching effects, for it has to do not only with immediate happiness, but eternal joy as well. It affects not only the two people involved, but their families and particularly their children and their children's children down through the many generations."[3]

The Right Place, the Right Authority

For a believing Latter-day Saint, there can be no question as to where and how to get married—in an LDS temple by someone holding the sealing power. President Gordon B. Hinckley said, "There is no substitute for marrying in the temple. It is the only place under the heavens where marriage can be solemnized for eternity."[4]

The Right Person

We suspect that most Latter-day Saints understand what we have written so far about the importance of the decision to marry and the decision to marry in the temple. A person committed to temple marriage must then ask themselves: "Whom should I marry?" "How do I identify the 'right person' for me?"

Everyone has advice for single people considering marriage. The rock group, the Beatles, sang: "All you need is love, love; love is all you need." Newsstand magazines claim: "Good communication is all you really need." Television and films seem to shout: "Find someone who is good-looking, someone who really 'turns you on,' then you'll be happy!"

Fortunately, we have a great deal of counsel from sources much better than the Beatles, magazines, or television and films. The words of the Savior in the scriptures and the teachings of inspired ancient and modern prophets set us on the right path. Not surprisingly, this divine and prophetic counsel is supported by more than 60 years of social science research on premarital predictors of later marital quality and stability.[5] In this section we look at what the scriptures and General Authorities have taught about spouse selection and offer as a "second witness" the results of research on premarital phenomena that influence later marital success.

But first, we need to clarify what is meant by "the right person." Latter-day Saints sometimes get led astray by the idea that there is a "one-and-only" somewhere out there with whom we made a covenant to marry in the premortal existence, one who is the only person with whom we could be happy. This romantic ideal, however, is not supported by the prophets. President Boyd K. Packer has said:

> While I am sure some young couples have some special guidance in getting together, I do not believe in predestined love. . . . You must do the choosing, rather than to seek for some one-and-only so-called soul mate, chosen for you by someone else and waiting for you.[6]

President Kimball said it even more forcefully:

> "Soulmates" are fiction and an illusion; and while every young man and young woman will seek with all diligence and prayerfulness to find a mate with whom

life can be most compatible and beautiful, yet it is certain that almost any good man and any good woman can have happiness and a successful marriage if both are willing to pay the price.[7]

Evidently, seeking for a mate is not a matter of waiting for that "one-and-only" to walk by and grab you. Indeed, President Packer and President Kimball make it clear that we are expected to choose our spouse wisely and prayerfully. Counsel from Church leaders and supportive ideas from the social sciences can help a person choose wisely. We also discuss in greater detail the issue of receiving a "spiritual confirmation" through prayer. Now, we return to how to be and find a "right person" to marry.[8]

Being a Right Person

One of the most important principles we learn from the scriptures to help us choose an eternal companion is articulated by the Savior in Matthew 7:3–5:

> And why beholdest thou the mote that is in thy brother's eye, but considerest not the beam that is in thine own eye? Or how wilt thou say to thy brother, Let me pull out the mote out of thine eye; and, behold, a beam is in thine own eye? Thou hypocrite, first cast out the beam out of thine own eye; and then shalt thou see clearly to cast out the mote out of thy brother's eye.

Elder Neal A. Maxwell spoke more specifically to those in families, including those in the courtship stage, when he said:

> If the choice is between reforming other Church members [including fiances, spouses, or children] or ourselves, is there really any question about where we should begin? The key is to have our eyes wide open to our own faults and partially closed to the faults of others—not the other way around! The imperfections of others never release us from the need to work on our own shortcomings.[9]

Thus, as we think about the prophetic counsel and the research cited below on choosing a spouse, we need first to apply the ideas and counsel to ourselves; then we can more appropriately evaluate another's rightness for us.

ESSENTIAL ATTRIBUTES OF AN ETERNAL COMPANION

Numerous apostles and prophets have spoken about the process of seeking an eternal companion. Elder Richard G. Scott suggested several "essential attributes that bring happiness," which we should look for in a potential mate: "a deep love of the Lord and of His commandments, a determination to live them, one that is kindly, understanding, forgiving of others, and willing to give of self, with the desire to have a family crowned with beautiful children and a commitment to teach them the principles of truth in the home."[10]

Elder Hugh B. Brown taught that we should marry someone "who has achieved physical, mental, emotional, and spiritual maturity." Someone "who has achieved self-control."[11]

President Hinckley taught: "Be true to yourselves, and your respect for yourself will increase. Know that yours is a divine birthright. Cultivate a good opinion of yourselves."[12]

The scriptures teach that this kind of self-respect, or confidence in oneself, comes from being charitable and virtuous in thought and not from comparing yourself to another or becoming conceited : "Let thy bowels also be full of charity towards all men, and to the household of faith, and let virtue garnish thy thoughts unceasingly; then shall thy confidence wax strong in the presence of God" (see D&C 121:45).

Social science research has also noted the importance of such personal characteristics. Some of the premarital personal characteristics that have the most influence on later marital success include impulse control, emotional/mental health, sociability, and self-esteem. Impulsive people act quickly before thinking. They fail to first consider the consequences of their actions on themselves or others. Emotional health is evidenced by the presence or absence of abnormally high anxiety, clinical depression, irritability, self-consciousness, and hostility. People with a good sense of who they are and their worth as individuals are more likely to be unselfish, considerate of others, and supportive. Low self-worth leads to the opposite conditions: selfishness, inconsiderateness, and an inability to support others emotionally. Another important resource to have in a marriage is a moderate degree of sociability. People who are moderately sociable, who relate fairly well with others and are fairly comfortable in social situations, tend to have the communication and conflict-management skills necessary to form long-term close personal relationships such as marriage.

Finally, attitudes or beliefs that researchers have identified that seem to have strong negative effects on marital satisfaction include beliefs that "people cannot change," that "marriage and family isn't all that important," or that "making money is the most important thing in life for me." Alternately, beliefs about the innate goodness of others, about the importance of marriage and family life, and beliefs that problems can be solved lead to stronger marriages.

The recent counsel of President Hinckley about choosing an eternal companion seems an appropriate way to summarize what prophets and Apostles teach us:

> Choose a companion you can always honor, you can always respect, one who will complement you in your own life, one to whom you can give your entire heart, your entire love, your entire allegiance, your entire loyalty.[13]

Thus, while research suggests the importance of personality, self-esteem, emotional health, values, attitudes, and beliefs, prophets counsel us to look more deeply into the spiritual attributes, dispositions, maturity, and commitment to gospel principles of our prospective companion and ourselves. They counsel us first and foremost to seek a man or woman of God, and to become one ourselves.

Before leaving this topic, we should mention that the Saints have been counseled to seek someone who is clearly on a righteous track, but we must be careful not to expect perfection in a potential mate. In his general conference talks to single adult men and women of the Church, President Ezra Taft Benson counseled both men and women "do not expect perfection in your choice of a mate."[14] Indeed, Elder Scott recently made this comment: "I suggest that you not ignore many possible candidates who are still developing these attributes, seeking the one who is perfected in them. You will likely not find that perfect person, and if you did, there would certainly be no interest in you. These attributes are best polished together as husband and wife."[15]

THE RIGHT RELATIONSHIP

We have received a great deal of counsel from Church leaders on the kind of couple relationship we need to establish before entering into an eternal marriage. Much of this counsel corresponds with the findings of social science research. Research has demonstrated, for example, that the more similar the backgrounds, the happier the marriage. President Kimball wrote:

> We recommend that people marry those who are of the same racial background generally, and of somewhat the same economic and social and educational

CHARACTERISTICS OF IMMATURE AND MATURE LOVE

ASPECTS OF LOVE	IMMATURE LOVE	MATURE LOVE
Emotional Part of Love	Possessiveness Jealousy Infatuation Preoccupation Anxiety	Lasting Passion Desire for Companionship Warm Feeling of Contentment
Belief Part of Love	"Love is blind" Love is external to us "Cupid's Arrow" Love is beyond our control	Love is something you have to "decide" Love means: Commitment Trust Sharing Sacrifice
Behavior Part of Love	Selfish Lustful Concern only for satisfying own needs Clinging Over-Dependent Demanding of obedience from partner	Creates an environment of growth and development Allows partner space for growth

Based on Patricia Noller's 1996 article, "What Is This Thing Called Love? Defining the Love That Supports Marriage and Family." *Personal Relationships, 3,* 97–115. Scriptural references: 1 Cor. 13; Col. 3:8; Mosiah 2:32; Alma 5:30–31; 12:14; 3 Ne. 11:29; Moro. 7:47–48; D&C 20:54; 88:124; 136:23.

Box 3.1

background. Some of those are not an absolute necessity, but preferred; and above all, the same religious background, without question.[16]

When we marry someone similar to us, especially one who is of our faith, we increase the likelihood that we will share many of the same values, attitudes, and beliefs about the importance of marriage and family life, children, and myriad other things. As President Kimball also stated, "The difficulties and hazards of marriage are greatly increased where backgrounds are different."[17]

While a good relationship begins with similarity of background and values, it deepens as couples learn to solve problems, resolve differences, and increase agreement on important issues. Two hallmarks of

good premarital relationships that Church leaders have stressed are love and communication. These two things help couples solve problems, resolve differences, and increase consensus on important issues. On love, Elder Marvin J. Ashton said:

True love is a process. True love requires personal action. Love must be continuing to be real. Love takes time. Too often expediency, infatuation, stimulation, persuasion, or lust are mistaken for love. How hollow, how empty if our love is no deeper than the arousal of momentary feeling or the expression in words of what is no more lasting than the time it takes to speak them.[18]

President Spencer W. Kimball helped a young couple on the verge of marriage with this counsel:

SELECTED SCRIPTURAL REFERENCES TO NEGATIVE AND POSITIVE COMMUNICATION

SPIRITUAL REFERENCE	NEGATIVE COMMUNICATION (That Which Destroys)	POSITIVE COMMUNICATION (That Which Builds)
Eph. 4:29, 31–32	Corrupt, bitter, angry, loud, malicious	Edifying, gracious, kind
Matt. 12:34–37	From an evil heart: idle words, resulting in condemnation	Tenderhearted, forgiving
Matt. 15:16–20	From an evil heart: a mouth that defiles. From evil thoughts: evil deeds	From a good heart: good things, resulting in being justified
Prov. 8:6–9	Wickedness, rudeness, perversion	
Prov. 15:1–2	Grievous words stir up anger. Fools speak foolishness	Excellent things, right things, truth, righteousness, plainness
Prov. 15:28		Heart of the righteous studieth his answer
Col. 4:6		Speech with grace, seasoned with salt
D&C 121:41–45	Reproving, correcting, without the Holy Ghost and without an increase in love	Speech with contrite spirit, meek language that edifies. Speech that demonstrates persuasion, long-suffering, meekness, love unfeigned, kindness, pure knowledge, without hypocrisy, without guile. Reproof or correction only when moved upon by the Holy Ghost and with an increase in love.

Box 3.2

Love in marriage transcends sex. Your love, like a flower, must be nourished. There will come a great love and interdependence between you, for your love is a divine one. It is deep, all-inclusive, most comprehensive. It is not like that association of the world which is misnamed love, but which is mostly physical attraction. . . . The love of which the Lord speaks is. . . . faith, confidence, understanding, and partnership. It is devotion and companionship, parenthood, common ideals and standards. It is cleanliness of life and sacrifice and unselfishness. This kind of love never tires nor wanes. It lives on through sickness and sorrow, through prosperity and privation, through accomplishment and disappointment, through time and eternity. . . . You must live and treat each other in a manner that your love will grow. Today it is a demonstrative love, but in the tomorrows of ten, thirty, fifty years it will be a far greater and more intensified love, grown quieter and more dignified with the years of sacrifice, suffering, joys, and consecration to each other, to your family, and to the kingdom of God.[19]

Researchers have also found that the greater the love couples have in their relationships before they marry, the more successful their marriages.[20] However, one researcher reviewed dozens of studies on love and found that there is both "immature love" and "mature love." Mature love, she declared, is the kind of love needed for successful "marriage and family life."[21] Love, whether immature or mature love, has three aspects—an emotional part, a belief part, and a behavioral part. Box 3.1 shows the characteristics of immature and mature love.

Notice how the characteristics of love spoken of by Elder Ashton and President Kimball mirror the characteristics that research has found to be the mature kind of love upon which stable, high-quality marriages and family life are built. But the love of which these Church leaders speak goes beyond the love even the best social science research has discovered. It includes, as President Kimball noted, a "consecration" to partner, to family, and also the kingdom of God. This kind of love is intimately connected to covenants and to our love of the Lord. It is a love "that binds them to each other and to the Lord."[22] This kind of love eschews the lust and selfishness of premarital sex and unlawful cohabitation. This kind of love cares more about the other person than the self.

This kind of love also leads to a high-quality communication that allows dating and engaged couples to build a strong foundation of agreement on important issues and a pattern of solving problems and resolving conflict that will serve them throughout their married lives. The research of social scientists makes it abundantly clear that high-quality communication, begun before marriage and continued into the marriage, is one of the most important aspects of success in marriage.[23] Church leaders make it no less clear. Elder A. Theodore Tuttle of the Seventy said: "Couples young and old must learn to communicate with one another. This one thing alone can solve most marital problems."[24]

Communication is largely a function of the heart. Jesus taught, "Out of the abundance of the heart the mouth speaketh" (Matt. 12:34). There are instances of both negative and positive communication in the scriptures. Negative communication can destroy relationships; positive communication builds and edifies. Box 3.2 shows what the scriptures teach us about negative and positive communication. Elder Ashton built upon these truths when he said, "If we would know true love and understanding one for another, we must realize that communication is more than a sharing of words. It is the *wise* sharing of emotions, feelings, and concerns. It is the sharing of oneself totally."[25]

The way we communicate in dating and courtship usually influences how our partner will feel about us and our relationship. Relationships are established upon the comfort and trust created by sincere communication. Positive communication, practiced in dating and courtship, increases the likelihood of greater commitment, better conflict resolution, and more love between partners. Good communication begins with a righteous heart that desires the welfare of the partner. However, a good heart with no communication skills may lead to misunderstandings. On the other hand, skillful communication from a selfish heart is generally just manipulation.

PERSONAL AND RELATIONSHIP CONTEXTS

When asked what constitutes a successful marriage, most people mention characteristics of the two people or characteristics of their relationship together. As we have pointed out, these things are important, but there are other things also. We have called these other things "contexts" and divided them between personal contexts and relationship contexts.

Personal contexts include family-of-origin influences like the degree of cohesion or unity in the family in which the person grew up, the quality of one's relationships with parents, and the quality of parents' marriage. Other personal context characteristics include your age, education level, and socioeconomic level at the time you marry. In general, in most industrialized societies, an older age at marriage (i.e., age 20 or greater), more education, and more financial resources help increase the chances of a happy and stable marriage.

Relationship context influences refer to the situation or environment in which the individuals and couple lives. Examples of premarital relationship context factors that will affect later marital satisfaction include (1) Parental approval of the marriage, (2) friends' approval, and (3) external and internal pressures to marry or barriers to getting married.

Parental and friend approval are positively related to later marital quality. Pressures may be self-induced internal pressure to get married (e.g., a person age 25 may feel that he or she "should be married by now") or external pressure (e.g., parental or peer pressure because parents want grandchildren or all of one's roommates are getting married). These pressures sometimes result in individuals marrying before they are emotionally, financially, or occupationally ready. Besides pressures to marry, there can also be barriers to marrying. Many couples feel pressure from others or from changing social norms to delay marriage because of career demands or to live together rather than marry.

Unfortunately, much social science theory and research treat these contextual issues as if these factors *determine* much of the course of marriage. The gospel of Jesus Christ, while acknowledging that factors external to ourselves or our relationship can influence what we can or cannot do, helps us see that we are not mere pawns of family, social, economic, or cultural pressures.

The gospel of Jesus Christ teaches that all of us possess the God-given gift of moral agency, the ability and responsibility to choose good or evil. The circumstances, or contexts, within which a relationship develops influence the array we have to choose from and the conditions under which we must exercise our agency. Elder Maxwell taught that "Of course our genes, circumstances, and environments matter very much, and they shape us significantly. Yet," he continued, "there remains an inner zone in which we are sovereign, unless we abdicate. In this zone lies the essence of our individuality and our personal accountability." Elder Maxwell further taught that "God thus takes into merciful account not only our desires and our performance, but also the degrees of difficulty which our varied circumstances impose upon us."[26]

Social science research has addressed some of those circumstances, or contexts, that influence us. One of the most important of those contexts is our family background. Much of who we are and how we act is shaped by the family we came from. While we can do little to change our "gene pool," we can choose how to respond to the events and conditions of our upbringing, and courtship is one of the most opportune times to do so. President David O. McKay said: "In our early youth, our environment is largely determined for us, but . . . in courtship and marriage we can modify, aye, can control to a very great extent, our environment. Morally speaking, we can carve the very atmosphere in which we live."[27]

What if our childhood included a parental divorce, poor-quality relations with parents, or even abuse? Are we doomed to suffer the consequences of our parents' iniquities "unto the third and fourth generation"? (Ex. 20:5; Deut. 5:9; D&C 124:50). The scriptures that warn of wickedness being passed on to the third and fourth generation also show the way out of a troubled family background. Doctrine and Covenants 124:50, for example, states that the iniquities of the fathers will be visited upon the head of the children "so long as they [the children] repent not, and hate me." Thus, repentance and loving the Lord can free us from the sins or weaknesses of our parents.

The Book of Mormon is replete with examples of how to deal with parental influences, and speaks of them as the "traditions of [the] fathers." The story of the Lamanites who responded to the teaching of Ammon and his brethren is a powerful example of a people who overcame generations of "wicked traditions of the fathers." In brief, the Book of Mormon teaches that we can overcome these negative effects by studying the scriptures, having faith in the Lord, allowing ourselves to be taught by one having the Spirit, suffering in patience the afflictions that parents have brought upon us, and by repenting of any of the unrighteous or unhelpful habits and behaviors of our parents that we have picked up (see Mosiah 1:5; Alma 9:16–17; Alma 17:9, 15; Alma 25:6; Hel. 15:7). People who have suffered severe abuse or trauma may benefit from adding therapy or counseling with a trustworthy professional to their efforts to increase their readiness.

Elder Richard L. Evans suggests another concern: not only is it important to have family (and friends) on our side and supportive of the upcoming marriage, it is also important to consult them concerning this most important decision. Even though premarital couples may be defensive about negative comments or views about their impending marriage, often the truth is that the parents or friends may see potential problems or weaknesses to which the couple is blind. "Don't let this choice [of a marriage partner] ever be made except with earnest, searching, prayerful consideration, confiding in parents, [and] in faithful, mature, trustworthy friends."[28]

Loving parents who genuinely want the best for their child, and "faithful, mature, trustworthy friends" can often act as a sounding board, help their child or friend see beyond the romance of the moment, and counsel how best to proceed.

PROBLEMS FACING LDS COUPLES ENTERING MARRIAGE

Before moving on to the next section we want to share some information available from the perspective of LDS professional counselors as to problems facing LDS couples entering marriage. From a list of 29 possible problem areas, LDS counselors, who were members of the Association of Mormon Counselors and Psychotherapists, were asked to estimate the percentage of LDS premarital couples who would have problems or complaints in each area. Six of the 29 potential problem areas were estimated to occur frequently (at least 50 percent of the time) in LDS couples entering first marriages.[29] These problem areas and estimated percent of couples facing each are: unrealistic expectations of marriage or spouse (71%), communication (69%), money management/finances (58%), decision making/problem solving (54%), power struggles (53%), and sex (50%).

We have already discussed several of these areas that counselors see as most frequently causing problems for premarital couples. We need to say just a few words about three more of them—money management/finances, power struggles, and sexual relations.

Financial Issues

Young couples often believe they can "live on love." Setting up housekeeping with deposits, rent, food expenses, car expenses, etc., quickly disabuses most couples of this romantic notion. Couples are wise to prepare before marriage by taking a class on money management or reading a book on finances, talking over their beliefs about money, and seeking counsel from parents, married friends, or financial professionals about preparing financially for marriage. Two of the most important things couples can do are save money and stay out of debt. A huge diamond ring or exotic honeymoon, for example, may be impressive, but the burden of several years of payments can dim the luster of the ring or the memories of the trip considerably.

Power Struggles

Power struggles in a marriage are often related to unresolved personal or couple issues or unhealthy personal characteristics. Such issues as marital roles and responsibilities must be clarified and worked out before marriage and during the early months of marriage. Increased ability for overall communication and decision making go a long way in resolving and preventing power struggles. It takes time for a couple to discover these potential problems, and it takes time to establish a good foundation to deal with them. Not knowing each other well and rushing into marriage with a short courtship and engagement greatly increases the likelihood that serious problems will not be discovered or dealt with until after the couple is married.

Sexual Intimacy

Being prepared for sexual intimacy was also identified as a frequently occurring problem area. Marriage counselors have found that sexual "problems" most often are not problems, but frustrations that occur in the normal development of a healthy marital sexual relationship. This is because the sexual aspect of marriage is closely linked to the emotional and personal elements in the relationship. In marriage, the couple wants and needs to achieve a sexual relationship that expresses, sustains, and renews their deepest and most tender feelings for each other. To fully understand each other in these intimate ways takes time. As President Kimball said, quoting Reverend Billy Graham:

> The Bible celebrates sex and its proper use, presenting it as God-created, God-ordained, God-blessed. It makes plain that God himself implanted the physical magnetism between the sexes for two reasons: for the propagation of the human race, and for the expression of that kind of love between man and wife that makes for true oneness. . . . It can be a creative force more powerful than any other in the fostering of a love, companionship, happiness or can be the most destructive of all life's forces.[30]

Readers will find additional discussions of marital intimacy issues in Chapter 4. It is sufficient for us to note that while sexually arousing discussions and situations must be avoided before marriage, a thorough understanding of sexuality and of each other's values, attitudes, beliefs, and desires about sexual matters important for couple consideration.

To summarize the last three sections, one needs to *be* a "right person" as well as *find* a "right person"; the quality of the couple relationship established before marriage influences the quality of the marriage; and circumstances from our past and our present

MYTHS ABOUT SELECTING A MATE

A myth is a widely held belief that is not supported by research evidence and inhibits individuals from solving life's problems and attaining happiness. These myths relate to selecting a person to marry. Read each myth and decide if you endorse it. Then, consider the alternative, more realistic, and functional belief that we encourage you to consider.

MYTH	ALTERNATIVE
1. There is a "one and only" right person in the world for me to marry.	1. I can be happy with one of several possible partners.
2. Until I find the perfect person to marry, I should not be satisfied.	2. No one is perfect. Selecting a partner based on the qualities that are most important to me and the ability to compromise when all the qualities are not present will guide my selection of a partner to marry.
3. I should feel totally competent as a future spouse before getting married.	3. Although I should feel competent to be a spouse, some anxiety about my competence is natural.
4. We should prove our relationship will work before getting married.	4. There is no way to prove a marriage will work before getting married. If we have good communication, commitment, and Christlike attitudes, we will likely be able to adjust to each other and solve issues.
5. I can be happy with anyone I choose to marry if I try hard enough.	5. It takes two mature and well-adjusted adults to make a marriage work.
6. Being in love with someone is sufficient reason to marry them.	6. Although love is important, similarity of values, individual maturity, realistic expectations, good couple communication skills, and other factors are at least as important to marital satisfaction.
7. It doesn't matter if we have known each other for only a short period of time as long as we know we are "right" for each other.	7. The longer you know each other before marriage, the better your chances for marital satisfaction.
8. The sign of a perfect relationship is the absence of conflict.	8. All couples will experience disagreements; it is *how* they resolve their differences that is important.
9. Marrying in the temple is a guarantee for marital satisfaction.	9. Temple covenants do not mean that one's marriage is guaranteed to work or that marriage will be easy, but living those covenants consistently will make resolving differences and coping with stress easier.

Reference for myths 1–6: J. J. Larson (1996), "Challenging Irrational Beliefs about Partner Selection," *Directions in Clinical and Counseling Psychology*, 6, 2–12. Reference for myths 7–9: T. Faddis and C. Faddis (1999), "Myths Commonly Held by Latter-day Saints upon Entering Marriage," unpublished paper, Brigham Young University.

Box 3.3

environments affect the way our relationships develop. Statements of Church leaders, the scriptures, and research all suggest the importance of each of these areas and provide insights into how to strengthen ourselves and our relationships relative to each area.

But we need to know more than where to marry, by what authority to marry, the characteristics of a good future marital partner and good premarital relationships, and how past and present circumstances affect relationship development. We also need to know when to get married. The question of when involves understanding how old (mature) we ought to be, plus how long or short the courtship and engagement period should be. The social sciences provide us some clues about timing and so do Church leaders. We now move on to a discussion of President Hinckley's counsel that we marry "at the right time."

THE RIGHT TIME

From Acquaintance to Commitment

In most cultures where people are allowed to seek out their future spouse on their own and decide together whether or not to get married, a process unfolds that G. Levinger describes with his A-B-C-D-E model.[31] He suggests that one begins with the Acquaintance/Attraction stage. This can be followed by the Buildup stage, the Commitment stage, a Deterioration stage, and an Ending stage. Not all couples, of course, go through all stages, nor do they necessarily go through them in order. In general, however, relationships that end up in marriage include at least the first three stages.

Speaking of initially finding or searching out a mate, numerous prophets have admonished the Saints to search among those who have similar backgrounds. As we previously noted, President Kimball and others recommend we marry within our own racial, social, educational, and especially religious group. This is, as President Kimball said a recommendation, and carries no connotation of sin if not followed. The counsel to choose a person of the same religious background is clearly of the upmost importance if one wishes to enjoy a happy, eternal marriage. President Hinckley explained it this way, "Choose a companion of your own faith. You are much more likely to be happy."[32]

The Acquaintance/Attraction phase for Latter-day Saints usually includes physical attraction. As

President Harold B. Lee said: "Our Creator has placed within the breast of every true man and woman a strong mutual attraction for each other, which acquaintance ripens in friendship, thence through the romance of courtship, and finally matures into happy marriage."[33]

But physical attraction alone is not enough. As President Hunter said, "Marriages do not endure when they have no ground except in physical attraction."[34] It must include getting to know each other, sharing feelings, core values, attitudes, ideals, and dreams. This initial attraction must lead to other attractions and sharing, otherwise we are inclined to forget to develop the friendship that is so important to stable marriage.

As Church leaders recognize, the love that is based on more than physical attraction or lust takes time to develop. A number of the prophets have counseled the Saints not to be too hasty in making the decision to marry a particular person, but also not to put marriage off too long. Said President Lee, speaking to returned missionaries:

> Now don't misunderstand me. I am not trying to urge you younger men to marry too early. I think therein is one of the hazards of today's living. We don't want a young man to think of marriage until he is able to take care of a family, to have an institution of his own, to be independent. He must make sure that he has found the girl of his choice, they have gone together long enough that they know each other, and that they know each other's faults and they still love each other. I have said to the mission presidents (some of whom have been reported to us as saying to missionaries, "Now, if you are not married in six months, you are a failure as a missionary"), "Don't you ever say that to one of your missionaries. Maybe in six months they will not have found a wife; and if they take you seriously, they may rush into a marriage that will be wrong for them." Please don't misunderstand what we are saying; but, brethren, think more seriously about the obligations of marriage for those who bear the holy priesthood at a time when marriage should be the expectation of every man who understands [his] responsibility.[35]

President Lee's counsel can apply as equally to young women as to the young men of the Church. Young men need not move too quickly after their missions to marry; young women need not move too quickly after high school, college, or missions to marry. Both young men and young women need to go together long enough to know each other well. They need to be sure they are not marrying in haste or for the wrong reasons, such as out of the desire to keep up with friends, roommates, or former missionary companions; or out of spite toward parents or to get out of an unhappy home environment; or "on the rebound" after a breakup; or simply because they have a strong physical attraction toward each other.

At the other end of the spectrum are those who move too slowly. When we reach the age when marriage should be our next priority, putting it off can lead to selfishness and unhappiness. "I hope," said President Hinckley, "you will not put off marriage too long. I do not speak so much to the young women as to the young men whose prerogative and responsibility it is to take the lead in this matter. Don't go on endlessly in a frivolous dating game. Look for a choice companion, one you can love, honor, and respect, and make a decision."[36]

"[A]nd make a decision" says President Hinckley. A study of American LDS couples showed that like other Americans, they believed the decision of whom to marry was theirs to make—not that of their parents or a matchmaker. But unlike other Americans, they tended to consult a higher source for the final decision—they sought through prayer to receive what they called "spiritual confirmation" of their decision to marry a particular person.[37] But getting spiritual confirmation is not a simple matter of asking.

Inspiration, Infatuation, or Desperation: Seeking Spiritual Confirmation

In other contexts we have already quoted prophets who have suggested the importance of making the marriage decision prayerfully. Latter-day Saints understand that we should seek the guidance of the Lord in all things, whether in the conduct of daily life or in major decisions. The scriptures and Church leaders demonstrate that in this "most important decision" several factors need to be kept in mind as we seek spiritual confirmation.

1. Live worthy of inspiration. Elder Boyd K. Packer reminds us that "if [we] desire the inspiration of the Lord in this crucial decision, [we] must live the standards of the Church."[38] Clearly, we must be worthy to receive the inspiration we need.

2. Exercise agency and inspiration. Elder Bruce R. McConkie notes that we need to understand the balance between agency and inspiration. On the one hand, we have been given the power to choose and we are expected to exercise that right. But, we have

also been told to seek guidance from the Lord in all things. The fundamental principle, he says, is this: "We're supposed to learn correct principles and then govern ourselves. We make our own choices, and then we present the matter to the Lord and get his approving, ratifying seal."[39]

A number of Presidents of the Church have suggested the same relationship between agency (doing all we can do) and inspiration. For example, President Kimball wrote:

In selecting a companion for life and for eternity, certainly the most careful planning and thinking and praying and fasting should be done to be sure that of all the decisions, this one must not be wrong.[40]

And President Gordon B. Hinckley said:

All of this [a good marriage and happy family life] can come to pass if you make this most important decision, one guided by prayer as well as instinct, of choosing a dear companion who will be yours through thick and thin forever, throughout all eternity.[41]

3. Ask in faith. We must believe that the Lord answers such petitions. In the Doctrine and Covenants Oliver Cowdery was told that if he asked in faith, with an honest heart, believing he would receive, and if he studied it out in his mind and then asked if the decision that he made was right, he would receive either a confirmation of the correctness of his choice or an indication that his decision was wrong: ". . . and if it is right I will cause that your bosom shall burn within you; therefore you shall feel that it is right. But if it be not right you shall have no such feelings, but you shall have a stupor of thought that shall cause you to forget the thing which is wrong" (D&C 9:8–9).

Some people expect this burning to come in a profound way, but the common ways of the Spirit, that is, a still, small voice that whispers that truth or confirmation to our hearts and minds, are more likely. The experience of one young man illustrates this:

There are two things in my life that I've always felt would be important: a career and marriage. Yet at the time I didn't feel like I was getting a response. I prayed, "Heavenly Father, this is so important, I need to know whether or not it's right." Then toward the end of our courtship, I went to the temple. I was so frustrated because I wasn't getting an answer either way. After praying and waiting for an answer, I got more frustrated and gave up. That was when an impression came to me: "You already know the

REMARRIAGE

- Marriage is popular and so is remarriage. Remarriage, whether the result of death of a spouse or divorce, is common. In the United States almost half (46%) of marriages performed on any day are remarriages for either the bride, the groom, or both.

- For couples entering any marriage there are often feelings of anxiety and apprehension, and this is true of remarriages also. Such feelings are normal and actually may enhance the likelihood that the remarriage will be satisfying and stable.

- It is important that the remarital couple (and any children) understand each other's past as they build the future together in their new marriage. The personal context of the remarrying couple will include the life experiences of at least one spouse having been previously married. Thus, there are family relationships and experiences from that marriage that can influence the remarriage.

- The study of LDS counselors, cited in the body of the chapter, identified two potential problem areas unique to remarrying couples—children and problems related to the previous marriage. In regard to children, when a couple begins a marriage where one spouse is not the biological or initial parent, there is the need for the couple to work out their roles and responsibilities in parenting children in the home. An example of problems related to the previous marriage that must be dealt with in a remarriage would be financial obligations such as previous debt, alimony, or child support payments.

- Especially in those remarriages where only one spouse has previous parenting experience, it is useful for the couple to participate in parent education or parent training before the wedding.

- Involving the couple (and children) in counseling and stepparent educational programs after the wedding are excellent ways to strengthen the "new" marriage and family. LDS Family Services would be a resource to assist in locating such counseling or educational services.

Box 3.4

answer." Then I realized that God had answered my prayers. The decision to marry Becky always made sense and felt right. I can see now that God had been telling me in my heart and in my mind that it was a good decision. And later, at the time of the ceremony, I had another confirmation that what I was doing was right.[42]

4. *Seek multiple witnesses.* The last sentence in the above quote from the young man illustrates our fourth point: Seek multiple witnesses. The scriptures teach us that "in the mouth of two or three witnesses shall every word be established" (2 Cor 13:1; D&C 6:28). A spiritual witness can be confirmed a second time in any number of circumstances.

5. *Discern between inspiration, infatuation, and desperation.* Inspiration comes as explained above—when one is living worthily, exercising agency and studying carefully, and when the answer is confirmed by multiple spiritual enlightenments and peaceful feelings (D&C 6:15, 22–23). Infatuation is usually manifest by the immature love we discussed above, including great anxiety, possessiveness, selfishness,

clinging, and over-dependence. Infatuation may be more likely with individuals who are somewhat lacking in emotional and spiritual maturity and in the personal characteristics discussed above such as self-respect, emotional health, impulse control, and realistic beliefs and expectations about relationships and marriage. Desperation is often associated with social or cultural contexts or circumstances that create an atmosphere (at least in the person's mind) of "now or never." Pressure from peers, family, and cultural norms may create a sense of desperation that leads to a hasty courtship and an unwise decision. A desire to get away from an unpleasant family situation or fear of failure in school or work can cause someone to look desperately to marriage as a way out of the problem. Such fears and anxieties may "speak" so loudly in our minds that we cannot hear the still, small whisperings and warnings of the Spirit.

6. *Confirmations should be sought by both.* One last point directly related to our third point is that the spiritual confirmation needs to come to both parties involved. A person should not feel that if his or her partner receives a confirmation, that he or she is

therefore released from the necessity of seeking a similar confirmation. Elder Dallin H. Oaks discussed this issue:

> If a revelation is outside the limits of stewardship, you know it is not from the Lord, and you are not bound by it. I have heard of cases where a young man told a young woman she should marry him because he had received a revelation that she was to be his eternal companion. If this is a true revelation, it will be confirmed directly to the woman if she seeks to know. In the meantime, she is under no obligation to heed it. She should seek her own guidance and make up her own mind. The man can receive revelation to guide his own actions, but he cannot properly receive revelation to direct hers. She is outside his stewardship.[43]

Engagement and Planning the Wedding

Once the decision is made to marry, then the couple must start planning their temple marriage. This is usually done during the engagement period, a time when the couple has formally announced their intention. The engagement period needs to be long enough to make all necessary plans for the wedding and all that surrounds it, but not so long as to create undue stress on the couple and their desire to be together as husband and wife. LDS couples in two different studies had engagements of three to four months on average, and most found that to be just about right.[44]

Planning for a temple marriage is important. In two *Ensign* articles on temple marriage by Elder Cree-L Kofford of the Seventy,[45] Elder Kofford helps us understand the importance of "marriage in the Lord's way," including how temple marriages are different from civil marriages, what the sealing ordinance entails, how to prepare to go to the temple, and many other issues surrounding temple marriage. We recommend these two articles to couples planning their temple marriage.

Among the important things that many North American couples also plan during the engagement are a wedding breakfast, reception, open house, and honeymoon. These things and others like them are often part of the couple's culture but are not a part of the actual temple marriage. Some couples seem to forget this and spend much of their time and energy worrying about dresses, tuxedos, rings, flowers, cakes, meals, invitations, and the like. While these things are important to many couples and their families, they may often become the "tail that wags the

dog." That is, the couple gets so caught up in those things that the sacred, holy, and simple sealing in the temple is lost in the rush. Elder Kofford and others have counseled couples to "focus on the spiritual" and to "remember that your wedding day is not a social experience with a tinge of the spiritual, but rather it is a spiritual experience with a tinge of the social."[46]

Besides a time for planning the temple wedding, the engagement period is also a final chance for the couple to make sure their impending marriage is right. There is no dishonor in breaking an engagement if it becomes clear that the approaching marriage is not right. In fact, it is the wise and courageous thing to do. One of us counseled a young woman who was in an abusive, unhappy marriage. Asked when she knew the marriage was in trouble, she admitted that she knew during the engagement that they were headed for trouble. When asked why she didn't back out at that point she replied, "The invitations had already gone out, so I had to get married!" The embarrassment and even expense of a broken engagement pale in comparison to the pain of an unhappy, abusive marriage. If a person feels strongly and persistently sad or troubled about the impending marriage, this may be a "stupor of thought" (D&C 9:9), and it seems prudent to discuss breaking up.

Deterioration and Ending: The Break-Up of a Premarital Relationship

The D (Deterioration) and E (Ending) phases of relationship development are possibly the most difficult to face. Relationships, of course, can "deteriorate" and "end" quickly—after only a few minutes of acquaintance—or at any stage of development. But breaking up a relationship that has grown toward a sense of interdependence and possible plans for marriage is very difficult. While the break-up of marriages has received a lot of attention in social science research, comparatively little research has been done to understand premarital relationship break-ups.

The most recent study of premarital break-ups is instructive for this chapter, because 70% of the sample were LDS.[47] These seriously dating or engaged couples all completed a questionnaire before they were married and then about six years later. Those who broke up before marriage scored generally lower in the areas we have discussed already as compared to those who married and were highly satisfied with their marriages. That is, the break-up group had poorer relationships with parents as children and as adults; they had lower emotional health, self-esteem, and impulse control; they had less support for the impending marriage from family and friends; and their communication, conflict-resolution skills, and sense of couple identity were all lower than those who eventually married and had very satisfying marriages. Interestingly, their premarital scores were not much different from those who married and eventually divorced or those who were still married but were very unhappy. Clearly, they were wise to break up their premarital relationships, since they were on course to end up in divorce or unhappy marriages.

Research like this and counsel from Church leaders suggest several reasons to break up, even after the engagement. Church leaders suggest that when there is a lack of love,[48] a partner who tempts you to break commandments and covenants[49] or does not inspire the best in you,[50] then it is appropriate for a couple to think seriously about ending the relationship. Certainly if one does not receive clear spiritual confirmation or if there are serious issues with personality traits, unresolved family background issues or continuing serious problems in the parent–adult child relationship, or personal and social context concerns, one should seriously consider whether the relationship is viable.

If it is right to break off a relationship, how can that be done so as to cause the least hurt? Certainly, the Proclamation principles that lead to successful marriages can be applied to relationships that should not proceed to marriage. The Proclamation principles of prayer, repentance, forgiveness, respect, love, compassion, and work seem especially appropriate. We also believe the counsel given by the Lord to Joseph Smith and contained in the 121st section of the Doctrine and Covenants provides excellent counsel not only for strengthening, but also ending, a relationship. Especially helpful is the counsel contained in verses 41–44:

> No power or influence can or ought to be maintained by virtue of the priesthood, only by persuasion, by long-suffering, by gentleness and meekness, and by love unfeigned; By kindness, and pure knowledge, which shall greatly enlarge the soul without hypocrisy, and without guile—Reproving betimes with sharpness, when moved upon by the Holy Ghost; and then showing forth afterwards an increase of love toward him whom thou hast reproved, lest he esteem thee to be his enemy; That he may know that thy faith-

fulness is stronger than the cords of death. (D&C 121:41–44)

Verses 41 and 42 teach us that we should not attempt to continue a relationship by any unrighteous means. A partner should not be coerced into staying in a relationship, nor should we ever feel coerced. Furthermore, when a relationship should end, the principles articulated in verses 41 and 42 can be a guide for dealing with the hurt and emotion that may result. One may need to be long-suffering, gentle, meek, and kind with a partner who does not understand or resists the change. The counsel given in verses 43 and 44 may seem extreme but, when considered carefully, is some of the best counsel we can get for ending a relationship. To *reprove* means to correct and *betimes* means immediately. Thus, when "pure knowledge," received by the Holy Ghost, helps us understand that a relationship must end, we should "correct" the situation (end the relationship) quickly and not let it drag on. The word *sharply* can mean "with clarity" (think of a sharp picture) rather than "with severity" as it is most often interpreted. Thus, while being as loving and kind as we can, we should make it clear that the relationship is ending and why, rather than "beating around the bush," hoping the partner will get the message. Again, this should be done with kindness, meekness, and love unfeigned; recognizing that even if the partner has hurt us in some way, she or he is a beloved child of God who must be treated in a Christlike manner. If one is the "breakee" rather than the "breaker," the same counsel applies: The breaking-up partner should not be coerced or forced in any way to continue if she or he does not want to continue. Even if the emotional hurt is strong, one needs to back off, not try to hurt the partner back in some way, and allow oneself time to heal.

Breaking up is nearly always difficult and painful, but it is not the end of the world. Great learning and maturity can come from surviving a premarital break-up.[51] If one initiates or endures a break-up with as much Christlike behavior and feelings as possible and allows himself or herself to be healed through the Spirit, that person is then more ready to create a relationship that can result in an eternal marriage.

The Honeymoon

In many cultures, the wedding is followed by a honeymoon. This is a time of seclusion for the couple, often in a romantic setting, where they can establish for themselves and others the legal and emotional

RESOURCES FOR COUPLES, PARENTS, AND CHURCH LEADERS

There are a number of resources for couples, parents who want to help prepare their children for marriage, and teachers or leaders of couples approaching marriage. Here are just a few.

1. The Church has prepared a student manual for use in the Religion 234 class taught in LDS Institutes of Religion. The manual is called *Achieving an Eternal Marriage and Family.* The manual contains a listing of selected teachings and complete talks from General Authorities on dozens of topics relevant to courtship and marriage.

2. A number of good books by General Authorities and LDS authors have been written on the topics of dating, courtship, mate selection, and the transition into marriage. Since books go out of print fairly quickly, we do not give any specific titles here. Many of the best books are available on Bookcraft's Infobase Library and Deseret Book's GospeLink CD-ROMs.

3. Several Internet sites provide excellent information. Bookcraft has a site at ***www.ldsworld.com*** that gives you access to much of the same material as on their Infobase Library CD-ROM. The Family Studies Center at Brigham Young University has a web site designed specifically to provide resources for couples preparing for marriage. Its URL is ***http://familycenter.byu.edu***

4. The Family Studies Center has also developed a questionnaire for couples to help them prepare for marriage or strengthen an existing marriage. It is called the RELATionship Evaluation, or RELATE. RELATE contains 271 questions about all of the factors research has shown to be predictive of later marital success. Both partners fill out a questionnaire. The couple receives a 20-page RELATE Report after their questionnaires have been scored. Paper versions of RELATE are available in English and Spanish and may be ordered by telephone (801.378.4359) or email (***relate@byu.edu***). RELATE can also be taken on the Internet at ***http://relate.byu.edu*** The cost is $5 per person for the paper or online version.

Box 3.5

boundaries around the new marriage. Because of the lore surrounding honeymoons, they are often not all they are hyped up to be. The emotional and physical drain caused by all the planning and preparing for the wedding and the anticipation of beginning the intimate aspects of the marriage can make the honeymoon less than a fulfilling experience. Couples need to take things slowly, be patient, and have a sense of humor. As couples learn together, draw on their love for and commitment to each other, and laugh together, the adjustments to the new marriage can be a wonderful and memorable time the couple will cherish all their lives.

CONCLUSION

Elder David B. Haight stated, "Considering the enormous importance of marriage, it is rather astonishing that we don't make better preparation for success. . . . Too many people are inadequately prepared for this lofty responsibility."[52] This chapter has helped you learn more about this most important of decisions for Latter-day Saints. Not only have prophets and apostles given counsel on this decision, the Lord's inspiration is available to everyone so that they need not fear this momentous decision, but rather be filled

with hope and peace concerning the process of choosing an eternal mate.

NOTES

1. Gordon B. Hinckley (1999, February). *Ensign, 29*(2), 2.

2. Bruce R. McConkie (1996), *Mormon doctrine* (Salt Lake City: Bookcraft), 118.

3. Spencer W. Kimball (1976), *Marriage and divorce* (Salt Lake City: Deseret Book), 2.

4. Gordon B. Hinckley (1995, November), Of missions, temples, and stewardship,. *Ensign, 25*(11), 51.

5. J. H. Larson and T. B. Holman (1994), Premarital prediction of marital quality and stability, *Family Relations, 43*(2), 228–237; T. B. Holman and Associates (2000), *Premarital Prediction of Marital Break-Up,* (New York: Plenum). [These two publications summarize the extensive research on premarital predictors of marital well-being.]

6. Boyd K. Packer (1973), *Eternal love* (Salt Lake City: Deseret Book), 11.

7. Kimball (1976), 16.

8. S. F. Gilliand (1997, June), I have a question, *Ensign, 27* (6), 39–42.

9. Neal A. Maxwell (1982, May), A brother offended, *Ensign, 12*(5), 39.

10. Richard G. Scott (1999, May), Receive the temple blessings, *Ensign, 29*(5), 26.

11. Hugh B. Brown (1960), *You and your marriage,* (Salt Lake City: Bookcraft), 38.

12. Gordon B. Hinckley (1996, May), Stand true and faithful, *Ensign, 26*(5), 92.

13. Hinckley (1999, February), 2.

14. Ezra Taft Benson (1988, May), To the single adult brethren of the Church, *Ensign, 18*(5), 53; Ezra Taft Benson (1988, May), To the single adult sisters of the Church, *Ensign, 18* (11), 96.

15. Scott (1999, May), 26.

16. Spencer W. Kimball (1976), 11.

17. Spencer W. Kimball (1982), *The teachings of Spencer W. Kimball* (Salt Lake City: Bookcraft), 302.

18. Marvin J. Ashton (1975, November), Love takes time, *Ensign, 5*(11), 108.

19. Spencer W. Kimball (1982), 248.

20. Holman et al. (2000).

21. P. Noller (1996), What is this thing called love? Defining the love that supports marriage and family, *Personal Relationships 3*, 97–115.

22. Bruce C. Hafen (1996, November), Covenant marriage, *Ensign, 26*(11), 28.

23. Holman et al. (2000).

24. A. Theodore Tuttle (1969, December), The home is to teach, *Improvement Era*, 108.

25. Marvin J. Ashton (1976, May), Family communications, *Ensign, 6*(5), 52.

26. Neal A. Maxwell (1996, November), According to the desire, *Ensign, 26*(11), 21.

27. David O. McKay (1953), *Gospel ideals* (Salt Lake City: The Improvement Era), 462.

28. Richard L. Evans (1969, December), This you can count on, *Improvement Era*, 73.

29. R. F. Stahmann and T. R. Adams (1997), LDS counselor ratings of problems occurring among LDS premarital and remarital couples, unpublished manuscript, BYU, in possession of author.

30. Spencer W. Kimball (1981, September), Thoughts on marriage compatibility, *Ensign, 11*(9), 45.

31. G. Levinger (1983), Development and change, in J. Wilson (Ed.), *Close relationships* (New York: W. H. Freeman and Company).

32. Hinckley (1999, February), 2.

33. Harold B. Lee (1996) *The teachings of Harold B. Lee* (Salt Lake City: Bookcraft), 169.

34. Howard W. Hunter (1967, December), Is a church necessary? *Improvement Era*, 46.

35. Harold B. Lee (1974, January), President Harold B. Lee's general priesthood address, *Ensign, 4*(1), 99–100.

36. Gordon B. Hinckley (1990, March), Thou shalt not covet, *Ensign, 20*(3), 6.

37. T. B. Holman (1996), Commitment making: Mate selection processes among active Mormon American couples, in D. J. Davies (Ed.), *Mormon identities in transition* (New York: Cassell).

38. Packer (1973), 11.

39. Bruce R. McConkie (1975, January), Agency or inspiration? *New Era*, 42.

40. Kimball (1976), 11.

41. Hinckley (1999, February), 4.

42. T. B. Holman et al. (2000).

43. Dallin H. Oaks (1981), Revelation, in *Fireside and devotional speeches, 1981–82* (Provo, UT: Brigham Young University), 25.

44. Holman (1996); G. B. Schallje and T. B. Holman, Courtship practices and marital timing among students at a Mormon university, unpublished manuscript in possession of author.

45. Cree-L Kofford (1998, June), Marriage in the Lord's way: Part one, *Ensign, 28*(6), 7–12; Cree-L Kofford (1998, July). Marriage in the Lord's way: Part two, *Ensign, 28*(7), 15–23.

46. Kofford (1998, July), 19; see also Scott (1999, May), 26.

47. T. B. Holman et al.

48. John A Widtsoe (1994), *An understandable religion* (Salt Lake City: Deseret Book).

49. A. Theodore Tuttle (1974, November), We haven't half enough missionaries—Prepare yourselves, you are needed, *Ensign, 4*(11), 71–72.

50. Benson (1980); McKay (1953).

51. Victor L. Brown (1992, April), Reluctant to marry, *Ensign, 22*(4); M. G. Wells (1982, June), Breaking up without going to pieces: When dating doesn't end in marriage, *Ensign, 12*(6).

52. David B. Haight (1984, May), Marriage and divorce, *Ensign, 14*(5), 13.

Helping Couples in Counseling Remain Committed to Their Marriage

Catherine E. Lundell

Originally, I planned on going into medicine as a profession. But as often happens to college students, along the way I changed my major to family science, which gave me a good foundation for training as a marriage and family therapist. My inability to stay awake in biochemistry class was only part of the reason for the switch. Some of my family experiences had left me wondering intently what makes marriage work. And I sensed promises in my patriarchal blessing that I would be blessed to help others with their family challenges.

My work as a marriage and family therapist is a great blessing and joy in my life. Yes, there are draining and discouraging moments. But most of the time my work is still as exciting and exhilarating as it was during my first year of graduate school training. I am awed and inspired by the strength and courage of individuals and couples striving to repair their relationships and rebuild a happy marriage.

I recently received a card from a couple I had worked with a few years ago.[1] They expressed their appreciation for my help. "Thanks for not giving up on us," the note simply said. "We're doing great." This temple-married couple first came to me with a set of common but serious problems. He had returned from his mission and quickly married a young woman whom his parents wanted him to marry. A baby came soon. He was feeling smothered and regretted his quick marriage and lack of freedom. He began

spending most of his time away with friends. She was needy, lonely, and depressed. They sought professional help and committed to six months of hard work on solving their problems. But if things were not better by spring, they planned on ending the marriage. After working with me for six months, however, there was little progress. As spring approached, it was as if the couple were begging me to acknowledge the failure of their marriage and justify their strong, mutual desire to get divorced. I think I was as frustrated as the couple by then. At that time I did not have a great deal of experience as a therapist and I did not know what else to do. I thought there was no way to save this marriage. Perhaps it *was* time to end marriage counseling and begin counseling for a "good divorce." But something stopped my natural response. Instead, I gently refused to provide the justification the couple wanted. As a good therapist should, I placed the burden back on them. "You are the ones who have to decide to break your covenants," I said. "You are the ones who will have to live with the decision."

The couple returned two weeks later. They were strangely affectionate and responsive to each other. I asked for an explanation. The husband responded: "I thought a lot about it. I just decided I was really going to be committed to this marriage. That's all." With that newfound commitment, they began working on their challenges together with my help and made great progress. It wasn't easy, but they made it. And as spring came, instead of breaking up their family they had decided to add another member.

There is nothing terribly unusual about this couple's problems. A lot of these problems can be prevented by better marriage preparation and education about how to keep marriages vital and happy. But I'm grateful to have the opportunity as a therapist to help some couples resolve difficult challenges before it's too late. And in this case, I can't help but wonder what another therapist, one who did not have a strong faith in the eternal nature of families, would have said at that critical moment when an eternal family hung in the balance. I am glad I was there to help. And I know that He who ordained marriage as a central part of the plan of happiness was there, as well.

NOTE

1. This story is used with the couple's permission.

Chapter 4

Chastity and Fidelity in Marriage and Family Relationships

Terrance D. Olson

*We further declare that God has commanded that the sacred powers of procreation
are to be employed only between man and woman, lawfully wedded as husband and wife.*
(The Family: A Proclamation to the World, ¶ 4)

Introduction

This chapter is written to those who are married or those who are going to be. More generally, it is written to members of families. Thus, when the term "we" is used, it refers to anyone who is a member of a family—especially to husbands, wives, and parents. The chapter is meant to encourage individuals and couples to accept chastity and fidelity as inescapable starting points for high-quality marriage and family relationships. This chapter invites the reader to a certain view—perhaps even vision— of where high-quality marital relationships "come from" and how such relationships are created and maintained. The hope, of course, is that the reader comes to see how chastity and fidelity are central to the Lord's divine plan of happiness and the reason our "sacred powers of procreation are to be employed only between man and woman, lawfully wedded as husband and wife" (Proclamation, ¶ 4) is because that is the way to bless ourselves, each other, and succeeding generations. An understanding of the concepts in this chapter will also assist the reader to articulate and defend the Proclamation principles of chastity and fidelity.

We have been granted the privilege of exercising the power to create life. That power is a gift from God, designed to be a blessing to us and across generations. The proper use of that power is central to God's plan for us. We live in a world that does not talk about sacred powers, but about sex. The language of the world stands in contrast to the language of the Lord in these matters and is symbolic of a chasm between the sacred principles upon which the Proclamation is based and the secular philosophies that guide worldly views.

The concepts of chastity, fidelity, and intimacy are intertwined. In many respects, to honor one of these qualities is to live them all. Alternatively, to be unchaste is also to destroy fidelity and intimacy. And while the sacred procreative powers granted by God to His offspring are an obvious focus of this chapter, those powers, and intimacy itself, are grounded in relationships that are, of necessity, more than physical. Chastity, fidelity, and intimacy are expressions of social, emotional, spiritual, and familial commitments and feelings. Without our granting that these qualities are more than physical, they cannot be fully understood. When philosophies of intimacy focus on the act, they miss the mark of understanding relationship-based and commitment-based intimacy.

Marriage and Our Procreative Powers

We marry *for.* Marriage is an act of being for. It may seem as though we marry for ourselves. But for marriage to be a blessing to us, we must give ourselves away. We actually marry for ourselves only to the extent we are committed to the other and to the next generation. Our best interests are served only when we are married for our mate and our children-to-be. This is because in marriage we are building something greater than ourselves. We are participating in an opportunity and an obligation. Thus, it seems obvious that a man and woman marry for each other. Moreover, those who marry for themselves without being for the other usually discover that marriage and family life leave much to be desired. It is precisely when we are trying to find something for ourselves in marriage that what we are seeking eludes us. Without fully giving our hearts to our spouse, we do not qualify ourselves for the blessings available to us when our mate gives his or her heart to us. This principle is especially pertinent regarding how we exercise the power to create life.

Human sexuality is presented in our culture as if it were the driving force—if not the ultimate need—behind all human endeavor. If the popular culture is right, sex is so compelling that societies must figure out ways to allow the regular, frequent expression of sex. Otherwise, individuals will be required to repress a need so basically human that when it is denied, unbearable—if not personality-changing—tensions are created that can lead to all sorts of aberrant and destructive sexual pursuits. Indeed, stories of sexual aggressiveness, incidents of rape, songs that celebrate losing control, and the philosophy behind legalizing prostitution suggest adequate evidence that the popular culture sees humans as victims of sexual needs and feelings.

This view that we are sexually driven makes marriage a convenient social solution, an approved outlet for our sexuality. However, this view cheapens the idea of marriage and invites subversive ideas to be carried into the marriage: If men are more sexually driven than women, then a mismatch of desire is inevitable. At best, much marital sexual interaction becomes a compromise between two people with unequal desires; at worse, marriage becomes a recurring emotional and physical bondage for that member of the couple who is less desirous. This view leaves little space for notions of romance, companionship, person-centeredness, or even love. It reduces all sexual interaction, including marital sex, to self-serving need, no matter how it may be dressed up in cultural notions of love or one person being "special." Moreover, this description of the human condition sweeps away any foundation for chastity, builds in an excuse for infidelity, and undermines the idea of person-centered intimacy.

In the restored gospel, the reality of sexual desire is acknowledged, without making that desire a force beyond our moral agency. As agents, we have the power to have our physical desires be expressions of our commitment to the well-being of another. When so directed, sexual drives and desires are expressions of a God-given gift and are even essential to the Creator's plan for us, His children. The Proclamation affirms that "the means by which mortal life is created [is] divinely appointed" (¶ 5). When something divine is perverted and misused, the consequences threaten the purposes for which we come to earth.

A gospel view of these matters stands in contrast to worldly views. The question is not whether we will be satisfied, but whether we will exercise the power to create life for the other, and within the bounds the Lord has set. Our sexual responsiveness in marriage is either an expression of being for the other, and therefore a means to our being mutually blessed, or of being for ourselves, and therefore a means to self-centered (selfish) activity. In either case, we will have our reward. Ironically, when we are sexually for the other, we are not seeking reward and are rewarded. When we are sexually for ourselves, the reward we receive seems insufficient, disappointing, never adequate. To make sense out of this requires that we examine what being human means and then look at a gospel view of the power to create life. It is out of these understandings that the case for chastity, fidelity, and intimacy can be made. It is out of gospel doctrine regarding our power to create that we discover the blessings of chastity and fidelity. Commandments regarding chastity and fidelity are from a loving God, and our obedience is a token of being for ourselves, for our spouse and our children (present or future), and for God, who has granted us the gift to be a blessing to us and a means of carrying out His work.

BEING HUMAN AND BEING MORAL AGENTS

We humans are unique on the earth. Our uniqueness is more than the gift of dominion over all other forms of life. It is not just that we have a superior brain or that we have developed oral and written language allowing us to transmit our culture—our lives—across generations. It is that we are offspring of God. We are made in His image: "In the image of his own body, male and female, created he them, and blessed them, and called their name Adam" (Moses 6:9; see also JST Gen. 6:9). God has granted us, as His offspring, a gift to be co-creators with Him, to provide bodies for His spirit children to come to earth and to participate in His work and His glory, which is "to bring to pass the immortality and eternal life of man" (Moses 1:39). The power to create life is a godly power. God does not use the power whimsically. We are expected to use our God-given power in godly ways. To be a person of chastity and fidelity is to be true to being a son or daughter of God, our Creator.

Thus it seems that to exercise the power to create life must be a matter of agency, and since the power can be profaned—can be used in ungodly ways—it must be a matter of moral agency. This stands in contrast to popular notions of human sexuality that cast it as a driving, motivating force that grounds human relationships in barely controllable physical desires. Such a view does not grant us our agency in matters of procreation, but places humans firmly as animals in an animal kingdom, driven by instinct. In the gospel, while sexual desires are understood as relatively strong and constant in the mature human, they hardly constitute an uncontrollable force. At least it is possible for the feelings not to be experienced as uncontrollable, which means they are not merely instincts that dictate our actions. Being human means we are capable of acting on the environment rather than being acted upon (see 2 Ne. 2:26–27), and this ability must extend to the power to create life.

BEING MORAL AGENTS AND OUR PROCREATIVE POWERS

If humans are moral agents, and sexual drives and desires are subject to our agency, then our sexual feelings are also a matter of morality. They are the kind of feelings that can be expressed honorably as well as dishonorably. Samuel the Lamanite declares how we are moral agents:

> ye are free; ye are permitted to act for yourselves; for behold, God hath given unto you a knowledge and he hath made you free. He hath given unto you that ye might know good from evil, and he hath given unto you that ye might choose life or death; and ye can do good and be restored unto that which is good, or have that which is good restored unto you; or ye can do evil and have that which is evil restored unto you. (Hel. 14:30–31)

For us to be held morally accountable for an action, we must have had the law to know it is moral, and we must have the ability to freely choose or reject a moral course of action. The gospel includes our sexual desires in our agency; thus we can be held accountable for our use or misuse of our procreative powers.

Worldly philosophies that make sexuality a matter of bodily need and sexual expression a necessity make the spirit subject to the body in matters of procreation and dismiss agency as irrelevant. But the quality or spirit of our procreative powers resides in the spirit, not in the body, and thus our sexual involvement is an expression of that spirit, and we are accountable for our actions, not mere victims of desires we can do nothing about. The body is likely to respond to what the spirit tells it to do.

Specifically, our sexual feelings and involvement must be a matter of agency, for the Lord issues commandments and sets boundaries for our exercise of our procreative power. For example, the Lord has always restricted sexual involvement to legal marriage. Thus, it has always been a moral issue. Sexual feelings are a matter of agency since "the Lord giveth no commandments unto the children of men, save he shall prepare a way for them that they may accomplish the thing which he commandeth them" (1 Ne. 3:7). This is a sign of hope for us and a signal that the Lord has great confidence in us to respond to the call to be chaste. The call to chastity and fidelity means we have the ability to obey, if we are willing to do so. We can not excuse ourselves from the commandment on the grounds that we are unable, or that the feelings are too strong, or that boundaries set by the Lord are unrealistic.

If we accept the idea that we are moral agents and that we can be true or false to the sexual moral boundaries the Lord has set, then why do we sometimes experience "a river of fire" that seems to go against what would be right to do or to be? Why does the Lord set limits that seem to make our feelings—or controlling them—such a burden? Here is one possible answer.

THE MORAL QUALITY OF FEELINGS AND EMOTIONS

The scriptures commend certain feelings, attitudes, and desires. Typical examples are: "And be ye kind one to another, tenderhearted, forgiving one another, even as God for Christ's sake hath forgiven you" (Eph. 4:32). Similarly, we are counseled to cultivate such feelings as persuasion, long-suffering, gentleness, meekness, kindness, and love unfeigned (see D&C 121:41–42). But the scriptures also condemn feelings of anger: "Can ye be angry and not sin? Let not the sun go down upon your wrath" (JST Eph. 4:26), and emotions of a similar quality: "Let all bitterness, and wrath, and anger, and clamour, and evil speaking, be put away from you, with all malice" (Eph. 4:31). This counsel reveals that emotions, too, have a moral quality inherent in them. If I am angry with you, I am in danger of God's judgment (see JST Matt. 5:24).

In contrast, if we express charity, if we mourn with others when they have cause to mourn (Mosiah 18:9), we are being as the Lord would be if He were with us. So some emotions are condemned outright and others are unequivocally commended. Our emotions, then, must be matters of agency, otherwise how could we give up those the Lord condemns? The truth about our lives is that the quality of our earthly experience is an expression of the moral quality of life we are living. The Book of Mormon's contribution to this understanding centers on how our experience changes when the Lord changes our hearts. Alma expresses this theme while reminding the people of Zarahemla of their ancestors: "Behold, he changed their hearts; yea, he awakened them out of a deep sleep, and they awoke unto God. Behold, they were in the midst of darkness; nevertheless, their souls were illuminated by the light of the everlasting word; . . . they humbled themselves and put their trust in the true and living God. . . . [They] received his image in [their] countenances . . . experienced this mighty change in [their] hearts" (Alma 5:7, 13, 14). To go from dark to light is a dramatic transformation. It describes the two ways we can experience life itself—and the two qualities of emotion that are inescapably a feature of having a hard or soft heart. Our heart condition can change from moment to moment.

Some who are used to thinking of emotions as characteristics of our personality are troubled by the seemingly black-and-white implications of these scriptures. They assume that if a person is angry with his brother, he is basically evil, or that if a person is charitable toward her brother, she is basically good. But the scriptures condemn a person's spiritual condition, not the person, and the scriptures simply reject emotions of a certain quality. Those emotions are symptoms of our spiritual condition at the moment, not some unchangeable feature of our

personality or inescapable characteristic of our "human nature." The quality of our emotions at any given moment expresses the condition of our hearts in that moment. When we are hard-hearted, we are hateful, resentful, or jealous. When we are soft-hearted, we are compassionate, meek, and humble. When we are hateful, it is a sign of being hard-hearted. It has almost nothing to do with personality, even though we can begin to live in the world and be so habitual in our hard-heartedness that our feelings seem to be just "what we are." If Book of Mormon peoples could have their hearts changed, then we can also. That emotions have a moral quality gives us hope, for it means, as moral agents, that as we turn our hearts to God our feelings can be transformed accordingly. We are not trapped by them. In the instant we are self-centered in our physical intimacies in marriage, we cheat ourselves of the emotions which attend self-forgetful loving.

So the dilemma is dissolved this way. When I walk in darkness, my attitudes, feelings, emotions—even my sexual feelings—are of a moral quality the Lord rejects. They are symptoms of living as "natural man" and constitute one of the reasons we can be described as "enemies to God." But when we walk in the light, when we walk with God, we put off the natural man, and heed the call of Mosiah 3:19, to become "as a child, submissive, meek, humble, patient, full of love." These feelings of humility or patience or love unfeigned (see D&C 121:41) are evidences of a mighty change in our hearts. The quality of our feelings when we are walking in the light is totally different than when we are walking in darkness. Even our sexual feelings change from being uncontrollable and self-centered to being linked in quality with all the feelings we experience in the light. Our desires are compatible with being meek, humble, patient, full of love. They are expressions of love unfeigned, of gentleness and kindness. A shorthand way of describing this is to cast it as the difference between lust and love. President Kimball offers the classic explanation of the difference. He had been talking with a young LDS couple who had justified sexual transgression by presenting themselves as in love:

> This young couple looked up rather startled when I postulated firmly, "No, my beloved young people, you did not *love* each other. Rather, you *lusted* for each other." . . . The beautiful and holy word of *love* they had defiled until it had degenerated to become a bedfellow with lust, its antithesis. As far back as Isaiah,

deceivers and rationalizers were condemned: "Woe unto them that call evil good, and good evil; that put darkness for light, and light for darkness; that put bitter for sweet, and sweet for bitter!" (Isaiah 5:20).

If one really loves another, one would rather die for that person than to injure him. At the hour of sin, pure love is pushed out of one door while lust sneaks in the other. Affection has then been replaced with desire of the flesh and uncontrolled passion. Accepted has been the doctrine which the devil is so eager to establish, that illicit sex relations are justified.[1]

So, evidently, our sexual feelings are dark and bitter when we exercise them outside the bounds the Lord has set and are light and sweet when exercised obediently. So perhaps there is no dilemma here except to those in lust. Otherwise, we understand our sexual feelings can be experienced in two different ways. When we live willingly within the bounds the Lord has set, we do not find ourselves experiencing such desires in a way that they are uncontrollable. We are aware of our feelings. We are not helpless or burdened by their presence. We are not driven by self-centered need. We find the counsel of Alma to his son Shiblon meaningful: "see that ye bridle all your passions, that ye may be filled with love" (Alma 38:12). To bridle is an act of love. Love includes a commitment to the well-being of another person and includes a sensibility about how that person should be treated. This would include all of the possible ways we could imagine wanting to be treated, and then we would do even so to others. How we treat another sexually would be especially relevant, important, and necessary. By bridling our passions, we are filled with love—with concern for, interest in, commitment to—the other person. To engage in sexual relations selfishly is to abandon our concerns for, interest in, or commitment to the other person. Love is of one quality; lust is the degenerated alternative.

Those who experience lustful feelings may experience them as if such feelings had a life, a call, an agency of their own, which only physical satisfaction could reduce. It is more likely that, by walking in darkness we are the author of our own lusts in a way that would be surprising even to ourselves. When we are in the dark, we experience our sexual feelings helplessly, as a great need, and self-gratification is the purpose of our sexual participation. In the dark we lose concern for the other person. Ultimately, solutions to problems of lust are found, not merely by controlling such feelings, but by giving them up, by asking God to change our hearts, by losing ourselves

in our desire to do right by another. Thus, perfect love casts out lust.

MARRIAGE: AN OBLIGATION AND AN OPPORTUNITY, BUT NOT A LICENSE

The power to create life is a godly gift. When we honor the gift, it is a blessing to us:

> In LDS life and thought, sexuality consists of attitudes, feelings, and desires that are God-given and central to God's plan for his children. . . . Sexual feelings are to be governed by each individual within boundaries the Lord has set. Sexuality is not characterized as a need, or a deprivation that must be satisfied, but as a desire that should be fulfilled only within marriage, with sensitive attention given to the well-being of one's heterosexual marriage partner.[2]

Proper sexual desire, then, is moral and relational—person-centered. And by divine design it is marital. Even in marriage, however, a husband and wife must approach each other with selflessness and with mutuality of feeling. Making marriage covenants makes us accessible and obligated to each other, but it does not legitimize lust. When lust characterizes marital sexual relations, it is likely that it is an expression of unrighteous dominion, and the intended blessings of the physical sharing are not realized. The man and woman are to be one in the Lord, and when lust characterizes marital interaction, husband and wife are not one, and "if ye are not one, ye are not mine" (D&C 38:27). Of course if they are not one they certainly are not each other's, either.

The Anti-Chastity Culture

We wish not only for ourselves to be chaste, but to teach our children to be so. Our children may be seduced first by the philosophies of the world before they succumb to worldly practices. Most of the time, people live in accordance with their beliefs. One contemporary example of this link is that several authors attribute the reduction in premarital sexual involvement in the 1990s to a variety of factors, including a more conservative philosophy (beliefs) about sexual involvement.[3] Parents can foster wise beliefs in their children by unraveling the philosophies of the world.

We live in a culture where the ideal of chastity has not only been lost, it invites ridicule. Generally, the move away from chastity has included abandoning marriage as the prerequisite for sexual involvement. It also has introduced the notion of responsible or irresponsible sex in premarital or even extramarital contexts. Not surprisingly, the rejection of chastity is usually accompanied by rationalizations. It seems even a culture cannot call good evil and evil good without presenting a philosophy in defense of sexual license. These defenses are far more fundamental than simple phrases such as "It can't be wrong if it feels so right," or "Even educated fleas do it." Typical is the line in the movie *While You Were Sleeping*. The heroine, having helped foster the false idea that she is engaged, explains to her co-worker regarding sex, that she and her "fiance" are "waiting." The response of the co-worker is a disbelieving stare and the comment, "Waiting? For what?!" The world's version of love or affection is deemed an adequate prerequisite to sexual involvement. This freedom of sexual access sometimes carries two restrictions, even in worldly philosophies: Your partner ought not to be married to someone else, and there must be mutual consent. Embedded in those ideas is the implication that sexual involvement is not an expression of something permanent, not a token of commitment, not a matter of activity in a legal relationship recognized by the community.

More recently, this philosophy of "sexual access with affection" has been extended to legal minors. Thus, individuals who are too young to qualify to sign financial contracts or exercise the right to vote are assumed to have a right to sexual access. One illustration of this is the United Nations' "Declaration on the Rights of the Child." Amid some otherwise worthy ideas and thoughts on the protection of children is the assertion that parents should not have the right to restrict an adolescent's autonomy in sexual decisions.

This philosophy is not unique to such august forums as the U.N. Several years ago I served on a national government committee designed to combat adolescent pregnancy. A debate over when an adolescent should be free to choose sexual involvement ensued, and the president of the National Council for Adoption challenged the liberal view of most of the 16 committee members by asking at what age should this freedom be extended to youth. He asked, "How young is too young for a girl? Is it 16, 15, 14, . . . is it 12?" The answer from several of the committee was, "That depends." Their ideas of what it depended on certainly did not include marriage. The person sitting next to me on the committee, who was the head of a national high school athletic association, turned to me and said, "Nobody restricted my sexual access when I was in high school, and I certainly wouldn't want to restrict anyone else's."

We must offer an alternative ideal to our children. Once sexual access is moved outside of marriage, outside most moral boundaries, and even extended as a "right" to legal minors, mutual consent becomes the only legal measure of the activity. Actually, one other practical necessity and more recent ethical boundary has reemerged. Given that sexual involvement can foster a host of sexually transmitted diseases, the most disastrous of which is AIDS, individuals owe it to themselves and others to behave in a way which reduces the risk of infection. Hence there is a notion of responsible versus irresponsible sex, which is available outside of marriage and usually to legal minors. This notion of "responsible sex" proceeds as if sexual involvement creates only physical consequences. Such involvement is considered completely unrelated to social, emotional, spiritual, relational, familial, psychological, and generational consequences that surely accompany sexuality.

So, our children deserve to respond to such philosophies with a gospel understanding of chastity—reserving sexual sharing until marriage—even in the face of a popular culture that has abandoned the idea. Major public organizations and private lobbying groups foster the granting of sexual access to legal minors. These cultural affirmations of sexual involvement spill forward from certain basic assumptions about the human condition and the implications of those assumptions regarding the meaning of human sexuality. Our children will be confronted, implicitly or explicitly, with these false ideas:

1. Sex is normal and natural for everyone. To be human is to be sexual.

2. Sexual involvement is to be expected among the sexually mature.

3. Sexual expression is a need.

4. The loss of virginity is an essential feature of growing up and an event to be celebrated.

5. Those who are sexually experienced are now "real" men and women.

6. Affection is a preferred, but not necessary prerequisite to sexual involvement.

7. Those who make premarital sexual involvement a moral issue create unnecessary guilt in adolescents and unnecessarily stigmatize them.

Gospel Foundations of Chastity

The Proclamation is straightforward: "God has commanded that the sacred powers of procreation are to be employed only between man and woman, lawfully wedded as husband and wife" (¶ 4). President Gordon B. Hinckley reminded us: "Notwithstanding the so-called new morality, notwithstanding the much-discussed changes in moral standards, there is no adequate substitute for virtue. God's standards may be challenged everywhere throughout the world, but God has not abrogated His commandments."[4]

Chastity and fidelity are more than sexual abstinence before marriage and physical fidelity after marriage. This is because human sexuality is not simply a physical matter, as the world often invites us to believe. Chastity and fidelity begin in the spirit, not in the body, and involve the giving of our hearts—our broken hearts, our softened hearts—to our mates unequivocally. We are, in fact, to have our "hearts knit together in unity and love one towards another" (Mosiah 18:21). For husbands and wives, there can be no fulfillment in any endeavor or activity without such willing, mutual commitment in love.

The threat, either to the chastity of the unmarried or the fidelity of the married, is in the quality of our spirit, of which our thoughts are just one expression. For example, "whosoever looketh on a woman to lust after her hath committed adultery with her already in his heart" (Matt. 5:28). When we harden our hearts, we have hardened our spirit against the light and truth we would otherwise see. When our sins include sexual impurity, our hard-heartedness makes us susceptible to temptation. Or, in Alma's words:

> Then if our hearts have been hardened, yea, if we have hardened our hearts against the word, insomuch that it has not been found in us, then will our state be awful, for then we shall be condemned.
>
> For our words will condemn us, yea, all our works will condemn us; we shall not be found spotless; and our thoughts will also condemn us. (Alma 12:13–14)

In other words, unchastity is not merely an act. It is an expression of the condition of the spirit. Our thoughts and our works can place us in jeopardy. But of course we have created the danger—and the thoughts—by what we seek and invite. And the impact and implications always go beyond the present moment and are not just physical. While we are unrepentant, the consequences of sexual sin can be found in the immediate relationship, in a lack of spiritual understanding, in our emotional troubles, and in the meaning of love itself. Chastity represents our commitments to, and our connections with, others. When we are unchaste, we are thinking only of ourselves. We are not thinking of the Lord; there is no place in our hearts for our mother, our father, our brothers and sisters, or our children, or children we someday will invite to the earth. In unchastity, we are not even thinking of our partner (so-called). We are focused only on ourselves. It is as if, in moments of unchastity, we have disconnected ourselves from the real world—from the reality of God and from the relationships that have nurtured us or to which we have given ourselves. Unchastity, which the world holds out as an act of freedom, fulfillment, and need, is actually an act that enslaves, leaves us unfulfilled, and, regarding "need," proves to be unsatiable. It has always been so with lust; it has always been so with selfishness. Lust is always a thought and act of the self-centered, the self-consumed.

Restoring the Obvious: Chastity Is Realistic in the Real World

What the Lord asks of us is to safeguard the power to create life precisely because it is so central to His plan for His children. We are His children. As our Creator, He offers to share all that He has with us. The fountains of life are sacred and to be exercised with love, reverence, commitment, and mutuality. To be chaste is to act in behalf of ourselves and our family and preserve the meaning and value of family commitment across generations. We come to earth as the Savior did, to do our Father's will, to bless others, to act in their behalf. We are to look to the Savior as our example. When we substitute our own will—and our licentious will at that—for the reason we came to earth, we are living a counterfeit life. Real life is beneficial, practical, and realistic in what it offers for human happiness. We taste those benefits to the extent we serve those we love. That happiness is linked to the quality of our relationships with others, especially in the family. "No other success can compensate for failure in the home,"[5] because home is where real life unfolds. When we are willing to lose our lives in family service and commitment, we find our lives. We are real people. When we are unchaste, we become "unreal" or counterfeit to our reason for being.

Elder Jeffrey R. Holland has noted at least three reasons chastity is fundamental to our mission on the earth and to our personal happiness. First, as noted in the Doctrine & Covenants, "the spirit and the body are the soul of man" (88:15). For our ultimate fulness of joy, we need both spirit and body. Misuse of the body is a threat to the soul. Second, chastity and fidelity are symbols of unity, of commitment, of total union. Forsaking all others is possible when we make and honor covenants. Finally, Elder Holland notes, "Sexual intimacy is not only a symbolic union between a man and a woman—the uniting of their very souls—but it is also symbolic of a union between mortals and deity, . . . uniting for a rare and special moment with God himself and all the powers by which he gives life in this wide universe of ours. In this latter sense, human intimacy is a sacrament, a very special kind of symbol."[6]

So we are unmarried. We are dating. What manner of men and women are we to be? We are to be those who are being, thinking, and acting for the person we are with. When we lose ourselves in their behalf, the Lord will take care of the rest. While dating, we can behave in ways that jeopardize the spiritual peace or future of our dating partner. We then invite them into a counterfeit world of experience, where we don't just call good evil and evil good. We become an expression of the evil we have been called to forsake, and we compound the sin by seeking someone as an accomplice. If, by the way we act, we jeopardize his or her spiritual future, we are collaborating in placing that person at risk. Unchastity is never a solitary sin (unless it is rape). And because the consequences go to the heart of our mission on the earth—to become mothers and fathers who raise children in the Lord, under the covenant—when we violate the law of chastity we send ripples of consequences across our past, present, and future family relationships.

The practical consequences of unchastity affect the couple and children. Recent research identifies risks of cohabitation without marriage that the cohabitants may not anticipate. These figures are particularly sobering because the risks occur irrespective of whether the couples cohabiting know the law of the Lord. In other words, whether the couples are living together in ignorance of the Lord's call to chastity, or are violating their own sense of what would be right for themselves or their children, the consequences are still the consequences. For example:

1. Living together before marriage increases the risk of breaking up after marriage.

2. Living together in a nonlegal marriage increases the risk to women and children of physical and sexual violence.

3. Unmarried couples report lower levels of happiness and general well-being than married couples report.

4. Cohabiting couples are more accepting of divorce than singles living alone or married couples.

5. Three-fourths of children born to cohabiting parents will see their parents split up before the children reach age 16.[7]

In summary, and as President Boyd K. Packer has pointed out regarding those who live together without marriage, "To suppose that one day they may nonchalantly change their habits and immediately claim all that might have been theirs had they not made a mockery of marriage is to suppose something that will not be. One day, when they come to themselves, they will reap disappointment. One cannot degrade marriage without tarnishing other words as well, such words as boy, girl, manhood, womanhood, husband, wife, father, mother, baby, children, family, home."[8]

Honoring the Necessary: Fidelity Is Essential and a Blessing

When we honor our covenants with each other, as spouses, fathers, mothers, sons, and daughters, we seek to obey the commandments, in part, because we see that we are in a network of relationships that we can make of high quality. Those who have so lived, across generations, can testify to the blessings of such a life. They can testify it is the happiest, most fulfilling, the most productive, safest, least harmful, most glorious, honorable, and best way to act in behalf of those we love.

A key feature of fidelity in marriage is chastity. That is, marriage partners not only refrain from sexual thoughts and desires regarding others, but their own relationship is not tinged by self-centered, lustful initiatives. The qualities of marital sexual involvement are exactly the same as those characterizing any nonsexual relationship that proceeds according to covenant: the qualities include patience, gentleness, kindness, love unfeigned, charity, and so on. The depth of the love and fulfillment in such a relationship is unbounded. The practices in marriage do, however, have boundaries. The marriage license is not a license for licentiousness.

It is an invitation to act in each other's behalf as the Lord intended and with the opportunity to continue generations of His sons and daughters on earth.

Adultery and fornication are virtual synonyms except for the marital status of the transgressor.

However, the degree of accountability of the adulterer may be greater, and usually the consequences are more immediate, influence more lives, and are more destructive of family bonds. Nothing threatens the purpose of marriage and parenting like infidelity. Unity, commitment, sacrifice, selflessness—so essential to both marriage and to the well-being of the next generation—are abandoned in the moment of infidelity. Lost to adultery are trust, unity, sacrifice, honesty, humility, covenant. Lost to unchastity are confidence, commitment, personhood, and promise. Sexual impurity is personally destructive, but the consequences can continue beyond the present moment, beyond the illicit relationship, and across generations. Individuals can repent. They must also seek forgiveness from others, lest their previous sins are visited on the heads of children and others who become hard-hearted and unforgiving themselves. We cannot isolate ourselves from others regarding the consequences of our sins. Mothers sorrow, fathers weep, siblings are horrified, children are visited with sins and consequences not of their making. Marriages are threatened or destroyed. We know that unchastity can have eternal consequences, yet the temporal, mortal consequences are immediate and real.

Those who have repented of sexual sin testify that their unchastity was the most painful, regretful, harmful, dangerous, despairing, false, subversive, destructive circumstance they ever invited into their experience. But only after they came out of the darkness of their wrongdoing could they see the truth of their circumstance. The truth didn't look like the truth to them when they were in the dark. They had to be willing to receive the light and then all is revealed. John described this kind of blindness this way: "If we say that we have fellowship with him [the Savior], and walk in darkness, we lie, and do not the truth: . . . If we say that we have no sin, we deceive ourselves, and the truth is not in us" (1 Jn. 2:6, 8).

If we could help those wavering in chastity and fidelity to imagine the quality of life their sin will create for themselves and others, we would reduce adultery dramatically. But precisely because pre-adulterers have their rationalizations in place in advance of the act, they are blind to the meaning of their infidelity. If Latter-day Saints would do nothing more than operate on faith, and turn to God in moments of temptation, they would be led out of the wilderness of lust and blindness. Obedience is the first law of heaven, in part, because only through obedience do we see the truth clearly.

Ultimately, it is in the faces of those we love where we see the call to righteousness, to fidelity, to love, to sacrifice, to commitment, to the giving of our best, to the fulfilling of our earthly missions. We do use symbols to remind us, but our strength is in our hearts. We can remember what the wedding ring is for. Perhaps it can serve a protective function, as a reminder of who we are and to whom we belong. We wear covenant clothing as a protection and a reminder. Perhaps our mothers said, "Remember who you are." What did they mean? Who are we? Why is the song "I am a child of God"[9] a song of chastity and fidelity? Ultimately, the answers to these questions are just outward signs of an inward commitment, and a person who is already intent on dishonoring fidelity and chastity will not think to ask the questions. But if the questions could even be an echo of invitation to be true to that which matters most, they serve as reminders of how essential fidelity is to the joy and blessing we believe we came to the earth to receive.

The Moral Sense and Sexual Sensibility

So human sexuality is understood only when sexual feelings are recognized as moral, marital, and mutual. This should not be a surprise. Virtually all human interaction is moral interaction. That is, we either treat each other as we ought to be treated, or we don't. In athletics, education, employment, business, government, and a host of human activities—even standing in line at movie theaters—we either behave in a seemly fashion, or we don't. In human relationships, especially marriage and family relationships, and in matters of human sexuality, the highest standards of ethical and moral treatment are central to the quality of those relationships. Sexual involvement is at the heart of our morality, because it involves the fountains of life. Is adultery a moral issue? Alma told Corianton it is less serious than only two other sins: murder and the denial of the Holy Ghost (see Alma 39:3–5). It is not to be taken lightly, even when our culture regards adultery as unremarkable in many jokes, plays, movies, and television shows that mock marital covenants and giggle at adultery. Failure to see adultery as an immoral, grave, and destructive act is the epitome of being lightminded. To see humans as driven by need, and not called by moral purpose, is to misunderstand completely the meaning of the power to create life. We begin our understanding of that power when we see ourselves as moral agents, able to honor the Lord's offer to become one with a covenanted spouse and to prepare a home for those spirits waiting to come to earth.

We May Lose Our Way But We Can Always Find the Path

The Savior lamented regarding those who were the chosen but rejected him: "O Jerusalem, Jerusalem which killest the prophets, and stonest them that are sent unto thee; how often would I have gathered thy children together, as a hen doth gather her brood under her wings, and ye would not!" (Luke 13:34; also Matt. 23:37).

Those who have walked the way of the unchaste or the adulterous can find their way back. Those who have run to the dark invitations of indulgence may feel either justified or helpless to return. Even their helplessness is a justification of sorts. When we see ourselves as helpless when we are not, we can be saying, "I would change if it were possible, but it is not possible; I cannot change." Not even the Savior in His condemnation of the murderous leaders in Jerusalem said they could not help it. The testimony is, "and ye *would* not" (Luke 13:34, emphasis added).

Although the return is hard, it is possible. Moreover, the people I know who have made their way back report later that, while the journey is not easy, it is easier than the alternative—to continue in sin, in rejection of covenant, in using others, in abandoning mate and children, past, present or future. To repent in the present moment is to make a new future. To insist that change is impossible is to accept the false idea that we are damned already. In order not to condemn and damn themselves, people must accept the truth that change is possible. Our self-condemnation starts with our refusal to see the truth—either regarding our sins, or regarding the possibility of repentance. Those who are unchaste will not progress as long as they cling to the idea that "I cannot help it," or "It is too late for me." They could be blessed by accepting the truth: "I *will* not help it."

The problem is not that they cannot change, but that they will not.

The Lord makes no idle promises: "Behold, I stand at the door, and knock: if any man hear my voice, and open the door, I will come in to him, and will sup with him, and he with me.

"To him that overcometh will I grant to sit with me in my throne . . ." (Rev. 3:20–21).

This hope is part of accepting the Atonement. To respond to the knock and answer the door is a matter of willingness, not ability. Grasping the iron rod is easier than wandering when we let go. The sustaining influence of the Spirit on the path of repentance and righteousness is a breath of blessing we can receive. To turn back to the correct path is to begin to see clearly once again. But the first step is always ours. The truth that makes us free is the Savior: the Way, the Truth, the Life (see John 14:6). Turn to Him and we have a beginning, and a restoration of light and truth about our own behavior and what we should do. To be willing to be gathered under His wings is the first step to being gathered, and restored, to the path of righteousness. It is always worth the walk.

NOTES

1. Spencer W. Kimball (1982), *The teachings of Spencer W. Kimball* (Salt Lake City: Bookcraft), 279.

2. D. H. Ludlow et al. (Eds.) (1992), *Encyclopedia of Mormonism,* (New York: Macmillan), 3:1306.

3. F. D. Cox (1996), Human intimacy: marriage, the family and its meaning (7ᵗʰ ed.) (St. Paul, MN: West), 167, 326.

4. Gordon B. Hinckley (1988, August), With all thy getting get understanding, *Ensign, 28*(8), 2.

5. David O. McKay (1935, April), in Conference Report, 116 (Quoting J. E. McCulloch (1924), in *Home, the Savior of Civilization,* 42).

6. Jeffrey R. Holland (1988), Of souls, symbols, and sacraments, *Devotional and fireside speeches, 1987–88* (Provo, UT: Brigham Young University), 12.

7. Data summarized from D. Popenoe and B. D. Whitehead (1999), *Should we live together?* (New Brunswick, NJ: National Marriage Project, Rutgers University).

8. Boyd K. Packer (1981, April), in Conference report, 15.

9. "I Am a Child of God," in *Children's Songbook,* 2–3.

PERSONAL PURITY AND MARITAL INTIMACY

WENDY L. WATSON

After twenty-five years of clinical research with individuals, couples, and families struggling to achieve greater intimacy, I believe that personal purity and a relationship with Christ are the keys to intimacy. I also believe that a personal relationship with the Savior is the only way to achieve true intimacy in our relationships with others. Only with a strong personal relationship with our Savior Jesus Christ will any and all of our interactions with others reach their full flowering. Without the Savior's touch, there is no staying power to loving words and actions. Without the Savior's tutoring, there is no ability to see beyond the obvious—to look deeper into the soul of another and to see the lovable, the redeemable, the possible.

We will find intimacy only in relationships that honor sacred marital covenants. Why? Because true intimacy of any kind in any relationship must involve the Savior, whose plan of salvation is crowned by the creation of each celestial being. And how can we forge a closer relationship with the Savior? By living to increase our personal purity. Personal purity increases intimacy with the Lord and with others. Keeping the Lord's commandments with ever-increasing devotion and precision increases our personal purity. Thus it follows that keeping the Lord's commandments increases intimacy. We can increase the experiences of intimacy in our lives by doing what the Lord has asked us to do.

The Savior has asked us to show love to Him by keeping His commandments (see John 14:15). And as we are faithful and diligent in keeping His commandments, He promises to "encircle [us] in the arms of [His] love" (D&C 6:20). Our closeness to the Savior fills us with love, increasing our ability to love others and to feel love from others. Truman Madsen in his *Four Essays on Love* said it well: "You cannot love until you are loved. You cannot be loved until you are Beloved, Beloved of God."[1] Thus:

- If you want to be filled with the love of the Lord, keep His commandments.
- If you want to feel loved, keep the Lord's commandments.
- If you truly love someone, keep the Lord's commandments.

If you truly want to experience intimacy and increase your personal purity, keep the Lord's commandments.

BROADENING OUR VISION OF PHYSICAL INTIMACY

True intimacy also involves vision. And vision is even more crucial when viewing physical intimacy. When we are seeking increased understanding about physical intimacy, which is so sacred and so powerful, we need wide-angle-eternal vision and

Spirit-enhanced depth perception. If our understanding of physical intimacy is presently based on a picture that is taken, developed, and framed by none other than the father of all lies himself, our experiences with physical intimacy will be deadly—unless mediated by the life-giving power in the Savior's Atonement.

As we strive with our loved ones for an increasingly intimate relationship, blessed by the presence of the Spirit, the distinction between the Lord's truth about intimacy and the adversary's lies will become increasingly clear. For truly it seems that if there is anything impure, defiling, of an illicit nature, or obscene, the adversary seeks to generate these things and seeks to convince us that such things are normal, good and part of intimacy. They are not.

Satan's vision of physical intimacy is cunning, counterfeiting, and contorting. Lucifer offers his skewed view of physical intimacy through any and all publications and productions known to humankind—from movies, magazines, music and stage plays to Internet chat rooms. When our vision clears and our frame is enlarged, we see the adversary's ploys for what they really are: elaborate and extensive maneuvers to capture our souls.

THE SANCTITY OF HUMAN INTIMACY

The Lord has not left us alone. He has provided His truth about intimacy through His scriptures and His prophets. The Proclamation declares "that God has commanded that the sacred powers of procreation are to be employed only between man and woman, lawfully wedded as husband and wife" (¶ 4). Could it be any clearer than that? Any and all other physical intimacies are outside of God's law. The fact that God intended physical intimacy only for husbands and wives to share speaks volumes about its sacred importance.

Elder Jeffrey R. Holland presented three eternal truths about physical intimacy in October 1998 general conference. First, physical intimacy is a soulful experience, involving the body and the spirit. We, as members of the Lord's Church, are doctrinally distinct in understanding that "the spirit and the body are the soul of man" (D&C 88:15). Physical intimacy should involve your soul—your body *and* your spirit—not just your body.

The second grand truth offered by Elder Holland is that physical intimacy is a symbol of the total commitment and union a husband and wife should have

for one another in all areas of their lives. If the only time a husband and his wife unite is during physical union, they are probably experiencing "counterfeit intimacy." Counterfeit intimacy occurs when we relate to each other in fragments—a fragment of a wife here, connecting with a fragment of her husband there.[2] Physical uniting is to be a symbol of spouses' total union, not the total and only occurrence of their union.

The third grand eternal truth is that physical intimacy is a kind of sacrament—a time to draw close to God, a time "when we quite literally unite our will with God's will, our spirit with His spirit, where communion through the veil becomes very real."[3]

This is a profound truth. Sadly, however, it is the exact opposite of what far too many have believed. Influenced by the adversary's lying lens of love, they have supposed that they were never further away from the Lord than when joining together in physical union. Nothing could be further from the truth. The truth is that physical intimacy is a sacramental moment. Elder Holland states that at sacramental moments "we not only acknowledge [God's] divinity but we quite literally take something of that divinity to ourselves."[4]

THE HOLY GHOST AND HUMAN INTIMACY

When marital intimacy is embedded in personal purity, love is co-created. Pure love. The kind of love Parley P. Pratt describes:

> I had loved before, but I knew not why. But now I loved—with a pureness—an intensity of elevated, exalted feeling, which would lift my soul from the transitory things of this groveling sphere and expand it as the ocean. I felt that God was my Heavenly Father indeed; that Jesus was my brother, and that the wife of my bosom was an immortal, eternal companion. . . . In short, I could now love with the spirit and with the understanding also.[5]

The Lord blesses spouses who love each other purely. Alma 38:12 reads, "bridle all your passions, that ye may be filled with love." Parley P. Pratt also taught: "The gift of the Holy Ghost . . . quickens all the intellectual faculties, increases, enlarges, expands and purifies all the natural passions and affections; and adapts them, by the gift of wisdom, to their lawful use."[6] As we increase our understandings of these truths about the Spirit, we will not worry that increased purity might decrease our God-given passions. Those natural passions (and the operative word is *natural*) will be increased, purified, and adapted to their lawful use. Spirit-magnified and purified natural passion will always be sweeter and more joyful than mere lust.

Whether married or unmarried, we need our natural passions and affections to be purified and we need the wisdom to use them lawfully. Think of the healing that is available for all of us—from those who struggle with the effects of their own moral sins to those who have been victims of others. Think of the possibilities for intimacy that are available to all of us as we seek to receive this blessing—this gift from the Holy Ghost.

CONCLUSION

As women and men of the latter days, we need to seek diligently to increase the purity in our lives by keeping the Lord's commandments with ever-increasing exactness. As men and women who have made sacred covenants with the Lord, we need to draw closer to Him and to invite others to come unto

Him. We, as spirit daughters and sons of heavenly parents, need to ensure that Satan is continually cast out of our hearts, minds, homes, and families. We, as men and women of God, need to forge intimate relationships with others that involve the Savior. We, as daughters of Eve and sons of Adam, need to distinguish good from evil and partake of physical intimacy only within the sacred ordinance of marriage. As we do so, we will co-create love in intimate relationships that are sanctified by the Lord.

NOTES

1. Truman G. Madsen (1971), *Four essays on love* (Salt Lake City: Bookcraft), 29.

2. Victor L. Brown Jr. (1981), *Human intimacy* (Salt Lake City: Publishers Press).

3. Jeffrey R. Holland (1998, November), Personal Purity, *Ensign, 28*(11), (298).

4. Holland (1998, November), 298.

5. Parley P. Pratt (1976), *Autobiography of Parley P. Pratt* (Salt Lake City: Deseret Book), 298.

6. Parley P. Pratt (1973), *Key to the science of theology* (10ᵗʰ ed.) (Salt Lake City: Deseret Book), 61.

Equal Partnership and the Sacred Responsibilities of Mothers and Fathers

Alan J. Hawkins, Diane L. Spangler, Valerie Hudson, David C. Dollahite, Shirley R. Klein, Susan Sessions Rugh, Camille A. Fronk, Richard D. Draper, A. Don Sorensen, Lynn D. Wardle, and E. Jeffrey Hill

By divine design, fathers are to preside over their families in love and righteousness and are responsible to provide the necessities of life and protection for their families. Mothers are primarily responsible for the nurture of their children. In these sacred responsibilities, fathers and mothers are obligated to help one another as equal partners.
(The Family: A Proclamation to the World, ¶ 7)

We begin this chapter by reviewing the underlying theology of this profound statement from the Proclamation, a theology that is sometimes incompletely grasped or even misunderstood. Next, we explore some of the rich meaning behind the concepts of paternal presiding and providing and maternal nurturing. Then, we investigate the concept of equal partnership. The concepts of equal partnership and sacred responsibilities for mothers and fathers are deeply interwoven; to separate them would likely damage the tapestry of truth they portray. Hence, they are combined in this chapter. We also look briefly at some historical changes that have supported building equal partnerships and overview the research that confirms how equality in marriage is associated with stronger relationships and happier individuals. At greater length, we look at some misunderstandings associated with equal partnership and distinctive gender responsibilities.

In all this, we are aware of the sensitive nature of the issues raised in this chapter and we acknowledge our imperfect understanding of these important truths. Our hope is to increase understanding and faith.

The Doctrine of Equal Partnership and Sacred Responsibilities of Mothers and Fathers

The scriptures teach that this mortal probation is a time for us to prepare ourselves to meet God and dwell with Him, (see Alma 34:32) where we will live together not solely as celestial individuals but as celestial couples (see D&C 132:19) and heirs of God (see Rom. 8:14–17). Our ultimate possibilities are realized in the context of an eternal marriage, like our heavenly parents. Thus the work of God, and of exalted persons, is carried out as women and men united in eternal marriages. To become heirs of God, couples must learn to abide a celestial law (see D&C 78:7; 132:22).

Adam and Eve and all their descendants were created spiritually and physically, male and female, in the image of our heavenly parents. The Proclamation states: "All human beings—male and female—are created in the image of God. Each is a beloved spirit son or daughter of heavenly parents" (¶ 2). But a physical likeness to God and our divine heritage are not sufficient for us to be full heirs; we must also be transformed spiritually to become like our heavenly parents through the Atonement of Jesus Christ. Righteous relationships between husbands and wives are indispensable in helping us achieve this spiritual transformation and fulfill God's ultimate purpose for us.

Eve's and Adam's Interdependence and Equality

To achieve this spiritual transformation and to fulfill God's ultimate purposes in this life and in the next, women and men are dependent on each other and must become one to fulfill their divine potential. One gender does not have greater eternal possibility than the other (see Moses 2:26–27; 2 Ne. 26:28, 33). In the scriptural account of Adam and Eve in the Garden of Eden, their interdependence is often missed; instead, the account is too often used to justify false inequalities between husbands and wives, mothers and fathers. In a state where they did not know good from evil (see 2 Ne. 2:23), Eve and Adam eventually understood the necessity to know God through faith, as mortality requires, become moral agents, pass through tribulation, experience mortal life, and die physically. To become heirs of their divine parents, they had to choose for themselves and for all their posterity to leave the Garden of Eden and the presence of God. This separation from God was necessary to allow Eve and Adam to become mortal, to be tempted, to obtain knowledge, and to walk by faith to see whether they would be obedient to the truths they had been taught. Eve was the first to choose this necessary course and partake of the fruit of the tree of knowledge of good and evil. She led the way for all into mortal life and opened the door to the attainment of agency, experience, and greater knowledge.[1] Adam also perceived that this course was good and necessary (see Gen. 3:6; Moses 4:12). As partners, Adam and Eve became mortal, moral agents.

The scriptural account suggests that Eve was given stewardship over nurturing mortal life, including providing physical bodies for God's spirit children and for guiding those in a state of innocence to a state of accountability and knowledge before God. Adam received a stewardship of bestowing ordinances and experiences that allowed all to return to the presence of God. In this way, Eve's and Adam's stewardships were interdependent; together these stewardships allowed for the separation from and reuniting with God. Through Eve and her daughters, we enter mortal life, a necessary step in the plan of salvation, and are nurtured in light and truth. Through Adam and his sons, we may receive the saving ordinances of the priesthood that help us return to our heavenly home and gain eternal life. There seems, then, an intentional interdependence and equality in the responsibilities given to mothers and fathers and a real way in which the man is not "without the woman, neither the woman without the man, in the Lord" (1 Cor. 11:11). Adam and Eve served each other as equals, with each performing acts of leadership and service for the other.

Equality, Not Hierarchy

Within a system of equal and interdependent partnership, some distinction in stewardship does not mean that one stewardship is superior to the other. Although in God's system of divine orderliness some distinctive stewardships have been assigned to husbands and wives, it is important to be clear about what this means and does not mean today and throughout history. Some have misinterpreted the biblical account of Eve's partaking of the fruit and her "beguiling" by Satan as indicating that women are spiritually inferior to men, and they wrongly assume that husbands are in a superior position to their wives. But prophets and apostles of The Church of Jesus Christ of Latter-day Saints have taught otherwise. Elder Dallin H. Oaks taught that Eve's act was "a glorious necessity to open the doorway toward eternal life" and that Eve did not sin "because God had decreed it," and that we are to "celebrate Eve's act and honor her wisdom and courage in the great episode called the Fall."[2] Eve made her choice for mortality in "wisdom and courage." Although Eve apparently was "beguiled" in some way, we do not know exactly how. Possibly she was deceived as to the true identity and motivations of Satan, or she was deceived as to how decisions were to be made (i.e., jointly as a couple and with God instead of alone).[3] Despite the ambiguous meaning of her beguiling, the scriptures clearly teach that Eve ultimately understood the goodness of choosing mortality, for she said, "Were it not for our transgression we never should have had seed, and never should have known good and evil, and the joy of our redemption, and the eternal life which God giveth unto all the obedient" (Moses 5:11).

Similarly, some misunderstand the scriptural phrase that Eve was to be an "help meet" for Adam (see Gen. 2:18; Moses 3:18) to mean that wives are in a subordinate position to their husbands. However, commenting on the meaning of "help meet," President Howard W. Hunter explained the word "*meet* means equal."[4] Furthermore, referring to the scripture that says Adam should rule over Eve (Gen. 3:16), President Gordon B. Hinckley said: "I regrettably recognize that some men have used this through centuries of time as justification for abusing and demeaning women. But . . . in so doing they have demeaned themselves and offended the Father of us all." Rather, President Hinckley interprets the scripture to mean that "the husband shall have a governing responsibility to provide for, to protect, to strengthen and shield the wife."[5]

In addition, we often forget about the other word in the phrase "help meet"—help. An understanding of the original Hebrew words gives insight into the meaning of the term and the reciprocal nature of men's and women's God-given stewardships. The first word, translated as "help," combines the meanings "to rescue or save" with the idea of "strength." Combined with the second word, "meet," or equal, help meet suggests one who has equal strength to rescue. In other words, Eve had equal capacity to help Adam as he had to help her. It is important to note that nowhere in scripture does the term *help mate* occur. Help mate wrongly suggests the Lord gave Adam a companion just to help him, quite a different meaning from what scripture and the Proclamation teach.

The stewardship over priesthood given to Adam and his worthy sons and the stewardship over bestowing and nurturing life given to Eve and her daughters both come with strict guidelines for how they are to be used to bless the lives of others. These stewardships do not entail domination and subordination; rather, they allow for a system of interdependent service and leadership for the purpose of redeeming souls. Stewardship over priesthood allows a father to open some doors to spiritual progression for his family just as stewardship over nurturing life allows a mother to open some doors to spiritual progression for her family. The Savior taught:

> Ye know that the princes of the Gentiles exercise dominion over them, and they that are great exercise authority upon them. But it shall not be so among you: but whosoever will be great among you, let him be your minister; and whosoever will be chief among you, let him be your servant. (Matt. 20:25–27).

Reciprocal service requires husbands and wives to stand as equals in their homes; neither husbands nor wives should exercise authority over the other.

The scriptures warn of the temptations to misuse the powers associated with stewardships over nurturing life and priesthood. "We have learned by sad experience that it is the nature and disposition of almost all men, as soon as they get a little authority, as they suppose, they will immediately begin to exercise unrighteous dominion" (D&C 121:39). Those who attempt to use their stewardship powers to "exercise control or dominion or compulsion upon the souls of the children of men, in any degree of unrighteousness" lose their power and authority (D&C

121:37). The righteous steward understands that "no power or influence can or ought to be maintained by virtue of the priesthood, only by persuasion, by longsuffering, by gentleness and meekness, and by love unfeigned; by kindness, and pure knowledge" (D&C 121:41).

Righteous husbands and wives do not try to rule over each other; rather, each submits to the principles of the gospel and allows these principles to govern (see D&C 58:20, 28; 2 Ne. 2:26–27). President Hunter said: "The Lord intended that the wife be. . . . a companion equal and necessary in full partnership . . . For a man to operate independent of or without regard to the feelings and counsel of his wife in governing the family is to exercise unrighteous dominion."[6] Elder Richard G. Scott specifically denounced cultural practices that condone husbands dominating their wives: "Is yours a culture where the husband exerts a domineering, authoritarian role? . . . That pattern needs to be tempered so that both husband and wife act as equal partners."[7] In blunter terms, President Gordon B. Hinckley said:

> Some men who are evidently unable to gain respect by the goodness of their lives use as justification for their actions the statement that Eve was told that Adam should rule over her. How much sadness, how much tragedy, how much heartbreak has been caused through centuries of time by weak men who have used that as a scriptural warrant for atrocious behavior! They do not recognize that the same account indicates that Eve was given as a helpmeet to Adam. The facts are that they stood side by side in the garden. They were expelled from the garden together, and they worked together, side by side.[8]

Family stewardships should be understood in terms of their responsibilities—obligations to one's spouse, not power over one's spouse. Moreover, contrary to scripture and the teachings of latter-day prophets, some have interpreted *presiding* to mean that after equal counsel, equal consent is not necessary because the presider (or husband) has the right of final say. A noted LDS marriage and family therapist, Carlfred Broderick, reports that he received pointed instruction from President Boyd K. Packer on this matter when he (Broderick) was sustained as a stake president: "When there is a [family] decision to be made that affects everyone, you and your wife together will seek whatever counsel you might need, and together you will prayerfully come to a unified decision. If you ever pull priesthood rank on her you will have failed."[9] On a later occasion, President Packer explained: "In the Church there is a distinct line of authority. We serve where called by those who preside over us. In the home it is a partnership with husband and wife equally yoked together, sharing in decisions, always working together."[10]

The stewardship of priesthood does not superimpose a hierarchical relationship over the God-ordained equality between husband and wife. President James E. Faust taught that "every father is to his family a patriarch and every mother a matriarch as coequals in their distinctive parental roles."[11] We emphasize that the patriarchal priesthood is not so called to imply a hierarchy between men and women. Instead, as President Ezra Taft Benson taught, it is called patriarchal because in ancient days it was handed down from faithful father to faithful son, and today frequently still is (see D&C 107:40–42). (*Patri* is Latin for father.) President Benson also taught that the patriarchal order is the family order of government, presided over by mothers and fathers.[12] One of the most revolutionary aspects of the restored gospel is its ability to help us envision difference without hierarchy, distinctiveness without inequality. This is what the Proclamation calls upon us to hold as the ideal relationship between husbands and wives.

Oneness

The importance for husbands and wives to be equal partners also derives from the commandment for eternal companions to be one (Gen. 2:22–24). The scriptures teach us that it is not good for man or woman to be alone; in God's plan of happiness, we are to be together and inseparable in body and heart in an eternal covenant of marriage. Adam expressed this truth when he exclaimed: "[Eve] is now bone of my bones, and flesh of my flesh. . . . Therefore shall a man leave his father and his mother, and shall cleave unto his wife: and they shall be one flesh" (Gen. 2:23–24). Note also that Adam was to "cleave unto" his wife, Eve. The Hebrew word translated here (*dâbaq*) means to stick to, cling to, adhere to. Similarly, the Greek word used in Matthew (*kollaó*) means to join together, bind, weld, and stresses the idea of making two things into one.[13] In marriage, God intends to create a new spiritual and physical relationship marked by the words "one flesh." Underscoring the point, Genesis 5:2 declares that God created male and female "and blessed them, and called *their name* Adam, (emphasis added)"[14]

suggesting God no longer regarded them just as two separate beings but rather as one unit.

The cause and purpose of marriage is to make man and woman one. In this unity, it is God's work to exalt us (see Moses 1:39). No wonder, then, marriage is ordained of God (see D&C 49:15). Properly conceived and practiced, marriage is deity in embryo. Like the two strands of a double helix that wind around each other in their connection to form the basis of physical life, when woman and man become one in marriage, their intertwining forms the seed of eternal lives.

The doctrine of equal partnership and sacred responsibilities for mothers and fathers beckons men and women to draw their families within the living circle of God's eternal purposes as they forever grow in glory. The Proclamation specifically counsels fathers to preside and provide and mothers to nurture. In this next section, we explore some reasons for this doctrine and ponder the rich meaning behind the principles of presiding, providing, and nurturing.

SACRED RESPONSIBILITIES OF FATHERS AND MOTHERS

Fathers Preside in and Provide for Their Families

The importance of fatherhood. From a spiritual perspective, fathering is both a joyous blessing and a challenging, sacred responsibility. Latter-day scripture and prophetic teaching strongly emphasize how important fathers are in God's plan of happiness for His children. In modern scripture the Lord states that "great things" would be required of fathers (D&C 29:48) and Elder Jeffrey R. Holland stated that "surely the greatest of those things will be to have done all they could for the happiness and spiritual safety of the children they are to nurture."[15] President Harold B. Lee stated to LDS men that "the most important of the Lord's work you and I will ever do will be within the walls of our own homes."[16] Similarly, President David O. McKay told the priesthood brethren that "no other success can compensate for failure in the home."[17] President Benson taught that, "Fathers, yours is an eternal calling from which you are never released. . . . A father's calling is eternal, and its importance transcends time."[18] These teachings remind us that family is the preeminent sphere of priesthood service in the Lord's kingdom and *husband* and *father* are the preeminent responsibilities priesthood holders have. Of note, recent research has shown how religious beliefs and practices can be especially helpful in promoting responsible fathering.[19]

In recent years, the negative consequences of fatherlessness and the positive contributions fathers make to their families have received considerable attention from researchers. Much of this attention on fathering has come as a result of learning about the consequences to women and children when fathers fail in their responsibilities. When a father is not present in the home, his children often do not receive the financial support they need. Accordingly, half of single-parent, mother-headed families live below the poverty line.[20] Without the financial and social support of a father, children, on average, do not do as well in school and have less educational achievement. There is much greater risk that adolescents in fatherless homes will commit crimes or become involved in delinquent behavior, as well as early sexual activity. The scholarly evidence on the negative consequences of fathers not living up to their divinely appointed responsibilities is sobering.[21] Such data provide support for the belief of some scholars that absent or inadequate fathering is "the most harmful demographic trend of this generation" and "the leading cause of declining child well-being in our society."[22] While some scholars continue to argue that fathers are not irreplaceable in terms of children's well-being and that marriage should not be privileged as a foundation for rearing children,[23] many scholars now are finding strong evidence that good fathering helps children in their cognitive, social, and moral development[24] and that marriage is a critical foundation for responsible fathering.[25]

Presiding in love and righteousness. President Benson stated, "Brethren, I say to you with all soberness, [Christ] is the model we must follow as we take the spiritual lead in our families. Particularly is this true in your relationship with your wife."[26] The scriptures make clear that the Savior treated all people—men, women and children—He knew and met, with perfect love, compassion, respect, and dignity (see Mark 10:13–16; 3 Ne. 17:11–25). The Apostle Paul taught, "Husbands, love your wives, even as Christ also loved the church, and gave himself for it" (Eph. 5:25). Thus, Jesus is our exemplar in what it means to preside in love and righteousness. For example, the Savior always sought to know and do His Father's will, not his own (see John 5:30; 6:38). A righteous father will constantly seek to know and do the will of God and will never assume that his call to preside is a license to impose his will on family members. Another aspect of Christ's righteous leadership was that he continually served others, often at significant personal sacrifice. In addition, Jesus always led with love and commanded his disciples to love as he loved (see John 15:12). Thus, the foundation for a father's stewardship to preside must be love for God, for his wife, and children.

Presiding requires following Christ and His authorized servants. A righteous father also seeks guidance from the Holy Spirit for the benefit of his family. He attempts to lead his family to Christ through his righteous example. Presiding in love and righteousness involves an eternal commitment to the well-being of one's family. It involves learning their needs, extending the blessings of the priesthood to them, leading family members in prayer, scripture study, family home evening, and other family devotional activities. A father uses the priesthood to open doors to gospel ordinances for family members. He blesses, teaches, counsels, prays for and with, and seeks revelation to help family members with their choices and challenges. Fathers should give their all to bless their families, as Christ gave His all for our eternal welfare.

President Benson said, "As the patriarch in your home, you have a serious responsibility to assume leadership in working with your children. You must help create a home where the Spirit of the Lord can abide. . . . Your homes should be havens of peace and joy for your family. Surely no child should fear his own father—especially a priesthood father."[27] President Faust taught that the sealing power restored by Elijah designed to turn the hearts of fathers to children and children to fathers (see D&C 110:15; Mal. 4:6) "reveals itself in family relationships, in attributes and virtues developed in a nurturing environment, and in loving service. These are the cords that bind families together, and the priesthood advances their development."[28] In short, presiding means leading by giving righteous, loving, Christlike, priesthood guidance and service (see Mark 9:35).

Leadership with love is difficult in any context, and the home is no exception. Thus, all priesthood holders will need to grow in their abilities to be righteous leaders in the home. A righteous husband and father will regularly seek counsel from his wife about how he is carrying out his responsibilities and how he can progress further. A wife who uses kindness, meekness, gentle persuasion, love unfeigned, and

TIPS FOR FATHERS TO HARMONIZE THEIR EMPLOYMENT AND FAMILY LIFE

Here are some ideas for fathers to think about as they strive to fulfill their joint duties to provide for their families and spend the time with them that is important to righteous priesthood leadership and service. This is a set of ideas, not a checklist; not every idea is applicable to every father. And some fathers have more freedom to implement these ideas than others. Individual adaptation to unique circumstances is necessary.

Be careful in selecting a vocation that fits with the needs of family life:
- Choose a vocation that energizes you and makes you excited about life.
- Be a good employee; it leads to much more flexible work opportunities in the long run.
- Choose a job that leaves you with enough time and energy for family life.
- Avoid vocations that require a lot of travel.

Allow your family to "be there" while you are in the workplace:
- Display a recent family picture prominently where you labor.
- Call home at lunch or during breaks just to say "I love you."
- Encourage your children to call you at work to talk about their school day.
- Bring your children to work on occasion to let them see firsthand what you do all day.

Use your commute time for personal and family development:
- Bring a tape recorder and record stories about your youth for your children.
- Sing or pray out loud to invite the Spirit into your car, especially on the way home as you prepare to be with family members.

Make the best of it when you have to travel out of town:
- Find a speaker phone, and call to have family prayer together morning and night.
- Use frequent flyer miles to occasionally bring your wife and/or older children on business trips.
- Select a different child each night and talk to him or her on the phone for an extended period of time.
- Have children fax you homework and pictures.
- Send e-mail to family members.
- Work longer and harder while away so that you can spend more time at home when you return.

Create family time by using flexible work options:
- Use flextime to create morning time for devotional, prayer, and breakfast with the family.
- Use parental leave to create quantity and quality family time when new babies come.
- Come to work early; then volunteer at your child's school once a month in the afternoon.

When you come home from work, really come home from work:
- Don't bring work pressures and frustrations into the sacred confines of your home.
- Listen to some classical or sacred music during the ride home.
- Mentally prepare yourself to walk through the door and be available for family members.

Box 5.1

pure knowledge (see D&C 121:41) can be of tremendous assistance in this growth process. LDS women are asked to sustain their husbands who preside in righteousness, just as LDS husbands are asked to sustain their wives in their nurturing. Fathers who are not living with their children due to divorce or other unfortunate circumstances still should strive to provide loving priesthood leadership and service to their children. Mothers in these circumstances should still respect and facilitate the righteous use of priesthood leadership by their former husbands as much as possible for the benefit of their children.

Providing the necessities of life. The Proclamation specifies that fathers are "responsible to provide the necessities of life . . . for their families" (¶ 7). This injunction was taught in ancient times (see 1 Tim. 5:8), and in modern revelation the Lord stated, "Verily

I say unto you, that every man who is obliged to provide for his own family, let him provide, and he shall in nowise lose his crown" (D&C 75:28). Also, "Women have claim on their husbands for their maintenance, until their husbands are taken" (D&C 83:2). President Packer said to fathers: "You are responsible, unless disabled, to provide temporal support for your wife and children."[29] Paradoxically, in a time of great economic and materialistic prosperity for so many, these reminders are more important than ever because too many fathers disregard this commandment, particularly when they are not living with their children. Again, fathers who are not living with their children due to divorce or other unfortunate circumstances are not excused from their obligation to do all they can to provide the necessities of life for their children.

Providing the necessities of life, however, should not be used as a justification for spending too much time at work to provide a high standard of living. The Lord's servants do not seek first for riches but for the kingdom of God (see Matt. 6:33; Jacob 2:18–19; 3 Ne. 13:33). In a culture that worships material things, as President Spencer W. Kimball warned,[30] some fathers spend so much time providing for things far beyond the necessities of life that they have little time to preside in love and righteousness. (See Box 5.1.)

Providing protection. Not only are fathers required to provide the necessities of life for their families, but the Proclamation teaches that fathers are also "responsible to provide . . . protection for their families" (¶ 7). What do families need protection from? And what can fathers do to provide this protection?

President Hunter taught: "A righteous father protects his children with his time and presence in their social, educational, and spiritual activities and responsibilities."[31] Consequently, a father should make spending time with his family a high priority. Good research confirms that when a father spends significant time with his children, his children are less likely to become involved in risk-taking and delinquent behavior.[32] In addition, President Hunter stated, "A man who holds the priesthood leads his family in Church participation so they will know the gospel and be under the protection of the covenants and ordinances."[33] Sacred covenants and ordinances provide the protection of God's presence and blessings to His covenant people (see Ex. 19:5; D&C 54:6).

We live in a world in which moral dangers confront children at earlier and earlier ages. Thus, the Lord's commandment for fathers to pray for their wives and children (see 3 Ne. 18:21; Alma 34:21) is more important than ever. This can protect children because "the effectual fervent prayer of a righteous man availeth much" (James 5:16). However, because faith without works is dead (James 2:17), fathers should actively protect their children by helping them to make wise choices about the literature they read, the movies they see, the television programs they watch, the Internet sites they visit, and the friendships they establish.

Physical protection is important, too. Fathers can take the lead in providing physical protection for their families in numerous ways. Although crime occurs in all locations, providing the family with a home in a safe neighborhood is important. A father may be able to provide in this way by getting a good education or vocational training that increases his earning power. Teaching children ways to be safe in various situations (e.g., water sports, biking, crossing streets, driving cars) can help them avoid serious injuries. Family preparedness is another way to protect the family from life's uncertainties, and fathers should take the lead insuring that principles of preparedness are taught and lived in their families. Recently, President Hinckley warned members that financial prosperity can be fleeting.[34] He encouraged members to be cautious and prepared. Getting out of debt, living modestly, and saving have been counseled regularly by Church leaders and help protect families from financial crisis.

Following the example of Heavenly Father. After discussing the sublime relationship between Heavenly Father and His Son Jesus Christ, Elder Jeffrey R. Holland asked: "As a father, I wonder if I and all other fathers could do more to build a sweeter, stronger relationship with our own sons and daughters here on earth. Dads, is it too bold to hope that our children might have some small portion of the feeling for us that the Divine Son felt for His Father? Might we earn more of that love by trying to be more of what God was to His child?"[35] One of the many ways the Father showed His love for Jesus was in the manner He spoke of His Son when Jesus was baptized (see Matt. 3:16–17), on the Mount of Transfiguration (see Matt. 17:5), when Jesus appeared to the Nephites (see 3 Ne. 11:7), and when the Father and the Son appeared to the Prophet Joseph Smith (see JS–H 1:17). On these occasions the Father said "my beloved Son" and also that He was "well pleased" with His Son. This is a divine pattern that all fathers can follow. Fathers who are actively involved and present with their children—especially at important times and events—show their children they care and that their hearts are turned to the children (Mal. 3:4–5). Fathers who frequently communicate both privately and publicly to their children of all ages that they love them and are pleased with them provide their children with a great blessing. Unfortunately, far too many children doubt whether their fathers love and are proud of them. If more fathers followed this divine pattern, more children would feel about their earthly fathers as Jesus felt about his Heavenly Father.

Regardless of where a father currently stands in his ability to preside joyfully in love and righteousness and to provide his family with temporal and spiritual blessings, he can progress. Elder Holland offered encouragement to all fathers when he said:

> And, brethren, even when we are *not* "the best of men," even in our limitations and inadequacy, we can keep making our way in the right direction because of the encouraging teachings set forth by a Divine Father and demonstrated by a Divine Son. With a Heavenly Father's help we can leave more of a parental legacy than we suppose.[36]

Mothers Nurture Their Children

The meaning and importance of nurturing. The Proclamation teaches that mothers have a divine responsibility to nurture their children. Defining such a broad term as *nurturance,* however, can be difficult. Looking at the scholarly literature on parenting can help us be more specific about the meaning of nurturing. It refers to a number of parenting behaviors including attachment, warmth, support, recognizing the individuality of each child, and attending to children's needs.[37] Since the early 1960s, social science researchers investigating the effects of nurturing on child development have noted numerous positive effects and concluded that "nurturance per se is more important than any particular method or technique of child-rearing."[38] Many studies of nurturance are based on a theory of bonding or attachment,[39] which posits that a child's attachment to a parent and development of a sense of security results from sensitive and responsive care during infancy and beyond. It may seem self-evident, but leading child development scholars acknowledge that nurturing is best done in a stable family context.[40]

Spiritual sources especially help to clarify the meaning of nurturance. Mother as nurturer means not only that mothers have a responsibility to oversee the physical growth of each child, but also to guide their children's full development during this mortal experience. The First Presidency explained this stewardship in 1942:

> Motherhood thus becomes a holy calling, a sacred dedication for carrying out the Lord's plans, a consecration of devotion to the uprearing and fostering, the nurturing in body, mind, and spirit, of those who kept their first estate and who come to this earth for the second estate "to see if they will do all things whatsoever the Lord their God shall command them" (Abraham 3:25). To lead them to keep their second estate is the work of motherhood, and they who keep their second estate shall have glory added upon their heads for ever and ever.[41]

A stewardship, or holy calling, to nurture body, mind, and spirit is thus the work of motherhood. It is a work that is comprehensive, complex, and constant. Clearly, the need for children to be nurtured by a loving mother is as strong as, if not stronger than, ever, yet we still hear voices arguing against this logic. Some seductive current thinking suggests that beyond our genes and the neighborhood we provide our children, differences in parental nurturing do not make much difference in children's development.[42] This is a misinterpretation of scientific studies; the evidence that parents make a critical contribution to children's development is strong but too voluminous to review here. Such thinking, supported by misapplication of scientific findings, may cause some mothers to discount the importance of their nurturing contributions. One of Satan's most effective approaches to draw us away from God's plan of happiness is to demean the work of a wife and mother in the home. Elder Scott cautioned that "this is an attack at the very heart of God's plan. . . . Don't be lured away from the plan of our God to the ways of the world, where motherhood is belittled, femininity is decried, and the divinely established role of wife and mother is mocked."[43]

Usually we associate the word *nurture* with gentleness and passiveness. The sense of power, leadership, and strength that are part of a mother's nurturance are too often overlooked. Just as real power and authority accompany a calling to the priesthood, the powers of godliness also accompany the holy calling of motherhood. The 1942 First Presidency statement proclaims: "Motherhood is near to divinity. It is the highest, holiest service to be assumed by mankind. It places her who honors its holy calling and service next to the angels."[44]

A mother's love awakens in young children a memory of the life, love, and goodness they experienced in the premortal existence from their heavenly parents. This awakening to goodness and hope prepares the new soul to recognize the moral law later in life because these things will be familiar and beloved. A mother's love prepares her children in such a way that these new souls will have "the work of the law written in their hearts" (Rom. 2:15). Knowing that our mothers know and love us helps us believe that God knows and loves us. Perhaps we better understand that Christ would suffer for us because our mothers did the same to enable our lives. Thus, our hope and faith in God is awakened by our mothers. Accordingly, motherhood is a "holy calling."

In the same way that we should honor and obey counsel that comes from priesthood leaders, Elder Russell M. Nelson asks children to honor and obey their mothers. "Remember that your mother is your *mother*. She should not need to issue orders. Her wish, her hope, her hint should provide direction that you would honor." Moreover, Elder Nelson said, "If one dishonors the commandments of God, one dishonors mother, and if one dishonors mother, one dishonors the commandments of God."[45] Similarly, President Thomas S. Monson said: "May each of us treasure this truth: One cannot forget mother and remember God. One cannot remember mother and forget God. Why? Because these two sacred persons, God and mother, partners in creation, in love, in sacrifice, in service, are as one."[46]

Elder Bruce C. Hafen argued that the importance of maternal nurturing goes beyond the well-being of one child; it matters terribly to the well-being of society. He discussed the importance of female nurturing and stated that it is the equivalent of moral influence, an influence that is increasingly devalued and lost. He believes we must reinstate the moral influence of women to help recapture peace, purpose, love, and human attachments:

> Men and women share all of the common traits of human nature and often perform the same tasks. But some of their strengths are gender specific. Women have certain unique gifts that have long fostered crucial civilizing functions. . . . [But] we are losing what these powerful female specialties contribute to cultural cohesiveness. . . . [W]omen['s] . . . influence begins in each society's very core—the home, where women have always taught and modeled what Alexis de

Tocqueville called "the habits of the heart"—the mores, or civilizing habits, that create a sense of personal and civic virtue, without which free and open societies can't exist.[47]

Elder Hafen argued that we must rebuild cultural support for female nurturing and influence. Important aspects of womanhood that enable nurturing behaviors include motherhood, sexual fidelity of both husbands and wives, marriage, and women's distinctive voices. These broad cultural supports have eroded dramatically in the past 30 years. Women's moral influence through nurturing activities is essential to restore the human and social capital of a free, democratic society.

Pressures that detract from nurturing. In addition to the erosion of broad cultural supports for nurturing, a number of pressures work against mothers' efforts to nurture on a daily basis. Time pressures, a consumer-oriented society, and opportunities in the workplace are some of the pressures women face today. Husbands and wives who are aware of these pressures can take steps to minimize their effects in their own homes.

One significant pressure comes from an acceleration of time that can blur our vision of life by its pace.[48] Time is as critical a currency for caring as love. Family sociologist Kerry Daly observes: "In our industrialized culture, we have a speed fetish that values expediency over processes that take a long time."[49] Nurturing children is one of those processes that takes sustained effort over a long time; it is not accomplished in short, irregular particles of time. Parental monitoring, general attentiveness, and being "at the crossroads" are time-intensive activities essential to nurturance (see Box 5.2). Some believe that "quality time" can substitute for "quantity time," but in many ways, quality is a direct function of quantity,[50] and parents—especially mothers—with their primary responsibility to nurture, must provide both.

In modern society we experience an accelerated sense of time in family life that can leave family members, especially children, feeling like a cog in some time machine rather than a loved individual.[52] In a recent representative national survey, 44% of children reported that their time with their mother was rushed, and feeling rushed was related to children's negative feelings about their mothers.[53] Children's time is not the same as adults' time; their pace is slower and less structured.[54] Mothers who remember the pressure of time and carefully guard against

TEN WAYS TO SPEND TIME WITH CHILDREN
PRESIDENT EZRA TAFT BENSON[51]

"Be at the Crossroads. . . . [T]ake time to always be at the crossroads when your children are either coming or going—when they leave and return from school, when they leave and return from dates, when they bring friends home.

"Be a Real Friend. . . . Listen to your children, really listen. Talk with them, laugh and joke with them, sing with them, play with them, cry with them, hug them, honestly praise them.

"Read to Your Children. . . . You will plant a love for good literature and a real love for the scriptures if you will read to your children regularly.

"Pray with Your Children. . . . Have your children feel of your faith as you call down the blessings of heaven upon them. Paraphrasing the words of James, 'The . . . fervent prayer of a righteous [mother] availeth much' (James 5:16).

"Have Weekly Home Evenings. . . . Participate in a spiritual and an uplifting home evening each week. . . . Make this one of your great family traditions.

"Be Together at Mealtimes. . . . Happy conversation, sharing of the day's plans and activities, and special teaching moments occur at mealtime because mothers and fathers and children work at it.

"Read Scriptures Daily. . . . Reading the Book of Mormon together as a family will especially bring increased spirituality into your home and will give both parents and children the power to resist temptation and to have the Holy Ghost as their constant companion.

"Do Things as a Family. . . . Make family outings and picnics and birthday celebrations and trips special times and memory builders. Whenever possible, attend, as a family, events where one of the family members is involved.

"Teach Your Family. . . . Catch the teaching moments. This can be done anytime during the day at mealtime, in casual settings, or at special sit-down times together, at the foot of the bed at the end of the day, or during an early morning walk together.

"Truly Love Your Children. . . . A mother's unqualified love approaches Christlike love."

Box 5.2

children may be devalued because of temptations to buy more and better things. President Hinckley and other Church leaders have cautioned Latter-day Saints about materialism and have counseled us to avoid it by not confusing needs with wants, not spoiling children with excessive spending and by living modestly, avoiding unnecessary debt, being generous, and sharing our surplus with others.[55] Families who heed this counsel can increase mothers' time devoted to nurturing. Beyond an adequate level of temporal well-being, caring, creativity, and time are more essential to nurturance than money and material goods.

Along with the pressure from a consumer-oriented society to have and spend more money, mothers may feel pressure from opportunities to employ their skills and talents in the workplace. The decision to forego a married mother's second income or her opportunity to work outside the home for a time can be a challenging one. How maternal employment affects children is a puzzle social scientists are still trying to solve. Research is mixed in terms of the effects of mothers' employment on children's development. Some reports suggest children suffer some ill effects, especially with prolonged daycare at early ages,[56] while other reports indicate no negative effects or even some benefits.[57] The best and most recent study on this issue suggests that more hours in outside child care were associated with somewhat more negative and less sensitive interactions between mothers and children.[58] This is not hard to understand given the time crunch that many employed mothers experience. Still, additional research is needed to disentangle the complicated links between maternal employment, nonmaternal child care, and child well-being.[59]

Amid the conflicting and inconclusive data from social scientists, prophets have consistently reinforced the importance of mothers devoting their full efforts to caring for their children and avoiding other commitments that seriously detract from this sacred responsibility of nurturing.[60] Recently, President Hinckley sensitively addressed this issue:

> Some years ago President Benson delivered a message to the women of the Church. He encouraged them to leave their employment and give their individual time to their children. I sustain the position which he took.
>
> Nevertheless, I recognize, as he recognized, that there are some women (it has become very many in fact) who have to work to provide for the needs of their families. To you I say, do the very best you can. I

overinvolvement in other activities can use time as a precious resource to spend for the benefit of their children.

Mothers today also may feel pressure from a consumer-oriented society. The time needed to nurture hope that if you are employed full-time you are doing it to ensure that basic needs are met and not simply to indulge a taste for an elaborate home, fancy cars, and other luxuries. The greatest job that any mother will ever do will be in nurturing, teaching, lifting, encouraging, and rearing her children in righteousness and truth. None other can adequately take her place.

It is well-nigh impossible to be a full-time homemaker and a full-time employee. I know how some of you struggle with decisions concerning this matter. I repeat, do the very best you can. You know your circumstances, and I know that you are deeply concerned for the welfare of your children. . . . [A]s the years pass, you will become increasingly grateful for that which you did in molding the lives of your children in the direction of righteousness and goodness, integrity and faith. That is most likely to happen if you can spend adequate time with them.[61]

Women without husbands to assist them in nurturing responsibilities can call on extended family for support. The Proclamation counsels "extended families should lend support when needed" (¶ 7). In addition, bishops, stake presidents, Relief Society presidents, and home and visiting teachers all have obligations to visit the fatherless and widows (James 1:27).[62] Former counselor in the General Relief Society Presidency Sister Cheiko Okazaki also encouraged women of the Church to be supportive and sharing, to refrain from judging one another, and to remember that circumstances often constrain choices.[63]

Personal development and prophetic promises. Nurturing responsibilities in the home should not overshadow the need for personal rejuvenation and development. One cannot serve from an empty plate. A mother who takes time for regular rejuvenation does not necessarily subtract from her ability to nurture. Instead, she adds to her reservoir of energy to care for her children. In addition, nurturing can be done without giving up individuality or righteous desires to bless the lives of others outside the family. A mother is a person too, a beloved daughter of God with unique gifts and blessings to offer, both to her children and the world. President Ezra Taft Benson counseled husbands to support their wives' opportunities "to grow intellectually, emotionally, and socially."[64] Sister Camilla Eyring Kimball encouraged women to continue to learn:

If we want to give effective service to our families and our neighbors, as we are commanded to do, we must develop ourselves to our full potential. We need

to enlarge our intellect and perfect our character. . . . My feeling is that each of us has the potential for special accomplishment in some field."[65]

President Faust reminds women that they have many opportunities in the various seasons of a full life:

Women today are being encouraged by some to have it all—generally, all simultaneously: money, travel, marriage, motherhood, and separate careers in the world. . . . Doing things sequentially—filling roles one at a time at different times—is not always possible, as we know, but it gives a woman the opportunity to do each thing well in its time and to fill a variety of roles in her life. . . . [A woman] may fit more than one career into the various seasons of life. She need not try to sing all the verses of her song at the same time.[66]

The amount of effort that needs to be devoted to specific gifts and stewardships will shift across time and circumstance. Flexibility and personal revelation are needed to accommodate to such changes and circumstances. Some mothers have special talents, circumstances, and inspired callings with divine help that allow them to contribute to their communities and professions at the same time they fulfill their primary responsibility to nurture their children.

In thinking about the need for personal development, however, we should not forget that "nurturing life is the most profoundly transforming experience in the range of human possibilities."[67] Researcher Ellen Galinsky eloquently describes the personal development found in nurturing in a way that echoes the great scriptural paradox that "whosoever will save [her] life shall lose it; but whosoever will lose [her] life for my sake, the same shall save it" (Luke 9:24):

Taking care of a small, dependent, growing person is transforming, because it . . . exposes our vulnerabilities as well as our nobility. We lose our sense of self, only to find it and have it change again and again. . . . We figure out how we want to interpret the wider world, and we learn to interact with all those who affect our children. . . . Often our fantasies are laid bare, our dreams are in a constant tug of war with realities. And perhaps we grow. In the end, we have learned more about ourselves, about the cycles of life, and humanity itself.[68]

Of course, sometimes the thought of such a sacred responsibility and the nearly constant demands of nurturing children can feel overwhelming. Nurturing is hard work; the pressures of modern life that tend to devalue nurturing activities can tempt

HOW HUSBANDS AND WIVES SUPPORT EACH OTHER IN THEIR SACRED RESPONSIBILITIES

A HUSBAND SUPPORTS HIS WIFE BY:	A WIFE SUPPORTS HER HUSBAND BY:
• getting a good education or strong vocational training to be able to provide for his family; being a wise steward in his family responsibilities.	• expressing appreciation for her husband's efforts to provide; gaining a good education; being a wise steward in her family responsibilities.
• honoring his wife and expressing reverence and respect for her motherhood and service in the home.	• supporting and expressing appreciation for her husband's fatherhood and his priesthood service.
• showing his children how much he loves their mother.	• showing her children how much she loves their father.
• sharing in child care, teaching children, and in management of the home.	• encouraging, expecting, and valuing the father's participation in daily family work.
• supporting his wife's regular rejuvenation and on-going personal development.	• supporting her husband's regular rejuvenation and on-going personal development.

Box 5.3

mothers to escape it all. Nurturing children is God's work, and according to President Benson, "there is no more noble work than that of a good and God-fearing mother."[69] Moreover, Sister Marjorie P. Hinckley reminds mothers to "have joy in your mothering . . . don't wish away your days of caring for . . . children. This is your great day."[70] The Lord has promised mothers great blessings for their efforts and promises them that He will be a partner in their divine labors. Elder Jeffrey R. Holland said:

> Mothers, we acknowledge and esteem your faith in every footstep. Please know that it is worth it then, now, and forever. . . . Yours is the work of salvation, and therefore you will be magnified, compensated, made more than you are and better than you have ever been as you try to make honest effort, however feeble you may sometimes feel that to be. . . . You are doing God's work. You are doing it wonderfully well. He is blessing you and He will bless you, even—no, *especially*—when your days and your nights may be the most challenging.[71]

EQUAL PARTNERSHIP: PROGRESS AND PROBLEMS

The Proclamation teaches that mothers and fathers are "obligated to help one another as *equal partners*" (¶ 7, emphasis added). Ideals of equality and

oneness have often been ignored and can be difficult to achieve; men and women across time and cultures have struggled to understand and live according to these principles. But God is merciful and has and always will strive to help men and women live according to principles of happiness. In this next section, we discuss historical and cultural changes that supported efforts to build equal partnerships in the American society generally. Then we explore the continuing contemporary struggles in our understanding and practice of equal partnerships. There are powerful secular ideologies that are inconsistent with the gospel. An understanding of the ideas in this section will assist in articulating and defending the related Proclamation principles of distinct gender responsibilities and equal partnership.

Progress

Some cultures now view marriage ideally as an equal partnership and many families are striving to implement this ideal. These harmonious strains of equal partnership in the lives of many women and men must be pleasing for the Lord to hear. In pre-industrial times, mothers and fathers were highly interdependent in their labors; that is, their working partnerships around the home and farm were critical to economic survival and prosperity. The dramatic changes to families that resulted from industrialization and urbanization actually diminished this kind of partnership between men and women. However, other changes over the same period of time helped to support greater marital equality. In recent times, some societies have eliminated many important legal, political, economic, and social barriers that hinder building equal partnerships.

Historical Perspective. Marital inequality has been a common characteristic of family relations across time and cultures, with the husband/father wielding power over the wife/mother. Recent trends toward equal partnership should be seen in the context of the gradual removal of substantial legal, political, economic, and social barriers to women's equality as individuals. Although here we focus on American history, a similar trend would be found in many other Western cultures. Because of limited space, what follows analyzes the trend for the American working and middle class and does not apply to the history of Native Americans and African-Americans (who were not legally granted full civil rights until the 1960s).

Early Americans inherited from their English forebears a hierarchical view of society, in which kings ruled men and men ruled women. The family was seen as a "little commonwealth," with the father as the benevolent ruler over wife, children, and servants. This hierarchical view of the family was upheld by English and early American law (see Box 5.4). Men used positions of authority in local government and in the church to uphold the marital hierarchy. While most early American women accepted marital hierarchy, and husbands and wives were economically interdependent partners, women had few legal, political, or economic rights.[72]

The gradual reduction of barriers to equality between husbands and wives began only after society accepted the goals of equality and liberty for which they fought in the American Revolutionary War (1776–1783). As the founding fathers were writing the Constitution, the new nation's citizens were thoroughly committed to ideas of liberty and equality.[73] Abigail Adams, wife of John Adams, architect of the Constitution, asked her husband to "Remember the Ladies, and be more generous and favorable to them than your ancestors. Do not put such unlimited power into the hands of the Husbands."[74] However, because wives had no legal standing, the privilege of voting was restricted to white males, and the second-class citizenship of women reinforced marital inequality.[75]

Industrialization and the growth of large cities in

LEGAL STATUS OF WIVES

Historically, women did not enjoy the same legal and economic rights as men. For instance, at common law, according to Blackstone, "the very being or legal existence of the woman [was] suspended during . . . marriage, or at least [was] incorporated and consolidated into that of the husband; under whose wing, protection and cover she perform[ed] everything." The husband was essentially the legal guardian of his wife. A married woman could not sue or be sued in her own name, but only by and in the name of her husband. She could not make contracts. Any land and much of the personal property that she owned at the time of marriage became the husband's property. In return, he was required to support her and pay her debts.

Today, there is a strong presumption that wives and husbands must be treated equally in the law and they generally enjoy the same rights and privileges in the law and in marriage. The U.S. Supreme Court has invalidated laws that give preference or control of marital property to husbands rather than wives, has invalidated laws that allow wives but not husbands to recover alimony, and state courts generally require the equal treatment of husbands and wives with regard to claims for custody of their children.

W. Blackstone (1915), *Commentaries on the Laws of England,* ed. W.C. Jones (San Francisco: Bancroft Whitney), vol. 1, book 1, 442. (Original work published 1765–1769).

Box 5.4

---

the early nineteenth century led to a separation of parental roles: men worked outside the home as breadwinners, and women remained in the home to nurture children. Motherhood was seen as so important that middle-class men expected a larger "family wage" so mothers could stay at home. Parents had fewer children and invested more in the training of each child.[76] With their removal from the home to the workplace, the authority of city-dwelling fathers diminished within the family.[77] The idea of equality in marriage began to take hold, but it was still not equal because women did not have the same basic legal rights as men.[78]

The trend toward equal partnership in marriage accelerated in the twentieth century with the emergence of companionate marriage as an ideal. In the 1920s, society began to recognize sexual intimacy as important to the marital bond, and the bearing and rearing of children became just one stage in a life-long marital companionship.[79] In addition, wives gained more rights to their property, and women became more active in the public sphere after they were granted the right to vote in 1920.[80]

Many contemporary ideas about happy families come from idealized media images of the 1950s suburbs, where mothers cared for the children and fathers commuted downtown to work. There are many admirable aspects of the 1950s family life, yet it was still a time when American husbands generally controlled household assets and dominated the decision-making processes in their families. Heavy breadwinning demands on fathers also meant many men had limited involvement with their children.[81]

Over the last 30 years, other forces have strengthened the ideal of marital equality in American society. The Civil Rights Movement furthered a belief in the inherent equality of all people. Moreover, fathers have increasingly sensed the value of and need for their daily involvement in the lives of their children.

While individual couples can build and maintain equal partnerships in marriage under many different legal, political, economic, and social systems, the changes that created greater equality between women and men in the ways discussed above have generally had a positive impact on marital equality. And although other parallel trends have had negative effects on marriage (e.g., privileging the self over family), we can appreciate those positive changes that have occurred to support marital equality.

Recent Research Perspectives. The Proclamation teaches the eternal importance of fathers and mothers helping each other as equal partners to raise a family. Given the importance that the Lord has placed on equal partnership in marriage, it is not surprising that research documents how marital equality is associated with stronger and happier marriages and greater individual well-being for both men and women. Recent reviews of research[82] in this area concluded that marital equality was moderately associated with greater couple intimacy (including physical and emotional intimacy) and more relationship satisfaction of both husbands and wives. In addition, better individual mental health is associated with greater marital equality, especially for wives.[83] Similarly, greater inequality is associated with less self-esteem for wives and more frequent feelings of hostility. Inequality is also costly for the more dominant partner—usually the husband—too. There is a loss of intimacy and openness in the relationship and less satisfaction with the marriage.

The encouraging news is that research generally confirms that marriages are happier for both husbands and wives when they report that they have equal say in making important decisions and when husbands take on significant, regular responsibilities in caring for the home and children. Excellent research also confirms that husbands who are accepting of their wives' influence are four times less likely to divorce or have an unhappy marriage.[84] Also, recent research confirms that today's fathers are significantly more involved in child care and household labor than in the past.[85]

Problems

Although such changes toward equality are encouraging, false ideologies from the past continue to influence unrighteous family behavior today. We continue to struggle to understand and live in a manner consistent with divine revelation regarding gender, marriage, and parenthood. Furthermore, new ideologies have been mixed with older, false traditions producing ever-new confusions, beliefs, and practices that are inconsistent with the Proclamation. Adherence to any ideology that is out of tune with the gospel results in some degree of disharmony in the family. We discuss only four core ideologies here. Of note, these four ideologies, like dissonant tones, overlap considerably with each other making it difficult to separate them intellectually.

1. Irrelevant gender versus eternal gender. LDS theology makes a crucial distinction between the full union of the sexes and complete gender sameness. The Proclamation makes clear that gender, like marriage (under the covenant), is eternal; that is, it predates and continues beyond mortality: "Gender is an essential characteristic of individual premortal, mortal, and eternal identity and purpose" (¶ 2). Marriage, parenting, and gender are not entirely mortal compositions or earthly institutions, but are "ordained of God" (D&C 49:15) and do not diminish but are augmented when mortality ends. Although we do not fully understand the eternal nature of gender, we should acknowledge its meaning and purpose, and humbly seek to understand and appreciate the nature of divine gender distinctions in God's plan for His children. President Boyd K. Packer stated:

> Be careful lest you unknowingly foster influences and activities which tend to erase the masculine and feminine differences nature has established. A man, a father, can do much of what is usually assumed to be a

woman's work. In turn, a wife and a mother can do much—and in time of need, most things—usually considered the responsibility of the man, without jeopardizing their distinct roles. Even so, leaders, and especially parents, should recognize that there is a distinct masculine nature and a distinct feminine nature essential to the foundation of the home and the family.[86]

Latter-day Saints should acknowledge meaning in and purpose to sacred gender distinctions. Of course, it is important to realize that marriage, parenthood, and gender *as currently defined and practiced on earth* does not necessarily constitute how they will be understood and experienced in celestial realms. Elder Neal A. Maxwell said: "We know so little about the reasons for the division of duties between womanhood and manhood as well as between motherhood and priesthood. These were divinely determined in another time and another place."[87] In these matters of eternal marriage, parenthood, and gender, we still "see through a glass darkly" (1 Cor. 13:12), and not all has been revealed to answer every question. On earth, marital, parental, and gender practices have varied a great deal over time and place and are influenced substantially by societal norms, culture, and the "traditions of their fathers" (D&C 93:39; 123:7). Thus, we should listen carefully to what the Spirit and the prophets can teach us on this subject rather than rely only on secular voices. Many current voices go "beyond the mark" (Jacob 4:14), modulating the doctrine of divine gender distinctions into strained beliefs of gender independence, separateness, and mistrust. We address these beliefs in the next three sections.

2. Independence versus interdependence. An "independence ideology" asserts that mothers and fathers operate as individual units with mutually exclusive, non-overlapping functions. This ideology can lead us to view mothering and fathering as separate endeavors with separate goals that do not overlap or intertwine and leads some parents to believe falsely that their family responsibilities end with their distinctive stewardship. In contrast, prophets have taught that the stewardships are not mutually exclusive; for instance, fathers are to be involved in the daily care of the home and children, as part of their obligations to preside and provide.[88] While mothers and fathers have been given some different leadership responsibilities within the family, overemphasizing their independence promotes reliance on rigid family roles and following the "traditions of men" rather than seeking for inspiration in fulfilling family responsibilities. The problems created by adherence

to this independence ideology include isolation and emptiness where husbands and wives feel they have grown apart and are working alone, unsupported, toward separate goals.[89]

This *in*-dependence ideology stands in contrast to the *inter*-dependent view espoused in the Proclamation, which states that "in these sacred responsibilities [of parenthood], fathers and mothers are obligated to help one another as equal partners" (¶ 7). Fathers and mothers should be united in a common goal of rearing righteous children. This joint responsibility and opportunity of fathers and mothers opens to each parent almost any activity that promotes the spiritual, emotional, intellectual, or physical growth of their children. Even within the context of specific stewardships given to women and men, the work of mothering and fathering is not mutually exclusive, nor does it function best in isolation. Rather, fathers' and mothers' hearts and hands are to be joined in accomplishing the work of parenthood by continually echoing and harmonizing with each other as it was in the beginning, when Eve and Adam labored together (see Moses 5:1). Thus, unlike the *in*-dependent ideology, an *inter*-dependent approach emphasizes shared purpose, mutual support, joint overall responsibility, and collaboration.

3. Separateness versus oneness. Recent secular writings have put a new twist on an old ideology of the relations between men and women. As the title of one popular book puts it, *Men Are from Mars, Women Are from Venus*.[90] A "separateness ideology" goes beyond the independence ideology discussed above by stating that (metaphorically) women and men are from different planets and their natures are alien to one another. Although books like this sometimes can be useful tools to help men and women learn to understand each other better, when the concept of gender difference is taken too far it supports a separateness ideology. Adherence to this false ideology risks family disharmony by setting the stage for such problems as stereotyping one's spouse or oneself as having particular characteristics based *solely* on gender; viewing men as inherently uncivilized brutes and spiritually deficient, and thus in need of social taming and spiritual tutoring by "naturally" spiritual women; viewing women as rationally inferior and unable to make important decisions without guidance from men who are "naturally" rational and decisive; not taking responsibility for changing unrighteous behaviors by excusing or justifying them as gender-appropriate (e.g., "boys will be boys"); and acceptance of marital contention as inevitable, mutual understanding as next to impossible, and emotional intimacy as unobtainable.

The seemingly universal human tendency to create separation by grouping individuals, and then negatively viewing those not belonging to one's own group, has been consistently documented in psychological research and is known as the *in-group, out-group bias*.[91] This bias involves exaggerating differences between members of one's own group and members of another group, exaggerating similarities within one's own group, assigning negative characteristics to the members of the other group, and assigning positive characteristics to members of one's own group. The in-group, out-group phenomenon occurs even when the distinction between groups is inconsequential, such as eye color or art preference,[92] and may underlie the development of prejudices such as racism and sexism.[93]

While the Proclamation points out that gender has a spiritual purpose and that God has given mothers and fathers specific family stewardships, it is not in accord with revealed truth that women and men come from different social planets and are alien to one another. Revelation teaches us our true origins are the same—"near unto" Kolob (Abr. 3:2–3), where our heavenly parents reside in celestial oneness. Accordingly, we are brothers and sisters, offspring of the same heavenly parents; we walk the same path to salvation. The divine attributes taught by our Elder Brother, Jesus Christ, are expected of both women and men.

It is not surprising, then, that well-conducted scientific research to date indicates relatively few significant sex-based differences in abilities, behaviors, or characteristics.[94] Clearly, basic physical differences between men and women contribute to their abilities to fulfill their distinct family responsibilities. But there is also a tendency to dichotomize differences between men and women. These dichotomies are not well supported by current research. For instance, in contrast to popular notions about different styles of communication, a recent review of research documents little gender difference in how men and women communicate, prompting the authors to write: "If men and women do originate from different cultures or worlds, they at least speak the same language about 99% of the time."[95] Sex-based differences, where found, are likely to be small, although small differences need not diminish their eternal significance, for "by small means the Lord can bring about great

things" (1 Ne. 16:29). In addition, research with children so far indicates that sex-based differences are usually due to socialization, rather than inherent traits.[96] Although advances in neuroscience may yet discover more gender differences within the human brain, there is a clear human tendency to exaggerate and stratify any differences. Hence, careful scrutiny of cultural roles and beliefs about gender are necessary to determine whether or not any proposed gender difference pertains to eternal purposes and the sacred, sex-specific responsibilities articulated in the Proclamation.

Perhaps in divine wisdom, God has composed differences in responsibilities between the genders in order to invoke or ensure collaboration and unity and to create shared, balanced power. This sharing of power may explain why only in the union of a woman and a man is godhood made possible. That is, it may be both the commonalties *and* distinctions between women and men that allow for interdependence, union, and the capacity to become like God. Because husbands and wives are commanded by God to become one, the righteous combination of male and female is ultimately more significant than any specific gender distinction. (See Box 5.5.)

4. Trust versus mistrust. A peculiar twist to the separateness ideology also exists today. While many worldly philosophies assent to the value of equal power in marriage, the means by which it is thought to be achieved may not be in accord with the Proclamation. That is, some argue that a certain amount of separateness between women and men is needed because there cannot be full trust between them. One example of how this lack of trust is manifested is in an ideology that insists on wives' economic independence from husbands.[97] Because wives' reliance on their husbands for economic support has been a factor in unrighteous dominion in too many families, it is understandable that modern ideologies that seek to improve women's lives discourage women from sacrificing their economic independence in marriage. Many recent studies include wives' contributions to the family income as a part of the definition of marital equality.[98] These studies assume that power is based on access to resources such as money and prestige and that equality cannot be achieved in relationships where only one individual is providing them. Moreover, this ideology of economic independence correctly observes that in a time and place of high divorce and paternal abandonment, many women and children suffer from economic reliance on men.

PRINCIPLES OF EQUAL PARTNERSHIP

Although the exact allocation and implementation of family responsibilities may differ between families and across time within the same family, the following principles of equal partnership should prevail at all times and places.

Equal and United in Power	Husbands and wives each have common and unique powers or stewardships that are balanced; each is essential to become like God.
Equal and United in Purpose	Wives and husbands work toward the same, equal purpose which is to aid in bringing to pass the immortality and eternal life of themselves, each other, and their children.
Equal and United in Possibility	Husbands and wives are yoked together as an interdependent unit. Their ultimate, eternal possibilities are as a joined couple, not as individuals.
Equal and United in Participation	Wives and husbands have equal levels of responsibility and participation in the plan of salvation and in the sacred work of family life. Husbands are as dependent on wives as wives are on husbands.
Equal and United in Prominence	There are no value hierarchies or value distinctions between women and men nor in the stewardships they fulfill as wives and husbands, mothers and fathers.

Box 5.5

Hence, from this perspective, married mothers should be engaged continuously in paid work in order to maintain economic independence and equality.

There are at least two falsehoods in this ideology, however. First, mothers are not the only ones who are reliant upon their spouse; fathers are equally reliant on mothers. That is, mothers who devote themselves to full-time homemaking contribute significantly to the economic (and spiritual) welfare of their families. If the wide range and full depth of services provided by homemakers were purchased in the market (and probably they could not be), they would likely consume all and more of the family income provided by fathers. Families that purchase some domestic services, such as child care, pay high prices for a lesser service compared to what mothers usually provide. Thus, fathers who provide income for their families through work outside the home are in a real sense reliant on the (unpaid) economic contributions that wives provide through work inside the home.

Moreover, husbands rely on their wives to nurture and rear children in righteousness, to do something that is crucial to fathers' own spiritual progression and to the welfare of their children whom they love. Thus, husbands trust and depend on wives to fulfill their stewardships faithfully, just as wives trust and depend on husbands to fulfill their stewardships faithfully.

A second falsehood is that marital equality cannot exist in marriages in which husbands trust wives to contribute to the family with full-time homemaking and wives trust husbands to contribute to the family with full-time employment. Granted, in a time and place of great family instability, when many individuals choose not to fulfill their sacred familial stewardships, trust and reliance on one's spouse can be an act of faith and courage. Touching directly on this subject, Elder Henry B. Eyring said: "It takes courage and faith to plan for what God holds before you as the ideal rather than what might be forced upon you by circumstances."[99]

In righteous, equal partnerships, wives' reliance on husbands does not imply subservience or devaluation of homemaking nor does husbands' reliance on wives imply subservience or devaluation of economic providing. To define power in terms of duties performed or worldly status is wrong. Developing trust in one's spouse goes far beyond believing he or she will fulfill specific duties. Rather, it involves identifying, sharing, and appreciating each other's gifts and stewardships and deciding together how best to implement or fulfill each set of gifts at specific points in time throughout life. Thus, it is never the case that developing one's gifts and talents demonstrates a lack of trust in one's spouse. Latter-day Saints must understand that inequality and mistrust result from unrighteous attitudes and behaviors, not from the nature of marriage or from a particular way that men and women allocate family responsibilities. In fact, one study[100] suggests that American couples are uncomfortable defining marital equality in such flat terms as the proportion of income or housework contributed. Rather, they stress marital processes and attitudes such as mutual respect, commitment, supportiveness, reciprocity, and most important, trust, in their personal definitions of marital equality. These are qualities needed for equal partnership regardless of how couples divide family tasks. Trusting one's spouse is an essential part of righteous marriage. To place complete trust in each other stretches our faith and tests our spiritual courage, which is, perhaps, another reason why marriage is ordained of God.

CONCLUSION

In this chapter, we have presented doctrine and prophetic teaching related to the Proclamation principles of equal partnership in marriage and parenting, and to the sacred stewardships given to mothers and fathers. A summary of the principles of equal partnership discussed in this chapter can be found in Box 5.5. Woven together, these principles are a tapestry of truth that beautifully portrays righteous relationships in families, helping husbands and wives to work together as equal partners and guiding mothers and fathers in their efforts to rear righteous children.

NOTES

1. Dallin H. Oaks (1993, November), The great plan of happiness, *Ensign, 23*(11), 72–75.

2. Oaks (1993), 73.

3. Hugh W. Nibley (1980), Patriarchy and matriarchy, in M. M. Mouritsen (Ed.), *Blueprints for living: Perspectives for Latter-day Saint women* (Provo: Brigham Young University Press), 44–61.

4. Howard W. Hunter (1994, November), Being a righteous husband and father, *Ensign, 24*(11), 51.

5. Gordon B. Hinckley (1991, November), Daughters of God, *Ensign, 21*(11), 99.

6. Hunter (1994, November), 51.

7. Richard G. Scott (1998, May), Removing barriers to happiness, *Ensign, 28*(5), 86.

8. Gordon B. Hinckley (1991, November), Our solemn responsibility, *Ensign, 21*(11), 51.

9. C. Broderick (1986), *One flesh, one heart: Putting celestial love into your temple marriage* (Salt Lake City: Deseret Book), 32.

10. Boyd K. Packer (1998, May), The Relief Society, *Ensign, 28*(5), 73.

11. James E. Faust (1996, May), The prophetic voice, *Ensign, 26*(5), 6.

12. Ezra Taft Benson (1985, August), What I hope you will teach your children about the temple, *Ensign, 15*(8), 610.

13. G. Kittle (Ed.) (1965), *Theological dictionary of the New Testament* (Grand Rapids, MI: Wm. B. Eerdmans Publishing), 822–823.

14. Gen. 5:2, "Male and female created he them; and blessed them, and called their name Adam, in the day when they were created."

15. Jeffrey R. Holland (1999, May), The hands of the fathers, *Ensign, 29*(5), 16.

16. Harold B. Lee (1974), *Stand ye in holy places* (Salt Lake City: Deseret Book), 225.

17. David O. McKay (1935, April) in Conference report, 116 (quoting J. E. McCulloch, in *Home, the Savior of Civilization,* [1924], 42).

18. Ezra Taft Benson (1987, November), To the fathers in Israel, *Ensign, 17*(11), 48.

19. D. C. Dollahite (1998), Fathering, faith, and spirituality, *The Journal of Men's Studies, 7,* 3–15; D. C. Dollahite, L. D. Marks, and M. M. Olson (1998), Faithful fathering in trying times: Religious beliefs and practices of Latter-day Saint fathers of children with special needs, *The Journal of Men's Studies, 7,* 71–93; D. C. Dollahite (1999, November), Faithful fathering: How religion fosters responsible and meaningful father involvement, paper presented at World Congress of Families II. Geneva, Switzerland. Available at http://www.worldcongress.org

20. D. Blankenhorn (1995), *Fatherless America* (New York: BasicBooks).

21. Blankenhorn (1995); D. Popenoe (1996), *Life without father* (New York: Free Press).

22. Blankenhorn (1995), 1.

23. L. B. Silverstein and C. F. Auerbach (1999), Deconstructing the essential father, *American Psychologist, 54,* 397–407.

24. H. B. Biller (1993), *Fathers and families: Parental factors in child development* (Westport, CT: Auburn House); B. J. Ellis, S. McFadyen-Ketchum, K. A. Dodge, G. S. Petit, and J. E. Bates (1999), Quality of early family relationships and individual differences in the timing of pubertal maturation in girls: A longitudinal test of an evolutionary model, *Journal of Personality of Social Psychology, 77,* 387–401; M. E. Lamb (1997), *The role of the father in child development* (3rd ed.) (New York: John Wiley & Sons).

25. W. J. Doherty, E. F. Kouneski, and M. F. Erickson

(1998), Responsible fathering: An overview and conceptual framework, *Journal of Marriage and the Family, 60,* 277–292.

26. Benson (1987, November), 50.

27. Benson (1987, November), 50.

28. James E. Faust (1993, May), Father, come home, *Ensign, 23*(5), 37.

29. Boyd K. Packer (1994, May), The father and the family, *Ensign, 24*(5), 21.

30. Spencer W. Kimball (1976, June), The false gods we worship, *Ensign, 6*(6), 3–6.

31. Hunter (1994, November), 51.

32. Blankenhorn (1995); Biller (1993).

33. Hunter (1994, November), 51.

34. Gordon B. Hinckley (1998, November), To the boys and to the men, *Ensign, 28*(11), 52–53.

35. Holland (1999, May), 15.

36. Holland (1999, May), 15.

37. G. W. Brock, M. Oertwein, and J. D. Coural (1993). Parent education: Theory, research, and practice, in M. E. Arcus, J. D. Schvaneveldt, and J. J. Moss (Eds.), *Handbook of family life education: Foundations of family life education* (Newbury Park, CA: Sage), 2:87–114.

38. Brock et al. (1993), 91.

39. J. Bowlby (1969), *Attachment and loss: Vol. 1. Attachment* (New York: BasicBooks).

40. U. Bronfenbrenner (1990), Discovering what families do, in D. Blankenhorn, S. Bayme, and J. Elshtain (Eds.), *Rebuilding the nest: A new commitment to the American family* (Milwaukee, WI: Family Service American), 27–38.

41. The First Presidency (1942, October), The message of the First Presidency, in Conference report, 759, 761.

42. J. R. Harris (1998), *The nurture assumption: Why children turn out the way they do* (New York: Free Press).

43. Richard G. Scott (1996, November), The joy of living the great plan of happiness, *Ensign, 26*(11), 74, 75.

44. The First Presidency (1942, October), 761.

45. Russell M. Nelson (1999, May), Our sacred duty to honor women, *Ensign, 29*(5), 38.

46. Thomas S. Monson (1998, April), Behold thy mother, *Ensign, 28*(4), 6.

47. Bruce C. Hafen (1999, November 17). The moral influence of women, paper presented at the World Congress of Families II, Geneva, Switzerland, 5, 6. Available on Internet at http://worldcongress.org

48. J. Gleick (1999), *Faster: The acceleration of just about everything* (New York: Pantheon).

49. K. Daly (1996), *Families and time: Keeping pace in a hurried culture* (Thousand Oaks, CA: Sage), 9.

50. A. R. Hochschild (1997), *The time bind: When work becomes home and home becomes work* (New York: Metropolitan Books).

51. Ezra Taft Benson (1987, February 22), To the mothers in Zion, address given at a fireside for parents (Salt Lake City: The Church of Jesus Christ of Latter-day Saints), 8–12.

52. Daly (1996).

53. E. Galinsky (1999), *Ask the children* (New York: William Morrow).

54. D. Elkind (1988), *The hurried child: Growing up too fast too soon* (Reading, MA: Addison-Wesley); J. Piaget (1963), *The origins of intelligence in children* (New York: W. W. Norton).

55. Joseph J. Christensen (1999, May), Greed, selfishness, and overindulgence, *Ensign, 29*(5), 9–11; Hinckley (1998, November).

56. J. E. Bates, D. Marvinney, T. Kelly, K. A. Dodge, D. S. Bennett, and G. S. Pettit (1994), Childcare history and kindergarten adjustment, *Developmental Psychology, 30,* 690–700; J. Belsky (1988), The "effects" of infant day care reconsidered, *Early Childhood Research Quarterly, 3,* 235–272.

57. E. Harvey (1999), Short-term and long-term effects of early parental employment on children of the National Longitudinal Survey of Youth, *Developmental Psychology, 2,* 445–459; NICHD Early Child Care Research Network (1998), Early child care and self-control, compliance, and problem behavior at twenty-four and thirty-six months, *Child Development, 69,* 1145–1170.

58. NICHD Early Child Care Research Network (1999), Child-care and mother-child interaction in the first 3 years of life, *Developmental Psychology, 35,* 1399–1433.

59. C. H. Hart, S. F. Olsen, C. C. Robinson, and B. L. Mandleco (1997), The development of social and communicative competence in childhood: Review and a model of personal, familial, and extrafamilial processes, *Communication Yearbook, 20,* 305–373; C. Howes, D. A. Phillips, and M. Whitebook (1992), Thresholds of quality: Implications for the social development of children in center-based child care, *Child Development, 63,* 449–460.

60. See Benson (1987, February 22).

61. Gordon B. Hinckley (1996, November), Women of the church, *Ensign, 26*(11), 67.

62. Hinckley (1996, November).

63. Cheiko N. Okazaki (1994, November), Rowing your boat, *Ensign, 24*(11), 92–94.

64. Benson (1987, November), 50.

65. Camilla E. Kimball (1986), Keys for a woman's progression, in *Woman to woman: Selected talks from the BYU Women's Conferences* (Salt Lake City: Deseret Book), 8, 9.

66. James E. Faust (1986, September), A message to my granddaughters: Becoming "great women," *Ensign, 16*(9), 18, 19.

67. M. K. Blakely (1983, August), Executive mothers: A cautionary tale, *Working mother,* 73.

68. E. Galinsky (1987), *The six stages of parenthood* (Reading MA: Addison-Wesley), 317.

69. Benson (1987, February 22), 1–2.

70. Marjorie Hinckley, quoted in Virginia H. Pearce (1999), *Glimpses into the life and heart of Marjorie Pay Hinckley* (Salt Lake City: Deseret Book), 52, 61.

71. Jeffrey R. Holland (1997, May), Because she is a mother. *Ensign, 27*(5), 35, 37.

72. J. Demos (1970), *A little commonwealth: Family life in Plymouth Colony* (New York: Oxford University Press); L. T. Ulrich (1983), *Good wives: Image and reality in the lives of women in northern New England, 1650–1750* (New York: Oxford University Press); C. H. Dayton (1995), *Women before the bar: Gender, law, and society in Connecticut, 1639–1789* (Chapel Hill: University of North Carolina Press).

73. G. S. Wood (1972), *The creation of the American Republic, 1776–1787* (New York: W. W. Norton).

74. L. H. Butterfield, M. Friedlaender, and M. Kline (1975), *The book of Abigail and John: Selected letters of the Adams family, 1762–1784* (Cambridge, MA: Harvard University Press), 121.

75. L. K. Kerber (1998), *No constitutional right to be ladies: Women and the obligations of citizenship* (New York: Hill & Wang).

76. M. P. Ryan (1981), *Cradle of the middle class: The family in Oneida County, New York, 1790–1865* (New York: Cambridge University Press); J. Boydston (1990), *Home and work: Housework, wages, and the ideology of labor in the early Republic* (New York: Oxford University Press); N. A. Hewitt (1990), *Women, families, and communities: Readings in American history, vols. 1 and 2* (Glenview, IL: Scott, Foresman/Little Brown).

77. R. Sennett (1970), *Families against the city: Middle-class homes of industrial Chicago, 1872–1890* (Cambridge, MA: Harvard University Press).

78. S. Mintz and S. Kellogg (1988), *Domestic revolutions: A social history of American family life* (New York: Free Press).

79. Mintz and Kellogg (1988).

80. Kerber (1998).

81. R. L. Griswold (1993), *Fatherhood in America: A history* (New York: BasicBooks); E. T. May (1988), *Homeward bound: American families in the cold war era* (New York: BasicBooks).

82. J. H. Larson, C. H. Hammond, and J. M. Harper (1998), Perceived equity and intimacy in marriage, *Journal of Marital and Family Therapy, 24,* 487–506; J. M. Steil (1997), *Marital equality: Its relationship to the well-being of husbands and wives* (Thousand Oaks, CA: Sage).

83. Steil (1997).

84. J. M. Gottman and N. Silver (1999), *The seven principles for making marriage work* (New York: Crown).

85. P. R. Amato and A. Booth (1997), *A generation at risk: Growing up in an era of family upheaval* (Cambridge, MA: Harvard University Press); J. H. Pleck (1997), Paternal involvement: Levels, sources, and consequences, in M. E. Lamb (Ed.), *The role of the father in child development* (3rd ed.) (New York: John Wiley & Sons), 66–103.

86. Packer (1989, May), 73.

87. Neal A. Maxwell (1979), The women of God, in *Women* (Salt Lake City: Deseret Book), 94.

88. See Benson (1987, November); Hunter (1994, November); Nelson (1999, May).

89. A. J. Hawkins, S. L. Christiansen, K. P. Sargent, and E. J. Hill (1993), Rethinking father involvement in child care: A developmental perspective, *Journal of Family Issues, 14,* 531–549.

90. J. Gray (1992). *Men are from Mars, women are from Venus* (New York: HarperCollins).

91. H. Tajfel (1982), Social psychology of intergroup relations, *Annual Review of Psychology, 33,* 1–39.

92. Tajfel and Billing (1974), Familiarity and categorization in intergroup behavior, *Journal of Experimental Social Psychology, 10,* 159–170.

93. A. Bettencourt, K. E. Dill, S. A. Greathouse, K. Charlton, and A. Mulholland (1997), Evaluations of ingroup and outgroup members: The role of category-based expectancy violation, *Journal of Experimental Social Psychology, 33,* 244–275; R. Vonk and M. Olde-Monnikhof (1998), Gender subgroups: Integroup bias within the sexes, *European Journal of Social Psychology, 28,* 37–47.

94. B. Lott (1996), Politics or science? The question of gender sameness/difference, *American Psychologist, 51,* 155–156; B. Lott (1997), The personal and social correlates of a gender difference ideology, *Journal of Social Issues, 53,* 279–297; E. E. Maccoby and C. N. Jacklin (1974), *The psychology of sex differences* (Stanford, CA: Stanford University Press); D. Spangler and D. D. Burns (1999), Is it true that men are from Mars and women are from Venus? A test of gender differences, independence, and perfectionism, *Journal of Cognitive Psychotherapy: An International Quarterly, 13*(4), 339–357.

95. D. J. Canary and T. M. Emmers-Sommer (1997), *Sex and gender differences in personal relationships* (New York: Guilford), vii.

96. E. E. Maccoby (1990), Gender and relationships: A developmental account, *American Psychologist, 45,* 513–520.

97. A. P. Mitchell (1995), The maternal bond, *American Journal of Family Law, 9,* 125–133; Steil (1997).

98. Steil (1997).

99. Henry B. Eyring (1998, February), The family, *Ensign, 28* (2), 16.

100. S. C. Rosenbluth, J. M. Steil, and J. H. Whitcomb (1998), Marital equality: What does it mean? *Journal of Family Issues, 19,* 227–244.

CHAPTER 6

HOME AS A SACRED CENTER FOR FAMILY LIFE

MARIBETH C. CLARKE, LORA BETH BROWN, CAROLYN GARRISON, JON D. GREEN, PEGGY HONEY, JERRY L. JACCARD, NORA NYLAND, CAROLINE PROHOSKY, MAXINE L. ROWLEY, MARY J. THOMPSON, AND RITA R. WRIGHT

Only the home can compare with the temple in sacredness.
(Bible Dictionary, 780–781)

This chapter considers some of the principles by which we may manage the material aspects of the sacred space we call "home." Accordingly, we will treat some of the priorities and contexts within which we care for each other, rear our children, and provide for the family's physical and spiritual needs. We begin with some reflections on the concepts "home" and "family." Then we review prophetic statements on how families can conduct home life in ways that protect its sanctity and fulfill its divine purposes. To the Lord, all things are spiritual, and thus the essential but ordinary tasks of family life are sacred responsibilities of transcendent importance (see D&C 29:34). In view of its inherent sanctity, it has been said that home is, or ought to be, like a temple. We consider what that comparison may mean and its implications for life at home. If there is divine purpose and high priority in the everyday activities necessary to maintain a home, what difference should that knowledge make in the ways we house, feed, and clothe ourselves? We conclude the chapter with a partial answer to that question, with a brief look at the meanings of food, clothing, home design, and cultural enrichment in the context of the ultimate purpose of home.

The home is sacred. It is a covenant institution, its sanctity based not only in the promises a couple makes at marriage, but in God's command that they should make and honor such promises. It is sacred because it is an earthly counterpart of our true home, the home from whence we come and to which we return when we pass from this life. The home is sacred because it is the privileged place, in space and time, from which and in which we fulfill the sacred responsibilities that accompany marriage and the bearing and rearing of children.

HOMES AND FAMILIES

The word home does not appear in the Proclamation. Instead, the specific components of home are singled out: marriage, husband and wife, parents, children, and family. Home is there implicitly, but it is to the family members that the principles of the Proclamation are directed. This approach is in harmony with a tendency by some Church leaders to use family and home interchangeably. Thus, Elder Carlos E. Asay writes that "marriage, family, home, and true religion are so interrelated that it might be said that they are one and the same. All are godly concepts, and each one builds the others."[1] In the following statement by President Stephen L Richards, home is a complete synonym for family:

> The home has an enlarged significance that is subordinate to nothing else in life, for it constitutes not only the source of our greatest happiness here in this life, but also the foundation of our exaltation and glory

in the life to come. After all, it is essentially a religious institution. It has its origin in religious ceremony. It is the fulfillment of divine command. Its government is of a religious nature and the finest of its products are spiritual.[2]

On the basis of dictionary definitions, one might argue that the combination of family and dwelling place makes a home. However, it is not just any dwelling place that may be combined with the presence of family members to generate home. Nowadays many of the dwelling places we occupy are mere temporary shells. None of them may attain the status of *home* in the sense that they embody the permanence, family history, affection, and identity that the term home signifies. Indeed, in the presence of family, the shell-house may not be necessary at all for home to exist. We need to keep our priorities clearly in view, so that investment in whatever place we happen to occupy does not distract us too much from attention to the people whose presence is the necessary and often sufficient basis of home. Three distinct definitions of home are relevant here, only one of which fits the popular notion that family plus house equals home.

Heaven Is Home

First, home is where we have our ultimate and eternal identity. Home is where God dwells, where we lived before we were born into our present families, and where we want to return to live. It is this home the poet William Wordsworth celebrates in his "Ode: Intimations of Immortality."

> *Our birth is but a sleep and a forgetting:*
> *The Soul that rises with us, our life's Star,*
> *Hath had elsewhere its setting,*
> *And cometh from afar. . . .*
> *Trailing clouds of glory do we come*
> *From God, who is our home:*[3]

It is of this home the prophet Alma speaks when he says "that the spirits of all men, as soon as they are departed from this mortal body . . . are taken home to that God who gave them life" (Alma 40:11). And it is this concept of home that is the reference point when President David O. McKay says "it is possible to make home a bit of heaven,"[4] or when President Spencer W. Kimball says he has glimpsed heaven in the homes of some families he has visited,[5] or when Elder Henry B. Eyring reminds us that "you, and I,

and all of our Father's children will someday know that being with God is being home—and that everywhere else, however beautiful it may be, will be a place where you long for home."[6]

Home Is Where We Belong

A second usage of "home" conveys the sense of fitting in or belonging. We say we are at home if we are comfortable somewhere, perhaps among people we like and who seem to be like us. In contrast, we feel out of place or not at home in unfamiliar, uncongenial, or threatening contexts. It is such displacement to which Elder Neal A. Maxwell refers when he says:

> We are never really at home in time. Alternately, we find ourselves wishing to hasten the passage of time or to hold back the dawn. We can do neither, of course, but whereas the fish is at home in the water, we are clearly not at home in time—because we belong to eternity. Time, as much as any one thing, whispers to us that we are strangers here.[7]

It is in this sense of home as belonging together that George MacDonald suggests that mankind is "always struggling to make our home in the world," but not succeeding "because we are not at home with the lord of the house, the father of the family, not one with our elder brother who is his right hand."[8] Stating the same principle, but with reference to our eternal home rather than this earth, Elder James E. Talmage declares that "any man may enter the highest degree of the celestial kingdom when his actions have been such that he can feel at home there."[9]

Home Is Where a Family Dwells

The third, more familiar use of home is as the family dwelling place. However, Church leaders make plain that the joining of house and family may not produce a home if the emotional and spiritual environment is not right. More than anything else, the presence of love makes a home. "Homes are made permanent through love," states President McKay, and "It is not home without love."[10] President McKay speaks even more explicitly on the relation of house and home: "The house is not the family. The wind may tear the roof off, blow out the windows; the hurricane may even sweep the house away; but the family remains, that which makes the home."[11] Elder Asay adds that "home is where your love is. So long as you are accompanied or surrounded by those who love you and whom you love, you are home. It is not so much a place as it is a way of loving and living."[12]

To judge from the statements of the prophets, we family members often need to be reminded that in homemaking for the eternities the essential building blocks are the parents and children of the family. The practices of the world sometimes encourage us to devote too much time and effort to the external, material aspects of our lives—the components of house and lifestyle—and to neglect the welfare of the family members who are the enduring elements of our homes. An example or two will make the prophetic point. President McKay stresses that while we should not ignore the "material and cultural needs which are indispensable to successful home life," still it is true that

> We need not power or splendor,
> Wide halls, or lordly dome,
> The good, the true, the tender—
> These form the wealth of home.[13]

President Gordon B. Hinckley, speaking to the women of the Church, admonishes :

> I hope that if you are employed full-time you are doing it to ensure that basic needs are met and not simply to indulge a taste for an elaborate home, fancy cars, and other luxuries. The greatest job that any mother will ever do will be in the nurturing, teaching, lifting, encouraging, and rearing her children in righteousness and truth. None other can adequately take her place.[14]

MAGNIFYING THE SACRED IN OUR HOMES

The family home is sacred in its essence, by its nature. It is the setting in which we cooperate with our Father in bringing to pass the immortality and eternal life of His children. Yet, as with other gifts of heavenly potential, by exercising our agency we may magnify that potential, or we may conduct our family life in ways that shroud or diminish its inherent sanctity.

What are the characteristics of a home that magnify and augment its essential sanctity? What can parents do to make their homes more sacred? President Hinckley gives a set of "four elements in building the environment of our homes" which include "(1) a spirit of service, (2) an atmosphere of growth, (3) the discipline of love, and (4) the practice of prayer."[15]

Below we list and discuss briefly, mostly in terms of inspired counsel, 10 aspects of sanctity in the home, including those taught by President Hinckley. These are sanctifying principles or processes inspired by scriptural references to temples, recommended by Church leaders, and exemplified in righteous Latter-day Saint homes. Several of these are treated in more detail in other chapters of this book. These aspects of family life include and build on the scriptural list of sanctifying characteristics of the Kirtland Temple, which the Lord said should be "a house of prayer, a house of fasting, a house of faith, a house of learning, a house of glory, a house of order, a house of God" (D&C 88:119). Many of these characteristics of the Lord's house also apply to our homes. In setting forth principles and activities that heighten the sense of the sacred in our homes, we state them in a form parallel to that used in describing the temple. Most of these are stated or implied in the Proclamation.

A House of Love

No single characteristic is more important than love in sanctifying the home. President McKay declares, "there is no true home when love does not abide."[16] President Kimball writes that "Great, overwhelming, natural love, as taught by the Church in its total program, should be the blessing of the child from conception to its death."[17]

A House of Prayer

The sanctity of home is fortified by prayer. Prayer is always on the short list of practices taught by the prophets as truly essential to saving ourselves and our families. Elder Hugh B. Brown states, "where the home is enveloped by love and hallowed by prayer, there is heaven on earth, and there eternal homes are in the making."[18] President Hinckley tells parents to "behold your little ones. Pray with them. Pray for them and bless them. . . . You can do nothing better for your children than to have them taking their turn in the family prayer, expressing gratitude for their blessings."[19]

A House of Children

The prophets have said that righteous family life must include children, if at all possible. President Harold B. Lee, speaking of exemplary homes he had visited, says: "If I were to name the first thing that impresses me always in these fine Latter-day Saint homes, I would say it was a love for and a desire for children."[20]

Describing a home visit that provided him a "glimpse of heaven," President Kimball writes:

> It was most refreshing to sit with a large family growing up in unselfishness. So content and comfortable were we in the heart of this sweet simplicity and wholesomeness that we gave no thought to the unmatched chairs, the worn rug, the inexpensive curtains, the numbers of souls that were to occupy the few rooms available.[21]

A House of Sacrifice and Service

"Sacrifice is the very essence of religion; it is the keystone of happy home life, the basis of true friendship, the foundation of peaceful community living," declares President Hinckley.[22] According to President Lee, "Great love is built on great sacrifice, and that home where the principle of sacrifice for the welfare of each other is daily expressed is that home where there abides a great love."[23]

Ours is a time of great public and personal selfishness, which we sometimes hide under the euphemisms "individualism" and "personal rights." President Hinckley counsels parents that "the antidote for selfishness is service, a reaching out to those about us—those in the home and those beyond the walls of the home. . . . A child who sees his father and mother forego comforts for themselves as they reach out to those in distress, will likely follow the same pattern when he or she grows to maturity."[24]

A House of Work

President Hinckley speaks of "the cultivation of home and family," and the term *cultivation* reminds us of the effort involved in maintaining our homes and working our way back home. He calls for work by both parents and children:

> Fathers and mothers . . . who will rise and stand upon their feet to make of their homes sanctuaries in which children will grow in a spirit of obedience, industry, and fidelity to tested standards of conduct. If our society is coming apart at the seams, it is because the tailor and the seamstress in the home are not producing the kind of stitching that will hold under stress.[25]

President Hinckley says the need to work is one of the things that makes home beautiful:

> How beautiful is that home where lives a man of godly manner, who loves those for whose nurture he is responsible, who stands before them as an example of integrity and goodness, who teaches industry and loyalty, not spoiling his children by indulging their every wish, but rather setting before them a pattern of work and service which will underpin their lives forever.[26]

A House of Happiness and Cheer

We are counseled in the scriptures and by our modern leaders to be a happy people. The love of God, as represented by the fruit of the tree of life in Lehi's dream, is "desirable to make one happy" (1 Ne. 8:10). In our time the Lord has instructed us to be of good cheer, to have glad hearts and cheerful countenances, and to "cheerfully do all things that lie in our power" (D&C 59:15, 17; 61:36; 68:6; 123:17).

To have glad hearts and cheerful countenances is to have the clear-sighted cheerfulness, the resilient good humor that recognizes that while life has its ups and downs, life is worth living and our ultimate purpose in life is glorious.[27]

President Ezra Taft Benson relates: "One great thing the Lord requires of each of us is to provide a home where a happy, positive influence for good exists. In future years the costliness of home furnishings or the number of bathrooms will not matter much, but what will matter significantly is whether there was happiness and laughter, or bickering and contention."[28] President McKay suggests that the "atmosphere" of home "might be and should be . . . joyous." He saw the ideal home as a place where children and young people were happy, indeed, where more happiness could be found than in any other place.[29] President Lee praises the home "made happy by the laughter of . . . little children."[30]

A House of Learning

The Lord has said, "Seek ye out of the best books words of wisdom; seek learning, even by study and also by faith" (D&C 88:118). Later, as part of instruction to "set in order the churches," Church leaders were commanded to "study and learn, and become acquainted with all good books, and with languages, tongues, and people" (D&C 90:15). President McKay urges parents to pay attention to the "body" of the home by meeting each family member's physical needs for food, space, sleep, exercise, recreation, and cultural development, while also devoting the necessary effort to the spiritual environment.[31] His definition of "home building" is instructive: "By the art of home building, I mean the inculcating in the lives of children a nobility of soul that leads them instinctively to love the beautiful, the genuine, the virtuous, and as instinctively to turn from the ugly, the spurious, and the vile."[32]

Home is the sacred place where we are first to be nourished by the good word of God. President Kimball reminds us that the most essential textbooks are the Holy Scriptures, but the Lord requires more, for home should be "a place for all that is good and enlightening and true . . . a climate for constant growth and learning for all who live there."[33] President Hinckley urges parents "to work at the matter of creating an atmosphere of learning in their homes. They need to let their children be exposed to great minds, great ideas, everlasting truth, and those things which will build and motivate for good."[34] Elder Maxwell advises that "every home ought to be a mini-school of the prophets, since so much learning can occur there. Indeed, so much learning (good or bad) does occur in a family whether we wish it to or not. It is simply a question of how righteously influential we want our family school to be."[35]

A House of Order

In 1833 the Lord instructed the leaders of the Church to "set in order your houses; keep slothfulness and uncleanness far from you" (D&C 90:18). In the revelation on the eternal nature of the marriage covenant, we read, "mine house is a house of order, saith the Lord God, and not a house of confusion" (D&C 132:8).

If our homes are to be sacred, there are many things to be set in order. The most important kind of order is that our goings and comings be in harmony with the commandments. That is, if our homes are "houses of order," they will be homes of obedience to the commandments, of discipline, of living according to the Lord's plan.

A home of order also implies it is a place where priesthood ordinances are given to family members since another name for the Melchizedek Priesthood is the "Holy Priesthood, after the Order of the Son of God" (D&C 107:3). That some elements of order-liness and good physical upkeep of the household are involved may be inferred from the reference to "slothfulness and uncleanness" quoted above, but plainly the Lord is concerned with cleanliness and order of a higher order—with moral cleanliness and keeping the commandments—for in his instruction to Frederick G. Williams he clarifies what is meant by the command to set things in order at home: "I have commanded you to bring up your children in light and truth. But . . . you have continued under this condemnation; You have not taught your children light and truth, according to the commandments; and that wicked one hath power, as yet, over you" (D&C 93:40–42).

How do we set our homes in order? We adopt divine priorities, we exercise discipline, we fit our desires and wishes into their appropriate place in the Lord's plan. We adjust to the "order" of our Father's will. We keep the commandments. Elder Maxwell points to the pivotal role of the family in helping us learn the proper order of things:

> One's style of giving and receiving is, as with so many things, shaped in the home. Apparently, the recurring challenge is to do things at the right time, for the right reasons, in the right spirit, and in the right way. Then there can be full closure in terms of human growth. Otherwise, though transactions may occur, though a ritual may transpire, a real spiritual outcome has not been achieved. How crucial the training in family life can be in this respect![36]

A House of Purity

President David O. McKay said that "pure hearts in a pure home are always in whispering distance of heaven,"[37] and President Hinckley writes:

> The Church lays great stress on the sanctity of the home and teaches that children are a blessing from the Lord. There is no principle on which the Latter-day Saints lay greater emphasis than the sacredness of the marriage covenant.[38]

A House of Reverence and Respect

Respect has to do with our attitude toward other persons and our surroundings. It contains elements of deference and appreciation for others, a recognition and acceptance of their integrity and worth, and a willingness to allow and assist them to reach their potential. President Hinckley ties respect to acknowledgment of the Savior's plan and self-discipline. "Good homes," he writes, "are not easily created or maintained."

> They require discipline, not so much of children as of self. They require respect for others, that respect

which comes best from acceptance of the revealed word of Lord concerning the purpose of life, of the importance and sacred nature of the family, and recognition of each member of the family as a child of God.[39]

Respect is related to reverence, the attitude of awe, honor, respect, appreciation, and deference to the holy. President Kimball said:

> True reverence involves happiness, as well as love, respect, gratitude, and godly fear. It is a virtue that should be part of our way of life. . . . The home is the key to reverence, as it is to every other godlike virtue. . . . True reverence is a vital quality, but one that is fast disappearing in the world as the forces of evil broaden their influences. We cannot fully comprehend the power for good we can wield if the millions of members of Christ's true church will serve as models of reverent behavior. . . . Perhaps even more important, we cannot foresee the great spiritual impact on our own families if we become the reverent people we know we should be.[40]

HOME AND TEMPLE: IN THESE HOLY PLACES

Many years ago the Church made an inspirational film about temples and the eternal nature of family covenants. It was entitled *In This Holy Place,* a title that could as aptly be applied to a film about the normal activities of good families. And while there would be some parallels—in both, prayers are offered, there are "backstage" and "frontstage" rooms, scriptures are read, loved ones gather together, sacred covenants are enacted, and the plan of salvation is taught. In the Bible Dictionary of the Latter-day Saint edition of the King James version of the Bible, the purpose and sanctity of the home are compared to those of the temple in these words: "A temple is literally a house of the Lord, a holy sanctuary. . . . A place where the Lord may come, it is the most holy of any place of worship on the earth. Only the home can compare with the temple in sacredness."[41]

This is not to say that the righteous home should look and be in all respects like a temple or that the place of the temple in the divine scheme of things is the same as that of the home. The nature of many of the activities that go into healthy home-life are not appropriate in the temple. The point is that holy places need not be alike in all respects to be holy. The functions they serve may differ greatly, yet both, or all,

may be holy. Also, while some LDS families choose to organize and decorate a special room in their homes to re-create in some way the quiet cleanliness and dignity of a celestial room, trying to make an entire house a "temple-like" décor might create confusion and frustration. The activities that are normal and appropriate at home, given the characteristics of small children or teenagers, cannot reasonably be carried out in the kinds of rooms that are appropriate for adult participation in sacred temple services. In other words, it may be positively inappropriate—it may be out of order—to expect the physical setting of one kind of sacred activity to be directly transferable as the appropriate context for another kind of sacred activity.

The personal reflections in Essay E (following chapter) illustrate one young mother's struggle for enlightenment as she tries to understand the sanctity of home and its relation to the sanctity of the temple. The account of her changing understanding of what constitutes "holiness" in the home is thought-provoking and relevant to the life of every parent and homemaker.

CARING FOR OUR FAMILIES WITH JUDGMENT AND THANKSGIVING

The Lord has promised that if we keep His commandments, "the fulness of the earth is yours . . . and the good things which come of the earth, whether for food or for raiment, or for houses, or for barns, or for orchards, or for gardens, or for vineyards; . . . for the benefit and the use of man, both to please the eye and to gladden the heart; . . . to be used, with judgment, not to excess, neither by extortion" (D&C 59:16–20).

His requirement that the "fulness of the earth," as we apply it to our nourishment, shelter, and clothing, be used with judgment suggests that some ways of caring for ourselves are better than others. Good judgment and the skills by which it is enacted are not instinctive.

Historically in Western culture, homemaking has been defined as largely the province of mothers. Within the families of the Church, the nurturing and homemaking aspects of family life are defined more as women's responsibilities than men's. However, modern prophets have also stressed that, while mothers may be the leading specialists in homemaking, fathers should share the responsibility and much of the performance. President Howard W. Hunter urges husbands to "honor your wife's unique and divinely appointed role as a mother in Israel and her special capacity to bear and nurture children." At the same time, he placed much of the homemaking responsibility directly upon husbands and fathers: "You share, as a loving partner, the care of the children. Help her to manage and keep up your home. Help teach, train, and discipline your children."[42] Elder James E. Faust, speaking on the challenges facing women, writes that "no doubt it would help if husbands would follow the counsel of the late Elder G. Homer Durham: 'Man, as well as woman, has obligations to learn the difficult art of fatherhood in homemaking. This is not a task just for the woman.'"[43]

The care and management of a home is both science and art. It requires the proper management of both spirits and bodies, and the use of material things according to spiritual principles. Families have a stewardship over what they possess (see D&C 42:32; 136:27), and the responsibility to take care of self and family is an important practical application of the gospel. Elder Maxwell has commented on the need for careful planning by parents:

> Deliberate decisions must be made in order to achieve that desirable condition, "love at home," such as budgeting enough time at home to, among other things, express love to children by adding to their storehouse of happy memories. Singing that song is not enough; it must be matched by wise scheduling to benefit the family, which is often victimized by our busyness.[44]

In the rest of this chapter, we look at four aspects of the organization and management of home, focusing on the meaning of each of these in the overall spiritual mission of the family. For instruction in each of these aspects of homemaking, most of us may draw upon the teachings of our parents and grandparents or upon specialists in our congregations and neighborhoods. More detailed, even technical, "how to" information is available in school classes, extension and adult education programs, and in books, magazines, and the publications of parenting and family organizations. Within the family, we may follow the Lord's counsel and "teach each other" the principles and skills by which our families may thrive both here and hereafter.

MEALS: FOOD AS THE FAMILY SACRAMENT

The ancient temples on the earth had altars called tables. Temple worshipers presented their sacrifices upon altars. Those going to the temple come together around the altar, as one, to focus on the Savior, the ultimate sacrifice.[45] When the Savior knew that His days upon the earth would end, He joined His Apostles, who had become like family, around a table for His last supper. "And he took bread, and gave thanks, and brake *it,* and gave unto them, saying, This is my body which is given for you: this do in remembrance of me. Likewise also the cup after supper, saying, This cup *is* the new testament of my blood, which is shed for you" (Luke 22:19–20).

Food for the family in the home, as a daily sacrifice, brings families together around the table to give gratitude for the harvest. Mealtime is an opportune time for families to redirect their efforts in becoming at one with each other and with the Savior, thus making home a sacred center for family life.

The Lord seems always to have been concerned about our relationship to food, from the earliest commandments forbidding certain foods (see Gen. 2:17; 9:4) through the dietary restrictions of the law of Moses down to the present-day Word of Wisdom (see D&C 89). Providing food is one of the tasks required of us in this life: "In the sweat of thy face shalt thou eat bread," Adam was told (Gen. 3:19). Caring for our bodies is part of our mortal stewardship. We need nutrients from a variety of foods in order to sustain life. If our food is to sustain us, we must understand and respect our bodies.

Enjoying food is one of the pleasures granted to us. The products of the earth are intended "for the benefit and the use of man, both to please the eye and to gladden the heart; . . . for taste and for smell, to strengthen the body and to enliven the soul" (D&C 59:18–19). Food preparation and family meals in the home provide creative, satisfying, and effective daily opportunities for parents to love and serve their children. Feeding the family meets physical needs, develops a variety of skills, and fosters family traditions and cultural appreciation. It teaches family members to love and serve one another with respect and compassion. Our need for food is a constant reminder of our mortality, and through the preparation and partaking of food, we learn moderation, control, and mastery.

CLOTHING, SANCTITY, AND THE FAMILY

Clothing is ordained of God. Man's first clothing was made by God (see Gen. 3:20–21).

Brother Joseph Fielding McConkie explains:

Before Adam and Eve left the Garden of Eden, the Lord taught them the law of sacrifice and placed them under covenant to live that law and all other principles necessary to return to his presence. A sacrificial offering was made, symbolizing the necessity of sacrifice by the shedding of blood. From the skin of that sacrifice, robes or garments were made for Adam and Eve, thus symbolizing the protection necessary in the world they would now enter. . . . Thus our first parents were "clothed with power and authority" and given promises of protection through righteousness, of which this sacred clothing, made by God himself, would be a constant reminder.[46]

Clothing protects our physical bodies from the elements. It is also intended to shield both our physical and spiritual bodies. The human body, made in the image of God, is sacred, and we have been commanded to treat it with respect. "Know ye not that your body is the temple of the Holy Ghost which is in you, which ye have of God?" wrote the Apostle Paul (1 Cor. 6:19). Immodest or inappropriate clothing manifests disrespect for our bodies and may also be disrespectful to persons we encounter while we are dressed inappropriately.

Our clothing is an aspect of our spirituality; it may also be an aspect of our disobedience and a useful tool for Satan. Men and women have agency over clothing choices that express, among other things, their age, interests, talents, gender, and resources, and perhaps also their humility or pride. Style represents the worldly emphasis on clothing, and it has been described as a powerful token that can be used positively or negatively.[47] Because of our clothing, we may succeed or fail, we may be ostracized or accepted (see Gen. 37:3–4).

Adorning ourselves and our children in expensive and ostentatious clothing may signify decadence and selfishness (see Jacob 2:13; D&C 42:40). Moroni indicts the people of our day who are lifted up in the pride of their hearts "unto the wearing of very fine apparel." Moroni asks: "Why do ye adorn yourselves with that which hath no life, and yet suffer the hungry, and the needy, and the naked, and the sick and the afflicted to pass by you, and notice them not?" (Morm. 8:36–39). In marked contrast is the clothing standard reported among the peaceful people of Alma, who cared for the poor and the needy among them and who "did not wear costly apparel, yet they were neat and comely" (Alma 1:27).

President Kimball affirms:

Wear modest, clean clothing. Your clothing doesn't need to be new and [it] should have some fashion of course, but [it] should be clean, modest, and neat. Be dignified in your outward manner and in your inward morality. . . . If we dress in a shabby or sloppy manner, we tend to think and act the same way. I am positive that personal grooming and cleanliness, as well as the clothes we wear, can be tremendous factors in the standards we set and follow on the pathway to immortality and eternal life.[48]

Clothing is one of the most powerful nonverbal spiritual messages that Latter-day Saint families have at their disposal. We must not underestimate the powerful connection between what we wear and how we behave. Clothing the family influences and is influenced by righteous living in the home. Ideally, the responsibility for clothing the family is realized in the privacy of a home where family members are taught that clothing is meaningful and should manifest respect for ourselves and others.

HOUSING, SANCTITY, AND THE FAMILY

Most of the experiences that create a home transpire within some kind of built environment, be it a house, apartment, hogan, or tent. We usually call this setting the "house," and it is there that the family meets to communicate with each other and with God. As the physical setting for important family processes and events, the house merits special attention. Whether we are able to design our houses or live in a house designed by someone else, we usually have some control over the organization and adornment of our dwelling space. The design of a home environment certainly does not necessarily determine the behavior of the people within, but it does facilitate or impede certain kinds of activities.[49] Parents should pay careful attention to the design (if possible), furnishing, and decoration of their living space, for the way that space is organized will encourage some kinds of activities and attitudes and make others more difficult.

President McKay emphasizes the importance of appropriate home design and decoration in the story of a newly married man who invited his father to visit the couple's new home:

The young son took the father from room to room and showed him the furnishings, the paintings on the walls and so forth, and the father said, "This is lovely. I congratulate you, but, Son, I have looked in vain for anything that indicates that you have a place here for God." In writing about it later, the young man said, "I went through the rooms later, and I found that Father was right. . . ." Let us go back to our homes and see whether the spirit of our homes is such that if an angel called, he would be pleased to remain.[50]

A former BYU interior design instructor, Ted Dansie, once was working with a family to design their house. The mother expressed her frustration over a lack of reverence in her children. She often had a hard time getting her children to calm down and say their prayers before bed. Brother Dansie thought about this problem for some time. He talked with the family and together they decided to display in the home art that depicted reverent themes. Pictures suggesting reverence were strategically placed in the hallway that led from the public areas of the house to the bedrooms. Each evening, as the children went to bed, they passed beautiful pictures of people in the attitude of prayer. As intended, the reverence represented in the art "spilled over" into the home. When the children grew up and had families of their own, they applied the same principle in their homes, quietly encouraging reverence through sensitive, thoughtfully placed artwork.[51]

In many homes today, the television set assumes the central place in the home. It is the focal point of the living room or family room, and in many homes it has even invaded the kitchen and the bedrooms. What message does it send when the television set takes the place of honor in a room, with all the furniture arranged around it, directed toward it? It is almost as if it were the altar at which the family worships. Families can control the television viewing that takes place in their homes, but many merely adjust to the TV, offering it significant power in the organization of their family life. Some families have exercised their collective agency and moved the television set from its place of central importance in the family environment. Others have banished it entirely. Its position and role in family activities is a crucial question for the family. In making that decision, parents should remember that if the set is centrally positioned, it is likely to dominate a room's activities.

If it is important that your children be comfortable bringing their friends home, then choose child-friendly furnishings and provide space for the clutter and activities children bring. If it is important that disabled friends and family are welcome in your home, make certain that at least one entrance is wheelchair-accessible. There are numerous ways in which families through conscious design decisions can provide greater opportunities for the activities that they value.

LEARNING AND CULTURAL ENRICHMENT IN THE HOME

To maintain home as the sacred center of family life, we need the cultural enrichment and entertainment in the home to be elevating and conducive to the Spirit. President Brigham Young writes: "Every art and science known and studied by the children of men is comprised within the Gospel. . . . It matters not what the subject be, if it tends to improve the mind, exalt the feelings, and enlarge the capacity."[52] These three characteristics are useful criteria for deciding the type of cultural nourishment that should be allowed into our minds and our homes.

While the eighteenth-century idea of "art" was broader than the contemporary idea, certainly the gospel includes the uplifting and educational works that Latter-day Saint families enjoy. When children are young, they love to sing, dance, draw, and act, and they are impulsive in their desires. Although they lack professional expertise, they do not lack passion. An accomplished Latter-day Saint writer, Orson Scott Card gave this timely counsel:

> To enter into children's lives, whatever their age, we must take their art as seriously as they do. To enhance our children's lives, we must provide them with opportunities to create and feel appreciated for what they have created. And in the process, we can use their very seriousness to instill in them a love for righteousness and truth that will not leave them when they are adults.[53]

As children mature, they may seem to outgrow their natural attachment to the arts, especially if cultural education at home is not encouraged. Negative influences in the home or community may stifle creative intent or heighten fears of inadequacy. Children's endeavors in music and the arts are closely tied to their sense of identity.[54] Encouragement of creativity at home is one way to help children weather the "identity crisis" that troubles many young people.

Encouraging children in uplifting aesthetic experiences in the home can balance the preponderance of rationalism in society, creating a lively attraction for the "higher tastes" so vital to the education of the heart. This can happen only if parents have learned to appreciate the arts themselves and are willing to take time to share with their children their love for good music, literature, art, and drama. A parent can feed a child's natural desire to create simply by inviting the child to dance to lively music in the home, making up the movements as they go along. Children can be involved in writing stories or poems about each other or encouraged to sketch pictures of their homes and friends. Dramatic creativity can occur as family members act out scriptural stories in family home evening. A child who shows interest in music or dance lessons, or whose teachers point out an apparent talent, should be encouraged as the family resources allow.

If parents want their children to read good books, they should read with them when they are young and set an example by reading good books themselves. President Hinckley has often urged parents to surround their children with good books:

> Begin early to expose children to books. The mother who fails to read to her small children does a disservice to them and a disservice to herself. It takes time, yes, much of it. It takes self-discipline. It takes organizing and budgeting the minutes and hours of the day. But it will never be a bore as you watch young minds come to know characters, expressions, and ideas. Good reading can become a love affair, far more fruitful in long-term effects than many other activities in which children use their time. . . . Parents need to work at the matter of creating an atmosphere of learning in their homes. They need to let their children be exposed to great minds, great ideas, everlasting truth, and those things which will build and motivate for good.[55]

Library story time, young people's concerts, school and Church choirs, children's theater, school music programs, writing and art contests, and cultural fairs can all provide families with enrichment and ideas to enjoy in the home. Another art that may enrich the home is dance. In dance there is a sense of unity, freedom, and joy that affirms the sacred realities that surround us. Few people think of dance when considering facets of the arts that would strengthen family life in the home, but sibling, marital, and intergenerational dance in the home has great potential to bind the hearts of family members together. One Latter-day Saint woman tells of tender experiences she had with dance in her home. She is not petite, nor is she glamorous, but she has a genuine sense of beauty and confidence. When she was young, her father used to place her feet on his and dance with her. She said that when they danced she felt the embodiment of her father's love and care for her. She said that when she became too heavy for his toes, they continued to dance. She traces much of her confidence in life to the experience of dancing with her dad in their home. In the Old Testament, dance is often associated with expressions of joy, in both sacred and secular contexts. Latter-day revelation also equates dance with joy. We read: "If thou art merry, praise the Lord with singing, with music, with dancing, and with a prayer of praise and thanksgiving" (D&C 136:28).

"Wholesome recreational activities" (Proclamation, ¶ 7) involving creation and experience with words, music, dance, drama, and the visual arts greatly enrich the members of our families. They also provide ways for us to show our love for our Heavenly Father and our Savior and are channels through which the Spirit may touch our hearts.

CONCLUSION

We close with two inspired statements by modern apostles, each a recital of the kinds of cultivation, both spiritual and temporal, necessary to maintain homes of sufficient sanctity to prepare us for our homes on high. First, President Faust portrays the emergence of heroism from the sanctity of home:

> For most . . . life is not a matter of legislative battles, judicial decrees and executive decisions. It is a fabric of helping hands and good neighbors; bedtime stories and shared prayers; lovingly-packed lunchboxes and household budget balancing; tears wiped away and a precious heritage passed along; it is hard work, and a little put away for the future. In a healthy society, heroes are the men, women, and children who hold the world together one home at a time.[56]

Finally, here is Elder Richard L. Evans's estimate of the acts of heroism necessary if parents are to lead their families home:

> It is an act of greatness and heroism to hold a family together, to set before them an example, to teach them in ways of truth, to live a life of consistency, to provide necessities, to nurse and serve in sickness, to wash, to cook, to clean, to make, to mend, to counsel, to love, to understand, to pray, to be patient, and to do the thousand other unnamed things that it takes to rear a family, to make a house a home—and to do it every day, sometimes without seeming gratitude—and to lead a family righteously unto eternal life.[57]

NOTES

1. Carlos E. Asay (1992), *Family pecan trees* (Salt Lake City: Deseret Book), 7.

2. Stephen L Richards (1955), *Where is wisdom?* (Salt Lake City: Deseret Book), 193.

3. W. Wordsworth (1802–1804). Ode: Intimations of immortality from recollections of early childhood, in O. Williams (Ed.) (1975), *Immortal poems of the English language: British and American poetry from Chaucer's time to the present day* (New York: Washington Square Press).

4. David O. McKay (1976), *Gospel ideals: Selections from the discourses of David O. McKay* (Salt Lake City: Deseret Book), 490.

5. Spencer W. Kimball (1972), *Faith precedes the miracle* (Salt Lake City: Deseret Book), 259–262.

6. Henry B. Eyring (1997), *To draw closer to God* (Salt Lake City: Deseret Book), 64.

7. Neal A. Maxwell (1997), *All these things shall give thee experience* (Salt Lake City: Deseret Book), 11.

8. G. MacDonald (1974), *Life essential* (Wheaton, IL: Harold Shaw Publishers), 29–30.

9. James E. Talmage, quoted in Hugh B. Brown (1961), *Continuing the quest* (Salt Lake City: Deseret Book), 135.

10. McKay (1976), 480, 484.

11. McKay (1976), 357.

12. Asay (1992), 47.

13. McKay (1976), 444.

14. Gordon B. Hinckley (1997), *Teachings of Gordon B. Hinckley* (Salt Lake City: Deseret Book), 392.

15. Gordon B. Hinckley (1981), *Be thou an example* (Salt Lake City: Deseret Book), 67.

16. McKay (1976), 484.

17. Spencer W. Kimball (1982), *The teachings of Spencer W. Kimball*, ed. Edward L. Kimball (Salt Lake City: Bookcraft), 340.

18. Brown (1961), 10.

19. Hinckley (1997), 215.

20. Harold B. Lee (1973), *Decisions for successful living* (Salt Lake City: Deseret Book), 244.

21. Kimball (1972), 262.

22. Hinckley (1997), 565.

23. Harold B. Lee (1947, April), in *Conference Report*, 49.

24. Hinckley (1997), 583–85.

25. Hinckley (1981), 13, 18.

26. Hinckley (1997), 419.

27. S. Ruddick (1984), Maternal thinking, in Joyce Trebilcot (Ed.), *Mothering: Essays in feminist theory* (Totwa, NJ: Rowman & Allanheld), 217–218.

28. Ezra Taft Benson (1981, April), *Ensign, 11*(4), 34, cited in Carlos E. Asay (1992), *Family pecan trees* (Salt Lake City: Deseret Book), 104.

29. McKay (1976), 477, 490.

30. Lee (1973), 114.

31. McKay (1976), 480–481.

32. McKay (1976), 478.

33. Spencer W. Kimball (1979), *My beloved sisters* (Salt Lake City: Deseret Book), 27.

34. Hinckley (1981), 68.

35. Neal A. Maxwell (1974), *That my family should partake* (Salt Lake City: Deseret Book), 97–98.

36. Maxwell (1974), 117.

37. Quoted in Harold B. Lee (1974), *Stand ye in holy places* (Salt Lake City: Deseret Book), 176.

38. Hinckley (1997), 5.

39. Hinckley (1997), 416.

40. Kimball (1982), 223–225.

41. Bible Dictionary, "Temple," 780–781.

42. Howard W. Hunter (1994, November), Being a righteous husband and father, *Ensign, 24*(11), 50.

43. James E. Faust (1986, September), Becoming great women: A message to my granddaughters, *Ensign, 16*(9), 19.

44. Neal A. Maxwell (1981), *Not withstanding my weakness* (Salt Lake City: Deseret Book).

45. J. F. McConkie (1985), *Gospel symbolism* (Salt Lake City: Bookcraft), 202.

46. McConkie (1985), 202.

47. E. Klench (1995), *Style* (New York: Berkley Publishing Group).

48. Kimball (1982), 379–380.

49. J. Lang (1987), *Creating architectural theory: The role of the behavioral sciences in environmental design* (New York: Van Nostrand Reinhold).

50. McKay (1976), 481.

51. E. Dansie (1977, Fall), Home: Laboratory for family growth and self-actualization, *Family Perspective 5*, 42–47.

52. Brigham Young (1854), *Journal of discourses* (Liverpool/London: F. D. and S. W. Richards), 12:257; 1:335.

53. O. S. Card (1977, July), Family art, *Ensign, 27*(7), 67.

54. Card (1977, July), 67.

55. Hinckley (1981), 68.

56. James E. Faust (1990), *Reach up for the light* (Salt Lake City: Deseret Book), 68.

57. Richard L. Evans (1964, October), in Conference Report, 136, cited in Carlos E. Asay (1992), *Family pecan trees* (Salt Lake City: Deseret Book), 33–34.

MY HOME AS A TEMPLE

KRISTINE MANWARING

I have spent too much time in my home discouraged. I want to rear my children in a celestial atmosphere. "With all my heart I believe that the best place to prepare for . . . eternal life is in the home," said President David O. McKay,[1] and his words resonate to the core of my being. Yet, believing something does not automatically make it happen. In the abstract, I love my family, I love my home, and I wouldn't want to be anywhere else. In the reality of three meals a day, soccer games, dirty laundry, reports on Spain, and strep throat, the connection between eternal life and daily life often escapes me.

"Only the home can compare with the temple in sacredness," the LDS Bible Dictionary (p. 781) tells me. When I think of "sacred" I think of temples. I picture white couches, hushed voices, crystal chandeliers, and uninterrupted worship. I cannot recall ever leaving the temple wishing I hadn't been there or begrudging the time I spent serving our ancestors. It seems everything in the temple runs according to plan and that everything I do there is part of a larger, meaningful whole. Homes, on the other hand, are noisy, messy, often disorganized, and characterized by nothing but interruptions. The demands during a single day are relentless, and it is not uncommon for both mother and father to feel used or spent. Even in the quiet moments, I usually find myself cooking, folding laundry, giving spelling quizzes, and playing Legos. These activities do not feel sacred to me, and, if the truth be told, I'd rather not be doing them so much of the time. What possible definition of the word *sacred* could apply to these two seemingly opposite experiences?

When I was first presented with the idea that homes should be sacred, I tried to make my home fit the kind of cleanliness and order I thought the temple represented. Instead of a temple-like home, I ended up with a growing resentment toward the things that homes exist for. Cooking and laundry became onerous because the tasks created disorder. I even developed an intolerance for the cheerful chaos that burst through the back door with my children as the school bus pulled away. I became confused. Is my home still sacred when it is messy? What about when it is loud? What if I have children or friends who do not want to be reverent? Do they still get to come into my home? The harder I pushed my family to fit my narrow definition of sacred, the more anxious and less temple-like we all felt.

Then I began walking in the mornings with a wise neighbor who has come to believe that the work of feeding, clothing, and nurturing one another is every bit as spiritual as it is physical. She feels strongly that when ordinary, life-sustaining tasks are done together as a family, they bind family members to one another in small but critical ways. I was startled to realize that she saw as "sacred" the tasks that I always thought were obstacles to sacredness.

And for evidence, she turned to the scriptures. The parable of the sheep and the goats found in Matthew 25 clearly shows that Christ will judge us according to our willingness to feed and clothe "the least of these my brethren" (verse 40). Does this include members of our own families? In fact, Christ used imagery of feeding and washing and cleaning throughout His parables and object lessons. "He shall feed his flock like a shepherd" (Isa. 40:11). He will wash "away the filth of the daughters of Zion" (2 Ne. 14:4) and "sweep away the bad out of [His] vineyard" (Jacob 5:66). He even likens Himself to a hen who "gathereth her chickens under her wings" (Matt. 23:37).

Even more striking to me, Christ not only spoke of these things, He personally did them. He fed multitudes with limited tangible resources in a miraculous example of His attention to our physical as well as spiritual hunger. He washed the feet of His disciples to illustrate the humble service required of a Master and to reveal what He was willing to do that we might be entirely clean. In the book of Moses, He states that He, Himself, made the coats of skins to clothe Adam and Eve. When seen in this new light, my perception of tasks like peeling potatoes and scrubbing floors began to turn upside down and inside out. It was becoming obvious to me that when we care for the physical as well as the spiritual needs of our families, we are patterning our lives after the Savior.

One morning my friend commented about the struggle mothers face when cleaning up after children. She worried that if mothers think they have to maintain temple-like standards of cleanliness, they will focus on the cleaning itself and miss out on the wonderful opportunity to work side-by-side with their children. "Are we doing a disservice to mothers if we hold out the temple as a standard for them to emulate?" she asked. Her question touched a raw nerve. It brought back painful memories of my own attempts to make my home like a temple, and I wanted to object. I went home and looked up the exact wording of the "Temple" entry in the Bible Dictionary. There it was again: "Only the home can compare with the temple in sacredness." There was no hint that we should try to make our homes sacred like the temple. The sacredness is somehow already there. For the rest of the day, parallels between my routines at home and those at the temple flooded my mind. In the temple, for instance, we worship as a group. The pace for the entire group is set by the slowest member. I thought of how family scripture

reading or dressing for church or even passing the food at dinner is almost always determined by our two-year-old. In the temple what we do with our hands is just as important as what we say with our lips. Certainly I show my love for my family with both my hands and my lips during the rituals of homemaking. I vocally tell my children I love them, but an understanding of the depth of my love comes when my hands clean up their vomit or gently scrub their backs or hang on to the seats of their bicycles or hold their hands as we cross the street. I even thought about what it is we are taught at the temple. In both settings we learn of our true identity and our connections and obligations to one another. Elder Boyd K. Packer stated, "Most of what I know about how our Father in Heaven really feels about us, His children, I have learned from the way I feel about my wife and my children and their children. This I have learned at home."[2]

Michael Wilcox, in his book *House of Glory*, states that "as we pray for understanding, we can be assured that everything in the temple is beautiful. . . . The temptation to reject a symbol as unedifying says much more about our ignorance of its meaning than about the symbol itself. If we understood it, it would be beautiful and powerful."[3] As I have prayed for an understanding and testimony of the sacredness of my home, I have learned to apply this same principle to the ceremonies of making a home. Only when I cease to feel "above" mundane tasks like taking out the garbage or sweeping the kitchen floor do I glimpse their symbolic and sacred nature. As I clean windows, for instance, I notice the sunlight shining through more clearly, affirming that Jesus Christ is the source of all light. When I choose to spend a particular moment serving my family in this way over the many other possibilities, I remember that Mosiah taught that "when [we] are in the service of [our] fellow beings" we are also in the service of our God (Mosiah 2:17).

I learn even more when I share these tasks with my children. One Saturday morning my nine-year-old daughter and I were cleaning our large kitchen window together. I was outside and she was inside. We both sprayed the entire window with cleaner and when I looked at the window, I couldn't see her at all. Gradually, as we both wiped away the spray, her image became clearer until, with both the dirt and the spray gone, I could see her with perfect clarity. Our relationship is sometimes stormy, and the incident reminded me of my need to constantly keep wiping away surface tensions, judgmental thoughts, and misunderstandings whenever her true identity and potential are temporarily clouded from my vision.

On the days I don't really feel like laboring for and with my family, my reluctance itself teaches me about my relationship with my Heavenly Father, His Son Jesus Christ, and my own progress toward Them. How much greater Their love for us must be than what I am capable of, for They never tire of listening to our prayers nor are They inconvenienced by our constant need for Their help.

Realizing something of the spiritual value of homemaking has made me more aware of the need to more fully involve my family in these tasks. My husband and I no longer simply delegate chores to our children each day. We wash dishes and make beds alongside them. By doing so, we have been blessed with opportunities to teach our children and be taught ourselves with a frequency and a depth we previously never imagined. A year ago, I spent most of my dishwashing time muttering under my breath and trying to jam too many dishes into the limited dishwasher space. Now, every time I invite a child to thrust his or her hands into the warm, soapy water with mine, I learn something new about that child's spirit and life. It is only when doing dishes together that my twelve-year-old son, who mostly speaks in monosyllables about his experiences at school, reveals who his friends are and why he has chosen them, the pressure he feels about his grades, how much he likes math, and what he thinks about his teacher. Paradoxically, what I previously labeled "mindless" and once thought of as interruptions to spiritual growth are becoming the core of what makes my home feel sacred. As I cook meals, wash dishes, make beds, and sweep floors, I am continually in the midst of both teaching and being taught about charity, humility, hope, and faith. I am exchanging independence and "everyone seeking after their own" for a mutual dependence and unity in purpose that surely is related to Zion. I feel the sacredness in my home not only when it is clean, but also when we are in the process of getting it that way. Some days I don't even mind that we will go through the process again the next day.

Much of my discouragement at home was due to a sense of failure I felt for not being able to create sacredness artificially there. How comforting it is to be released from that burden. With joy and gratitude I now realize I need only look for the way sacredness already surrounds me.

NOTES

1. David O. McKay (1963, April), Blueprint for family living, *Improvement Era,* 252.

2. Boyd K. Packer (1998, November), Parents in Zion, *Ensign, 28*(11), 24.

3. Michael S. Wilcox (1995), *House of glory: Finding personal meaning in the temple* (Salt Lake City: Deseret Book), 32.

MEETING THE TEMPORAL NEEDS OF THE FAMILY

BERNARD PODUSKA

Parents have a sacred duty to rear their children in love and righteousness,
to provide for their physical and spiritual needs.
(The Family: A Proclamation to the World, ¶ 6)

When we take time to think about the great responsibility that this statement entails, it can be quite daunting. By consenting to become parents, by agreeing to create the physical bodies needed to allow our Heavenly Father's spirit children to come to earth, we are actually consenting to assume temporal and spiritual stewardship over Jesus Christ's brothers and sisters. Our Heavenly Father is entrusting us with the general welfare of His children. We, in turn covenant to rear these children in love and righteousness, and to provide for both their physical and spiritual needs. In other words, we are assuming both temporal and spiritual responsibilities. With this in mind, Brigham Young admonished: "We cannot talk about spiritual things without connecting with them temporal things, neither can we talk about temporal things without connecting spiritual things with them."[1]

The temporal and spiritual connection in financial matters can be found throughout the scriptures, such as in the parable of the talents (see Matt. 25:14–30), or in the situation when Jesus asked the rich man to "sell whatsoever thou hast, and give to the poor, and thou shalt have treasure in heaven: and come, take up thy cross, and follow me" (Mark 10:21). Similarly, the law of consecration (see D&C 42:30–33) and the law of tithing are presented, in which we are asked, "Will a man rob God? Yet ye

have robbed me. But ye say, Wherein have we robbed thee? In tithes and offerings" (Mal. 3:8).

Sometimes we forget that the earth that we stand on was created by the Lord; the cotton that clothes us is from the plants He created, the wool and leather that we so often take for granted are from the animals that He asked Adam to name. Blessed with a life of relative plenty, we often forget the source of our temporal blessings even though we are admonished by Paul to give "thanks always for all things unto God and the Father in the name of our Lord Jesus Christ" (Eph. 5:20).

Paying tithing is one of the ways in which we can express our thanks—one way of showing our gratitude for all that we have been given. Making a commitment to pay tithing and teach children to do so, even during the hard times, is one of the most important financial decisions we can make. During the middle of a financial crisis, our faith can be severely tested, and some Church members may be tempted to decrease expenses by not paying their tithing. President Spencer W. Kimball took special care in teaching the Saints about how important it was for us to exercise our faith and to establish spiritual and temporal priorities:

Few men have ever knowingly and deliberately chosen to reject God and his blessings. Rather, we learn from the scriptures that because the exercise of faith has always appeared to be more difficult than relying on things more immediately at hand, carnal man has tended to transfer his trust in God to material things. Therefore, in all ages when men have fallen under the power of Satan and lost the faith, they have put in its place a hope in the "arm of flesh" and in "gods of silver, and gold, of brass, iron, wood, and stone, which see not, nor hear, nor know" (Daniel 5:23)—that is, in idols. This I find to be a dominant theme in the Old Testament. Whatever thing a man sets his heart and his trust in most is his god; and if his god doesn't also happen to be the true and living God of Israel, that man is laboring in idolatry.[2]

Paying a full tithe is an act of faith and a declaration of where we place our trust. In addition to paying a full tithe, however, many Latter-day Saints also assume the extra cost of traveling to and from temples, maintaining food-storage programs, making substantial contributions to fast offerings, and supporting ward missionary funds or paying for their own missions and missionaries. Charitable contributions are an integral part of a Latter-day Saint family's budget. Our first stewardship is the welfare of our families, but we also recognize that this does not excuse us from our obligation to be our brothers' keepers and, in the true spirit of Christian charity, to give what we can to those in need.

"By divine design, fathers . . . are responsible to provide the necessities of life and protection for their families" (Proclamation, ¶ 7). In June 1965, President David O. McKay, while conversing with some brethren, admonished:

> Let me assure you, brethren, that some day you will have a personal priesthood interview with the Savior, Himself. If you are interested, I will tell you the order in which He will ask you to account for your earthly responsibilities.
>
> First, He will request an accountability report about your relationship with your wife. Have you actively been engaged in making her happy and ensuring that her needs have been met as an individual?
>
> Second, He will want an accountability report about each of your children. . . .
>
> Third, He will want to know what you personally have done with the talents you were given in the pre-existence.
>
> Fourth, He will want a summary of your activity in your Church assignment. . . .
>
> Fifth, He will have *no* interest in how you earned your living, but if you were honest in all your dealings.
>
> Sixth, He will ask for an accountability on what you

have done to contribute in a positive manner to your community.[3]

The fifth item in President McKay's outline states, "He will have *no* interest in how you earned your living, but if you were honest in all your dealings." No financial gain is worth sacrificing valued family relationships, self-respect, or our standing with our Heavenly Father. Those that depend on their husbands and fathers for their subsistence have every right to expect these resources to be gained honestly.

Disability, death, or other circumstances may necessitate individual adaptation (Proclamation, ¶ 7). Life is full of surprises; some are pleasant and some are unpleasant, but by their very nature they are unexpected. Factories can close, economies can go bust, health conditions can change in an instant, reputations can become suspect overnight, and our Heavenly Father can call us or one of our loved ones home at any time. In an attempt to temper the impact of such tragedies we save funds to be used in an emergency; we buy medical, disability, and life insurance; and we submit names to the prayer rolls of the temple. Unfortunately, far too many believe that they will be able to meet life's challenges by simply earning more money, believing that if they only had a higher income, they would be able to cope with whatever emergencies might arise. This trust in money, however, all too often proves to be futile.

Responsible financial planning requires husband and wife to set common goals and frequently consult one another about budgets, the use or investment of increased income, plans for emergencies, long-term family needs, and if possible, help for less fortunate members of the extended family. Planning and wise use of money and other resources will not bring peace of mind in the absence of faith—the essential oil in our lamps. Faith is not something that can be stored in the basement or thawed out in a microwave oven when needed. It must be fed and nurtured over time with prayer and knowledge, and is the main ingredient in satisfying our temporal needs.

THE CHALLENGES OF DEBT

For centuries, the ability to gratify our desires was, for the most part, limited by people's ability to generate the means of gratifying them—their ability to earn the money needed to pay for their desires. However, once the world of credit was introduced, the ability to gratify desires seemed at last to be without limit. People no longer had to earn enough money to pay for something, they could buy it on time or "pay" for it with a credit card. In an attempt to gratify their desires, families soon began to live beyond their means. They began consuming at a voracious rate, but no matter how much they bought, it never seemed to be enough. As a consequence, today many families find themselves burdened with overwhelming debt. In this regard, it would be wise for the stewards of these families to heed the counsel given by President Joseph F. Smith:

> It is highly proper for the Latter-day Saints to get out of debt. . . . Wherever I have had the opportunity of speaking, I have scarcely ever forgotten to hold out to the people the necessity—that I feel, at least—of our settling our obligations and freeing ourselves from debt. . . . I would say, in connection with this subject, that one of the best ways that I know of to pay my obligations to my brother, my neighbor, or business associate, is for me first to pay my obligations to the Lord. I can pay more of my debts to my neighbors, if I have contracted them, after I have met my honest obligations with the Lord, than I can by neglecting the latter; and you can do the same. If you desire to prosper, and to be free men and women and a free people, first meet your just obligations to God, and then meet your obligations to your fellowman.[4]

However, since financial problems are usually behavior problems rather than money problems, after paying off their old debts, many will soon find themselves burdened with a newly acquired set of debts. They buy and buy and yet there is always a desire for more.

There is an old adage that says, "You can never get enough of what you don't need because what you don't need can never satisfy you." And so the question arises, what is enough? What is enough house, car, or income? Hugh Nibley quotes both scriptures and Brigham Young in his attempt to declare "enough is enough":

> "Having food and raiment," says Paul to Timothy, "let us be therewith content" (1 Timothy 6:8). We must have sufficient for our needs in life's journey, but to go after more is forbidden, though you have your God-given free agency to do so. "Our real wants are very limited," says Brigham; "When you have what you wish to eat and sufficient clothing to make you comfortable you have all that you need; I have all that I need." How many people need to eat two lunches a day? We all eat too much, wear too much, and work

too much. Brigham says if we all "work less, wear less, eat less, . . . we shall be a great deal wiser, healthier, and wealthier people than by taking the course we now do."[5]

But if we were to follow such counsel, how would we ever be able to "keep up with the Joneses"? The Lord Himself aids us in knowing where and how our resources are to be spent. To begin with, He teaches: "Thou shalt not covet thy neighbour's house, thou shalt not covet thy neighbour's wife, nor his manservant, nor his maidservant, nor his ox, nor his ass, nor any thing that *is* thy neighbour's" (Ex. 20:17).

In spite of such teachings, envy is still with us. We see what others have and suddenly we too must have it. Envy is based on selfishness. A selfish person's desires are centered on self-gratification rather than on the needs of others and as such have no place in an eternal family.

An eternal marriage means being willing to commit oneself totally to another. It means unceasing devotion, a total consecration of one's time and resources, and a willingness to sacrifice in behalf of those we love. President Spencer W. Kimball, in his description of what it means to provide for the physical and spiritual *needs* of a family, wrote:

> Marriage is not a legal cover-all; but it means sacrifice, sharing, and even a reduction of some personal liberties. It means long, hard economizing. It means children who bring with them financial burdens, service burdens, care and worry burdens; but it also means the deepest and sweetest emotions of all.[6]

NOTES

1. Brigham Young (1864), Address, in *Journal of discourses* 10:329.

2. Spencer W. Kimball (1982), *Teachings of Spencer W. Kimball* (Salt Lake City: Bookcraft), 76.

3. David O. McKay (1965), unpublished manuscript sheet in author's personal file.

4. Joseph F. Smith (1977), *Gospel doctrine* (Salt Lake City: Deseret Book), 259.

5. H. Nibley (1989), *Approaching Zion* (Salt Lake City: Deseret Book; Provo, UT: Foundation for Ancient Research and Mormon Studies), 235.

6. Spencer W. Kimball (1982); see also Spencer W. Kimball (1974), Marriage is honorable, in *1973 Speeches of the year*, Provo, UT: Brigham Young University and Spencer W. Kimball (1980), *Marriage* (Salt Lake City: Deseret Book).

PROCLAMATION-BASED PRINCIPLES OF PARENTING AND SUPPORTIVE SCHOLARSHIP

CRAIG H. HART AND LLOYD D. NEWELL[1]
AND LISA L. SINE

Parents have a sacred duty to rear their children in love and righteousness.
(The Family: A Proclamation to the World, ¶ 6)

INTRODUCTION

How parents view the nature of a child and their own role as parents has great influence over the life of that child. Many perspectives about the nature of children have arisen in the course of Western Civilization that have shaped child-rearing practices for centuries, including the increasingly accepted scholarly view that parents matter relatively little in children's lives.[2] This chapter emphasizes inspired, eternal principles that are supported by empirical and conceptual scholarship, which suggests that optimal parenting does indeed matter in children's lives.

The purpose of this chapter is fourfold. First, to help readers learn about divergent worldviews on the nature of children and the role of parents, so that they will come to better appreciate the enlightened perspective of the Proclamation and prophetic counsel. Second, to understand how revelation from God as reflected in the Proclamation and the restored gospel emphasizes the divine centrality and responsibility of parents in children's lives. Third, to understand and apply inspired counsel and supportive research, so that readers will be able to strengthen and improve their own parenting skills in ways that will bless the lives of their children. Fourth, to internalize this knowledge, so that readers will be empowered to articulate the principles of the Proclamation in ways

that defend Proclamation-based ideals about parenting and help others incorporate them into their lives. In essence, this chapter focuses on how revelation from God vitally expands our understanding of children and child-rearing.

To begin, we discuss Proclamation-based views of child nature and child-rearing as compared and contrasted with other perspectives. Next, we consider how biological and spiritual components of child nature interplay with parental nurture in ways that can enhance or diminish inborn childhood predispositions. This will be followed by prophetic counsel on parenting and supportive scientific research regarding parenting styles. Child and teenage outcomes associated with different child-rearing patterns will be presented, along with some practical tips for parenting. We conclude the chapter by considering our Heavenly Father's perfect example of parenting and discussing wayward children.

PROCLAMATION-BASED VIEWS OF CHILD-REARING

Understanding the nature of children is critical to the study of parent–child interactions. Consider the succinct declaration and unique understanding of the nature of both parents and children in the Proclamation:

All human beings—male and female—are created in the image of God. Each is a beloved spirit son or daughter of heavenly parents, and, as such, each has a divine nature and destiny. . . . In the premortal realm, spirit sons and daughters knew and worshiped God as their Eternal Father and accepted His plan by which His children could obtain a physical body and gain earthly experience to progress toward perfection and ultimately realize his or her divine destiny as an heir of eternal life. (¶¶ 2–3)

Divine inheritance is a vital component of every person's makeup. Thus, while children are entrusted to earthly parents, they remain the spirit sons and daughters of God. The Proclamation expounds on this stewardship:

Husband and wife have a solemn responsibility to love and care for each other and for their children. "Children are an heritage of the Lord" (Psalm 127:3). Parents have a sacred duty to rear their children in love and righteousness, to provide for their physical and spiritual needs, to teach them to love and serve one another, to observe the commandments of God and to be law-abiding citizens wherever they live. Husbands and wives—mothers and fathers—will be held accountable before God for the discharge of these obligations. (¶ 6)

Children are dependent upon parents to meet their physical, emotional, and spiritual needs (see D&C 75:28; 83:4–5; Mosiah 4:14). Thus, parents are charged with teaching the gospel to their children and nurturing their souls with all that "is good and acceptable before God" (1 Tim. 5:4). As such, they will be held accountable before God as stewards of

His children (see D&C 68:25–28). A brief review of the religious and philosophical views of childhood and child-rearing will enlarge our appreciation for the truth of the restored gospel as it pertains to childhood and child-rearing.

At the outset, we acknowledge that the challenges and stresses unique to each family clearly influence parent–child interactions. Also, the many variations of parenting structures and "nontraditional" families—single parents, foster parents, stepparents, old and young parents, parents and children who move a lot, and so forth—make each parenting experience unlike any other. This chapter and the next are intended to present the various approaches and models of parenting, paying particular attention to the kind of parenting the Lord through his prophets has counseled and commanded parents to provide. Our focus is on parenting and the principles that can be applied to many different types of parenting for mothers and fathers, not on any particular situation in which parents operate. As Joseph Smith said, "I teach them correct principles, and they govern themselves."[5] Therefore, mothers and fathers are responsible for applying the general principles of effective Proclamation-based parenting to their individual circumstances.

RELIGIOUS AND PHILOSOPHICAL VIEWS OF CHILDHOOD

During the seventeenth and eighteenth centuries in Western societies, both positive and negative views about human nature at birth became solidified in ways that still influence modern-day thinking.[6] These typically break down into three categories: innately evil, blank slate, and innately good.

Innately Evil

The innately evil perspective is rooted in the Judeo-Christian view of children born in original sin as a consequence of Adam and Eve's transgression in the Garden of Eden. In this view of "fallen" humanity, children were characterized as being prone to wrongdoing and in need of strict discipline so that their innately evil natures might be subdued. Many parents believed they needed to "beat the devil" out of their children.[7] Because of this belief proposed by Protestant theologians such as John Calvin, harsh child punishment was often legitimized and displays of affection were sometimes thought to be harmful for the child.[8]

Of all the joys of life, none other equals that of happy parenthood. Of all the responsibilities with which we struggle, none other is so serious. To rear children in an atmosphere of love, security, and faith is the most rewarding of all challenges. The good result from such effort becomes life's most satisfying compensation.

President Gordon B. Hinckley.[3]

Parents are directly responsible for the righteous rearing of their children, and this responsibility cannot be safely delegated to relatives, friends, neighbors, the school, the church, or the state.

Elder Ezra Taft Benson[4]

Box 7.1

Paradoxically, the Judeo-Christian view of children also adopted Old Testament teachings that children were gifts from God and a source of family honor. This apparent contradiction is extended in New Testament writings where, in order to enter the kingdom of heaven, adults are invited to "become as little children" (Matt 18:3). As Borstelmann noted, these paradoxical viewpoints of the nature of children in scripture set the stage for "an antipathy between parental control for and affection for the child that has persisted to the present day."[9]

The LDS Perspective Compared and Contrasted with the Innately Evil View

The doctrine of original sin and thus the innately evil view is rejected in the restored gospel: "We believe that men will be punished for their own sins, and not for Adam's transgression" (2nd Article of Faith). Latter-day Saints view the fall of Adam and Eve not as a curse but rather as the gateway to mortality: "Adam fell that men might be" (2 Ne. 2:25). Also, Mormon, quoting the words of Christ, teaches us that little children have no need for repentance or baptism because "little children are whole, for they are not capable of committing sin; wherefore the curse of Adam is taken from them in me, that it hath no power over them. . . . Little children need no repentance neither baptism . . . Little children are alive in Christ, even from the foundation of the world" (cf. Moro. 8:8–12). Further, in 1833 the Lord revealed to the Prophet Joseph Smith, "Every spirit of man was innocent in the beginning; and God having redeemed man from the fall, men became again, in their infant state, innocent before God" (D&C 93:38).

That is why we are commanded to become again as little children: dependent, submissive, teachable, trusting, humble, patient, pure. Why are they pure? Robert Millet, BYU Dean of Religious Education, reveals the doctrine of Christ with this response:

> It is a false doctrine which prevails in the world that children have to be cleansed from original sin. The posterity of Adam in no way whatever is subject to original sin. Even should parents be guilty, that does not place any sin on the soul of the child. Little children are not under the cloud of sin.[10]
>
> Joseph Fielding Smith
>
> Box 7.2

The humanist might answer: "A child is pure because he or she is just that way by nature. They are innately good." But the scriptures teach otherwise. An angel taught Benjamin that "even if it were possible that little children could sin they could not be saved" if there were no Atonement; "but I say unto you they are blessed; for behold, as in Adam, or by nature, they fall, even so the blood of Christ atoneth for their sins" (Mosiah 3:16). Here is the sum and substance of the whole matter: little children are saved by Christ; they are pure because our Master has decreed them so, as an unconditional benefit of his atonement. "Little children are holy, being sanctified through the atonement of Jesus Christ; and this is what the scriptures mean" (D&C 74:7). God has instructed us that "little children are redeemed from the foundation of the world through mine Only Begotten" (D&C 29:46).[11]

In light of the truth of the restored gospel that we are not born innately sinful, modern-day prophets have spoken against "breaking the will of the child" by harsh discipline that relies on the "rod of correction" or severe physical punishment.

Blank Slate

In contrast to the traditional Judeo-Christian perspective that emphasized the evil child, John Locke (1632–1704), the father of British Empiricism, promoted the blank slate (or *tabula rasa*) view that what a child becomes is a function of his or her experiences. Thus, children are not born good or evil but are molded by their upbringing. Locke therefore encouraged parents to be good role models and to exercise affectionate and sensitive authority in terms of gently controlling children's impulses. More recently, psychologists John B. Watson and later B. F. Skinner saw humans as blank slates on which the experiences of life shape behavior. Watson went so far as to suggest that he could take a dozen healthy infants and make them into any kind of person he wanted as long as he had control of their environment.[12] In this view, parents, teachers, and others are wholly responsible for the fate of children.

The LDS Perspective Compared and Contrasted with the Blank-slate View

As the blank slate view connotes, the type of environment children are reared in is extremely important to Latter-day Saints as well. In the Proclamation, parents are admonished to provide an environment in which they "love and care for each other and for their children" (¶ 6). Parents are to do all they can to create an atmosphere of love and learning in the home.

Notwithstanding parental influence for good or ill, the restored gospel teaches that individuals have agency to choose their own destiny (see 2 Ne. 2:27–29; Hel. 14:30–31). Thus teachings of prophets and examples in scripture of "good parents" (e.g., Adam and Eve, Lehi and Sariah) who, despite their best efforts, had rebellious children, demonstrate that environment cannot account for everything a child becomes. Even with the sacred child-rearing responsibilities entrusted to parents and despite their most dedicated and sincere efforts, they cannot guarantee their children will grow to be "steadfast and immovable" in the faith (Mosiah 5:15). Ultimately children are free to choose.

Innately Good

French philosopher Jean-Jacques Rousseau (1712–1778) offered a parallel view: the child is innately well motivated, only to be corruptible by a corrupted adult society. He suggested that children are born innately pure, with an intuitive sense of right and wrong; and if children were left more to themselves, they would achieve their greatest potential. Parents were encouraged to allow their children to learn from experience and to follow inherently positive inclinations under well-regulated liberty. Carl Rogers, Abraham Maslow, and others of the humanistic tradition also saw human nature as fundamentally good.

The LDS Perspective Compared and Contrasted with the Innately Good View

"Children are an heritage of the Lord" (Ps. 127:3). The restored gospel teaches that every individual has a "divine nature and destiny" (Proclamation, ¶ 2) and that we are the spiritual offspring of God. Each child had a premortal life. And every person is endowed with spiritual gifts (see D&C 46; Moro. 10; 1 Cor. 12–14) that can be refined, developed, and enlarged as a result of earthly experiences. Even though a child comes into the world, as President David O. McKay said, "like a pure angel living in a little body,"[13] parents have a responsibility to teach that child right from wrong. Unlike Rousseau's innate-goodness view, in which children are left to their own devices to develop according to their intuitive sense of right and wrong, parents in the restored gospel are admonished to teach and guide children. While it is true that every

person born into the world receives the light of Christ, or conscience, to help guide him or her (see Moro. 7:16; D&C 88:6–13), the Lord directly commands parents, "But I have commanded you to bring up your children in light and truth" (D&C 93:40). Elder Joseph Fielding Smith taught:

> Every soul is precious in the sight of God. We are all his children and he desires our salvation. . . . [God] has placed the obligation upon all parents that they must teach the first principles of the Gospel to their children, teach them to pray, and see that they are baptized when they are eight years of age. Parents cannot shirk or neglect this great responsibility without incurring the displeasure of a righteous God.[14]

The Uniqueness of the LDS Perspective on Child Nature and Child-rearing

A comparison and contrast of these three views of children and child-rearing with Latter-day Saint doctrine is enlightening. These secular and religious views remain to this day because each contains some element of truth. However, they have never been fully reconciled; the debate among innately evil, blank-slate, and innately good viewpoints still rages among many people. But the light of the restored gospel dispels the confusing and contradictory darkness with a fulness of truth.

Which view is correct? Perhaps the best answer is none of them. The restored gospel does not advocate a singular view of innate goodness, blank slate, or innate evil. President McKay summarized the nature of humankind, and thereby children: "Man has a dual nature: one, related to the earthly or animal life; the other, akin to the Divine."[15] Thus, children of God have both goodness and fleshly susceptibilities within them. All receive the light of Christ to discern good from evil (see Moro. 7:15–19). We come from the heavenly realm and are born into a world of sin beset with temptations for the "natural man," but also full of spiritual opportunities for growth for the "divine" (see Mosiah 3:19; 16:5).

Being born innocent (see D&C 93:38) is being born neither good nor evil but having the potential for both. The "natural man" in us grows as a result of sin and our rejection of the promptings of the Spirit, whereas our divine nature is manifest when we heed those spiritual promptings and reject sin (see Mosiah 5:2). The restored gospel teaches that children are innocent and pure of any sin or evil; and while they have the capacity for transgression, they are not evil by nature but succumb to sin when they (1) are given wrong direction or no direction, or (2) when they willfully choose evil over good after the age of accountability. Therefore, we must guide our children to understand their eternal possibilities and internal potential for choosing good and fulfilling their own unique missions in life.[16]

Children are not accountable before God in overcoming the natural man until they arrive at the age of

---

I believe that I am a child of God endowed with a divine birthright. I believe that there is something of divinity within me and within each of you. I believe that we have a godly inheritance and that it is our responsibility, our obligation, and our opportunity to cultivate and nurture the very best of these qualities within us.

Gordon B. Hinckley[17]

The responsibilities of parenthood are of the greatest importance. The results of our efforts will have eternal consequences for us and the boys and girls we raise. Anyone who becomes a parent is under strict obligation to protect and love his children and assist them to return to their Heavenly Father. All parents should understand that the Lord will not hold guiltless those who neglect these responsibilities."

Howard W. Hunter[18]

Box 7.3

---

accountability (age eight, barring mental disability). Researchers have found, interestingly, that it is about this age when a variety of intellectual and reasoning capabilities emerge that help children make moral decisions.[19] The light of Christ and, then after baptism, the gift of the Holy Ghost are available to assist children. Before age eight and beyond, parents have a responsibility "to rear their children in love and righteousness" (Proclamation, ¶ 6) and to provide a loving home environment that allows them ample opportunity to search and find the truths that will help them "return to the presence of God" (¶ 3). Parents are to teach children to discern between good and evil and to use their agency so that their lives become an expression of their noble and eternal natures (see Moro. 7:19). Parents are to teach their children to love and serve each other and the Lord. "Humanness" is not the child's basic, fundamental, eternal nature. The truest description of their nature

is as the children of light (see 1 Thes. 5:5; Mosiah 5:7; D&C 106:5), sons and daughters of God. This understanding should influence powerfully the way we treat, guide, and view our children.

"In the premortal realm, spirit sons and daughters knew and worshiped God as their Eternal Father" (Proclamation, ¶ 3). Knowledge of premortal life that has come through the restoration provides a unique perspective on individual growth and development. The Proclamation's response to the age-old "nature or nurture" question would be an enlightened "yes"— both the nature and the nurture of a child contribute to his or her identity.

Nature and Nurture [20]

Spiritual identity and spiritual gifts cultivated in the premortal realm (see D&C 46; Abr. 3) interact with genetic individuality in ways that influence how children respond to their earthly environments. Thus, children reared in the same home will likely display different interests, personalities, and behavior because of unique biological blueprints provided by parents,[21] coupled with spiritual predispositions, talents, and desires. These characteristics are further refined by environmental factors in and out of the home (e.g., parents, peers, siblings, school, culture) and by the ways that children respond to them.[22] In order to succeed in adapting to the individual nature of each child, Brigham Young encouraged parents to "study their [children's] dispositions and their temperaments, and deal with them accordingly."[23] Elder Neal A. Maxwell stated: "Of course our genes, circumstances, and environments matter very much, and they shape us significantly. Yet there remains an inner zone in which we are sovereign unless we abdicate. In this zone lies the essence of our individuality and our personal accountability."[24]

Biological Characteristics

A growing body of evidence suggests that biological characteristics play a role in children's dispositions and temperaments. These include tendencies toward inhibition/shyness, sociability,[25] impulsiveness and "thrill-seeking,"[26] activity level (degree of lively energetic behavior and perpetual motion), aggression, behavior problems stemming from psychiatric disorders,[27] emotionality (e.g., intensity of arousal related to fear, anger, elation), and religiosity.[28]

There is also evidence that different genetically based characteristics can turn on or turn off at different points in development in ways that may be partially influenced by environmental factors.[29] Thus it may well be that some children cycle in and out of more easy and difficult developmental periods as they grow. Some biological/genetic tendencies may make up part of the "natural man" that must be overcome throughout life (Mosiah 3:19).

Fitting Nature with Nurture

Research exploring genetic contributions to children's development suggests that children select, modify, and even create their own environments according to their biological predispositions.[30] For example, a more sociable child may by nature seek out opportunities to interact with peers,[31] but may be less academically motivated. Alternatively, a more socially passive child in the same family may actively avoid social gatherings and prefer to spend time in solitary activities (such as coin or stamp collecting) and be more academically inclined.

In the same way, some children with more spirited dispositions (e.g., aggressive, highly emotional, or thrill-seeking tendencies) may raise concerns and evoke more formal intervention by parents in terms of rules, redirection, punishment, and monitoring than children who are "easier" to rear.[32] This can be particularly true when child behavior falls outside cultural norms and family expectations.[33] Thus, even though there are shared parenting influences,[34] children by their very natures can foster different parenting behaviors for different siblings in the same family.[35] Even children understand that parents adjust their styles to different needs and personality characteristics of their siblings.[36] These findings are confirmed in research as well as in the experience of parents with more than one child.

Children may also respond to similar parenting styles in different ways according to how experiences are filtered through their perceptions. For example, a temperamentally anxious/fearful child may view parental coercion (e.g., yelling and commanding) as threatening. He or she may respond by dutifully submitting to parental demands, yet harbor feelings of anger and resentment that are later manifest in feelings of loneliness and depression. Alternatively, a more spirited sibling may perceive parental coercion as confrontational and might often react by mouthing off and acting out in more openly defiant and angry ways. Yet other children may perceive warm and supportive parents as having little authority, may have little regard for their input, and may take advantage of a parent's good nature by trying to get away with everything that they can.

In essence, *nonshared* experiences that children in the same family have—in concert with individual genetic influences—often influence the many different personality characteristics found among siblings.[37] There is also scientific evidence that *shared* family influences, stemming from parental modeling and encouragement of the same moral, religious, and political interests and values, are as important or even more important than genes in creating likenesses between brothers and sisters.[38] Thus, the impact of rearing children in gospel-centered homes should not be underestimated.

Spiritual Capacities

Some children may be more difficult or easy to raise due, in part, to inherent personality characteristics that stem from spiritual predispositions. As President Brigham Young noted: "Some spirits are more noble than others; some are capable of receiving more than others. There is the same variety in the spirit world that you behold here, yet they are of the same parentage, of one Father, one God."[39]

God referred to Cain, for example, as "the father of lies, . . . for thou wast also [a liar] before the world (Moses 5:24). Alternatively, there were many "noble and great ones" who "were good" from before the world (Abr. 3:22–23). Nephi was likely one of those valiant ones who exercised his agency in responsible ways. He had "great desires to know of the mysteries of God . . . [and] did not rebel" (1 Ne. 2:16) against his father, as his brethren Laman and Lemuel did. Yet all three brothers were "born of goodly parents" (1 Ne. 1:1). Or perhaps Lehi and Sariah parented each of their children differently, according to the unique desires, dispositions, and abilities of each child. Wise parents work to adjust, relate to, and rear each child in a manner that is somewhat tempered to individual needs.

Whatever the nature and disposition of a given child, the Proclamation teaches the principle that parents should "rear their children in love and righteousness" (¶ 6). How this is done in practice for each child may vary according to his or her individual nature. Without attempting to offer a complete instruction manual, some of the principles and practices noted in this chapter can be helpful in further enhancing positive child characteristics and providing growth in areas where spiritual and genetic attributes may be less than complete. Weaknesses can foster humility and can eventually become strengths (see Ether 12:27). Parents can play a supportive role by helping children overcome weaknesses and build upon natural strengths in ways that enhance "individual premortal, mortal, and eternal identity and purpose" (¶ 2).

REARING CHILDREN IN LOVE AND RIGHTEOUSNESS

The Proclamation admonishes respect for the divine and individual nature of children as parents love, teach, and guide them. The emphasis of the Proclamation is on teaching and preparing children rather than on unrighteously controlling their wills.[40] Consistent with this, Brigham Young taught:

> God has placed within us will, and we should be satisfied to have it controlled by the will of the Almighty. . . . It has been the custom of parents to break the will until it is weakened, and the noble, God-like powers of the child are reduced to a comparative state of imbecility and cowardice. Let that heaven-born property of human agents be properly tempered and wisely directed. Parents should never drive their children, but lead them along, giving them knowledge as their minds are prepared to receive it. Chastening may be necessary betimes, but parents should govern their children by faith rather than by the rod, leading them kindly by good example into all truth and holiness.[41]

Parents are to rear their children in righteousness as emphasized in the Proclamation (¶ 7). This involves a process of teaching children to act for themselves in responsible ways by regulating their own wills in accordance with righteous values, beliefs, and understandings. It means respecting children's needs and wishes and responding to their inborn desire for autonomy.[42] Parental righteous dominion emphasizes charity, gentleness, kindness, long-suffering, persuasion, and appropriate discipline in a warm and nurturing relationship (see D&C 121: 39–46). It *invites* children to decide to adopt the parent's perspective on many issues. Unrighteous dominion centers around coercion, dominion, and compulsion "upon the souls of the children of men" (D&C 121:36–37) and can also include neglectful and indulgent parenting in ways that will be explained later.

To help children become masters of themselves

Consider the following words of modern-day prophets that shed additional light on what it means to rear children in love and righteousness. Scientific support for their counsel is noted later in this chapter:

"Use no lash and no violence, but approach them with reason, with persuasion and love unfeigned. . . . The man that will be angry at his boy, and try to correct him while he is in anger, is in the greatest fault . . . You can only correct your children by love, in kindness, by love unfeigned, by persuasion, and reason."

Joseph F. Smith[43]

"Setting limits to what a child can do means to that child that you love and respect him."

Spencer W. Kimball[44]

"Fathers, be kind to your children. Be companionable with them."

Gordon B. Hinckley[45]

"I believe those marvelous and simple words set forth the spirit in which we should stand as fathers (see D&C 121: 41–42). Do they mean that we should not exercise discipline, that we should not reprove? Listen to these further words: 'Reproving betimes with sharpness [When? While angry or in a fit of temper? No–] when moved upon by the Holy Ghost; and then showing forth afterwards an increase of love . . .' (D&C 121:43). I commend these words to every man within the sound of my voice . . ."

Gordon B. Hinckley[46]

Box 7.4

and to exercise their agency in accordance with correct principles, the Proclamation enjoins parents to "*teach* [their children] to love and serve one another, to observe the commandments of God and to be law-abiding citizens wherever they live" (¶ 6, emphasis added). Teaching these principles can be accomplished, in part, by parents setting a righteous example. President David O. McKay noted accordingly: "Children are more influenced by the sermons you act than by the sermons you preach."[47] Acting the sermons requires self-discipline on the part of parents and most fall short from time to time. As President Brigham Young observed, "I have seen more parents who were unable to control themselves than I ever saw who were unable to control their children."[48]

As these and statements in Box 7.4 make clear,

children require a balance of the following from their parents in order to promote optimal development:

- Love, warmth, and support
- Clear and reasonable expectations for competent behavior
- Limits and boundaries with some room for negotiation and compromise
- Reasoning and developmentally appropriate consequences and punishments for breaching established limits
- Opportunities to perform competently
- Absence of coercive, hostile forms of discipline, such as harsh physical punishment
- Models of appropriate behavior that are consistent with self-control, positive values, and positive attitudes

PARENTING STYLES AND CHILDREN'S DEVELOPMENT

How might parents best exercise righteous dominion? And if they do, will they really have a positive influence on their children's lives? Interestingly, the social science literature is full of debate over how important mothers and fathers actually are to their children's development. Recent interpretations of scientific research have lead to three contradictory conclusions:

(a) Parents are not essential to children's development;[49]

(b) An "average expectable" environment provided by parents is all that is needed;[50]

(c) "Optimal" rather than "good enough" parenting is essential for children's optimal development.[51]

The Proclamation, scriptures, and modern prophets confirm this view (c), teaching that there is a connection between the quality of parenting and what children become (e.g., Deut. 6:7; Prov. 22:6; Mosiah 4:15). Research has documented that changes in parenting behavior are reflected in corresponding changes in how children interact with others inside and outside of the home.[52]

While this connection is clear for the Latter-day Saint, social science has yet to confirm many of the positive and spiritual outcomes that parents in Zion most cherish. Part of the difficulty is the shortcomings of social science. It may well be that the essence of charity, kindness, righteousness, humility, testimony, and other crucial spiritual qualities can never really be adequately quantified. Few researchers have

attempted to examine such spiritual attributes. Further, can cause and effect as it relates to parents and their children ever be accurately and completely measured?

Despite these limitations, scientific evidence suggests that parents respond to the characteristics of their children in more and in less adaptable ways, thus influencing in positive and negative directions what children become.[53] Research also indicates that the predispositions with which children come into the world interact with ways that parents structure the child-rearing environment.[54] And still other research points to the correlation between the quality of the parents' marriage and the quality of their parenting.[55] To be sure, these are complex and multifaceted issues.

PARENTING STYLES

In Diana Baumrind's widely accepted research-based parenting model, three distinct styles of parenting are conceptualized:

- *coercive* [56]
- *permissive*
- *authoritative*

Of these three, the parenting style most consistent with the Proclamation, scripture, and what prophets have taught is the more responsive and flexible style, *authoritative child-rearing.*[57] Our discussion here attempts to provide meaningful direction to parents. Some of the problems with coercive and permissive styles will also be noted.

Coercive Parenting

Hostile parenting that derides, demeans, or diminishes children and teens by continually putting them in their place, putting them down, mocking them, or holding power over them via punitive or psychologically controlling means is called *coercive parenting.* It takes place in homes where there is a climate of hostility manifest by frequent spanking, yelling, criticizing, and forcing and has been linked to many forms of antisocial, withdrawn, and delinquent behaviors in children and adolescents.[58] It has also been associated with children coming to think they will get their way by using force with peers.[59] Likewise, psychological control designed to manipulate children's psychological and emotional experience and expression has also been associated with children's "externalizing" (e.g., aggressive, disruptive, delinquent behavior) and "internalizing" (e.g., anxiety, depression) disorders in childhood and adolescence.[60]

Psychologically controlling behaviors may include communicating disinterest in what a child is saying, invalidating or discounting a child's feelings, attacking a child in a condescending or patronizing way, and using guilt induction, love withdrawal, or erratic emotional behavior as means of control and manipulation.[61] Love withdrawal (e.g., angrily refusing to talk to or look at a child after he or she misbehaves), in particular, runs contrary to ways that God deals with his disobedient children. The Lord assures: "[My] hand is stretched out still" (Isa. 5:25; see also "Our Heavenly Father's Example" section later in this chapter).

From the beginning, unrighteous dominion has centered on control, dominion, and compulsion (see D&C 121). In gospel terms, it was Satan who wanted to destroy agency and achieve obedience through compulsion (see Moses 4:3). His motivation for doing so was self-aggrandizement by bringing honor unto himself (see Moses 4:1). Although exclusive reliance on coercion may result in immediate compliance in children, it often comes with a cost to children's abilities to learn how to regulate their own behavior from within.[62] Certainly, it shows little respect for the divine and individual nature of a child and corresponds with the innately evil and blank-slate child views. These views promote parents as controllers of all aspects of children's development.

Spare the rod? Parenting practices that include physical punishment ("the rod") have been advocated on the basis of biblical interpretations.[63] However, President Gordon B. Hinckley, echoing the counsel of President Brigham Young and other prophets, said, "I have never accepted the principle of 'spare the rod and spoil the child.' . . . Children don't need beating. They need love and encouragement."[64]

In support of this view, a good shepherd guides his sheep by gathering the lambs in his arms, carrying them in his bosom, and gently leading them along (see Isa. 40:11). The shepherd's rod is never used for beating sheep. It is used instead to ward off intruders, to count sheep as they "pass under the rod" (Lev. 27:32; Ezek. 20:37), to part the wool to examine for defects, disease, or wounds, and to nudge sheep gently from going in the wrong direction. The rod is viewed as a protection and is also translated from the Hebrew in other places as "the word of God" (e.g., Micah 6:9; Isa. 11:4). It is also interesting to note that

the rod is referred to as "the word of God" in the Book of Mormon (1 Ne. 15:23–24). Note that David, himself once a shepherd, said "thy rod and thy staff they *comfort* me" (Ps. 23:4).

As with many Old Testament scriptures used to support the view that "sparing the rod will spoil the child," a viable alternate translation from the Hebrew for Proverbs 13:24 ("He that spareth his rod hateth his son; but he that loveth him chasteneth him betimes") is "He who withholds the word of God, hateth his son: He who loveth his son, corrects (or teaches) him early on (when he is young)." Likewise, Proverbs 23:13–14 ("Withhold not correction from the child: for if thou beatest him with the rod, he shall not die. Thou shalt beat him with the rod, and shalt deliver his soul from hell") could be translated as "Withhold not correction from a child; for if you regulate him with the word of God, he will not die. Regulate him with the word of God, and you will deliver his soul from hell." Consider Proverbs 22:15, "Foolishness is bound in the heart of a child; but the rod of correction shall drive it far from him." This could be translated as "Folly conspires in the heart of the child, but the word of God casts it far from him." Finally, "the rod and reproof give wisdom" in Proverbs 29:15 could just as well read "the word of God imparts wise correction."[65]

Spanking. Parents are often confused by the contradictory evidence for and against spanking that is reported in the national media.[66] On one side, Diana Baumrind, a leading researcher in the study of parenting effects on children, states that "a blanket injunction against disciplinary spanking . . . is not scientifically supportable."[67] A body of scientific literature suggests that "nonabusive" spanking consisting of one or two mild slaps on the buttocks in limited situations (e.g., out-of-control behavior that poses danger to the child or others) can be beneficial as a last resort, but only for children between two and six years of age.[68] It can be particularly beneficial when backing up other discipline measures that have failed (e.g., reasoning with child or withdrawing privileges), or when conducted infrequently in the context of a warm and responsive relationship.[69]

Within this perspective, it has also been argued that parents need to take the child's nature into account. Whereas a more spirited youngster may benefit at times from stronger measures, a more sensitive child who comes to tears from a single disapproving word may not require any such discipline at all.

Another body of sophisticated research supports the notion that even though limited spanking may immediately stop a child from misbehaving and willfully defying in the short term, it actually increases the likelihood of greater disobedience and antisocial behavior later on.[70] It is also more likely to be done in anger.[71] So what are we to make of all this, particularly in light of Proclamation principles and restored gospel perspectives? Because of the inherent limitations associated with the scientific studies supporting both sides of the argument,[72] the debate over whether to spank, the severity of the practice, and how much spanking at what ages is appropriate will likely continue.

As will be noted later in the section on authoritative parenting, there are usually better alternatives to physical punishment. President Hinckley has observed, "I have tremendous respect for fathers and mothers who are nurturing their children in light and truth, . . . who spare the rod and govern with love, who look upon their little ones as their most valued assets to be protected, trained, and blessed."[73] In the biography of President Hinckley it states, "Gordon liked to say that his father never laid a hand on him except to bless him, and he intended to follow suit."[74]

Permissive Parenting

Permissive parenting, that which indulges children in their every whim and desire or that neglects children by leaving them to their own devices, could be considered another form of unrighteous dominion because parents are shirking their divine duties. The counsel of modern-day prophets has been that children need regulation and limits set. Parents are responsible for teaching their children the bounds of acceptable and unacceptable behavior.

In contrast to coercive parenting, permissive parents believe that children will flourish in their development if allowed to explore and engage in life unfettered by parental demands and restrictions. This is somewhat akin to Rousseau's "innately good" view, noted earlier. It is a child-centered perspective with an emphasis on the child's "agency." Children are considered parental equals in terms of rights, but not in terms of responsibilities.[75] Permissive parents do exert a degree of control over their children, but to a much lesser degree than coercive and authoritative. Permissive parents tend to avoid using their authority at all costs, being tolerant of children's impulses (including aggression), encouraging children to make their own decisions without providing parameters

within which they can be made, and refraining from imposing structure on children's time (i.e., bedtime, mealtime, TV watching). They also keep at a minimum restrictions, demands for mature behavior, and consequences for misbehavior.[76]

Social science research suggests that children raised by permissive parents may have greater difficulty respecting others, coping with frustration, delaying gratification for a greater goal, and following through with their plans.[77] Unlike coercive parenting, in which child outcomes are predominately negative, permissive parenting produces mixed results. Children of permissive parents have been found to be quite social and to have a low rate of internalized problems (e.g., depression, anxiety), but they tend to do less well academically, are more defiant of authority figures, and have a higher rate of adolescent sexual activity and drug and alcohol use.[78]

Indulging children is another form of permissiveness that requires careful consideration. Elder Joe J. Christensen counseled: . . . "we should avoid spoiling children by giving them too much. In our day, many children grow up with distorted values because we as parents overindulge them. . . . One of the most important things we can teach our children is to deny themselves. Instant gratification generally makes for weak people."[79]

Elder Neal A. Maxwell taught:

A few of our wonderful youth and young adults in the Church are unstretched. They have almost a free pass. Perks are provided, including cars complete with fuel and insurance—all paid for by parents who sometimes listen in vain for a few courteous and appreciative words. What is thus taken for granted . . . tends to underwrite selfishness and a sense of entitlement.[80]

Permissive parenting does not fit well in the Proclamation-based parenting model. As has been noted, parents are charged with the responsibility to guide and teach the principles of the gospel to their children by example and precept. Elder Ezra Taft Benson, quoting President J. Reuben Clark Jr., said:

I appeal to you parents, take nothing for granted about your children. The great bulk of them, of course, are good, but some of us do not know when they begin to go away from the path of truth and righteousness. Be watchful every day and hour. Never relax your care, your solicitude. Rule kindly in the spirit of the gospel and the spirit of the priesthood, but rule, if you wish your children to follow the right path.

President Benson continued by saying, "Permissive parents are part of the problem."[81]

Authoritative Parenting

Parenting that fosters a positive emotional connection with children, provides for regulation that places fair and consistent limits on child behavior, and allows for reasonable child autonomy in decision-making is typically referred to by researchers as *authoritative*.[82] This style has been documented to create a positive emotional climate that helps children be more open to parental input and direction.[83] Children and adolescents reared by authoritative parents tend to be better adjusted to school, are less aggressive and delinquent, less likely to abuse drugs, more friendly and accepted by peers, more communicative, self-motivated, academically inclined, and willing to abide by laws.[84] They are also more capable of moral reasoning[85] and are more self-controlled.[86] For the Latter-day Saint, the implication is that such children are more willing to abide by and reap the blessings of spiritual laws as well. Positive parenting styles are likely more effective when parents are unified in their parenting efforts.[87] Characteristics of this style are discussed below.

Connection. One of the major features of good parent-child relationships includes being responsive to and "companionable" with children, as noted by President Hinckley. Brigham Young counseled, "Kind looks, kind actions, kind words, and a lovely, holy deportment towards them will bind our children to us with bands that cannot be easily broken; while abuse and unkindness will drive them from us." Prophetic statements such as these supported by research suggest that warm and responsive parenting tends to promote lasting bonds with parents and "felt security" within children.[88] This, in turn, has been linked to better behavior now[89] and in the future.[90] Warm and responsive child rearing also helps prevent hostility, resentment, and anger in children,[91] all of which has been admonished in holy writ through the ages: ". . . provoke not your children to wrath: but bring them up in the nurture and admonition of the Lord" (Eph. 6:4).

Specifically, research has documented that children are less aggressive and more sociable and empathetic if they have parents (particularly fathers) who are more loving, patient, playful, responsive, and sympathetic to children's feelings and needs.[92] Similarly, mothers who take the time to engage in mutually enjoyable activities with their children more effectively convey values and rules to them.[93] Children are less likely to push limits and seek attention through misbehavior when they feel that they are of high priority in their parents' lives.

A recent study showed that Latter-day Saint parents who are emotionally connected with their teens, set regulatory limits, and foster autonomy in ways described later are far more likely to have adolescents who are more careful in their selection of peers, regardless of what part of the country they live in. Children reared in these types of family environments, where prayer, scripture study, and religious values are stressed, were also more likely to internalize religiosity. Personal prayer and scripture study as well as private spiritual experiences were found to be a strong deterrent to delinquent behavior.[94]

> Every child is entitled to grow up in a home where there is warm and secure companionship, where there is love in the family relationship, where appreciation one for another is taught and exemplified, and where God is acknowledged and His peace and blessings invoked before the family altar.[95]
>
> Gordon B. Hinckley
>
> Box 7.5

Regulation. Finding ways to effectively help children learn how to regulate their own behavior in noncoercive ways is one of the most challenging parts of parenting. Like riding a horse, knowing how and when to tighten or loosen the reins requires considerable creativity, effort, and inspiration. There are no recipe books, but there are principles that can be helpful. In authoritative homes, parents are clear and firm about rules and expectations. Unlike coercive parents who administer harsh, arbitrary punishments, authoritative parents proactively explain reasons for setting rules and administer corrective measures promptly when children do not abide by them. Correction is motivated by a sincere interest in teaching children correct principles rather than merely to control, exercise dominion, or vent anger. In so doing, authoritative parents make a conscious effort to also take into consideration the developmental level of the child and the child's individual temperament. In an effort to make the home a place of security, they build a safety net of appropriate limits for their children and generously communicate their approval of desirable behavior. With all of this, a premium is placed on helping children understand how to regulate themselves in a parent–child interaction context that is friendly as well as tutorial and disciplinary. Research has shown that when firm habits of good behavior are established early in life through parental regulatory practices that include ingredients of limit setting, a judicious use of punishment, positive reinforcement, and reasoning, parents are better able to relax control as their children grow older.[96]

Setting limits and following through with pre-established consequences when rules are violated is one way that parents can help children learn to be self-regulating. Just as the rod is used to gently nudge sheep away from dangerous places, setting limits around potentially harmful influences (e.g., inappropriate media and early dating) helps children feel more safe and secure. As the scripture reassures, " . . . thy rod and thy staff they comfort me" (Ps. 23:4). For example, carefully monitoring adolescent whereabouts and behavior as well as helping them adhere to parental expectations is a form of limit setting that can go far in reducing delinquent activity.[97]

Authoritative parents take responsibility for setting the appropriate number of rules for regulating children's behavior that can be realistically remembered and enforced. Some children may require more and varying types of rules and punishments than others, depending on their individual natures. Some rules may be implicit and just part of the family routine (e.g., family prayer is daily at 7:00 A.M.). Others may be more explicit with consequences attached (e.g., roller-blading in the house will result in the roller blades being put away for several days). When rules and their accompanying consequences that have been explained in advance are violated, authoritative parents are firm and consistent when following through in a calm and clear-headed manner, particularly after a sufficient number of warnings adapted to the child's ability for self-regulation have been given. Examples could include temporarily suspending teen driving privileges for traffic violations, calmly showing up at a son or daughter's teen party when curfew is violated, enforcing time-out when a child is angry and hurting others and then discussing alternative methods for dealing with anger, or letting the stove timer determine whether chores are completed in a reasonable time frame so that certain privileges can be earned. Being consistent in administering corrective discipline provides opportunities for children to experience the negative consequences of poor choices. It

also allows subsequent opportunities for children to "rehearse" better behavior, by arming them with new information about how to handle the situation more appropriately in the future.

There are times when chastisement or other forms of punishment are necessary (see D&C 121: 43; Heb. 12:5–11). Indeed, punishment is an eternal principle (e.g., Alma 42:16, 18–21; 2 Ne. 2:13). However, as noted earlier, there are usually better alternatives than physical punishment. Alternatives can include reproving, withdrawing privileges, setting up opportunities to make restitution, or following through on predetermined consequences for breaking rules. To be most effective, punishments should be logically tied to the misbehavior, accompanied by reasoning, and administered in a prompt, rational manner. Seeking guidance from the Spirit will assist parents in finding ways to discipline in a context of love, respect, consistency, justice, and sensitivity to the child's developmental level and individual personality.

Negative side effects for the child and the parent-child relationship can occur when punishment is arbitrarily and coercively administered as a way to vent parental anger or to brandish authority, rather than as a way to calmly emphasize an important message. These can include children feeling hostility and resentment towards parents, or conforming out of fear rather than acting out of respect for parental leadership and an increasing desire to do right for intrinsic reasons.

Punishment is not always the answer. It is important to try to understand the underlying causes of misbehavior and deal with them first. Challenging behavior can sometimes be associated with a biologically based mood, thought, behavioral, or learning disorder that might require professional help. It can also be tied to an unfulfilled need (e.g., being tired, hungry, or lacking in parental attention), a stage of growth (e.g., teething or natural striving for autonomy during the wonderful twos/threes and again during the teen-age years), something going awry in the present environment (e.g., friends being mean; fear of the dark at bedtime), or a child just simply not knowing any better (e.g., animals can get hurt when mistreated).[98]

For example, punishment may be ineffective for an out-of-control child who is acting out due to lack of sleep. Adequate rest will likely be a better solution. When less capable of understanding the reasons behind rules and related consequences for misbehavior, young children sometimes respond better to simply being redirected to more acceptable behaviors (e.g., being shown how to gently pet a cat rather than strangle it). Planning ahead can also eliminate problems before they occur (e.g., putting safety latches on cupboards for curious toddlers, providing a watch with a beeper alarm so children won't forget to come home in the midst of play with friends).

When consequences need to be enforced, the scriptures teach the principle of "showing forth afterwards an increase of love toward him whom thou hast reproved" (D&C 121:43). When the child has been corrected in a calm, controlled manner, that same Spirit which prompted it can create a sense of compassion, charity, and forgiveness towards the child. These are moments when children have a particularly intense and immediate need to feel the strength of parental love after the consequence has been administered. Authoritative parents will take action to assure the child of their love and genuine concern in a way that is suited to the age and individual needs of the child. For example, with a young child who requires concrete experiences, physical affection, such as hugging them or holding them lovingly helps to calm the quivering lip and restore a sense of inner security (e.g., "Maybe you can sit here on my lap for a while until you feel like playing with your sister again"). Ignoring misbehavior that is not harmful to self or others may be an appropriate consequence at times for young children when followed up by love and acceptance (e.g., calmly ignoring whining and then responding positively to normal speech). Affirming verbal statements are important at all ages (e.g., "Even when I need to punish, you can be sure that I love you very much"; "I know that as a child of God, you will choose the right"). Often humor can be used to break the tension (e.g., "Better watch out, I think a tickle monster is coming to get you!"; "Okay, enough of this serious stuff, time for a group hug!"). A change in activity may help, particularly when it gives children a chance to positively interact with their parent (e.g., "Hey, where's that football I promised to toss around with you when I got some time?"; "Will you be my helper in the kitchen? I need a junior chef to help me whip up some cornbread.") Finally, expressing confidence in children can help alleviate their concerns (e.g., "It's been a hard day. We all make mistakes. I know you'll do better next time").

While confrontations and conflicts are inevitable in family life, parents can work diligently to nurture relationships and keep a positive tone in the home.

This can be accomplished, in part, by responding to children's natural desire to please and to be accepted. Frequent, affirming, and sincere statements that identify children's strengths or draw attention to a specific aspect of the child's behavior or performance can be encouraging and promote the child's desire to maintain a high standard of behavior (e.g., "John, the lawn sure looks good since you mowed it—Thanks for sweeping the sidewalks as well"; "I'll bet it felt good to get your homework done right after school so you could play with friends"; "Thanks for being quiet while I was on the phone"). Also, periodically surprising a child with extra privileges or providing ways to "earn benefits" associated with desirable behavior can also encourage good performance (e.g., "You have worked so hard on your piano practicing over the last month that I'd like to go on a daddy–daughter date with you to the concert this weekend"; "How about after your chores are done going to the movie you wanted to see ?"). Rewarding good behavior and framing expectations in a positive manner can go far in inviting children to regulate their behavior in desirable ways (see the entry "Reward," pp. 430–31 in the Topical Guide of the LDS scriptures).

As noted earlier, prophets have emphasized that reason and persuasion are important when working with children. For example, when regulating behavior parents can say things like, "If you only do what you want to do when playing with Johnny, he probably won't want to play with you anymore. What things do you think he would like to do when you get together?" This helps keep parental focus more on teaching and preparing children for acceptable ways of behaving rather than on directing and controlling misbehavior. Telling young children things like "Yes, Tom, I can understand why you are angry, and that's okay, but I won't let you hit Jim. Remember next time to use your words when you want your trike back so that there will be no hitting. Hitting hurts." This type of approach communicates clear limits, acknowledges emotions being felt, emphasizes consequences to others for hurtful behavior, and presents more acceptable strategies for dealing with conflict. Following up with role-plays, perhaps in a Family Home Evening, can go far in helping children rehearse acceptable behavior. Although not required for every situation, consistent efforts to provide simple rationales that are often repeated eventually sink in and can win voluntary obedience even in two- to three-year-old children.[99]

Numerous studies have documented positive ways that reasoning with children (especially in advance of a problem) can help them willingly regulate their own behavior, resulting in more confident, empathetic, helpful and happy children.[100] For example, parents who plan ahead and predispose their young children before going into a store that "we are not buying treats to eat right now so there will be lots of room in our tummies for healthy foods at dinner" are more likely to avoid temper tantrums in the checkout line.

How children respond to reasoning oriented parental input depends on a variety of factors, including the age of the children, their relationship with the parent, their receptiveness to instruction, and their ability to understand.[101] As Father Lehi demonstrated when reasoning with older children (i.e., Laman and Lemuel), there are times to back off, particularly after a point has been made or the message is clearly not getting through. "And he did exhort them then with all the feeling of a tender parent, that they would hearken to his words . . . and after he had preached unto them, and also prophesied unto them of many things, he bade them to keep the commandments of the Lord; and he did cease speaking unto them" (1 Ne. 8:37–38).

For adolescents and older children, reasoning can often come across as preachments and may provoke more opposition and testiness if not carefully worded. Also, wise parents remember that the tone of voice, a loving touch, and the sincere feeling behind the words parents use often communicate much more than the words themselves. Playing a "consultant role" often works better.[102] This involves (a) reflective listening (e.g., saying something like "So it sounds like you're feeling angry because your teacher doesn't explain math very well and you are suffering for it"), (b) using less directive "I" rather than more intrusive "you" statements ("I am confused about why you want to drop algebra. You've seemed really excited about a career in electrical engineering" rather than "You will never be an electrical engineer without algebra"), (c) musing and wondering aloud about potential consequences and alternatives (e.g., saying "I am just wondering how you are going to graduate from high school if you drop algebra" rather than saying "You need to take algebra in order to graduate"), and (d) leaving more ownership for problem solving to the child (e.g., "What do you want to have happen here?" "Which alternative that we have discussed do you think would be best for your future?" or "What are you going to do about it?").

Parents can also reason and persuade by teaching the simple truths of the gospel. President Boyd K. Packer has said, "True doctrine, understood, changes attitudes and behavior. The study of the doctrines of the gospel will improve behavior quicker than a study of behavior will improve behavior."[103] As parents focus on emulating and teaching the "plan of happiness" (Alma 42:16) and the doctrines of the kingdom to their children, and helping those within their stewardship to deeply understand and internalize eternal truths, children will more likely embrace the "correct principles" of their parents. Through the loving reasoning and gentle persuasion of parents as well as personal religious experiences and public religious behavior, children will more likely "lay hold upon the word of God" (Hel. 3:29) and remain faithful.[104]

I was blessed with a good father and mother. I can never remember their laying a hand on me or [on] any of their other children. We probably deserved it, but they did not do it. They sat us down and talked with us. That was enough.

Gordon B. Hinckley[105]

Rear [your children] in love. You don't have to kick them around. You don't have to get angry with them. You just have to love them. If they make mistakes, forgive them and help them to avoid repetition.

Gordon B. Hinckley[106]

Box 7.6

Autonomy. Children also benefit from making the choices that authoritative parents offer them and being allowed to make their own decisions in a variety of domains.[107] By developing decision-making skills and learning how to make choices within limits that are acceptable to parents (e.g., allowing a child the option of taking the trash out in the evening or in the morning before school; asking if a child would prefer hot or cold cereal, etc.), children learn and grow. Whenever possible, supporting children's autonomy in this manner helps children view adults as providers of information and guidance rather than as deliverers of messages of control.[108] Psychological control and other aspects of coercive parenting, as described earlier, work against this important aspect of children's development.[109] Positive psychological interventions entailed in devising options and providing reasoning or gentle persuasion do not lend themselves to the rebellion that unrighteous dominion may often provoke. Elder Robert D. Hales has counseled:

> Act with faith; don't react with fear. When our teenagers begin testing family values, parents need to go to the Lord for guidance on the specific needs of each family member. This is the time for added love and support and to reinforce your teachings on how to make choices. It is frightening to allow our children to learn from the mistakes they may make, but their willingness to choose the Lord's way and family values is greater when the choice comes from within than when we attempt to force those values upon them. The Lord's way of love and acceptance is better than Satan's way of force and coercion, especially in rearing teenagers.[110]

Indeed, from the enlightened perspective of the restored gospel, we know that moral agency is an eternal principle. Also, every person born into this world is given the light of Christ (and then, later, if he or she enters the covenant and remains faithful, the gift of the Holy Ghost), which facilitates the making of right choices (see Moro. 7:13–19). When children have been taught and then internalize correct principles (doctrine) and have had opportunities to make choices (good and bad) within an environment of unfailing love and concern, they are more likely to choose wisely.

Authoritative parents teach with warmth and responsiveness thereby allowing for a "give-and-take" in their relationship with their children.[111] Differences are respected and valued. Parental communication is open and nonjudgmental, with more emphasis on listening to understand rather than on talking. Respect for authority and independent thinking and feeling are valued, rather than viewed as being mutually exclusive. Research has shown that children are more likely to be respectful to parents and others when there is reciprocity and a degree of power-sharing in their relationships with parents.[112]

Reciprocity comes into play in areas where firm rules and restrictions are deemed unnecessary or unreasonable and parents model and encourage negotiation and compromise (e.g., allowing the child's input into when to take the trash out). Finding ways to say yes more often than no to a child's requests lends more credence when a parent has to say no. When children and teens are given latitude for decision-making in areas that matter less, they are more likely to feel trusted and empowered to choose

rightly and conform to parental expectations in areas that matter more.

Developmental stages and needs are also considered in reciprocal relationships. As children grow older and more mature, they are granted more autonomy and a greater share in family decision-making.[113] Provided that a pattern of choice-giving, limit-setting, follow-through, and reasoning is established early in children's lives, parent-child relationships and positive child development will more likely be enhanced.

Advantages of Authoritative Parenting

Because authoritative parenting is flexible, it appears to provide the best fit for children with varying temperamental dispositions. In other words, each child is guided in a balanced style of connection, regulation, and autonomy that best matches his or her unique set of strengths and weaknesses. For example, some teenagers are self-motivated to engage in appropriate activities, do not require curfews, and are home at reasonable hours. Without restrictions, many teens lose control of their lives. Yet others rebel when locked into tightly controlled curfews and expectations. Sometimes a middle-of-the-road approach that balances granting autonomy with imposing regulation works best with more spirited teenagers.[114] They often become surprisingly responsible when the general expectation is that they inform parents about where they are, who they are with, and when they will be home (within reasonable limits), as well as being allowed to compromise with parents when there is a disagreement. Creativity and inspiration are required to know how to work best with each child and teen.

Parental input is important for enhancing or diminishing more and less desirable characteristics in children.[115] Finding a "good fit" between child temperament and child rearing[116] is a challenging and creative adventure that requires considerable time, patience, energy, and commitment. Permissive parents do little to create optimal growing opportunities for children because they are less actively involved and may overindulge or neglect their children, thus robbing them of vital life lessons. Conversely, when parents become locked into an "all-fits-one" coercive approach, relying solely on hostile forms of punishment, isolation, or restriction, there is far less latitude for seeking after and receiving divine inspiration that can help individual children develop in optimal ways. In contrast, "authoritative" parents actively seek inspiration in order to teach and prepare children—

through positive communication, encouragement, and individualization—to succeed in life. They realize that every child is unique and requires, to a certain extent, an individualized parenting approach wherein each child is treated fairly, although not always equally. Authoritative parents understand their divine charge to teach and guide their children in light and truth. Parents often find that direction and insight for how to approach their children "authoritatively" in any given situation comes best from humbly seeking the guidance of the Spirit. Because authoritative parenting has both an open window of learning and a solid framework of teaching, divine direction and strength can be more readily sought, found, and implemented.

> Child rearing is so individualistic. Every child is different and unique. What works with one may not work with another. I do not know who is wise enough to say what discipline is too harsh or what is too lenient except the parents of the children themselves, who love them most. It is a matter of prayerful discernment for the parents. Certainly the overarching and undergirding principle is that the discipline of children must be motivated more by love than by punishment.
>
> James E. Faust[117]
>
> Box 7.7

President Hinckley has summarized well the distinctiveness of parenting that aligns with Proclamation principles and the lasting ramifications of the parenting styles we employ:

> As children grow through the years, their lives, in large measure, become an extension and a reflection of family teaching. If there is harshness, abuse, uncontrolled anger, disloyalty, the fruits will be certain and discernible, and in all likelihood they will be repeated in the generation that follows. If, on the other hand, there is forbearance, forgiveness, respect, consideration, kindness, mercy, and compassion, the fruits again will be discernible, and they will be eternally rewarding. They will be positive and sweet and wonderful. And as mercy is given and taught by parents, it will be repeated in the lives and actions of the next generation.[118]

Parenting is difficult work. Parents get fatigued and stressed and are not always at "100 percent peak operating efficiency." Like a river that ebbs and flows, parents are not always authoritative and never permissive or coercive.[119] Even the most wonderful, responsive parents will, from time to time and under difficult circumstances, lose patience with demanding children.[120] Parents who admit mistakes and say they are sorry model sincere efforts to change and overcome human weaknesses. At one moment parents may be more permissive because of various external and internal factors, at another moment more coercive. However, most parents tend to be more one way than another. It is the pattern of interaction or the climate of parenting style in the home that makes the difference. When parents try to be unified and consistent in employing an authoritative style that balances characteristics of connection, regulation, and autonomy, children have more chance at optimal growth and joy. When children are reared in a home where parents are striving to lead and guide with love, patience, respect, and humility, children will more likely respond in positive ways.

At some point, most parents feel as if they could have done better or more. However, most have also felt some success as parents when they handled a situation well, didn't lose their temper, and were loving but firm. Just as children grow, learn, make mistakes, and ask for forgiveness, so do parents. In a covenant family, when parents ask forgiveness of their children and humbly seek the Lord's help in overcoming personal weaknesses, parenting becomes a sanctifying process. As they lead and guide their little ones back to Heavenly Father, they become more like Him.

OUR HEAVENLY FATHER'S EXAMPLE

Our Father in Heaven has given us a perfect example of how we should parent through the ways that He parents us. He gives us commandments, outlining the limits and boundaries within which we should conduct our lives. The boundaries are clear, as are His expectations of us. He has high expectations (see Moses 1:39) and provides us the warmth and support necessary to meet those expectations. The loving gift of His "great plan of happiness" (Alma 42:8)—so that we may learn and progress in this life and throughout eternity as well as experience untold joy—is evident in the atoning sacrifice of His Son for us (see John 3:16).

When we fail to meet His expectations, we face consequences and punishments according to eternal laws that are consistent with our transgressions, and

His rebukes are accompanied and motivated by His unfailing love. He will not withdraw His perfect and constant love from us, although we may withdraw from Him at times. His capacity to bless is constrained by our righteousness and obedience (see D&C 82:10; 130: 20–21). He is always there for us when we earnestly seek Him in humility and righteousness (see D&C 88: 63, 83). Because He *is* love (see 1 Jn. 4:16), nothing we do or don't do will alter His complete capacity to love us. He loves perfectly. The more we draw near unto Him, the more we will be filled with His love.

Parents become more like Him as they learn to love as He loves. They love not as their children become more lovable, but as the parents are increasingly filled with His love. President Benson has reminded us that "above all else, children need to know and feel they are loved, wanted, and appreciated. They need to be assured of that often."[121] The more parents purely love their children, the more likely those children will become more loveable. It is not so much that the children have changed, but that the parents have changed.

It is also important for parents to show this kind of love to each other. Indeed, President Benson and other prophets have stated that children need to know that parents love one another: "One of the greatest things a man can do for his children is to love his wife and let them know he loves her."[122] As parents unfailingly love each other and each child with fulness of heart, relationships can change, miracles of forgiveness and understanding can take place, and family solidarity and closeness can result.

Like loving parents with children, our Father in Heaven's love can soften our defenses and help us hear the counsel we need to hear. He is the Master at listening and He communicates with us in ways that we can hear and understand. He allows us our autonomy and agency, encouraging us to make decisions according to that which we know to be good and true, and to study it out in our minds first before coming to Him for help (see D&C 9:7–8), rather than expecting Him to make our decisions for us. He wants us to grow into spiritual adulthood, becoming even as He is (see 3 Ne. 12:48). He does everything He can to help us to do so, including allowing us to make mistakes and rectify them. Though limits and boundaries are set, there are endless possibilities of good choices within those boundaries. Our Father in Heaven allows us the use of our agency in choosing among these possibilities, recognizing that doing so is essential if we are to grow and progress.

Our Father in Heaven also teaches us by His loving example. Not only through His example in His interactions with us and the plan of salvation He has provided, but also by sending His Son, Jesus Christ, to model His expectations of the attributes we should be actively working towards acquiring. As President Spencer W. Kimball has explained:

> Jesus lived and taught the virtues of love and kindness and patience. He also taught the virtues of firmness and resolution and persistence and courageous indignation. These two sets of virtues seem to clash with each other . . . yet both are necessary. If there were but one, love without discipline, love without deep conviction of right and wrong, without courage to fight the wrong, such love becomes sentimentalism. Conversely, the virtues of righteous indignation without love can be harsh and cruel.[123]

The model of parenting our Father in Heaven has outlined for us through His example, through the example of the Savior, and through the words of the prophets, promotes children's optimal development spiritually, psychologically, emotionally, and intellectually. It fosters children's development of internal motivation to live in accordance with their personal beliefs, convictions, and correct principles rather than acquiescing to the desires of others who would have them go against their values. It fortifies them against the trials of this life, promoting their resiliency, and blesses them to experience the joy life has to offer.

Accountability

Parents "will be held accountable before God for the discharge of [their] obligations" and their "sacred duty" and "solemn responsibility" to rear their children in love and righteousness, to provide for them, and to teach them the principles of righteousness (Proclamation, ¶ 6). In the Father's stewardship relationship to us He has as His work and glory "to bring to pass the immortality and eternal life of man" (Moses 1:39). Earthly parents also have a sacred stewardship relationship with their children. They are entrusted with the precious spirit children of the Father and as such are duty bound to love, care, nurture, teach, and rear those children in righteousness, with gentleness, meekness, love, kindness, charity, faith, and virtue (see D&C 121:41–46).[124]

When fathers and mothers parent in humility and sincerity by the model and commandments of the

Father, the Holy Ghost will be their companion and will guide, comfort, and instruct. In partnership with God, parents seek for the vital divine assistance and guidance that will enhance their own natural abilities and inclinations. President Gordon B. Hinckley summarizes well this sacred stewardship:

> Never forget that these little ones are the sons and daughters of God and that yours is a custodial relationship to them, that He was a parent before you were parents and that He has not relinquished His parental rights or interest in these His little ones. Now, love them, take care of them. Fathers, control your tempers, now and in all the years to come. Mothers, control your voices, keep them down. Rear your children in love, in the nurture and admonition of the Lord. Take care of your little ones, welcome them into your homes, and nurture and love them with all of your hearts. They may do, in the years that come, some things you would not want them to do, but be patient, be patient. You have not failed as long as you have tried. Never forget that.[125]

When a Child Wanders

The scriptural admonition in Proverbs 22:6, "Train up a child in the way he should go: and when he is old, he will not depart from it," can cut two ways. Good teaching and training can help to set children on a path that leads to an abundant life in both temporal and eternal domains. Alternatively, children raised in unrighteous ways may not depart from habits and paths that are harmful to themselves and others unless, at some point, they experience a "mighty change [of] heart" (see Alma 5:12–14). Notwithstanding parental influence for good or ill, the restored gospel teaches that individuals have agency to choose their own destiny (see 2 Ne. 2:21–30; Mosiah 2:21; Hel. 14:30–31; Alma 12:31; Moses 6:56). Sometimes, despite the best efforts of parents, children exercise their agency in irresponsible ways and wander into forbidden paths (see Luke 15:11–32). However, parents would do well not to berate themselves for what they think could have been. One should also not think there is a foolproof, "100 percent guaranteed" method for raising good and faithful children. Just as surely as parents cannot take all the blame for unrighteous and rebellious offspring, parents cannot take all the credit for faithful offspring. All parents fall short of perfection, even in ways they know better, for energy and patience do not always last to the limits of knowledge. As

> A successful parent is one who has loved, one who has sacrificed, and one who has cared for, taught, and ministered to the needs of a child. If you have done all of these and your child is still wayward or troublesome or worldly, it could well be that you are, nevertheless, a successful parent. Perhaps there are children who have come into the world that would challenge any set of parents under any set of circumstances. Likewise, perhaps there are others who would bless the lives of, and be a joy to almost any father or mother.
>
> My concern is that there are parents who may be pronouncing harsh judgement upon themselves and may be allowing these feelings to destroy their lives, when in fact they have done their best and should continue in the faith.
>
> Howard W. Hunter[126]
>
> Box 7.8

evidenced by the challenges that Adam and Eve had, as well as Lehi and Sariah (to name but two of many righteous couples), who faced some wayward children, children's agency is a God-given gift over which parents have limited control. Even our Heavenly Father, although perfect, was not spared the disaffection of Lucifer and one-third of the spirit host of His sons and daughters (see D&C 76:26; Moses 4:1–3; Rev. 12:4, 9).

For children who kept their first, premortal, estate and are sealed to their parents in this life, even if they wander, there is hope for their return when they are ready.[127] Proclamation principles of "faith, prayer, repentance, forgiveness, respect, love, [and] compassion" (¶ 7) can go far in extending an invitation for a wayward child to come back to the fold of God.

An Eternal Perspective

The restored gospel teaches that parents play a central role in Heavenly Father's plan of happiness by providing children with the foundation upon which they will make choices that enhance or diminish their earthly and eternal opportunities and possibilities. Children are born innocent, with the potential for both good and evil. As the Proclamation declares, parents should maintain a high priority on teaching children the principles of righteousness. This is best done in authoritative, rather than in coercive or permissive ways.[128] By studying their children's individual temperaments, which stem from each child's genetic and spiritual natures, parents can create the best environment for optimal growth and development. Where better than in a righteous home that is imbued with the Spirit can children learn to discern between good and evil (see Moro. 7:13–19; D&C 84:44–46) and to develop in optimal ways? Living in harmony with Proclamation principles maximizes the possibilities that children will make choices that will help them "return to the presence of God and for families to be united eternally" (¶ 3).

NOTES

1. The first two authors contributed equally to the chapter and are co-lead authors.

2. J. R. Harris (1998), *The nurture assumption: Why children turn out the way they do* (New York: Free Press); D. C. Rowe (1994), *The limits of family influence: Genes, experience, and behavior* (New York: Guilford Press); S. Scarr (1992), Developmental theories for the 1990s: Development and individual differences, *Child Development, 63,* 1–19; L. G. Silverstein and C. F. Auerbach (1999), Deconstructing the essential father, *American Psychologist, 54,* 397–407.

3. Gordon B. Hinckley (1997), *Teachings of Gordon B. Hinckley* (Salt Lake City: Deseret Book), 421.

4. Ezra Taft Benson (1970, October), in Conference report, 21.

5. Joseph Smith (1865, November 15), *Millennial Star, 13(22),* 339.

6. P. Greven (1990), *Spare the child* (New York: Vintage Books); W. Kessen (1965), *The child* (New York: John Wiley & Sons); E. E. Maccoby (1980), *Social development: Psychological growth and the parent–child relationship* (New York: Harcourt Brace Jovanovich); J. Trawick-Smith (2000), *Early childhood development: A multicultural perspective* (Upper Saddle River, NJ: Prentice Hall).

7. M. A. Straus (1994), *Beating the devil out of them: Corporal punishment in American families* (New York: Lexington Books).

8. Maccoby (1980).

9. L. J. Borstelmann (1983), Children before psychology: Ideas about children from antiquity to the late 1800s, in P. H. Mussen (Ed.), *Handbook of child psychology vol. 1* (New York: John Wiley & Sons), 36.

10. Joseph Fielding Smith (1972–1973). Selections from *Answers to gospel questions* [Melchizedek Priesthood course of study] (Salt Lake City: The Church of Jesus Christ of Latter-day Saints), 124.

11. R. L. Millet (1997), *Alive in Christ: The miracle of spiritual rebirth* (Salt Lake City: Deseret Book), 70–71.

12. J. B. Watson (1926), Experimental studies on the growth of the emotions, in C. Murchison (Ed.), *Psychologies of 1925* (Worcester, MA: Clark University Press).

13. David O. McKay (1965, October), The worth of a child. *Improvement Era,* 853.

14. Joseph Fielding Smith (1998), *Church history and modern revelation, vol. 2* (Salt Lake City: The Church of Jesus Christ of Latter-day Saints), 2:31.

15. David O. McKay (1976), *Gospel ideals: Selections from the discourses of David O. McKay* (Salt Lake City: Deseret Book), 347–348.

16. Daniel Judd is greatly acknowledged for his insights on this topic. For exammple, see D. Judd (1996), The Lord's plan for parents and children, *Eternal Families,* 66–89.

17. Hinckley (1997), 159.

18. Howard W. Hunter (1997), *The teachings of Howard W. Hunter,* ed. C. J. Williams (Salt Lake City: Bookcraft), 148.

19. D. Elkind (1994), *A sympathetic understanding of the child: Birth to sixteen* (Boston: Allyn and Bacon); J. Piaget and B. Inhelder (1969), *The psychology of the child,* trans. H. Weaver (New York: BasicBooks); D. Wood (1988), *How children think and learn* (Oxford: Basil Blackwell).

20. For an expanded overview of scientific research pertaining to nature/nurture issues, see C. H. Hart and L. D. Newell (in press), Parenting skills and social/communicative competence in childhood, in J. O. Greene and B. R. Burleson (Eds.), *Handbook of communication and social interaction skill* (Mahwah, NJ: Lawrence Erlbaum Associates).

21. R. Plomin and M. Rutter (1998), Child development, molecular genetics, and what to do with genes once they are found, *Child Development, 69,* 1223–1242.

22. C. H. Hart, S. F. Olsen, C. C. Robinson, and B. L. Mandleco (1997), The development of social and communicative competence in childhood: Review and a model of personal, familial, and extra familial processes, in B. R. Burleson (Ed.), *Communication yearbook,* (Thousand Oaks, CA: Sage), 20:305–373; C. H. Hart, D. C. Burts, M. A. Durland, R. Charlesworth, M. DeWolf, and P. O. Fleege (1998), Stress behaviors and activity type participation of preschoolers in more and less developmentally appropriate classrooms: SES and sex differences, *Journal of Research in Childhood Education, 12,* 176–196; G. W. Ladd and C. H. Hart (1992), Creating informal play opportunities: Are parents' and preschoolers' initiations related to children's competence with peers? *Developmental Psychology, 28,* 1179–1187; K. H. Rubin, W. Bukowski, and J. G. Parker (1998), Peer interactions, relationships, and groups, in W. Damon (Series Ed.) and N. Eisenberg (Ed.), *Handbook of child psychology, vol. 3: Social, emotional, and personality development* (New York: John Wiley & Sons), 619–700.

23. Brigham Young (1998), *Discourses of Brigham Young,* ed. John A. Widtsoe (Salt Lake City: Deseret Book), 207.

24. Neal A. Maxwell (1996, November), in Conference report, 26.

25. A. H. Buss and R. Plomin (1984), *Temperament: Early developing personality traits* (Hillsdale, NJ: Lawrence Erlbaum Associates); N. A. Fox, K. H. Rubin, S. D. Calkins, T. R. Marshall, R. J. Coplan, S. W. Porges, and J. M. Long (1995), Frontal activation asymmetry and social competence at four years of age: Left frontal hyper and hypo activation as correlates of social behavior in preschool children, *Child Development, 66,* 1770–1784; J. Kagan (1997), Temperament and reactions to unfamiliarity. *Child Development, 68,* 139–143.

26. J. E. Bates and T. D. Wachs (1994), *Temperament: Individual differences at the interface of biology and behavior* (Washington, DC: American Psychological Association); Plomin and Rutter (1998).

27. E. J. Van den Oord, I. Boomsma, and F. C. Verhulst (1994), A study of problem behavior in 10- to 15-year-old biologically related and unrelated international adoptees, *Behavior Genetics, 24,* 193–205; K. Deater-Deckard and R. Plomin (1999). An adoption study of the etiology of teacher and parent reports

of externalizing behavior problems in middle childhood, *Child Development, 70,* 144–154; Plomin and Rutter (1998).

28. N. G. Waller, B. A. Kojetin, T. J. Bouchard Jr., D. T. Lykken, and A. Tellegen (1990), *Psychological Science, 1,* 138–142.

29. R. Plomin, J. DeFries, G. McClearn, and M. Rutter (1997), *Behavioral genetics* (3rd ed.), (New York: Freeman).

30. R. Plomin, D. E. Reiss, M. Hetherington, and G. W. Howe (1994), Nature and nurture: Genetic contributions to measures of the family environment, *Developmental Psychology, 30,* 32–43; M. K. Rothbart and J. E. Bates (1998), Temperament, in Damon and Eisenberg, 105–176; T. D. Wachs (in press), The what, why, and how of temperament: A piece of the action, *Child psychology: A handbook of contemporary issues* (New York: Garland).

31. C. H. Hart, C. Yang, D. Nelson, S. Jin, and L. Nelson (1998), Peer contact patterns, parenting practices, and preschoolers' social competence in China, Russia, and the United States, in P. Slee and K. Rigby (Eds.), *Peer relations amongst children: Current issues and future directions* (London: Routledge), 1–30.

32. Hart et al. (1998); G. W. Ladd and B. S. Golter (1988), Parents' management of preschoolers' peer relations: Is it related to children's social competence? *Developmental Psychology, 24,* 109–117; J. Mize, G. S. Pettit, and G. Brown (1995), Mothers' supervision of their children's peer play: Relations with beliefs, perceptions, and knowledge, *Developmental Psychology, 31,* 311–321; T. G. O'Connor, K. Deater-Deckard, D. Fulker, M. Rutter, and R. Plomin (1998), Genotype-environment correlations in late childhood and early adolescence: Antisocial behavioral problems and coercive parenting, *Developmental Psychology, 34,* 970–981; S. M. Profilet and G. W. Ladd (1994), Do mothers' perceptions and concerns about preschoolers' peer competence predict their peer-management practices? *Social Development.* (Cambridge, MA: Basil Blackwell Publishers).

33. R. Q. Bell and M. Chapman (1986), Child effects in studies using experimental or brief longitudinal approaches to socialization, *Developmental Psychology, 22,* 595–603; Wachs (in press).

34. A. Russell and G. Russell (1994), Coparenting early school-age children: An examination of mother–father interdependence within families, *Developmental Psychology, 30,* 757–770.

35. G. W. Holden and P. C. Miller (1999), Enduring and different: A meta-analysis of the similarity in parents' child rearing, *Psychological Bulletin, 125,* 223–254; A. Sanson and M. K. Rothbart (1995), Child temperament and parenting, in M. H. Bornstein (Ed.), *Handbook of parenting, vol. 4: Applied and practical parenting* (Mahwah, NJ: Lawrence Erlbaum), 299–321.

36. A. Kowal and L. Kramer (1997), Children's understanding of parental differential treatment, *Child Development, 68,* 113–126.

37. Plomin et al. (1997); M. McGue, A. Sharma, and P. Benson (1996), The effect of common rearing on adolescent development: Evidence from a U.S. adoption court. *Developmental Psychology, 32,* 604–613; A. Pike, S. McGuire, E. M. Hetherington, D. Reiss, and R. Plomin (1996), Family environment and adolescent depressive symptoms and antisocial behavior: A multivariate genetic analysis, *Developmental Psychology, 32,* 590–603.

38. L. W. Hoffman (1991), The influence of the family environment on personality: Accounting for sibling differences, *Psychological Bulletin, 108,* 187–203; L. W. Hoffman (1994), Commentary on Plomin, R. (1994): A proof and a disproof questioned, *Social Development, 3,* 60–63; R. Plomin (1990), *Nature and nurture* (Pacific Grove, CA: Brooks/Cole).

39. Young in John A. Widtsoe, (Ed.), 391.

40. A. L. Scoresby (1996), *Focus on the children: A developmental approach to highly effective families* (Orem, UT: Knowledge Gain Publications).

41. Young in Widtsoe, (Ed.), (1998), 264, 208.

42. D. B. Rodgers (1998, May), Supporting autonomy in young children, *Young Children,* 75–80.

43. Joseph F. Smith (1963), *Gospel doctrine* (13th ed.) (Salt Lake City: Deseret Book), 316–317.

44. Spencer W. Kimball (1982), *The teachings of Spencer W. Kimball,* ed. Edward L. Kimball (Salt Lake City: Bookcraft), 341.

45. Gordon B. Hinckley (1997, November), Some thoughts on temples, retention of converts, and missionary service, *Ensign* 27(11), 52.

46. Gordon B. Hinckley (1967, November), in Conference report, 91–92.

47. David O. McKay (1955, April), in Conference report, 26; L. Okagaki, K. A. Hammond, and L. Seamon (1999), Socialization of Religious Beliefs, *Journal of Applied Developmental Psychology, 20,* 273–294; L. Okagaki and C. Bevis (1999), Transmission of religious values: Relations between parents' and daughters' beliefs, *Journal of Genetic Psychology, 160,* 303–318.

48. Brigham Young (1870, July 12), *Teachings of Presidents of the Church, Brigham Young,* 338; Brigham Young (1870, July 12), *Deseret News Semi-Weekly,* 2.

49. Harris (1998); Silverstein, and Auerbach (1999).

50. Scarr (1992); Rowe (1994).

51. D. Baumrind (1993), The average expectable environment is not good enough: A response to Scarr, *Child Development, 64,* 1299–1317; D. Baumrind (1997), Necessary distinctions. *Psychological Inquiry,* 8(3), 176–229; J. Gottman and J. DeClaire (1997), *The heart of parenting: How to raise an emotionally intelligent child* (New York: Simon & Schuster).

52. G. R. Patterson (1986), Performance models for antisocial boys, *American Psychologist, 41,* 432–444; G. R. Patterson, B. D. DeBaryshe, and E. Ramsey (1989). A developmental perspective on antisocial behavior, *American Psychologist, 44,* 329–335; R. E. Tremblay, E. Vitaro, L. Bertrand, M. LeBlanc, H. Beauchesne, H. Boileau, and L. David (1992), Parent and child training to prevent early onset of delinquency: The Montreal longitudinal study, in J. McCord and R. E. Tremblay (Eds.), *Preventing anti-social behavior: Interventions from birth through adolescence* (New York: Guilford Press), 117–138; C. Webster-Stratton and M. Hammond (1997), Treating children with early-onset conduct problems: A comparison of child and parent training interventions, *Journal of Consulting and Clinical Psychology, 65,* 93–109; S. Vuchinich, L. Bank, and G. R. Patterson (1992), Parenting, peers, and the stability of antisocial behavior in preadolescent boys, *Developmental Psychology, 28,* 510–521; H. Yoshikawa (1994), Prevention as cumulative protection: Effects of early family support and education on chronic delinquency and its risks, *Psychological Bulletin, 115,* 28–54; see Hart and Newell (in press) and W. A. Collins, E. E. Maccoby, L. Steinberg, E. M. Hetherington, and M. H. Bornstein (2000, February), Contemporary research on parenting: The case for nature and nurture,

American Psychologist, for expanded scholarly critiques of the notion that parents don't matter.

53. See Hart et al. (1997); K. H. Rubin, L. J. Nelson, P. Hastings, and J. Asendorpf (1998), The transaction between parents' perceptions of their children's shyness and their parenting styles, *International Journal of Behavioral Development, 22,* 1–22; Vuchinich et al. (1992).

54. See Hart et al. (1997); P. D. Hastings and K. H. Rubin (1999), Predicting mothers' beliefs about preschool-aged children's social behavior: Evidence for maternal attitudes moderating child effects, *Child Development, 70,* 722–741.

55. F. D. Fincham (1998), Child development and marital relations, *Child Development, 69,* 543–574.

56. The term *coercive* replaces the term *authoritarian,* which is more typically used in the research literature but is easily confused with *authoritative.*

57. C. C. Robinson, B. Mandleco, S. F. Olsen, and C. H. Hart (1995). Authoritative, authoritarian, and permissive parenting practices: Development of a new measure, *Psychological Reports, 77,* 819–830.

58. J. D. Coie and K. A. Dodge (1998), Aggression and antisocial behavior, in W. Damon and Eisenberg, 779–862; T. J. Dishion, T. E. Duncan, J. M. Eddy, B. I. Fagot, and R. Fetrow (1994), The world of parents and peers: Coercive exchanges and children's social adaption, *Social Development, 3,* 255–268; Hart et al. (1997); G. S. Pettit, M.A. Clawson, K. A. Dodge, and J. E. Bates (1996), Stability and change in peer-rejected status: The role of child behavior, parenting, and family ecology, *Merrill-Palmer Quarterly, 42,* 267–294; R. L. Nix, E. E. Pinderhughes, K. A. Dodge, J. E. Bates, G. S. Pettit, and S. A. McFadyen-Ketchum (1999), The relation between mothers' hostile attribution tendencies and children's externalizing behavior problems: The mediating role of mothers' harsh discipline practices, *Child Development, 70,* 896–909; D. Schwartz, K. A. Dodge, G. S. Pettit, and J. E. Bates (1997), The early socialization of aggressive victims of bullying, *Child Development, 68,* 665–675; R. L. Simons, D. Johnson, and R. D. Conger (1994), Harsh corporal punishment versus quality of parental involvement as an explanation of adolescent maladjustment, *Journal of Marriage and Family, 56,* 591–607.

59. C. H. Hart, G. W. Ladd, and B. R. Burleson (1990), Children's expectations of the outcomes of social strategies: Relations with sociometric status and maternal disciplinary styles, *Child Development, 61,*127–137; C. H. Hart, M. D. DeWolf, and D.C. Burts (1992), Linkages among preschoolers' playground behavior, outcome expectations, and parental disciplinary strategies, *Early Education and Development, 3,* 265–283.

60. B. K. Barber (1996), Parental psychological control: Revisiting a neglected construct, *Child Development, 67,* 3296–3319; C. H. Hart, D. A. Nelson, C. C. Robinson, S. F. Olsen, and M. K. McNeilly-Choque (1998), Overt and relational aggression in Russian nursery-school-age children: Parenting style and marital linkages, *Developmental Psychology, 34,* 687–697; S. F. Olsen, C. Yang, C. H. Hart, C. C. Robinson, P. Wu, D. A. Nelson, L. J. Nelson, S. Jin, and W. Jianzhong (in press), Mothers' psychological control and preschool children's behavioral outcomes in China, Russia, and the United States, in B. Barber (Ed.), *Psychological control of children and adolescents* (Washington, DC: American Psychological Association).

61. Barber (1996); S. F. Olsen et al. (in press).

62. Rodgers (1998, May).

63. J. C. Dobson (1992), *The new dare to discipline* (Wheaton, IL: Tyndale House Publications); J. MacArthur (1998), *Successful Christian parenting* (Bedford, TX: Word Books).

64. Gordon B. Hinckley (1994, November), Save the children, *Ensign, 24*(11), 53. Brigham Young said, "I will say here to parents, that kind words and loving actions towards children, will subdue their uneducated nature a great deal better than the rod, or, in other words, than physical punishment" (*Deseret News Weekly,* December 7, 1864, 2). He also said, "Let the child have a mild training until it has judgment and sense to guide it. I differ with Solomon's recorded saying as to spoiling the child by sparing the rod" (*Journal of Discourses,* 9:195–196).

65. J. R. Kohlenberger III (Ed.) (1982), *NIV Interlinear Hebrew-English Old Testament* (Grand Rapids, MI: Zondervan Publishing House); F. Brown Sr., C. Driver, and A. Briggs (1996), *The Brown–Driver–Briggs Hebrew and English lexicon: With an appendix containing the Biblical Aramaic* (Peabody, MA: Hendrickson); and J. Strong (1984), *The new Strong's exhaustive concordance of the Bible* (Nashville, TN: Thomas Nelson Publishers for comparable word translations).

66. Spare the rod? Maybe (1997, August 25), *Time Magazine;* When to spank (1998, April 13), *U.S. News and World Report.*

67. D. Baumrind (1996), A blanket injunction against disciplinary use of spanking is not warranted by the data, *Pediatrics, 98*(4), 828.

68. See R. S. Larzelere (1996), A review of the outcomes of parental use of nonabusive or customary physical punishment, *Pediatrics, 98*(4), 824–828.

69. D. Baumrind (1996b). The discipline controversy revisited, *Family Relations, 45,* 405–414; Baumrind (1997); K. Deater-Deckard and K. A. Dodge (1997), Externalizing behavior problems and discipline revisited: Nonlinear effects and variation by culture, context, and gender, *Psychological Inquiry, 8,* 161–175; R. E. Lazelere, P. R. Sather, W. N. Schneider, D. B. Larson, and P. L. Pike (1998), Punishment enhances reasoning's effectiveness as a disciplinary response to toddlers, *Journal of Marriage and the Family, 60,* 388–403.

70. See Z. Strassberg, K. A. Dodge, G. S. Pettit, and J. E. Bates (1994), Spanking in the home and children's subsequent aggression toward kindergarten peers, *Development and Psychopathology, 6,* 445–461; M. A. Straus, D. B. Sugarman, and J. Giles-Sims (1997), Spanking by parents and subsequent antisocial behavior of children, *Archives of Pediatrics and Adolescent Medicine, 151,* 761–767; I. A. Hyman (1997), *The case against spanking: How to discipline your child without hitting* (San Francisco: Jossey-Bass Publishers).

71. G. W. Holden, S. M. Coleman, and K. L. Schmidt (1995), Why 3-year-old children get spanked: Parent and child determinants as reported by college-age mothers, *Merrill-Palmer Quarterly, 41,* 431–449.

72. See Lazerle (1996); or When to spank (1998, April 13), *U.S. News and World Report,* for a simplified overview.

73. Gordon B. Hinckley (1995, May), This is the work of the Master, *Ensign 25*(5), 70.

74. Sheri L. Dew (1996), *Go forward with faith: The biography of Gordon B. Hinckley* (Salt Lake City: Deseret Book), 141.

75. Baumrind (1996).

76. E. E. Maccoby and J. A. Martin (1983), Socialization in the context of the family: Parent–child interaction, in

P. H. Mussen (Series Ed.) and E. M. Hetherington (Vol. Ed.), *Handbook of child psychology, vol. 4: Socialization, personality and social development* (New York: John Wiley & Sons), 1–102.

77. Maccoby and Martin (1983).

78. B. K. Barber and J. A. Olsen (1997), Socialization in context: Connection, regulation, and autonomy in the family, school, and neighborhood, and with peers, *Journal of Adolescent Research, 12,* 287–315; S. D. Lamborn, N. S. Mounts, L. Steinberg, and S. M. Dornbusch (1991), Patterns of competence and adjustment among adolescents from authoritative, authoritarian, indulgent, and neglectful families, *Child Development, 62,* 1049–1065; L. Steinberg, S. D. Lamborn, N. Darling, N. S. Mounts, and S. M. Dornbusch (1994), Over-time changes in adjustment and competence among adolescents from authoritative, authoritarian, indulgent, and neglectful families, *Child Development, 65,* 754–770.

79. Joe J. Christensen (1999, May), Greed, selfishness, and overindulgence, *Ensign 29(5),* 9.

80. Neal A. Maxwell (1999, January 12), Address given at BYU devotional. Online. Available: http://advance.byu.edu/devo/98–99/maxwellw99.html

81. J. Reuben Clark Jr., quoted by Ezra Taft Benson (1974), *God, Family, Country* (Salt Lake City: Deseret Book), 499–500.

82. Baumrind (1996); Barber and Olsen (1997); P. Bronstein, P. Duncan, A. D'Ari, J. Pieniadz, M. Fitzgerald, C. L. Abrams, B. Frankowski, O. Franco, C. Hunt, and S. Oh Cha (1996), Family and parenting behaviors predicting middle school adjustment: A longitudinal study, *Family Relations, 45,* 415–425; M. R. Gray and L. Steinberg (1999), Unpacking authoritative parenting: Reassessing a multidimensional construct, *Journal of Marriage and the Family,* 61, 574–587; Maccoby and Martin (1983); L. Steinberg (1990), Autonomy, conflict, and harmony in the family relationship, in S. S. Feldman and G. R. Elliott (Eds.), *At the threshold: The developing adolescent* (Cambridge, MA: Harvard University Press), 255–276; L. Steinberg, J. D. Elmen, and N. S. Mounts (1989); Authoritative parenting, psychosocial maturity, and academic success among adolescents, *Child Development, 60,* 1424–1436.

83. N. Darling and L. Steinberg (1993), Parenting style as context: An integrative model, *Psychological Bulletin, 113,* 487–496; J. E. Grusec and J. J. Goodnow (1994), Impact of parental discipline methods on the child's internalization of values: A reconceptualization, *Developmental Psychology, 30,* 4–19; J. Mize and G. S. Pettit (1997), Mothers' social coaching, mother–child relationship style and children's peer competence: Is the medium the message? *Child Development, 68,* 291–311.

84. Bronstein et al. (1996); K. Bogenschneider, M. Wu, M. Raffaellil, and J. C. Tsay (1998), Parent influences on adolescent peer orientation and substance use: The interface of parenting practices and values, *Child Development, 69,* 1672–2688; M. Dekovic and J. M. A. Janssens (1992), Parents' child-rearing style and child's sociometric status, *Developmental Psychology, 28,* 925–932; K. L. Glasgow, S. M. Dornbusch, L. Troyer, L. Steinberg, and P. Ritter (1997), Parenting styles, adolescents' attributions, and educational outcomes in nine heterogeneous high schools, *Child Development, 68,* 507–529; Hart et al. (1990); Hart, DeWolf et al. (1992); Hart, Olsen et al. (1997); Hart, Nelson et al. (1998); C. H. Hart, D. A. Nelson, C. C. Robinson, S. F. Olsen, M. K. McNeilly-Choque, C. L. Porter, and T. R. McKee (2000), Russian parenting styles and family processes: Linkages with subtypes of

victimization and aggression, in K. A. Kerns, J. M. Contreras, and A. M. Neal-Barnett (Eds.), *Family and peers: Linking two social worlds, 47–48* (Westport, CT: Praeger Publishers); Steinberg et al. (1994); Maccoby and Martin (1983); M. D. Resnick et al. (1997), Protecting adolescents from harm: Findings from the national longitudinal study on adolescent health, *Journal of the American Medical Association, 278,* 823–832.

85. E. Turiel (1998), Development of morality, in Damon and Eisenberg, 779–862; L. J. Walker and J. H. Taylor (1991), Family interactions and the development of moral reasoning, *Child Development, 62,* 264–283.

86. G. Kochanska and N. Aksan (1995), Mother–child mutually positive affect: The quality of child compliance to requests and prohibitions, and maternal control as correlates of early internalization, *Child Development, 66,* 236–254.

87. J. Belsky, K. Crnic, and S. Gable (1995), The determinants of coparenting in families with toddler boys: Spousal differences and daily hassles, *Child Development, 66,* 629–642; Russell and Russell (1994).

88. Hart et al. (1997); Brigham Young stated, "Kind looks, kind actions, kind words, and a lovely, holy deportment towards them will bind our children to us with bands that cannot be easily broken; while abuse and unkindness will drive them from us." (*Deseret News Weekly,* December 7, 1864, 2).

89. S. L. Isley, R. O'Neil, D. Clatfelter, and R. D. Parke (1999), Parent and child expressed affect and children's social competence: Modeling direct and indirect pathways. *Developmental Psychology, 35,* 547–560; Hart, Nelson et al. (1998); Hart, Nelson et al. (2000); N. B. Miller, P. A. Cowan, C. P. Cowan, E. M. Hetherington, and W. G. Clingempeel (1993), Externalizing in preschoolers and early adolescents: A cross-study replication of a family model, *Developmental Psychology, 29,* 3–18; G. S. Pettit, J. E. Bates, and K. A. Dodge (1997), Supportive parenting, ecological context, and children's adjustment: A seven-year longitudinal study, *Child Development, 68,* 908–923.

90. C. L. Booth, L. Rose-Krasnor, J. McKinnon, and K. H. Rubin (1994), Predicting social adjustment in middle childhood: The role of preschool attachment security and maternal style, *Social Development, 3,* 189–204; J. Elicker, B. Egeland, and L. A. Stroufe (1992), Predicting peer competence and peer relationships in childhood from early parent–child relationships, in R. D. Parke and G. W. Ladd (Eds.), *Family-peer-relationships: Modes of linkage* (Hillsdale, NJ: Lawrence Erlabaum), 77–106; G. Kochanska, N. Aksan, A. L. Koenig (1995), A longitudinal study of the roots of preschoolers' conscience: Committed compliance and emerging internalization, *Child Development, 66,* 1752–1769; Pettit, Bates, and Dodge (1997); Rubin, Bukowski, and Parker (1998); Resnick et al. (1997); L. S. Wakschlag and S. L. Hans (1999), Relation of maternal responsiveness during infancy to the development of behavior problems in high-risk youths, *Developmental Psychology, 35,* 569–579.

91. M. L. Hoffman (1983), Affective and cognitive processes in moral internalization, in E. T. Higgins, D. Ruble, and W. Hartup (Eds.), *Social cognition and social development: A sociocultural perspective* (New York: Cambridge University Press) 236–274; M. R. Lepper (1981), Intrinsic and extrinsic motivation in children: Detrimental effects of superfluous social controls, in W. A. Collins (Ed.), *Minnesota Symposium on Child Psychology* (Minneapolis: University of Minnesota Press), 155–214; E. E. Maccoby (1983), Let's not overattribute to the attribution

process: Comments on social cognition and behavior, in E. T. Higgins, D. N. Ruble, and W. W. Hartup (Eds.), *Social cognition and social development: A sociocultural perspective* (Cambridge: Cambridge University Press).

92. S. L. Isley, R. O'Neil, D. Clatfelter, and R. D. Parke (1999), Parent and child expressed affect and children's social competence: Modeling direct and indirect pathways, *Developmental Psychology, 35,* 547–560; L. Carson and R. Parke (1996), Reciprocal negative affect in parent–child interactions and children's peer competency, *Child Development, 67,* 2217–2226; J. Gottman (1997); Hart, Nelson et al. (1998).

93. G. Kochanska (1997), Mutually responsive orientation between mothers and their children: Implications for early socialization, *Child Development, 68,* 94–112.

94. B. L. Top and B. A. Chadwick (1998), Raising righteous children in a wicked world, *Brigham Young Magazine*; B. L. Top and B. A. Chadwick (March 1999), Helping teens stay strong, *Ensign 29*(3), 26–34; See Okagaki et al. (1999) for related findings.

95. Hinckley (1997), 416.

96. Baumrind (1996); G. S. Pettit, J. E. Bates, and K. A. Dodge (1997), Supportive parenting, ecological context and children's adjustment: A seven-year study, *Child Development, 68,* 908–923; see C. M Rehme (April 2000), The truth of consequences, *Ensign 30*(4), 31–33, for practical application ideas associated with regulation principles noted below.

97. Barber (1996).

98. See Coping with disturbing behavior (August 1986), *Ensign, 16,* 34–37 for practical ways of dealing with underlying causes of misbehavior.

99. C. H. Hart, M. D. DeWolf, and D. C. Burts (1993), Parental disciplinary strategies and preschoolers' play behavior in playground settings, in C. H. Hart (Ed.), *Children on playgrounds: Research perspectives and applications* (Albany, NY: SUNY Press), 271–313.

100. M. L. Hoffman (1994), Discipline and internalization, *Developmental Psychology, 30,* 26–28; Hart, Ladd, and Burleson (1990); C. H. Hart, M. D. DeWolf, P. Wozniak, and D. C. Burts (1992), Maternal and paternal disciplinary styles: Relations with preschoolers' playground behavioral orientations and peer status. *Child Development, 63,* 879–892; Hart, DeWolf, and D. C. Burts (1992); G. Kochanska (1995), Children's temperament, mothers' discipline, and security of attachment: Multiple pathways to emerging internalization, *Child Development, 66,* 597–615; J. Krevans and J. C. Gibbs (1996), Parents' use of inductive discipline: Relations to childrens' empathy and prosocial behavior, *Child Development, 67,* 3263–3277; G. S. Pettit, J. E. Bates, and K. A. Dodge (1997).

101. Grusec and Goodnow (1994).

102. F. Cline and J. Fay (1990), *Parenting with love and logic: Teaching children responsibility* (Colorado Springs: Pinon Press); F. Cline and J. Fay (1992), *Parenting teens with love and logic: Preparing adolescents for responsible adulthood* (Colorado Springs: Pinon Press).

103. Boyd K. Packer (1986, November), Little children, *Ensign 16*(11), 17.

104. See Top and Chadwick (1998); see also Okagaki et al. (1999).

105. Hinckley (1997), 422.

106. Gordon B. Hinckley (1999, February), Life's obligations, *Ensign, 29*(2), 4.

107. L. Nucci and J. G. Smetana (1996), Mothers' concepts of young childrens' areas of personal freedom, *Child Development, 67,* 1870–1886; L. P. Nucci and E. K. Weber (1995), Social interactions in the home and the development of young children's conceptions of the personal, *Child Development, 66,* 1438–1452.

108. E. L. Deci, H. Eghrari, B. C. Patrick, and D. R. Leone (1994), Facilitating internalization: The self-determination theory perspective, *Journal of Personality, 62*(1), 119–142.

109. Barber (1996); Olsen et al. (in press).

110. Robert D. Hales (May 1999), Strengthening families: Our sacred duty, *Ensign 29*(5), 34.

111. A. Russell, G. S. Pettit, and J. Mize (1998), Horizontal qualities in parent-child relationships: Parallels with and possible consequences for children's peer relationships, *Developmental Review, 18,* 313–352.

112. J. E. Dumas, P. J. LaFreniere, and W. J. Serketich (1995), Balance of power: A transactional analysis of control in mother–child dyads involving socially competent, aggressive, and anxious children. *Journal of Abnormal Psychology, 104,* 104–113; L. Kuczynski and S. Lollis (in press), Four foundations for a dynamic model of parenting, in J. R. M. Gerris (Ed.), *Dynamics of Parenting* (Hillsdale, NJ: Erlbaum); G. S. Pettit and S. Lollis (1997), Reciprocity and bidirectionality in parent–child relationships, *Journal of Social and Personal Relationships, 14,* 435–440; L. Siqueland, P. C. Kendall, and L. Steinberg (1996), Anxiety in children: Perceived family environments and observed family interaction, *Journal of Clinical Child Psychology, 25,* 225–237.

113. Baumrind (1996).

114. D. Chapman (February 2000), The Three Questions, *The New Era 30*(2), 26–27.

115. J. Belsky (1997), Theory testing, effect-size evaluation, and differential susceptibility to rearing influence: The case of mothering and attachment, *Child Development, 64,* 598–600; J. Belsky, K. Hsieh, and K. Crnic (1998), Mothering, fathering, and infant negativity as antecedents of boys' externalizing problems and inhibition at age 3 years: Differential susceptibility to rearing experience? *Development and Psychopathology, 10,* 301–319; U. Bronfenbrenner and S. J. Ceci (1994), Nature-nurture reconceptualized in developmental perspective: A bioecological model, *Psychological Review, 4,* 468–586; S. P. Hinshaw, B. A. Zupan, C. Simmel, J. T. Nigg, and S. Melnick (1997), Peer status in boys with and without attention-deficit hyperactivity disorder: Predictions from overt and covert antisocial behavior, social isolation, and authoritative parenting beliefs, *Child Development, 68,* 880–896; G. Kochanska (1993), Toward a synthesis of parental socialization and child temperament in early development of conscience, *Child Development, 64,* 325–347; S. A. McFadyen-Ketchum, J. E. Bates, K. A. Dodge, and G. S. Pettit (1996), Patterns of change in early childhood aggressive-disruptive behavior: Gender difference in predictions from early coercive and affectionate mother–child interactions, *Child Development, 67,* 2417–2433; L. Woodward, E. Taylor, and L. Dowdney (1998), The parenting and family functioning of children with hyperactivity, *Journal of Child Psychology and Psychiatry, 39,* 161–169.

116. A. Thomas and S. Chess (1986), The New York longitudinal study: From infancy to early adult life, in R. Plomin and J. Dunn (Eds.), *The study of temperament: Changes, continuities, and*

challenges (Hillsdale, NJ: Erlbaum); G. Paterson and A. Sanson (1999), The association of behavioral adjustment to temperament, parenting, and family characteristics among 5-year-old children, *Social Development, 8,* 293–309.

117. James E. Faust (1990, October), in Conference report, 41.

118. Hinckley (1997), 204.

119. Holden and Miller (1999).

120. Holden (1995), Parental attitudes toward childrearing, in M. H. Bornstein (Ed.), *Handbook of parenting, vol. 3: Status and social conditions of parenting* (Mahwah, NJ: Lawrence Erlbaum), 359–392; Holden et al. (1995).

121. Ezra Taft Benson (1982, November), Fundamentals of enduring family relationships, *Ensign 12*(11), 60.

122. Ezra Taft Benson (1988), *The teachings of Ezra Taft Benson* (Salt Lake City: Bookcraft), 505.

123. Kimball (1982), 245.

124. There is also, in this regard, a covenant relationship of family. Covenant parents, by bringing children into the world, commit to do all they can to fulfill their sacred duty to nurture their children in light and truth; children, in a covenant family, promise to honor and obey their parents in righteousness.

125. Hinckley (1997), 422.

126. Hunter (1997), 148.

127. See R. L. Millett (1996), *When a child wanders* (Salt Lake City: Deseret Book).

128. See *A parents guide* (1985) (Salt Lake City: Corporation of the President of The Church of Jesus Christ of Latter-day Saints).

CHAPTER 8

UNDERSTANDING AND APPLYING PROCLAMATION PRINCIPLES OF PARENTING

H. WALLACE GODDARD AND LARRY C. JENSEN

Children are an heritage of the Lord (Ps. 127:3). Parents have a sacred duty to rear their children in love and
righteousness, to provide for their physical and spiritual needs, to teach them to love and serve one another,
to observe the commandments of God and to be law-abiding citizens wherever they live.
(The Family: A Proclamation to the World, ¶ 6)

We are greatly blessed by the clear statements of principle in the Proclamation on the family. Those declarations, together with the teachings of scripture and prophets, allow us to sort through the numerous discoveries and theories of family scholars in order to arrive at answers to the challenges of family life. In the latter-days, the Lord has "pour[ed] down knowledge from heaven upon the heads of the Latter-day Saints" (D&C 121:33). That knowledge can help us be the kind of parents He would have us be.

As Latter-day Saints, we turn to the scriptures as the sure source of truth to guide us in life's decisions. Yet the scriptures never undertake to provide a paint-by-numbers process for the full life. Rather, they provide statements of principle and hundreds of stories of people struggling to apply the principles to their lives. This chapter will review the principles, spirit, and practices that underlie effective parenting. In addition, there are ideas on how you can be preparing now to be a more effective parent. It is intended to help you be better prepared for the surprises and challenges of parenthood (see Box 8.1).

Parenting Principles

An eternal perspective can make an eternal difference in family relationships. Elder Boyd K. Packer has taught that "true doctrine, understood, changes attitudes and behavior. The study of the doctrines of the gospel will improve behavior quicker than a study of behavior will improve behavior. . . . That is why we stress so forcefully the study of the doctrines of the gospel."[1] "Happiness in family life is most likely to be achieved when founded upon the teachings of the Lord Jesus Christ" (Proclamation, ¶ 7).

The commandment taught by Jesus shortly before His crucifixion was: "A new commandment I give unto you, That ye love one another; as I have loved you, that ye also love one another" (John 13:34). Love is the core of the gospel of Jesus Christ. Love, also called nurturance, affection, warmth, and support, is consistently the most predictive variable for favorable child outcomes in research on parenting.[2] *Nurturance* is defined as behavior that helps the child feel safe, valued, and accepted. Effective loving is the most important thing a parent can do for a child.

Our Divine Parent has set an example for parents in His commitment to His children: "He doeth not anything save it be for the benefit of the world; for he loveth the world, even that he layeth down his own life that he may draw all men unto him" (2 Ne. 26:24).

Heavenly Father's example teaches us to establish family priorities in life. As we get an education, plan a career, accept or decline a job, and consider housing, the impact of those decisions on our ability to love and bless each other in the family should be a central

Nancy and I were both BYU students when our first child was born. We prepared for the birth by borrowing a crib, buying blankets and clothes, and starting a scrapbook. We were excited to welcome the first child to our family. Nine months of pregnancy passed. One August evening, labor began. Between pains Nancy sat at the sewing machine to stitch up a new nightgown to wear after the birth.

We went to the hospital but were sent back home for the labor to progress further before being admitted. About midnight we returned to the hospital. Through the long hours of the night Nancy labored and I rubbed her back. The contractions and rubbing continued through all of the morning and into the afternoon. This was taking longer than I had expected. Our firstborn arrived at 3:10 P.M. Our exhaustion turned to exhilaration as we held little Emily in our arms. Over the months of pregnancy we had looked forward to her arrival, but nothing could have prepared us for the sheer wonder and joy as we looked into our little girl's face for the first time. That unprecedented joy may have been the biggest surprise of my life.

But there were far more surprises to follow. We were surprised at the way our lives changed. Nancy and I could no longer jump on our motorcycle and run to a movie like we used to. We were surprised after the birth of our second-born, Andy, that Nancy started having miscarriages. Unable for a time to add to our family we chose to take foster children. A string of angry teenagers taught us how hard it is to change a pained person's outlook on life. We were surprised that the doctors did not take the miscarriages seriously until we had had almost a dozen. We were surprised and delighted when Sara was added to our family. Now, decades later, I am surprised by all the silly things I believed and unhelpful things I did in my effort to be a parent to three growing children and over twenty confused foster children.

Box 8.1

consideration. "Why not require family impact studies before proceeding with this program or that remedy, since of all environmental concerns the family should be first?"[3]

LOVING IS MORE THAN WORDS

Effective loving is far more than regularly announcing our affection to our children. Effective loving helps the child feel safe, valued, and accepted. We cannot nurture effectively unless we have taken

the time to discover what is important to the people we are striving to love. "For the Lord God giveth light unto the understanding; for he speaketh unto men according to their language, unto their understanding" (2 Ne. 31:3). We should follow Heavenly Father's remarkable example and customize our messages and actions of love to the language and understanding of our family members. Even years before we become parents, we can study how to show caring and support to the people with whom we interact.

Parents do not always feel loving toward their children. But love is more than a feeling. It may be considered a commitment to act in the best interest of another person. Even when we are feeling disagreeable, we can alert our loved ones and can call on Heavenly Father for the wisdom to act helpfully.

The greatest human example of gentleness and compassion for children was Jesus. While his companions were bothered by the intrusion of children, Jesus was attentive, appreciative, tender, patient, and loving (see 3 Ne. 17:11–12, 21–23; Mark 10:13–16; Luke 18:15–17).

SOME KINDS OF CONTROL ARE BETTER THAN OTHER KINDS

The Latter-day Saints have been taught by the Prophet Joseph Smith an inspired doctrine of governance or control. "I teach the people correct principles, and they govern themselves."[4] Such an approach makes a unique combination of teaching and agency. Some researchers have divided parental control techniques into three broad categories: coercion, love withdrawal, and induction.[5]

Coercion

Coercion is any use of power to control children. It might include such techniques as grounding, yelling, punishing, and hitting children. It seems that coercion is most likely to be used by parents who believe that their children are basically bad or by parents whose own lives are troubled. While coercion may get compliance from children, regular use tends to result in children who lack social ability, are withdrawn, lack spontaneity, are more aggressive, and have an underdeveloped conscience.[6] It also violates the principle of agency. In the council in heaven, it was Satan who proposed to compel righteousness (see Moses 4:3). Heavenly Father teaches that "no power or influence can or ought to be maintained by virtue of the priesthood" (D&C 121:41) and, presumably, parenthood. Coercion is not effective and should not be used.

Love withdrawal

Love withdrawal is parent behavior that shows disapproval and suggests that the relationship is suspended until the child changes behavior or makes amends. Refusing to talk with or acknowledge a child is one form of love withdrawal. Time-out may or may not be a love withdrawal technique depending on how it is interpreted by the child. If it suggests to the child that the parent wants nothing to do with the child, it is love withdrawal. If, on the other hand, it suggests to the child that both parent and child might benefit from some cooling off before discussing their differences, then it probably does not qualify as love withdrawal. Research has shown mixed results on the effectiveness of love withdrawal in controlling children's behavior. Some researchers have suggested that even when love withdrawal is effective in controlling behavior it may result in children who often feel excessive guilt. Love withdrawal seems to be at odds with the actions of a God who repeatedly said to His disobedient children: "[My] hand is stretched out still" (e.g., Isa. 5:25).

Induction

The third control technique is called induction, which is behavior that attempts to win voluntary compliance from children. It includes reasoning with the child and helping the child understand the effects of his or her behavior on others. The message of induction is that the parent believes that the child is oriented toward goodness and needs only guidance and instruction in order to behave well. Parents who regularly use induction have children who are more socially competent, responsible, independent, confident, achievement-oriented, and have better-developed consciences. It is clear from research that this gentle and persuasive approach to control is the most effective in developing well-balanced children. It honors the agency of the child while urging toward proper behavior. It is very much like the control efforts recommended by the Lord: "by persuasion, by long-suffering, by gentleness and meekness, and by love unfeigned; By kindness, and pure knowledge, which shall greatly enlarge the soul without hypocrisy, and without guile" (D&C 121:41–42). There may never have been wiser counsel for parental control.

Induction is not the same thing as begging or bargaining. It comes from a remarkable position of strength: "I love you deeply. I want what is best for you. I respect your agency. I will frame options and use influence rather than power to help you." The choices are framed according to the age and personality of the child. For example, a young child would not normally be allowed to pick his or her own bedtime but might be asked to choose, "Do you want Mom or Dad to tuck you in?" The Lord does not rewrite eternal law to suit our preference. He provides us options and invites and encourages righteous choices.

There are also times when we must speak with sharpness or directness. But notice the requirements for using such strong measures: "Reproving betimes with sharpness, *when moved upon by the Holy Ghost;* and then *showing forth afterwards an increase of love* toward him whom thou hast reproved, lest he esteem thee to be his enemy; That *he may know that thy faithfulness is stronger than the cords of death*" (D&C 121:43–44; emphasis added). Reproof requires specific divine permission. And we must be willing to demonstrate our profound love afterwards. Judging by such a high standard, one would expect appropriate reproof to be rare in families.

Family life is seldom as tidy as research makes it sound. Children have different temperaments, including difficult ones. Parents have many stresses and demands. The young person who wants to be a good parent one day has many opportunities to prepare for the work. We can exercise patience with co-workers or customers, we can negotiate with roommates, we can be loving with our siblings. There will be unexpected challenges. Yet we can be better prepared if we are cultivating our wisdom, sensitivity, and goodness.

Parents can set children up for success by tailoring efforts to their readiness and capacity. Some parents use distraction to prevent problems by redirecting a child toward acceptable behavior when they are tempted by unacceptable behavior. Some parents use attention and encouragement to keep children pointed toward positive behavior. Some parents use understanding and caring to build a strong relationship with the child in order to prevent serious problems. Some parents are skillful at forming alternatives for younger children so that the children have a choice but the options are acceptable to the parent. Some parents use consistency and natural consequences to help a child discover the lawfulness of their experience. There are many positive and sensitive ways that different parents support growth in each child.

Before Elder Dallin H. Oaks was eight years old, he lost his father. Yet his father left him a great legacy that illustrates the power of love. "The strong impression I have of my relationship with my father I cannot document with any event or any words I can recall. . . . Based on words and actions long since lost to mind, this feeling persists with all the clarity of perfect faith. He loved me and he was proud of me. . . . That is the kind of memory a boy can treasure, and also a man."[7]

Parents who build positive relationships with their children, appreciate their good behavior, plan ahead to prevent problems, allow children developmentally appropriate freedom, and stay in tune with their children's needs and interests are more likely to have healthy children and to enjoy strong relationships with their children than parents who neglect such practices.

When parenting is set in a spiritual perspective, an overarching parental responsibility becomes clear. Parents should activate the spiritual nature in their children. They should minimize the role of the "natural man" (Mosiah 3:19), that part of us and our children unrefined by or in opposition to the Spirit of

One Sunday at dinner our teenage daughter Emily was troubled. She asked about the stake conference we had attended that morning. "When we stood to sing 'I Know that My Redeemer Lives,' I felt so happy that I cried. What is wrong with me?" Nancy and I realized that we had not taught our children to recognize the messages of the Spirit. We began a practice of taking time at Sunday dinner to share our best experiences of the day. The experiences ranged from an insight in priesthood, to a feeling of love for a struggling Saint, or a palpable sense of peace during the sacrament. The sharing of spiritual experiences has increased our appreciation for each family member's spiritual gifts and it has sensitized us to spiritual experiences.

Box 8.2

God. The implications of this simple idea are monumental (see Box 8.2).

When we are critical and unkind or dwell on the negative, we are acting to strengthen the influence of

Satan in our families. The irony of using harshness to compel good behavior is evident. Our concern for righteous behavior does not justify harsh measures. Accusing and injuring our children's tender spirits block eternal learning and eternal blessings.

When we are filled with love, when we respect agency, when we teach and invite with the Spirit, we are speaking the language understood by our children's spiritual natures. The power of sitting peacefully with our children and helping them discover their own eternal identities and to act on them is certain. That is why Satan would do anything to prevent us from acting as heavenly messengers and helpers for our children. All the great discoveries in parenting research can be summarized in Heavenly Father's command: "bring up your children in light and truth" (D&C 93:40).

THE SPIRIT OF PARENTING

In most ways, parent-child relationships and the skills that strengthen the relationships are like those in other relationships. However, parenting provides a unique opportunity for us to enlarge our goodness beyond that developed in most other relationships in two ways. As parents we have a more serious power imbalance than in any other relationship. The newborn is entirely dependent upon our good will. We may bless or abuse. We may serve or neglect. Heavenly Father has entrusted us with an opportunity to appreciate His remarkable power. No mortal has as much power as He. Yet no one uses power as graciously as He. Parenting provides us an opportunity to learn "that the powers of heaven cannot be controlled nor handled only upon the principles of righteousness" (D&C 121:36).

The other way in which family relationships are unique is that they are intimate and continuing. Family intimacy provides the severest test of our claims to be disciples of Jesus Christ. "Therefore if any man be in Christ, he is a new creature: old things are passed away; behold, all things are become new" (2 Cor. 5:17). Will we respond to the same old mistakes in family members with judgment, impatience, and punishment? Will we ritualize and automate our patterns of unkindness? Or will we let God make our family relationships new again every day? Korihor, the anti-Christ, taught, that "every man fared in this life according to the management of the creature; therefore every man prospered according to his genius, and that every man conquered according to his strength"

(Alma 30:17). It is anti-Christ doctrine that we can be as good as we should be on our own. The truth is that we simply cannot be as wise or loving as we need to be without divine help. When the believing parent feels flooded with ungracious impulses, he or she can call out for divine mercy. We join the many who have been healed by Him in calling out "Jesus, Master, have mercy on us" (Luke 17:13; see also Matt. 9:27; 15:22; 17:15; 20:30).

The young adult who would prepare for the parental role can practice being humble, repenting gladly, loving even the disagreeable, and helping with menial tasks. There is room for growth in even the best of us. Jesus was the perfect example of submission, service, and love. Christian parenting can be done only in partnership with Him who is called Life, Light, Bread, Water, Shepherd, Counselor, Redeemer, and Savior. It is the kind of parenting that a perfect Father uses and the kind that we should strive to implement in our families.

SPECIFIC PARENTING PRACTICES

Languages of Love

Gospel principles of parenting must be translated into specific practices if they are to be useful. Nurturing is the heart of parenting. Each child needs to know that the parent's "faithfulness is stronger than the cords of death" (D&C 121:44). If a parent is to express love to a child in a language clearly understood by the child, the parent must study the child's language of love. What are the ways that each child prefers to be shown love? There are sensible ways to discover each child's preferences. The sensitive parent notices what methods have been most effective in the past. Does the child love to cuddle? Does the child respond best to being told? Does the child prefer actions, such as working on projects together? The child's preference for nurturing may change form as he or she matures, but the history of the relationship has vital clues for helping us love effectively.

We can also learn about a child's preference for nurturing by noticing how she or he shows love. Children often show love in the language they prefer to receive it. There are two languages of love that are universally effective if used appropriately. The first is *taking time*. When we take time to be with children, doing things that they value, they feel loved. Of course the key is that we are sensitive to their preferences. A second universally effective language of love

is *understanding or compassion*. It is most difficult and most important when our children are emotionally injured. Most of us suffer from the human tendency to lecture those who are in trouble: "When are you going to learn?" "What is wrong with you?" "What you need to do is . . ." There is healing balm in simply showing an appreciation of the person's pain or difficulty. We help people heal by showing compassion: "The house seems so empty without Susie around." "You must feel very disappointed." "You were really hoping that would work out."

Each of us has a lifetime of experience that can help us learn to be better nurturers. Who are the people who have shown us love most effectively? What did they do that was most effective? Answers to those questions can help us to be more effective in loving.

But what about correction, teaching, and discipline? We do not have the right to correct anyone we do not love. Even when we are annoyed by their actions, we are wise to see them as innocent and earnest.

The Value of Prevention

The single most important tool of correction is prevention. Prevention has wide application in child-rearing. For example, sometimes a parent can anticipate sibling contention at times of hunger and tiredness and can preempt it with wise redirection. Rather than leaving children to squabble over toys during that frightful hour before dinner, Susie might be invited to run an errand while Johnny sets the table. Experience is our friend only if we learn from our mistakes (see Box 8.3).

A parent can set a child up for success by structuring tasks that are sensitive to the personality,

When Nancy was weary of Andy's loud banging of the pans, she did not react angrily and demandingly. She got out the play dough. She found cookie cutters and plastic utensils. She began to sculpt with the brightly colored material. Andy became curious. "What are you doing, Mom?" "I'm making animals with play dough." Andy hardly dared hope—"Can I make some too?" "Sure. Come join me." Taking a walk or getting out stuffed animals might have worked just as well. The principle is the same: An ounce of prevention is worth a ton of correction.

Box 8.3

development, and mood of the child. A prime example is a trip to the grocery store. When a parent takes a child to the store without planning ahead, the parent can expect frustration. The normal child needs to be busy. A parent can provide toys, conversation, or tasks for the child. A child might be invited to pick a fruit juice or to pick among vegetables. A mature child might be invited to get cornflakes for the family. But the savvy parent sets limits on choices. Rather than allowing a child to pick any cereal for the week and getting a sugar-coated cereal, the parent may invite the child to pick between plain granola or granola with raisins. A younger child riding in the cart might be provided with a head of broccoli to handle—rather than waiting for him or her to reach for something fragile.

Our job as parents is to help children have the experiences that will help them grow and develop their agency. Children need many opportunities to explore and to make choices. Parents can customize many situations to maximize the learning while minimizing the misery.

Effective guidance includes teaching children how to deal with life. When a child reports being picked on at the bus stop, both compassion and strategy are called for. Compassion helps the child get past the pain. "You must have felt hurt and humiliated." When the child is feeling peaceful, the parent can pose, "I wonder what you could do to prevent being picked on in the future?" Every idea by the child should be valued. The parent can suggest possibilities the child might not have considered. "You might walk to the bus stop with a friend." "You might invite the person who has teased you over after school and make cookies." "You might find a way to use humor to change the mood." The parent is an advisor to the child, providing ideas and encouragement.

Every child needs to be taught. In this delicate area of correction, discipline, and reproof, our need for the Lord's example is especially keen. First, it seems that the Lord favors teaching over punishment. For many human beings, punishment is intended to make people suffer. But the perfect parent asks, "Have I any pleasure at all that the wicked should die? saith the Lord God: and not that he should return from his ways, and live?" (Ezek. 18:23). He does allow us to bear the consequences of bad decisions. But He takes no delight in our suffering. President J. Reuben Clark taught: "I believe that in his justice and mercy he will give us the maximum reward for our acts, give us all that he can give, and in the reverse, I believe that he

will impose upon us the minimum penalty which it is possible for him to impose."[8]

Likewise, as parents we should attempt to gain compliance from our children using as little punishment as possible. Our Heavenly Father, like the father of the prodigal son, waits patiently for each of us to tire of fighting swine for leftover husks (see Luke 15:11–32). When we do no more than turn toward home, He runs to us with open arms. He embraces each of us with His encouraging vision of our eternal possibilities.

This is not a minor point. It is the tendency of mortals to judge and condemn each other. The tendency is nowhere more evident than in the close relationships of family. If our families are to transcend the petty ways of the world, we must take Him as our model and guide. There is no other way to live in charity.

The Use of Consequences

In this context, consider the use of consequences with children. Parents sometimes impose consequences that are so harsh that their punishing intent is obvious; they are often delivered with a coldness that confirms the child's sense of isolation and desperation. That is not how Heavenly Father delivers consequences. "He'll call, persuade, direct aright, And bless with wisdom, love and light; In nameless ways be good and kind But never force the human mind."[9] Even as we stubbornly insist on doing things our way,

---

PRINCIPLES FOR THE USE OF CONSEQUENCES

1. Consequences can be effectively overseen only by a parent who feels love for the child, who yearns for the peace and happiness of that child. If we want the child to suffer "for his or her own good," we probably do not have the right spirit.

2. Consequences should be naturally and logically connected to the child's actions. The connection between arguing with a sibling and being kept home from a school activity is probably not clear to most children. When the consequence is not clearly connected to the transgression, we are punishing rather than teaching.

3. Consequences should teach children that behaviors have consequences while never removing hope and while teaching redemption through repentance.

Box 8.4

He continues to invite us to do it His better way. If we choose to act contrary to His counsel, He does not stomp off and sulk in a corner of the universe. He does not scold us. He waits. He waits patiently and lovingly until we come to our senses.

One mother demonstrated the third principle of consequences (see Box 8.4) admirably. On the way home from church her two boys were quarreling. The younger one, about ten years of age, attacked his brother with a string of obscenities. Mother was horrified and angry. When they arrived home she confronted the offender and said, "I can't believe I heard what I did. I'm so angry I don't know what to do. I want you to go to your room and think about what happened while I go to my room and try to decide how to respond." That wise mother made excellent use of time-out. Properly used, it gives us time to find our best selves. When children are forced to "sit in the corner" they may use time-out only to ruminate on their injuries and to plot revenge. That isn't helpful.

After the mother had found her best self through prayer and reflection, she joined her son in his room. She taught him why the words he used were so offensive to her. She expressed her love and hopes for him to be an honorable priesthood bearer. He seemed genuinely penitent. She told him that he had a choice. He could suffer for his mistake through a period of grounding or he could repent. He wanted to know more about the repentance option.

"Repentance is where we fix what we have broken," the mother taught. "You have hurt your relationship with your brother and with your Heavenly Father." The boy was mortified. "Mom, how can I fix it?" With the mother's guidance he developed and delivered an apology to his brother. Then he knelt by his bed and, with his mother's help, apologized to his Heavenly Father. On that day that young man learned vital lessons about repentance and redemption.

In different circumstances with a different child, other responses may have been more appropriate. One child might need consequences. Another might need parental soothing. There is no simple formula. Wisdom and inspiration are essential.

It is not easy for mortal parents to apply consequences helpfully. We are likely to become vengeful when children are disobedient, unlike the exemplary Lord who never varies from His redemptive intent. He always wants to bless and teach. But there are times when blessings must be delayed until the requisite maturity is in place. We do not let a child walk to town alone unless she has demonstrated her ability to be careful. We do not let a child bake cookies alone unless he has demonstrated his knowledge and carefulness. But we always work to help them get ready for the opportunities of life. We, like Moses, should always seek to bring our children into the presence of God (D&C 84:23).

The Blessing of Housework

Household responsibilities can teach children both the necessity and the satisfaction of contributing. That usually does not happen without wise and patient supervision. Demanding that children weed for an hour per day may teach them only to hate gardens. Providing children an area in the garden to care for with periodic inspections and appropriate training may be more beneficial.

Parents can assign children to tasks where they are likely to be successful. Wise parents also comment supportively: "I didn't know the grass could look so good." "The bathroom looks so much tidier." "Thank you for taking out the trash." Chore charts can be useful reminders. But nagging can set up a negative interaction. It is better to use humor and kindness. For instance, a note on the child's door might say, "Boy, am I hungry. (Signed) Your faithful dog, Fido."

Cleaning can be a source of continuing friction when parents impose their standards and preferences on their children without regard for the children's preferences. Parents should discern between principle and preference. Many parents have discovered the advantages of ignoring some messiness in children's rooms rather than damaging their relationship with relentless nagging. On the other hand, when a child fails to wash dishes or feed the dog, a parent may take a firmer stand. "You may go out and play as soon as the dishes are washed."

For the person who wants to be prepared to be a parent, there are immediate opportunities. You can learn to do laundry, wash dishes, mop floors, and clean bathrooms. Working and helping is good preparation for the daily demands of family life.

Strengthening Parent-Child Bonds through Celebrations, Traditions, and Ordinances

The Lord has commanded that our religious practices be woven intimately into our personal and family life. Family scholars are increasingly seeing the importance of family ritual. In *The Intentional Family,* family counselor and scholar William Doherty challenges modern families to establish rituals of connection and meaning. He recommends family meals, comings and goings, holiday rituals, and special-day rituals. According to Doherty, as family connections are crowded out by busy lifestyles, only intentional effort will keep us connected. "At heart, the Intentional Family is a ritualizing family. It creates patterns of connecting through everyday family rituals, seasonal celebrations, special occasions, and community involvement."[10]

Latter-day Saints are blessed to have a rich network of connecting rituals that include family prayer, family worship, family home evening, family scripture study, priesthood blessings, and sacred ordinances. In the Church it is often taken for granted that families will worship together. This ideal is painfully unavailable to many families in the Church, but the opportunity to build family meaning through joint worship is the goal. The sharing of hymns, sermons, and the blessed sacrament can bring renewal and power to families. Parents who work to establish and maintain important family traditions bless their children greatly.

Service also plays a vital role in the family. "Parents have a sacred duty . . . to teach [their children] to love and serve one another" (Proclamation, ¶ 6). Not only do we help each other within the family, but we take part in ward and family service efforts. This is another area in which something as simple as taking part in a ward service project while in college can ripple into later family life. To prepare to be a good parent, serve.

The objective of family scripture study is to create a living presence of the divine in the lives of family members. English professor Neal Lambert has compared scripture study for Latter-day Saints to the Liahona for ancient Nephites; they point us in a sure course back to our eternal home.[11] Sister Michaelene P. Grassli, former general Primary President, has recommended that we do more than "dip our toes" in the scriptures: "Immerse the children in the stories of Jesus so that they can know him and can imagine what it might have been like to have lived when he was on earth. Tell them how he took the children on his knee and blessed them and prayed for them. Tell them how the people knew he was the Son of God."[12]

The temple points us to our eternal and glorious destiny joined in family work with Heavenly Father. Priesthood blessings and fathers' blessings connect family members in faith and love.

"Only an Intentional Family has a fighting chance to maintain and increase its sense of connection, meaning, and community over the years."[13] For decades the prophets have encouraged the practices that family scientists now acknowledge as essential. In the crush of family time demands, it is probably the rare Latter-day Saint family that never misses family prayer or home evening. Yet there are rich rewards for the families that continue to bring the divine into their family lives.

We counsel parents and children to give highest priority to family prayer, family home evening, gospel study and instruction, and wholesome family activities. However worthy and appropriate other demands or activities may be, they must not be permitted to displace the divinely appointed duties that only parents and families can adequately perform.[14]

Loving and inspired family practices can be more than a ritual; they can build the connections that tie family members to each other and to God throughout eternity.

PREPARING NOW FOR FUTURE PARENTAL ROLES

For those who are not already parents, all of these principles and practices may seem natural enough. It is easy to picture their yet-future family days as blissful and loving. Others imagine that they will never be ready for all the challenges and stresses of parenting and family life. Neither glibness nor anxiety is useful. Preparation is.

The best preparation for your future family life is probably learning to have loving relationships with people in your life such as your roommates, siblings, and parents. You can be grateful for the challenges you currently have in those relationships. They provide a laboratory for you to enlarge your skills.

The most important quality you can develop is charity. This pure love from Christ does not come naturally to us. It is so difficult for us that we are instructed to "pray unto the Father with all the energy of heart, that ye may be filled with this love, which he hath bestowed upon all who are true followers of his Son, Jesus Christ; that ye may become the sons of God" (Moro. 7:48). As with all cherished gifts, charity comes from God and is obtained through earnest seeking.

When you have a misunderstanding with a roommate or family member, you can suspend your instinctive reactions and seek to see that person as Jesus sees him or her. Then you can seek to see the world as that person sees it. All along the way you can pray for the divine gift that transforms you from a natural person into a saint, from a judge into a helper, from an observer into a supporter. The best preparation for parenting is to be growing in the light of God.

"Children are entitled to birth within the bonds of matrimony, and to be reared by a father and a mother who honor marital vows with complete fidelity" (Proclamation, ¶ 7). Latter-day Saints uphold the lofty standard of sexual abstinence before marriage and absolute fidelity after marriage. Preparation for parenting should include keeping our minds free of degrading images and our souls free of any immorality. That is a challenge in a world sated with cynicism and carnality. Church leaders have taught that not only are necking and petting wrong, but the feelings stirred by sexually oriented movies, magazines, and music are forbidden by the Lord. Moral cleanliness is excellent preparation for marriage and parenting.

Research on adult relationships suggests that many people get stuck in their relationships with parents. Some resent them and wish to punish them. Some idealize and idolize them. Healthy people are more realistic. They recognize that their parents have faults and shortcomings as well as strengths and aspirations. We can appreciate our parents for their efforts and forgive them for their sins and shortcomings and strengthen our relationship with them as preparation for our future parenting.

GETTING ADDITIONAL HELP WITH PARENTING

There are many resources to prepare us for our parental responsibilities. The best print resources are the scriptures and the teachings of living prophets. We often approach the scriptures looking for point-by-point advice. The Lord counsels otherwise: "Look unto me in every thought; doubt not, fear not" (D&C 6:36). We study the scriptures so that we can come to know our divine and perfect parent. It is from knowing Him that we find our answers. We can learn how to teach from the remarkable way He taught Elijah. We can learn to love from the compassionate way Jesus embraced the children in both the Old and the New Worlds. We can learn how to teach hope, joy, and redemption by studying the exquisite message of the Atonement in chapters He inspired in the Book of Mormon. It is from His example and especially from His direct teaching through the Spirit that we learn the essential lessons of parenting. The teachings of the

living prophets on parenting found in Church magazines and books are invaluable because they give the word of the Lord for this generation.

There is both practical and inspiring advice as well as unwise and unhelpful advice for parents among the books written by both Latter-day Saints and non–Latter-day Saints. Sometimes it is difficult to tell what advice is wise and helpful. As you examine any parenting advice, you should consider, "Does this agree with the messages of scripture, the example of Jesus, and the impressions from the Spirit? Does it encourage me to be more tender, more compassionate, and more wise?" Even when the parenting advice you are testing is frankly secular, the same tests can be applied. But remember, no one has written a parenting manual that gives you step-by-step instructions for rearing your particular children.

Almost all people would benefit from classes and workshops on child development or child guidance. The good research discussed in such classes can help us better understand children and their needs. The best research supports and harmonizes with the gospel of Jesus Christ.

Mentors can provide additional help as you prepare for the sacred role of parent. Look around your family and your community for those people who love their children and work harmoniously with them. Look in particular for those who listen to their children, who treat them with respect, and whose children seem peaceful and happy. You can learn much from such examples. Study their actions. Ask them how they handle difficult situations or how they teach their children. Ask them to teach you. If your family life has been negative and painful, you are especially likely to benefit from mentoring by wise and able parents. All of us can learn from those humble Saints who have learned to follow Jesus' example of compassion and love in their family lives. We also learn a lot by listening to our children. Box 8.5 reports what a group of Latter-day Saint teens said they would like their parents to do and not do. As suggested in the Box, this list can serve to initiate discussion between parents and children.

The most skilled of earthly parents is not good enough without divine help. The most troubled and confused parent is not beyond the reach of His tutoring goodness. The Lord provides an unexpected perspective on our shortcomings when He tells us that He gives us weakness so that we may be humble. But His grace is sufficient. If we will humble ourselves

50 TIPS FOR PARENTS—FROM TEENS

This list of "tips for parents" was created by 112 teenage students of Chad P. Conrad in five of his Jr. High classes in Orem, Utah. It gives parents the collective wisdom of a group of thoughtful teens. As an activity, parents and kids might each read through individual copies of this list and mark the five or ten tips they think need attention. Then they could meet together and compare the items marked. For a home evening activity, parents and kids could come up with their own "Tips for Parents" and "Tips for Kids" lists and discuss them.

1. Trust us. If we lose your trust, make us earn it back.
2. Teach us our responsibilities, then let us suffer the consequences or the rewards.
3. See that we eat meals together as a family.
4. Treat us with respect and expect the same from us.
5. Talk with us and listen sincerely to our ideas.
6. Teach us money management skills.
7. Provide everyone work to do around the home.
8. In addition to allowances, let us earn money by doing extra chores.
9. Pay older siblings for lengthy babysitting.
10. Recognize all your children's accomplishments.
11. Encourage participation in many different activities, but don't force them.
12. Go to our ball games and performances.
13. Read books together as a family.
14. Stick up for us, but don't fight all our battles for us.
15. Spend individual time with each child in the family.
16. Have daddy–daughter dates and father–son activities often.
17. Have fun family home evenings.
18. Have short family prayers and scripture study.
19. Encourage good grades, but don't overdo their importance.
20. Don't ground us. It only makes us mad and encourages rebellion.
21. Let us help set up the rules and the consequences for breaking them.
22. Be flexible and willing to compromise.
23. Don't preach to us too much. Tell us why principles are important to you, then let us choose for ourselves.
24. Don't have too many rules. The fewer rules the better—but stick to them.
25. Give us the benefit of the doubt and hear our side of the story before judging.
26. Teach us the value of work and the value of money.
27. Help us with our homework.
28. Talk with us about the birds and the bees.
29. Practice what you preach or we won't have any reason to follow you.
30. Mom and Dad should work together on discipline— don't let us pit you against each other.
31. Don't use guilt trips. Just tell us honestly how you feel about our mistakes.
32. Encourage us to explore and respect mother nature.
33. Avoid just saying "no" when possible. Give us alternatives.
34. Use the "three strikes and you're out" rule for discipline.
35. Don't tell us the sins you committed as a kid; we'll think that if you could do it and turn out all right, then so can we. Just tell us the lessons you learned.
36. Give us the right to make mistakes sometimes. We're still trying to figure life out.
37. Play lots of good music to us when we're young.
38. Don't yell at us or let us yell at you.
39. Give us advice, but don't say, "This is the way it is because I'm the parent" about everything.
40. Don't allow yourselves to "burn out" on parenting with the last children. They deserve your best, too.
41. Expose us to things and places outside our local culture.
42. Take lots of family trips and vacations. We want to feel part of a family.
43. Take us on family church history tours when possible.
44. Admit to us when you're wrong.
45. Teach us self-reliance and reliance on the Lord.
46. Be sure your expectations for us are clearly defined. Sometimes we mess up because we genuinely don't understand what you want from us.
47. Treat all the children in the family fairly. If you treat one child differently than another, be certain we understand why.
48. Don't compare us with our siblings. All of us are unique and need to be accepted for who we are.
49. Remember what it was like to be a kid and try to empathize with us.
50. Have faith in us.

Box 8.5

and have faith, He will turn our weaknesses into strengths (see Ether 12:27).

But there are no guarantees of perfect children. Parents as great as Adam and Eve and Lehi and Sariah had wayward children. The only guarantee is that if we seek Him, the Lord will teach us His ways.

NOTES

1. Boyd K. Packer (1986, November), Little children, *Ensign, 16*(11), 17.

2. E. E. Maccoby and J. A. Martin (1983), Socialization in the context of the family: Parent–child interaction, in P. H. Mussen (Ed.), *Handbook of child psychology, vol. 4* (New York: John Wiley), 1–101; B. C. Rollins and D. L. Thomas (1979), Parental support, power, and control techniques in the socialization of children, in W. R. Burr, R. Hill, F. I. Nye, and I. L. Reiss (Eds.), *Contemporary theories about the family, vol. 1* (New York: Free Press), 317–364.

3. Neal A. Maxwell (1997), *The Neal A. Maxwell quote book* ed. C. H. Maxwell (Salt Lake City: Bookcraft), 116.

4. Quoted in John Taylor (1987), *The gospel kingdom* (Salt Lake City: Bookcraft), 323.

5. Rollins and Thomas (1979).

6. Maccoby and Martin (1983).

7. Dallin H. Oaks (1995, November), Powerful ideas, *Ensign, 25*(11), 25.

8. J. Reuben Clark (1953, October), in Conference report, 84.

9. Know this, that every soul is free, *Hymns*, no. 240.

10. W. J. Doherty (1997), *The intentional family: How to build family ties in our modern world* (New York: Addison-Wesley), 8.

11. N. E. Lambert (1999), The Liahona experience: Getting directions through the scriptures, in H. W. Goddard and R. H. Cracroft (Eds.), *My soul delighteth in the scriptures: Personal and family applications* (Salt Lake City: Bookcraft).

12. Michaelene P. Grassli (1988, November), Children at peace, *Ensign, 18*(11), 79.

13. Doherty (1997), 8.

14. Letter from The First Presidency to Members of the Church throughout the World (February 11, 1999).

INTERGENERATIONAL TIES, GRANDPARENTING, AND EXTENDED FAMILY SUPPORT

SUSANNE FROST OLSEN, ALAN C. TAYLOR, AND KELLY DISPIRITO TAYLOR

Extended families should lend support when needed.
(The Family: A Proclamation to the World, ¶ 7)

Typically when individuals think about parenting, they focus on parent–child relationships when offspring are children or adolescents. Today, because of increased life expectancy, parent–child relationships endure much longer than in the past.[1] Although adult children may or may not reside in parents' households, principles of the Proclamation apply in these relationships, as parents continue to "teach [children] to love and serve one another, to observe the commandments of God and to be law-abiding citizens wherever they live" (¶ 6). In addition, the Proclamation provides counsel regarding potential sources of support available to parents, whatever the age of their children, stating that "extended families should lend support when needed" (¶ 7). Thus, family members such as grandparents, aunts, uncles, and cousins may provide much-needed assistance to parents.

This chapter takes into consideration issues associated with parent-adult child relationships and the intergenerational transmission of parenting. We also discuss how individuals outside the immediate family, including grandparents and the extended family, can support parents in raising their children in righteousness.

PARENT-ADULT CHILD RELATIONSHIPS

As adolescent children grow and develop into young adults, the parent–child relationship often changes. Research indicates that the quality of relationships tends to improve, often because young adult children are out of the house and there are not as many disagreements over everyday matters.[2]

Most research studies report that parent-adult child relationships are quite positive[3] and that in conflict situations, constructive approaches are used more frequently than other approaches.[4] Recently, however, some theorists in the field of family studies have argued that parent–adult child relationships may be characterized by ambivalence or alternating positive and negative feelings about the relationship.[5]

Elder Marvin J. Ashton counsels parents regarding their relationships with adult children. He states, "Wise parents, whose children have left to start their own families, realize their family role still continues, not in a realm of domination, control, regulation, supervision, or imposition, but in love, concern, and encouragement."[6] Since some estimates are that relationships between parents and their adult children may last for over half a century,[7] it is important to nurture positive relationships such as those mentioned by Elder Ashton.

In addition, the scriptures provide an example of parent-adult child relationships in the parable of the Prodigal Son. Even though the son had squandered his inheritance in "riotous living," his father welcomed him home, showing love and compassion (see Luke 15: 11–32).

Even though the quality of parent-adult child relationships may vary, past histories in the family of origin (the family we grew up in) generally influence current associations in some way.[8] For instance, research has shown that adult children who remember a lack of affection from their parents as a child have less close relationships with them when they are adults.[9] In addition, adult children who believe that their parents treated them unfairly in childhood in relation to their siblings also report higher levels of conflict and lower levels of affection in parent-adult child relationships.[10]

> All are free to choose, of course, and we would not have it otherwise. Unfortunately, however, when some choose slackness, they are choosing not only for themselves, but for the next generation and the next. Small equivocations in parents can produce large deviations in their children! Earlier generations in a family may have reflected dedication, while some in the current generation evidence equivocation. Sadly, in the next, some may choose dissension, as erosion takes its toll.
>
> Elder Neal A. Maxwell
> Oct. 1992 general conference
>
> Box 9.1

Regardless of how a person has been treated, or believes he has been treated, as a child by his or her parents, President Ezra Taft Benson provides insightful counsel regarding how one should think about the parenting experienced as children in our families of origin. He states, "Let us also learn to be forgiving of our parents, who, perhaps having made mistakes as they reared us, almost always did the best they knew how. May we ever forgive them as we would likewise wish to be forgiven by our own children for mistakes we make."[11]

As parents grow older, adult children may also need to become a caregiver for an aging parent. Research indicates that when elderly parents decline in health and, as a result, need additional assistance, it is typically family members who provide help.[12] One group of researchers argues that caregiving relationships will be of better quality when they are motivated by emotional attachment to parents, rather than obligation.[13] As mentioned previously, the Proclamation states that parents have a sacred obligation to care for their children and that "extended families should lend support when needed" (¶ 7). It seems

that this counsel would also apply to children caring for the needs of their parents. Indeed, Christ provided the ultimate example regarding the care of parents when, as He hung on the cross, He was concerned about the welfare of His mother (see John 19: 25–27). Some principles for strengthening parent-adult child relationships are listed in Box 9.2.

> ### PRINCIPLES FOR STRENGTHENING PARENT–ADULT CHILD RELATIONSHIPS
>
> 1. Parents should be genuinely concerned but not overinvolved in young adult children's lives.
> 2. Parents should continue to avoid favoring individual children in the family.
> 3. Parents and children should be willing to forgive each other of past mistakes.
> 4. Adult children should provide opportunities for grandchildren to develop close relationships with their grandparents.
> 5. Adult children should allow their aging parents to be independent as long as possible, but offer assistance when needed.
>
> Box 9.2

THE TRANSMISSION OF PARENTING AND VALUES ACROSS GENERATIONS

Ideas about parenting and values are often learned in our homes, frequently as a part of our cultural heritage. Research has shown that both positive and negative parenting styles may be transmitted across generations.[14] For example, children whose mothers and fathers engage in harsh, coercive, or abusive parenting may be more likely to engage in similar types of parent–child interactions.[15] On the other hand, if fathers and mothers use authoritative parenting styles, characterized by support and reasoning combined with firm limits, their children will be more apt to use these more positive methods.[16]

In the scriptures we read that the sins of the fathers may be visited upon their children in subsequent generations (see Deut. 5:9). In regards to parenting, some people may interpret this scripture as implying that if children have parents who engage in less positive types of parenting, the logical consequence is that the children will be just like the parents. President Joseph Fielding Smith clarifies the scripture, describing under what conditions the sins of the fathers are visited upon children in subsequent generations, as well as the role of agency in this process. He explains that the Lord never punishes or holds children responsible for the sins or transgressions of their parents; instead, "when a man transgresses he teaches his children to transgress, and they follow his teachings. It is natural for children to follow in the practices of their fathers and by doing so suffer for the parents' iniquity which they have voluntarily brought upon themselves."[17]

The Proclamation underscores the importance of breaking unhealthy parenting patterns in families, stating that "individuals who . . . abuse spouse or offspring, or who fail to fulfill family responsibilities will one day stand accountable before God" (¶ 8). Both scientific research and Church teachings support the notion that change is possible through the use of agency and forgiveness. For example, research findings generally demonstrate that cycles of abuse can often be interrupted when an individual receives a high level of support from a spouse or a nonabusive, emotionally supportive adult. Thus, if a person has been involved in difficult relationships in the family of origin, relationships that he or she chooses in adulthood may be corrective.[18] Findings from sibling research also support the notion that it is possible to break unhealthy family patterns. For instance, mothers who reported having negative relationships with their siblings were more likely to have children who related positively with one another. Apparently, these mothers selected methods of child rearing that included less differential treatment of their children.[19]

Another way that negative parenting patterns can be broken is if an individual becomes a transitional character, or a person who refuses to pass on family patterns he or she has encountered. Carlfred B. Broderick, a well-respected Latter-day Saint family therapist and scholar, stated, "A transitional character is one who, in a single generation, changes the entire course of a lineage. The changes might be for good or ill, but . . . they break the mold. They refute the observation that abused children become abusive parents. . . . Their contribution to humanity is to filter the destructiveness out of their own lineage so that the generations downstream will have a supportive foundation upon which to build productive lives."[20]

Even individuals who have themselves engaged in unhealthy parenting patterns have the opportunity, afforded to all, to repent and become transitional

characters. Elder Boyd K. Packer provides insight into this process:

> To you adults who repeat the pattern of neglect and abuse you endured as little children, believing that you are entrapped in a cycle of behavior from which there is no escape, I say: It is contrary to the order of heaven for any soul to be locked into compulsive, immoral behavior with no way out! . . . I gratefully acknowledge that transgressions . . . yield to sincere repentance. I testify with all my soul that the doctrine of repentance is true and has a miraculous, liberating effect upon behavior. . . . For we are all children of the same Heavenly Father. May not each of his children, of any age, claim the redeeming sacrifice of Jesus Christ, and in so doing, through complete repentance, be cleansed and renewed to childlike innocence?[21]

Thus, through the process of repentance, each of us has the opportunity to change and reach our divine potential as parents.

> To you I say with all of the energy of which I am capable, do not become a weak link in the chain of your generations. You come to the world with a marvelous inheritance. You come of great men and women. . . . Never let them down. Never do anything which would weaken the chain of which you are a fundamental part.
>
> President Gordon B. Hinckley
> Ricks College Devotional, 1999
>
> Box 9.3

GRANDPARENTS AND PARENTING

The parent–child relationship is both sacred and infinitely necessary; however, every individual in a family should be involved in supporting parents—especially parents that are rearing children alone. Grandparents and other extended family members can be influential in supporting and strengthening parents.

With the current trends in family life concerning divorce, unwed motherhood, and dual-earner families, many more grandparents are finding themselves assuming more parental-type roles with their grandchildren. For example, when adult children return home to live or when they work a great deal, they may rely on their parents, the grandparents, as caregivers for their children.[22] However, even though the scenarios mentioned above are becoming more prevalent, many grandparents still support their adult children by playing influential roles in the lives of their grandchildren that are similar to the relationships they shared with their own progenitors.

Historically, the functioning family unit included more than just the traditional nuclear family. Elder J. Richard Clarke comments, "In earliest biblical culture, the family was more than a parent and child unit. It included all who were related by blood and marriage. This kindred family, as I prefer to call it, was strongly linked by natural affection and the patriarchal priesthood. The elderly were venerated for their experience and wisdom. There were strength and safety in numbers, and, through love and support, members established solidarity and continuity."[23]

Positive Influences of Grandparents

Grandparents have been found to be influential in some of the fundamental aspects of their grandchildren's lives, namely in helping them form their identities and in transmitting values, ideals, and beliefs to them. These areas have been described in family research over several decades.[24]

One potential way that grandparents can influence their grandchildren's lives is by influencing their sense of identity. For example, when an individual does not have intergenerational family relationships, he or she may lack a cultural and historical sense of self. A lack of bonds, especially at the intergenerational level, may yield a less-developed sense of identity. Through relationships with those of previous generations, we can gain a better grasp of who we are and where we came from.[25] To further illustrate this point, Stone theorized that the particular human chain we belong to is central to our individual identity.[26] In addition, research with adolescents and young adults shows that transmitting knowledge about cultural and familial roots may be the most important and influential way grandparents can influence an adolescent's search for identity.[27]

In addition to influencing identity, grandparents are influential in the transmission of values, ideals, and beliefs to grandchildren. Certain traits are more commonly transmitted intergenerationally than are others. These may include religious affiliation, education, and occupational achievement.[28] In addition, sexual, moral, and educational beliefs have also been associated with grandparental influence.[29]

Interestingly, some research shows that grandmothers are especially influential in their grandchildren's value development.[30] Work ethics, however, seem to be equally influenced by both grandmothers and grandfathers.

Potential Roles Grandparents Play in Grandchildren's Lives

Grandparents may influence their grandchildren through the various roles they assume in their grandchildren's lives. Based on interviews of 300 grandchildren, Kornhaber and Woodward suggested a number of direct roles played by grandparents,[31] including family historian or a link to the past, mentor or teacher, nurturer of emotional and physical well-being, role model for the family and society, and playmate.[32]

Family historians. Grandparents who act as family historians inform current generations about the experiences of their progenitors and the origins of their family lineage. Grandparents often remember more about family history and are able to provide continuity in family traditions.[33] This is a particularly important role given the Church's strong emphasis on genealogy and the knowledge that families will have the opportunity to be united beyond this life into the eternities. Bill R. Linder wrote in the *Improvement Era* concerning grandparents: "They serve as a link between the child and the preceding generation, bringing continuity to the family and knowledge of previous eras. . . . Through grandparent companionship, the child learns the humanness and early experiences of his parents. The child has something on which to build his own personality and attitudes— different and separate, yet part of his family units. . . . Without the past there is no future—and if we close the connecting links we will not only find the past, but we will be prepared for the future also."[34]

Mentor-teacher. Just as being a family historian is an important role of grandparents, the role of mentor and teacher is also significant to familial well-being. Grandparents acting as mentors or teachers will take time to teach a moral principle or skill or instruct in some meaningful way. For example, President Ezra Taft Benson encouraged grandparents to take time to read with their grandchildren and to tell them stories. Through this type of interaction, "children then obtain a perspective of life which is not only rewarding but can bring them security, peace, and strength."[35] In addition, grandchildren may emulate grandparents' examples observed through one-on-one interactions. Mentorship can also involve demonstrating leadership skills and assuming patriarchal and matriarchal responsibilities within the extended family unit. President Benson emphasized this idea when he stated, "We urge all senior members, when possible, to call their families together. Organize them into cohesive units. Give leadership to family gatherings. Establish family reunions where fellowship and family heritage can be felt and learned."[36]

Nurturers of emotional and physical and emotional well-being. Another role that provides important opportunities for grandparents is that of being nurturers of grandchildren's emotional and physical well-being. Even though a small percentage of grandparents find themselves having primary responsibility for their underage grandchildren, a much larger portion will occasionally assume a nurturing role in the lives of their grandchildren.[37] Many grandparents feel a need to assure themselves of the physical and emotional well-being of their posterity, which makes this role a vital one in many families.

Role models. With the state of today's deteriorating society, a grandchild is often in need of positive role models in his or her life. Adolescents and young adults are continually searching for people to emulate. Elder Monte J. Brough commented on this topic when he stated, "Most of us, with relatively little effort . . . can provide for our families a veritable list of important role models. This list can be created from a modest search into the lives of our ancestors."[38] Grandparents can serve this function for families and society simply by living honorable and respectable lives. They can be the heroes that many children seek to pattern their lives after. Most grandchildren are observant and will strive to emulate specific qualities they find admirable in the adults with whom they associate—especially their parents and grandparents. Related to this, in a study of Latter-day Saint grandfathers and their adult grandchildren, many of the grandchildren interviewed respected and acknowledged their grandfathers as the patriarchs of their families, and consequently, many felt that they wanted to emulate the ways in which their grandfathers fulfilled this role in their families.[39]

Playmates. Finally, grandparents can serve as playmates in the lives of their grandchildren. Sometimes parents are busy with jobs and the responsibilities of other children; however, grandparents are free from some of these obligations. For example, in a study of Latter-day Saint grandfathers, recreational activities

were a dominant theme discussed by adult grandchildren as a source of bonding between grandfathers and their grandchildren.[40]

Activities That Strengthen Intergenerational Ties

Most people acknowledge that strengthening relationships between grandparents and grandchildren is important to family well-being, but the question that continually surfaces is: What are the best means of building these intergenerational ties? Activities between grandparents and grandchildren provide the setting for meaningful interactions. In my talking with grandfathers and their adult grandchildren, several categories of activities were identified as effective in strengthening intergenerational bonds. Such activities include family get-togethers, working and doing chores, recreational activities, phone calls and conversations, family- and church-oriented activities. Grandparents were also sought out as advice-givers by their grandchildren[41] (see Box 9.4).

ACTIVITIES GRANDPARENTS CAN DO
WITH GRANDCHILDREN TO STRENGTHEN
INTERGENERATIONAL TIES

1. Family get-togethers (reunions, birthday and holiday celebrations)
2. Working and doing chores together (chores, running errands, community service, paid employment)
3. Recreational activities (board games, puzzles, playing catch, hunting and fishing, shopping, taking walks and drives)
4. Church-oriented activities (attending church services and socials together) and participating in religious ceremonies (baby blessings, priesthood ordinations, baptisms, temple endowments and sealings, etc.)
5. Family-oriented activities (writing and sharing personal histories, visiting extended family, visiting cemeteries, and discussing one's childhood and ancestors)
6. Conversation and phone calls
7. Offering advice and counsel when requested

Box 9.4

Regarding parenting, the Proclamation states, "Disability, death, or other circumstances may necessitate individual adaptation. Extended families should lend support when needed" (¶ 7). Grandparents can support parents in myriad ways. They can be influential and ultimately strengthen their intergenerational family ties.

SUPPORT OF PARENTS BY OTHER MEMBERS OF THE EXTENDED FAMILY

In addition to grandparents, other members of the extended family such as aunts, uncles, stepparents, cousins, and other relatives can serve as an important source of support to parents. Relatives may offer emotional or spiritual support, as well as provide information and material or other types of assistance. Such support may help to buffer the effect of stressful events experienced by parents or assist them in coping with difficult parent–child relationships.[42] This type of support may be especially helpful to a parent who is raising children by her or himself.

In addition, extended family members may also reinforce traditional parenting values and child-rearing practices.[43] Indeed, child development researchers have found that parents who receive support from spouses, relatives, or friends are more likely to engage in positive parent–child relationships and less likely to be authoritarian (domineering) in the parenting of their children.[44]

Extended family members should be sensitive in determining the amount and type of support to provide to parents. A "goodness-of-fit" should exist between the amount of support desired by parents and the amount of support received. Support or contact from extended family members, if excessive and unwanted, could serve as a source of stress to parents.[45]

Elder Robert D. Hales has underscored the importance of the extended family in supporting parents. He states, "Unmarried adult members can often lend a special kind of strength to the family, becoming a tremendous source of support, acceptance, and love to their families and the families of those around them. Many adult members of the extended family do much parenting in their own right. Grandparents, aunts and uncles, brothers and sisters, nieces and nephews, cousins, and other family members can have great impact on the family." Elder Hale continues, "Sometimes extended family members can say things parents cannot say without starting an argument. After a long heart-to-heart discussion with her mother, one young woman said: 'It would be awful to tell you and Dad I had done something wrong. But it

would be worse to tell Aunt Susan. I just couldn't let her down.'"[46]

In summary, grandparents and extended family can be an integral support system to parents. Elder L. Tom Perry stated:

> To build a foundation strong enough to support a family in our troubled world today requires the best effort of each of us—father, mother, brother, sister, grandmother, grandfather, aunts, uncles, cousins, and so on. Each must contribute energy and effort in driving piles right down to the bedrock of the gospel until the foundation is strong enough to endure through the eternities. The Lord has promised us in the Doctrine and Covenants that "he that buildeth upon this rock shall never fall."[47] (See D&C 50:44.)

NOTES

1. G. O. Hagestad (1984), The continuous bond: A dynamic, multigenerational perspective on parent–child relations between adults, in M. Perlmutter (Ed.), The Minnesota symposia on child psychology, vol. 17: *Parent–child interaction and parent–child relations in child development* (Hillsdale, NJ: Lawrence Erlbaum Associates), 129–158; G. O. Hagestad (1987), Parent–child relations in later life: Trends and gaps in past research, in J. B. Lancaster, J. Altmann, A. S. Rossi, and L. R. Sherrod (Eds.), *Parenting across the life span: Biosocial dimensions* (New York: Aldine De Gruyter), 405–433.

2. A. Ambert (1997), *Parents, children, and adolescents: Interactive relationships and development in context* (New York: Haworth Press).

3. V. Bengtson, C. Rosenthal, and L. Burton (1990), Families and aging: Diversity and heterogeneity, in R. H. Binstock and L. K. George (Eds.), *Handbook of aging and the social sciences* (3rd ed.) (New York: Academic Press), 263–287.

4. K. L. Fingerman (1995), Aging mothers and their adult daughters' perceptions of conflict behaviors, *Psychology and Aging, 10,* 639–649.

5. K. Luescher and K. Pillemer (1998), Intergenerational ambivalence: A new approach to the study of parent–child relations in later life, *Journal of Marriage and the Family, 60,* 413–425.

6. Marvin J. Ashton (1974, January), He took him by the hand. *Ensign, 4*(1), 104.

7. Bengston et al. (1990).

8. A. Rossi and P. Rossi (1990), *Of human bonding: Parent–child relationships across the life course* (Hawthorne, NY: Aldine de Gruyter).

9. L. B. Whitbeck, D. R. Hoyt, and S. Huck (1994), Early family relationships, intergenerational solidarity, and support provided to parents by their adult children, *Journal of Gerontology, 49,* S85–S94; L. B. Whitbeck, R. L. Simons, and R. D. Conger (1991), The effects of early family relationships on contemporary relationships and assistance patterns between adult children and their parents, *Journal of Gerontology, 46,* S330–S337.

10. V. H. Bedford (1992), Memories of parental favoritism and the quality of parent–child ties in adulthood, *Journal of Gerontology, 47,* S149–S155.

11. Ezra Taft Benson (1989, November), To the elderly in the Church. *Ensign 19*(11), 6–7.

12. M. Gatz, V. L. Bengtson, and M. J. Blum (1990), Caregiving families, in J. E. Birren and K. W. Schaie (Eds.), *Handbook of the psychology of aging* (3rd ed.) (New York: Academic Press), 404–426.

13. J. J. Suitor, K. Pillemer, S. Keeton, and J. Robison (1995), Aged parents and aging children: Determinants of relationship quality, in R. Blieszner and V. H. Bedford (Eds.), *Handbook of aging and the family* (Westport, CT: Greenwood Press), 223–242.

14. S. F. Olsen, P. Martin, and C. Halverson (1999), Personality, marital relationships, and parenting in two generations of mothers, *International Journal of Behavioral Development, 23,* 457–476.

15. R. L. Simons, L. B. Whitbeck, R. D. Conger, and W. Chyin (1991), Intergenerational transmission of harsh parenting, *Developmental Psychology, 27,* 159–171; L. B. Whitbeck, D. R. Hoyt, R. L. Simons, R. D. Conger, G. H. Elder, F. O. Lorenz, and S. Huck (1992), Intergenerational continuity of parental rejection and depressed affect, *Journal of Personality and Social Psychology, 63,* 1036–1045.

16. R. L. Simons, J. Beaman, R. D. Conger, and W. Chao (1993), Childhood experience, conceptions of parenting, and attitudes of spouse as determinants of parental behavior, *Journal of Marriage and the Family, 55,* 91–106; A. A. Vermulst, A. J. L. L. de Brock, and R. A. H. van Zutphen (1991), Transmission of parenting across generations, in P. K. Smith (Ed.), *The psychology of grandparenthood: An international perspective* (New York: Routledge), 100–122.

17. Joseph Fielding Smith (1957), *Answers to gospel questions* (Salt Lake City: Deseret Book), 83.

18. J. Belsky and E. Pensky (1988), Developmental history, personality, and family relationships: Toward an emergent family system, in R. Hinde and J. Stevenson-Hinde (Eds.), *Relationships within families* (Oxford: Oxford University Press), 193–217.

19. L. Kramer and L. A. Baron (1995), Intergenerational linkages: How experiences with siblings relate to the parenting of siblings, *Journal of Social and Personal Relationships, 12,* 67–87.

20. C. B. Broderick (1988), *Marriage and the family* (Englewood Cliffs, NJ: Prentice Hall), 14.

21. Boyd K. Packer (1986, November), Little children, *Ensign 16*(11), 16–18.

22. B. A. Hirshorn (1998), Grandparents as caregivers, in M. E. Szinovacz (Ed.), *Handbook on grandparenthood* (Westport, CT: Greenwood Press), 184–199.

23. J. Richard Clarke (1989, May), Our kindred family—Expression of eternal love, *Ensign 19*(5), 60.

24. A. M. Tomlin (1998), Grandparents' influences on grandchildren, in M. E. Szinovacz (Ed.), *Handbook on grandparenthood* (Westport, Ct: Greenwood Press), 159–170.

25. C. Ramirez-Barranti (1985), The grandparent/grandchild relationship: Family resource in an era of voluntary bonds, *Family Relations, 34,* 343–352.

26. E. Stone (1988), *Black sheep and kissing cousins: How family stories shape us* (New York: Times Books).

27. J. F. Robertson (1976), The significance of grandparents: Perceptions of young adult grandchildren, *Gerontologist, 42,* 137–140.

28. J. Aldous and R. Hill (1965), Social cohesion, lineage type, and intergenerational transmission, *Social Forces, 43,* 471–482.

29. Tomlin (1998).

30. K. A. Roberto and J. Stroes (1992), Grandchildren and grandparents: Roles, influences, and relationships, *International Journal of Aging and Human Development, 34*(3), 227–239.

31. A. Kornhaber and K. L. Woodward (1981), *Grandparent/grandchildren: The vital connection* (Garden City, NY: Doubleday).

32. A. Kornhaber (1996), *Contemporary grandparenting* (Thousand Oaks, CA: Sage).

33. P. K. Smith (1995), Grandparenthood, in M. H. Bornstein (Ed.), *Handbook of parenting, vol. 3: Status and social conditions of parenting* (Mahwah, NJ: Erlbaum), 89–112.

34. B. R. Linder (1969, October), Bring on the grandparents, *Improvement Era,* 22.

35. Benson (1989, November), 7.

36. Benson (1989, November), 5.

37. B. A. Hirshorn (1998).

38. Monte J. Brough (1995, May), Search for identity, *Ensign, 25*(5), 41.

39. A. C. Taylor (1998), *Perceptions of intergenerational bonding: A comparison between grandfathers and their adult grandchildren,* unpublished doctoral dissertation, Virginia Tech, Blacksburg, VA.

40. Taylor (1998).

41. Taylor (1998).

42. M. Cochran and S. Niego (1995), Parenting and social networks, in M. H. Bornstein, *Handbook of parenting, vol. 3: Status and social conditions of parenting* (Mahwah, NJ: Erlbaum), 393–418.

43. M. Cochran (1993), Parenting and personal social networks, in T. Luster and L. Okagaki (Eds.), *Parenting: An ecological perspective* (Hillsdale, NJ: Erlbaum), 149–178.

44. J. Belsky (1984), The determinants of parenting: A process model, *Child Development, 55,* 83–96; Cochran and Niego (1995).

45. J. Belsky (1984).

46. Robert D. Hales (1999, May), Strengthening families: Our sacred duty, *Ensign, 29*(5), 34.

47. L. Tom Perry (1985, May), Born of goodly parents, *Ensign, 15*(5), 23.

FAITH AND PRAYER IN A CHRIST-CENTERED FAMILY

BRENT D. SLIFE, MELINDA J. PETERSEN, AND DANIEL K JUDD

Happiness in family life is most likely to be achieved when founded upon the teachings of the Lord Jesus Christ.
(The Family: A Proclamation to the World, ¶ 7)

This chapter discusses how we make Christ the center of our family life through faith in Him and through prayer. Secular philosophies, such as hedonism, moralism, and relativism can displace Christ and lead to a misunderstanding and misapplication of the gospel of Jesus Christ in family life, and so this chapter discusses them as well.

Many scriptures and stories from the prophets emphasize the importance of joy and happiness. In the Book of Mormon, the prophet Lehi tells us that "men are, that they might have joy" (2 Ne. 2:25). We all want to experience such joy. The Proclamation instructs us in how to discover this type of happiness by centering our lives in the gospel of Jesus Christ. When we place Christ at the center of our families, happiness should follow. That seems simple enough. So why is it that many who are striving to follow the Savior's teachings do not find the promised joy? Why are so many young people filled with strife? Why are spouses distracted and distant? Why is it hard for so many children to really talk to their parents?

Not surprisingly, there are many philosophies and secular understandings that are available to replace Christ as the center of our families. The Apostle Paul warns us: "Beware lest any man spoil you through philosophy . . . after the tradition of men . . . and not after Christ" (Col. 2:8). These philosophies are powerful, yet can be deceptively subtle because they are so much a part of the society we live in. But subtle or

not, they can color even our well-meaning understanding of gospel principles and carry us away from Christ and His teachings. They can even harm our relationships with family members. Elder Merrill J. Bateman emphasized the importance of examining human philosophy in the light of gospel truth when he stated, "It is particularly revealing to compare the teachings of the Proclamation with contrasting philosophies of the world."[1]

In this chapter, we will talk about three of these philosophies: hedonism, moralism, and relativism. The first involves our understanding of happiness and how happiness is manifested in our lives. Often we see happiness as the world sees happiness: the fulfillment of our worldly needs, satisfactions, and pleasures. Sometimes we try to make the gospel a means to fulfilling our worldly sense of happiness and comfort. The fictional story of John and Linda Pleasant will illustrate one family's struggle to distinguish hedonism from spiritual joy.

The second secular philosophy we find invading our lives—moralism—is an understanding of gospel principles that is influenced by Greek notions of truth. The Greeks understood truth as a set of propositions that were static, lifeless, and isolated. However, gospel principles as found in the gospel of Jesus Christ are constantly informed by revelation and thus constantly open to new meaning, understanding, and application. They are a part of our living relationship with a living Father in Heaven and a living Jesus Christ. They breathe meaning into our actions only within the context of those relationships. Tony and Beth Morall, another fictional couple, will evidence the struggles that well-meaning families can have with moralism.

Tony's and Beth's struggles will ultimately raise another concern and another secular philosophy: relativism. Relativism—a philosophy that denies truth because of changing circumstances—is a justified concern of many religious families, as we will show. The temptation to turn the gospel into a set of unchanging rules often stems from our fear of change: if application of gospel principles can change in the context of our relationship with God, then we can never count on anything being stable and real. Our fear of this instability may propel us into what is seemingly the only alternative—Greek-type principles that are static and lifeless. However, we believe that the Lord has and will guide us around these dangerous and sometimes subtle philosophies. We believe that there is a way of understanding our families that helps us steer completely clear of hedonism, moralism, and relativism so that we can truly understand and live the principles of happiness outlined in the Proclamation.

Ultimately, what we will find is that only when the Lord Jesus Christ is the foundation of our families can we be happy in the way that Heavenly Father wants us to be happy (see Hel. 5:12). Only in cultivating our relationships with Heavenly Father and Jesus Christ can we truly follow gospel principles with the right spirit. As we will show, the central way to follow Christ is to be "drawn out in prayer unto [God] continually" (Alma 34:27). Prayer brings the Savior into our homes in a way that allows our hearts to be changed. It allows us to center our lives on Him and His gospel, rather than on the vain and foolish philosophies distracting us (see 2 Ne. 28:9).

THE PLEASANT FAMILY

Linda and John have been married for eighteen years. Both grew up in the Church and have been consistently active in their wards. Both are concerned with making their children and each other happy. They have two teenage girls and two boys soon to be teenagers. The Pleasants hold weekly family home evening, but it is getting more and more difficult to convince their daughters that it is worth their time. With all the busy schedules of sports, play practice,

and homework too, Linda has come to dread Monday nights and the complaints or stern silence that consume much of the evening. The Pleasants persevere because they believe that holding family home evening will bring happiness to their family. Linda and John both know many different kinds of activities build children's talents and help them to be happy and well adjusted. After all, their girls get more leading parts and more game time than any of the other girls their age.

Linda is trying to keep her children happy, but they seem to be increasingly resentful and distant. Linda sees herself as the peacemaker, trying to keep angry tempers from bubbling over into the arguments and fights that seem to be lying beneath her children's silence. She wants her children to learn to be kind and not to "fight and quarrel one with another" (Mosiah 4:14). Linda also wants her home to be easy and happy for John, so that he will spend more time with the family. She believes that if John can be spared the tedious and difficult parts of family life, then he can be free from worry while at home.

John often has to work overtime to help offset the costs of all the children's activities. But he tries to be involved with the children when he gets home. Many of the boys in the neighborhood race model cars, and John tries to spend as much time with his son Tom, refining and polishing their latest creation, as work and church callings will allow. John believes this is quality time with Tom, where he can teach him the value of good, clean competition and hard work. John takes great pride in his shop and the happiness that he's worked so hard to obtain for his family. He tries to be a good dad to his daughters, too.

John and Linda love each other. They've had their problems but they have always worked through them. What Linda cannot understand is, if they love each other, why isn't she really happy? Her conversations with John are not carefree and intimate, as Linda expects. If marriage and family are a part of her divine calling, and if they are supposed to bring her so much joy and happiness, why are they so hard? Why does it seem like the harder she tries to make her husband and children happy, the further away they seem and the emptier she feels? Somehow, she wonders if she has not been obedient enough to the laws of God. Linda seems to find confirmation of this in her reading of Doctrine and Covenants 130:21: "And when we obtain any blessing from God, it is by obedience to that law upon which it is predicated." "So," Linda reasons, "if we can find ways to be obedient, then the Lord will *have* to bless us with happiness."

The Pleasants are working hard and they love the Lord. Things are going pretty well for them. They may not be perfect and they may have things to work on, but so do all of us. They want to live the gospel and be worthy of the blessings of the Lord. However, apostate philosophies, such as hedonism, stand as a road block to the Pleasants' attempts to make Christ the center of their family.

Hedonism in Its Many Manifestations

In order to understand what the Proclamation teaches us about families, we need to distinguish secular philosophy from the gospel of Jesus Christ. The Pleasant family is trying to seek the happiness and joy of the gospel. However, the joy promised as a result of our relationship with Christ must be carefully separated from the pleasure, happiness, and fulfillment depicted in the popular culture.

The philosophy of hedonism teaches that it is human nature to seek pleasure and avoid pain. We often think of a hedonistic lifestyle as promoting the "eat, drink, and be merry" conception of daily life (2 Ne. 28:7–8). However, there are many other, less obvious ways to get caught in this hedonistic trap. Pursuing material things is certainly one culturally acceptable way of getting trapped. President Spencer W. Kimball talked about modern-day idols that find their way into our lives. He warned that "many people spend most of their time working in the service of a self-image that includes sufficient money, stocks, . . . credit cards, furnishings, automobiles, and the like to *guarantee* carnal security throughout, it is hoped, a long and happy life."[2] When we place our trust in such worldly comforts they become our "gods of silver, and gold, of brass, iron, wood, and stone, which see not, nor hear, nor know" (Dan. 5:23).

Placing hope for happiness in such worldly goals is easy to do. We want to provide for our families and bless their lives. Looking to the world for ways to provide happiness, however, comes between us and our families as we devote more and more time to gaining the things of the world. We can forget that what will really bless our family has nothing to do with money or worldly achievements. Just as we want God to know and understand us, our family members want us to know and understand them. When all is said and done, what we remember most about our families is the time we spend together. The things we

possess seem unimportant compared to the activities and associations we share with each other.

All too often, we think we are working extra hard for our families when actually we are working hard mainly for our own status and pride. If, for example, John Pleasant were honest with himself, he would know that the time he spends on Tom's car isn't purely about being with Tom. John knows that others in the neighborhood, including other fathers, pay attention to how well Tom's car performs. John feels that to make Tom happy, John has to make the fastest, slickest car in town. The time spent in the shop with Tom, and all the equipment his hobby requires, is as much about keeping up with the Joneses as it is about his son Tom. Certainly, it is good to spend time with Tom, but how much better would it be if Tom were himself the end, instead of the means to John's status in the neighborhood?

President Kimball reminds us that all our resources are to be used "in our families and quorums to build up the kingdom of God . . . to raise our children up as fruitful servants unto the Lord; to bless others in every way, that they may also be fruitful."[3] We must be trying to bless others, rather than trying to accrue things and find our worth in them. The harder we run after the world, the further we will leave our families behind. And when our families see us chasing after the world, we cannot be preparing them to serve the Lord. In truth, John knows that Tom cares a lot more about winning than he does about spending time with Dad. Perhaps that is because John has taught Tom to care so much about winning.

Unlike John, Linda Pleasant, is not stuck so much in the world of possessions or competition—she is really trying to live the gospel and regularly prays and reads her scriptures. Still, she feels that she is coming up short of the happiness she reads about in the scriptures.

Her well-intentioned actions on behalf of her family don't seem to be working. In a vain search for an artificial peace and happiness, Linda is pushing her family away. She stifles her children's feelings because she fears that those feelings might cause her family not to be happy. Any negative feelings, she reasons, bring unhappiness, so they must be controlled or avoided. As a result, her children feel that their mom doesn't care about what they feel. Rather than strengthening family relationships by dealing directly with her children's feelings, Linda is forcing her family to turn away from each other and deal with their feelings alone. She is robbing herself and her family of experiences that would allow Christ to heal their angry feelings and harmful behavior.

Linda's relationship with her children is strained because the lines of communication are being closed down. Most teenagers feel, at some point, that their parents don't understand them. The same lack of communication Linda experiences with her children is distancing her from her husband. Linda cannot expect to keep John away from the trials and tribulations of rearing a family and at the same time expect him to feel close and committed to the family. It is *in* struggles that relationships are fired and polished and strengthened. As the Book of Mormon states, "For it must needs be, that there is an opposition in all things" (2 Ne. 2:11). But Linda cannot find meaning in the struggles of her life, so she tries to avoid them. "Making others happy" gets translated into hedonism, where avoiding pain and ultimately finding ways to help others avoid pain becomes the goal of life.

This means that Linda inevitably isolates herself, because she will not trust in the Lord (and thus her family or friends) to pull together and openly work through struggles. She is chasing a worldly idea of happiness in which difficulties have no place and suffering can only be something from which to flee. Linda confuses happiness with freedom from conflict and thus when crisis or trouble appears, as they always will, Linda cannot see a way to be happy. If she is supposed to be happy in the gospel, why doesn't the Lord fix things so that she would be able to be happy? Just as she isolates herself from her family and friends, Linda pulls away from the Lord in her struggles by insisting that the only help Christ can give is to take her problems away. Short of that, she cannot see how to be happy.

By including Heavenly Father in opening the lines of communication, Linda and John would invite Him into their family, as we can invite Him into our families through prayer. By doing so we can ask Heavenly Father to send us direction through the Holy Ghost so that we have His Spirit to guide us in our family struggles. Just as communication strengthens family relationships, it strengthens our relationship with our Heavenly Father: "As soon as we learn the true relationship in which we stand toward God (namely, God is our Father, and we are His children), then at once prayer becomes natural and instinctive on our part."[4] If the Pleasants could pour out their hearts to their Heavenly Father, including their pain, He could help them in a merciful, healing way.

Prayer is also an important way to emphasize Christ's central role in our families. Our families are healed in Christ just as we are healed in Him. He will heal even our broken hearts (2 Kgs. 20:5). Christ pleads with us to come unto Him that He may heal us (see 3 Ne. 9:13) as our mediator with the Father (see John 14:6). When we recognize prayer as a way to bring our family closer to our Father in Heaven and to the Savior, we are strengthening our relationships with and faith in Them by inviting Them to help us communicate better with our family members.

Most would agree that we will not find happiness by doing things that are contrary to the commandments of God. The Pleasants also know intellectually that they cannot look to the world for the happiness they seek. Samuel the Lamanite lamented that the Nephites had "sought for happiness in doing iniquity, which thing is contrary to the nature of that righteousness which is in our great and Eternal Head" (Hel. 13:38). We know that wickedness will not bring us happiness (see Alma 41:10). But does this mean that living the gospel will always take away our trials, which is Linda's understanding of happiness? The Pleasants seem to take this approach in many of their church-related activities. For instance, family home evening is a program they follow because it is supposed to make them happy. Linda wants to be obedient in hopes that it will make her happy. The problem is that these approaches make the gospel the means to her own selfish ends. Family home evening and obedience become methods for meeting her own needs rather than ways to serve the Lord.

The Pleasants are making a common mistake that is often difficult to recognize—turning the gospel into a mere vehicle for their own happiness. After all, no one would claim that happiness is wicked in and of itself or that those who keep the commandments do not report a type of happiness (see Mosiah 2:41). The Lord wants us to be happy. However, the happiness spoken of by the Lord is not the same kind of happiness talked about in the world (see John 14:27). The Lord promises to be with us in our tribulations; He promises to be with us forever in righteousness (D&C 122:9). He promises that the Holy Ghost will be our "constant companion," even in our pain (see D&C 121:46). He also promises that if we are righteous, if we love the Lord, we will have confidence as we are privileged to be in His presence (see D&C 121:45).

This is the kind of happiness promised to the Prophet Joseph Smith as he suffered the many trials and tribulations leading to his eventual martyrdom.

This is the kind of peace of soul that allowed Job to say, "though he slay me, yet will I trust in him" (Job 13:15). Job's friends could not understand this type of happiness, nor is it a happiness that the world can comprehend. But this is the never-ending happiness that comes from dwelling with the Lord and having His Spirit (see Mosiah 2:41). This is a happiness which, rather than distracting us from Christ and His Gospel, is "the peace of God, which passeth all understanding, [and] shall keep your hearts and minds through Christ Jesus" (Philip. 4:7).

Part of why this peace "passeth all understanding" is that it cannot be pursued by us. That is, it cannot be controlled completely by us, nor can it be our ultimate goal. Happiness and peace can develop only from our relationship with God. At six different times in the Doctrine and Covenants the Lord reminds us to keep our "eye single to the glory of God" (see D&C 4:5; 27:2; 55:1; 59:1; 82:19; 88:67). When we try to use the gospel as a means to simply gain our own happiness, we have taken our eye off the Lord and turned it toward ourselves. The Lord becomes a means rather than an end. In seeking our own happiness we have failed to follow the first two commandments of the gospel: to love God with all your heart, might, mind, and strength and to love your neighbor (Matt. 22:36–40).

Linda Pleasant might ask, "But doesn't the Book of Mormon teach us that we should seek happiness?" The Book of Mormon teaches, "Behold, this is joy which none receiveth save it be the truly penitent and humble seeker of happiness" (Alma 27:18). But the nature of Ammon's seeking for happiness described in this verse already put him into a particular kind of relationship with his Heavenly Father and Jesus Christ. Ammon was humble and penitent. That already means that Ammon was working for the glory of his God rather than for himself. In fact, he describes his happiness as being "swallowed up in the joy of his God" (Alma 27:17). He felt this joy as he was working to bring the gospel to all the people he could reach, even if that meant going into the land of his enemies, without regard for his own safety. His eye was single to the glory of his God, and joy ensued as a result. He felt happiness only in seeking the glory of the Lord.

The Lord repeatedly promises us happiness and joy in the scriptures. To enter His kingdom and live with Him for eternity is described as "never-ending happiness" (Mosiah 2:41). But if we follow the commandments or live the gospel just so that we can make ourselves happy, happiness will elude us. Happiness that comes from the Lord cannot be separated from loving the Lord and doing His will. As such, that happiness cannot be pursued in itself. Christ made this clear when speaking of Lot's wife. Recall that she perished because her heart was not with the Lord but with her own happiness and worldly possessions: Remember Lot's wife. "Whosoever shall seek to save his life shall lose it; and whosoever shall lose his life shall preserve it" (Luke 17:32–33). Christ clarifies in other scriptures what truly "preserving life" means—it means that those who lose their lives for His sake shall find them (see Matt. 10:39). Seeking or pursuing happiness for ourselves, even if it is through what we think are gospel principles, does not bring happiness. Only seeking to serve the Lord brings true happiness.

Hedonism is a philosophy that claims it is human nature to seek happiness and pleasure. However, the happiness of hedonism will never bring us the happiness found in the gospel of Jesus Christ. Hedonism deceptively points us toward the happiness of the world through possessions, status, and self, and away from our Heavenly Father, Jesus Christ, and our families. Hedonism also says that pain should and must be avoided in order for us to be happy. Christ, on the other hand, teaches us that we can find meaning in our trials. His own life is evidence of this. Our trials can strengthen our relationships with Heavenly Father, Jesus Christ, and our families. Hedonism ignores Christ's active and saving role in our lives and teaches us instead to seek our own comfort and happiness.

THE MORALL FAMILY

The Morall family illustrates a second philosophy that conflicts with the gospel of Jesus Christ. This philosophy involves a misunderstanding of gospel principles that leads to an overemphasis on rules and laws and ultimately interferes with our relationship to Christ, including our faith in Him. This is another instance in which the "philosophies of men" taint our good intentions, as we see with the Moralls.

Tony Morall is one of the Pleasant family's home teachers. On a recent visit to the Pleasant household, Linda confided in Tony and his companion some of her questions concerning happiness and the gospel. Tony couldn't help but wonder if the Pleasants were having family scripture study or daily family prayer. After all, those activities are the bedrock of his own family. From Tony's perspective, Linda would have no questions or problems of any kind if she understood the scriptures properly and were obeying the commandments. Because of their knowledge of gospel principles gained through scripture study and their considerable experience in the Church, Tony and Beth Morall believe they know what to do at all times.

Beth and Tony Morall were married in the temple 10 years ago and have three young children. Tony works hard at his career and is the elder's quorum president. Beth has loved being a mother and running the household with efficiency. Dinner is always ready at 6:30 P.M., with kids washed and seated at the table. Beth and Tony decided early in their marriage that eating together is important and that this would be a family rule. This rule has been difficult to maintain with Tony's many church duties, but Tony and Beth are determined: if it is a family rule, they will do whatever they have to do to follow it.

Tony and Beth put great care into teaching their children the principles and rules of the gospel. The family has lists of rules posted on the fridge and in children's bedrooms. They emphasize memorizing scriptures and the Articles of Faith. Beth teaches the children to make their beds and clean their rooms, and the children do pretty well. She hears many women complain about their messy homes, but Beth has taught her children that "cleanliness is next to godliness" and they are obedient. Tony has taken the lead in teaching his children about Jesus Christ and how one must forgive everyone and always repent when one does something wrong. His children know all the steps of repentance. Even little Ben, who is only four years old, knows what to pray about when he has been naughty.

Repentance and forgiveness are important principles in the Morall home. Beth and Tony have vowed never to go to bed angry, because they have been taught that it is bad for their marriage. They pray together and repent every night, even if Tony has come home late from his meetings. It's an important rule that they pray together about forgiveness in their relationship and in their individual lives. Beth feels close to Tony when she hears him pray openly in front of her about his weaknesses. It helps Beth to remember that she doesn't have to be perfect for Tony to continue to love her.

The Moralls are a good family with many strengths. However, they often seem focused on the rules and schedules of running their household and sometimes this emphasis causes problems. Of course,

there is nothing wrong with having rules and guidelines within the family. However, rules can take on too great an importance—without the family realizing it—and become the family's primary anchor and way of relating. Indeed, enforcing the rules and managing the schedule can take the place of loving relationships. If rules become the focus of our lives, we will know better how to follow the rules than we will know how to form meaningful relationships with our siblings, parents, and children.

Rules and schedules can even take the place of relationships with our Heavenly Father and Jesus Christ. Gospel principles can even be turned into idols—rules or laws to rigidly follow, instead of ways to create a direct relationship with God. We can turn principles into a mediator between us and our Heavenly Father and Jesus Christ—something we have to do before we can approach the Lord in prayer or receive any communication from Him. If we are not careful, principles can be turned into substitutes for Christ—just as the Pharisees of old did with the law of Moses. In this way, we depend on ourselves alone to follow the rules and prove ourselves. We forget our need for the mercy of our Heavenly Father through the Atonement of the Lord Jesus Christ.

Principles and Propositions

Why would some be tempted to insert a mediator or an obstacle between themselves and Christ? Why focus on a set of pharisaic rules and propositions instead of Christ? How is it that some seem to worship "the law" more than the "Lawgiver"? There is actually a long philosophical tradition that may lead many in Western culture to do this. This tradition requires truth and knowledge to be seen in a particular, philosophical way, and this view has been, sometimes unknowingly, transferred into our religious understanding.

This tradition assumes that truth must exist separately and apart from our everyday lives. Truth is thought to exist in some eternal and elusive, abstract sphere, forever apart from us, where it cannot change and can only make contact with our lives if we translate it into our particular situations. If truth were to change, according to this philosophy, then it would not be perfect—it would not be truth.

When we apply this philosophical tradition to our understanding of gospel principles, we separate them from our lives and the situations in which we live. Gospel principles, according to this moralistic philosophical tradition, must be abstract propositions or immutable codes that stand apart from us and wait to be applied in our lives. By thinking of them as standing apart from us, we think they have the advantage of resisting the changes that occur in our changing situations; they can be applied universally across changing times and situations. However, this separation has two important disadvantages: it can put the focus on obedience to these commandments rather than on a relationship with the Lord who gave the commandments, and it can make it seem as if we are left to our own devices in applying these abstract propositions.

From this moralistic tradition, Christ is seen as perfect not because He is the Only Begotten of the Father or because of His relationship with the Father, but because He perfectly applied all the right laws. Christ is seen as the perfect example and teacher of the moral code. To follow Christ is to model His behaviors and discern the codes and rules behind His sermons and teachings. From this perspective, families follow Christ when they adopt His principles, like they adopt a secular legal or moral code.

Tony and Beth Morall seem to take this perspective as they teach their children about Christ. For them, learning about Christ is learning about the steps and rules He gave us. They teach their children about Christ and repentance by teaching them steps to follow in all situations. By following the rules of repentance, which are always the same, their children will have obeyed the law and, from their perspective, followed the principle. Thus the children will have satisfied the gospel in their eyes.

The problem with this philosophy is this: Christ did not say that He *knew* the way, the truth, and the life. He said that He *is* the way, the truth, and the life (see John 14:6). This means that Christians have an embodied Truth rather than a principled truth. We can have a relationship with a living, loving Savior—who *is* Truth. Christ can lead and guide us in our changing situations. Gospel principles, in this sense, are to lead us to Him. Keeping His commandments is not a substitute for knowing Him, but a way to know Him (see 1 Jn. 2:3).

Principles and rules seem to be the main way that Beth and Tony relate to their children. From the moralistic philosophical perspective, the main task and role of the parent is that of instiller of principles and rules. Parents are considered successful when their children exhibit these unchanging principles in their own behavior.

In this sense, it is easy for Tony and Beth to look to the principle or law first and the Lawgiver second, or always to relate to the Lawgiver through the laws. Beth knows that she is a good mother because she follows the family schedule, and Tony makes sure his children can articulate the rules of the gospel. Their successes include children who know how to pick up their toys and know the steps of repentance. Furthermore, for Tony and Beth, these principles and rules are universal—they take away all their questions because they cannot conceive of a situation in which the principles would not apply. They become expert at applying the principles to ensure that they might never misapply them. The net effect is that the living Christ has been removed from their decisions and activities. Only the historical Christ of scripture is relevant, because He provided an example of good ways to apply good principles.

This is not to say that following principles is always easy for Tony and Beth. But Beth's and Tony's main motivation is to satisfy the principle or law rather than to follow the moment by moment counsel and commands of a loving Father through His chosen representative. Indeed, the responsibility of training and rearing their children, Heavenly Father's children, weighs heavily upon them. What if they cannot help their children learn everything they need to know? What if the children are faced with a decision and Beth's and Tony's training fails them? If the children make a mistake, then Beth and Tony have failed as parents. The burden of parents caught in a moralistic approach is huge. Would a parent centered more on Christ be as burdened? As Christ ministered to the overburdened, He said, "Come unto me all *ye* that labour and are heavy laden, and I will give you rest" (Matt. 11:28). In other words, those families who make Christ the center of their family will not be so burdened. Parents and children continue to have other responsibilities, to be sure, but their main responsibility is to acknowledge and facilitate the inclusion of Christ in their family lives—where they can "rest" and receive the "peace of God which passeth all understanding" (Philip. 4:7).

Beth and Tony also struggle with the way an overemphasis on principles, rules, or laws can interfere with family relationships. Tony feels that he is always pressed for time; it is only the family rules that force him out of the office and into the home to see his family. In this sense he is grateful for the rules. He knows, for instance, he needs to be there for dinner and prayer. He also understands that he must be home for family home evening. Sometimes, however, Tony senses that he is just following the rules and going through the motions more than he is relating to his family. After all, he has to check his calendar and plan some "family time" just to talk to his children or learn about their lives. The rules hold sway over his actions. The rules stand as a mediator between Tony and his family—it is the rules that bring him to his family and the rules that undermine some of the value of family time.

All too often we treat Christ the way Tony treats his family. We assume that our acceptance of Christ requires mediating principles. Some might say that following Christ is itself a principle to be followed. However, this understanding would assume that we first look to this principle, and only then attempt to follow Christ. Actually, the gospel teaches that we must first come unto the Father through the Atonement of Christ and only then hope to know, let alone follow, divinely inspired principles. Some of these well-meaning principles could be our own human inventions, our own structures, instead of His truths.

The point is that we should not follow the laws or principles of the gospel as if they were ends in themselves. The scriptures tell us that principles are given to point the way to Christ (see Gal. 3:24; Jacob 4:5; Mosiah 13:30; Alma 13:16, 34:14). Laws or principles do not bring us to the Father. Faith in Christ brings us to the Father. In this sense, Christ can be the only mediator.

It is through prayer that we can most vividly understand how Christ is our mediator with the Father. It is not prayer for the sake of praying that brings us to Heavenly Father, but it is praying in faith in the name of Christ. The Bible Dictionary states that "we pray in Christ's name when our mind is the mind of Christ, and our wishes the wishes of Christ—when his words abide in us (John 15:7). . . . Many prayers remain unanswered because they are not in Christ's name at all; they in no way represent his mind."[5] To be of the same mind as Christ is to know Christ—to be in a relationship where He can communicate with and change us through the Holy Ghost. Then we can change our family relationships. Following the command to "pray always" (see 2 Ne. 32:9; Alma 34:27; 3 Ne. 18:15, 21; 20:1; D&C 10:5, 14:8, 46:30; 2 Chr. 7:14; Luke 11:1, 18:1; Rom. 8:26) is not enough if that prayer does not truly involve faith in the risen and living Lord.

Three of the four Gospels in the New Testament tell of a young man who approached Christ and asked how to gain eternal life. (See Matt. 19:16–22; Mark 10:17–22; Luke 18: 18–23.) Christ answered that he should keep the commandments, or the law. The man said that he had done this since he was young. Christ told him to then sell everything he had and give it to the poor and follow Him. The young man could not and went away sorry. This demonstrates not only a youth whose heart was set on the things of the world, but also a man who has kept the commandments without establishing a relationship with Christ. He wanted to hear that keeping the laws was the whole of the gospel and that by keeping the commandments he was done. However, when confronted with Christ, his living, speaking Savior, the man did not follow Him because all of his law-keeping had not brought him to know Christ (see John 17:3).

All this does not mean principles are unimportant. We need them because they lead us to Christ. Without such principles, we would be bereft of any guidance or grounding in how to seek and maintain a redeeming relationship with the Savior. Indeed, we come to cherish these principles even more because they bring us to Christ. Perhaps this fuller understanding of principles would help to ease Tony's and Beth's burden in parenting. They desire to teach their children the gospel (see D&C 68: 25–28), but the gospel is not a set of rules and principles for children to memorize and recite so that they can call up the rules in their memory and try to apply them to their individual situations. Instead, the doctrines of repentance and faith, and all principles of the gospel, are pointing a person or family toward Christ. If Beth and Tony can teach their children to have faith in Him, then the principles will have meaning. Beth and Tony should first teach their children how to look to Christ and only then how principles help to strengthen their relationships with Him.

To do this, Tony and Beth must first realize that their relationship to their children also involves a relationship with Heavenly Father and Christ. They fear the burden of parenting because they feel as though they are solely responsible for teaching their children. If Beth and Tony could see themselves as partners with the Lord in rearing their children, then He could give them confidence and lead them by His Spirit. By praying together, they could invite their Heavenly Father to guide them as parents.

What about Relativism?

One of the less obvious implications of a truly Christ-centered family is a kind of sensitivity to the changing situations and relationships of our lives. If we no longer focus on philosophized principles that supposedly exist in a realm outside our lives, we can focus on the relationships that occur in our lives, including our relationship with the living Savior. The problem is that these relationships often change, as the situations involved in these relationships themselves change. As the Prophet Joseph Smith taught, "That which is wrong under one circumstance, may be, and often is, right under another."[6] Even what is right for one person in a given situation may not be right for that same person in another situation. For those caught in a moralist tradition, this changeableness of relationships and situations is frightening, because it seems to imply relativism and no firm grounding for our values or our actions.

Recall that Tony and Beth have a ready answer for everyone, because they believe that their principles are unchangeable. They do not need to hear about particular relationships and situations because these things do not matter in an ultimate sense—what matters to Tony and Beth are the principles. What if, however, principles were secondary to the will of God? What if what is right and truthful depends to some degree on the situation? Clearly, they would feel groundless because right and wrong could change from situation to situation. They might even feel as if they would have to give up on truth altogether.

This is the relativist position. If knowledge and morality are solely relative to the situation (e.g., family, culture, era), then truth cannot exist. Ultimately, anything goes; there is no absolute right or wrong, because no one can say what is right for someone else. Tony and Beth are properly concerned about this position, because it obliterates right and wrong in any type of absolute sense. The most that Jesus Christ can be, in this relativist sense, is the Supreme Tolerator of all value systems. Because there is no truth, He cannot stand for a particular truth.

Christ, however, *is* the Truth. Just because His counsel might change across situations does not mean we are without the Truth. Our Father in Heaven, manifesting His will through Jesus Christ and the Holy Ghost, can provide needed wisdom in any particular situation. As even Tony and Beth know, there are times in which the right thing to do is to violate the family rule. How do they know this? How can she be sure that their son, say, should be allowed to miss family home evening on a particular occasion? Our Heavenly Father knows our situation and if we are open to Him, He will counsel us through the Holy Ghost and even intervene on our behalf.

This means, however, that as our situations change, His counsel or interventions might change. For example, His counsel not to kill or murder, as the sixth commandment makes clear, is in force for almost all situations. However, we know that Nephi was commanded to take the life of Laban (see 1 Ne. 4), and Abraham was commanded to sacrifice his son Isaac (see Gen. 22). Such extreme examples of God commanding us to disobey a commandment are rare. But these scriptural accounts dramatically teach that we must depend on the Lawgiver, not simply the law.

The point is that we must place faith in God, who is omniscient. We ultimately must rely on His endless and living wisdom, not an abstract principle. We must be constantly open to and dependent on Him and His wisdom. He is sovereign, not the commandments, and so we must rely on more than our understanding of any principles; we must rely on Him.

Paul said to the Saints scattered throughout Galatia: "But if ye be led of the Spirit, ye are not under the law" (Gal. 5:18). That does not mean that there is no law, or that the law is unimportant and you can do whatever you want. It means that the law does not stand above you when you are led by the Spirit. When you have the Spirit, the law is a means to an end—coming unto Christ. Christ makes it clear that principles are given to lead us into a relationship with Him when He says, "For, behold, I say unto you, that it mattereth not what ye shall eat or what ye shall drink when ye partake of the sacrament, if it so be that ye do it with an eye single to my glory—remembering unto the Father my body which was laid down for you, and my blood which was shed for the remission of your sins" (D&C 27:2).

More important than even the rules and principles of the sacrament ordinance is our communion with and faith in Heavenly Father and Jesus Christ. If that were not so, Paul says, Christ would have died (and lived) in vain (see Gal. 2:21). God sometimes asks his servants to do things differently from the previous commandments He had given His children, as He did with Abraham and Nephi. Constant revelation is vital to the Church and our lives, because we are changing, our situations are changing and our understanding of the Lord is changing. But this does not change God's eternal nature. God can be relied on to make and keep His covenants with His children, because of who He is. Christ says, "I, the Lord, am bound when ye do what I say" (D&C 82:10). The Lawgiver can be counted on to be completely faithful to His children, keeping His promises to them and fulfilling His covenants with them.

CONCLUSION

Our hope is that this discussion about secular philosophies—hedonism, moralism, and relativism—will help families ultimately to center themselves on Christ and His teachings. We have seen from the Pleasants that seeking after happiness in all the different ways in which the world can define happiness will only take us further away from Christ. Making happiness our ultimate goal turns us toward ourselves and away from God. The joy that comes from the Lord can only come as a result of following Christ.

We also have seen from the Moralls that we cannot replace Christ's active role in our lives and families with principles and rules. Gospel principles are, instead, given to help us recognize and facilitate this active role. Prayer is a vital instrument in this sense, both in strengthening our relationships and in bringing Christ into our lives and families. Without it, we are adrift in a sea of secular philosophies, concerned with others only insofar as these others affect our well-being. We are self-centered or rule-centered rather than Christ-centered. With prayer, however, we are freed of such pride. With constant, searching prayer, the Pleasants and the Moralls will be brought to Christ, who will, by His Spirit, help them to obtain their deepest, righteous desires. Prayer allows the children of God to take their place in the most loving and giving relationship imaginable—the relationship offered through the Atonement of Jesus Christ by a loving Heavenly Father. And when the Lord Jesus Christ is the sacred center of our marriages and families, He will help us draw close to one another, serve one another, comfort one another, and grow in faith together.

NOTES

1. Merrill J. Bateman (1998), The eternal family, *Brigham Young Magazine*, 52(4), 26.

2. Spencer W. Kimball (1976), The false gods we worship. *Ensign, 6,* 4.

3. Kimball (1976), 4.

4. Bible Dictionary, "Prayer," 752.

5. Bible Dictionary, "Prayer," 753.

6. Joseph Smith (1938), *Teachings of the Prophet Joseph Smith,* ed. and comp. Joseph Fielding Smith (Salt Lake City: Deseret Book).

Let Us Gather in a Circle and Join in Family Prayer

Mary K. Dollahite

Prayer is central to worship. We come to know our Heavenly Father through prayer. We exercise faith in the Lord Jesus Christ when we pray. We repent when we pray. We receive direction from the Holy Ghost through prayer. But how do we first learn how to pray? We learn best by doing; we learn best when we are taught in love. Primary children learn to sing the invitation, "Let us gather in a circle/And kneel in fam'ly prayer/To thank our Heav'nly Father/For the blessings we all share."[1] In short, the parent teaches and guides the child.

Latter-day Saint children learn when they are young that prayer is not a spectator activity. Regardless of the number in a family, each person gets a turn. First we are coached, praying as an echo, then we remember some phrases (such as, "We thank thee for the food" and "In the name of Jesus Christ. Amen"). At some point, each child branches out to have his or her own individual prayers, using what they have learned in family prayer, and learning, too, that they need to be completely honest with God. Then daily they return to share in family prayer, where they do more exploring and learning. Family prayer often centers on the well-being of individual family members (present, as well as distant) and other things the family cares about, such as missionaries and leaders of the Church.

By the time we are adults and ready to marry, many of us have had quite a bit of experience with personal and family prayer. We have recognized that prayer creates a bonding with others, especially family, that can only come through joint prayer and the presence of the Holy Ghost. Still, how many single adults have considered or experienced couple prayer? Not until I had already met my husband-to-be did the thought enter my mind that I would be sharing daily family prayer with this man, by no means a stranger, but not yet family. We realized that to have a strong marriage and family we would want to establish both couple and family prayer. The challenge was that we had each witnessed as many couple prayers as we had others' private prayers—that is, none.

In the temple, couples begin their married life in the house of God, on their knees, holding hands. There is profound sacredness felt kneeling across the altar holding hands, being sealed as one. That sacredness can be retained as a couple kneels daily in couple and family prayer.

The first years of marriage are devoted to couple prayer: mealtime prayer is couple prayer, family prayer is couple prayer, prayers of gratitude and for safety are couple prayers. Many prayers are kneeling prayers; most newlyweds naturally hold hands. Prayer takes on a new dimension while listening to each other giving thanks—maybe for something the other hadn't thought of, or for the other as a spouse—hearing each other's pleas—making commitments to work together to increase faith to achieve those pleas—sharing each other's phrases, giving a freshness and a bonding at the same time.

Couple prayer is basic to an eternal family, continuing as a constant through the whole of marriage. Family prayer will include children. Individual prayer will increase in focus and effectiveness as one strives to learn how to improve individually to become a better spouse and family member, especially while learning from ongoing family life how important those relationships are. Couple prayer is jointly coming before our Heavenly Father to give thanks for the blessings of family life and to learn from the Eternal Father better ways to love and personally prepare for parenthood.

A baby born in the covenant of temple marriage emerges from the safe encircling of the womb and soon is brought to a sacred, prayerful circle of blessing where usually father, grandfathers, uncles, and caring leaders surround the child in the loving and lifting embrace of priesthood power. The newborn, tenderly cradled by strong hands, is presented to Heavenly Father, named, and blessed.

The newborn joins the family prayer circle in a parent's arms, where it is hoped that he or she experiences a sense of belonging, a sense of safety and security. There is something to the feeling of connectedness, the warmth, the joining of the generations in a circle holding hands and calling upon our Heavenly Father in the name of Jesus Christ. Two could be a circle. Three is more definitely a circle. As the number of children increases in a family, the circle of two that began at the altar simply enlarges.

When the first child begins to speak and mimic words, many couples find the child spontaneously joining in the parent's prayer. Parents feel great joy when a child follows the words of her earthly father or mother to learn communication with her Heavenly Father. And then, the blessed, sweet prayers of a child join in the family harmony. I would wish that joy on every person in this world. The gratitude for the sandbox, for Dad coming home, for snow to sled on; the requests for not being scared at night or for a scraped knee to not hurt anymore. Always to the Father in the name of Jesus Christ. Faith comes early, in a circle, holding hands.

Hugging is natural and easy to do after prayer. It might be enough to join hands in a family circle. Still, there is added security when each person is also individually encircled.

Family prayer continues, including in the prayer itself those at home and those away—even as those away become more than those at home. Family prayer will naturally become couple prayer again, couple prayer that is the result of the circle begun at the altar. There is a centering in couple and family prayer that brings the spirit and power of the eternal into our lives and into our families. Where there is a couple in prayer, there is a sacred place. Where there is a family in prayer, there is a sacred circle in a sacred place.

NOTES

1. "Family Prayer," *Children's Songbook* (Salt Lake City: The Church of Jesus Christ of Latter-day Saints), 189.

CHAPTER 11

REPENTANCE, FORGIVENESS, AND PROGRESSION IN MARRIAGES AND FAMILIES

JAMES M. HARPER AND MARK H. BUTLER

Successful marriages and families are established and maintained on principles of . . . repentance, forgiveness. . . .
[S]pirit sons and daughters . . . accepted His plan by which His children could obtain a physical body and gain earthly
experience to progress toward perfection and ultimately realize his or her divine destiny as an heir of eternal life.
(The Family: A Proclamation to the World, ¶¶ 7, 3)

Principles and practice of repentance, forgiveness, and progression are central to our happiness and successful relationships in this life and throughout eternity. This chapter considers each of these principles in secular and spiritual perspective. We begin with some discussion of the doctrines of repentance, forgiveness, and progression. Then we present ways to apply these doctrines in our personal lives and in marriage and family relationships. Because of the personal, internal nature of repentance and forgiveness, parts of the chapter are more individually oriented. However, the crucial familial aspects of repentance, forgiveness, and reconciliation are addressed—particularly in the later parts of the chapter.

Repentance, forgiveness, and progression each occur within a specific context that must be understood and experienced before our practice of these principles attains its redemptive power. The context in which repentance occurs is justice—the eternal justice of God and the justice requisite in human relationships. The enabling spiritual context of forgiveness is our own experience of repentance and forgiven-ness—through the Father's and Christ's infinite mercy and atoning sacrifice. In turn, progression is enabled through repentance, forgiveness, and grace—both God's grace and the help we offer to and receive from one another.

THE CONTEXT OF REPENTANCE

The context in which repentance occurs is justice. Or, in other words, while salvation is freely given (see 2 Ne. 26:27), it is not free, since someone must pay the penalty for sins (see D&C 19:16). The cost of mercy we receive is the price of justice, paid by someone *else*—whether that be a friend, a parent, a brother or sister, a child, and ultimately, Jesus Christ. In our heavenly family our elder brother Jesus Christ elected to suffer beyond imagination to prevent the rest of us from having to suffer and to offer us the opportunity for exaltation in God's kingdom. Heavenly Father stood by, allowing Jesus to make that choice just as an earthly father might allow his son or daughter to sacrifice, even take risks if need be, to help other children in the family.

In accordance with God's eternal plan for the happiness and progression of His children, "God himself [Jesus Christ] atoneth for the sins of the world, to bring about the plan of mercy, to appease the demands of justice, that God might be a perfect, just God, and a merciful God also" (Alma 42:15). Our avoidance of sin, our repentance, and our forsaking of sin should always be drenched in the humility, sincerity, and reverence of our remembrance that Christ suffered so we might repent.

Spiritual perspective on repentance also leads us to understand that we change for the ones we love as well as for ourselves. However, almost universally, secular models of change are self-focused models.[1] Clearly, both the method and the motive for change is different in secular models. Self-focused change is optional change. Consequently, the moral imperative for change may be relatively lacking in a secular perspective, while in a spiritual/gospel perspective, it is central. Repentance in spiritual context is fundamentally about relationships and reconciliation—first and foremost with God—and about caring for ourselves and one another, especially family members. In marriages and families, we move at the heart of one another's lives. Marriage and family life require repentance, seeking forgiveness, and being forgiven to be successful.

THE CONTEXT OF FORGIVENESS

Family therapists such as Madanes and others[2] advocate "good will" and "moral responsibility" in marriages and families, but the basis of enduring, even eternal relationships is anchored in *self*-sacrifice, the demands of which include willingly suffering for one another. Such demands extend beyond the reach of secular concepts. Embedding repentance, forgiveness, and progression in a spiritual context brings the greater understanding needed. "For God so loved the world, that he gave his only begotten Son, that whosoever believeth in him should not perish, but have everlasting life" (John 3:16). "Beloved, if God so loved us, we ought also to love one another" (1 Jn. 4:11). Thus, our own experience of God's love and our forgiven-ness, through the Atonement that love inspired, is the context for the development of our own forgiving natures.

According to forgiveness researchers M. E. McCullough and his colleagues, in all families, family members must humbly seek forgiveness and be forgiving in order for their relationships to survive.[3] Beyond personal progression, then, forgiveness and forgiving facilitates quality family relationships. When mothers and fathers can be humble and do not have to portray an image of always being right, they are able to seek forgiveness from their children. When parental example teaches children to seek forgiveness, they protect the heart and spirit of their relationships with each other and with their parents. Repentance and forgiveness are a regular daily process between family members, and a binding influence. Even when we seek to be forgiven by God, the restoration we seek is a family one—to be restored again to our Eternal Father, through the merits of His Son and to return to our heavenly parents.

Jesus Christ offers the gift of forgiveness in all family relationships through our continual recognition of God's forgiving love for each of us. His gift and gospel allow family members to live out their own forgiven-ness through their own love and forgiving, and form the basic foundation of our interpersonal relationships.[4]

The Atonement and our forgiven-ness. Our forgiven-ness is anchored in the Atonement of Jesus Christ. We may elect to forgive one another, and we may be forgiven by another, but complete healing and reconciliation—with our Father in Heaven and with one another—come only through the Savior. Christ alone can fully succor and heal both the offender and the offended, enabling enduring, even eternal relationships.

In life and in Gethsemane, Christ took upon Himself more than just our sins (see Heb. 4:15). He bore "the pains and the sicknesses of his people," "suffering pains and afflictions and temptations of every kind" (Alma 7:11). By "tak[ing] upon him [our] infirmities, . . . he . . . know[s] according to the flesh how to succor his people" (Alma 7:12). Without the kind of forgiveness that stems from the Atonement—that pays the demands of justice and fully heals all family members—there is no eternal family; living families petrify and hearts turn to stone under the gradually accumulating layers of hurt and pain over the years. The Atonement of Christ redeems us individually and redeems our relationships.

THE CONTEXT OF PROGRESSION

The context of progression is grace. Real progression, sanctifying progression, occurs only through grace. Thus, "we labor diligently to write, to persuade our children, and also our brethren, to believe in Christ, and to be reconciled to God; for we know that it is by grace that we are saved, after all we can do" (2 Ne. 25:23). Our receipt of God's gift of grace requires persistent spiritual labor and yielding our hearts to God, but ultimately it yields to us the joy and consolation of sanctification and reconciliation (see Mosiah 3:19; Hel. 3:35).

Repentance and forgiveness are also prerequisite to receiving a fulness of God's grace. Repentance is change of behavior and change of heart. Repentance, forgiveness, and grace are essential for progression to exaltation in an eternal family. Grace is the receipt of divine strength and temporal assistance for both repentance and forgiving. Real progression is sanctifying progression, and God's grace and the help we receive from one another are necessary for sanctifying progression.

This process, however, is fundamentally spiritual, and all who experience it will ultimately testify, "It is by grace that we are saved, after all we can do" (2 Ne. 25:23). Women and men signify their acceptance of God's invitation to sanctification—through grace—by their humble submission, yielding their hearts to God (see Hel. 3:35). Grace, brought into operation by our faith in Christ, is the spiritual context of progression.

In the next three sections, we will consider in a practical way the processes and practice of repentance, forgiveness, and progression in family relationships.

THE PROCESS AND PRACTICE OF REPENTANCE

Repentance is soul change, not mere behavior change. The Bible teaches that repentance involves feeling sorrow (see 2 Cor. 7:10), changing behavior or ceasing to do evil, and ceasing to transgress (see Isa. 1:16; Ezek. 18:30; Prov. 28:13). Repentance involves a change of belief, a change of heart, and a change in behavior—especially behavior in our relationships.

Mere time does not cancel sin.[5] Nor, as Elder Richard G. Scott teaches, can our sincere efforts or our personal suffering alone bring reconciliation with God or others, or cleanse and heal.[6] Jesus Christ is the author of our repentance and our own and others' healing. Faith in Jesus Christ and His Atonement are the keys that unlock our access to His healing, redeeming love and power.

In a devotional address to Brigham Young University about repentance, LDS clinical psychologist Allen Bergin placed the elements required for repentance into three broad categories—self-confrontation, self-control, and self-sacrifice (see Box 11.1).[7]

Self-confrontation

A well-known psychiatrist, Karl Menninger, devoted an entire book to his concerns about the disappearance of the word *sin* from the modern vocabulary.[8] Self-confrontation requires awareness that we live in a moral context, where immoral decisions lead

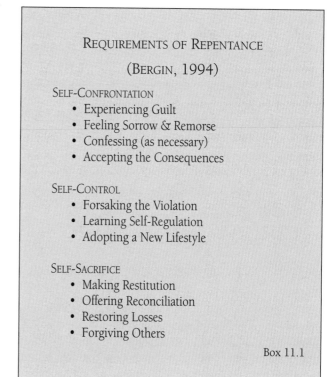

REQUIREMENTS OF REPENTANCE

(BERGIN, 1994)

SELF-CONFRONTATION
- Experiencing Guilt
- Feeling Sorrow & Remorse
- Confessing (as necessary)
- Accepting the Consequences

SELF-CONTROL
- Forsaking the Violation
- Learning Self-Regulation
- Adopting a New Lifestyle

SELF-SACRIFICE
- Making Restitution
- Offering Reconciliation
- Restoring Losses
- Forgiving Others

Box 11.1

to harm, and where harm is sin. Ours is not Korihor's morally relative world where whatsoever we do there is no sin (see Alma 30:17). Rather, "if we say that we have [or there is] no sin, we deceive ourselves, and the truth is not in us" (1 Jn. 1:8).

Experiencing Guilt

One view promoted in secular psychology has been that shame and guilt represent a dysfunctional experience, and unnecessary, oppressive psychological bondage, even as Korihor the anti-Christ once asserted (see Alma 30). Secular psychologist Albert Ellis argued that guilt was detrimental to people and an irrational experience.[9] Such views risk engendering a guilt-free or "shameless" society, drenched in the euphemisms of "alternative lifestyles," oblivious to sin, and incapable of feeling guilt.

Latter-day Saint scholars James Harper and Margaret Hoopes described characteristics of healthy guilt. They defined healthy guilt as a recognition that one's behavior has violated a personal standard or a standard of someone who is important. These standards or moral sensibilities arise from social interaction and discourse. In this view, people who are by nature good, experience guilt that leads them to change their behavior. Guilt is necessary in the repentance process.[10] Shame, which arises in social interaction, can also motivate change.

Unhealthy guilt or shame, however, is a belief or message, with attendant negative feelings, that one is bad at his or her very core, that one can "never get it right." Persons struggling with overwhelming guilt or shame may conclude that changing behavior does not help them feel differently, so they may stop trying to live up to either personal or society's standards. Thus, excessive or worldly guilt or shame may lead to discouragement, despair, and surrender to sin, rather than repentance.

Extremes of guilt and shame—either shamelessness or chronic shame—are not spiritually inspired. Clearly, to rob people and society of appropriate guilt deprives them of emotions that are crucial motivators of repentance. Guilt is the natural fruit of moral feeling and responsibility. Through the personal and social embarrassment of guilt we are lead to avoid choices and acts with shameful consequences. When we do err, these same experiences provoke repentance. Guilt, fully understood and spiritually experienced, is a healing experience, not a destructive one. Our own and others' guilt must always be kept in "healing perspective."[11]

Feeling Sorrow and Remorse

Godly sorrow and remorse are spiritually inspired. They are, quite literally, gifts from a loving Father in Heaven. Elder Boyd K. Packer taught that "consequences, even painful ones, protect us. So simple a thing as a child's cry of pain when his finger touches fire can teach us that. Except for the pain, the child might be consumed."[12]

President Spencer W. Kimball taught that some degree of suffering is part of the repentance process.[13] As with guilt, the appropriate measure of sorrow and remorse for sin is defined by its intended outcome—repentance. Repentant Alma the Younger counseled his rebellious son Corianton, clearly delineating the proper parameters of guilt and godly sorrow. He urged Corianton to "only let your sins trouble you, with that trouble which shall bring you down unto repentance" (Alma 42:29). Specifically, persons block the way to repentance through erasing guilt or hardening their hearts against spiritually prompted remorse. Alternatively, persons also block the way for repentance by succumbing to excessive shame and its paralyzing guilt. Yet, at times, our attentiveness and commitment to repentance follows our being "harrowed up" by a more acute awareness of the tragic and terrible consequences of our actions. "Harrowing" may well begin with a clear spiritual, emotional, and cognitive comprehension (even empathic experience) of specific personal and relationship effects flowing from our choices. For those hardened by the consequences of sin, a "bright recollection of all our guilt" (Alma 11:43) may prove a blessing. Such confrontation, however, is the work of the Spirit and must be spiritually prompted and guided (see D&C 121:43–45). The Spirit "strives" with men and women to encourage repentance (see 1 Ne. 7:14; Morm. 5:16; Ether 2:15; 15:19; Moro. 8:28; 9:4).

One might sense an apparent contradiction in the criticism of excessive guilt followed by our extolling of needful "harrowing up" or cultivating an appropriate sense of guilt. The critical distinction between "harrowing up" on the one hand and unhealthy shame or excessive guilt on the other is that Alma's teaching of being "brought down to repentance" (Alma 42:29) drew his son's attention to the horribleness of his *behavior*, while shame leads us to believe it's *us, the person,* who is horrible. Consequently, the former motivates repentance and leads to life, while the latter immobilizes and kills one's spirit.

In summary, godly sorrow leads good people to repent from doing bad things and to change their behavior, feelings, and thoughts, and this change confirms their goodness. President Gordon B. Hinckley stated, "He [God the Father] never intended that you should be less than the crowning glory of His creations. . . . What marvelous potential lies within you."[14] Godly sorrow, then, actually inspires us to rise to the stature of our divine potential through a change in heart, belief, and behavior.

Confessing and Accepting Consequences

Spiritual perspective enlightens our understanding of confession. Our willingness to completely confess to authorized servants of the Lord signifies a broken heart and depth of contrition that is essential to repentance. Confession is humble submission; it is "unconditional surrender" to the Lord. It signifies that we are "humbly . . . willing to submit to all things which the Lord seeth fit to inflict upon [us], even as a child doth submit to his father" (Mosiah 3:19).

SELF-CONTROL

Forsaking the Violation, Learning Self-regulation, and Adopting a New Lifestyle.

Achieving self-control is a life-long task and extremely important in both marriages and families. According to the social science literature, changing habits and gaining self-control is a matter of "pattern interruption" or changing the context or place in which the behavior occurs, or changing the sequence of behaviors in which the habit occurs, or speeding up or slowing down the behavior.[15] Ideas about changing habitual behavior integrated with the central ingredient of the Atonement invite self-control with its accompanying characteristics of forsaking the sin, regulating oneself, and developing a new lifestyle or becoming a new person.

SELF-SACRIFICE

Making Restitution, Offering Reconciliation, Restoring Losses, Forgiving Others, Obeying God, Serving Others

The last broad category of the repentance processes is self-sacrifice. Restitution requires that we make every effort to be better in our relationships. Often this requires us to work extra hard to mend broken trusts and sometimes broken covenants. Reconciliation and restoration imply that we become aware of the harm, alienation, and bad example we have created, and—like Alma, Paul, the sons of Mosiah, and so many others—be filled with anxious desire and willingness to labor all our days to "repair unto [God's children] the wrongs which [we have] done" (Hel. 5:17). We must also give up our inclination to judge others who have sinned and serve others with greater diligence.[16] Admitting we are wrong, expressing an apology, offering reconciliation (except when the possibility of ongoing abuse is present), and increasing service become important components of the process of repentance and forgiveness.

Building from the Positive: The Special Power of Obedience, Service, Virtue

If our transgression is all we "see" about ourselves, we may become disheartened. This can at times actually weaken us and diminish our ability to resist temptation. This possibility may be partly reflected in Elder Boyd K. Packer's statement that "[d]octrine *can* change behavior quicker than talking about behavior will."[17] Immersion in the inspiring word of God is more helpful than analytic dissection of the problem.

Elder Packer taught that the mind is like a stage and that the easiest way to sweep it clean of dark, loathsome elements is to fill it with virtuous ones.[18] Elder Marvin J. Ashton encourages us: "There are no restrictions on participating in good works. There are no reasons to wait while God's children are in need of your love and service. Love should be a vehicle allowed to travel without limitations."[19] Repentance is most effective when we fill our life with things that are "virtuous, lovely, or of good report, or praiseworthy" (13th Article of Faith), instead of merely trying to keep it swept clean of evil. We ought to so busy ourselves in doing good that there is no empty place or empty inclination in our lives for weakness to reenter and set up house. Clearly, repentance is a lifelong process of becoming.

DIFFICULTIES IN REPENTING

Self-confrontation is generally difficult because it requires us to examine how we avoid the truth about ourselves.[20] Psychological research indicates that recognizing errors and feeling sorrow creates a threat to people's self-image and that it is the general nature of human beings to protect their self-concept from full disclosure of faults and weaknesses.[21] Perhaps this is why the illumination of a loving Father and Savior, which both precedes and accompanies our repentance and our restoration to divine perspective, is given to us "line upon line, precept upon precept" (2 Ne. 28:30; D&C 98:12; 128:21; Isa. 28:9–10). Anything more than partial illumination of the distance left to travel would risk overwhelming us, and the Lord, unswervingly loving and committed to our growth, would not do that (see 1 Cor. 10:13).

Elder Neal A. Maxwell counsels in this regard: "We can contemplate how far we have already come in the climb along the pathway to perfection; it is usually much further than we acknowledge, and such reflections restore resolve. . . . We can allow for the reality that God is still more concerned with growth than with geography. . . . This is a gospel of grand expectations, but God's grace is sufficient for each of us if we remember that there are no *instant* Christians."[22] The crucial test of mortality may not be to reach our destination, but to irrevocably establish

MECHANISMS OF MORAL DISENGAGEMENT

Justification. Convincing yourself that an action against a personal standard fulfills some kind of higher moral law; e.g., "Violence against people who hold different beliefs than I do is all right because solidifying the beliefs I hold is important to saving the world."

Language Labeling. Use of language that minimizes the immorality of our actions; e.g., "It was sort of like sin," or in a confession, "We kissed and you know, did other stuff."

Advantageous Comparison. Comparing one's actions against worse actions of others; e.g., "What I did is small compared to someone in my ward."

Entitlement. Convincing oneself that you are entitled to the action that violates standards because you are emotionally low and feel vulnerable; e.g., "I deserve to party; it's been a hard week."

Displacement of Responsibility. Viewing one's actions as the responsibility of an authority; e.g., a prison guard feeling little responsibility for misconduct to prisoners because "I was just doing my job."

Diffusion of Responsibility. Seeing one's actions as the responsibility of group decision-making; e.g., "It was okay to drink beer because everyone that was with me decided to do it."

Ignoring or Distorting Consequences. Purposely not thinking about consequences or minimizing the effects of one's actions on others; e.g., "No one else is hurt by my actions."

Dehumanization. Viewing those who are hurt by our actions as divested of human qualities; e.g., "He's just a kid—what does it matter?"

Failing to See Others as Divine. Avoiding viewing someone who could be hurt by our actions as a child of Heavenly Father; e.g., "They're not one of us."

Attributing Blame to the Victim. Blaming those who are hurt by our actions as responsible for our violation of personal standards; e.g., "If she hadn't _____, I wouldn't have _____."

Box 11.2

and unswervingly maintain our *direction* and our *desire.*[23]

At times, however, we may flinch and backslide from even incremental illumination and the painful clarity of our self-concept seen in heaven's light. Bergin identified processes of moral disengagement that serve to protect a person's view of him- or herself, but it is protection that forecloses on repentance and progress. Thus, we are stifled and unable to realize the joy of coming closer, in reality, to those ideals.[24]

Bergin and his colleagues examined fears and conflicts provoked by self-confrontation in 60 college students who were members of The Church of Jesus Christ of Latter-day Saints. Those who avoided this part of the repentance process employed several different mechanisms, including avoiding feeling for a time until their guilt subsided, convincing themselves that what they had done was not really bad, promising themselves they would never do it again, doing something righteous to balance their account, deriding and calling themselves names for a period of time, avoid thinking about the action, and avoiding spiritual contexts for a time. Each of these can be classified as either defense mechanisms of denial, suppression, or rationalization.[25]

According to Bergin, "the process of spiritual reform requires overcoming these defenses and accepting painful self-awareness. It is an exercise in honesty guided by the Spirit of Truth. . . . This process involves suffering, and we have a natural inclination to shrink from it."[26] However, perhaps one of the purposes of suffering is to give us a taste of the suffering that the Savior endured for us, which instills both gratitude and a vivid memory of the consequences of our misdeeds.

THE PROCESS AND PRACTICE OF FORGIVENESS

The suggestions that follow will prove helpful in seeking forgiveness from Heavenly Father, in seeking forgiveness from others, and in forgiving ourselves.

Remember the Atonement

A first step in forgiving others is accepting the Atonement into our lives and, following our repentance, forgiving ourselves. As we experience the infinite love that redeems us, and the hope that comes from forgiveness, divine love fills our hearts and we extend love, hope, and forgiveness to all God's children (see Moro. 7:44–48). "Forgiveness is mortality's mirror image of the mercy of God."[27] Joseph Smith taught, "The nearer we get to our heavenly Father, the more we are disposed to look with compassion on perishing souls; we feel that we want to take them upon our shoulders, and cast their sins behind our backs."[28]

SEEKING AND OFFERING FORGIVENESS

SEEKING FORGIVENESS FROM GOD AND FORGIVING OURSELVES
- Study and experience Christ's Atonement—it is the foundation.
- Strengthen your testimony that you are a child of God.
- Offer complete confession as needed.
- Practice mighty prayer (Enos 1).
- Develop increased obedience and service.
- When repentance is complete, ask for forgiveness, and forgive yourself.

SEEKING FORGIVENESS FROM OTHERS
- Engage in self-confrontation—regularly examine your actions and motives.
- Ask "Is it I?"—be the first to confess, apologize, and invite reconciliation.
- Self-disclose—share your feelings and story with family members.
- Avoid backhanded confessions.
- Search for solutions instead of blame.

FORGIVING OTHERS
- Live your own *forgiven-ness*—Christ's Atonement is the foundation.
- Remember that every person is a child of God and our brother or sister—mirror God's mercy (your forgiven-ness) through your own forgiving.
- Pray mightily for understanding and to have anger lifted.
- Develop empathy and emotional understanding of the situation of your offender.
- Avoid unnecessary retelling of the offense—ruminating reinforces an unforgiving heart.
- Remember that forgiving rarely entails memory loss, but freedom from preoccupation with the offense—do not let your thoughts, emotions, and reactions be consumed by the offense. You are a child of God, and the Atonement applies to you.

Box 11.3

Forgiving and being forgiven is usually not a momentary event but a process worked out over time. Elder Neal A. Maxwell declared, "[Repentance] is too little understood, too little applied by us all, as if it were merely a word on a bumper sticker" and went on to teach that the Lord requires more of His disciples than "cheap repentance or superficial forgiveness."[29] Forsaking the sin, turning to Christ, making appropriate confession, experiencing a broken heart, and developing a contrite spirit without guile or pride are requirements for approaching God and asking for forgiveness.

For those who believe that God cannot forgive them, a greater understanding and faith in the Atonement are necessary. This can be facilitated through deeper study of the scriptures and other good books such as President Spencer W. Kimball's classic book on repentance, *The Miracle of Forgiveness*,[30] frequent and sincere prayer, the influence of the Spirit, and the help of priesthood leaders. Hope in the Atonement is required of each of us, and Christ's out-stretched arms beg us to not be pessimistic about being forgiven.

Seeking Forgiveness from God and Forgiving Yourself

In his *Handbook of Self-Forgiveness*, Ruteledge describes forgiving yourself as a difficult struggle.[31] Difficulty forgiving ourselves is often related to patterns of thinking within us. Negative beliefs about ourselves, misguided perfectionism, and unhealthy shame can keep us from recognizing our divine worth.

SEEKING FORGIVENESS FROM OTHERS

Self-confrontation—Regularly Examine Your Actions and Motives

McCullough and his colleagues suggest that it might be helpful to switch roles (in your imagination) with family members. This can help you see how they might have felt and how they were affected by what you did and said.[32] Straightforward examination of your intent and motives is also helpful: Did your anger camouflage your fear or hurt so that family members only saw an angry person and not your pain? Did you use anger or rage, blaming or humiliation to avoid facing personal feelings of inadequacy, inconvenience, fear, hurt, or fatigue? Did you blame other family members for your negative feelings, thereby precluding personal responsibility and repentance? Is pride an obstacle, preventing you from admitting that you sometimes offend people and need to apologize and seek their forgiveness?

Be the First to Confess, Apologize, and Invite Reconciliation

Though we may feel that we are owed an apology, we should look first to ourselves (See Matt. 26:20–22). Don't withdraw your love or interaction and hold out hoping that another family member will seek you out to apologize and admit his or her mistake. Be the first to confess and say you are sorry, and make it a personal priority (see Matt. 5:23–24).

Self-disclose—Tell Your Story and Include Your Feelings

In seeking forgiveness, it can help to share our story—not to excuse ourselves, but to provide relevant context that may help ameliorate others' perceptions of motive and cause and, subsequently, their measure of hurt. Children learn about the hurts that their parents received in their families-of-origin. Parents listen to children's explanations of their behavior. Again, this is not an excuse for hurting people, but relating such stories helps others develop empathy for us which in turn helps them forgive.

We may feel that expressing vulnerability at such times is a sign of weakness and may compromise our "position." Ironically, in disclosing our own weakness and vulnerability, we actually reveal our strength and courage, and others are likely to respond in kind, leading to resolution and reconciliation.

Don't Make Backhanded Confessions

"Yeah, it was wrong, but it made so much sense considering that you . . ." We undermine forgiveness and reconciliation when we hint that our spouse, our child, or our parent should be confessing to us.[33] Simply describe what you did wrong and communicate that you feel bad about it.

Search for Solutions Instead of Blame

When we find ourselves blaming, it is a signal that we need to spend more time in self-examination and self-confrontation. When you feel like blaming and attacking a family member, ask yourself what you are avoiding in yourself. We often attack those things in others that we find it difficult to accept in ourselves. Blaming is not helpful in marriage or family relationships. Rather than blaming, brainstorm together how to resolve the issue.

FORGIVING OTHERS

During a discussion about conflict and offense in personal relationships, Peter asked Jesus, "How oft shall my brother sin against me, and I forgive him? till seven times?" Jesus answered, "I say not unto thee, until seven times; but until seventy times seven" (Matt. 18: 21–22). Did he really mean 490 times? Peter thought seven times was gracious, a generous outpouring of his heart and his patience to even consider forgiving seven times. But Christ's answer was 70 times more than what Peter had offered. This suggests that forgiveness is not an act, but a way of life.

Thus, are we required to forgive even mean, bad people who may never repent and may never come asking for forgiveness from us? Are we required to forgive even those who have knowingly sinned and in the process wounded our heart, our very soul? Yes (see D&C 64:10)—especially since forgiving is as much a gift we give ourselves as one we give the other person. Faith in the Atonement gives us the strength, and love gives us the desire to unlock the prison door through forgiving, that all who will heal may heal, and none of us—neither the offended nor the offender—need remain a prisoner of our past.[34]

So how then do we do this? Several things can help. A correct understanding of forgiving—what it is and what it isn't—is probably the first step.

Correct Understanding of Forgiving

Though the Lord tells us he will forgive repentant people and remember their sins no more (see D&C 58:42), remembering may refer more to our accountability in the day of judgment than to the presence or absence of historical recollection. Thus, though "forgive and forget" is often heard, forgiving rarely entails memory loss. Rather, it represents that one's sins will no longer be remembered in judgment. Such common misconceptions, however, may lead to futile attempts at forgetting that in the end obstruct rather than promote forgiving. Inappropriate forgetting can also jeopardize one's safety. "Letting go" seems a more appropriate characterization of forgiving than does "forgetting." It is possible that over time our memory of a hurtful event may fade, but it is not necessary for us to lose our memory of an event to transform our hearts to forgiveness.

Better definitions of forgiveness have been offered by many.[35] We like Enright's definition of forgiveness: "willingness to abandon one's resentment, condemnation, and subtle revenge toward an offender who acts unjustly, while fostering the undeserved qualities of compassion, generosity, and even love toward him or her."[36] Forgiving means we are not preoccupied with the offense or obsessed with resentment, condemnation, and revenge. It means that we are able to put the offense in the broad perspective of the totality of our lives, and the offender's. Certainly all of us are much more than simply someone who has been hurt, and the offender more than one who inflicted the hurt. When we forgive, we can remember the offense, but the memory does not come loaded with the heavy baggage of negative emotions and thoughts it once did. The offense no longer distracts us from doing other important things. We do not spend time harboring fantasies of revenge. Forgiving also frees us from creeping cynicism about the world in general (see Matt. 24:12). We become less focused on blame, judgment, and punishment and more focused on transforming our own hearts (see John 8:10–11). We develop a mature understanding of what happened and leave judgment and punishment to a wise and loving Heavenly Father.

The above definition also implies that the offended person chooses to forgive. Forgiveness from this perspective is primarily one person's response, attitude, or mindset toward the other. It does not require that one seek out an offender and express forgiveness. This would be especially difficult in relationships where doing so might invite further harm. The forgiver can unconditionally offer the gift regardless of the offender's current attitude.

Reconciliation

Reconciliation is another important and complex issue related to forgiveness. Reconciliation means restoration of the relationship with our offender. In some cases this may be a worthy goal, but in other cases, seeking out a relationship with a perpetrator of sexual or physical abuse can be dangerous and may invite further harm. Reconciliation is a worthwhile outcome when the offender is fully repentant and the forgiver can be confident that he or she will not be further harmed. Because forgiving is not forgetting, nor does it imply a restoration of trust—it does not lead to or require endangering ourselves or acting uncautiously as though the behavior had never happened.

Once a healthy understanding of forgiving is in place, we are prepared to adopt it as a way of life. We soon find, though, that correct doctrine is the easiest and the only easy part. Is it difficult to eliminate blame and judgment from your relationships with your parents, siblings, spouse, or even your children? Do you find yourself fantasizing how "they'll get theirs" and then imagining fitting punishments they might receive? Perhaps you even hope to be the one to inflict the punishment, so as to make sure they hurt as much as you and to "make yourself feel better." So how do we make this comprehensive change of heart called forgiving? How do we bring about the context where our mercy (forgiveness) overshadows our demands or desires for justice and retribution? An important part of the answer may be our faith that through the Atonement of Christ no harm or injury is permanent or cannot be healed (see Isa. 53:4–5; Heb. 4:15–16; Alma 7:12). This faith can help us to forgive.

Remember our Forgiven-ness, Practice Pleading Prayer

Again, the context of forgiving is remembering our own forgiven-ness. Studying and working to develop feelings about the Atonement form the foundation for a forgiving heart. Next, pleading prayer can help transform our grieving, angry hearts into forgiving hearts.

If anyone ever had reason to be bitter, it was the Prophet Joseph Smith. Yet his heart was forgiving. At one time William Smith, the Prophet's brother and a member of the Quorum of the Twelve, had become embittered. He had said vicious and vile things against Joseph. His was a distracted, vengeful heart, and he had even physically attacked his brother. In the midst of all of this, Daniel Tyler, a member of the Church recorded in his journal this description of the Prophet Joseph:

> I attended a meeting "on the flats" where Joseph presided. . . . I perceived sadness in his countenance and tears trickling down his cheeks. . . . he opened the

meeting by prayer. Instead of facing the audience, however, he turned his back and bowed upon his knees, facing the wall. . . . that prayer, which was to a considerable extent in behalf of those who accused him of having gone astray and fallen into sin, was that the Lord would forgive them and open their eyes that they might see aright. That prayer . . . partook of the learning and eloquence of heaven. . . . It was the crowning of all the prayers I ever heard.[37]

The prophet Joseph used prayer to soften hearts, his own first, and others to follow.[38]

Expand Your Vision

Third, see others as children of God and try to develop an understanding or empathy for them, even your offenders. Several authors believe this is the most crucial step. We greatly improve our ability to forgive by increasing our understanding of others' circumstances, their feelings, their situation—in short, by empathizing with them. Studies have shown that when people learn to be more empathic with others, they automatically develop more forgiving temperaments.[39] Likewise, marital partners who have more empathy for each other are more forgiving, more committed, report more trust, and are happier.[40] Perhaps this intimate understanding of one another, and this compassion, is why one recent study found more acceptance of forgiveness among married couples than has been previously found among single adults.[41] In a relationship context of unconditional love, our experience of the offense is diminished and our capacity to forgive is enlarged. The sacrifice—of the demands of justice, which we pay in part ourselves—requisite to forgiving is made possible by our attaining Christlike love.

Enlarging our temporal and eternal vision about those who offend us can help us develop greater empathy. Consider someone who has recently offended you. First, remember his or her divine nature and potential. Where is the child of God in that person? Can Christ's blood cleanse him or her as it can me? Forgiveness is a relational stance in which we accept the inherent worth of another person even after judging their actions to be wrong.[42] In an address to the Twelve in 1839 the Prophet Joseph Smith encouraged, "Ever keep in exercise the principle of mercy, and be ready to forgive our brother on the first intimations of repentance, and asking forgiveness; and should we even forgive our brother, or even our

---

COMPONENTS OF FORGIVENESS TRAINING PROGRAMS FOR MARRIED COUPLES

- Discussion of what forgiveness really is—that it does not involve condoning, does not have to involve reconciliation, and does not mean suppressing the offending event
- Discussion of forgiving as letting go so one is not obsessed with detail—telling of the offending event or feelings about it
- Empathy training involving understanding the deep feelings of another
- Reattribution training involving a process of gaining a new perspective taken by the offended toward the offender
- Training for overcoming pride and learning to be quick to apologize

Box 11.4

---

enemy, before he repent or ask forgiveness, our heavenly Father would be equally merciful unto us."[43]

Interest in Forgiveness in Mental Health Literature

Prior to about 1985, it was difficult to find any literature on forgiveness.[44] Since that time, however, forgiveness studies have increased dramatically in the mental health literature.[45] In the last decade, forgiveness interventions have been used successfully for a variety of different issues, including alcoholism, help with cancer patients,[46] anger and depression,[47] sexual abuse and compulsions,[48] drug abuse,[49] personality disorders,[50] family-of-origin issues,[51] and marital problems.[52] A variety of different types of articles have been published in professional journals. These include reviews and critiques of forgiveness,[53] religious and conceptual ideas about forgiveness,[54] development of clinical interventions using forgiveness,[55] and the development of forgiveness scales and measures.[56] These many studies have identified several common steps in forgiving.

BENEFITS OF BEING FORGIVING

Husbands and wives who have forgiving temperaments or who develop them have happier marriages. Woodman studied marriages and compared the qualities of relationships such as commitment, trust, liking and loving each other, agreeing with each other, and the balance of positive to negative emotions in couples who were more forgiving with those who were not as forgiving. She discovered that husbands and wives who were forgiving experience more trust, agreement, positive emotion, commitment, liking and loving, and greater overall marital satisfaction.[57] Nelson examined college students who were dating or married. Similar to Woodman's findings, she concluded that forgiving relationships were stronger and more stable.[58] McCullough and his colleagues studied processes of forgiving in couples and concluded that forgiveness—as evidenced by stopping rumination about the offending event and increased empathy for their partner—was predictive of relationship closeness, commitment, and overall satisfaction with the relationship.[59] In a study of long-term first marriages, Fenell identified 10 characteristics of satisfying, enduring marriages. Willingness to forgive and be forgiven was one of the 10.[60]

Other studies have developed marriage education programs that center exclusively on developing forgiveness among husbands and wives. Married people who participated in these programs reported an increase in overall marital satisfaction and happiness.[61] The major components of these programs are listed in Box 11.4

In families the need for forgiving lifestyles is equally important. How many adult children harbor pent-up resentment toward their parents? How many parents have cut their children out of their lives because they cannot bring themselves to forgive them for some offense? A pioneer in family therapy, Ivan Boszormenyi-Nagy, examined the relationships between generations of families and found that people feel a strong need for justice and fairness in family relationships. He believes that a moral ledger is kept between generations. When parents are loving and caring and generally meet their children's needs, moral "credits" are passed on to their children. In such cases children will be able to be loyal to their parents and grandparents and pass on moral credits to their children. When neglect, abuse, or failure to meet needs is evident, moral "debits" are passed on. In these cases children experience injustice and have pain and resentment toward their parents.

Almost all parents "fail" their children in some way. Boszormeny-Nagy recommends that the solution is for adult children to exonerate their parents from moral guilt for imperfections. This means that children recognize the moral debt their parents owe them, but they willfully decide to let their parents off

the hook—to forgive. To do this, adult children must develop empathy for their parents through trying to understand their parents' upbringing and circumstances in their families of origin.[62] The components of the forgiveness training program for marriages mentioned in Box 11.4 may also be helpful to adult children who need to forgive their parents.

Research shows that people who are forgiving have better emotional and physical health. Neuman and Chi found that individuals who were forgiving had lower levels of anger and hostility.[63] In three different studies, researchers concluded that forgiving someone who has offended you led to a reduction of behaviors related to cardiovascular disease such as anger and stress responses.[64] Strasser found that forgiveness is related to better health in older adults.[65] Another scholar, Trainer, studied divorced people and concluded that those who were able to truly forgive their spouses experienced greater adjustment and personal power. True forgiving meant that they did not ruminate over the failed events of their marriage; they did not blame their spouse; they did not seek revenge.[66]

CONCLUSION: FORGIVENESS, REPENTANCE, AND ETERNAL PROGRESSION

Repentance and forgiveness allow for the eternal progression of individuals, couples, and families. Eternal progression is Heavenly Father's plan of happiness for men and women and is inherent in each of us as children of God. The concepts of repentance and forgiveness are inseparably linked to the plan of eternal progression. Repentance, forgiveness, and progression are critical concepts in understanding personal growth and how people change their behavior and their nature (see Mosiah 3:19; Hel. 3:35) and the relationships in which individual growth optimally occurs.

The doctrine of progression, that men and women as eternal couples and families may become like God, is much more visionary than any concepts of individual growth espoused in behavioral and social science. The doctrines of the gospel, as attested in the Proclamation, increase our loving commitment to one another and give us hope that family members can repent, be forgiven, forgive others, and progress eternally in these most sacred of all relationships—eternal families.

NOTES

1. W. Doherty (1995), *Soul searching: Why psychotherapy must promote moral responsibility* (New York: Basic Books).

2. Doherty (1995).

3. M. E. McCullough, S. J. Sandage, and E. L. Worthington (1997), *To forgive is human: How to put your past in the past* (Downers Grove, IL: InterVarsity Press).

4. McCullough et al. (1997), 16.

5. C. S. Lewis (1962), *The problem of pain* (New York: Macmillan).

6. Richard G. Scott (1986, May), We love you—please come back, *Ensign 16*(5), 10.

7. A. E. Bergin (1994), The psychology of repentance, *Brigham Young University devotional and fireside speeches, 1994–1995* (Provo, UT: Brigham Young University Press).

8. K. Menninger (1973), *Whatever became of sin?* (New York: Hawthorn).

9. A. L. Ellis (1995), My response to "Don't throw the baby out with the holy water": Helpful and hurtful elements of religion, *Journal of Psychology and Christianity, 3,* 323–326.

10. J. M. Harper and M. H. Hoopes (1990), *Uncovering shame: Integrating individuals with their family systems* (New York: W. W. Norton).

11. F. Enzio Busche (1982, May), Love is the power that will cure the family *Ensign 12*(5), 70.

12. Boyd K. Packer (1988, May), Atonement, agency, accountability, *Ensign 18*(5), 71.

13. Spencer W. Kimball (1974, May), What is true repentance? *New Era,* 7.

14. Gordon B. Hinckley (1995, November), Stand strong against the wiles of the world, *Ensign, 25*(11), 98.

15. W. O'Hanlon (1987), *Taproots: Underlying principles of Milton Erickson's therapy and hypnosis* (New York: Norton).

16. Bergin (1994).

17. Boyd K. Packer (1997, May), Washed clean, *Ensign 27*(5), 10.

18. Boyd K. Packer (1974, January), Inspiring music and worthy thoughts, *Ensign, 4*(1), 25–28.

19. Marvin J. Ashton (1988, May), While they are waiting, *Ensign, 18*(5), 62–64.

20. Bergin (1994).

21. A. Bandura (1996), Mechanisms of moral disengagement in exercise of moral agency, *Journal of Personality and Social Psychology, 71,* 364–374.

22. Neal A. Maxwell (1981), *Notwithstanding my weakness* (Salt Lake City: Deseret Book), 9, 11.

23. Marvin J. Ashton (1987, May), I am an adult now, *Ensign, 17*(5), 67.

24. Bergin (1994).

25. A. E. Bergin, R. D. Stinchfield, T. A. Gaskin, K. S. Masters, and C. E. Sullivan (1988), Religious lifestyles and mental health: An exploratory study, *Journal of Counseling Psychology, 35,* 97.

26. Bergin (1994), 29.

27. Dallin H. Oaks (1989, November), Modern pioneers, *Ensign, 19*(11), 66.

28. Joseph Smith (1938). *Teachings of the Prophet Joseph Smith,* ed. and comp. Joseph Fielding Smith (Salt Lake City: Deseret Book), 241.

29. Neal A. Maxwell (1991, November), Repentance, *Ensign, 21*(11), 30–32.

30. Spencer W. Kimball (1969), *The miracle of forgiveness* (Salt Lake City: Bookcraft).

31. T. Rutledge (1997), *The self-forgiveness handbook: A practical and empowering guide* (Oakland, CA: New Harbinger).

32. McCullough et al. (1997).

33. McCullough et al. (1997).

34. Neal A. Maxwell (1982, July), Thanks be to God, *Ensign 12*(17), 52.

35. D. S. Davenport (1991), The functions of anger and forgiveness: Guidelines for psychotherapy with victims, *Psychotherapy, 28,* 140–153; R. D. Enright, D. L. Eastin, S. Golden, I. Sarinopoulos, and S. Freedman (1992). Interpersonal forgiveness within the helping professions: An attempt to resolve differences of opinion, *Counseling and Values, 36,* 84–103; S. R. Freedman and R. D. Enright (1996), Forgiveness as an intervention goal with incest survivors, *Journal of Consulting and Clinical Psychology, 64,* 983–992; J. North (1987), Wrongdoing and forgiveness, *Philosophy, 61,* 499–508; J. P. Pingleton (1989), The role and function of forgiveness in the psychotherapeutic process, *Journal of Psychology and Theology, 17,* 27–35.

36. R. D. Enright (1996), Counseling within the forgiveness triad: On forgiving, receiving forgiveness, and self-forgiveness, *Counseling and Values, 40,* 107–127, esp. 108.

37. Quoted in H. L. Andrus and H. M. Andrus (1974), *They knew the Prophet* (Salt Lake City: Bookcraft), 51–52.

38. See M. H. Butler (May 1997), *Strengthening families through the couple–God relationship: A triadic process model,* presentation at the spring conference of the Association of Mormon Counselors and Psychotherapists, Salt Lake City, UT; M. H. Butler, B. C. Gardner, and M. H. Bird (1998), Not just a time-out: Change dynamics of prayer for religious couples in conflict situations, *Family Process, 37*(4), 451–478.

39. McCullough et al. (1997).

40. T. Woodman (1992), The role of forgiveness in marriage and marital adjustment, unpublished dissertation, Fuller Graduate School of Psychology.

41. S. K. Dahlin and M. H. Butler (1999), Language of forgiveness and treatment acceptability, unpublished manuscript, Provo, UT.

42. McCullough et al. (1997), 27.

43. Smith (1938), 155.

44. Freedman and Enright (1996).

45. S. Walrond-Skinner (1998), The function and role of forgiveness in working with couples and families: Clearing the ground, *Journal of Family Therapy, 20,* 3–19.

46. L. J. Phillips and J. W. Osborne (1989), Cancer patients' experiences of forgiveness therapy, *Canadian Journal of Counseling, 23,* 236–251.

47. R. P. Fitzgibbons (1986), The cognitive and emotive uses of forgiveness in the treatment of anger, *Psychotherapy, 23,* 629–633.

48. Freedman and Enright (1996); C. Madanes (1991), *Sex, love, and violence* (New York: W. W. Norton); Schneider (1989), Alcoholic day treatment: Rational, research, and resistance, *Journal of Drug Issues, 19,* 437–449.

49. B. Flanigan (1996), *Forgiving yourself: A step-by-step guide to making peace with your mistakes and getting on with your life* (New York: Macmillan).

50. S. F. Fisher (1985), Identity of the two: The phenomenology of shame in borderline development and treatment, *Psychotherapy, 22,* 101–109.

51. D. Hope (1987), The healing paradox of forgiveness, *Psychotherapy, 24,* 240–244.

52. E. L. Worthington and F. A. DiBlasio (1990), Promoting mutual forgiveness within the fractured relationship, *Psychotherapy, 27,* 219–223.

53. Enright et al. (1992); M. E. McCullough and E. L. Worthington (1994), Encouraging clients to forgive people who have hurt them: Review, critique, and research prospectus, *Journal of Psychology and Theology, 22,* 3–20; M. E. McCullough and E. L. Worthington (1994), Models of interpersonal forgiveness and their applications to counseling: Review and critique, *Counseling and Values, 39,* 2–14; J. N. Sells and T. D. Hargrave (1998), Forgiveness: A review of the theoretical and empirical literature, *Journal of Family Therapy, 20,* 21–36.

54. R. H. Al-Mabuk, C. V. Dedrick, and K. M. Vanderah (1998), Attribution retraining in forgiveness therapy, *Journal of Family Psychotherapy, 9,* 11–30; H. J. Aponte (1998), Love, the spiritual wellspring of forgiveness: An example of spirituality in therapy, *Journal of Family Therapy, 20,* 37–58; C. K. Benson (1992), Forgiveness and the psychotherapeutic process, *Journal of Psychology and Christianity, 11,* 76–81; Enright et al. (1992); R. D. Enright and the Human Development Study Group (1994), Piaget on the moral development of forgiveness: Identity or reciprocity? *Human Development, 37,* 63–80; Fitzgibbons (1986); Hope (1987); J. P. Pingleton (1989), The role and function of forgiveness in the psychotherapeutic process, *Journal of Psychology and Theology: An evangelical forum for the integration of psychology and theology, 17,* 27–35; C. M. Rosenak and G. M. Harden (1992), Forgiveness in the psychotherapeutic process: Clinical applications, *Journal of Psychology and Christianity, 11,* 188–197; H. Wahking (1992), Spiritual growth through grace and forgiveness, *Journal of Psychology and Christianity, 11,* 198–206; Walrond-Skinner (1998).

55. B. B. Cunningham (1985), The will to forgive: A pastoral theological view of forgiving, *The Journal of Pastoral Care, 49,* 141–149; F. A. DiBlasio (1998), The use of a decision-based forgiveness intervention within intergenerational family therapy, *Journal of Family Therapy, 20,* 77–94; G. Veenstra (1992), Psychological concepts of forgiveness, *Journal of Psychology and Christianity, 11,* 160–169; Worthington and DiBlasio (1990); E. L. Worthington (1998), An empathy–humility–commitment model

of forgiveness applied within family dyads, *Journal of Family Therapy, 20,* 59–76.

56. T. D. Hargrave and J. N. Sells (1997), The development of a forgiveness scale, *Journal of Marital and Family Therapy, 23,* 41–62; P. A. Mauger, T. Freeman, J. E. Perry, D. C. Grove, A. G. McBride, and K. E. McKinney (1992), The measurement of forgiveness: Preliminary research, *Journal of Psychology and Christianity, 11,* 170–180; M. E. McCullough, K. E. Rachel, S. T. Sandage, E. L. Worthington, S. W. Brown, and T. L. Hight (1998), Interpersonal forgiving in close relationships: II Theoretical elaboration and measurement, *Journal of Personality and Social Psychology, 75,* 1586–1603; M. W. Pollard, R. A. Anderson, W. T. Anderson, and G. Jennings (1998), The development of a family forgiveness scale, *Journal of Family Therapy, 20,* 95–109.

57. Woodman (1992).

58. M. K. Nelson (1992), A new theory of forgiveness, unpublished dissertation, Purdue University.

59. McCullough et al. (1998).

60. D. L. Fenell (1993), Characteristics of longer-term first marriages, *Journal of Mental Health and Counseling, 15,* 446–460.

61. Fitzgibbon (1986); McCullough and Worthington (1994); M. E. McCullough and E. L. Worthington (1995), Promoting forgiveness: A comparison of two brief psychoeducational group interventions with a waiting list control, *Counseling and Values, 40,* 55–68; Worthington and DiBlasio (1990); Worthington (1998).

62. I. Boszormenyi-Nagy and B. R. Krasner (1986), *Between give and take: A clinical guide to contextual therapy* (New York: Burnner/Mazel).

63. J. K. Neumann and D. S. Chi (1993, April), Total T-cells and forgiveness, paper presented at the annual meeting of the Christian Association for Psychological Studies, Kansas City, MO.

64. Freedman and Enright (1996); B. H. Kaplan (1992), Social health and the forgiving heart: The type B story, *Journal of Behavioral Medicine, 15,* 3–14; R. B. Williams and V. Williams (1993), *Anger kills: Seventeen strategies for controlling hostility that can harm your health* (New York: HarperCollins).

65. J. A. Strasser (1984), The relation of general forgiveness and forgiveness type to reported health in the elderly, unpublished dissertation, Catholic University of America.

66. M. F. Trainer (1981), Forgiveness: Intrinsic, role-expected, expedient, in the context of divorce, unpublished dissertation, Boston University.

Love, Respect, and Compassion in Families

Howard M. Bahr, A. Scott Loveless, Ivan F. Beutler

Husband and wife have a solemn responsibility to love and care for each other and for their children. . . .
Parents have a sacred duty to rear their children in love and righteousness, to provide for their physical and spiritual
needs, to teach them to love and serve one another. . . . Successful marriages and families are established and
maintained on principles of . . . respect, love, compassion, . . . By divine design, fathers are to preside over their
families in love and righteousness.
(The Family: A Proclamation to the World, ¶¶ 6, 7)

The word *love* appears five times in the Proclamation on the family. Each time it is combined with one or more action terms, as in "to love and care" or "to love and serve." Love is portrayed as solemn responsibility, sacred duty, practice to be taught, principle of family establishment, and aspect of family leadership. The language of the Proclamation suggests that love is something we may *do,* that we have some choice about and can direct. In contrast, much modern usage suggests that love is something we "fall into" and "out of," something that "hits us." In fact, the idea of love as a "solemn responsibility" seems strange in a society where love is often portrayed as mindless irresponsibility or subordination of head to heart.

In this chapter we explore the meaning of love as it is used in the scriptures and elsewhere, and we look at love in families, including issues of why love is so important and principles that may be applied to make our families more loving. Finally, we consider the related principles of respect and compassion in families.

Definitions: What Is Love?

When the rich young man asked Jesus, "What good thing shall I do, that I may have eternal life?" (Matt. 19:16), part of Jesus' answer was the command to love his neighbor. In order to understand this

commandment we must know what Jesus meant by the word *love,* for in today's world it has many meanings. It may express exalted or romantic feeling, strong affection or interest, commitment, concern, satisfaction, preference, or mere sexual gratification. Plainly, until we understand the Savior's definition of love, we may have difficulty obeying Him. President Gordon B. Hinckley describes love and its fruits in family life this way:

> Love is the very essence of life. It is the pot of gold at the end of the rainbow. Yet it is more than the end of the rainbow. Love is at the beginning also, and from it springs the beauty that arches across the sky on a stormy day. Love is the security for which children weep, the yearning of youth, the adhesive that binds marriage, and the lubricant that prevents devastating friction in the home; it is the peace of old age, the sunlight of hope shining through death. How rich are those who enjoy it in their associations with family, friends, church, and neighbors. . . . love, like faith, is a gift of God.[1]

Aspects of Love: Heart, Might, Mind, Strength, Soul

Love is multidimensional, involving different aspects of our being. The scriptural commandments to love are rarely stated in a simple, one-verb form. Instead a more complex form is used that combines

EXAMPLES OF LOVE AND ACTION
IN THE COMMANDMENTS

Ex. 20:5–6: . . . for I the Lord thy God am a jealous God . . . shewing mercy unto thousands of them that *love me, and keep my commandments.*

Lev. 19:18–19: . . . thou shalt *love thy neighbour* as thyself: I am the Lord. Ye shall *keep my statutes.*

Deut. 10:12–13: . . . what doth the Lord thy God require of thee, but *to fear the Lord thy God, to walk* in all his ways, *and to love him, and to serve* the Lord thy God with all thy heart and with all thy soul, *to keep the commandments of the Lord?*

Deut. 13:3–4: . . . for the Lord your God proveth you, *to know whether ye love* the Lord your God with all your heart and with all your soul. *Ye shall walk* after the Lord your God, *and fear* him, *and keep* his commandments, *and obey* his voice, *and ye shall serve* him, *and cleave* unto him.

Neh. 1:5: . . . O Lord God of heaven . . . that keepeth covenant and mercy for them *that love* him *and observe* his commandments.

Mosiah 4:15: But ye will teach them [children] *to walk* in the ways of truth and soberness; ye will teach them *to love* one another, *and to serve* one another.

D&C 20:19: And gave unto them commandments that they should *love and serve* him, the only living and true God.

D&C 42:22: *Thou shalt love* thy wife with all thy heart, *and shalt cleave* unto her and none else. (Emphasis added.)

Box 12.1

"thou shalt love" with a verb or noun phrase denoting action of some kind. Several such combinations are shown in Box 12.1.

God commands us to love in language that teaches us that love is more than interior feeling, that heart, might, mind, and strength are all united in love. Over and over, in "love and serve," "walk and keep," "love and obey," and "love and cleave," the point is made that genuine love requires each aspect of self, not just part of us. The heart is essential, as is the mind, and so is the "might" of physical activity, of doing as the love-filled heart directs. There is no choice but to act if we truly love, for He has said that if we love Him we will keep His commandments (John 14:15). In our marriages and families, we must love with our heart, our minds, our spirit, and our hands.

While love may reside in heart or mind, and

therefore may partake of the emotions, it is more than emotion, for it also is manifest in other parts of the self. Love is a feeling, but not *only* a feeling. It is behavior, but not *only* behavior. And our capacity to love and our behavior in loving is subject to our control, or God could not command us to love, nor could we teach love to our children.

THE OBJECTS OF OUR LOVE

We will now consider three dominant perspectives on love, beginning with the "self-love" of modern self-esteem psychology. Then we examine the commandment to "love thy neighbor," both as the "royal law" of neighbor-as-self and in light of the Savior's "new commandment" of celestial altruism.

Self-Love and Self-Esteem

The self-esteem movement of popular psychology is a dominant, widely accepted modern worldview. It has reshaped social priorities across a wide range of topics ranging from what makes a healthy childhood to what constitutes a meaningful life. It has even redefined the objects toward which we direct our love. The self-esteem literature frequently places love of self in priority over love of God and love of neighbor. Little wonder that Latter-day Saint philosopher James Faulconer expresses concern that many in the LDS community seem to have accepted the worldly philosophy of self-priority.[2]

Some have accepted the notion that "you have to love yourself before you can love others" as if it were part of the gospel. Yet this is a modern idea based in secular psychology. Self-esteem is not part of the scriptural or historic Christian heritage. Indeed, Faulconer argues, the whole notion of "self-image" as something we should focus on, evaluate, polish, work to improve, and in effect serve, verges on the love of other gods forbidden in the first commandment and the idolatry forbidden in the second.

Alleged scriptural justifications for the acclaimed self-priority of our time have helped to skirt its hedonistic underpinnings and to promote its general acceptance. The Savior's statement, "Thou shalt love thy neighbour as thyself" (Lev. 19:18) is often cited as if love of self is an important part of the equation. But remember that Jesus was quoting the Mosaic Law, using the "as thyself" to say, in effect, treat your neighbor at least as well as you treat yourself. In Faulconer's words:

The scripture assumes that those to whom it is addressed love themselves, but it doesn't command them to do so. . . . the command to love another as myself is not a command to love myself. It assumes I do, and it tells me to use that as a standard for loving others. Without adding something to it that isn't there, it says no more than that. . . . As such, it sets a minimum standard for conduct; it doesn't tell us that we ought to think of ourselves, either first or at all.[3]

We are commanded to be perfect, even as our Father is perfect (Matt. 5:48). Yet there are no scriptural references to His self-esteem: "When the scriptures speak of God's love, it is always his love of something other than himself."[4]

Nowhere in scripture are we told to love ourselves, but we are repeatedly commanded to love and serve God and our fellow beings. Love of self is explicitly condemned as wickedness to be avoided. Paul warned that "in the last days perilous times shall come. For men shall be lovers of their own selves, covetous, boasters, proud . . . lovers of pleasure more than lovers of God; . . . from such turn away" (2 Tim. 3:1–5). Jesus condemned untoward attention to self-image: "For whosoever exalteth himself shall be abased; and he that humbleth himself shall be exalted" (Luke 14:11). Paul counseled the Corinthians that "we dare not make ourselves of the number, or compare ourselves with some that commend themselves: but they measuring themselves by themselves, and comparing themselves among themselves, are not wise. . . . But he that glorieth, let him glory in the Lord" (2 Cor. 10:12, 17). In our day the Lord commands, "Exalt not yourselves " and "thou shalt not be proud in thy heart" (D&C 112:15; 42:40).

The traits named by the Savior as fitting for His people differ greatly from those sought by many of the secular proponents of self-esteem. The Lord asks us to be gentle, humble, unassertive enough to turn the other cheek, long-suffering, meek, and lowly of heart. Our hearts are to be broken, our spirits contrite, and "part of the sacrifice of a broken heart and a contrite spirit is a willingness to sacrifice the love affair so many of us have with our own egos."[5]

Anciently, Paul cautioned members of the Church that we "be not conformed to this world" (Rom. 12:2), and he specifically singled out pride in self for criticism. Each of us, he said, ought "not to think of *himself* more highly than he ought to think" (Rom. 12:3), and "if a man think himself to be something, when he is nothing, he deceiveth himself"(Gal 6:3; see 1 Cor. 8:1–2; 10:12).

We must not allow the eternal worth of a soul the gospel acknowledges as deriving from our celestial parentage to be twisted into the self-centered, pride-based "self-esteem" of the world, which is, in fact, its opposite.

The Royal Law: "Thy Neighbor As Thyself"

There are three scriptural accounts of the episode in which a Pharisaical antagonist, trying to catch the Savior in his words, asks him to choose from the Mosaic Law the greatest commandment (Matt. 22:34–40; Mark 12:28–31; Luke 10:25–37). In each, the answer is the same: "Thou shalt love the Lord God with all thy heart and with all thy soul, and with all thy strength, and with all thy mind; and thy neighbour as thyself" (Luke 10:27). The question dealt directly with the Law, and the Savior quoted the Law in his response (cf. Lev. 19:18, 34). This commandment to love neighbor as self was repeated many times by Jesus and his disciples, and the apostle James called it "the royal law" (James 2:8). The Law of Moses specified love for brethren, neighbors, and strangers, but not necessarily for enemies. Jesus amended the Law to include everyone, especially those whom one might not be disposed to love such as enemies or persons at whose hands one had suffered. He applied this principle of love not to a limited special group, but to all of mankind.

The Higher Law: "As I Have Loved You"

Near the end of His earthly ministry, the Savior gave a new principle of love that went beyond the Mosaic "neighbor as self" equivalence. His new commandment (John 13:34) set a higher standard for Christian love. We were now commanded to "love one another as I have loved you," and the potential sacrifice required was clarified in Jesus' statement that "greater love hath no man than this, that a man lay down his life for his friends" (John 15:13). In our obedience to this law, the sacrifice that is required is often, in Elder Hafen's memorable phrase, having the strength to "lay down her life for her sheep, even an hour at a time."[6] In our marriages and families we can joyfully make the daily sacrifices and do the daily service that Jesus exemplified in His life.

LOVE IN FAMILIES

Although the Savior's teachings clarified and extended the Mosaic commandments on love, Jesus did not deny the priorities of responsibility that derive from kinship and proximity. We too must be careful that our concern for humanity in the abstract does not impede our love for those near to us. The Savior's command that we love our neighbor implies proximity. Those close to us, both in kinship and physical proximity, have a special call upon our thoughts and attentions.

The Prophet Joseph Smith taught that people who had experienced God's love would be anxious to share it far and wide, beginning with their own families: "Love is one of the chief characteristics of Deity, and ought to be manifested by those who aspire to be the sons of God. A man filled with the love of God is not content with blessing his family alone, but ranges through the whole world, anxious to bless the whole human race."[7]

In a similar vein, Elder Carlos E. Asay assures us that "We fulfill both the letter and the spirit of the law when we love each other and serve each other, beginning within the family circle and reaching beyond to all people."[8]

Families occupy a special place in the divine economy of love. In addition to the general commandments that we are to love God and our neighbors, there are specific directives about love in families.

The commandment that husbands and wives are to live together in harmony and love goes back to God's instruction to Adam and Eve whereby they were to cleave to each other and be one.

The prophet Jacob, calling the Nephites to repentance, reminded them of the exemplary family devotion among the Lamanites: "Behold, their husbands love their wives, and their wives love their husbands; and their husbands and their wives love their children" (Jacob 3:7). Paul urged husbands to "love your wives, even as Christ also loved the church, and gave himself for it" (Eph. 5:25), and wives were "to love their husbands, [and] to love their children" (Titus 2:4).

Fathers and mothers are commanded to love their children, care for them, and teach them to love God and obey His commandments. In the Book of Mormon, Jacob pleads with wayward parents to "remember your children" (Jacob 3:10), lest the sins of the parents destroy their children. King Benjamin exhorts us to nurture our children both physically and spiritually. We are neither to neglect their physical care, nor permit them to "transgress the laws of God, and fight and quarrel one with another, and serve the devil." Instead, parents are to "teach them to

walk in the ways of truth and soberness . . . to love one another, and to serve one another" (Mosiah 4:14–15).

Sociologist Robert Bellah and his associates have shown that nowadays many people's ideas about family love tend to be grounded in a pervasive individualism that minimizes obligation, responsibility, and sacrifice. In this prevailing philosophy, finding "self-fulfillment" is the meaning of life, and it is said that people ought to be free to find their "true selves," independent of social constraints and cultural influence.[9] The main alternative to such individualism, Bellah says, is "altruistic commitment" based on traditional Judeo-Christian values. In this perspective:

> Love . . . becomes a matter of will and action rather than of feelings. While one cannot coerce one's feelings, one can learn to obey God's commands and to love others in a selfless way. . . . In Christian love, free choice and duty can be combined, but it is obligation that comes first. Then love of God can make one want to do what one is obligated to do. . . . Christian love is, in the view of its practitioners, built of solider stuff than personal happiness or enjoyment. It is, first, a commitment, a form of obedience to God's word. In addition, love rests less on feeling than on decision and action. Real love may even, at times, require emotional self-denial, pushing feelings to the back in order to live up to one's commitments.[10]

Such altruistic commitment still exists in our society, but it is far less visible than it once was. Indeed, "the spirit of the 1990s seems to tell us we are not fully free until we break loose from all relationships and commitments that tie us down. Belonging, in the modern view, seems to enslave rather than to enrich. . . . Ours is the age of the waning of belonging."[11]

Learning to Love in Families

Love is the most fundamental principle of the gospel. How do we learn to love, and how can we teach its practice? It is well established, both in modern revelation and by secular authority, that no group or social institution is more suited to teaching love than the human family. Elder Bruce Hafen writes that love is "nowhere more potent or more significant than in marriage and family life,"[12] and Elder Neal Maxwell says that it is in the family "wherein we can learn, first and best, about love, taking turns, negotiating, and restraining selfishness."[13] It is "the most efficient means for producing human happiness and human

SELF-CENTERED VERSUS OTHER-CENTERED LOVE

Every decision we make inescapably reveals our motivation, "for thee" or "for me." The consequences of each such moment-to-moment choice in life are far more profound than we are accustomed to believing, for when we approach others with love, we literally see the world in a different, healing way. For example, one evening several years ago I came home from a difficult day at work to find our house in shambles. We had four children under the age of eight, and they had strewn toys, clothes, blankets, papers, and even food from one end of the house to the other.

Ignoring my first thought that perhaps something was wrong and I should check with my wife, I became angry. My mental accusations were directed toward my wife (who obviously had fallen down in her "duties"), but I took my frustration out on the kids. I can still hear my words, louder than appropriate, "What's going on? You know the rules! No eating outside the kitchen! Don't you kids care what the house looks like? Now if this stuff isn't put where it belongs in the next ten minutes, I'm going to throw it in the trash!"

The children scattered to begin the clean-up. I cleared a spot on the edge of the couch and sat with my face in my hands, deep in exasperation and self-pity. When I looked up, there stood our six-year-old daughter, silently looking at me with tears in her eyes. Instantly, my world was transformed. *She* suddenly mattered, not I. My anger and self-pity vanished, and in that same moment I somehow knew that what she needed was to hear me acknowledge that she was trying to be a good girl. When I did so, she beamed, hugged me around the neck, and ran off to help in the cleaning. For my part, I sought out each child, held each one while I apologized, and then helped them straighten the house.

At the time I did not realize what had happened. Looking back now, I understand that my concern had shifted from myself, from the problems these people were causing me, to my daughter and the other children. In that moment of change, I again was loving them, and their needs far outweighed my own need for a restful evening in a spotless house. My *heart* had changed, and with it my way of seeing and being in the world with others. When we love, we no longer view personal preferences as needs and we are replenished not by seeking to acquire but by giving. As I experienced that day, when another's needs came first, meeting those needs became my need. My self-centered "needs" disappeared, as did all of the accompanying and incredibly draining negative emotions.[37]

A. Scott Loveless

Box 12.2

goodness," the place where "God's extraordinary work is most often done by ordinary people."[14]

James Q. Wilson devotes an entire book to the proposition that "people have a natural moral sense, a sense that is formed out of the interaction of their innate dispositions with their earliest familial experiences."[15] He concludes:

> Families are the world in which we shape and manage our emotions. . . . The family is a continuous locus of reciprocal obligations that constitute an unending school for moral instruction. . . . We learn to cope with the people of this world because we learn to cope with the members of our family. Those who flee the family flee the world; bereft of the former's affection, tutelage, and challenges, they are unprepared for the latter's tests, judgments, and demands.[16]

Families are also the environment in which many of our failures to love occur, and where much of the struggle to learn patience, meekness, and long-suffering takes place. If we are to learn the practice of love in the family, then the family must be a family of love. "Wickedness never was happiness" (Alma 41:10), and love does not flow from contention or neglect. President Gordon B. Hinckley warns that "the warm sunlight of love will not rise out of a swamp of immorality."[17]

The tension between the two competing worldviews, individualism or self-priority versus altruistic commitment or other-orientation, is not merely a struggle between people committed to different values. It is also a struggle *within* each of us, an ongoing series of choices in which we decide whose interests or "needs" will be granted priority, ours or the others in or out of our circle. The nature of this internal struggle, and the kinds of family outcomes that flow from each priority, are treated in Box 12.2.

While we are commanded to love and serve with every part of our being, sometimes we will be better in some dimensions than others. One aspect of our love may lag; our spirits may be willing, but our flesh weak; our hearts in tune, but our strength lacking. Presumably, growth in the exercise of love in one dimension of our being may foster growth in the other dimensions. How, then, shall we teach our children to love? How do we practice love together? Here are five love-creating principles that apply to family life.

1. Family love grows as we serve and sacrifice for each other. In this scenario, we become what we do. That is, we become loving people as we serve and sacrifice. Our capacities to love are increased by bearing each other's burdens. The experience of sorrow and joy in living with, caring for, and serving others can increase our capacity to love. Speaking of the Savior, Elder Bruce and Sister Marie Hafen write that "the height of his infinite capacity for joy is the inverse, mirror image of the depth of his capacity to bear our burdens." And as it is with Him, so it can be for us. Our sorrows and sacrifices "carve and stretch" the "caverns of feeling within our own hearts," and as these caverns are enlarged "they expand our soul's capacity for joy."[18]

Where does love come from? Elder Henry B. Eyring promises that "the Atonement working in our lives will produce in us the love and tenderness we need." In simple, practical terms, he asks us to seek opportunities to work in behalf of others. He illustrates the principle with this experience:

> Not long ago . . . my wife and I were in a hurry, getting ready to go somewhere. We were both under pressure, and I was pretty much turned inward toward myself, but I thought a thought. It's the thought I'd suggest you try: "Everything I have that's good is a gift from God. How would he have me use my gifts to serve someone?" And I simply asked my wife if there was anything I could do for her. It turned out that there was—I made the bed. It was such a small thing that I'm sure it doesn't sound very impressive to you, and it probably wasn't very impressive to her either. I could have done more. But as I did that simple little thing, I felt something that I've felt before. When I gave of my time in a way I thought the Savior would want me to for my wife, not only did my love for her increase—I also felt *His* love for her.
>
> I promise you that if you'll use your gifts to serve someone else, you'll feel the Lord's love for that person. You'll also feel his love for you. And you'll be preparing for times when you will be called to serve people and to love them.[19]

President Hinckley emphasizes the power of service to create enduring love between husband and wife: "Any man who will make his wife's comfort his first concern will stay in love with her throughout their lives and through the eternity yet to come."[20] That love is created by mutual support and sacrifice is implicit in the statement by a Papago Indian woman about the source of her affection for her husband: "I had grown fond of him. We had starved together so much."[21]

Under the heading "family love is action-oriented," a recent family text contained this wise counsel: "Among a parent's kindest acts of love are creating opportunities for children to learn love, by service and sacrifice, for example is an inadequate teacher of love. One learns to love by loving, not by being loved; and to serve by serving, not by being served. If children are always served, without the opportunity of serving in return, they learn to take, not to give."[22]

2. Love produces love: Loving acts generate love among the recipients of love. Not only does our love increase as a natural consequence of our service to others, but if we are sensitive and receptive to the Spirit, we come to love those who have served and sacrificed for us. In some measure, we become what is done to us. In this context, it is not enough that another makes declarations of love: action is the key to positive change. Relevant here is the Apostle James's challenge to faith without works. It applies as well to love: "If a brother or sister be naked, and destitute of daily food, And one of you say unto them, Depart in peace, be *ye* warmed and filled; notwithstanding ye give them not those things which are needful to the body; what *doth* it profit? Even so faith [or love], if it hath not works, is dead, being alone" (James 2:15–17). Here the proof of love is the visible fruit of that emotion, in behavior we can see.

3. Love produces love: Acts of love generate love among those who see and hear. Loving acts may also produce love among those who observe the interaction of love, even though they themselves are neither the givers nor the recipients. In this situation, we become what we see. As we perceive the loving acts of others, we internalize the virtues of love and are influenced to emulate them. This scenario for the generation of love is particularly relevant in our media culture of vicarious viewing, both of good and evil. Example alone may be an inadequate teacher, but it is a beginning.

If we become what we see, then parents can create love among their children by modeling love in their lives. Thus, President Benson counseled mothers, "Do nothing in your life to cause your daughters to stumble because of your example. . . . Teach them to love home because you love home."[23]

4. Love produces obedience, and obedience invites the promptings of the Spirit, which enhance love. Our obedience and humility open us to the influence of the Spirit, and as we feel the Spirit, we are increasingly open to divine grants of love. Here, we become what we feel, but the feelings themselves derive in part from our showing obedience to gospel principles, especially prayer, fasting, reading the scriptures, and honestly seeking to follow the Savior in our families.

Take family prayer as an example. President Hinckley promises that if we remember to pray for the poor and the needy, there grows within us "a love for others above self, a respect for others, a desire to serve the needs of others." How, then, to teach our children love and respect for their neighbors? Pray for the neighbors, for, "One cannot ask God to help a neighbor in distress without feeling motivated to do something toward helping that neighbor." In like manner, praying in our families for heads of government increases our love of country, and praying for leaders of the Church increases our love and respect for them.[24]

5. After all we can do, love is a gift of God. We pray for love, to be "filled" with it, in general terms, and most especially when we are having difficulty with a particular "neighbor." Our efforts to build love into our families would fail were it not for the infusions of divine love that we are granted along the way. Like Lehi, having partaken of the love of God and found it to be sweet above all earthly sweetness, we desire that our families also may partake. Here, the prophet Mormon can be our guide:

> Wherefore, my beloved brethren, pray unto the Father with all the energy of heart, that ye may be filled with this love, which he hath bestowed upon all who are true followers of his Son, Jesus Christ; that ye may become the sons of God; that when he shall appear we shall be like him, for we shall see him as he is; that we may have this hope; that we may be purified even as he is pure. (Moro. 7:48)

RESPECT AND LOVE IN FAMILIES

Respect seems to accompany love, either as an attitude that fosters love or as an outgrowth of love. Like love, respect manifests itself both as feeling and action. Its Latin roots suggest a looking back or a second look. In English usage it refers to feelings of honor or esteem, expressed in deference and courtesy. Respect is shown in acts of concern, consideration, deference, regard, and honor. It denotes an appreciation of worth, a regard and esteem that see beyond appearances, a "seeing through" that appreciates the sanctity of things, persons, or life itself. We may also understand respect by thinking about its opposite: "To treat the sacred without respecting its

---

A PARENT'S PLEA: "CAN'T YOU SEE WHO HE REALLY IS?"

We arrived home from the ball game after 9:00 P.M. There was a message on the answering machine from an anxious customer who had not received his newspaper. Joshua felt sure he had delivered the paper to Mr. Wood's box, but for two weeks now there had been an irregular and annoying disappearance of this neighbor's paper. The evening was clear as we biked across our neighborhood to deliver Mr. Wood's paper. Joshua appreciated my company on the errand, but wanted to feel some independence and asked me to wait at the corner of the house. I could hear his knock, and anticipated a greeting of appreciation for a second effort rendered on this cool winter night. Instead Mr. Wood responded with impatience and contempt, "Well, it's about time! I'm not sure why I put up with this lack of service. You have ruined my entire evening and I'm reporting this to your supervisor."

I was surprised at my response. I remained silent, but I actually felt pity for this brother, a full-grown man who thought only of himself, and hadn't thought enough of this child to inquire about the circumstances. Worse yet, he had no idea whom he was addressing in such derogatory terms. I knew Joshua to be a chosen son of our Father in Heaven. I was present at his birth and felt, as other fathers have, the magnitude of this child's worth in the courts on high. The preceding summer we had hiked the high Uintahs and I had listened to the tender voice of this eight-year-old as from memory he sang for hours the hymns he had learned in Primary and at his mother's knee, more than the rest of our group combined could recall. I had been voice for priesthood blessings and knew something of this lad's remarkable life's mission. This was the young man that I knew, and so it was regrettable that a neighbor of mature years was speaking to him so harshly. Surely, he did not know to whom he spoke.

Ivan F. Beutler

Box 12.3

---

sacredness—this is the heart of what traditionally has been called sin."[25]

In its components of deference and regard, respect is related to reverence. President David O. McKay linked reverence to respect and love when he defined reverence as "profound respect mingled with love."[26] President Hinckley promises that we would enjoy more peace, security, and love in our homes "if husbands and wives would cultivate the discipline of speaking softly one to another, and if both would so speak to their children."[27] "Quiet talk," he says, "is the language of love. It is the language of peace. It is the language of God. . . . The voice of heaven is a still small voice. The voice of peace in the home is a quiet voice."[28]

Why is there a connection between respect and family love? The behavior we call respectful is based on an awareness of who our spouse and children really are, of our "seeing beyond" the present moment. That "seeing beyond" which is the essence of respect is illustrated in the experience recorded in Box 12.3.

The ordinariness of our daily comings and goings may make us forget how special our families are. To be disrespectful is to be "blind to the meaning of things."[29] Often our blindness is greatest when we are at home with our families. We need to be reminded of the holiness of that which we take for granted. One such reminder is C. S. Lewis's insight that there are no ordinary people:

> It is a serious thing to live in a society [or family] of possible gods and goddesses, to remember that the dullest and most uninteresting person you can talk to may one day be a creature which, if you saw it now, you would be strongly tempted to worship, or else a horror and a corruption such as you now meet, if at all, only in a nightmare. All day long we are, in some degree, helping each other to one or other of these destinations. It is in the light of these overwhelming possibilities, it is with the awe and the circumspection proper to them, that we should conduct all our dealing with one another, all friendships, all loves, all play, all politics. There are no *ordinary* people.[30]

Respect relates to love for one's neighbor as reverence relates to one's love for God. Just as Moses' communication with God depended, in part, on an initial demonstration of his respect for holy ground, so does successful, loving communication in the home depend on our truthful recognition of who and where we are. Elder Neal A. Maxwell says that our reverence (or respect) for others, grounded in the knowledge of our eternal relationships to God and His children, is the foundation of our capacity to love.[31]

Respect accompanies love in successful families. President Hinckley maintains that strong family life comes of parents who love and respect one another, and who love and respect and nurture their children in the ways of the Lord. He urges fathers and mothers to respect their children, for "they are children of God, sons and daughters of God. They are His. . . .

Let love prevail between you and your children." He identifies "love, a spirit of sacrifice, [and] an attitude of respect for one another" as characteristics of "great homes" and predicts that "there will be need for greater emphasis of these qualities in the future."[32] If respect is essential to love, what happens to a society that disdains respect? If family love is inseparable from respect, might some of the contemporary disintegration of the family be attributable to the decline of respect?

How do we build respect? Do we remember that our children are really children of God? Do we remind them of their celestial heritage? Our success in helping them to appreciate their divine ancestry depends on how we treat them. Their respect for their own sanctity grows as they are treated as noble children of God, and their respect for home increases as parents treat it as an outpost of heaven.

COMPASSION AND LOVE IN FAMILIES

The word *compassion* literally means "to suffer together." It suggests a love for others strong enough to make us willing to share their suffering, "to mourn with those that mourn" and "comfort those that stand in need of comfort" (Mosiah 18:9). In addition to an empathy such that we resonate to another's pain, compassion includes a desire to aid and comfort the suffering one. If we are to become like God, we too must be "full of compassion," being moved upon to help as we confront someone's need (see Luke 10:33; Mark 6:34–42; Luke 7:11–14; 3 Ne. 17:6–9).

The Lord teaches us of compassion in two striking biblical images involving parents. In Isaiah, He offers perhaps the strongest image of loving family commitment, the nursing mother: "Can a woman forget her sucking child, that she should not have compassion on the son of her womb?" He asks, then assures us that His love for us far exceeds that mortal standard: "Yea, they may forget, yet will I not forget thee" (Isa. 49:15). In the parable of the prodigal son, the image is that of the compassionate father. The disgraced, wastrel son returns home, expecting little, but "when he was yet a great way off, his father saw him, and had compassion, and ran, and fell on his neck, and kissed him" (Luke 15:20).

Our practice of compassion may be informed by examining instances in the scriptural account of the Savior's ministry when the term *compassion* is used. Jesus spoke of compassion in three parables: the unjust servant, the good Samaritan, and the prodigal son. In addition, Jesus is described as having compassion toward the multitudes, whom He teaches, heals, and feeds. Finally, there are the instances in which the term is used to describe the Savior's responses to pleas for help.

These episodes of compassion shed light on the practice of compassion in our own lives. First, compassion moves us. It is not passive. Compassion moves the father of the prodigal to rejoice, impels the Samaritan to minister to the wounded, and prompts Jesus to raise the widow's son. Facing a famished multitude or answering a leper's plea, Jesus is "moved with compassion" (Matt. 9:36; 14:14; Mark 1:41). We conclude that compassion necessarily involves action; the urge to help must produce more than mere sympathy. The good Samaritan's compassion is shown in his willingness to delay his journey and help, rather than simply passing by with a wish that the poor fellow had eluded his assailants.

Second, moved by compassion, the Savior responded with personal involvement: He touched the blind man's eyes, reached out to the leper, put His hand to the funeral bier, took children one by one into His arms and blessed them (see Matt. 19:13–15; 20:34; Mark 1:41; 10:16; Luke 7:13–14; 3 Ne. 17:21). Here we must conclude that the compassion approved by heaven involves much of hands-on, "getting hands dirty" effort. The Savior's example prompts us to answer need with personal action—reaching, touching, rubbing shoulders, and sharing tasks. During His earthly ministry, Jesus did not attempt to solve the problems or heal the suffering of the whole world. His Atonement would, in fact, do that, but during His ministry, His hands could reach only so far. But wherever He was, He reached out and touched, listened, and healed.

The tears of deity are instructive, revealing more of compassion. The Savior's deep emotional involvement is manifest in His tears for the fate of Jerusalem (Luke 19:41), His empathetic "groanings within" for those who mourned Lazarus (John 11:44–38), His tears and groanings for the suffering and sins of the world (Moses 7:28; 3 Ne. 17:14), and His tears of joy and love for the faithful Nephites and their children (3 Ne. 17:21–22). Looking for parallels among us mortals, we remember Paul's testimony "that by the space of three years I ceased not to warn every one night and day with tears" (Acts 21:31), and the Lord's statement that the Prophet Joseph Smith's prayers and "weeping for Zion" had been heard and accepted (D&C 21:8). One wonders whether our own compassion is measured by our supplications and tears for others, and especially the tears that accompany the challenges, loves and losses of family life.

"Marriage," writes Elder Jeffrey R. Holland, "is the highest and holiest of all human relationships. . . . It offers never-ending opportunities for the practice of every Christian virtue and for the demonstration of truly divine love."[33] The family is not the only place where we may learn compassion, but for most of us the experience of love and sacrifice in our family life presents the occasions in which we confront the needs of others, and suffer, comfort, and mourn with them. As parents we have recognizable, visceral experience with compassion, indicated in the hollowness in our stomachs as we yearn to help a child who performs, the sick feelings within as we search for a lost child, the anguish we experience in the face of a child's affliction. Indeed, many aspects of our parenting may be seen as mortal versions of the "unlimited parental commitment" the Savior feels for those who are His sons and daughters because they have been born again spiritually through Him. Like the Savior, we grow in compassion through the sacrifices of parenthood:

> A mother descends into the dark valley of pain and death, risking her life to bring forth the life of her child. And when the child is born, she feels the awesome limitlessness of maternal bonds that are stronger than the cords of death. This sacrifice, understandable to any parent, yet most understandable to mothers, mirrors both the Savior's sacrifice and his everlasting commitment to nourish and cherish the children of Christ for whom he offered his body and his blood.[34]

Elder and Sister Hafen have suggested that the "bonds" of marriage and family life are really liberating opportunities to serve and grow. Without such "bonds," they say, we might never be "forced" to "tap into the reservoirs of strength and compassion we carry within ourselves."

> The demanding intimacy of familistic commitments tests us and teaches us in ways that are impossible in short-term, casual relationships. It isn't that difficult to be polite and fair toward church, business, and social acquaintances. But it requires real compassion to be patient and unselfish with those who, over many years, share the same possessions, the same checkbook, and the same name. . . . If we can't learn to be compassionate in the bonds of family life, we are probably not compassionate—Christlike—in any

important sense. But if we let ourselves become what our bonds demand of us, we will develop the capacity to be compassionate not only with family companions but also with everyone else. That will be our spiritual liberation.[35]

CONCLUSION

We have said that family love grows as we serve and sacrifice for each other, and our loving acts generate love among those we love and serve. Acts of love generate love among those who see our loving behavior, and our obedience to the loving example of the Savior opens our lives to the influence of the Holy Spirit and to divine grants of love. For in the last analysis we may obtain a love like the pure love of the Savior—the love that is called charity in the scriptures—only as a gift from God (Moro. 7:47–48). Elder Hafen states that "Charity in its full-blown sense is '*bestowed* upon' Christ's righteous followers. Its source, like all other blessings of the Atonement, is the grace of God."[36] All family members have access to this gift of charity and should seek it, that they might truly manifest divine love, respect, and compassion for each other, and for our Heavenly Father's other children.

NOTES

1. Gordon B. Hinckley (1989), *Faith: The essence of true religion.* (Salt Lake City: Deseret Book), 44.

2. James Faulconer (1993, June), Self-love, self-image, and salvation, *Latter-day Digest, 2*(3), 7–26.

3. Faulconer (1993, June), 13.

4. Faulconer (1993, June), 12.

5. Bruce C. Hafen (1989), *The broken heart: Applying the Atonement to life's experiences* (Salt Lake City: Deseret Book), 119.

6. Bruce C. Hafen (1996, November), Covenant marriage, *Ensign, 26*(11), 27.

7. Joseph Smith, quoted in George Q. Cannon (1986), *Life of Joseph Smith, the Prophet* (Salt Lake City: Deseret Book), 330.

8. Carlos E. Asay (1992), *Family pecan trees* (Salt Lake City: Deseret Book), 170.

9. Robert N. Bellah, Richard Madsen, William M. Sullivan, Ann Swidler, and Steven M. Tipton (1985), *Habits of the heart: Individualism and commitment in American life* (New York: Harper & Row), 108, 109, 150.

10. Bellah et al. (1985), 94, 97.

11. Bruce C. Hafen and Marie K. Hafen (1994), *The belonging heart: The Atonement and relationships with God and family* (Salt Lake City: Deseret Book), 42–43.

12. Bruce C. Hafen (1990), *The believing heart: Nourishing the seed of faith* (2nd ed.) (Salt Lake City: Deseret Book), 87.

13. Neal A. Maxwell (1982), *We will prove them herewith* (Salt Lake City: Deseret Book), 90.

14. Neal A. Maxwell (1974), *That my family should partake* (Salt Lake City: Deseret Book), 7, 122.

15. James Q. Wilson (1993), *The moral sense* (New York: Free Press), 2.

16. Wilson (1993), 162–163.

17. Gordon B. Hinckley (1997), *The teachings of Gordon B. Hinckley* (Salt Lake City: Deseret Book), 202.

18. Hafen and Hafen (1994), 315–316.

19. Henry B. Eyring (1997), *To draw closer to God* (Salt Lake City: Deseret Book), 88.

20. Hinckley (1997), 329.

21. C. Niethammer (1977), *Daughters of the earth: The lives and legends of American Indian women* (New York: Collier Books), 90.

22. W. R. Burr, R. D. Day, and K. S. Bahr (1993), *Family science* (Pacific Grove, CA: Brooks/Cole), 122.

23. Ezra Taft Benson (1990), *Come, listen to a prophet's voice* (Salt Lake City: Deseret Book), 23.

24. Gordon B. Hinckley (1981), *Be thou an example* (Salt Lake City: Deseret Book), 31; Gordon B. Hinckley (1989), 71.

25. A. B. Schmookler (1993), *Fool's gold: The fate of values in a world of goods* (New York: Harper), 11.

26. David O. McKay (1967, April), in Conference report, 86–87.

27. Hinckley (1997), 201.

28. Hinckley (1997), 324–325.

29. Schmookler (1993), 1.

30. C. S. Lewis (1996). *The weight of glory* (New York: Simon & Schuster), 39.

31. Neal A. Maxwell (1979), *All these things shall give thee experience* (Salt Lake City: Deseret Book), 67–68.

32. Hinckley (1997), 202–203, 205, 405.

33. Jeffrey R. Holland (1985), 99.

34. Hafen and Hafen (1994), 144.

35. Hafen and Hafen (1994), 183–184.

36. Bruce C. Hafen (1989), 195.

37. A. S. Loveless (1994), What in the world is love? *This People,* Holiday issue, 40–48.

CHAPTER 13

THE MEANING AND BLESSINGS OF FAMILY WORK

KATHLEEN SLAUGH BAHR, CHERI A. LOVELESS, KRISTINE MANWARING,
MAUREEN RICE, AND VAUGHN E. WORTHEN

Successful marriages and families are established and maintained on principles of . . . work . . . .
(The Family: A Proclamation to the World, ¶ 7)

One day a week we deep-clean the house together. My parents divide us into teams. We hate this. They force us to work together. We get along much better when we aren't working so close together. Usually it ends up in a yelling match, and then my parents freak out. My mom starts crying because we aren't getting along, and therefore we aren't righteous enough and she's failed as a mother. Then my dad gets upset because Mom is upset. The result: We are forced to spend more time with each other to prepare us for eternal life as a family. Cleaning the house is a miserable experience for everyone.[1]

So wrote one BYU student, and her feelings are not uncommon. Family work—the necessary, hands-on labor of sustaining life, such as feeding, clothing, and sheltering a family—has become the work that no one wants to do. Usually referred to as "housework," it has also become a major source of contention between the sexes. One study found that six months into marriage, disagreement over allocation of household chores was the number one source of conflict between husband and wife and remained so after five years.[2]

In stark contrast, the Proclamation states that caring for a spouse and children is "a solemn responsibility" and that providing for the physical needs of one's children is "a sacred duty" (¶ 6). The Proclamation also adds "work" to the list of principles on which "successful marriages and families are established and maintained," in the same context as faith, prayer, repentance, and compassion (¶ 7). President Gordon B. Hinckley states that families working together are part of the antidote for society's worst ills:

> The observance of four simple things on the part of parents would in a generation or two turn our societies around in terms of their moral values.
>
> They are simply these: Let parents and children (1) teach and learn goodness together, (2) *work together,* (3) read good books together, and (4) pray together.[3]

Have we lost sight of the true nature of work? Is it possible for families to develop a strong family work ethic in a day when many consider household work a waste of time? If so, how? These and related questions will be explored in this chapter.

FAMILY WORK IS ESSENTIAL TO A JOYFUL FAMILY LIFE

When Adam and Eve left the Garden, they exchanged an existence where life was sustained without effort for a life of work and trials. Traditionally, Christians think of such labor as a curse, but a close reading of the scriptures reveals otherwise. God cursed *the ground* to bring forth thorns and thistles, which in turn forced Adam to labor. And yet Adam was told, "Cursed shall be the ground *for thy sake*" (Moses 4:23; emphasis added). In other words, the hard work of eating bread "By the sweat of thy face" (Moses 4:25) was meant to be a blessing.

According to Paul, so was the work of bearing and rearing children: "[Eve] *shall be saved* in childbearing, if they continue in faith and charity and holiness with sobriety" (I Tim. 2:15; emphasis added). Significantly, Joseph Smith revised this verse to read, "*They* shall be saved in childbearing" (JST; emphasis added), indicating that more than sparing Eve's physical life was at issue. Somehow both Adam and Eve would be privileged to return to their Heavenly Father through the labor of bringing forth and caring for their offspring.

What does such ordinary, family-centered work have to do with salvation? The answer is so obvious in common experience that it has become obscure: Family work links people. It does so by providing endless opportunities to recognize and fill the needs of others. In every dispensation of time, in every culture, whether in poverty or prosperity, people need to be fed, clothed, sheltered, and succored. Family work is universal and, by its nature, can bind us to one another.

Note that although Adam and Eve were each given a specific stewardship, they helped one another in their labors. Adam brought forth the fruit of the earth with Eve working by his side (see Moses 5:1); Eve bore children, but Adam joined her in teaching them (see Moses 5:12). When family members work side by side in the right spirit, a foundation of caring and commitment grows out of their shared daily experience. The most ordinary tasks, like fixing meals or doing laundry, hold great potential for connecting us to those we serve and those with whom we serve. One young man described it this way: "I never realized why my older brother and I were such good friends. When we were in our early teens, we helped my dad build our house, install the sprinklers, landscape the yard, and do all sorts of odds-and-ends jobs. I remember many times when we would have to cooperate to accomplish many of our work goals. . . . Now that we are older, there is a bond that we share because we worked side by side in our developing years."[4]*

Ironically, the things commonly disliked about family work offer the greatest possibilities for nurturing close relationships. For instance, our larger culture suggests that family work is mindless. Yet, chores that can be done with a minimum of concentration

leave our minds free to focus on one another while we labor. Unlike playing together, which often requires mental as well as physical involvement, sharing an everyday task seems to dissolve feelings of hierarchy, inviting intimate conversation that otherwise might not take place.

One college student wrote, "Some of the best times with my dad were when I would help him do yard work. . . . We'd have some of our best talks about life as we raked leaves or hauled wood."[5] Another stated, "I think picking strawberries and string beans was especially productive as a family because the work was long and mundane. The quiet, almost mentally effortless work is fertile soil for conversation. I sometimes miss those days."*

We also tend to think of household work as menial; and much of it is. Yet, because it is menial, even the smallest child can make a meaningful contribution. Preschoolers can learn to fold laundry, wash walls, or sort silverware with sufficient skill to feel valued as part of the family. Since daily tasks range from the simple (chopping, folding, scrubbing) to the complex (prioritizing, organizing, training others), participants at every level can feel competent yet challenged, including the parents with their overall responsibility for coordinating tasks, people, and projects into a cooperative, working whole.

Another aspect of family work that bothers many people is its repetitiveness, especially when the same labor must be performed several times a day. However, each rendering of a task is a new invitation for all to enter the family circle. The most ordinary chores can become daily rituals of family love and belonging. One young man from a family that "rarely does any activities together" and "has never gone on vacation together nor [has] ever once had family home evening" fondly remembers cooking together:

> The most fun thing we would prepare together was enchiladas. It was definitely a group project because we would always form an assembly line. My dad would prepare the tortillas, and next, someone would be in charge of dipping them in the sauce. That person gives it to someone to be in charge of adding in the meat. Down the line we have people in charge of cheese, olives, and the rolling and putting them in the pan. There was a job for everybody, and we spent more time talking and laughing than preparing food.[6]

Family identity is built moment by moment amidst the talking and teasing, the singing and storytelling that often attend such work sessions. Daily repetition of tasks allow the words and actions that accompany each day's labor to gradually form our most basic beliefs. Often family members remain unaware of the cumulative impact of these small moments. A young woman writes:

> While I was growing up, my family had a wood burning stove, and each summer we would have to go cut enough wood to heat our home for the winter. For as long as I can remember, my immediate family and my grandparents would make a trip into the forest each summer. . . . For all those years, I watched my grandmother working alongside my grandfather and my mom working alongside my dad in the hard and tiresome task of cutting firewood. The thought never crossed my mind that perhaps it wasn't "usual" for women to do such work. It was simply a way of life that was embedded in me from the beginning.*

Finally, some people insist that family work is demeaning because it involves cleaning up after others in the most personal manner. Yet, in so doing, we observe their vulnerability and weaknesses in a way that forces us to admit that life is possible day-to-day only by the grace of God. We are reminded that when we are fed, we could be hungry; when we are clean, we could be dirty; and when we are healthy and strong, we could be feeble and dependent. Family work is thus humbling work, helping us to acknowledge our unavoidable interdependence; encouraging (even requiring) us to sacrifice "self" for the good of the whole in the pattern of our Savior.

Sometimes the sacrifices are small, like this one made by a young man who helped care for his much younger twin sisters. He reflects:

> I learned to love those I served. My sisters almost became part of me and my life. For example, when my soccer game had finished on a sweltering hot day, I was given some ice cold juice to cool me off. Just as I was about to drink it, I saw that one of my sisters was hot and had nothing to drink. So I gave her my drink. For me this was a big step, because at this time my sister and I did not get along very well. I attribute this act of kindness to the hours of care and babysitting I had spent with her.*

Other times the sacrifices are great, revealing the most profound potential of family work: the power not only to strengthen, but to heal relationships. Doing the mundane yet essential for those who cannot do it for themselves can create, in the absence of pride, a precious connection between giver and receiver. As we figuratively touch one another at this simple level of everyday need, the most routine act of service can surmount any breach. Writes Kristine Manwaring, a mother of four:

> When my mother was twelve, her mother abandoned her and left her with an alcoholic, abusive father. My mother knew why my grandmother left, but still felt cheated. She resented the fact that her mother had never helped her, not even after the births of her children.
>
> Their relationship had been strained for years when my grandmother was diagnosed with terminal cancer. But my mother decided to care for her mother as she died. At first, she resented her mother's constant demands. She had to say a silent prayer at the door of Granny's bedroom every time she entered and at each stoplight as she drove her to doctor appointments.
>
> But something happened during the five months that my mother gave round-the-clock service to my grandmother. One day I got a phone call. My mother said, "You have to visit us. You have to see us together like this. You have to see that I love my mother."
>
> Later my mother explained to me, "When I took care of her, I could see who she was. When I would bathe her or see her in a vulnerable moment, my whole body would fill with love and warmth, and I would just feel for her."
>
> It seemed backwards. But when I asked my mother what my grandmother had given her, she just kept saying, "She took care of me by appreciating everything that I did. I got back more than I gave."*

Thus family work is a link to one another, a link to the Lord, a stepping-stone toward salvation that is always available. This daily work of feeding, clothing, and sheltering each other has the power to transform us spiritually as we transform others physically. Perhaps this is why Jesus, when preparing His apostles for His imminent death and instructing them to become one, chose the sacred ordinance of washing feet—a task ordinarily done in His time by the most humble of servants:

> [Jesus] riseth from supper, and laid aside his garments; and took a towel, and girded himself.
>
> After that he poureth water into a bason, and began to wash the disciples' feet, and to wipe *them* with the towel wherewith he was girded. (John 13:4–5)

Peter objected, thinking that such work was beneath someone of Christ's earthly—and eternal—stature. However, Christ made clear the importance of participating: "If I wash thee not, thou hast no part with me."

So after he had washed their feet, and had taken his garments, and was set down again, he said unto them, Know ye what I have done to you?

Ye call me Master and Lord: and ye say well; for so I am.

If I then, *your* Lord and Master, have washed your feet; ye also ought to wash one another's feet.

For I have given you an example, that ye should do as I have done to you. (John 13:8, 12–15)

And so this work exists *for our sakes.*

But if family work is so essential to our relationships with each other, and thus to a happy family life and our salvation, why is it such a burden? Why does running a household, even with modern conveniences, take an inordinate amount of time and get in the way of what we really want to do? In particular, if cooperating as a family is the ideal, why is it easier for a parent to do family work alone than to involve children or even a spouse? Answers to such questions require stepping outside of our own experience to glimpse family work in other places and times. Not all cultures feel about family work as North Americans do, nor has our North American society always viewed family work as it does now.

WHY DOES FAMILY WORK FEEL LIKE A BURDEN?

Adam and Eve found "joy" in leaving the Garden to face the labors of this life (see Moses 5:11). Ironically, the tendency today is to do the reverse: seek happiness by avoiding the work of mortality and searching for an Eden-like ease. This concept of an ideal life directly conflicts with the first commandments given to Adam (to till the soil) and Eve (to bear children). The more distant a man's work from the fields, the more he is admired. The more removed from home and children a woman's work, the more she is thought to contribute to the world. Popular culture encourages us to enjoy life's bounties without working for them, preferably without the "interruption" of children—in other words, to desire the life Adam and Eve left behind.

As Latter-day Saints, we know that by remaining in the Garden, we could not have grown towards godhood (2 Ne. 2:22–25). We understand that instead of turning back to Eden, we should press forward towards Zion. Regrettably, much we do still follows the pattern of the world. Without thinking, we run households that emphasize comfort and ease. We attempt to avoid the call of our everyday obligations,

or we disdain them. President Joseph F. Smith responded to our devaluing of family work this way:

We should never be discouraged in those daily tasks which God has ordained to the common lot of man. Each day's labor should be undertaken in a joyous spirit and with the thought and conviction that our happiness and eternal welfare depend upon doing well that which we ought to do, that which God has made it our duty to do. Many are unhappy because they imagine that they should be doing something unusual or something phenomenal. . . . Let us not be trying to substitute an artificial life for the true one. He is truly happy who can see and appreciate the beauty with which God has ordained the commonplace things of life.[7]

Contrast our society's penchant for hiring out or efficiently minimizing "those daily tasks which God has ordained" with the practices of the Arapesh of New Guinea:

The Arapesh would have driven a welfare department or any efficiency expert completely mad. . . . The Arapesh terrain is mountainous, so rugged that there is almost no level land. The small garden plots might be separated from the hamlet by miles of difficult territory. The most economical way to cultivate them would have been to have one gardener working alone; yet up to six men would work on a small plot, often with their wives and children, traveling over forbidding territory from plot to distant plot, enjoying each other's society and the sharing of work. . . . A man walked miles with his coconut saplings to plant them on the house sites of others, he gave his pigs to relatives in distant hamlets to feed and tend for him, he hunted only to give his kill away.[8]

American families used to be much more like the Arapesh than they are today. Family work was what one naturally did all day, and family members valued interacting with one another as they did it. "How I would love to go with my father when he would hook up the old ox team and go to get sagebrush for wood," wrote Florence Willis, looking back at her girlhood in Utah in the 1880s. "I would pick flowers, hunt for pretty rocks, and play in the sand while he was loading. My father was such a happy, good-natured fellow. I think he got as much joy out of it as we did."[9]

Like most children in the United States in the early 1900s, Florence grew up in a home sustained by hands-on labor. Most of her chores literally helped keep her family alive. The work of the household was strenuous and required the involvement of every family member for most of each day. Yet, there appears to have been little rush to get the work "out of the way" so that everyone could "get on with life." Work *was* life—so much so that in Florence's account, it is sometimes difficult to distinguish work from play:

> Our parents very seldom allowed us to go play in the day time. We were taught to sew and knit, and I knitted two pair of stockings the winter I was eight years old. Mother allowed me to stripe my pair, and oh, the beautiful stripes of red and green and black I had in them.
>
> A few of the things we used to do that I remember so well were things like . . . corn husking bees, the apple cuttings, and washing each other's faces in apple and peach peelings. Oh! I can feel the sticky mess now![10]

Over the century that separates Florence's life from ours, events combined to essentially reverse the American concept of family work. In response to industrialization, many families abandoned the hands-on labor of farm life to seek more dependable work in factories. The resulting inner city squalor motivated various groups of reformers to seek "scientific solutions" to "home problems."[11] There were efforts to replace traditional family authority with that of scientific expertise. At the same time, daily work lost its tie to the earth, and the spheres of work for men and women became separated. Homes produced less while consuming more. The work that provided food, clothing, and shelter for families became divided from the actual tasks of feeding, clothing, and sheltering family members. Eventually, these changes altered the roles of men, women, and children within the family unit.

The Changing Role of Fathers

Before industrialization, most men learned the trade of their fathers. This does not mean they necessarily felt stifled.[12] To them, freedom came not from choosing what they wanted from many options, but from choosing to do well the work they were called to do. Indeed, the word *vocation* is derived from *vocatio,* a Latin term for *a calling.*[13]

As fathers began earning a living away from the household, the notion of work as a calling began to disappear. Where a son once forged ties with his father working side by side as he learned farming or the family business, he now followed his father's example by distancing himself from the daily work of the household. Historian John Demos notes:

> The wrenching apart of work and home-life is one of the great themes in social history. And for fathers, in particular, the consequences can hardly be over-estimated. . . .
>
> Of course, fathers had always been involved in the provision of goods and services to their families; but before the nineteenth century such activity was embedded in a larger matrix of domestic sharing. . . . Now, for the first time, the central activity of fatherhood was cited outside one's immediate household. Now, being fully a father meant being separated from one's children for a considerable part of every working day.[14]

By the 1950s, fathers had so fully left the domestic circle that they became like guests in their own homes. Now the natural connection between fathers and their children was supposed to be preserved and strengthened mostly by playing together. However, play, like work, also had changed over the course of the century, becoming more structured, more costly, and less interactive. "It could well be argued," concludes Demos, "that men's experience of domestic life has changed more deeply than that of all the other [family members] combined."[15]

The Changing Role of Mothers

For a time, the role of women in the family appeared to remain static because the kind of work they did remained the same. Yet, the way they did their work changed drastically over the century, influenced by the modernization of America's factories and businesses. In 1912, Frank B. Gilbreth told readers of the *Journal of Home Economics:* "It would seem that principles that have proved of use in the scientific management of commercial industries might have an application to the business of housekeeping."[16] The fact that business goals (increasing production and profits) might not fit the purpose of a home seemed not to concern those who encouraged "housewives" to organize, sterilize, and modernize.

Women were told that applying methods of factory and business management to their homes would ease their burdens and raise the status of household work by "professionalizing" it. Surprisingly, these innovations did neither. Because machines tended to replace tasks once performed by husbands and children, mothers carried out the same basic duties. Yet, houses and wardrobes expanded, standards for cleanliness increased, and new appliances encouraged more elaborate meal preparation. New tasks, like shopping and driving children to activities, were added. With husbands at work and older children in school, care of the house and young children now fell almost exclusively to mothers, actually lengthening their work day.[17] Work that was once enjoyable when done alongside family and friends often became lonely, boring, and monotonous.

Meanwhile, experts urged women to replace physical, hands-on labor with the supposedly more important work of the mind, thereby reducing the value of work done by hand. A leading home economics educator declared in 1901: "The woman who today makes her own soap instead of taking advantage of machinery for its production enslaves herself to ignorance by limiting her time for study."[18]

Because nurturing and housework required the labor of one's hands and received no monetary compensation, they lost value in the eyes of society. Later efforts to raise their status by calculating the market value of homemaking tasks inadvertently fed the growing concept that "time is money" and helped push the highly demanding nurture side of family work into near invisibility. Motherhood now meant spending long hours doing work that society said mattered little and should be "managed" to take almost no time at all.

The Changing Role of Children

As homes shifted from centers of production to centers of consumption, the role of children reversed. Prior to modernization, children shared much of the hard work of family life, laboring alongside their fathers and mothers. This work was considered good for them; it was part of their education for adulthood. When the workplace shifted, many children accompanied their parents to the factory. In fact, it became more common for children to provide additional family income than for mothers to do so.

As manufacturers became more profit driven, children—who were a source of cheaper labor—could often find work when fathers could not. Many youngsters ended up working long hours in factories to put food on the family table. However, when children no longer worked under the supervision of their parents, they were subject to great abuse. The child labor movement was organized to protect the "thousands of boys and girls once employed in sweat shops and factories" from "the grasping greed of business."[19]

However, child labor laws, designed to end the abuses, nearly ended all child labor, even in the home.[20]

At the same time that expectations for children to work were diminishing, new trends in child-rearing dictated that children should have their own money and be trained to spend it wisely. Soon the role of children had shifted from economic asset to pampered consumer. Now the "experts" taught that children needed advantages in life. Parents who allowed children to contribute labor and income to the support of the family were no longer seen as truly loving. Child-rearing experts were advising that the only legitimate reason to require work of children was educational, and even then they recommended it have a playlike quality:

> When an article appearing in *Home Progress* advised parents, "Let your children work," the work referred to "some little household task," not too difficult of course, "for their tender bodies." . . .
>
> House chores were therefore not intended to be "real" work, but lessons in helpfulness, order, and unselfishness. . . . Above all, warned *Parents Magazine*, one should "never give . . . children cause to suspect us of making use of them to save ourselves work."[21]

According to the new ideology, play was a child's "work." By 1970, Kenneth Keniston could state in the report of the Carnegie Council on Children that "[t]oday children rarely work at all."[22] Recent time-use studies show that although children do some work around the home, it is primarily work that benefits themselves, such as cleaning their own bedrooms, doing their own laundry, and fixing their own snacks (though not usually cleaning up the mess). The role change for children in the family was thus just as dramatic as that of fathers and mothers.

In combination, these role changes promoted a new ideal where family members were physically isolated from one another much of the time—father working away from home, mother (whether in the workforce or not) efficiently running the home alone, and children at school or at play. Unfortunately, when family members no longer cooperate to feed, clothe, and care for one another, they tend to grow further apart.

As a remedy, some suggest returning to a theoretically simpler and happier era, thinking technology itself is to blame. President Hinckley differs: "I have a profound feeling of gratitude for life in this remarkable age. What great technical progress has been made—in communications, in travel, in medicine, in conveniences for home and work. I stand in respect, almost reverence, for the men and women of science who have made life better for each of us."[23]

It is not modern technologies and work methods themselves that are the problem. It is how we have chosen to use them. Innovations have made it possible to do alone jobs that once required the help of others. But these innovations do not require us to work alone. Technology can bless our lives, if we use it wisely.

The work we are called to do in this generation is not that of our ancestors. It may even depend upon scientific advancements like those that have increased missionary and genealogical work. We must move forward, aware of the potential of family work to link us to one another, yet open to how new technologies and methods can help us better bear one another's burdens.

LIVING THE LORD'S WORK ETHIC IN TODAY'S WORLD

How, then, do we cultivate spiritual growth and family unity through family work in today's world? Essentially, each family must find and follow a blueprint unique to its circumstances. This is possible only with conscious effort and the guidance of our Father in Heaven. There is no substitute for kneeling humbly before our Creator and admitting that we lack wisdom to find our way. We must do so, however, remaining open to changing our personal perspective towards work and willing to live what we learn.

Sociologist Robert N. Bellah notes, "The problem is not so much the presence or absence of a 'work ethic' as [it is] the meaning of work and the ways it links, or fails to link, individuals to one another."[24] We will discuss here three concepts that are basic to forging such unifying links through family work: transcending a business mentality at home, helping children recognize need, and sharing the responsibility of caring for home and family.

Transcending a Business Mentality at Home

In contemporary society, we are encouraged, in fact expected, to apply business principles at home. We are taught to seek measurable results (a clean house), to employ efficient use of resources (no wasting time or money), and to manage by maintaining control (reward good workers, penalize shirkers). The "bottom line"—money—guides much of our thinking. For example, we are told to consider the dollar value of a mother's time to decide how much family work to do. Why make a dress when we can buy one, or cook a meal when it is "more economical" to serve convenience foods? One father refused to care for his children while his wife took a class because during that hour he could earn the money to pay a babysitter plus some.

But business thinking is not necessarily effective in a gospel-centered home. How does one divide "striving to be of one heart and mind" into applicable tasks? How does one measure progress towards "serving the Lord with all of our might, mind, and strength"? President Spencer W. Kimball addressed the fallacy of assessing the value of family work by temporal standards:

> I hope that we understand that, while having a garden, for instance, is often useful in reducing food costs and making available delicious fresh fruits and vegetables, it does much more than this. Who can gauge the value of that special chat between daughter and Dad as they weed or water the garden? . . . And how do we measure the family togetherness and cooperating that must accompany successful canning? . . . [P]erhaps the greater good is contained in the lessons of life we learn. . . . Even if the tomato you eat is a $2.00 tomato, it will bring satisfaction anyway and remind us all of the law of the harvest which is relentless in life. . . . [W]e do reap what we sow.[25]

The purpose of a home—to foster growth, forge unity, and learn charity—far exceeds mere economic profit. Certain business principles may sometimes apply, but as a daily *modus operandi* for a home, market economy thinking falls short. Before modernization, deadlines imposed on family work were rarely contrived. Work was done in response to the natural demands of life: cows had to be milked, eggs gathered, stoves fired up, meals prepared. Most of these tasks did not lend themselves to rushing. Making cows run to their stalls would mean less milk, and so one walked slowly, at the pace of the cows.

By the 1940s, textbooks for high school home economics courses were advising, "A home should be managed as smoothly and as well as any factory or business. The profitable business is one which has a definite routine and permits only a minimum of waste."[26] With this new perspective, the events of family life, from laundry to infant feedings, became subject to the clock; unavoidable and unpredictable needs that defy advance planning, like an illness, a child's curiosity, or a friend stopping by, were reduced to interruptions.

There are times when conforming to a schedule has legitimate advantages. But when sticking to the plan becomes an end in itself rather than a means, it may get in the way of loving attention to the real needs of children.[27] When children are playful while they work, they may thwart the plan, but not the larger purpose. Linking people has less to do with *what* gets done than *how* it gets done.

An overemphasis on efficiency and scheduling, for instance, is not conducive to experiences like this one described by a student: "My favorite [work experience] is singing at the top of our lungs with my sisters while we do the dishes. We sing all the songs we know and sometimes teach each other new ones. We sing in parts: soprano, alto, tenor, and whatever else we can make up. It probably takes longer to do dishes that way, but it sure is fun!"*

There will be times when we feel impressed to push a child to meet a high standard, when the product will take precedence over the process. Sometimes it will be appropriate to impose short-term goals. However, order that is based in love responds more to the rhythm of the needs of daily life than to the artificial demands of the planner or the clock. Anthropologist Dorothy Lee once observed:

> We have allowed the new technology to run ahead of our concern for a meaningful life. . . . Somehow we forgot to build a home for a zestful, boisterous, untidy existence; full of the opportunity and invitation to real talk and quarreling and anguish and absorbing spontaneous activities. Does my pale wall-to-wall carpeting encourage the tracking of autumn leaves as my children come home? Perhaps I have taken the precaution of building a special door, so that they can go directly to the rumpus room or their own rooms, leaving me to my efficient meal preparation and my living room intact, with its tomb-like perfection undisturbed. Does my kitchen invite a rush of noisy feet to find out what is cooking, to batter me with excited accounts of the day's happenings or even with offers of help? Or have I planned it so successfully, with such step-saving, muscle-bound efficiency, that it freezes out my husband and my children?[28]

She compares our culture of family work to that of a Polynesian group:

> Work among the Tikopia is . . . socially conceived and structured; and if a man has to work alone, he will probably try to take a little child along. . . .
>
> To the Tikopia, an American kitchen, with the mother mainly concerned with having everything within reach and no one under foot, would be an atrocity. When they prepare the meal, after they have returned from their gardening and other food-getting occupations, the whole Tikopia household works together. Nothing is within reach, and children fill this gap, fetching and carrying and running errands, forming a bridge between adult and adult. Father and mother, the unmarried aunt, the grandmother, the brother-in-law, all work together. . . . Jokes and anecdotes fly back and forth. No one apparently wants to be alone so as to concentrate or to work more efficiently.[29]

Our economic thinking is so ingrained that leaving it behind raises other issues. For example, does giving up a business mentality mean we should forgo a clean house, toss out scheduling, and live moment to moment? Of course not. Our eternal example is a Father who does not exert undue control, yet certainly creates order. But how will we ever get our children to work if we don't have a plan and methods to enforce it?

Helping Children Recognize and Respond to Need

It is a myth that children don't want to work. Most children, especially young children, love to work and often offer to help. What most children resent and resist is being asked to work alone. "Go clean your room" sounds overwhelming. "Let's go clean your room" says something quite different. This does not mean that efforts to train children to share in the family work will be easy or will always go smoothly. What it does mean is that we can reject the popular idea that children must be prodded, enticed, or supplied with some external motivation to participate in family chores.

When we speak of motivating others, we accept a nearly universal belief among social scientists that all action begins with the self. Supposedly, a person's needs (for food, shelter, safety, etc.) and desires (for acceptance, achievement, ease) prompt them to act in their own interest. In theory, then, the way to alter another person's behavior is to appeal to that self-interest by dangling rewards in front of them or by threatening unpleasant consequences for noncompliance.

There are, however, ways of conceptualizing why people take action. Mother Teresa once said, "I wouldn't touch a leper for a thousand pounds; yet I willingly cure him for the love of God."[30] In

CHILDREN WHO SERVE LEARN TO WORK

Even when family members work alone, their work should feel vital—a service to the entire family. This contrasts with most parenting advice today, which usually supports teaching self-reliance through chores, like having each child take responsibility for his or her own laundry. By contrast, children who do the laundry for the whole family or who take care of one aspect of the family laundry, like towels or bedding or folding clothes, experience an interdependency that links them to every other member of the family.

Canadian scholars who compared children who do "self-care tasks" (defined as "attention [focused] on what is one's 'own,'" such as "looking after one's 'own space'") and children who participate in "family-care tasks" (defined as having an "emphasis beyond what is one's own")[39] found "an overall pattern of results suggesting that beneficial effects of household work occur . . . when that work involves assistance to others, when it is required on a routine or self-regulating basis, and when the outcome variable is concern for others revealed in the family context."[40] In other words, children learn to care for others by doing work that helps them think about others.

Another study found that African children who fetched wood and water, watched siblings, and ran errands for parents had a high incidence of helpfulness toward others, while children in the Northeast United States, whose main chore was to clean their own room, were the "least helpful" of all children in the six-culture study.[41] Still another researcher found that "participation in the work of others . . . produces benefits ranging from sound work habits to the development of a sense of helping others, responsibility for the welfare of others, belief in oneself as a helpful person, a sense of agency or personal efficacy and an appreciation of the needs and feelings of others."[42]

Box 13.1

Doctrine & Covenants 82:19, we learn that a Zion society is "every man seeking the interest of his neighbor, and doing all things with an eye single to the glory of God." In other words, our actions can also begin with a concern for the well-being of others and a desire to honor and be like our Father in Heaven. This basis for action means forgetting self and working without regard for our own convenience.

When we train children to work by paying them, whether with money or privileges, we reinforce self-interest. While this approach may have positive results in the short term, it often disintegrates into manipulative attempts by both parent and child to outmaneuver one another.[31] Rather than "motivate" children, we should open their eyes to the needs that naturally surround them.

First, children must learn to recognize that life itself creates need and calls upon us to help. For example, the cry of a baby indicates that the baby is hungry or cold or in pain. Some needs are less obvious, but are no less real. When the lawn is long, it needs mowing. When the floor is dirty, it needs washing. When the trash is full, life is inviting us to take action, calling us to empty the container so that the family may enjoy a clean, healthy environment.

A Pueblo grandmother recalls learning to see need because she was told to look for it: "I remember the times that my mother would say to me, go see if your aunt so and so has water. Go see if they need water. And then go to your aunt and uncle to see if they need anything."[32] One of the authors of this chapter decided to try the Pueblo method with her seven-year-old daughter. When the girl left the dinner table without her plate, the mother said, "Go look at the table and see what needs to be done before someone else sits down to use it." Expecting only to retrieve the dirty plate, the mother was surprised when her daughter exclaimed, "A lot needs to be done!" Without further direction, the girl cleared all remaining dishes, took a cloth, and wiped the table clean.

Next, children must learn that when a need calls to them, it is their moral duty to respond. The crying baby cannot feed himself, the mother must do it, and she must feed him when he needs food, not at her convenience. The lawn, the floor, the trash must be tended to when the need is manifest, not when we feel like getting around to it. Although we each have agency and, as a technical matter, can choose to put off or not do what needs to be done, family work is not a matter of preference. The moral, right, and necessary choice, when we recognize genuine need, is to extend assistance.

This brings us to the trickiest part of teaching children to live these principles. As crucial as it is that children participate in family work, they should not be forced nor manipulated to do so. Here, as ever, the Lord is our example. Like Him, we must honor moral agency without excusing indolence. The Lord makes known that the Ten Commandments are not optional. He will not force us to obey them, but the expectation is clear.

> ### FAMILY WORK PREPARES CHILDREN FOR OTHER WORK
>
> Are the principles expounded in this chapter just ideals isolated to raising righteous families? Ponder the impact on missionary work of young men and women entering the mission field who can recognize and respond to need and who are familiar with working cooperatively as a team. Consider employers who look for people who can see needs and respond, enjoy teamwork, and can look beyond the short-term "bottom line" to the long-term value of a project or activity. The application of gospel-centered family work principles can succeed and generate rich blessings in any setting.
>
> Box 13.2

Fortunately, small children respond naturally to need. When mother is preparing a meal, the activity invites their participation. As children get older, though, they may become convinced by society's norms that they are free to shut out the call of another's need, especially if helping seems not in their self-interest. Without resorting to bribes and punishments, parents can find ways to gently insist that children acknowledge and respond to the needs of the household. "I need your help" says "I need *you*." Most children will not turn down a sincere request for help, especially if the task is small and shared—and out of small beginnings grows that which is great (see D&C 64:33). Occasionally, the Spirit will tell us not to press a child, and those promptings should be heeded. Overall, however, parents can clarify that family members are expected to put aside selfishness and learn to work in harmony with one another.[33]

Of course, families striving to become of one heart and one mind still experience disorder and conflict. Learning to patiently and lovingly work out disagreements is a vital part of linking family members through family work. One student recalls working with her brother:

> When I was in the fourth grade, my mom started a bakery business selling breads and cinnamon rolls to bring in some extra money. . . . As children, it was our job to wash the containers everyday. . . . We dreaded [it] but we did it anyway. I remember laughing so hard on some days, and I remember being so mad at my brother on other days that I knew I could never forgive him (until two minutes later when he would do

something that would be so funny and make me laugh). . . . I've always felt especially close to my brother, and I have believed for a long time that it is because we had to work and spend so much time together while growing up.*

Elder Russell M. Nelson explained: "The home is the great laboratory of love. There the raw chemicals of selfishness and greed are melded in the crucible of cooperation to yield compassionate concern and love one for another."[34]

Sharing the Responsibility of Caring for Home and Family

Children are not the only ones who dislike working alone. Feeling isolated in family work is exhausting for adults as well, especially when others think the work is unimportant and easy. Above all, family work is lonely when one spouse remains uninvolved. The loss a couple suffers when they do not work side-by-side—a loss of happy memories, of earnest conversation, of overcoming differences and learning to work well with one another—is truly a tragedy. Said a man who labored 25 years with his wife creating an extraordinary Japanese garden, "I wanted to build the garden to keep Mitsuko from getting homesick, but to me, the important thing is that in the years of collaboration on this work-in-progress, the friendship between the two of us has grown."[35]

Much has been written about spouses sharing family work. Today's model couple follows a "fair-share" method for dividing tasks: "I'll take out the garbage and vacuum, you do the dishes. I'll do the lawn, you do the flower garden." The emphasis is more often on making certain one partner is not overly burdened rather than on growing closer through shared participation in the ongoing work of the household.

Once again, what may seem good in the eyes of society may not apply in a gospel-centered home. The issue of dividing chores can become so central that it leads to "score keeping," which damages the marital relationship. Even when each spouse nobly fulfills his or her separate obligations as agreed, the husband and wife are robbed of the kind of interaction that creates unity. They may be "equal," but they are not "partners" (Proclamation, ¶ 7).

Research indicates that most wives, including those who work outside the home, do more of the family work than their husbands.[36] One result of this division of labor is that mothers may have a different view than fathers of what is needed. Some mothers express feelings such as: "I have a vision of family work unifying the family, but my husband does not. I don't want to pay the children; he does. I want everyone to work together. He never has time." A wise husband will realize that the insights and impressions a mother receives in her part of the family work stewardship are vital to the success of the family. He will honor the stewardship of Eve and be willing to learn from his wife in her capacity just as she is expected to honor and learn from him in his. Still, a mother may have to carry out her labors in patience. In most families, truths about working together as husband and wife are learned little by little, and progress is made over an extended period of time.

A couple who learns to "bear one another's burdens" (Mos. 18:8) at home will reap great blessings. In an incident recorded by Jesse Crosby, a neighbor of Joseph Smith, we glimpse the Prophet's feelings as he shared the burden of family work with Emma:

> Some of the home habits of the Prophet—such as building kitchen fires, carrying out ashes, carrying in wood and water, assisting in the care of the children, etc.—were not in accord with my idea of a great man's self-respect. [An occasion when] the Prophet [returned a] sack of flour gave me the opportunity to give him some corrective advice which I had desired to do for a long time. I reminded him of every phase of his greatness and called to his mind the multitude of tasks he performed that were too menial for such as he; to fetch and carry flour was too great a humiliation. "Too terrible a humiliation," I repeated, "for you who are the head, and you should not do it."
>
> The Prophet listened quietly to all I had to say, then made his answer in these words: "If there be humiliation in a man's house, who but the head of that house should or could bear that humiliation?"
>
> Sister Crosby was a very hardworking woman, taking much more responsibility in her home than most women take. Thinking to give the Prophet some light on home management, I said to him, "Brother Joseph, my wife does much more hard work than does your wife."
>
> Brother Joseph replied by telling me that if a man cannot learn in this life to appreciate a wife and do his duty by her, in properly taking care of her, he need not expect to be given one in the hereafter.

Brother Crosby concluded his account by saying,

> "His words shut my mouth as tight as a clam. I took them as terrible reproof. After that I tried to do better by the good wife I had and tried to lighten her labors."[37]

More recently, President Harold B. Lee directed this statement to fathers who spent long hours in church service while needs remained unmet at home:

> I find some of our brethren who are engaged in some leadership position justify their neglect of their family because they say that they are engaged in the Lord's work. I say to them, "My dear brother, do you realize that the most important part of the Lord's work that you will do is the work that you do within the walls of your own home? That is the most important work of the Lord. Don't get your sense of values mixed up."[38]

FAMILY WORK IS BOTH TEMPORAL AND SPIRITUAL

The fact that we must eat, stay warm, and keep clean to survive may seem strictly a temporal matter, but according to the Lord, it is not: "Wherefore, verily I say unto you that all things unto me are spiritual, and not at any time have I given unto you a law which was temporal; neither any man, nor the children of men; neither Adam, your father, whom I created" (D&C 29:34).

Let us look again at the Proclamation and the list of principles upon which "successful marriages and families are established and maintained" (¶ 7): "faith, prayer, repentance, forgiveness, respect, love, compassion, work, and wholesome recreation." At first, it may seem odd to see "work" listed among such important spiritual attributes. But the essence of family work is firmly entwined with these spiritual qualities in both the Proclamation and the scriptures, perhaps because it is while doing this work that we both learn and teach faith, respect, love, compassion, and more.

In the scriptures, the most fundamental gospel truths are tied to service that is no more and no less than homemaking: feeding the hungry, clothing the naked, and tending the sick, all of which nurture relationships. Isaiah tells us that a true fast is "to deal thy bread to the hungry . . . when thou seest the naked, that thou cover him; and that thou hide not thyself from thine own flesh" (Isa. 58:7). Alma and Amulek explain that this work is necessary to receive an answer to prayer, for after praying in our fields, our houses, and our closets, and praying at all times in our hearts: "[D]o not suppose that this is all; for after ye have done all these things, if ye turn away the needy, and the naked, and visit not the sick and afflicted . . . behold, your prayer is vain, and availeth you nothing, and ye are as hypocrites who do deny the faith" (Alma 34:28).

King Benjamin relates this work to repentance:

[F]or the sake of retaining a remission of your sins from day to day, that ye may walk guiltless before God—I would that ye should impart of your substance to the poor, every man according to that which he hath, such as feeding the hungry, clothing the naked, visiting the sick and administering to their relief, both spiritually and temporally, according to their wants. (Mosiah 4:26)

Finally, Jesus Christ, the source of all life, taught that our willingness to perform life-sustaining tasks for one another (not just for ourselves) will actually separate the sheep from the goats at the time of judgment (Matt. 25:31–33):

For I was an hungered, and ye gave me meat: I was thirsty, and ye gave me drink: I was a stranger, and ye took me in:

Naked, and ye clothed me: I was sick, and ye visited me: I was in prison, and ye came unto me. (Matt. 25:35, 36)

Then shall the righteous answer him, saying, Lord, when saw we thee an hungered, and fed thee? or thirsty, and gave thee drink?

When saw we thee a stranger, and took thee in? or naked, and clothed thee?

Or when saw we thee sick, or in prison, and came unto thee?

And the King shall answer and say unto them, Verily I say unto you, Inasmuch as ye have done it unto one of the least of these my brethren, ye have done it unto me. (Matt. 25:35–40)

In a world that rewards and glorifies the work we do for the masses before the eyes of all men, where do we feed, clothe, and care for "the least of Christ's brothers and sisters?" Perhaps it is as simple and as meaningful as noting the needs of our parents, our siblings, and our children in our own homes.

NOTES

1. All quotes with an asterisk (*) are from unpublished data from D. Smith.

2. F. D. Cox (1996), *Human intimacy: Marriage, the family, and its meaning* (7th ed.) (St. Paul, MN: West Publishing Co.), 207; couples were interviewed during engagement, then again six months, one year, and five years after marriage.

3. Gordon B. Hinckley (1996, September), First Presidency message: Four simple things to help our families and our nations, *Ensign, 26*(9), 7; emphasis added.

4. All student comments marked with an asterisk (*) are from student papers collected by K. S. Bahr.

5. D. Smith, unpublished data.

6. From a personal interview conducted by C. Loveless.

7. Joseph F. Smith (1971), *Gospel doctrine* (Salt Lake City: Desert Book), 285–286.

8. D. Lee (1976), *Valuing the self* (Prospect Heights, IL: Waveland Press), 7, 9.

9. F. M. S. Willis, *The story of my life,* unpublished, 14 pages.

10. Willis, *The story of my life.*

11. E. Richards (1910, February), *Journal of Home Economics, 2,* 17–18.

12. As early as 1701, the idea was expounded that every Christian had both a general calling to serve Jesus Christ and "a personal calling, or a certain particular employment, by which his usefulness in his neighborhood is distinguished," Cotton Mather [1701], *A Christian at his calling* (Boston: B. Green & J. Allen), 38.

13. *Webster's New World dictionary of the American language* (2nd col. ed.) (1974), The World Publishing Company.

14. Demos (1986), The changing faces of fatherhood, in *Past, present, personal: The family and the life course in American history* (New York: Oxford University Press), 51–52.

15. Demos (1986), 41.

16. F. B. Gilbreth (1912, December), Scientific management in the household, *Journal of Home Economics, 4,* 438–447.

17. R. S. Cowan (1983), *More work for mother: The ironies of household technology from the open hearth to the microwave* (New York: Basic Books).

18. C. L. Hunt (1929), *Revaluations* (Baltimore, MD: Np.), 18–19.

19. W. A. McKeever (1913, April), The new child labor movement, *Journal of Home Economics, 5,* 137–139.

20. Historian Viviana A. Zelizer charts these changes in child labor from instrumental to instructional in her 1985 book *Pricing the priceless child* (New York: Basic Books).

21. Zelizer (1985), 98–99.

22. Keniston and The Carnegie Council on Children (1977), *All our children: The American family under pressure* (New York: Harcourt Brace Javonovich), 14.

23. Hinckley (1996, September), 7

24. R. N. Bellah, R. Madsen, W. M. Sullivan, A. Swidler, and S. M. Tipton (1985), *Habits of the heart* (Berkeley: University of California Press), 56.

25. Spencer W. Kimball (1977, November), Welfare services: The gospel in action, *Ensign, 7*(11), 76–79.

26. A. L. Van Duzer, E. M. Andrix, E. L. Bobenmyer, E. M. Hawkins, M. E. Hemmersbaugh, and E. P. Page (1951), *The girl's daily life* (Philadelphia: Lippincott), 424.

27. S. Ruddick (1989), *Maternal thinking: Towards a politics of peace* (Boston: Beacon Press).

28. D. Lee (1964, Spring/Summer), Home economics in a changing world, *Penney's Fashions and Fabrics, 13,* 45.

29. D. Lee (1959), *Freedom and culture* (Englewood Cliffs, NJ: Prentice-Hall), 32.

30. Mother Teresa (1975), *A gift for God: Prayers and meditations* (London: Collins), 52.

31. A. Kohn (1993), *Punished by rewards* (New York: Houghton Mifflin).

32. I. M. W. Wong (2000), The influence of changing

patterns of living on the transmission of culture and values: A study with Pueblo Indians, Master's thesis, Brigham Young University.

33. Spencer W. Kimball (1978 May), Becoming the pure in heart, *Ensign, 8*(5), 81.

34. Russell M. Nelson (1999, May), Our sacred duty to honor women, *Ensign, 29*(5), 40.

35. C. S. Black (1999, July), Simple and serene: A garden with its roots in the past, *Better Homes and Gardens, 77*(7), 150.

36. A. Hochschild (1989), *The second shift* (New York: Avon Books).

37. Jesse W. Crosby, quoted in H. L. Andrus and H. M. Andrus (Comps.) (1974), *They knew the Prophet* (Salt Lake City: Bookcraft), 144–145.

38. Harold B. Lee (1961, April 19), Doing the right thing for the right reasons, in *BYU Speeches of the Year, 1960–1961,* 5.

39. J. E. Grusec, J. J. Goodnow, and L. Cohen (1996), Household work and the development of concern for others, *Developmental Psychology, 32,* 1000.

40. Grusec et al. (1996), 1006.

41. Grusec et al. (1996), 999.

42. Grusec et al. (1966), 999.

WHOLESOME FAMILY RECREATION

MARK A. WIDMER, DAVID J. CHERRINGTON, E. JEFFREY HILL, AND BRIAN J. HILL

Successful marriages and families are established and maintained on principles of . . .
wholesome recreational activities.
(The Family: A Proclamation to the World, ¶ 7)

On a Monday evening the Jensen family sat around the living room as they read and discussed the Proclamation. Aaron, an energetic teenager, was hardly listening until Dad read " . . . wholesome recreational activities." Aaron perked up and interrupted, "Dad, read that again!" Brother Jensen then read "Successful marriages and families are established and maintained on principles of faith, prayer, repentance, forgiveness, respect, love, compassion, work, and wholesome recreational activities" (Proclamation, ¶ 7). Aaron gleefully stated, "Did you hear that? The prophet wants us to have fun!"

For 31 years our extended family has vacationed at Lake Tahoe, thanks to Grandpa's foresight. We do many traditional activities every year—boating, hiking, family home evening, and family dinners. Our week together at Tahoe has tied our families together over four generations. I'm closer to my aunts and uncles than some of my friends are to their parents. And as cousins we share bonds of love and support in spite of the miles that separate us. We talk frequently about missions because Grandpa established a mission fund that helped support all the grandsons and more than half the granddaughters. This experience has influenced our extended family and now my own family, in ways that are immeasurable.

Wholesome recreation plays an important role in creating successful marriages and families. This chapter provides ideas from a variety of perspectives to assist families in creating wholesome recreational experiences. Recreational opportunities have expanded dramatically during the past century and these changes have important implications for developing personal values and creating happy families. Learning to find meaning and enjoyment in our free time requires both forethought and spontaneity, both careful planning and the willingness to modify plans to enjoy the moment. Couples who take time for recreation renew their marriages. Parents who provide opportunities for wholesome recreational activity lay a foundation on which their children can build virtuous, happy lives. Wholesome recreation also creates loving memories that lay the foundation for eternal relationships. Fostering wholesome recreational activities is not always an easy task. Wholesome family recreation does not always mean that every family member participates in every activity. Rather, it may involve couples or smaller groups of family members, such as a father and daughter, going on a date.

This chapter explains four primary principles regarding wholesome recreation.

1. Wholesome recreation is not the same as idleness or aimless leisure.

2. Wholesome recreation is not just spontaneous play.

3. Wholesome recreation helps to establish family rituals that create bonding experiences.

> Now, what about our leisure time? How we use our leisure is equally as important to our joy as our occupational pursuits. Proper use of leisure requires discriminating judgment. Our leisure provides opportunity for renewal of spirit, mind, and body. It is a time for worship, for family, for service, for study, for wholesome recreation. It brings harmony into our life.
>
> Leisure is not idleness. The Lord condemns idleness. He said, 'Thou shalt not idle away thy time, neither shalt thou bury thy talent' (D&C 60:13). Idleness in any form produces boredom, conflict, and unhappiness. It creates a vacancy of worth, a seedbed for mischief and evil. It is the enemy of progress and salvation.
>
> J. Richard Clarke[1]
>
> Box 14.1

4. Wholesome recreation needs to be balanced with our obligation to work.

AIMLESS LEISURE VS. WHOLESOME RECREATION

Leisure consists of free, unoccupied time when we can rest and engage in recreation; we often think of it as spare time or time that is not occupied with work or other obligations. Watching television, gardening, reading novels, playing computer games, visiting with friends, hiking in the mountains, and picnicking in a park are common examples of leisure activities.

Not all leisure activities are equally valuable. Some leisure activities are rejuvenating and contribute to personal development, marital enrichment, and family unity; some seem to neither help or hurt; while other leisure activities are destructive, undermining personal and family joy. Aimless leisure is much different than wholesome recreation. While wholesome recreation strengthens marriages and families and is consistent with gospel-centered living, aimless leisure is the opposite. This contrast is illustrated in Box 14.2.

Aimless leisure should not be confused with rest. Rest refers to the relaxation required by our bodies for physical recuperation and mental rejuvenation. Periods of rest and sleep are essential for our physical and mental health and we should not feel guilty when we need to rest. However, the temptation to excessive relaxation is ever present. Surveys indicate that most

Americans spend almost one-half of their free time watching television,[2] which seems to go well beyond needed rest and recuperation. This research suggests that many Americans are idle. Idleness is condemned throughout the scriptures, including the Old Testament (see Prov. 19:15, Ezek. 16:49–50), the New Testament (see 1 Tim. 5:8, 13), the Book of Mormon (see 1 Ne. 12:22–23; 2 Ne. 5:24; Alma 38:12), and the Doctrine & Covenants (see 42:42; 60:13; 68:30–31; 88:69; 88:124).

Wholesome Recreation

Although certain leisure activities have been repeatedly criticized by Church leaders, especially card-playing and gambling, we should not expect to find an official list of acceptable activities. Wholesome recreational activities cannot be prescribed in the abstract. Whether a particular activity qualifies as wholesome recreation depends partially on the activity itself—its purpose, its focus, and the outcome of the activity—and partially on the needs of family members for personal development and diversion from work.

Recreation in the Restored Church

The scriptures contain few references to recreation and leisure as we think of it today. Occasional references are made to dancing and celebrating activities that often had a sacred dimension (e.g., 2 Sam. 6:14; Ps. 149:3; 150:4; D&C 136:28). Latter-day Church leaders, however, have actively taught the vital role recreation should play in the lives of Latter-day Saints.[3] President Ezra Taft Benson instructed fathers to give spiritual leadership through recreation: "Go on daddy-daughter dates and father and sons' outings with your children. As a family, go on camp-outs and picnics, to ball games and recitals, to school programs. . . . Build traditions of family vacations and trips and outings. These memories will never be forgotten by your children."[4] Elder Bruce R. McConkie wrote that "recreation is an essential and vital part of the gospel of salvation . . . wholesome recreation may include parties, banquets, dinners, games, athletic endeavors and contests, dramas, dances, concerts, radio and television programs, picnics, outings, camping trips, hunting and fishing trips, and vacations in general."[5]

Joseph Smith enjoyed wrestling and playing other sports. He said that his mind was like a bow that would lose its spring if it were constantly strung.[6]

AIMLESS LEISURE VS. WHOLESOME RECREATION

	AIMLESS LEISURE ACTIVITIES	**WHOLESOME RECREATION**
Purpose:	Diversion, idleness, mindlessness, or pleasure "To forget the drudgery of life"	Personal growth and development Genuine enjoyment Meaningful interactions with others "To engage in life's purpose"
Focus:	Inward: self-concern, self-indulgence, self-oriented individualism Am I happy? Do I feel good?	Outward: being virtuous and oriented to others—especially one's spouse, family, and neighbors Am I obedient? Am I doing good? Am I serving others? Am I strengthening my family?
Outcome of the Activities:	Activities that serve to create transient psychological states of satisfaction and well-being. Pleasurable, but not enjoyable or meaningful	Activities that produce social, emotional, physical, moral, intellectual, and spiritual development in oneself, one's spouse, and one's children Activities that nurture family members and serve others Activities that provide a needed diversion Activities that are consistent with obedience and correct principles

Box 14.2

Brigham Young also encouraged recreation. In spite of extremely adverse circumstances that included crossing a frozen Mississippi River and a muddy Iowa prairie, Brigham Young encouraged the pioneers to dance and sing in the evenings. "[T]he trumpet by the order of Brigham Young called the camp out to a concert in the open air, and the Nauvoo Brass Band performed its best selections, after which the pilgrims joined in the dance and the music was as joyous as at a merrymaking."[7] The pioneers suffered many difficulties in their trek to the Salt Lake Valley, but throughout the migration evenings were filled with stories, music, recitations, and dance.

Recreation continued to play an important part in the lifestyles of the Saints after they reached the Salt Lake Valley. Their recreation involved entire families in such activities as dancing, playing musical instruments, singing, telling stories, cutting wood, quilting, and playing games. One of the first buildings constructed in the valley was the Social Hall, where the Saints enjoyed dances and theatrical performances. Brigham Young also organized holiday celebrations where thousands of Saints would vacation for a week in Big Cottonwood Canyon. In some respects, general conference each April and October became a week-long holiday where people came to worship.[8]

Although other nineteenth-century religions generally frowned on recreation, Latter-day Saint Church leaders encouraged recreation for at least four reasons. First, recreation contributed to improved physical health and greater spiritual well-being. Second, social events helped create a sense of community among the Saints who had separated themselves from the world. Third, persecution and other hardships created a need for an emotional relief from suffering. Fourth, recreation helped to fellowship converts who came from many different cultures.[9]

The importance of recreation is reflected in the design of church meeting houses. Early chapels had movable pews that could be cleared for dances and plays. Cultural halls with stages for performances were constructed in meeting houses at least as early as 1888. In 1946, the Church building committee authorized the inclusion of basketball facilities in all cultural halls.[10]

Church programs also reflect a commitment to wholesome recreation. The Mutual Improvement Association (MIA) was organized in 1875 to provide cultural refinement activities in music, dance, drama, speech, and athletics for the youth of the Church. The Church also adopted the Boy Scout program for young men because its activities provide a laboratory for applying priesthood concepts and its forms of wholesome enjoyment build character. Each ward is expected to have members called as "activity directors" to plan ward socials and outings. Wards and stakes sponsor sporting activities such as softball and basketball. The Relief Society also sponsors wholesome recreational activities where specific skills are taught.

THE HISTORY OF WORK AND RECREATION

A good life is one in which joy is found in both work and recreation. Parents have the opportunity to teach their children through example to love work and to intentionally seek wholesome recreation. The demands of life, however, make achieving an appropriate balance of work and recreation a difficult task. Unless we carefully shape our work and recreation we risk becoming disconnected from personal values and core activities that define the purpose of life.

Revealed gospel principles regarding work and recreation are clear: work is a divine obligation that serves to bless our lives; wholesome recreation enriches life and is not the opposite of work; and wholesome recreation serves a crucial role in rearing moral children and building successful families. These principles recognize that work is more than paid employment and wholesome recreation is more than entertainment or diversion. Work refers to worthwhile activities that provide useful products or services for our family or others. The value of work and wholesome recreation becomes clear when we understand the meaning of work and the principles underlying wholesome recreation.

Early Americans had no uncertainty about the work ethic and its importance: it was the only sure pathway to eternal salvation and worldly success. The moral preeminence of work stood unchallenged among all the early moralists: influential statesmen, clergy, and authors all taught that success came through hard work, diligence, perseverance, honesty, and thrift. Young people were confronted on all sides with advice about dedicated work, the wise use of leisure time, and the importance of good character.

The work ethic was extolled for many reasons, but above all a devotion to work was accepted as a divine commandment and was considered essential to eternal salvation.[11] The hours of work were from sunrise until sundown. Free time for recreation was scarce. While there was an implicit value attached to being busy and constantly at work, there was a greater value attached to being efficient and productive. The purpose of efficiency was to allow for recreational activities; but recreation was to be spent in education and other worthwhile pursuits rather than in idleness or fanciful play.[12] Early Americans enjoyed holiday celebrations, yet most of their recreation occurred when they worked together on projects like quilting bees, husking bees, or building cabins.

Between 1850 and 1920, technological advances reduced the work week from six to five days—from an average of 66 to 48 hours per week. This reduction contributed to the rapid rise in leisure-time activities, such as bicycling, picnicking, camping, vaudeville, movies, amusement parks, dance halls, and a host of new participant and spectator sports.[13] Between 1850 and 1920, the United States population tripled while the volume of manufactured goods increased about 14-fold. This efficiency changed ideas about the moral importance of work. Excess capacity made it harder and harder to insist that diligence, thrift, and long hours were among life's highest goals.[14]

The ultimate effect of excess capacity was to create a materialistic society with more leisure time and abundant consumer products. The importance of working hard diminished and the importance of enjoying the fruits of one's labors increased.[15] Leisure activities became a source of personal identification; owning expensive leisure materials, such as sporting goods, clothes, vehicles, and boats, became a source of social status and was called conspicuous consumption.[16] Economic improvements during the past century have enticed us to question the moral importance of work and led to the glorification of leisure pursuits. These advances provide us with the time and resources to enjoy unprecedented opportunities for leisure activities.

With such abundant leisure opportunities, we might expect to be the happiest people of all time, but research indicates that this is not the case. During the past century, depression has increased tenfold. It has been suggested that the glorification of the *self*, highlighted by excessive materialism and abundant leisure opportunities, has created unrealistic expectations for personal happiness.[17] Research has shown that happiness is not derived from pleasurable activities themselves; it is a by-product of more meaningful activities, such as service or working toward a goal or purpose larger than one's self.[18]

CHARACTERISTICS OF WHOLESOME RECREATION

Wholesome recreation can be either spontaneous or intentional. Spontaneous recreation, which is typically called play, is an excellent source of fun and enjoyment that may cost nothing and require only a small investment of time. Wrestling with Mom or Dad on the floor, reading a story together, or playing ball in the backyard are examples of play that might be the most meaningful highlight of a child's day. Play is a valuable and developmentally critical part of life, especially for children.[19]

Many forms of wholesome recreation, however, require thoughtful planning, creativity, and effort—they are intentional, deliberate activities. The rewards for planning and organizing a meaningful recreational activity are generally worth the effort. Family vacations, camping, hiking, teaching a child to swim, or participating in a community celebration all require planning. Consequently, creating wholesome recreation is not always an easy task and it is especially difficult for parents with heavy demands on their time and resources, such as single parents, parents of children with disabilities, or those struggling financially.

The characteristics of wholesome recreation may be amplified by integrating the teachings of Church leaders with two secular perspectives, one ancient and the other recent. The first secular perspective comes from Aristotle's philosophical analysis of what makes a good life, while the second is based on research regarding optimal experiences.

Wholesome Recreation and "The Good Life"

Nearly 2400 years ago, Aristotle described his philosophy regarding the meaning of life and the pursuit of happiness in his classical treatise *Nicomachean Ethics*. According to Aristotle, happiness is not a state of self-gratification or transient states of pleasure. Happiness, or the good life, which he called *eudaemonia*, is living and acting well; it is the habit of virtuous actions. Happiness comes from thoughtfully choosing the right way to live.[20] Much of his philosophy focuses on deciding what is right and wrong. His ideas continue to be highly respected today.

Aristotle's description of the good life contributes greatly to understanding the attributes of wholesome recreation. A central principle of the good life is the golden mean, or moderation; overindulgence hinders the attainment of the good life. According to this principle, it is possible to fish too much, ski too much, or watch too much television. Exceptions to this rule are gaining wisdom and understanding, which Aristotle described as limitless goods.

To Aristotle, the crowning virtue of the good life is leisure. But leisure does not refer to idleness or napping; it refers to activities by which human beings learn and acquire intellectual virtues. The intellectual virtues, such as art, knowledge, understanding, and wisdom, are the highest virtues of the good life. For Aristotle, thinking or using our minds is a distinctly human activity and the ultimate purpose of leisure.[21] To Aristotle, then, ethical leisure activities must include thinking and reasoning. These activities may be as practical as gardening, cooking, or cabinet making—all of which require skill or art—or as complex as scientific research, musical composition, and philosophical thought.

Four characteristics of ethical leisure have been derived from Aristotle's description of the good life: intellectual activity, creative activity, meaningful relationships, and moral behavior.[22] In summary, Aristotle's good life is a life of reflection, a life of seeking that which is good and lasting. It is not a thoughtless life of idleness and passivity or a hedonistic life of seeking thrills and pleasure through artificial stimulants or exotic activities. Parents may wish to consider these principles as they select wholesome recreational activities for their families.

Wholesome Recreation as "Optimal" Experience

Our understanding of wholesome recreation is enhanced by research on the conditions that lead to optimal, or "flow," experiences.[23] This research, which is based on the reports of thousands of subjects from diverse cultures regarding the best moments of their lives, identified eight factors that create optimal experiences. According to Mihaly Csikszentmihalyi, a psychologist and leading scholar on the topic, these experiences occur "when a person's body or mind is stretched to its limits in a voluntary effort to accomplish something difficult and worthwhile."[24]

An optimal experience requires time and effort to cultivate the necessary conditions; it is something that we make happen, rather than something that happens to us. For a child it may be reading a book for the first time to his mother or learning to ride a bike with his father. For a teenager it may be rock-climbing or performing a musical instrument in public. For a family, it may be rafting a river or backpacking in the mountains. The eight characteristics of flow experiences are described in Box 14.3.

1. We face a challenging task that we are capable of completing.

2. We concentrate on what we are doing.

3. We have clear goals.

4. We receive clear and immediate feedback regarding our progress.

5. We participate effortlessly with a deep involvement that eliminates awareness of concerns.

6. We experience a sense of control.

7. We lose our sense of self-concern during the activity, yet our self-awareness becomes stronger after the experience.

8. Our perception of the passage of time is altered.[25]

Box 14.3

The characteristics of flow are congruent with wholesome recreation and can be illustrated with a family ski outing. Imagine that you and your 15-year-old daughter are highly skilled skiers, but your spouse and 12-year-old son are just beginners. If you all go to the top of a mountain and attempt to ski down its steep slopes, you and your daughter will likely have an exhilarating experience while your spouse and son suffer frustration, failure, and perhaps injury. When they arrive at the bottom tired and cold they will want to go home. However, if you all go to the beginner's slope for the benefit of your spouse and son, you and your daughter will be bored and want to go home.

This illustration demonstrates the importance of matching a person's skill level with the challenge of the activity. Because of varying skill levels among family members trying to participate in the same activity, some can be totally absorbed while others are either bored because the task is too easy or frustrated because it is too difficult. The research on flow suggests that when people engage in activities that provide challenges equal to their skill levels they report that the experience is meaningful and enjoyable, while an imbalance results in a lack of enjoyment.

Csikszentmihalyi says that although flow experiences may be pleasurable, pleasure is not the motivating force, nor is it always present. Meaningful and satisfying flow experiences typically require self-discipline and intense mental or physical effort.[26] Research suggests, ironically, that optimal experiences occur more often at work than during leisure activities because the structure of work provides many of the elements necessary for flow, such as clear goals and feedback, while leisure time is unstructured.

The principles of flow help us understand how family activities must be adapted to make them meaningful for family members of different ages and skill levels. In general, activities need to be less challenging for younger children and more challenging for older children. At a family bowling activity, for example, young children become frustrated when they repeatedly roll the ball into the gutter and miss all of the pins. Placing bumpers in the gutters allows younger children to compete with the older children and parents.

It is uncommon for families to experience flow together. When it occurs, however, it can be a strong bonding experience. One father remembers when he introduced his three adolescents to backpacking in a beautiful rain forest. All of the flow components coalesced and the family members shared an optimal experience, one that they remember, talk about, and relive through the years. Another family spent time preparing and planting a garden together. Each family member had a different responsibility and they laughed and sang together as they worked toward their goal.

Many families participating in the Sesquicentennial Mormon Trail Wagon Train experienced flow as family members were stretched to their limits of physical and emotional endurance. Children walked until they became exhausted and were then placed in handcarts. Despite the hardships, families speak of this experience as the most meaningful event of their lives. Virtually all of the elements of flow were present in this experience.

Parents may feel overwhelmed when they consider planning family activities that promote flow experiences or integrate the principles of Aristotle's good life. Not every wholesome recreational activity will be extremely challenging; some is spontaneous activity, such as play. Research suggests, however, that almost half of an American's typical leisure time is spent in sedentary activities with the media.[27] Most Americans and most families would benefit from spending less time with the media and more time seeking greater challenge, novelty, and learning through creating wholesome family recreation.

CONCERNS WITH TELEVISON AS A SOURCE OF WHOLESOME RECREATION

Television has been criticized because it does not promote flow experiences and lacks other characteristics of wholesome recreation. Television is highly appealing because it provides immensely diverse entertainment, including sports, drama, news, education, weather, shopping, pornography, politics, and religion. Yet, research indicates that most television produces minimal enjoyment because it provides no physical challenge and often only limited intellectual challenge. It is pleasurable, but not enjoyable. Extensive research suggests that the more we watch, the worse we feel.[28] Unfortunately, many people spend more time watching television than any other leisure activity and the consequences are mostly undesirable. Excessive television viewing has been blamed for decreased physical health, increased violence among children, and diminished interests in other wholesome pursuits.[29]

Many television programs and commercials contain unhealthy messages that should be avoided entirely. Other programs communicate excellent information, such as the telecasts of LDS general

---

It may be tempting to use television, movies, and video games to keep your child busy, but your child needs to spend as much time growing and learning as possible. Playing, reading, and spending time with friends and family are much healthier than sitting in front of a TV screen.

American Academy of Pediatrics, 1999[31]

Box 14.5

---

conference and special programs on the arts, nature, history, and learning channels, as well as public broadcasting services. But even good programs and movies usually fail to offer families the benefits that are available through other activities. Television viewing is almost always inferior to other forms of family recreation.

Television viewing requires little creative thought or imagination and usually inhibits communication between viewers. The qualitative difference between watching television and other types of recreational activities is an important difference that parents need to understand. The benefits of reading a book together as a family, for instance, are vastly superior to seeing the same story as a TV movie. For example, the children's classic *Where the Red Fern Grows*[32] is a story that explores the joys, challenges, and deep disappointments of a young boy. The television production of this story is entertaining and moving. But watching it on television as a family in a two-hour period does not allow a family to explore important issues as meaningfully as they could while reading the story. Reading together provides opportunities to discuss the meaning of death, the importance of work, the value of money, and the need to obey parents. While reading a book, parents have time to answer children's questions and help them better understand difficult issues. These discussions bring families together in ways that simply cannot occur while watching television. When families watch television together, parents are more likely to ask children to stop talking so everyone can hear than to engage in conversation. While reading a good book, family members share an emotional experience that they continue to share for a lifetime, bringing feelings of connectedness. Reading a book also allows family members to use their own imaginations to create visions of people, places, and events, while television provides these images and thereby stifles imagination.

The leisure time of children must be constructively directed to wholesome, positive, pursuits. Too much television can be destructive, and pornography in this medium should not be tolerated.[30]

Ezra Taft Benson

Box 14.4

USING WHOLESOME RECREATION TO BUILD FAMILIES

Wholesome recreation makes an important contribution to building successful, organized families when these activities are part of family rituals. Family rituals have been defined as "repeated and coordinated activities that have significance."[34] For a recreational activity to be a family ritual it must be repeated, predictable, and include at least two family members. A husband and wife who go on a date every Friday night are participating in a family ritual. Likewise, an annual camping trip would be a ritual.

Family rituals may be very brief. Elder Dallin Oaks explains how he stayed emotionally close to his little girls in spite of a hectic law school schedule by the way he greeted them. "When I came home from my studies for a few minutes at lunch and dinnertime, I would set my books on the table and drop down on all fours on the linoleum. Then, making the most terrible growls, I would crawl around the floor after the children, who fled with screams, but always begged for more."[35] This greeting is a good example of an intentional and predictable family ritual.

When President Gordon B. Hinckley was raising his children, the time commitment demanded by his work with the Church was extensive. Summer vacations became annual rituals that were important to his wife Marjorie and the children. "One issue over which the children prayed each summer was that nothing

would come up to postpone, or worse, cancel their annual family vacation."[36]

By using wholesome recreational activities to establish family rituals families can reap four important blessings:

1. *Wholesome recreational activities will occur more frequently.* One busy father of a large family has a ritual of going on a date of the child's choosing on the Saturday before each birthday. During their time together he focuses on understanding and relating to the child. Because of this ritual the father has more frequent wholesome recreation with each child than he would otherwise.

2. *Families will have closer relationships.* One family has an annual tradition of preparing a Christmas program and presenting it at several retirement homes. The process of planning the program, learning the parts, rehearsing the songs, preparing the goodies, and finally presenting the program helps to forge more intimate family ties.

3. *Families will have a clearer sense of identity.* A family that has established rituals around camping, hiking, and fishing will be identified as an "outdoor family." A family that sings and performs together might be identified as a "musical family." A family that likes to tell jokes might be identified as a "fun family."

4. *Families will develop strong values.* One family has a standing tradition of going to a homeless shelter every Thanksgiving to prepare and serve food. This family ritual has helped members learn compassion and the value of service. A mother has the ritual of taking a brisk walk with one of her children each evening. She finds that it allows her to clarify important values with her children.

Choosing Age-Appropriate Recreation

A developmental perspective helps parents select appropriate wholesome recreational activities for children of differing ages. Lev Vygotsky, a noted Russian child development scholar, uses the term "zone of proximal development" to refer to what a child is capable of learning or mastering with the help of a mentor.[38] Parents should understand the successive steps that occur as their children develop and select appropriate activities for each stage of development.

Many families have children in various developmental stages, which challenges parents to select activities for a wide range of developmental needs. Some families have found that out-of-doors activities include a wide variety of tasks that provide something challenging for everyone, such as finding insects, watching birds, carving a whistle, pitching a tent, building a fire without matches, cooking a meal with or without utensils, marking a trail, and surviving in the wilderness. On a camping trip toddlers can explore with their senses, preschoolers can create their own imaginary games, older children can develop new skills (such as building fires and gathering wood), and teenagers can assume some adult responsibilities (such as preparing food and pitching tents).

Good literature can appeal to family members of different ages. One parent found that while reading *The Chronicles of Narnia*[39] together as a family, younger children could listen and follow the obvious story line, while older children and adults could listen and reflect on the deeper meaning and symbolism in the books.

As parents select wholesome recreational activities they should view them through the eyes of their children. Charles Francis Adams, the grandson of the second president of the United States, was a successful lawyer, a member of the U.S. House of Representatives, and the U.S. ambassador to Britain. Although he had little free time, he kept a diary. One day he wrote, "Went fishing with my son today—a day wasted!" On that same date, Charles's son, Brooks Adams, had printed in his own diary, "Went fishing with my father today—the most wonderful day of my life."[40]

Balancing Work and Recreation

The appropriate balance of work and recreation depends on the value of each and how they contribute to a meaningful and balanced life. No one can prescribe the exact number of hours that we should spend in work or recreation. This crucial choice is ultimately a personal moral decision. Both work and recreation must be tied to a broader perspective of the meaning of life and its purposes. Both should

contribute to personal and family development without distorting other important values or becoming an obsession.

People who spend excessive time in work or leisure activities miss valuable opportunities to strengthen their families and to serve others. The balance between work and recreation is not between two opposing values or activities, but rather between two complementary activities that have the potential to bless our lives and the lives of our families. Both activities are goal directed and challenging; they each require attention and effort, usually mental and physical. When we approach them enthusiastically, work and wholesome recreation help us develop our skills and we become completely absorbed in the activity. After work and wholesome recreation, family members share genuine feelings of accomplishment.

While people are encouraged to be anxiously engaged in good causes (see D&C 58:26–28), they are also encouraged to pursue cultural arts, music, dance, and literature (Ps. 33:1–3; 147:7; D&C 88:118; 136:28). President Brigham Young taught that "Life is best enjoyed when time periods are evenly divided between labour, sleep, and recreation . . . all people should spend one-third of their time in recreation which is rebuilding, voluntary activity— never idleness."[41]

People can become imbalanced in either work or leisure activities. One indication of imbalance is when work or leisure activities become addictive and keep us from spending time with our families. People who are too absorbed in work become workaholics and are literally addicted to their work—they experience anxiety and withdrawal when they are not working.[42] Conversely, people can also become addicted to leisure if their lives begin to revolve around those activities and they drift from important anchors such as family, work, and friends. People addicted to leisure spend most of their free time engaging in their hobby and when they are not doing it, they are thinking and talking about it.

To decide whether you have a proper balance of work and recreation, you should ask yourself such questions as: Is my life challenging? What do we do as a family that is exciting or meaningful? Do we have a passion for something? Is my work meaningful? Am I fulfilling my responsibilities to my family? Are we holding family home evenings regularly? Do my children or spouse feel ignored? Am I missing important family events? Are we scheduling meaningful family time together? Are we creating debt and financial

TIPS FOR ENCOURAGING WHOLESOME FAMILY RECREATION

Plan your recreational activities—fun doesn't just happen.
- For family home evening make a list of "100 things we want to do as a family in the next 100 years."
- Get a five-year calendar and block out two weeks each year for family vacation.
- Plan a fun date with your spouse once a week.
- Enjoy spontaneous fun when your plans go awry.

Plan age-appropriate recreational activities for your family.
- For infants, provide a safe environment where they can explore with their senses.
- For preschoolers, provide make-believe tools (such as old clothes) for imaginative activities.
- For school-age kids, plan activities that will encourage skill development (sports, sewing, etc.).
- For adolescents, provide grown-up activities to steer them away from aimless leisure.
- If it suits your family, try camping and hiking; there is something for all ages in nature.

Plan recreational activities that will foster the development of family members.
- Read bedtime stories to your children. Read in the car on family trips.
- Engage in musical activities (singing together, duets on the piano and playing an instrument).
- Play worthwhile music in your home and monitor use of headphones, radios, and CD players.
- Attend concerts, games, recitals of children. Let them know you care about their progress.
- Learn a new skill as a family (such as sewing, small engine repair, and orienteering).
- Learn as a family the etiquette of fine dining, theatre/concert enjoyment, enjoyment of and respect for the outdoors, and practice in the appropriate setting.
- Take family members who are old enough to appropriate concerts, operas, plays, ballets, art and natural history museums, and historical sites in your locale or while on vacation.

Limit your consumption of media (such as TV, Internet, radio, and movies).
- Hold a family media fast (no media for a day/week/month). See your family flourish.
- Plan TV viewing a week ahead. Watch only those shows you have planned to watch.
- Record TV on a VCR in absentia. Fast-forward through commercials and pause to discuss the show with the family.
- Monitor Internet access carefully. Place any computer with Internet access in the family room or other high-traffic area.
- Establish a rule that, regardless of rating, a parent must see a movie before children are allowed to see it. Cooperate with the parents of your children's friends so that parents will know if videos will be viewed at a party or other gathering and which videos will be viewed.

Intentionally establish rituals that connect family members and foster family love.
- Each evening read bedtime stories and sing songs to your children.
- Each week eat treats together after family home evening.
- Each quarter go on an overnight date with your spouse, and leave the kids at home.
- Each summer go camping or backpacking or hiking at a favorite secluded location.
- Each year take each child on a fun date the week before his or her birthday.
- Choose a family hymn and sing it at baptisms, missionary farewells, and on other special occasions.
- Create rituals involving care of a family member who is ill (such as a special story, a special blanket, favorite Jell-O or other suitable food and rewards for bravery).

Create one-on-one time with each family member through your recreation.
- Invite a child on your daily walk.
- Play chess or other board games with your children.
- Read a special bedtime story to just one of your children.
- Take a child to a sporting event, a musical presentation, or the theatre.

Be of service as part of wholesome family recreation.
- Plan a Christmas program with parts, music, and treats to be presented at nursing homes.
- Identify a family or person in need and anonymously carry out activities to provide help.
- Invite individuals with developmental disabilities to take part in a family activity.
- Take a hike in a pristine area and remove litter.

Box 14.8

stress to support our leisure pursuits? Most people who are imbalanced fail to recognize their plight and need to seek feedback from other family members or friends. The criticisms of loved ones regarding how you focus your time should be carefully considered rather than casually dismissed.

SUGGESTIONS FOR WHOLESOME RECREATION

Meaningful recreation requires knowledge, effort, and planning; it has been suggested that free time is more difficult to enjoy than work.[43] The following principles should be considered when planning wholesome recreational activities:

1. *Select recreation that builds meaningful relationships.* Spending time with others and devoting attention to them builds meaningful relationships.

2. *Regularly choose challenging activities that stretch each family member.* Activities that are too easy will be boring, while activities that are too difficult will be frustrating.

3. *Clarify the purpose of the activity.* Activities should be designed so that participants know what they are trying to accomplish. Goal accomplishment produces feelings of enjoyment and satisfaction.

4. *Select activities in which participants can acquire a sense of mastery and competence.* Activities that allow participants to develop and practice their skills provide a sense of control and accomplishment.

5. *Incorporate intellectual and creative elements.* The more we are intellectually challenged and the more we learn, the better our lives become; most wholesome recreational activities require some form of mental involvement.

6. *Look for opportunities to promote moral behavior.* Wholesome recreation encourages moral behavior. Competitive athletics should teach the value of sportsmanship, cooperation, and a genuine concern for others. Winning should not be promoted as the ultimate value. Volunteerism or service is another important aspect of moral behavior.

7. *Select activities that will rejuvenate both the mind and body.* Recreation serves to restore the mind and body and rejuvenate us for work.

Many recreational activities can be improved by following these principles. For example, canoeing, sewing, playing chess, cooking, reading, and performing service projects may all be structured to produce the desired outcomes of wholesome recreation.

Canoeing

Families that enjoy canoeing may learn about the history of canoes in different cultures and how they are built. They may also have the goal to design and build a canoe as a family. Working together to build a canoe and then planning and completing a trip as a family facilitates the type of interaction that will build relationships and fond memories that will last a lifetime. Canoeing offers different levels of challenge depending on the technical difficulty of the water and the position one occupies in the canoe. Goals may be established, such as learning how to paddle or completing the entire length of a river. Learning to control a canoe provides a sense of mastery and competence that may be shared by family members. While completing a trip, a family may learn about protecting the environment by not littering and thus create a sense of stewardship toward the earth.

Sewing

One spouse might teach the other or a child to sew, quilt, or cook and together they could make something for someone in need. After making it together, the couple could find a way to give it anonymously. Working together can build and strengthen the relationship while at the same time promote moral behavior. This could be the beginning of a family holiday tradition.

Chess

Playing chess will encourage creativity by helping their children find new strategies for starting the game and setting their defense. Chess has clear goals: it requires intellect and memory, it requires concentration and patience, and it has a generally accepted etiquette. The game also provides a context to teach fair play, honesty, and sportsmanship. Time spent together playing chess will foster stronger relationships. As children's skills improve, they will gain a sense of competence and mastery.

Reading

Reading good books is one of the most valuable forms of wholesome recreation. Both the scriptures and latter-day prophets extol the virtue of learning. We are commanded to read good books (see D&C 88:118) and pursue both religious and secular learning (see D&C 88:77–80). Reading together as a family is a wonderful way to instill in children a love for good literature and a desire to learn. Regular family visits to the public library can help children and parents discover books they are eager to read.

A careful analysis of these examples illustrates how activities can be designed to incorporate the principles of wholesome recreation. If we make the effort to plan and engage in wholesome recreation, we will be happier and achieve greater success in strengthening our families. How we choose to spend our time is a moral decision that reflects our commitment to our marriage and our family. These decisions also influence our growth and development and the quality of our lives both here and hereafter.

NOTES

1. J. Richard Clarke (1982, May), The value of work, *Ensign, 12*(5), 78.

2. J. Robinson and G. Godbey (1997), *Time for life: The surprising way Americans use their time* (University Park, PA: Penn State).

3. L. Holbrook (1975), Dancing as an aspect of early Mormon and Utah culture, *Brigham Young University Studies, 16*(1), 117–138.

4. Ezra Taft Benson (1988), *The teachings of Ezra Taft Benson.* (Salt Lake City: Bookcraft), 511.

5. Bruce R. McConkie (1966), *Mormon doctrine.* (Salt Lake City: Bookcraft), 622.

6. W. Allred (1892), Recollections, *Juvenile instructor, 27,* 471.

7. S. Y. Gates (1930), *The life story of Brigham Young* (New York: Macmillan), 253.

8. Gates (1930).

9. Holbrook (1975).

10. R. Jackson (1999, January 31), Personal correspondence.

11. R. M. Huber (1971), *The American Idea of Success* (New York: McGraw-Hill).

12. O. Seavey (Ed.) (1993), *Benjamin Franklin: Autobiography and other writings* (New York: Oxford University Press).

13. D. T. Rodgers (1978), *The work ethic in industrial America, 1850–1920* (Chicago: University of Chicago Press).

14. Huber (1971).

15. Rodgers (1978).

16. W. Rybczynski (1991), *Waiting for the weekend* (New York: Penguin); T. B. Veblen (1899), *The theory of the leisure class* (New York: Macmillan).

17. M. Seligman (1991), *Learned optimism* (New York: Knopf).

18. M. Csikszentmihalyi (1990), *Flow: The psychology of optimal experience* (New York: Harper & Row); M. Csikszentmihalyi (1997), *Finding flow: The psychology of engagement with everyday life* (New York: BasicBooks); D. Hudson (1992), Contemporary views of happiness, in J. Van Doren (Ed.), *The great ideas today* (Chicago: Encyclopaedia Brittanica), 171–216; Seligman (1991); A. Waterman (1993), Two conceptions of happiness: Contrasts of personal expressiveness (eudaemonia) and hedonic enjoyment, *Journal of Personality and Social Psychology, 64*(4), 678–691.

19. M. Ellis (1973), *Why people play* (Englewood Cliffs, NJ: Prentice Hall); J. N. Lieberman (1977), *Playfulness: Its relationship to imagination and creativity* (New York: Academic Press).

20. Aristotle (1982), *Aristotle: Selected works,* trans. H. G. Apostle and L. P. Gerson (Grinnell, IA: Peripatetic).

21. M. Adler (1991), *Desires, right and wrong: The ethics of enough* (New York: Macmillan).

22. M. Widmer and G. Ellis (1998), The Aristotelian good life model: Integration of values into therapeutic recreation service delivery, *Therapeutic Recreation Journal, 33*(4), 290–302; M. Widmer and G. Ellis (1997), Facilitating the Aristotelian good life through therapeutic recreation: Challenges of building an ethical dimension in the therapeutic recreation service model, in D. Compton (Ed.), *Issues in therapeutic recreation: Toward the new millennium,* 2nd ed. (Champaign, IL.: Sagamore).

23. Csikszentmihalyi (1990); Csikszentmihalyi (1997).

24. Csikszentmihalyi (1990), 3.

25. Csikszentmihalyi (1990), 49.

26. Csikszentmihalyi (1990).

27. J. Robinson and G. Godbey (1997).

28. Csikszentmihalyi (1990).

29. Robinson and Godbey (1997); J. Garbarino (1999), *Lost boys: Why our sons turn violent and how we can save them* (New York: Free Press).

30. Ezra Taft Benson (1984, May), Counsel to the Saints, *Ensign, 14*(5), 6–8.

31. *Pediatrics* (1999, August), 104(2), 341–343.

32. W. Rawls (1961), *Where the red fern grows: The story of two dogs and a boy* (Garden City, NY: Doubleday).

33. *Pediatrics* (1999).

34. W. Doherty (1997), *The intentional family: How to build family ties in our modern world* (New York: Addison-Wesley), 11.

35. Dallin H. Oaks (1975), *Speeches of the year: 1975* (Provo, UT: Brigham Young University Press), 225.

36. Sheri L. Dew (1996), *Go forward with faith: The biography of Gordon B. Hinckley* (Salt Lake City: Deseret Book), 167.

37. Robert D. Hales (1999, May), in Conference report, 33.

38. L. S. Vygotsky (1978), *Mind in society: The development of higher psychological processes* (Cambridge, MA: Harvard University Press).

39. C. S. Lewis (1988), *The Chronicles of Narnia* (New York: Macmillan).

40. S. Walker (1994), *Daily guideposts* (Carmel, NY: Guideposts Associates), cited in Rex D. Pinegar (1994, November), The simple things, *Ensign, 24*(11), 82.

41. Brigham Young, quoted in S. Y. Gates (1930), 251.

42. D. J. Cherrington (1980), *The work ethic: Working values and values that work* (New York: AMACOM), 189–196.

43. Csikszentmihalyi (1990).

BALANCING FAMILY AND WORK

E. JEFFREY HILL

In my professional career I study balance: not the balance of a gymnast, nor the balance sheet of an executive, but the balance men and women report between their jobs and their home life. Research shows many are spending more time in paid work and less time at home, and they are feeling more out-of-balance than ever. In light of the sacred duty of parents as outlined in the Proclamation, LDS members with large families, time-consuming jobs, and responsible priesthood/auxiliary stewardships have special challenges.

Our family has a special interest in this topic because my wife Juanita and I have nine children and we have struggled through 23 years of marriage to find balance in our lives. In this essay I will share our journey as we have sometimes succeeded and sometimes failed to find harmony among so many different demanding roles. I recognize that our path will be different than your path, but I hope you may garner some common principles and ideas that may be useful as you attempt to provide and nurture your family, while faithfully serving in the kingdom.

To provide for my family, I have worked for IBM for more than 20 years. When I was recruited, "I.B.M." stood for "I've Been Moved." The common practice at many companies was to relocate new employees about every two years to positions of increasing responsibility. In my first 10 years, I had five different IBM jobs and we lived in Washington, Utah, New York, Georgia, and Arizona. In marketing and human resources positions, I traveled extensively and worked long hours. In the Church, I served on the high council, in two bishoprics, as the high priest group instructor, early-morning seminary teacher, and in the stake mission presidency. Juanita chose not to work for pay, but stayed at home to nurture our kids. Six children were born while she served in the Primary presidency three times and in Relief Society and Young Women's presidencies.

Like many young LDS fathers who earnestly strive for career and church success, I found myself becoming a casual occupant in our home with not nearly enough connection to the day-to-day activities of our children. My waking hours were mostly spent away from home, doing IBM and church work. Many times the kids would be asleep when I left for work in the morning and would already be in bed by the time I got home at night. I was out of town several days each month. I missed birthdays, ball games, plays, concerts, recitals, and parent–teacher conferences. Family prayer, scripture reading, family home evening, getting chores done, and informal play became less frequent. A fog seemed to descend upon my family life. The little time I was at home seemed more prone to misunderstandings.

But I loved my family and yearned to be more involved in my wife's and children's lives. I began to worry I was living to work, instead of working to live.

I even got frustrated and discouraged when my church work would take me out of the home so often. And Juanita was feeling overwhelmed with so many little children at home and so little help from me. We struggled with this. We had many late-night discussions. With tears, we pled with God to help us build an eternal marriage relationship and to raise His children in righteousness. After a time we felt a sense of peace that God was with us and if we did our best He would provide a way.

Late in 1988 we discovered Juanita was unexpectedly expecting our seventh child. She had given birth to twins less than a year before, and the responsibility for this new baby on top of everything else would be too much. Early one morning an impression, which I attribute to the Spirit, came that we ought to request a parenting leave from IBM. This was a new program that enabled fathers and mothers to take time off for their children, without risk of losing their jobs. Thousands of female IBM employees took leave each year, but only a few men ever asked for parenting leave.

Early in 1989, I approached my new manager with the leave request. He chuckled and thought I was playing a practical joke on him. I convinced him I was serious. He apologized and, after some give-and-take, my leave was approved. My manager explained I could take up to six months leave without pay.

After a difficult labor and delivery, our 10-pound, 11-ounce Emily was born during the first week of June. My first day on leave was a great eye-opener. During my entire career I had never before been present when my children came home from school. I could not believe the kids' energy as they burst through the door anxious to share the experiences of the day. Listening to them was like opening a fire hydrant of enthusiastic information. I came to realize I must have missed most of their school lives by never being there at the crossroads before.

We defined new duties. Juanita was now responsible for the baby, and I was now responsible for the rest of the children. We shared the household chores. The haphazard rhythm of life in this environment was much different than the regular cadence at IBM. I would just get started with breakfast when Hannah would need her diaper changed and Aaron would be yelling that his older brother Jeffrey wouldn't give him back his toy car. I was suddenly baptized with a great wave of appreciation for what Juanita had being doing all these years.

In the past, Juanita had often talked to me about the kids, saying things like, "We've got to do something about Jeffrey . . . or Aaron . . . or Abigail . . ." and my standard reply was, "Don't worry—they'll grow out of it." Now, when I saw Jeffrey do the same obnoxious thing 50 times in one day, I understood her exasperation. Before, I had been the easygoing parent, the one the kids came to when Juanita's patience had worn thin. Now the kids would say, "Oh, Dad, you're just like Mom!" Juanita smiled at me. Sometimes I'd respond, "It's not funny," and walk away.

While Juanita was caring for the baby, I took the responsibility for toddler Hannah. We jogged together an hour every day; I was pounding the pavement and she was taking in the world from the vantage point of her stroller. She would excitedly give me a play-by-play description of her view: a dog here, a cat there, a flock of birds in the sky. In just a few weeks, Hannah began to display almost constant exuberance toward me. It warmed my heart and soothed my soul.

During the leave I kept a low profile to the outside world. I did not tell anyone at church or in the neighborhood that I was staying home full time. I refrained from answering the phone during the day. Sometimes I would forget, and the person on the line would say something like, "Jeff, is that you? What are you doing at home this time of day?" I felt a sense of guilt—as if I should look over my shoulder for the truant officer who might try to haul me back to work. I felt better when I overheard Abigail talking to one of her friends: "Why is your daddy home?" the friend asked. "He's taking a leave," Abby responded cheerfully, "because he loves me."

As my leave drew to an end in late November, I met with my manager to discuss my return to IBM. I realized how pale the work world was compared to the richness of the family realm. I didn't want to go back to work—I wanted to stay home forever. I realized that though I had taken the leave because I felt my family needed it, really I was the one who had needed it.

When I discuss this leave with others, many say something like, "Oh, that's nice, but I could never do that." That may or may not be true. When I took paternity leave in 1989 very few companies offered it. Now, the law in the United States requires that all companies with more than 50 employees offer fathers at least 12 weeks of unpaid leave in conjunction with the birth or adoption of a new baby. The principle that all can follow is to commit to do whatever it takes to rear a righteous family. The Lord opened this door for us, and He will open this or another door for you.

Shortly after returning to work, IBM offered me a job doing employee surveys. But the position was in New York, the commute would be horrendous, and the cost of living out of sight. Still, I hated to turn down this opportunity. Again an impression, which I feel came from the Spirit, came to accept the job with conditions. Instead of moving back to New York, I proposed that I telecommute instead. I reasoned with my future boss that I could better design surveys and analyze results through a 1200 bps modem from my home in the West than from an expensive office in the East. She agreed to let me do it on a trial basis.

Initially I was required to fly to New York every other week and work from the Phoenix office the rest of the time. However, within a few months I was traveling to New York only every other month and working from home most of the rest of the time. Though we entered this arrangement to accommodate my family needs, it quickly became apparent that flexibility in when and where I worked also helped me on the job. I found that by being liberated from the commute, unscheduled interruptions of co-workers, and office politics, I became much more productive. Telecommuting worked so well for me that soon four of my colleagues were working from homes in three states with similarly positive results.

Of course, this flexibility was wonderful for my family as well. I'm a morning person, and so I would often do IBM work from about 4:30 to 6:30 A.M. The kids would get up and between about 6:30 and 8:00 A.M. we had time for an unhurried family devotional, breakfast together, and dishes, and then the children would go off to school. I could then exercise, shower, and work the rest of the morning. Instead of eating lunch with work colleagues, I was able to eat with my preschoolers and Juanita. Mid-afternoon I tried to take about 30 minutes off to visit with the kids at the "crossroads" time when they came home from school. Jeffrey and I would often play a 10-minute game of one-on-one basketball. Now that he's off on his mission, I particularly value the hours we were able to spend together. On a typical telework day I found myself with more quality family time and just as much quality work time.

One benefit of this flexibility came when Juanita gave birth to our eighth child, Amanda, in 1992. With me working at home, Juanita could put the baby down for a nap and go shopping, to aerobics, or run errands. Being a new mother was much less taxing. We were able to use job flexibility to maximize my time with the children. In my home office, we set up three computers side-by-side, downstairs, so the kids could rub shoulders with me while they did their homework.

In 1993 I was excited to accept the work responsibility to research the effect of telecommuting on work and family. IBM saw telecommuting as a way to save millions of dollars in office costs and wanted to find out about it. After extensive interviews and surveys, the results indicated that almost all IBMers were more productive when given flexibility in the location and scheduling of their work. Though some went overboard and worked too many hours, many were able to use this flexibility to strengthen their families as well. The research confirmed flextime and flexplace to be a "win-win" proposition for employees and employers.

Beginning in 1994, IBM implemented flexibility on a grand scale. Between 1994 and 1996 they adopted what was called the "virtual office" for marketing and services employees in the United States. By the end of 1996, more than 25,000 IBMers no longer had dedicated IBM offices but were given laptops, cell phones, pagers, and given the charge to work wherever and whenever it made sense. They could work from home, a customer location, a hotel, an airport, at IBM, or anywhere else as long as they did a high-quality job in a timely basis. These flexible workers responded by achieving better results and have been critical to IBM's recent success.

For my family and me, flexibility in the timing and location of work was just the tool we needed to find balance in our lives. The Lord saw our situation and helped us create that solution, even though when I started working, that kind of flexibility was not common. It may be that job flexibility is not an option for you. However, if you do your best, the Lord will help you find the option that will work best for you.

Principles of Balancing Family and Work

This essay as been entirely personal. However, I would like to conclude with a few principles that we have gleaned that I feel apply to you:

Commit to the Family Stewardship: Commit to do your very best to love and care for your spouse and to fulfill your sacred duty to rear your children in love and righteousness and ask for the Lord's help.

Nothing is too hard for the Lord. He will help you see many creative opportunities for life balance.

Accept Trade-Offs: To be a better parent, it is likely you will have to make life choices with potentially negative career consequences. You may have to choose between climbing the career ladder and being involved in the home. Recognize and accept the fact that work and family trade-offs are real and make them gladly.

Be Flexible: Many jobs now have flexibility in when and where they are done. In order to create more quality family time be willing to use that flexibility (e.g., come in early so you can leave early, work from home, job share).

Prudent Personal Finance: Many opportunities for balance (e.g., leave and part-time work) are available to families who can live on reduced income for several months. Live below your means, be free of debt, and acquire a reserve of cash that can be traded for future family time.

Strong Work Performance: If you are a top performer, companies are likely to accommodate personal requests.

Successfully balancing the demands of work, church, and family is still a hard thing to do. However, "Is any thing too hard for the Lord?" (Gen. 18:14). I am convinced that if we clearly know where our priorities are, the Lord will help us compose a symphony of a life filled with rich service to our families and our religion and where we can provide sufficient resources for the needs of our families.

CHAPTER 15

THE SANCTITY AND IMPORTANCE OF HUMAN LIFE

CYNTHIA L. HALLEN

We affirm the sanctity of life and its importance in God's eternal plan.
(The Family: A Proclamation to the World, ¶ 5)

In academic circles and public forums, the phrase "sanctity of life" is used by people who have concerns about life-related issues such as abortion on demand, birth control, capital punishment, and euthanasia. When leaders of The Church of Jesus Christ of Latter-day Saints speak about the "sanctity of life" in conference talks and official statements, they usually focus on the issue of elective abortion, although other life-related topics are also occasionally addressed.

In 1991, the First Presidency of the Church issued a comprehensive statement on abortion, reaffirming the "sanctity of human life":

> In view of the widespread public interest in the issue of abortion, we reaffirm that The Church of Jesus Christ of Latter-day Saints has consistently opposed elective abortion. More than a century ago, the First Presidency of the Church warned against this evil. We have repeatedly counseled people everywhere to turn from the devastating practice of abortion for personal or social convenience.
>
> The Church recognizes that there may be rare cases in which abortion may be justified—cases involving pregnancy by incest or rape; when the life or health of the woman is adjudged by competent medical authority to be in serious jeopardy; or when the fetus is known by competent medical authority to have severe defects that will not allow the baby to survive beyond birth. But these are not automatic reasons for abortion.

> Even in these cases, the couple should consider abortion only after consulting with each other, and their bishop, and receiving divine confirmation through prayer. The practice of elective abortion is fundamentally contrary to the Lord's injunction, "Thou shalt not steal; neither commit adultery, nor kill, nor do anything like unto it" (D&C 59:6). We urge all to preserve the sanctity of human life and thereby realize the happiness promised to those who keep the commandments of the Lord.

> The Church of Jesus Christ of Latter-day Saints as an institution has not favored or opposed specific legislative proposals or public demonstrations concerning abortion.

> Inasmuch as this issue is likely to arise in all states in the United States of America and in many other nations of the world in which the Church is established, it is impractical for the Church to take a position on specific legislative proposals on this important subject. However, we continue to encourage our members as citizens to let their voices be heard in appropriate and legal ways that will evidence their belief in the sacredness of life.[1]

The introduction of a brain-extraction (D&X) abortion method, used on partially delivered viable babies prompted further comment from Church leaders in a 1997 statement:

> The Church of Jesus Christ of Latter-day Saints declares the sanctity of human life. We deplore the

practice of partial-birth abortion which destroys innocent life, and we condemn and oppose it as one of the most revolting and sinful practices of our day. It is abhorrent to God and is fundamentally contrary to his injunction, "Thou shalt not kill . . . nor do anything like unto it" (Doctrine and Covenants 59:6).[2]

When President Gordon B. Hinckley presented the Proclamation at the General Women's Meeting in 1995, he reaffirmed "the sanctity of life and of its importance in God's eternal plan" (¶ 5). Two weeks later in general conference, Elder Durrel A. Woolsey stressed that "we must hold fast to forceful proclamations from God regarding the sanctity of life, His eternal and never-ending instruction to be chaste and pure."[3] A careful look at the language of such teachings can help us understand why life is so sacred and so important.

What Is Life? Why Is Life Sacred? Why Is Life Important in God's Eternal Plan?

Life. The Old English etymology of the word *lif* includes meanings such as "body" and "person," or that which "remains" and "continues."[4] Life can be defined as a condition of sustained regenerative activity, energy, expression, or power that human beings and other animate creatures experience. Emily Dickinson said, "To be alive—is Power."[5] Her definition suggests that life is empowerment, in spite of the risks and difficulties that human beings may experience in mortality. Respect for the sanctity of life increases when we remember that "life" is one of the titles by which Jesus identifies himself: "I am the way, the truth, and the life: no man cometh unto the Father, but by me" (John 14:6).

Sacred. The earliest meanings of the word *sacre* in English have to do with the consecration of the body and blood of Christ in the sacrament.[6] Life is sacred because Jesus Christ is the ultimate source or fountain of life through His work in the Creation and through His sacrifice in the Atonement. Human life is sacred because human bodies are temples (see 1 Cor. 3:16), and all flesh is in the Lord's hands (see D&C 101:16). Our bodies belong to the Lord: "What? know ye not that your body is the temple of the Holy Ghost which is in you, which ye have of God, and ye are not your own? For ye are bought with a price: therefore glorify God in your body, and in your spirit, which are God's" (1 Cor. 6:19–20).

Each individual human being is sacred because each one reflects the divine image of the Creator (see Gen. 1:26–27; Col. 1:13–16; Moses 2:27). The Proclamation confirms that "all human beings—male and female—are created in the image of God" (¶ 2). Elder Lynn A. Michelsen elaborates on the importance of this principle: "We are created in the image of God. The union of the flesh with the spirit can bring us a fullness of joy. Teach your children to respect the sanctity of human life, to revere it and cherish it. Human life is the precious stepping-stone to eternal life, and we must jealously guard it from the moment of conception."[7]

From conception to resurrection, mortal life is a gift from God (see Job 33:4; Acts 17:25; Alma 40:11). Elder Russell M. Nelson explains why we should have respect for the gift of life: "As sons and daughters of God, we cherish life as a gift from him. . . . Life comes from life. It is a gift from our Heavenly Father. It is eternal, as he is eternal. Innocent life is not sent by him to be destroyed! This doctrine is not of me, but is that of the living God and of his divine Son."[8]

Each human being, no matter how young or how small, is a "beloved spirit son or daughter of heavenly parents, and, as such, each has a divine nature and destiny" (Proclamation, ¶ 2). To welcome children into our lives is one of the most important ways to follow Christ, who invited little children to come unto him (see Luke 18:16). Elder Nelson testifies of the value of a child's life: "Yes, life is precious! No one can cuddle a cherished newborn baby, look into those beautiful eyes, feel the little fingers, and caress that miraculous creation without deepening reverence for life and for our Creator."[9]

The gift of human life in the plan of salvation gives individuals a time and place to seek the face of the Lord—he who "shall gather [us] with his arm, and carry [us] in his bosom, and shall gently lead those that are with young" (Isa. 40:11).

What Is Abortion?

The English word *abort* comes from Latin *ab-* "off, away" and *or-ri,* "arise, appear, come into being"; so to abort literally means to "cut off the existence of someone" or to "cause someone to disappear."[10] Abortion can generally be defined as the natural or deliberate termination of the life of a prenatal, or partially born child by forcible removal from the womb.

To better understand public attitudes and Church policies on abortion, it is useful to distinguish between two types of abortion: (1) spontaneous or natural abortion, and (2) nonspontaneous or induced abortion. The phrase "spontaneous abortion" is a synonym for miscarriage: the premature, involuntary expulsion of a fetus from its mother by natural causes. While a miscarriage may cause significant grief for the mother and family members, spontaneous abortions are not considered a moral issue.

Nonspontaneous or induced abortion can be divided into two subcategories: (a) emergency abortion and (b) elective abortion. The more advanced a pregnancy is, the greater the danger is to the mother who undergoes an emergency or elective abortion. Methods of abortion correspond to various stages of fetal development in order to reduce risk factors for women who abort. All methods of induced abortion involve the violent destruction of at least one human life—the life of a child. All methods of abortion pose potential health risks to the mother, such as infertility, bleeding, increased susceptibility to breast cancer, and problematic future pregnancies. Whether legal or illegal, an elective abortion may also be fatal to the mother. John Willke, M.D., and his wife Barbara Willke, R.N., provide further information about the methods and risks of abortion in a handbook entitled *Love Them Both: Questions and Answers about Abortion.*[11]

The term "emergency abortion" refers to cases in which a fetus is intentionally expelled from the womb of its mother because of critical circumstances attending the mother, the child, or both. Such "hard cases" include serious health problems for the mother, and severe health problems for the baby.[12] For example, in medical emergencies such as ectopic, or tubal pregnancy, the life of the unborn child is taken because both the mother and the child would die if the pregnancy were to continue.[13]

In other cases, a woman may wish to abort a child conceived as a result of incest or rape because of the severe trauma that she has already experienced as a victim. However, the woman may not wish to experience aborting the child because she may see it as an extension or reenactment of the trauma she experienced as a victim of rape or incest.[14] Although emergency abortions raise moral questions, they are not at the heart of the abortion debate in society, because the number of emergency abortions is very low in comparison to the vast number of nonemergency elective abortions performed each year.

The phrase "elective abortion" is synonymous with terms such as "nontherapeutic abortion" or "abortion-on-demand." Elective abortion is the voluntary destruction of the fetus in the womb of its mother for nonemergency purposes or nonmedical reasons. Elective abortion is a serious moral problem because it pits the social, emotional, personal, psychological, or financial concerns of adults against the innocent lives of unborn children. Women cite financial trouble and pregnancy outside of marriage as the most frequent reasons for having an elective abortion.[15]

Due to increasingly broad judicial interpretations of the U. S. Supreme Court's 1973 decision in *Roe v. Wade*,[16] it is now legal for a woman to abort her child for almost any reason at almost any time. *Roe vs. Wade* judicially created a federal abortion "law" that was unlike the laws of the states, most of which tended to protect the unborn child, with exceptions for health emergencies. In a handful of states, a woman could obtain an abortion for reasons that did not rise to the level of an emergency, but often the law required her to obtain permission from a doctor who felt her reasons were justified. Some of these consultations were, for the most part, a matter of form.

Under *Roe vs. Wade's* trimester system, the states could not interfere with the abortion decision during the first three months of pregnancy. During the fourth, fifth, and sixth months—the second trimester—the states could regulate abortion in the interest of maternal health. For example, laws could require people performing abortions to be licensed appropriately. Finally, when the unborn child was "potentially viable" (able to live outside the mother's womb, with or without assistance,[17]) the state could regulate or prevent abortion unless a doctor found the mother's life or health to be in danger.[18]

Roe's trimester system created problems, and later cases aggravated them. First, *Roe's* trimester system did not allow for advances in medical science. "Potential viability" has medically moved from about 30 weeks' gestation to about 20 weeks. But the legal definition remains unchanged. It is hoped that the medical definition will continue its progress back to earlier and earlier stages of prenatal development; when that happens, the difference between the legal and medical definitions will increase.

Second, the difference between legal and medical definitions of "potential viability" creates a situation where babies who could survive with medical help are aborted. The methods used for abortion often make survival impossible, but babies are sometimes aborted alive. However, the U.S. Supreme Court has ruled that a state may not require a doctor to care for a baby that is aborted alive rather than born alive. That is, babies who survive abortion procedures usually receive no medical attention and are left to die. Nor may the state require a doctor to use the method that is least likely to harm the unborn child when removing it from the mother, all other factors being equal (e.g. cost, effect on maternal health, and so forth).[19]

Finally, the day it was announced, the *Roe* system was undermined by its companion decision, *Doe v. Bolton*.[20] If *Roe* provided an exception to a state's third-trimester prohibition of abortion for the mother's life and health, *Doe* made the exception swallow the rule when it defined *health* as: all factors—physical, emotional, psychological, familial, and the woman's age—relevant to the well-being of the patient.[21] The result was a barely regulated industry that essentially provided abortion on demand (at almost any time during a pregnancy for nearly any reason).

The number of abortions performed in the United States since 1973 has increased dramatically, to more than 1.5 million per year during the 1980s and 1990s.[22] In the late 1990s the rate and number of abortions has decreased somewhat, although they remain tragically high. The *Webster* and *Casey* Supreme Court decisions reinstated the right of states to place some limitations on the practice of abortion.[23] Some states are now working on laws that provide informed consent for women, parental notification for minors, abortion clinic safety regulations, limits on fetal-tissue experimentation, adoption education, and bans on the partial-birth abortion method.[24] Abortion rates have dropped significantly in states where informed consent laws have enabled women to obtain information about fetal development, adoption, and the risks of abortion.

WHY HAS THE CHURCH CONSISTENTLY OPPOSED ELECTIVE ABORTION?

Abortion on demand has become one of the gravest moral controversies of our time because it undermines the sanctity of life and undercuts traditional family roles: motherhood, fatherhood, childhood, brotherhood, sisterhood. According to Elder Neal A. Maxwell, an understanding of the sanctity of life in God's eternal plan gives a unique perspective on the difficult issue of abortion: "We sometimes fail to realize how illuminating gospel truths are with regard to so many issues of the day. For instance, given the plan of salvation—with our need to experi-ence this mortal school, and to acquire a mortal body—and the very preciousness of human life, we see the awful practice of widespread abortion differently."[25]

The doctrine of premortal existence teaches that all children exist as individual spiritual beings before they receive mortal bodies (Proclamation, ¶ 3). Elective abortion interferes with the plan of salvation because (1) it prevents spirit children from receiving mortal bodies, (2) it disregards the mortal body as a temple of the spirit, and (3) it prevents prospective parents from taking responsibility for the gift of procreation.

Latter-day Saints who disregard the teachings of the prophets with regard to abortion on demand are subject to disciplinary action in the Church. LDS men and women who have encouraged, performed, procured, or participated in an elective abortion typically are not eligible to serve as full-time missionaries of The Church of Jesus Christ of Latter-day Saints. Converts who may have been party to a non-emergency abortion before joining the Church, and who have fully repented, may be exempt from this restriction on a case-by-case basis as determined by priesthood leaders.[26]

Elective abortion mocks the mission of Jesus Christ, who laid down His life to give us spiritual birth, like a mother suffering to give us physical birth: "Can a woman forget her sucking child, that she should not have compassion on the [child] of her womb? yea, they may forget, yet will I not forget thee. Behold, I have graven thee upon the palms of my hands" (Isa. 49:15–16).

The Lord wants His children to experience "the happiness promised to those who keep the commandments of the Lord."[27] Church leaders want us to avoid the sorrow that comes from defiling the sacred fountains of life. President Boyd K. Packer explains that living the gospel means seeking purity and shunning unholy practices: "The doctrine we teach has no provision for lying or stealing, for pornography, immoralities, for child abuse, for abortion, or murder."[28]

In a 1976 Church produced filmstrip, President Spencer W. Kimball gave a loving but solemn warning against the use of abortion to avoid the consequences of promiscuous sexual behavior:

My dear young people, there are two very important things I need to say to you about abortion. First, abortion is wrong. Abortion is one of the most revolting and sinful practices in this day, when we are witnessing a frightening increase in permissiveness leading to sexual immorality. How could anyone submit to, encourage, or participate in any way in such an evil act? Second, to those who have so sinned, there may be a way back, not easy, but there may be a way. While forgiveness may be possible, the road back is long and difficult. Do not be deceived—wickedness never will lead to happiness. Some of God's most sacred commandments are violated when a person trifles or interferes with any of the processes of reproduction.[29]

Because life is sacred and not something to be trifled with, Church leaders have counseled couples to be prayerful and reverent about the processes of reproduction in marriage. Husbands and wives should ask the Lord for wisdom to help them make righteous decisions about the timing and spacing of children in their families (see Essay I).

APPROPRIATE AND LEGAL WAYS TO SUPPORT THE SACREDNESS OF LIFE

The Proclamation concludes with a call to action: "We call upon responsible citizens and officers of government everywhere to promote those measures designed to maintain and strengthen the family . . ." (¶ 9). Although the Church maintains strict neutrality with regard to candidates and political parties, Elder Joseph B. Wirthlin affirms that the Church has a right to speak out on moral issues such as abortion and to support public policy that coincides with moral beliefs.[30] An *Ensign* article on "Preparing Children for Their Community Roles" lists opposition to abortion as a valid contribution to community service:

> In recent years the First Presidency has frequently urged Church members *as citizens* to join with their neighbors in vigorously opposing such evils as pornography, abortion, and the availability of liquor to youth. Acting as concerned citizens (*not* as Church representatives) members have in many cases helped achieve tighter abortion laws.[31]

Latter-day Saints share a reverence for human life with people of many other faiths. Perhaps the best-known champion for unborn children was Mother Teresa, the beloved Catholic humanitarian and Nobel Peace Prize recipient:

> Many people are deeply concerned with the children of India, with the children of Africa where quite a few die of hunger. Many people are also concerned about all the violence in this great country of the United States. These concerns are very good. But often these same people are not concerned with the millions who are being killed by the deliberate decision of their own mothers. And this is what is the greatest destroyer of peace today—abortion, which brings people to such blindness.
>
> By abortion, the mother kills even her own child to solve her problems. And, by abortion, the father is told that he does not have to take any responsibility at all for the child he has brought into the world. That father is likely to put other women into the same trouble. So abortion leads to abortion. Any country that accepts abortion is not teaching its people to love but to use violence to get what they want. This is why the greatest destroyer of love and peace is abortion.[32]

The 1991 First Presidency statement on abortion encourages Church members as citizens "to let their voices be heard in appropriate and legal ways that will evidence their belief in the sacredness of life."[33] The following are a few suggestions for preserving and defending the sanctity of life in legal and appropriate ways:

1. Since unwed pregnancy is one of the chief motives behind elective abortion, the most important thing anyone can do to uphold the sanctity of life is to maintain sexual chastity before marriage and marital fidelity after marriage: "Marriage between man and woman is essential to [God's] eternal plan" (Proclamation, ¶ 7). Moreover, supporting measures that help individuals make and keep commitments of sexual chastity will help promote the sanctity of life.

2. Since financial problems are another common motive behind elective abortion, another important way to protect the sanctity of life is to provide help for women and men who find themselves facing parenthood out of wedlock. The United States has approximately 4,000 crisis pregnancy agencies.[34] These nonprofit organizations help women and their partners choose constructive solutions, such as adoption, when a problem pregnancy occurs. LDS Family Services provides such aid for unwed parents and their families regardless of religious affiliation or economic status. Competent, compassionate, and confidential help from LDS Family Services can be obtained by dialing the following toll-free number: 1–800–537–2229.

3. We can also help by becoming better informed about life-related issues. Research on the topic of elective abortion enables us to build persuasive arguments for promoting the sacredness of life. LDS legal scholars

ARGUMENTS FOR ELECTIVE ABORTION AND CONTRASTING STATEMENTS
FROM CHURCH LEADERS ON THE SANCTITY OF LIFE

1. Abortion is an option if the pregnancy affects the health of the mother; health may be defined in personal, physical, mental, emotional, social, or financial terms.

"When deemed by competent medical authorities that the life of one must be terminated in order to save the life of the other, many agree that it is better to spare the mother. But these circumstances are rare" (Russell M. Nelson (1985, May). Reverence for life. *Ensign, 15*[5], 12).

"Our leaders have taught that the only possible exceptions [to abortion] are when the pregnancy resulted from rape or incest, or a competent physician has determined that the life or health of the mother is in serious jeopardy, or the fetus has severe defects that will not allow the baby to survive beyond birth. But even these exceptions do not justify abortion automatically. Because abortion is a most serious matter, we are counseled that it should be considered only after the persons responsible have consulted with their bishops and received divine confirmation through prayer" (Dallin H. Oaks [1999, February 9]. BYU Devotional, find on Internet at http://speeches.byu.edu/devo/98–99/OaksW99.html).

2. Abortion is an option if the pregnancy is the result of rape or incest.

"Abortion is an ugly thing, a debasing thing. . . . While we denounce it, we make allowance in such circumstances as when pregnancy is the result of incest or rape. . . . But such instances are rare, and there is only a negligible probability of their occurring. In these circumstances those who face the question are asked to consult with their local ecclesiastical leaders and to pray in great earnestness, receiving a confirmation through prayer before proceeding" (Gordon B. Hinckley [1998, November], What are people asking about us? *Ensign, 28*[11], 71).

3. Abortion is an option if the child will be born with a physical disability or a mental deficiency.

"If one is to be deprived of life because of potential for developing physical problems, consistency would dictate that those who already have such deficiencies should likewise be terminated . . . those who are either infirm, incompetent, or inconvenient should be eliminated by those in power. Such irreverence for life is unthinkable!" (Russell M. Nelson [1985, May], Reverence for life, *Ensign, 15*[5], 13).

4. A woman should be free to choose what she does with her own body: "I would not have an abortion, but I believe that others should have freedom to choose abortion."

"The woman's choice for her own body does not validate choice for the body of another. . . . The consequence of terminating the fetus therein involves the body and very life of another. These two individuals have separate brains, separate hearts, and separate circulatory systems. To pretend that there is no child and no life there is to deny reality" (Russell M. Nelson [1985, May], Reverence for life, *Ensign, 15*[5], 13).

"The advocates for lifting all restraints excuse themselves from responsibility by saying, 'I do not intend to do any of these things myself, but I think everyone should be free to choose what they want to do without any moral or legal interference.' With that same logic one could argue that all traffic signs and barriers set to keep the careless from falling to their death should be pulled down on the theory that each individual has the moral right to choose how close to the edge he will go" (Boyd K. Packer [1992, March 29], The fountain of life, BYU 18-Stake Fireside, p. 7).

"I have been fascinated with how cleverly those who sought and now defend legalized abortion on demand have moved the issue away from a debate on the moral, ethical, and medical pros and cons of legal restrictions on abortion and focused the debate on the slogan or issue of choice. . . . Pro-choice slogans have been particularly seductive to Latter-day Saints because we know that moral agency, which can be described as the power of choice, is a fundamental necessity in the gospel plan. . . . Choice is a method, not the ultimate goal . . . we are not true to our teachings if we are merely pro-choice. We must stand up for the *right* choice. Those who persist in refusing to think beyond slogans and sound bites like pro-choice wander from the goals they pretend to espouse and wind up giving their support to results they might not support if those results were presented without disguise. . . . If we say we are anti-abortion in our personal life but pro-choice in public policy, we are saying that we will not use our influence to establish public policies that encourage righteous choices on matters God's servants have defined as serious sins. I urge Latter-day Saints who have taken that position to ask themselves which other grievous sins should be decriminalized or smiled on by the law. . . . Should we decriminalize or lighten the legal consequences of child abuse?" (Dallin H. Oaks [1999, February 9], BYU Devotional, find on Internet at http://speeches.byu.edu/devo/98–99/OaksW99.html).

"Some Latter-day Saints say they deplore abortion, but they give . . . exceptional circumstances as a basis for their pro-choice position that the law should allow abortion on demand in all circumstances. Such persons should face the reality that the circumstances described in these three exceptions are extremely rare. For example, conception by incest or rape—the circumstance most commonly cited by those who use exceptions to argue for abortion on demand—are involved only in a tiny minority of abortions. More than 95 percent of the millions of abortions performed each year that extinguish the life of a fetus are conceived by consensual relations. Thus the effect in over 95 percent of abortions is not to vindicate choice but to avoid its consequences" (Dallin H. Oaks [1999, February 9], BYU Devotional, find on Internet at http://speeches.byu.edu/devo/98–99/OaksW99.html).

5. Abortion is an option because we do not know exactly when life begins or when the spirit enters the body.

"It is not a question of when 'meaningful life' begins or when the spirit 'quickens' the body. In the biological sciences, it is known that life begins when two germ cells unite to become one cell, bringing together twenty-three chromosomes from both the father and from the mother. . . . A continuum of growth results in a new human being. . . . At twenty-six days the circulation of blood begins. Scripture declares that the 'life of the flesh is in the blood.' (Lev. 17:11) Abortion sheds that innocent blood" (Russell M. Nelson [1985, May]. Reverence for life, *Ensign, 15*[5], 13).

"Once a life is conceived, to inflict death, even before birth, is a major transgression, save conception results from rape, the mother's life hangs in the balance, or the life of the unborn is certified to be hopeless. We do not know all about when a spirit enters the body but we do know that life, in any form, is very precious. While we are given the power to generate life and commanded to do so, we have no license to destroy it" (Boyd K. Packer [1992, March 29], The fountain of life, BYU 18-Stake Fireside, p. 4).

6. Abortion should be used to reduce the number of people born because the earth is overpopulated. Abortion is necessary to stop poverty and to protect the environment.

"Many in developing nations unknowingly ascribe their lack of prosperity to overpopulation. While they grovel in ignorance of God and his commandments, they may worship objects of their own creation (or nothing at all), while unsuccessfully attempting to limit their population by the rampant practice of abortion" (Russell M. Nelson [1985, May], Reverence for life, *Ensign, 15*[5], 13).

"Today I speak to members of the Church as an environmentalist. . . . The deliberate pollution of the fountain of life now clouds our moral environment. The gift of mortal life and the capacity to kindle other lives is a supernal blessing. . . . While we pass laws to reduce pollution of the earth, any proposal to protect the moral and spiritual environment is shouted down and marched against as infringing upon liberty, agency, freedom, the right to choose" (Boyd K. Packer [1992, May], Our moral environment, *Ensign, 22*[5], 66).

7. Abortion is a means of empowering women; abortion improves the status of women.

"For the wrath of God is provoked by governments that sponsor gambling, condone pornography, or legalize abortion. These forces serve to denigrate women now, just as they did in the days of Sodom and Gomorrah" (Russell M. Nelson [1987, November], Lessons from Eve, *Ensign, 17*[11], 89).

8. Reproductive freedom through abortion is a fundamental human right.

"The rights of any individual bump up against the rights of another. And the simple truth is that we cannot be happy, nor saved, nor exalted, without one another. . . . Nowhere is the right of choice defended with more vigor than with abortion. . . . In or out of marriage, abortion is not an individual choice. At a minimum, three lives are involved" (Boyd K. Packer [1990, November], Covenants, *Ensign, 20*[11], 84–85).

9. Abortion is a moral issue; morality cannot be legislated.

"Life is a moral issue. When morality is involved, we have both the *right* and the *obligation* to raise a warning voice" (Boyd K. Packer [1992, May], Our moral environment, *Ensign, 22*[5], 67).

"Some reach the pro-choice position by saying that we should not legislate morality. Those who take this position should realize that the law of crimes legislates nothing but morality. Should we repeal all laws with a moral basis so our government will not punish any choices some persons consider immoral? Such an action would wipe out virtually all of the laws against crimes" (Dallin H. Oaks [1999, February 9], BYU Devotional).

10. Abortion is now legal. Abortion is "politically correct."

"Whatever the laws of man may come to tolerate, the misuse of the power of procreation, the destroying of innocent life through abortion, and the abuse of little children are transgressions of enormous proportion" (Boyd K. Packer [1986, November], Little children, *Ensign, 16*[11], 18).

"Hence we view pornography as an awful and enslaving thing. We cannot feel otherwise concerning such practices as abortion and pornography, even if practices such as abortion and pornography are legally and politically protected" (Neal A. Maxwell [1993, April], The inexhaustible gospel, *Ensign, 23*[4], 72).

"During a prayer breakfast in Washington on 3 February 1994, Mother Teresa gave the most honest and powerful proclamation of truth on this subject I have ever heard . . . Mother Teresa had tied abortion to growing violence and murder in the streets by saying, 'If we accept that a mother can kill even her own child, how can we tell other people not to kill each other? . . . Any country that accepts abortion is not teaching its people to love, but to use any violence to get what they want' . . . What consummate spiritual courage this remarkable aged woman [Mother Teresa] demonstrated. How the devil must have been offended! Her remarkable declaration, however, was not generally picked up by the press or the editorial writers. Perhaps they felt more comfortable being politically or socially correct. After all, they can justify their stance by asserting that everyone does it or that it is legal. Fortunately the scriptures and the message of the prophets cannot be so revised" (James E. Faust [1995, September], Serving the Lord and resisting the Devil, *Ensign, 25*[9], 5).

11. Abortion is acceptable because the unborn fetus is not really a person, or is not a baby, or is not a child.

"Abortion, which has increased enormously, causes one to ask, 'Have we strayed so far from God's second great commandment—love thy neighbor—that a baby in a womb no longer qualifies to be loved—at least as a mother's neighbor?'" (Neal A. Maxwell [1993, May], Behold the enemy is combined, *Ensign, 23*[5], 76).

12. Abortion is a solution for teen pregnancy and unwed parents.

"There will be those who . . . discover to their shock and dismay that they are to become parents, while they are scarcely older than children themselves. Abortion is not the answer. This only compounds the problem. It is an evil and repulsive escape that will someday bring regret and remorse. . . . When marriage is not possible, experience has shown that adoption, difficult though this may be for the young mother, may afford a greater opportunity for the child to live a life of happiness" (Gordon B. Hinckley [1994, November], Save the children, *Ensign, 24*[11], 53).

"There is a far better way. If there is no prospect of marriage to the man involved, leaving the mother alone, there remains the very welcome option of placing the child for adoption by parents who will love it and care for it. There are many such couples in good homes who long for a child and cannot have one" (Gordon B. Hinckley [1998, November], What are people asking about us? *Ensign, 28*[11], 71).

13. Every child should be a wanted child. If a pregnant mother does not want the child or is not able to rear the child, then the child should be aborted.

"Mother Teresa pled for pregnant women who don't want their children to give them to her. She said, 'I am willing to accept any child who would be aborted and to give that child to a married couple who will love the child and be loved by the child'" (James E. Faust [1995, September], Serving the Lord and resisting the Devil, *Ensign, 25*[9], 4).

Box 15.1

have published many useful studies on this topic from the perspective of Family Law.[35] Professional organizations such as Americans United for Life (AUL) http://www.unitedforlife.org); Feminists for Life of America (FLA) http://www.serve.com/fem4life); and University Faculty for Life (UFL) http://www.marquette.edu/ufl/ can also be a source of reliable information on abortion and other sanctity of life issues.

4. Members of the Church must not condone violent or illegal means for opposing elective abortion. Just mentioning the topic of abortion can stir up controversy because the issue has become so sensitive and volatile in modern society. Therefore, Latter-day Saints should seek the Spirit in order to discuss the sanctity of life in ways that will help others gain accurate information about elective abortion and its consequences. The vast majority of people who oppose abortion use peaceful means to express their concern. In a few highly publicized incidents, some individuals have chosen to fight abortion on demand with terrorist tactics. Elder Neal A. Maxwell has warned that "violence to an unborn child does not justify other violence."[36] All reputable "pro-life" advocates and organizations are opposed to the use of violence to end the violence of abortion.

5. We need to recognize the grief and psychological pain that may come to women, men, and families who have been affected by elective abortion.

Through "Project Rachel" workshops, the Catholic Church has made great strides in addressing postabortion trauma and the effects of abortion on individuals and families. Women Exploited by Abortion (WEBA) provides support for the living victims of the abortion industry. Other groups help men deal with abortion-related grief issues.

6. Latter-day Saints should prayerfully strive to strengthen their testimonies of the sanctity of life, their resolve to oppose elective abortion, and their ability to articulate and defend gospel principles relating to the sanctity of life. Box 15.1 provides prophetic responses to the common arguments used to justify legal elective abortion. Upholding the sanctity of life is not only a defense for prenatal children but also a shelter for individuals and families whose lives might otherwise be devastated by elective abortion. The Proclamation invites us to counteract the violence of abortion by peacefully upholding the sanctity of life.

NOTES

1. The First Presidency (1991, January 19), in *Church News*, 5; *Ensign* (1991, March), 21(3), 78.

2. *Deseret News* (1997, April 12), E8.

3. Durrel A. Woolsey (1995, November), A strategy for war, *Ensign*, 25(11), 85.

4. *Oxford English dictionary* (1989), Cd-Rom ed. (Clarendon: Oxford University Press), 260–262.

5. Dickinson (1960). Poem 677, *The complete poems of Emily Dickinson*. Thomas H. Johnson (Ed.). Boston: Little, Brown, and Co.

6. *Oxford English Dictionary* (1989).

7. Lynn A. Michelsen (1995, November), Eternal laws of happiness. *Ensign*, 25(11), 79.

8. Russell M. Nelson (1985, May), Reverence for life, *Ensign*, 15(5), 11, 14.

9. Russell M. Nelson (1985, May), 14.

10. *Oxford English Dictionary* (1989).

11. J. C. Willke and B. H. Willke (1997), *Love them both: Questions and answers about abortion* (Cincinnati: Hayes Publishing Co.).

12. A. Torres and J. D. Forrest (1988, July/August), Why do women have abortions? *Family Planning Perspectives*, 20(4), 170.

13. Willke and Willke (1997), 124.

14. Willke and Willke (1997), 234–246.

15. D. C. Reardon (1992), *Life stories* (Wheaton, IL: Crossway Books), 35.

16. U. S. 111 (1973).

17. U. S. at 160.

18. L. A. Wardle and M. A. Wood (1982), *A lawyer looks at abortion* (Provo, UT: Brigham Young University Press), 52–53.

19. *Colautti v. Franklin* (1980), 439 U. S. 379 (1979); see M. A. Wood and L. B. Hawkins. State regulation of late abortion and the physician's duty of care to the viable fetus, *Missouri Law Review*, 45(3), 394.

20. U. S. 179 (1973).

21. U. S. at 192.

22. Wardle and Wood (1982), 7; Willke and Willke (1997), 112.

23. L. D. Wardle, "Time enough": *Webster vs. Reproductive Health Services* and the prudent pace of justice, *Florida Law Review*, 41(5), 88; L. D. Wardle (1984, Summer), *Thomas Casey Human Life Review*, 20(3) 49–58.

24. Willke and Willke (1997), 41.

25. Neal A. Maxwell (1993, April), The inexhaustible gospel, *Ensign*, 23(4), 68–73.

26. Cheryl Higginson (1990), *What every LDS girl needs to know about abortion* (American Fork, UT: Covenant Communications), 5–6.

27. First Presidency (1991, January 19), Statement on abortion, *Church News*, 5; First Presidency (1991, March), Statement on abortion, *Ensign*, 21(3), 78.

28. Boyd K. Packer (1984, November), The pattern of our parentage, *Ensign*, 14(11), 66–69.

29. Spencer W. Kimball (1976), *Very much alive* [filmstrip cassette] (Salt Lake City, UT: The Church of Jesus Christ of Latter-day Saints).

30. Joseph B. Wirthlin (1992, May), Seeking the good, *Ensign*, 22(5), 87.

31. Preparing children for their community roles (1988, August), *Ensign*, 18(8), 60.

32. Mother Teresa (1996), *The joy in loving: A guide to daily living with Mother Teresa*, ed. Jaya Chaliha and Edward Le Joly (New York: Viking), 313–371.

33. First Presidency (1991, March), Statement on abortion, *Ensign*, 21(3), 78.

34. J. C. Willke, cited in J. W. Koterski (1997, June), *Life and learning VII: Proceedings of the Seventh University Faculty for Life Conference*, Loyola College (Washington, DC: Georgetown University), 7.

35. Wardle and Wood (1982); R. G. Wilkins, R. Sherlock, and S. Clark (1991), Mediating the polar extremes: A guide to post-*Webster* abortion policy, *Brigham Young University Law Review*, 1, 403–488.

36. Neal A. Maxwell (1993, May), Behold, the enemy is combined, *Ensign*, 23(5), 76.

PROCREATION AND THE SANCTITY OF LIFE

JOSEPH B. STANFORD, M.D.

We declare the means by which mortal life is created to be divinely appointed.
(The Family: A Proclamation to the World, ¶ 5)

One of the most significant and sacred gifts of God to His children is the power to procreate. The Lord has mandated that the sacred powers of procreation are to be used only within marriage, where they form the foundation of virtuous and holy families and enhance the bonds between husband and wife.[1] Married couples have been entrusted with a divine stewardship with regard to sexuality and procreation. While much of the world takes a casual, often recreational approach to human sexuality, the Church encourages husbands and wives to pray and counsel together in making decisions about the sacred powers of procreation. In making these decisions, couples should also have access to relevant, current medical knowledge. This brief essay about procreation and the beginning of human life emphasizes the need for prayer and discussion between husband and wife and, where appropriate, a competent health professional about relevant health and moral issues.

THE FIRST MAJOR ISSUE

Two major issues confront most married couples in their stewardship over procreation. The first is the decision of when to seek to have children. The commandment to "multiply and replenish the earth" is in force for Latter-day Saint married couples, who are encouraged to have as many children as they can reasonably care for and not to unduly delay having children for selfish reasons.[2] Nevertheless, a variety of circumstances, including the physical and emotional health of the mother and father, as well as the capacity to provide for children, indicates the need for wisdom and inspiration in determining whether to have a child and the time interval between the birth of children.[3] These are personal choices that should be left to the couple, who should not be judged by other Church members for their apparent choices or circumstances.

THE SECOND MAJOR ISSUE

If a couple prayerfully decides that it is wise for them to delay having a first child or another child for a time, a second major issue is choosing how to prevent pregnancy. Medical science has developed a variety of means to regulate fertility, commonly referred to in secular contexts as "contraception," "birth control," or "family planning."[4] The Church of Jesus Christ of Latter-day Saints has not taken an official position prohibiting or endorsing any particular reversible method of birth regulation. The Church has clearly condemned elective abortion, except in special, rare circumstances,[5] and has also strongly discouraged nonreversible birth control methods (sterilization) unless serious medical conditions threaten the life or health of the mother.[6]

No method of birth regulation is 100 percent effective in avoiding pregnancy (except complete abstinence). Prominent voices in the world consider a "contraceptive failure" (pregnancy) as a legitimate and sometimes compelling justification for elective abortion.[7] However, married Latter-day Saint couples should consider any pregnancy, even an unexpected one, as a sacred trust from God.[8] Thus, faithful Latter-day Saint couples will accept responsibility for all children that may result from sexual intercourse. It is not the purpose of this essay to discuss the effectiveness, risks, benefits, mechanisms of action, or side effects of the many means of birth regulation, although couples making decisions about these matters should seek such information from a competent health care professional whose values on procreative matters are consistent with those of the couple.

Infertility

Some Latter-day Saint couples who seek to have children find that they have difficulty doing so. Infertility affects at least 10 percent of couples in the United States.[9] While some infertility is the result of sexually transmitted diseases or other lifestyle factors such as smoking, more often infertility is due to health conditions that are not under control of the couple. Analogous to choices about birth control, choices about which medical treatments to pursue for infertility are not prescribed by the Church, but are the responsibility of the couple to consider prayerfully. Because of the complex nature of infertility treatments and the implications that some infertility treatments may have for the divinely appointed and unique relationship of husband and wife in creating mortal human life, it is wise for a couple faced with infertility to consult with a competent health professional who is sensitive to the moral values of the couple about human life and the sacredness of marriage. In considering some procedures for treating infertility, a couple may also wish to seek spiritual guidance from their bishop.

Conclusion

Decisions about procreation are among the most sacred and significant parts of married life. Latter-day Saints should not treat these decisions casually, nor rely on the prevailing attitudes and practices of the world to make these decisions, but should seek reliable health information relevant to their situation, counsel together as married couples, and most importantly, seek the inspiration and guidance of the Lord.

NOTES

1. Boyd K. Packer (1972, July), Why stay morally clean, *Ensign*, 2(7), 111–113.

2. Dallin H. Oaks (1993, November), The great plan of happiness, *Ensign*, 23(11), 72–75.

3. H. S. Ellsworth (1992), Birth control, in Daniel H. Ludlow (Ed.), *The Encyclopedia of Mormonism* (New York: Macmillan), 1:116–117.

4. J. B. Stanford, W. L. Larimore (1999), Birth control, in *The Encyclopedia of Christianity*, vol. 1 (A–D), ed. Fahlbusch, et al. (Grand Rapids, MI, Wm B. Eerdmans), 257–262.

5. M. K. Beard (1992), Abortion, in Daniel H. Ludlow (Ed.), *The Encyclopedia of Mormonism*, 1:7.

6. L. E. Rytting (1992), Sterilization, in Daniel H. Ludlow (Ed.), *The Encyclopedia of Mormonism*, 3:1417–1418.

7. *Planned Parenthood vs. Casey*, 505 U. S. 833 (1992), 835. "The *Roe* rule's limitation on state power could not be repudiated without serious inequity to people who, for two decades of economic and social developments, have organized intimate relationships and made choices that define their views of themselves and their places in society, in reliance on the availability of abortion in the event that contraception would fail."

8. Russell M. Nelson (1985, May), Reverence for life, *Ensign*, 15(5), 11–14.

9. A. Chandra and E. H. Stephen (1998), Impaired fecundity in the United States: 1982–1995, *Family Planning Perspectives*, 30, 34–42.

CHAPTER 16

THE DIVINE NATURE OF EACH INDIVIDUAL

BARBARA DAY LOCKHART AND SHIRLEY E. COX

All human beings—male and female—are created in the image of God. Each is a beloved spirit
son or daughter of heavenly parents, and, as such, each has a divine nature and destiny.
(The Family: A Proclamation to the World, ¶ 2)

This chapter focuses on the divine nature of each individual and on the eternal nature of gender. "All human beings—male and female—are created in the image of God. Each is a beloved spirit son or daughter of heavenly parents, and, as such, each has a divine nature and destiny" (The Family: A Proclamation to the World, ¶ 2). As the above quotation suggests, the family Proclamation also teaches great truth about the individual. Throughout the scriptures, the Lord emphasizes how precious each soul is to Him (see Ps. 49:8; D&C 18:10; Alma 31:35). The Lord Jesus Christ gave His life so that every person might live in joy forever (see 2 Ne. 2:6–7).

Eternal life is the Lord's life and His way is to join each individual with others to constitute an eternal family. The family, then, "is central to the Creator's plan for the eternal destiny of His children" (¶ 1). The family does not negate the importance of the individual but rather is Heavenly Father's way to eternally bless each individual. Thus, we focus not just on individuals but on individuals in family relationships.

In this chapter we explore specific aspects of the divine nature of each person. We examine the worth of the soul as distinct from personal worthiness. In addition, we discuss several absolutes taught in the Proclamation relevant to the divine worth of souls. Also, the Proclamation affirmation regarding the eternal nature of gender will be discussed in relation to

same-sex attraction. We conclude with ideas about knowing the sacredness of each individual and how that may help every person be more grateful for life and truth and contribute to a healthier and happier family.

HUMAN BEINGS ARE OFFSPRING OF GOD

In many faiths, God's creation of human life is said to have occured *ex nihilo,* "out of nothing." This erroneous idea is contrary to latter-day revelations and creates confusion regarding who we really are. Every individual is eternal. Intelligence or spirits "have no beginning; they existed before, they shall have no end, they shall exist after, for they are . . . eternal" (Abr. 3:18). "Man was also in the beginning with God. Intelligence, or the light of truth, was not created or made, neither indeed can be" (D&C 93:29). These scriptures make it clear that the substance of our being is eternal and does not come "out of nothing." We are actually immortals although we often casually refer to ourselves as mortals.

The Proclamation boldly pronounces that human beings are the literal offspring of God (¶ 2). While little has been revealed about the premortal creative process, we understand that our heavenly parents created spiritual bodies for each of us as their own sons and daughters and placed in these spirit bodies spirits—immortal beings made from existing, eternal intelligence. In Abraham 3:22, we learn that the intelligences "were organized before the world was." Joseph Smith taught that "if men do not comprehend the character God, they do not comprehend themselves."[1] President John Taylor beautifully describes humans as being of the same species as God.

> If we take man, he is said to have been made in the image of God, for the simple reason that he is a son of God; and being His son, he is, of course, His offspring, an emanation from God, in whose likeness, we are told, he is made. He did not originate from a chaotic mass of matter, moving or inert, but came forth possessing, in an embryotic state, all the faculties and powers of a God. And when he shall be perfected, and have progressed to maturity, he will be like his Father—a God; being indeed His offspring.[2]

EFFECT OF THE HOLY GHOST ON THE INDIVIDUAL

An intelligent being, in the image of God, possesses every organ, attribute, sense, sympathy, affection, of will, wisdom, love, power and gift, which is possessed by God himself. But these are possessed by man in his rudimental state in a subordinate sense of the word. Or, in other words, these attributes are in embryo, and are to be gradually developed. They resemble a bud, a germ, which gradually develops into bloom, and then, by progress, produces the mature fruit after its own kind.[3]

Elder Parley P. Pratt

Box 16.1

Recognizing that we are literal sons and daughters of heavenly parents is one of the most sacred truths we can know. Knowing this truth has a profound impact on how we regard ourselves and others as well as on how we choose to live. President Boyd K. Packer has forcefully taught how spiritually harmful to individuals and families is the deception that they are not literal children of God:

"No greater ideal has been revealed than the supernal truth that we are the children of God, and we differ, by virtue of our creation, from all other living things (see Moses 6:8–10, 22, 59). No idea has been more *destructive* of happiness, no philosophy has produced more sorrow, more heartbreak and mischief; no idea has done more to destroy the family than the idea that we are not the offspring of God,

only advanced animals, compelled to yield to every carnal urge."[4]

Gaining a testimony that we are literal sons and daughters of God is essential to truly understanding our divine nature and potential. It is both humbling and inspiring to have a testimony that our divine heritage is real and our divine nature is eternal.

THE SACREDNESS OF THE PHYSICAL BODY

Understanding the sacredness of the body gives further insight into the reality of the divine nature of human beings. The definition of what constitutes the soul is given in the Doctrine and Covenants: "the spirit and the body are the soul of man" (D&C 88:15). The Proclamation states, "In the premortal realm, spirit sons and daughters knew and worshiped God as their Eternal Father and accepted His plan by which His children could obtain a physical body and gain earthly experience to progress toward perfection and ultimately realize his or her divine destiny as an heir of eternal life" (¶ 3).

Understanding this doctrine gives us a deeper

THE BLESSINGS OF A PHYSICAL BODY

Nothing should be held in greater sacredness and honor than the covenant by which the spirits of men, the offspring of God in the spirit, are privileged to come into this world in mortal tabernacles. It is through this principle that the blessing of immortal glory is made possible. The importance of these mortal tabernacles is apparent from the knowledge we have of eternal life. Spirits cannot be made perfect without a body of flesh and bones. This body and its spirit are brought to immortality and blessings of salvation through the resurrection. After the resurrection there can be no separation again; body and spirit become inseparably connected that man may receive a fullness of joy. In no other way, other than through birth into this life and the resurrection, can spirits become like our Eternal Father.[5]

President Joseph Fielding Smith

Box 16.2

---

sense of the significance of the body as a temple. Just as temple ordinances are a necessity to exaltation, so is the body.

The greatest curse of all, the greatest punishment

given, is to not have a body. We should reverence our bodies and be grateful for who we are as we have been created. There is tremendous power in having a body, any body. The world would have us think that we must alter our bodies to make them ideal, suited for other's eyes, that we are not good as we are. But the Prophet Joseph Smith taught of the power of the physical body in regard to that which is really important—eternal progression:

> That which is without body, parts and passions is nothing. . . . We came to this earth that we might have a body and present it pure before God in the celestial kingdom. The great principle of happiness consists in having a body. The devil has no body, and herein is his punishment. He is pleased when he can obtain the tabernacle of man, and when cast out by the Savior he asked to go into the herd of swine, showing that he would prefer a swine's body to having none. All beings who have bodies have power over those who have not. The devil has no power over us only as we permit him. The moment we revolt at anything which comes from God, the devil takes power.[6]

The Prophet Joseph Smith in this statement equated happiness and power with having a body. Because we are embodied we have power over Satan and his hosts. We are more like Heavenly Father now that we are embodied. Our bodies are evidence of our eternal progression, of our love for the Savior, of our commitment to that which is right and true. President Boyd K. Packer has taught that as premortal spirits we yearned to come to this life to gain a body so we could be more like our glorious Heavenly Parents. "It is my conviction that in the spirit world prior to mortal birth, we waited anxiously for our time to enter mortality. I also believe that we were willing to accept whatever conditions would prevail in life. Perhaps we knew that nature might impose limits on the mind or on the body or on life itself. I believe that we nevertheless anxiously awaited our turn."[7]

We yearned for a body, even knowing the conditions here in mortality would not be ideal. The world would have us think that we must have a perfect body now, or that there is something inherently evil about the body, or that we can use our bodies however we please. Satan, having no body, uses a myriad of ploys to keep us from having reverence for our own body. Thus, understandably, one of the main purposes of the Proclamation is to teach the divine nature and eternal destiny of each of God's children and that having a body is one of our greatest blessings. The body is an ally for the spirit, a means of advancing the spirit. Human life is sacred, meaning all of human life—spirit and body. Jesus died so that we might live forever with our spirit and body together. And knowing the sacredness of our whole soul—body and spirit—is crucial to understanding our true, divine nature. Knowing we are like Jesus Christ, by nature, and that we are His—for He has bought us with a price (see 1 Cor. 6:20)—will greatly motivate us to want to be like Him and to realize our divine destiny.

ETERNAL, ABSOLUTE TRUTHS

Latter-day Saints have a gospel-based eternal perspective of truth that is a positive force for good. The perspective of the restored gospel on truth is absolute, not relative. Relativism is the perspective that prevails in society today. An absolute perspective of reality is one that looks to an authority beyond itself for truth, for the knowledge of what is real. A relative perspective assumes that what is real and what is true is relative to each individual—is authored by each individual. In the relative perspective there is no authority, no universal right and wrong, no reality beyond what the individual creates. Relative truths, such as scientific discoveries, may well be a consistent part of an absolute perspective, yet are different from relativism. Relativism and absolutism are at opposite ends of the continuum of identifying the source of reality. It would be philosophically impossible to subscribe to both an absolute and a relative perspective within one philosophy of life.

Although many authorities claim to be absolute, God is the ultimate, true reality and source of truth. Truth in this context is more than knowledge; it is reality. The restored gospel of Jesus Christ is the source of knowing truth and reality, which is knowledge "of things as they really are, and of things as they really will be" (Jacob 4:13). This does not preclude truths being found in other sources. These additional truths will be consistent with the truths of the gospel. As we embrace the gospel perspective, God blesses us with eternal truths and we can make these truths our own. But we do not create truth or reality.[8]

ABSOLUTE TRUTHS TAUGHT IN THE PROCLAMATION

The most important absolute truths are found in the plan of salvation and pertain to the exaltation of each individual human being. The Proclamation

A COMPARISON OF A TESTIMONY OF THE TRUTHS IN
THE PROCLAMATION WITH A RELATIVISTIC PERSPECTIVE

GOSPEL ABSOLUTE PERSPECTIVE

A1. I am a spirit child of heavenly parents and created in their image. This gives me an eternal, divine nature and destiny. I will make and keep covenants that make it possible to live with Heavenly Father, Jesus Christ, and my family for eternity.

B1. My gender is an essential characteristic of individual premortal, mortal, and eternal identity and purpose. I am grateful my gender is eternal and that I am who I am.

C1. My physical body is a blessing and an essential part of my being that helps me to progress toward perfection and ultimately realize my divine destiny as an heir of eternal life. Knowing my body is sacred helps me to make wise choices in many facets of my life.

RELATIVISTIC PERSPECTIVE

A2. I am born of earthly parents. Most likely we randomly evolved over millions of years from another life form. What I make of my life is up to me. What matters most is what I accomplish in this life.

B2. Gender is "socially constructed" and mostly related to life experiences. I may or may not be comfortable with my gender as it appears and am not bound by rules or traditional social mores with respect to my gender.

C2. My physical body is for this mortal life only. I have the right to use it as I please. I decide what is right and wrong for me to do.

Box 16.3

presents several of these absolutes. Among these are (1) each individual is born of heavenly parents and has a divine nature and destiny; (2) gender is eternal; and (3) the physical body is requisite to eternal life. What difference can knowing these truths make in a person's life? To help comprehend the impact of knowing these absolutes, we compare in Box 16.3 a testimony of the absolutes in the Proclamation with attitudes from a relative perspective that are found in society.

As we analyze the beliefs accompanying commitment to gospel principles, we realize these beliefs are based on absolute truths, truths that will never change and are in no way affected by life's circumstances. We can have complete trust and confidence in Jesus Christ, whose gospel will be constant and universal. Whether or not a person knows that he or she is a beloved spirit son or daughter of heavenly parents with a divine nature and destiny, it is still real. Absolutes are eternal, divine principles about all people, yet are not affected by people. This concept was expressed forthrightly by President Wilford Woodruff. "Principles which have been revealed for the salvation and exaltation of the children of men . . . are principles you cannot annihilate. *They are principles that no combination of men or [women] can*

destroy. They are principles that can never die. They are beyond the reach of man to handle or to destroy . . . It is not in the power of the whole world put together to destroy those principles. . . . Not one jot or tittle of these principles will ever be destroyed."[9] The absolute reality of our divine nature and destiny will not be altered by mortal conditions. Heavenly Father is an unchangeable God (see Moro. 8:18). We are ever His sons and daughters, His work and His glory (see Moses 1:39).

Elder Richard G. Scott testified: "Our Father's love, his perfections, and his perfect righteousness are absolute guarantees that we will ever exist as an individual entity, an intelligence clothed with spirit and body with latent divine capacities that mature and flower through obedience to his plan and his commandments."[10]

Does recognition of absolutes regarding human life, however, make individuality irrelevant? Does a belief in an absolute reality nullify the existence, purpose, or recognition of individuality? Elder Neal A. Maxwell has provided marvelous insight into this potential dilemma. "Righteousness increases the uniqueness of our presence, but sin sinks us into sameness."[11] Individual creation is fully compatible with absolute reality. The more one is true to Jesus

Christ, the more that person is the unique individual he or she is destined to be. If one is not obedient, that person loses sight of his or her uniqueness and becomes more like others. Jesus Christ is omniscient; He knows each of us perfectly. He is the true source of knowing exactly who we are. Through our righteousness, through serving Him and doing His will and because of His power in our lives, we become the unique individuals He desires us to be. The irony is this: absolutes actually bring about uniqueness, whereas relativism, in its highly individualized creation of supposed reality, brings about sameness.

Some might wonder how the commandment for us to be one relates to the reality of our individual uniqueness. The Lord tells us to be one: "I say unto you, be one; and if ye are not one ye are not mine" (D&C 38:27). Just as Jesus is one with His Father, He would have us be one with Him. Jesus and the Father are two unique individuals; however, they are one in purpose. Our oneness with Christ is being one in purpose, not losing our individual reality or self. Elder Maxwell reinforces the absolute nature of individuality while teaching us the meaning of the concept of losing oneself:

> Losing oneself means losing concern over getting credit; by knowing our true identity we need not be concerned about seeming anonymity. It likewise means losing our desire to be in the driver's seat; putting our shoulder to the wheel is enough. It means that eagles meekly serve under sparrows—without worrying over comparative wingspans or plumage. . . . Losing oneself means yielding the substance of one's own agendum if it does not match the agendum of the Lord.[12]

Losing ourselves is doing His will, willing to serve in any capacity, not having pride. Losing ourselves does not mean losing our individuality or individual self.

THE WORTH OF EACH SOUL IS ABSOLUTE

Because of the eternal heritage and destiny of each individual, denying or ignoring the worth of any soul contradicts the work and glory of Christ which is "to bring to pass the immortality and eternal life of man" (Moses 1:39). The worth of each and every soul is absolute. The worth of each individual is the same as every other individual since, a prophet has taught, "one being is as precious in his sight as the other"

(Jacob 2:21). The Atonement of Christ is an individual thing. Christ atoned for each individual and would have suffered and died for you had you been the only individual alive.

"Remember the worth of souls is great in the sight of God; For, behold, the Lord your Redeemer suffered death in the flesh; wherefore he suffered the pain of all men, that all men might repent and come unto him. And he hath risen again from the dead, that he might bring all men unto him, on conditions of repentance. And how great is his joy in the soul that repenteth!" (D&C 18:10–13).

Because it is an eternal absolute, the importance or worth of each individual cannot be affected by people. Worth cannot be increased or decreased, it cannot be annihilated or destroyed. Worthlessness is not an option. Feeling worthless is quite common but it is a feeling based on a false premise. It is erroneous thinking; nothing can make these feelings correct since no person is without eternal worth.

Worth is not of this life and therefore cannot be earned or affected by this life. The worth of each individual is a divine given. It is an inherent aspect of each life. Worth is constant and unchanging. Recognizing our great worth in the sight of God is humbling and, in fact, is just the opposite of pride. According to Elder Maxwell, "Humility is not the disavowal of our worth; rather, it is the sober realization of how much we are valued by God."[13] Sorting out these truths cognitively is only the first step. We must pray for a testimony, by the Spirit, of our eternal worth—that we are of such great value to Christ that He died for us personally (see D&C 18:10–13). By way of the Holy Ghost, we can know for certain that our worth, which is great in the sight of God, is absolute and can never be changed—no matter what we or anyone else thinks, believes, feels, or does.

Worthiness and Worth

Worthiness, however, is different from worth. Worthiness is dependent on what we do in our lives, how we use our agency, coupled with the Lord's grace. Worthiness is dependent on our love for the Savior and our obedience to His commandments. But worthiness does not determine worth. Worth is always a part of us, whether we are good or bad. Heavenly Father always loves us whether we are good or bad. However, having a testimony of our worth or importance to Heavenly Father does have a great impact on our worthiness. If we feel that we are "no good" or "worthless," and that Heavenly Father couldn't possibly love us, the tendency is to give up or to do things that affect our worthiness. If we have a testimony of our worth, when we make a mistake we want to repent. We are able to distinguish between who we are and what we do. We can view ourselves similarly to the way our Heavenly Father views us. We can love the sinner—ourselves—but not the sin. We want to repent because we want to please and commune with our Father, whom we know loves us perfectly, individually, and personally.

God's Love Is Absolute

Because we know our individual worth is absolute and eternal, we are able to have reverence for our own lives. This reverence has everything to do with who we are, literal sons and daughters of heavenly parents. We do not create our worth, rather we discover it by way of the Spirit. We gain a testimony of our worth. Then with the help of the Spirit we can come to "recognize how much we are valued by God" and realize, as Elder Jeffrey R. Holland has testified, that He always loves us with all His heart, might, mind and strength.[14] Understanding our value to God and valuing ourselves is pertinent to our progress toward exaltation. The absolute worth of our souls is the basis for having justifiable self-esteem. Elder Maxwell taught: "Since self-esteem controls ultimately our ability to love God, to love others, and to love life, nothing is more central than our need to build justifiable self-esteem. Self-contempt is of Satan; there is none of it in heaven."[15] Elder Maxwell also taught: "We can also come to know, through obedience, how much God loves us as his immortal children. If we can get that witness for ourselves that we are his and that he loves us, then we can cope with and endure well whatever comes in the varied tactical situations of life."[16] President Gordon B. Hinckley often teaches that "this principle of love is the basic essence of the gospel of Jesus Christ. Without love of God and love of neighbor there is little else to commend the gospel to us as a way of life."[17]

Moral Agency and Individuality

Moral agency, another eternal absolute, is also verification of the importance of each individual soul. Moral agency is fundamental to individuality and individual progress. Moral agency places on each of us the right and responsibility to choose our course in life (see 2 Ne. 2:27).

Of course, our Heavenly Father and Jesus Christ hope that we choose righteousness rather than evil. Indeed, choosing evil reduces our individuality, according to Elder Maxwell: "Wrong choices will make us less free. Furthermore, erosive error gradually makes one less and less of an individual. God and his prophets would spare us that shrinkage."[18]

Beautiful absolutes in the plan of salvation, including agency and the worth of each soul, teach us who we really are as individuals and whose we really are.

CHRIST OUR REDEEMER

One of the most profound absolute truths is our complete dependence on Jesus Christ for eternal life. And yet this dependence does not diminish our individual worth. Instead, it testifies how profoundly God loves us because He prepared a way for us to enjoy eternal life (see John 3:16). Elder Dallin H. Oaks teaches our total dependence on Jesus Christ in a discussion on the Atonement. We are all dependent upon the mercy God the Father extended to all humankind through the atoning sacrifice of our Lord and Savior, Jesus Christ. This is the central reality of the Gospel. This is why "we talk of Christ, we rejoice in Christ, we preach of Christ . . . that our children may know to what source they may look for a remission of their sins" (2 Ne. 25:26). The reality of our total dependence upon Jesus Christ for the attainment of our goals of immortality and eternal life should dominate every teaching and every testimony and every action of every soul touched by the light of the restored gospel.[19]

It is harmful to our understanding of the nature of human life if we do not accurately understand the Fall and the Atonement. Men and women by nature are like God. And yet, because of the eternal principle of moral agency, we are also subject to sin. The natural man is an enemy to God (Mosiah 3:19). But the natural man is not our divine heritage; the natural man is who we are as a result of sin. Through repentance and the Atonement of Christ, we can put off the natural man (Mosiah 3:19).

As we have reverence for our divine identity, we will love our Creator and His creations more deeply. We will treat all of creation, especially ourselves, our spouses, and the children we bear, with utmost respect. Our faith will be strengthened in our God, and in our capacity as His sons and daughters. "Wherefore, whoso believeth in God might with surety hope for a better world, yea, even a place at the right hand of God, which hope cometh of faith, maketh an anchor to the souls of men, which would make them sure and steadfast, always abounding in good works, being led to glorify God" (Ether 12:4).

Having a kind of hope that is the assurance of being on the right hand of God, trusting in the goodness of our own being, and desiring and striving to bring others to our eternal home, are all outgrowths of discovering who we really are. Our natures are holy, and eternal life is our destiny. In all of the grandeur of God's creations, men and women are supreme. James E. Talmage's description of the purpose of the universe gives us a perspective of man in relation to God: "What is man in this boundless setting of sublime splendor? I answer you: Potentially now, actually to be, he is greater and grander, more precious in the arithmetic of God, than all the planets and suns of space. For him were they created; they are the handiwork of God; man is his son. In this world man is given dominion over a few things. It is his privilege to achieve supremacy over many things. 'The heavens declare the glory of God; and the firmament sheweth his handiwork' (Ps. 19:1)."[20]

Only as we understand God, can we understand who we really are and our divine nature. Gaining a testimony of these truths will help us truly appreciate the profound message of the Proclamation which testifies that each of us "is a beloved spirit son or daughter of heavenly parents" (¶ 2).

GENDER IS AN ESSENTIAL CHARACTERISTIC OF ETERNAL IDENTITY

Understanding our individual worth is an important foundation for understanding gender, which is an essential characteristic of our eternal identity. The Proclamation states that "all human beings—male and female—are created in the image of God. . . . Gender is an essential characteristic of individual premortal, mortal, and eternal identity and purpose" (¶ 2). Today many proclaim a different message—gender is socially constructed; it can be deconstructed and reconstructed in any way that suits our purpose. President James E. Faust, however, taught:

> Our designation as men or women began before this world was. In contrast to the socially accepted doctrine that homosexuality is inborn, a number of respectable authorities contend that homosexuality is not acquired by birth. The false belief of inborn homosexual orientation denies to repentant souls the opportunity to change and will ultimately lead to discouragement, disappointment, and despair.[21]

God created us male and female. This is not a mistake or a variety of genetic or hormonal chance. What we call gender is an essential characteristic of our existence prior to our birth. Gender is part of our eternal identity and essential to our eternal progression. Although we may not know all the reasons why this is so, we do know some of the reasons why gender is essential to our eternal progression. To achieve our exaltation, an eternal marriage between a man and a woman is necessary. That marriage must be done in the Lord's way. Moreover, as stated in the Proclamation, "God's commandment for His children to multiply and replenish the earth remains in force. . . . God has commanded that the sacred powers of procreation are to be employed only between man and woman, lawfully wedded as husband and wife" (¶ 4). The sexual union between a married man and woman is, among other things, the means God has ordained to bring His spirit children into mortality, which is an essential step in the plan of salvation. God needs mortal tabernacles for His premortal spirit children in order for them to progress. As a result, sexual relations of any kind with an individual of the same gender will never be sanctioned by the Lord's church.

Unfortunately, there are men and women who experience same-sex attraction. Of course, we know that we are given many trials in this life. To accomplish the purposes of mortal life, it is essential that we be tested against opposition to see if we will keep the commandments of God (see 2 Ne. 2:11; Abr. 3:25–26). We are given our free agency, the power to choose between good—the path of life—and evil—the path of spiritual death and destruction (see 2 Ne. 2:27; Moses 4:3). Those who struggle with same-sex attraction, like those who struggle with other temptations, can call upon the power of Christ's Atonement to help them. They should also be able to call upon family members and friends for help.

Elder Oaks voiced concern for Latter-day Saints who face the confusion and pain that result when a loved one engages in sexual behavior with a person of the same gender, or even when a person has erotic feelings that could lead toward such behavior. In answer to the question how Church leaders, parents, and other members of the Church should react in these situations, he offered specific direction and advice. First, Elder Oaks reminds us of the First Presidency message, November 14, 1991, which

ELDER DALLIN H. OAKS ON SAME-GENDER ATTRACTION

Because Satan desires that "all men might be miserable like unto himself" (2 Ne. 2:27), his most strenuous efforts are directed at encouraging those choices and actions that will thwart God's plan for his children. Many people, including some members of the Church, believe that because we are born with homosexual attractions we can have no choice about our actions or sexual behavior. This clearly is not true. Some individuals struggling with same-gender attraction assert there is no way out of their cycle of frustration; however, there are numerous cases of individuals who have changed their life-style and behavior. In each case (and in other examples that could be given) the feelings or other characteristics that increase susceptibility to certain behavior may have some relationship to inheritance. But the relationship is probably very complex. The inherited element may be nothing more than an increased likelihood that an individual will acquire certain feelings if he or she encounters particular influences during the developmental years. But regardless of our different susceptibilities or vulnerabilities, which represent only variations on our mortal freedom (in mortality we are only "free according to the flesh" (2 Ne. 2:27), we remain responsible for the exercise of our agency in the thoughts we entertain and the behavior we choose . . .

Most of us are born with [or develop] thorns in the flesh, some more visible, some more serious than others. We all seem to have susceptibilities to one disorder or another, but whatever our susceptibilities, we have the will and the power to control our thoughts and our actions. This must be so. God has said that he holds us accountable for what we do and what we think, so our thoughts and actions must be controllable by our agency. Once we have reached the age or condition of accountability, the claim "I was born that way" does not excuse actions or thoughts that fail to conform to the commandments of God. We need to learn how to live so that a weakness that is mortal will not prevent us from achieving the goal that is eternal.

God has promised that he will consecrate our afflictions for our gain (see 2 Ne. 2:2). The efforts we expend in overcoming any inherited [or developed] weakness build a spiritual strength that will serve us throughout eternity.

Beware the argument that because a person has strong drives toward a particular act, he has no power of choice and therefore no responsibility for his actions. This contention runs counter to the most fundamental premises of the gospel of Jesus Christ.

Satan would like us to believe that we are not responsible in this life. That is the result he tried to achieve by his contest in the pre-existence. A person who insists that he is not responsible for the exercise of his free agency because he was 'born that way' is trying to ignore the outcome of the War in Heaven. We *are* responsible, and if we argue otherwise, our efforts become part of the propaganda of the Adversary.[22]

Box 16.4

makes an important distinction: "There is a distinction between [1] immoral thoughts and feelings and [2] participating in either immoral heterosexual or any homosexual behavior."[23] Elder Oaks clarifies there is no Church discipline for improper thoughts or feelings. All of us have some feelings we did not choose. Still, Elder Oaks counsels: "Although immoral thoughts are less serious than immoral behavior, such thoughts also need to be resisted and repented of because we know that 'our thoughts will also condemn us' (Alma 12:14). Immoral thoughts (and the less serious feelings that lead to them) can bring about behavior that is sinful."[24]

Our most important responsibility in these situations is to show forth love. Elder Oaks gave an important address on same-gender attraction that helps Latter-day Saints understand this challenging issue. (See Box 16.4.)

The First Presidency in their 1995 Easter Greeting reiterated what Jesus Christ has taught about loving one another: "We are asked to be kinder with one another, more gentle and forgiving. We are asked to be slower to anger and more prompt to help. We are asked to extend the hand of friendship and resist the hand of retribution. We are called upon to be true disciples of Christ, to love one another with genuine compassion."[25]

In our families and in relationships with other individuals with whom we work and associate, we should follow the admonition of our Savior, Jesus Christ, to extend compassion to all who suffer gender confusion or same-gender attraction. Elder Oaks admonishes that we should never engage in or encourage "gay-bashing"—physical or verbal attacks on persons thought to be involved in homosexual or lesbian behavior.[26] Rather, we should invite them to explore and expand their gospel knowledge and understanding. We should let them know of our unconditional love for who they are, children of our Father in Heaven. As parents, we need to maintain contact and emotional support. As siblings and friends, we need to communicate our appreciation of their eternal potentials and strengths. Those individuals who are working to resist homosexual tendencies ought not to feel like pariahs. We should be ever ready to love and to teach true doctrine to those who struggle.

Loving brothers and sisters, who have signified by covenant their willingness to "bear one another's burdens" (Mosiah 18:8), can provide invaluable assistance to family members and other persons struggling with the burden of same–sex attraction. While, as parents, we cannot accept or condone our children's homosexual behavior, we can still reach out to them in love and "so fulfil the law of Christ" (Gal. 6:2). As fellow children of God, we can love and maintain communication with those who struggle and we can hold out hope that with the help of the Lord they can overcome. We can become the means whereby the scriptural promise is fulfilled: "There hath no temptation taken you but such as is common to man: but God is faithful, who will not suffer you to be tempted above that ye are able: but will with the temptation also make a way to escape, that ye may be able to bear it" (1 Cor. 10:13).

Even though some of our brothers and sisters have lost their way, they are in the process, as we are, of working toward their eternal goals. We are all struggling to become all we are destined to be. Jesus Christ has commanded us to be perfect, and He shed His blood to provide us the opportunity to claim our divine destiny. "His confidence in our ability to achieve eternal life is manifest in his incredible invitation: 'What manner of men ought ye to be? Verily I say unto you, even as I am'" (3 Ne. 27:27).[27]

On occasion, individuals who struggle with these problems are counseled to marry an individual of the opposite sex as a means to healing or overcoming same–sex attraction. This is not wise. President Hinckley has declared that "marriage should not be viewed as a therapeutic step to solve problems such as homosexual inclinations or practices."[28] The problems go much deeper than heterosexual marriage can, by itself, solve. Those who struggle can obtain help through the truths of the gospel, through church attendance and service, through the counsel of inspired leaders, and frequently through professional assistance.

In all our attempts to help those who struggle with same–sex attraction, we must not forget that any sexual relations outside legal and lawful marriage are wrong and limit God's blessings. But change and repentance are possible. Research demonstrates that individuals struggling with same–sex attraction and behavior can be helped to change.[29] And repentance is always possible.

CONCLUSION

The doctrines taught in the Proclamation make it clear that each individual has a divine origin and destiny. We are literally children of heavenly parents, and we are imbued with characteristics of these divine parents. Indeed, the divine inheritance of each individual makes us all sacred beings. We have discussed the sacredness of the whole being, body and spirit. Gender is eternal, not a social construct of this mortal phase of our existence.

A testimony of these eternal, absolute truths and a testimony of our absolute worth will be the foundation to help make us personally secure. This personal security, which is founded in Christ, is the basis for being an emotionally mature individual. This quality is prerequisite to being a strong family member. This quality of personal security will help alleviate problems such as addictions, controlling behaviors, and selfishness that are so destructive to the family.

The more we understand our divine nature and believe and trust in it, the better we can contribute to forming a sacred, eternal family. We will be able to love our spouse and children with a Christlike love. We will love each person while not condoning sin. Our lives will be patterned after the glorious wisdom in Doctrine and Covenants 121:40–46, and our confidence will "wax strong in the presence of God."

NOTES

1. Joseph Smith (1938), *Teachings of the Prophet Joseph Smith,* ed. and comp. Joseph Fielding Smith (Salt Lake City: Deseret Book), 343.

2. John Taylor (1882), *The mediation and atonement* (Salt Lake City: Deseret News), 164–165.

3. Parley P. Pratt, *Key to the science of theology* (4th ed.), as quoted in James E. Talmage (1909), *The Articles of Faith* (Salt Lake City: Deseret News), appendix 8, 48.

4. Boyd K. Packer (1992, May), Our moral environment, *Ensign,* 22(5), 67.

5. Joseph Fielding Smith (1965, October), Conference report, 27–28.

6. Joseph Smith (1938), *Teachings,* ed. and comp. Joseph Fielding Smith, 181.

7. Boyd K. Packer (1988, November), Funerals—A time for reverence, *Ensign, 18*(11), 19.

8. See Spencer W. Kimball (1977, September 6), Absolute truth, Devotional address given at Brigham Young University.

9. Wilford Woodruff, quoted in Boyd K. Packer (1993, November), For time and all eternity, *Ensign, 23*(11), 22.

10. Richard G. Scott (1997, August 19), Finding happiness, BYU Education Week.

11. Neal A. Maxwell (1975), *Of one heart* (Salt Lake City: Deseret Book), 42.

12. Neal A. Maxwell (1990), *A wonderful flood of light* (Salt Lake City: Bookcraft), 99.

13. Neal A. Maxwell (1979), *All these things shall give thee experience* (Salt Lake City: Deseret Book), 127.

14. Jeffrey R. Holland (1993, November), Look to God and live, *Ensign, 23*(11), 14.

15. Neal A. Maxwell (1997), *The Neal A. Maxwell quote book* (Salt Lake City: Bookcraft), 306.

16. Neal A. Maxwell (1998, September), The pathway of discipleship, *Ensign, 28*(9), 7–13.

17. Gordon B. Hinckley (1984, March), And the greatest of these is love, *Ensign, 14*(3), 5.

18. Neal A. Maxwell (1988, November), Answer me, *Ensign, 18*(11), 32.

19. Dallin H. Oaks (1992, February), Sins, crimes, and atonement, CES Symposium, 4.

20. James E. Talmage, as quoted by Hugh B. Brown (1965, April), in Conference Report, 41.

21. James E. Faust (1995, September), Serving the Lord while resisting the Devil, *Ensign, 25*(9), 2–7.

22. Dallin H. Oaks (1988), Free agency and freedom, *Brigham Young University 1987–88 Devotional and Fireside Speeches* (Provo, UT: BYU Publications), 46–47; also in M. Nyman and C. D. Tate, Jr. (Eds.) (1989), *The Book of Mormon: Second Nephi, the doctrinal structure* (Provo, UT: BYU Religious Studies Center), 13–15, cited in Oaks (1995, October), 8, 9–10.

23. Letter of the First Presidency (1991, November 14), Cited in Dallin H. Oaks (1995, October), Same gender attraction, *Ensign, 25*(9), 8.

24. Dallin H. Oaks (1995, October), 8.

25. The First Presidency (1995, April 15), An Easter greeting from the First Presidency, *Church News,* 1.

26. Oaks (1995, October), 9.

27. Oaks (1995, October), 7.

28. Gordon B. Hinckley (1987, May), Reverence and morality, *Ensign, 17*(5), 47.

29. J. Satinover (1996), *Homosexuality and the politics of truth,* (Grand Rapids, MI: Baker Books), 179, 186.

Single Adults and Family Life

Cynthia Doxey, Douglas E. Brinley, Mary Jane Woodger, Mae Blanch, Richard K. Meeves, Maxine Lewis Rowley, and Pearl Raynes Philipps

All human beings—male and female—are created in the image of God.
Each is a beloved spirit son or daughter of heavenly parents,
and, as such, each has a divine nature and destiny.
(The Family: A Proclamation to the World, ¶ 2)

The Family: A Proclamation to the World states that "marriage between a man and a woman is ordained of God and that the family is central to the Creator's plan for the eternal destiny of His children" (¶ 1). This statement demonstrates the vital role that families have in the work of the Lord to "bring to pass the immortality and eternal life of man" (Moses 1:39), because "in order to obtain the highest [degree of the celestial kingdom], a man must enter into . . . the new and everlasting covenant of marriage" (D&C 131:2). The Proclamation was given "to the world" and does not exclude any person, including those who might not yet be a spouse or parent.

For those of God's children who are currently single adults, there are times when the blessings of family life seem distant and difficult to attain. Single individuals may feel they do not fit into the prescribed mold of the Church's programs. They may feel that the emphasis on families and marriage in the Proclamation does not apply to them because they are not currently married. The purpose of this chapter is to help each person recognize that all individuals, whether currently single, married, divorced, or widowed, are part of God's eternal family and thus can live the principles of the Proclamation throughout their lives.

In the Proclamation, we are instructed concerning the eternal nature of each individual: "all human beings—male and female—are created in the image of God. Each is a beloved spirit son or daughter of heavenly parents, and, as such, each has a divine nature and destiny" (¶ 2). From this statement, we understand that each individual is one of God's children, each one has the potential to inherit eternal life in "the presence of God," and our families can be "united eternally" (¶ 3). In other words, even though singles may not presently be members of what is considered a "traditional" family, they are part of Heavenly Father's eternal family. Single members of The Church of Jesus Christ of Latter-day Saints may be strengthened by that knowledge and eternal perspective. Many principles of the Proclamation can be applied in relationships with others throughout life, whether individuals are married or single.

In a single adult fireside address, President Gordon B. Hinckley stated that we have unfortunately grouped together all people who are not married into one category called "singles," thus making them seem different from other adults. He told singles, "You are just as important as any others in the scheme of our Father in Heaven."[1] In the same fireside, President Howard W. Hunter expressed his feelings about singles in the Church:

> This is the church of Jesus Christ, not the church of marrieds or singles or any other group or individual. The gospel we preach is the gospel of Jesus Christ, which encompasses all the saving ordinances and

covenants necessary to save and exalt every individual who is willing to accept Christ and keep the commandments that he and our Father in Heaven have given.[2]

While acknowledging diversity among single adults, both prophets emphasized the unifying influence of the gospel that brings us to Christ through commandments, covenants, and ordinances.

We must remember that each individual is responsible for working out his or her salvation through the Atonement of Jesus Christ.[3] "Each man and each woman sealed in an eternal relationship must be individually worthy" of exaltation in the celestial kingdom.[4] Thus, while the Proclamation focuses on families, all people are individually accountable for living its principles.[5]

SINGLE ADULTS IN THE CHURCH

For the purpose of this chapter, we define single adults as individuals over age 18 who are not currently married. This group comprises those who have not yet married and those who are divorced or widowed. Although sometimes we group all singles together for the purpose of discussion, we recognize a wide variation among them.

While the Proclamation does not directly discuss being single, approximately one-third of Church members over 18 years of age are not married.[6] However, singles must certainly be included with those to whom the Proclamation to the world applies. Considering the gospel's emphasis on family life, there are perhaps more single adults in the Church than one would expect. Church statistical projections in 1981 indicated that only a small percentage (3 percent) of men and women between 18 and 30 would not marry by age 60, but there is a sizeable proportion of the adult Church membership that is single at any given time due to never marrying, divorce, or widowhood.[7]

Box 17.1, below, based on research done in 1995 for the Relief Society, indicates that the vast majority of women will be single for some portion of their lives between age 18 and death. This phenomenon occurs in part because most women marry later than age 18 and also because most women live longer than their husbands. We do not have similar statistics for men in the Church, but we can assume that the pattern for men may be similar to the pattern for women. Until age 26, most individuals are single; the proportion of single individuals decreases as the group ages. One difference between women and men in the later years is that men will be less likely to be single as a result of the death of their wives.

When we contemplate the number of Heavenly Father's children who have not been sealed in the covenant of eternal marriage, we may recognize more fully the great extent of singleness in the Church. Many of God's children will require time beyond mortality to obtain the blessings of an eternal

MARITAL STATUS OF LDS WOMEN IN THE UNITED STATES AND CANADA (AS OF DECEMBER 31, 1995)			
AGE	NEVER MARRIED	DIVORCED/WIDOWED	MARRIED
18–25	67%	1%	32%
26–30	28%	1%	71%
31–45	12%	9%	79%
46–64	4%	19%	77%
65+ years	2%	47%	51%

Source: The Church of Jesus Christ of Latter-day Saints Research Information Division

Box 17.1

marriage. They include, but are not limited to, the following:

- Men and women who have been faithful to the principles of the gospel who were divorced or widowed prior to being sealed to a spouse, or those who have not yet married.
- Individuals who died at a young age before they were able to marry and are presently living as adult males and females in the spirit world.
- Individuals who were mentally or physically incapable of marriage in mortality, but who, at death, regain their status as healthy adult spirit sons or daughters of God.

In addition, among married individuals, where one spouse is unworthy to marry in the temple, or unfaithful to temple covenants, the faithful spouse will have an opportunity to be sealed at some time in the future. As stated by President Hunter, "No blessing, including that of eternal marriage and an eternal family, will be denied to any worthy individual."[8] If we take into account all of God's children who fit into one of the categories above, only a small percentage have actually been sealed to a spouse while in mortality.

Prophetic Promises for Single Adults

Faithful single adults who die before they marry or remarry have been promised that they will have the opportunity to marry in the next life if they remain worthy. The Prophet Joseph Smith promised faithful individuals: "All your losses will be made up to you in the resurrection, provided you continue faithful."[9] Elder Dallin H. Oaks emphasized that an eternal perspective is important in dealing with difficulties of life. "Singleness, childlessness, death, and divorce frustrate ideals and postpone the fulfillment of promised blessings. . . . But these frustrations are only temporary. . . . Many of the most important deprivations of mortality will be set right in the Millennium."[10] Similarly, President Lorenzo Snow taught:

> There is no Latter-day Saint who dies after having lived a faithful life who will lose anything because . . . opportunities were not furnished him or her. In other words, if a young man or a young woman has no opportunity of getting married, and they live faithful lives up to the time of their death, they will have all the blessings, exaltation, and glory that any man or

woman will have who had this opportunity and improved it. That is sure and positive.[11]

All people should remember that the frustrations of this life are only temporary, even though to our finite minds they may appear interminable. Eventually, all faithful singles who worthily live the gospel principles and covenants will obtain all blessings pertaining to marriage that they may not have received in mortality.

Responsibilities along with the Promises

While single individuals can take comfort in the promises of future eternal blessings that may be theirs, they must not be complacent about their responsibilities with respect to marriage in this life. As is stated in the Proclamation, "marriage between a man and a woman is ordained of God" (¶ 1). The Lord requires His children to keep all the commandments in order to be eligible for the blessings He desires to bestow (see D&C 130:20–21).

Church leaders are concerned about the growing number of Latter-day Saints who put off marriage until later life, or who are too picky in choosing a spouse.[12] Prophets have provided guidance about the responsibility to marry. President Ezra Taft Benson, in a talk to single brethren, discussed the need to examine their priorities and motives for marriage. Citing Genesis 2:18, "It is not good that the man should be alone," he counseled:

> Understand that temple marriage is essential to your salvation and exaltation. . . . Postponing marriage unduly often means limiting your posterity . . . I can assure you that the greatest responsibility and the greatest joys in life are centered in the family, honorable marriage, and rearing a righteous posterity. And the older you become, the less likely you are to marry, and then you may lose these eternal blessings altogether.[13]

President Benson, while reminding single males of their responsibility to marry, also invited them to have faith in themselves and in the Lord. He told single brethren they can overcome their fear of being able to support a wife and family by putting their trust in the Lord.[14] In a Devotional address at Brigham Young University, Elder Jeffrey R. Holland also expressed his concern that too many individuals draw back from marriage because of fear. He suggested that we should all be cautious and prayerful in making the significant decision of marriage, "but once there has been genuine illumination," i.e., inspiration that the decision is correct, "beware the temptation to retreat from a good thing."[15] Fear often holds individuals back from important decisions and blessings.

Responsibilities of Brethren

President Benson recommends that single males evaluate the qualities they seek in a mate: "Now brethren, do not expect perfection in your choice of a mate. Do not be so particular that you overlook her most important qualities."[16] Elder Richard G. Scott provided a list of important qualities of a prospective spouse, including "a deep love of the Lord and of His commandments, a determination to live them, one that is kindly, understanding, forgiving of others, and willing to give of self." He suggests that singles should: "not ignore many possible candidates who are still developing these attributes, seeking the one who is perfected in them. You will likely not find that perfect person, and if you did, there would certainly be no interest in you. These attributes are best polished together as husband and wife."[17]

President Hinckley has also counseled singles concerning their responsibility to marry: "My heart reaches out to those among us, especially our single sisters, who long for marriage and cannot seem to find it. Our Father in Heaven reserves for them every promised blessing. I have far less sympathy for the young men, who under the customs of our society, have the prerogative to take the initiative in these matters but in so many cases fail to do so."[18]

Church leaders lay much of the responsibility for marrying upon the shoulders of priesthood holders. This obligation may seem unfair because a marriage requires both a man and woman. Perhaps a good metaphor is the similar responsibility men have in comparison to women with respect to going on missions. President Hinckley, in a general conference priesthood meeting stated that "missionary work is essentially a priesthood responsibility. As such, our young men must carry the major burden."[19] In a similar manner, men in Western culture often carry a greater responsibility to take the initiative in pursuing marriage. For some individuals, courting can be somewhat like missionary work. Those who have experienced pain and rejection in courtship may be tempted to give up. But just as missionaries continue their work in the face of constant rejection, unmarried priesthood holders have a responsibility to continue the courtship process.

Responsibilities of Sisters

Despite the fact that prophets have admonished men to take the responsibility for finding an eternal companion, women also have responsibilities to prepare for and seek marriage. President Benson affirmed that single sisters should "never lose sight of this sacred goal [of marriage]. Prayerfully prepare for it and live for it." In addition, he counseled women to maintain high standards for themselves and those they marry, but not to expect perfection or be too concerned "about his physical appearance and his bank account."[20] He cautioned women against becoming "so independent and self-reliant that you decide marriage isn't worth it."[21] Elder Scott also told single members who "haven't identified a solid prospect for celestial marriage" to "live for it. Pray for it. Expect it in the timetable of the Lord. Do not compromise your standards in any way that would rule out that blessing [of eternal marriage] on this or the other side of the veil."[22]

Wisdom and intelligence must accompany the sense of responsibility for marriage. President Hinckley suggested, "Do not lose hope. But do not become obsessed with ambition to find a companion."[23] He also stated, "Don't rush it unduly and don't delay it unduly. 'Marry in haste and repent at leisure' is an old proverb that still has meaning in our time. But do not dally along in a fruitless, frustrating, and frivolous dating game."[24] President Joseph Fielding Smith also cautioned singles with the following: "You . . . who are single and alone, do not fear, do not feel that blessings are going to be withheld from you. You are not under any obligation or necessity of accepting some proposal . . . which is distasteful for fear you will come under condemnation."[25]

Marriage is a commandment that requires intelligent choice. Marriage was designed to bring joy and opportunity, as well as the kind of personal growth that prepares a couple for exaltation. It would be better to remain single rather than make an unwise marital choice.

These statements from Church leaders indicate that while there are promises for all of God's worthy children to receive the blessings of eternal life and companionship, our worthiness may in part be predicated on our desire and willingness to marry. While we should not marry simply to be married, neither should we wait until we find "perfection" in a companion.

CHALLENGES OF SINGLE LIFE

Single adults face a number of unique challenges. Even though the Church rightfully is family-oriented, being single is not an anomaly. The hope is that individuals will understand and recognize the various challenges of singleness, so all will go forward with renewed faith to overcome difficulties and enjoy life.

Challenges Experienced by Single Adults

Social science literature has focused on single adult life from the perspective that singles may have difficulties associated with isolation or loneliness. Much of the theory and practice for helping singles, who "are perhaps the biggest consumers of therapy"[26] focuses on the issues of overcoming feelings of isolation. Two such theories that can be applied to single adult life are human developmental theorist Erik Erikson's model of psychosocial development and therapist Karen Gail Lewis' framework of Nonsequential Developmental Tasks for Adult Singlehood. These theories will be briefly summarized here. Erikson and Lewis used research and observation to formulate a framework for understanding the feelings and challenges that singles face when they are not involved in a committed relationship.

The Erikson Model of Development. A central concept of Erikson's model is that each of his eight stages of life-cycle development focuses on coming to terms with a crisis associated with the individual's interaction with the social world. For example, according to Erikson, infants' interactions with their caregivers promote either trust or the alternative, mistrust. Infants who learn to trust others develop the basic strength Erickson labels hope. Each child's ability to cope with the current developmental crisis influences their beliefs, attitudes, behaviors, well-being, and future ways of dealing with crises at later developmental stages.

Erikson's stage most relevant to single adulthood is Stage VI: Intimacy vs. Isolation. The key challenge in this stage is to develop love within the context of interpersonal relationships. Attaining such relationships requires reaching out to others, disclosing feelings, thoughts, and dreams, and opening oneself up to pain should the relationship end. The developmental crisis in this stage comes in adjusting to and coping with the loss of close relationships or in not forming these types of relationships.[27]

For adult singles who do not marry, or do not marry until later in life, the absence of a close, intimate marriage partner may bring a feeling of isolation. Church doctrine rightly places a high value on marriage, but unfortunately, Church culture may include stigmatization of those who are not married, adding to their loneliness. Rather than separating singles from the rest of the Church, members should live the principle stated by Alma that we should mutually support each other as we "comfort those who stand in need of comfort" (Mosiah 18:9).

The Lewis Model of Developmental Tasks for Adult Singles. The other theory, developed by a therapist and researcher of single women's experiences,[28] provides a more pragmatic set of developmental tasks for adult singles. She suggests eight tasks that are important in adjusting to life as an adult single. Each task is significant and could be a guide for what singles may accomplish during their lives. While there is no exact sequence for these tasks to be carried out, they will be presented in the order Lewis listed them.

The majority of the nonsequential tasks focuses on fulfilling one's own needs in the circumstance of not having a committed relationship. The first four tasks are grounding (or feeling securely established within a home, community, and career), having close friendships (emotional intimacy), meeting basic needs (including daily contact with others), and nurturance (having opportunities to help others and to be nurtured by them). These tasks and needs can often be met through the relationships singles develop within the Church as ward or branch families provide opportunities for being with others, participating in temple and family history work, fulfilling church callings, and serving others.

Lewis's fifth task is to acknowledge sexual feelings and either express affection in an appropriate way, numb such feelings, or deny them completely. As the Proclamation states, "God has commanded that the sacred powers of procreation are to be employed only between man and woman, lawfully wedded as husband and wife" (¶ 4). Because of the importance of the law of chastity, many single individuals' concerns or difficulties with their sexual feelings may not be recognized or understood. The world may view the law of chastity as merely a numbing, denial, or stifling of "natural" feelings. However, the Proclamation and the prophets have declared that the "spiritual man" can overcome the "natural man" (see Mosiah 3:19), that we can and should "bridle all [our] passions, that [we] may be filled with love" (Alma 38:12). Thus, the gospel brings comfort and strength to those who are living the law of chastity.

The last three tasks from Lewis's model are concerned with accepting and dealing with the delay or loss of the dreams of a lasting and committed marriage: grieving (recognizing and accepting the ambiguities associated with being single), making peace with parents and family members (resolving parent–child relationships and helping family members to treat the single individual as an adult), and maintaining a positive image of oneself while preparing for old age. As mentioned earlier, the prophets counseled against losing hope for an eternal companion, but many singles do experience grief in recognizing that their opportunities for marriage are diminishing. Living singly is usually not the desired goal for most people, but the adult single must cope with his or her singleness by making decisions and plans without support from an eternal companion.

The gospel plan helps singles overcome difficulties associated with loneliness through service to others.[29] By living the principles of the Proclamation, individuals become less concerned about themselves and focus more on promoting the Lord's work of providing opportunities of eternal life for all of Heavenly Father's children.

Specific Challenges for Single Parents

Single-parent families have become an increasingly prevalent family form in the United States with 32 percent of families with children under 18 years old headed by single parents.[30] Often we think of divorce and widowhood as being the reasons why people become single parents, but included in this group are unmarried parents, as well as those parents who in effect function somewhat as a single parent because their spouse may consistently be away from home or debilitated by disease or other disability. There is a need to address the links between the Proclamation and strong, single parent families. The Proclamation states that "other circumstances may necessitate individual adaptation" (¶ 7). One of the "other circumstances" is living in a single parent family. President Benson told single parents, "Counsel with your priesthood leaders. Let them know of your needs and wants. Single parenthood is understood by the Lord. He knows the special challenges that are yours."[31]

Being a single parent is not a new phenomenon, although it seems more prevalent in our current society. Within the Church we have a unique cultural heritage when it comes to single parents. Consider the

women in the early history of the Church who parented families alone while their husbands were away for years, serving missions. Prophets and Apostles (e.g., Joseph F. Smith, Heber C. Kimball, David B. Haight, Dallin H. Oaks), great leaders, and humble, valiant people have been reared by single parents. Families headed by single parents can be successful, despite the challenges they have.[32]

Single parents have a unique set of difficulties that are different from those of singles without children. Single parents' responsibilities towards their children include their day-to-day care, along with the financial and emotional support that parents (including non-custodial parents) must give. Some specific challenges that single parents face include:

Providing for the physical needs of their children. Research shows that single parents experience role and task overload.[33] President Hinckley also addressed this issue by saying, "Most of you . . . carry exhausting burdens in fighting the daily battles that go with rearing children and seeing that their needs are met. This is a lonely duty."[34]

Financial difficulties. Financial worries are a universal and pervasive source of stress for single parents.[35] A related yet critical problem for one-parent families is finding adequate child care at a reasonable cost while the parent works to provide for the temporal needs of the family.

Supporting the children emotionally. While many children in single-parent families enjoy happy childhoods and grow up to be well-adjusted adults, some may struggle with emotional distress, depression, difficulty forming lasting relationships, difficulties in school, and the requirement to take on adult responsibilities at an early age.[36] Single parents must be available emotionally and physically to help their children, while also coping with any difficulties they themselves may be having.

Getting involved in a social life with other adults. One of the added difficulties for singles with children is that if they want to be involved socially with other adults they must be concerned not only about child care while they are gone, but also about the reactions of the children to a potential spouse, and reactions of the potential spouse to the children.

Single parents can be effective parents when they are able to assume a positive attitude toward their parental role and are determined to have a healthy family.[37] Successful single parents also make parenting a priority in their lives.[38] In their commitment to children, parents have found they must also include their own personal development, since there is a connection between the parent's own emotional and physical well-being and the children's well-being.[39] President Benson encouraged singles to "always be improving yourself. . . . Improve yourself physically, socially, mentally, and spiritually. . . . Keep growing and learning and progressing and serving others."[40]

As all families are strengthened, single parents will find they are also fortified through living the gospel. As President Gordon B. Hinckley described a single mother's difficulties and her need for divine help, he stated, "She recognizes a divine power available to her."[41] On another occasion, President Hinckley suggested that the Church has a great obligation to help those who are single parents:

> I hope that every woman who finds herself in [these] circumstances . . . is . . . blessed with an understanding and helpful bishop, with a Relief Society president who knows how to assist her, with home teachers who know where their duty lies and how to fulfill it, and with a host of ward members who are helpful without being intrusive.[42]

President Hunter, in a fireside for single adults, provided suggestions about how single parents, their extended families, and church community can help each other and find joy in their difficult circumstances. His counsel is summarized in Box 17.2.[43]

Many times the counsel for single parents is directed toward single mothers, but single fathers also play an important role in the lives of their children. Often, single fathers do not share in the custody of their children and may not appear to need help from the ward and community. However, they also need support for their role as a father, especially when their children do not live with them. Of course, single custodial fathers usually deal with many of the same difficulties as single mothers, except they tend to have fewer financial challenges.

LIVING THE PRINCIPLES OF THE PROCLAMATION

Elder Robert D. Hales posed the following question in a general conference address on strengthening families: "What if you are single or have not been blessed with children? Do you need to be concerned about the counsel regarding families? Yes. It is something we all need to learn in earth life."[44] Elder Scott suggested an overall objective for singles when applying the plan of happiness explained in the Proclamation: "Even if

---

PRESIDENT HOWARD W. HUNTER'S COUNSEL TO CHURCH MEMBERS

To you who have experienced divorce:
- Don't let disappointment or a sense of failure color your perception of marriage or of life.
- Do not lose faith in marriage or allow bitterness to canker your soul and destroy you or those you love or have loved.

To you who are widowed:
- The most important part of your life is *not* over.
- [You] may have opportunities for further companionship and remarriage.
- There can still be marvelous opportunities in life for personal growth and service to others.

To you priesthood and auxiliary leaders:
- Follow the scriptural counsel to look after the widows and the fatherless (see D&C 83:6).
- Take a prayerful interest in those who are single or in single-parent homes.
- Remember: the Church is for *all* members.

To each Church member:
- Practice the pure religion which is "to visit the fatherless and widows" (James 1:27).
- Be kind and considerate of all members. Be thoughtful.
- Be careful in what you say. Don't allow an insensitive remark or action to harm another.

Box 17.2

---

important parts of it aren't fulfilled in your life now, they will be yours in the Lord's due time. . . . As a daughter or son of God, live whatever portion of the plan you can to the best of your ability."[45] As Elder Scott and Elder Hales suggested, single adult members of the Church should heed the counsel of the prophets regarding family life, and they can apply the Proclamation to their present life situation.

The three dimensions of the mission of The Church of Jesus Christ of Latter-day Saints are to preach the gospel, perfect the Saints, and redeem the dead.[46] In living the principles of the Proclamation, single adults could focus their efforts in those three areas. "To every thing there is a season, and a time to every purpose under the heaven" (Eccl. 3:1). During the season of being single, individuals may be able to spend more time and energy in strengthening eternal family ties through missionary work, temple work, and family history work. While serving the Lord in these ways, individuals also develop more Christlike attributes.

Developing Christlike Characteristics

The goal of single members should be "not to wait successfully but to live richly, fully, joyfully."[47] Single members of The Church of Jesus Christ of Latter-day Saints "will discover compensatory blessings when [they] willingly accept the will of the Lord and exercise faith in Him."[48] Such blessings are produced when cultivating lives based on "faith, prayer, repentance, forgiveness, respect, love, compassion, work, and wholesome recreational activities" (¶ 7). The same characteristics that bless a marriage or family can bless any relationship. As President Hinckley has said, "The chances are that if you forget about [marriage] and become anxiously engaged in other activities, the prospects will brighten immeasurably. . . . The best medicine for loneliness is work, service in behalf of others."[49] Through service, unmarried members find close relationships with others in which they can develop the same characteristics they will need when they become part of successful family units.

President Hunter gave similar counsel to Latter-day Saint singles: "While waiting for promised blessings, one should not mark time, for to fail to move forward is to some degree a retrogression. Be anxiously engaged in good causes, including your own development."[50] There are many good causes in which all people can become engaged, including serving in our families, church, and communities. Each individual child of God can and should be developing the characteristics of faith, prayer, repentance, forgiveness, respect, love, compassion, work, and wholesome recreation listed in the Proclamation in their relationships throughout their lives, whatever their marital status.

Living Happily as a Single Adult

Although being single may not be someone's first choice, the Proclamation and the prophets show how singles can approach life. First, singles should discard attitudes that result only in misery. For example, it is tempting for a single adult to feel God is punishing her or him for some unrecognized sin or that he or she does not deserve the happiness of a good marriage. While each of God's children carries responsibility for his or her life, no one controls all circumstances and consequences. However, we can control our reaction to them. We can drown in self-pity or we can accept our present state and get on with making the best life possible. Box 17.3 contains suggestions about being happy in single life.

BEING SINGLE, BEING HAPPY

- Recognize that being single is not a punishment from God, but may be a "customized trial" that "can 'enlarge the soul,' including an enlarged capacity for joy."[51]
- Recognize the blessings available to singles:
  - Being single allows for more control over time, talents, and resources.
  - Singles often can participate in sharing the gospel and in family history and temple work because they do not have other family responsibilities.
  - Singles have greater freedom in finding satisfying work that makes an honorable contribution to society.
- Establish a home where you live. A home gives roots, a place in the community, and a wider acquaintance with neighbors. The spirit of God can be present there, and you and others can delight to be there.
- Cultivate and increase faith. As President Spencer W. Kimball has said, "One does not need to be married . . . in order to keep the first and second great commandments—those of loving God and our fellow men—on which Jesus said hang all the law and all the prophets."[52]

Box 17.3

Strengthening Families

Singles can strengthen families around them by serving in their own extended families, wards or branches, and in the wider community. President James E. Faust stated, "All society, including the adult single members, . . . have a vested interest in . . . families."[53] As part of our vested interest, unmarried individuals can have a positive influence on communities, church units, and nations. Elder Neal A. Maxwell explains: those "who cannot now enrich the institution of their own marriage so often enrich other institutions in society."[54] Similarly, Elder Robert D. Hales counsels, "Unmarried adult members can often lend a special strength to the family, becoming a tremendous source of support, acceptance, and love."[55] In this way, singles live the injunction at the end of the Proclamation "to maintain and strengthen the family as the fundamental unit of society" (¶ 9). Suggestions for ways singles can strengthen other families are included in Box 17.4

Being involved in church congregations and

activities can create a sense of belonging for the single adult and can provide opportunities for service he or she would not otherwise have. At times, single adults may feel like a "stow-away on Noah's ark" in a church where two-by-two is the ideal order of things, but they must recognize that they are valued members of the crew, essential to the captain and the other passengers. President Benson told singles:

> We see you as a vital part of the mainstream body of the Church. We pray that the emphasis we naturally place on families will not make you feel less needed or less valuable to the Lord or to His Church. The sacred bonds of Church membership go far beyond marital status, age, or present circumstance. Your individual worth as a [child] of God transcends all.[56]

SUPPORT FROM OTHERS TO LIVE PROCLAMATION PRINCIPLES

Extended Families

Because "family relationships [are] perpetuated beyond the grave" (¶ 3), eternal relationships, including those of son, daughter, aunt, uncle, brother, sister, niece, nephew, kindred spirit, and nurturing Saint will continue after this life. Single people are part of larger family units. The Lord "sent us to live with and be nurtured spiritually and temporally by a family."[58] If present circumstances do not provide a nurturing setting in a husband and wife relationship, there is much that an extended family, church unit, or friend can do to nurture and provide support for single members as an integral part of these family institutions.

Extended family members can provide essential support to those in their families who have not yet been blessed to be sealed as a husband or wife. Participating in the important life events of the single member is vital in helping them to feel important, loved, and supported. Extended family members can be especially sensitive during holidays, when emphasis is often placed on family activities. Including unmarried family members in these festivities enhances extended family relationships and gives those who are alone a sense of belonging. Further ideas on supporting singles can be found in Box 17.5.

Friends and Church Families

Though the Proclamation has clearly defined marriage as a husband and wife partnership, friends can be a nurturing influence in the lives of single members. Couples and singles can reach out to each other and provide support, concern, interest, and love that may be missing in the life of an unmarried Latter-day Saint. An understanding heart is an important characteristic in a friend who does not prejudge a single individual's circumstances. Refraining from accusatory or negative attitudes about why individuals are single is the first step to providing an atmosphere of love and support to those who need it. It is wise to remember that there are few Latter-day Saints who do not desire the blessings of marriage and children and who have not made real efforts to marry. Some negative perceptions about unmarried adults and positive solutions are mentioned in Box 17.6.

CONCLUSION

The Family: A Proclamation to the World is applicable to all people, married or single. "All of us, single or married, are eternally part of some family—someway, somewhere, somehow—and much of our joy in life comes as we correctly recognize and properly develop those family relationships."[59] Therefore, no Latter-day Saint should believe that the principles

---

NONSUPPORTIVE ATTITUDES ABOUT SINGLES

Many single adults, particularly those over 30 years of age, have had experiences where insensitive comments or negative attitudes towards them have perhaps led to hurt or anger.[59] The following are negative attitudes and comments that might hurt others:

- Singles are too picky or do not try hard enough to find a spouse.
- Singles lack faith and are not living the commandments.
- Singles are always fully responsible for their singleness.
- Singles do not like to associate with couples or families.
- Singles somehow need to be repaired or changed.

These perceptions should be avoided. Many people, in wanting to avoid negative attitudes, however, may not recognize that the following well-meant statements are discouraging:

- "What's wrong with all those women [or men] that nobody has found you yet?"
- "You are so good that there is no one good enough for you."
- "Maybe if you changed your appearance a little, people would notice you more."
- "I know someone who was just like you, and he just got married! You might get married, too!"

Suggestions for positive attitudes and statements towards singles:

- Instead of focusing on marital status, express appreciation for qualities you admire. In other words, most singles would appreciate not having to discuss their "singleness" at all, unless they bring up the topic themselves.
- Be sensitive to people's feelings, even if you do not understand or cannot relate to their circumstances. Simply telling stories about other people who got married could be discouraging since it may not currently apply in a single individual's life.
- Instead of assuming that all singles need to be matched up with each other, get to know them well first, and then ask them how they feel about meeting someone you know. When singles can trust the "matchmaker," they may be more open to suggestions.

Most single adults do not want to be singled out from the crowd due to their marital status. Usually, singles enjoy being around families who accept them for who they are and include them in their lives, not just because they are "the lonely service project."

Box 17.6

from the Proclamation do not apply to him or her. Much can be done to teach, support, inspire, and strengthen members of the Church whose family circumstances are less than ideal. Faithfully following the word of God is what will bring joy throughout this life and in eternity. Circumstances alone do not create happiness. There is the possibility and hope for a good life, whatever one's marital status.

Singles can take comfort in the promises made to them by the prophets concerning the eternities, and be assured that the gospel plan includes all of Heavenly Father's children. All are important to Him regardless of marital status. As President Hunter taught, "All of us, single or married, have individual identities and needs, among which is the desire to be seen as a worthwhile individual child of God."[61] The gospel plan helps each to feel worthwhile as a son or daughter of God.

NOTES

1. Gordon B. Hinckley (1989, June), To single adults, *Ensign, 19*(6), 72.

2. Howard W. Hunter (1989, June), The Church is for all people, *Ensign, 19*(6), 76.

3. See Articles of Faith 3; Howard W. Hunter (1989, June).

4. Hunter (1989, June), 76.

5. See Articles of Faith 2.

6. L. A. Young (1992), Single adults, in Daniel H. Ludlow (Ed.), *Encyclopedia of Mormonism* (New York: Macmillan), 3:1316–1319.

7. Young (1992).

8. Hunter (1989, June), 76.

9. Joseph Smith (1938), *Teachings of the Prophet Joseph Smith* ed. and comp. Joseph Fielding Smith (Salt Lake City: Deseret Book), 296.

10. Dallin H. Oaks (1993, November), The great plan of happiness, *Ensign, 23*(11), 75.

11. Lorenzo Snow (1984), *The teachings of Lorenzo Snow* comp. Clyde J. Williams (Salt Lake City: Bookcraft), 138.

12. Ezra Taft Benson (1988, April). To the single adult brethren of the Church, *Ensign, 28*(4), 51–53; Ezra Taft Benson (1988, November), To the single adult sisters of the Church, *Ensign, 28*(11), 96–97.

13. Benson (1988, April), 51, 52.

14. Benson (1988, April).

15. Jeffrey R. Holland (1999), Cast not away therefore your confidence, in *Brigham Young University 1998–1999 Speeches* (Provo, UT: Brigham Young University), 158.

16. Benson (1988, April), 53.

17. Richard G. Scott (1999, May), Receive the temple blessings, *Ensign, 29*(5), 26.

18. Gordon B. Hinckley (1991, May), What God hath joined together, *Ensign, 21*(5), 71.

19. Gordon B. Hinckley (1997, November), Some thoughts on temples, retention of converts, and missionary service, *Ensign, 27*(11), 52.

20. Benson (1988, November), 96.

21. Benson (1988, November), 97.

22. Scott (1999, May), 27.

23. Gordon B. Hinckley (1983, November), Live up to your inheritance, *Ensign, 13*(11), 83.

24. Hinckley (1989, June), 72.

25. Joseph Fielding Smith (1955), *Doctrines of salvation, volume II* (Salt Lake City: Bookcraft), 76.

26. K. G. Lewis (1994), Single heterosexual women through the life cycle, in M. P. Mirkin (Ed.), *Women in context: Toward a feminist reconstruction of psychotherapy* (New York: Guilford Press), 170.

27. E. H. Erikson (1950), *Childhood and society* (New York: Norton).

28. Lewis, (1994).

29. Gordon B. Hinckley (1996, November), Women of the Church, *Ensign, 26*(11), 67–70.

30. U.S. Bureau of the Census (1998), *Statistical abstract of the United States: 1998* (118th ed.) (Washington, DC: GPO).

31. Benson (1988, November), 97.

32. A. Barry (1979), A research project on successful single-parent families, *American Journal of Family Therapy, 7*(3), 65–73.

33. A. Barry (1979); M. M. Sanik and T. Mauldin (1986), Single versus two parent families: A comparison of mothers' time, *Family Relations, 35*, 53–56.

34. Hinckley (1989, June), 74.

35. M. L. Campbell and P. Moen (1992), Job-family role strain among employed single mothers of preschoolers, *Family Relations, 41*, 205–211; L. N. Richards and C. J. Schmiege (1993), Problems and strengths of single-parent families, *Family Relations, 42*(3) 277–285.

36. M. R. Olson and J. A. Haynes (1993), Successful single parents, *Families in Society, 74*(5), 259–267; L. N. Richards and Schmiege (1993).

37. Barry (1979).

38. Olson and Haynes (1993).

39. S. M. H. Hanson (1986), Healthy single parent families, *Family Relations, 35*, 125–132.

40. Ezra Taft Benson (1988, November), 97.

41. Hinckley (1991, May), 73.

42. Hinckley (1996, November), 69.

43. Hunter (1989, June).

44. Robert D. Hales (1999, May), Strengthening families: Our sacred duty, *Ensign, 29*(5), 34.

45. Richard G. Scott (1996, November), The joy of living the great plan of happiness, *Ensign, 26*(11), 75.

46. Spencer W. Kimball (1981, May), A report of my stewardship, *Ensign, 11*(5), 87.

47. C. Clark (1974), *A singular life: Perspectives for the single woman* (Salt Lake City: Deseret Book), 9.

48. Richard G. Scott (1996, May), Finding joy in life, *Ensign, 26*(5), 25.

49. Hinckley (1996, November), 68.

50. Hunter (1989, June), 77.

51. Neal A. Maxwell (1997, November), Apply the atoning blood of Christ, *Ensign, 27*(11), 22.

52. Spencer W. Kimball (1997, November), The role of righteous women, *Ensign, 27*(11), 103.

53. James E. Faust (1974, January), Happiness is having a father who cares, *Ensign, 4*(1), 23.

54. Neal A. Maxwell (1978, May), The women of God, *Ensign, 8*(5), 11.

55. Hales (1999, May), 34.

56. Benson (1988, November), 96.

57. Jeanette C. Hales (1992, September 5), Marriage is a righteous goal for singles, *Church News,* 4.

58. Gene R. Cook (1984, May), Home and family: A divine eternal pattern, *Ensign, 14*(5), 31.

59. John H. Groberg (1982, May), The power of family prayer, *Ensign, 12*(5), 50.

60. Don L. Searle (1987, September), Single in a family church, *Ensign, 17*(9), 21.

61. Hunter (1989, June), 76.

Moving Forward after Divorce

Linda Hunter Adams

As a member of a general Church committee, headed by Elder Russell M. Nelson, for singles in the Church, I brought the experiences of more than 20 years as a single parent and nearly a dozen years as the counselor over singles in the Young Special Interest presidency of Utah Valley. In connection with my YSI calling, in addition to helping plan the first conference for single adults in the Church, I had for years run a hotline for singles and heard the painful stories of the consequences of divorce, but also the moving stories as lives began to heal. In this essay, I would like to share with you some ideas that helped us move on after divorce.

The Church rightly places great importance on marriage and success in the home. A family offers the best place to progress and to develop our talents and gifts. It offers opportunities for giving love and being loved, for sacrificing for others' welfare. Most Church members take the responsibilities of marriage very seriously. So when a marriage is no longer a safe spiritual or physical place, it is difficult for members to move on. By the time of a divorce, the amount of damage to a person's feeling of self-worth usually is extensive and a sense of failure and of worthlessness prevails. Ward members, attentive visiting and home teachers, and a sensitive bishop can be of great support during this period.

Although many of the effects of divorce are the same for both men and women, some effects differ. Women usually end up financially worse off, often in poverty, and usually are left to do most of the child rearing. Because children usually live with the mothers, fathers more often lose the joy of seeing their children every day and of sharing in all their experiences as they mature. Perhaps because fathers are not with their children they find it harder to maintain Church activity. Sometimes divorced fathers distance themselves from their families because they cannot bear the loss, or after remarriage attention to a new family takes away from the fathers' involvement with his original family. Fathers need to put forth extra effort to remain involved. And mothers need to encourage, not just allow, the involvement of fathers in the children's lives.

As divorced people, we need to be careful not to criticize our former mate in the children's presence. The child is made up of both the father and the mother; when we criticize our spouse, we are tearing at half of the child. Single parents also need to be careful not to use children as pawns or as weapons in their relationship with a former spouse. The greatest gift we have to avoid these problems is forgiveness. Forgiving is difficult and takes time, but the Lord commands us "to forgive all men" (D&C 64:10).

Because after marriage most of your friends are couples, as a single person you may feel like you no longer fit in. And as a divorced person (particularly one with children), you don't really fit naturally into the "singles" lifestyle. A divorce may cause an awkward situation for the divorced couple and for their friends and acquaintances. Oftentimes friends of the couple don't know what to say or don't want to choose sides, so they drop the friendship at a time when friends are most needed. With a little added thought and care, friends can remain friends, rather than become former friends.

Being divorced and single is lonely. This loneliness can be alleviated, to some degree, by getting involved with worthwhile activities and serving others. When a divorce takes place, the ward family can help the divorced person move on. Following are some suggestions of service I found helpful as a divorced single parent:

1. Give emotional support and assurance to the divorced person that he or she is a good person, a beloved son or daughter of our Heavenly Father.

2. Express your sincere love and friendship with the assurance that the change in marital status has not affected your feelings about the person.

3. Make an effort to greet the person when he or she comes to church. It is uncomfortable for a divorced person to try to find someone to sit with, a place where we don't feel we are intruding. A simple "Come sit with us" can mean a lot.

4. Make sure the divorced person has a church calling. We are more involved when we serve and feel part of the ward. We feel more worthy when we are entrusted with a calling. Ideally, the calling would involve meaningful interaction with other adults. If the divorced person has just moved into the ward, a calling may help keep him or her from "disappearing." This may be particularly important for divorced men.

5. Invite the divorced person to attend the temple with you. It is hard to go to the temple alone. And after a divorce, the person especially needs the blessings of the temple.

6. Offer to tend young children to give a single mother or father a break. Having children come to your home with your children for a little while after school can ease a single parent's burden, especially a working single parent.

7. Offer help with a specific project such as mowing the lawn, working in the yard for spring cleanup, or fixing a leaky faucet, rather than saying, "If you need any help, let me know."

8. When a father or mother in a single-parent family is not available to take a child to events such as a Daddy–Daughter Night or a ward camp-out, offer to take the child along with your child.

9. As a Primary or Sunday School teacher, when helping a child make a gift for the parents, provide enough materials for the child to make two presents so he or she is not put in the painful position of choosing which parent to honor.

10. Have the visiting teachers and the home teachers drawn from the same married couple, so that the single parent and the children can have a sense of a family caring about them and including them.

11. Occasionally invite single-parent families to your family home evening so the children can see how the priesthood functions in the home and how loving couples treat one another.

12. Single-parent families can join together once a month for family home evening. The peer support helps a divorced person feel that he or she is not the only person in the world to go through a divorce and to see that one can heal. And it helps children to know that theirs is not the only family with just one parent. Invite

priesthood holders to attend the home evening.

13. As a ward, be creative in helping single parents with their financial struggles. One ward's elders quorum finished the basement of a single parent's home so that she could rent it and thus have some added income to enable her to stay at home with her young children.

14. A stake or ward could have a periodic Single Parent's Night Out and the Young Adults could care for children while the single mothers or fathers take a much-need break.

Together as a ward family and as individual friends and family we can bless the lives of our brothers and sisters who are moving forward after divorce.

CHAPTER 18

GOSPEL IDEALS AND ADVERSITY IN FAMILY LIFE

KYLE L. PEHRSON, JACQUELINE S. THURSBY, AND TERRANCE D. OLSON

"Children are an heritage of the Lord" (Psalms 127:3). Parents have a sacred duty to rear their children in love and righteousness . . . to teach them to love and serve one another.
(The Family: A Proclamation to the World, ¶ 6)

INTRODUCTION

The focus of this chapter is on living gospel ideals when confronted with adversities in family life—especially the adversity of children wandering from gospel ideals. For Latter-day Saints, the ideals and values of righteous family life are based on the plan of salvation. After a brief discussion of the importance of gospel ideals and an articulation of four core gospel ideals, we will discuss how to live gospel ideals when a child wanders from or rejects gospel-centered ideals cherished by other family members.

Patterning mortal family life according to gospel-centered ideals means learning to consistently be our best selves, performing or doing the best we can in every situation, and learning to become one in thought and action with our Heavenly Father. Gospel ideals influence the family goals we strive to reach and are the worthy concepts we hold close to our hearts and transfer from generation to generation. The ultimate gospel ideals are to become the perfected souls our Heavenly Father knows we can be and to be united with God and our family members eternally.

Although there are many gospel ideals that could be mentioned here, the following are four considered important by the authors: having an honest heart, being responsible moment-by-moment, being constant in service, and becoming one with Heavenly Father. These ideals can serve as guides and measures of wisdom in our daily lives and interactions with our families and others. Most important, living these ideals will not only invite a sweet atmosphere and close family unity, but can also cement the family covenants made in the temple, and eventually lead to the blessing of an eternal family in the celestial kingdom. After a brief discussion of each of these ideals, we will discuss some of the principles that apply when families reject or abandon the family's gospel-centered ideals.

HAVING AN HONEST HEART

The ideal of having an honest heart is fundamental to other ideal concepts. Jesus Christ said: "O ye house of Israel whom I have spared, how oft will I gather you as a hen gathereth her chickens under her wing; if ye will repent and return unto me with full purpose of heart" (3 Ne. 10:6). "Full purpose of heart" means having the pure intent of an honest heart. Hold to the ideal of having an honest heart, and teach your children to have an honest heart. The intrinsic nature of an ideal Christian family is not dependent on external circumstances such as material goods or secular knowledge. An honest heart filled with love and compassion is the key to Christian living, and these concepts can and must be taught in the home. In Luke 8:15 we are reminded that " . . . an honest and good heart, having heard the word, keep[s] it, and bring[s] forth fruit with patience." We are to follow the voice of the prophet and follow the inward light of the Holy Ghost. Although no family is perfect, the family setting is the ideal training ground for the ideal of an honest heart.

BEING RESPONSIBLE MOMENT TO MOMENT

To be responsible for our choices moment-to-moment has much to do with being respectful. Elder Bruce R. McConkie reminds us that "every person, both great and small, should be treated equally and impartially.[1] "Thou shall not avenge, nor bear any grudge against the children of thy people, but thou shalt love thy neighbour as thyself: I *am* the Lord" (Lev. 19:18). Often, people live in a family without honoring the ideal of being respectful of others. We are responsible to teach one another, but respect sometimes lags when a comment like "I love you but I don't love your choices" is repeated too often. Such reminders can be perceived as pointed condemnation.

Sometimes people believe their agency or accountability can be suspended when experiencing the heat of an emotion. However, we are still agents, even when we experience life as though we were victims of our emotions. Fortunately, repentance is always available to us—even when repentance is necessary to transform our destructive feelings to emotions that draw us properly to others. To be Christlike requires self-regulation. Self-regulation is always available to us. That is, in part, the meaning of being agents and being accountable. Further, our character, the reputation by which we are known in this world and in the next, can be defined by our willingness to live our ideals and to honor our beliefs and commitments.

To teach this in the family requires the righteous parents' example in their own lives and constant modeling of respectful behavior towards their children and others. Nurturing parents teach the ideal attributes of Heavenly Father by honoring the sacred covenants they have made, by example, and by living and teaching gospel principles. Respect for others must include not only people outside the family, but most especially each family member. Respect, as a family ideal, is synonymous with courtesy and consideration. Each family member is to be treated with honor and esteem. Teaching this process in the home provides children with a model to practice outside of the home as well; it places a value on treating other people as they would like to be treated themselves.

BEING CONSTANT IN SERVICE

To be "called his people" we must embrace the idea of service. We must be "willing to bear one another's burdens, that they may be light" (Mosiah 18:8). In a service-oriented family, children learn the sensitivity to recognize needs of others and act upon those needs. How can we teach our children to do this? How can we help them to understand, truly, "Whatsoever ye would that men should do to you, do ye even so to them"? (Matt. 7:12; Luke 6:31; 3 Ne. 14:12) Is that too ideal in this age? We live in a world designed for us to learn eternal principles; it is here, in mortality, that we truly learn to give ourselves to service and to choose between right and wrong. Elder Neal A. Maxwell reminds us that

> Even after all the careful, wise, premortal tutorials, the only way to tame the raw self with finality was to place it in a mortal environment. Therein we are free to choose. Therein we can experience the sour and the sweet. Therein we learn about consequences. This process is the only way to bring about final and fundamental changes, even in those who are spiritually submissive.[2]

It is here, in mortality, that we learn the consequences of service to one another, and ultimately we "learn that when ye are in the service of your fellow beings, ye are only in the service of your God" (Mosiah 2:17). Parents, servants of the Lord, can seek to provide consistent, responsible behavior in *all* interactions with their children. That is a service ideal, and it can be internalized by all family members through simple family activities that range from chores to celebrations, from dinner dishes to Saturday cleaning, from holiday traditions to reunions. As the children grow older, and their worlds grow larger, their service can be expanded to the extended family, the neighborhood, and the broader community. Service leads to wisdom through experience. Learning to recognize a need and doing something responsible about it becomes easier with experience.

BECOMING ONE WITH HEAVENLY FATHER

The ideal principle of becoming one with Heavenly Father implies becoming one as a family and may be the most important principle of all. As Elder Robert D. Hales stated, "Being one in a family carries a great responsibility."[3] Hope is imbedded in the concept of *becoming*, and our families can be blessed with knowledge that we are becoming one with Heavenly Father in thought and actions. Becoming one with our Heavenly Father helps us to understand the need to become one with one another. Sheri L. Dew stated that "He [Jesus Christ] knows how to succor *all* of us. But *we* activate the power of the Atonement in our lives . . . by seeking after Him."[4]

An example of empathy, or understanding the principle of becoming one with another, is demonstrated in the following story.

Ten-year-old Amanda traveled to St. Louis with her grandmother to visit extended family, her great-grandparents, and to meet her young cousins for the first time. At a family supper held outside on a hot summer evening, she noticed that her invalid uncle, sitting apart and alone, had nothing to drink. Without saying anything, she went inside to the kitchen, got a glass of ice water for him, and sat down at his feet. She told him that if he wanted more, she would get it for him. She saw a need, and she responded to it. When her grandmother praised her later for her thoughtfulness, she said simply, "He looked thirsty, so I got him some water." For a few moments, Amanda became one with the needs of her uncle—she practiced empathy.

Rhetorically speaking, how is the principle of empathy, the practice of putting oneself mentally in another's place, taught? Perhaps by example; that is, by carefully attending to one another's needs we teach others to care. Perhaps children need to be reminded occasionally when their needs are being met that Christ loves them and provided them with loving caretakers. Perhaps simply teaching them to say "thank you" with sincerity and saying "thank you" back to them can awaken an awareness of becoming one with another.

By studying and incorporating gospel-oriented ideals into the fabric of our families, we can accomplish many things entirely impossible for us without those principles. We can teach our children to embrace openly and eagerly all that is good in this world; we can help them to understand that an honest heart, being constantly responsible, giving service, and seeking to become one with their Heavenly Father and their family members will create loving personalities and characters for them. The consequence of those loving behaviors will be joy. The

ideals spoken of here of having an honest heart, being respectful of others, doing service for others and becoming one with Heavenly Father will lead us toward the capacity to truly soften our hearts and live as beings of love and joy. Thereby, families are empowered to love one another more deeply and honestly by welcoming Jesus Christ to the center of our families. The depth of family love is an indicator of the pain and sorrow we feel when children do not embrace family ideals, and of the great joy we feel when a wanderer returns to family ideals.

When Children Wander

Few family challenges are of more dramatic magnitude and have long-term implications than when family members fall away from correct principles and even eventually become involved in serious transgressions. There can be no assurance that individual family members will hold to the family ideals revealed in the Proclamation on the family. This is true even in the best of families. Most Latter-day Saint parents would willingly sacrifice their own resources, security, safety, or well-being if it would assure their children's health, happiness, and testimony. Elder Boyd K. Packer reminds us, "It is a great challenge to raise a family in the darkening mists of our moral environment."[5] Despite the sincere efforts of loving and dedicated parents who want nothing more than to teach their children true principles, some of those children may still stray and be drawn away by forces well beyond the control of their parents.

Lehi, in fear of losing Laman and Lemuel, "did exhort them then with all the feeling of a tender parent . . ." (I Ne. 8:37). His tender entreaties, incidentally, stand in contrast to seeking to reclaim children by means of harshness or anger. The scriptures include counsel to cultivate certain emotions: love unfeigned, patience, long-suffering, and so on (see Mosiah 3:19; D&C 121:41–42) and warn against emotions such as anger, hate, resentment, envy, jealousy, and so on (see 2 Ne. 26:32; 3 Ne. 30:2; Lev. 19:17–18; Ps. 37:8; Eph. 4:31). Such counsel implies that, as accountable beings, we are responsible in some way for the emotions we experience.

The scriptures stand in contrast to much of contemporary social science, which views emotions or attitudes as neither right nor wrong. Generally, emotions are considered to have a life of their own and the best we poor imperfect mortals can do is control them. Such a view suggests we are victims of our emotions. Anger is a typical feeling that can be destructive. Traditional psychology views emotions as not to be evaluated morally. R. C. Solomon summarizes a common view: "It is clear that anger is neither a 'good' nor a 'bad' emotion, neither 'positive' nor 'negative,' but depends, in any particular case, upon the circumstances and the individual, the nature of the 'offense' and its background."[6]

Solomon also notes that George Bach, author of *The intimate enemy* "argues that anger is an apt means to intimacy as well as one of its necessary results."[7]

Latter-day Saints are particularly sensitized to the issue of anger, for not only are they aware of how anger is condemned by the Savior—"whosoever is angry with his brother without a cause shall be in danger of the judgment" (Matt. 5:22)—they are aware that Joseph Smith, in his translation of the verse, deleted the words "without a cause."

The point of this discussion is that those qualities of feeling that the scriptures, the Savior, and we ourselves believe in—such as love, joy and sorrow—are not of the same quality as the destructive alternatives such as envy, hate, anger, mocking, and so on. And in family relationships, our path to the attitudes and emotions we believe are right is to live righteously. The moral quality of our emotions will be an expression of the moral quality of the life we are living. Thus, love and joy and sorrow are inextricably bound up in our own obedience, our personal faithfulness, and our individual willingness to walk in the light of the gospel.

So it makes sense that in the Proclamation, love is virtually commanded and tied to moral commitment and obligation, even toward family members who seem committed to breaking God's commandments. The command is "Husband and wife have a solemn responsibility to love and care for each other and for their children" and "parents have a sacred duty to rear their children in love and righteousness, . . . to teach them to love and serve one another" (¶ 6). Success in family life is deemed to be grounded in honoring principles such as "forgiveness, respect, love, compassion" and so on (¶ 7). To observe such counsel, mothers and fathers would embrace and nurture forgiving attitudes, loving emotions, and compassionate feelings. Such quality of experience requires a meek and lowly heart (see Matt. 11:29).

In any given moment of everyday life, we either live obediently, righteously, humbly and meekly and experience the love, respect, forgiveness, and compassion called for by the Proclamation, or we

don't. We can respond to our obligations, duties, and beliefs with feelings of love and joy, or with feelings of resentment and a sense of burden. One quality of feeling is an expression of a soft heart; the other quality evidence of a hard heart. A story demonstrates this truth.

Derek's Story

Derek ran away from home and was gone two days before his parents realized he wasn't just staying at a friend's house. Derek had occasionally, after some bitter argument with his parents, retreated to some buddy's home. But in checking with the retreats Derek had used previously, his parents discovered nobody else had seen the boy all week. Upon discovery of a large withdrawal from a joint savings account, the parents realized Derek had bolted. He was 16—old enough to think he knows everything and young enough to be swallowed by the world.

At first, Derek's parents said things to themselves such as, "Fine! If he can't handle the rules here, let him find out how cold and cruel the world really is. I am sick and tired of his selfishness and ingratitude!" But at some point, Derek's parents experienced what the Book of Mormon calls a change of heart. They went from resentment to sorrow. They abandoned bitterness in favor of compassion. Their new emotions were not attempts to excuse Derek for whatever his follies and sins might be nor to relieve him of responsibility for his own life choices. Rather, they were expressions of taking gospel ideals seriously, and they began seeking a starting point to invite him to return and to reconsider his ways. Only in love could they contemplate such a possibility. Whereas their previous harshness had been incompatible with the counsel of the Proclamation, their compassion, concern, love—and even personal repentance—all worked toward a longing to find him safe and to do what would be right to point Derek toward a nondestructive future.

Derek's parents' first task was to figure out where he might be. They considered filing a missing persons report. Just as they decided to call, they heard a scraping noise in the garage. Derek's dad opened the door to the garage and saw Derek, with a surly attitude, sitting on his backpack, peeking out from under the wave of hair that always hid his forehead and most of his eyes. Derek expected the standard lecture from his father, which always included the opening line "I hope you know you have worried your mother sick!" (Derek always wondered why his father never seemed to be worried sick.)

But Derek was unprepared for what his father actually said: "Oh, thank goodness. You made it just in time." That seemed a bizarre greeting to a son who had been on the road for almost three days. Where was the rage, the resentment, the hostile rebuke? But what his father said next was even more odd: "Derek, the clam chowder is ready. You got here while it is still warm." Aside from the fact that clam chowder was Derek's favorite, he couldn't quite track what this conversation had to do with his having run away. He tensely blurted, "O.K., Dad, what are you trying to pull here?" At this moment Derek's mother appeared in the doorway and said, "We were so worried about you that we thought if we made some clam chowder you would smell it and come home." As irrational as that comment was, Derek's immediate thought was more relevant to the situation. He thought, "How do you fight with these people?" Exactly. How do you defend yourself when there are no accusations? What do you do when there is no rage in those you have decided are your enemies? What is the response to the absence of hostility?

In a way, Derek's parents—in their worry over his absence and in some guilt regarding how harsh they had been with him, which helped provoke his flight—had changed their hearts and gone from resentful anger at his having run off and "worried them," to a concern about how, as described in scriptural language, to invite and entice him to do good (see Moro. 7:13). They had not yet figured out what to do that would be inviting and enticing, but at least the harshness in them that Derek had used to justify running away was not in their hearts now. Three days earlier, they had met every impudent, demeaning, even yelling accusation from Derek with their own hostile retorts. This proved to them, at the time, that they had the better argument. This hard-hearted attitude simply gave Derek ammunition to justify in his heart that his parents were absolutely unreasonable and out of control.

Now Derek's parents were being challenged with the same arrogance, but their response was not something Derek could even conceive. His parents had given up an unforgiving attitude and what they had left was love and concern for their son, even when he was being resentful against them. This by no means meant the problem was solved, but it did mean that Derek's parents had quit being a part of the problem. More specifically, Derek's parents had changed their

hearts. Responding to Derek in love gave them a starting point to address their problems. If Derek's response continues to be a hard-hearted one, he will continue in resentment, and their response will be parental sorrow of the same quality as godly sorrow. But if he softens also, the beginning of joy is at hand. Both Derek and his parents are agents regarding the quality of their emotions.

This way of understanding how it is possible for us to respond to God's commands to be loving, compassionate, respectful, and repentant, is evidence that gospel ideals are realistic. Only by living them do we discover how realistic they are. The best place to demonstrate that reality is in everyday life, as was the experience for Derek's parents.

Possibly, after all our trials, we can feel as though we cannot bear the loss of a child or the injustice of a parent, spouse, child, or employer or myriad other bitter realities. However, we cannot avoid such circumstances altogether; we are forced to confront them. Whether we confront them with or without our ideals is up to each of us. When we have clear ideals and sincerely strive to be true to them we have hope. When we reject or ignore our ideals, or in other words, let go of the iron rod, we are lost, and our feelings truly can include being overwhelmed or in despair. As mortals, we will on occasion, let go of the iron rod, but the solution to that problem is not to be found in any superficial excuses we may make or in trying to reduce our guilt by saying we are only human. It is to be found only in restoring our grasp on the iron rod.

Many good and faithful families in The Church of Jesus Christ of Latter-day Saints face relentless attacks of the adversary, which can lead to feelings of fear, frustration, inadequacy and failure. Through no fault of their own, people are called upon to experience less than ideal circumstances: lack of opportunity for marriage; infidelity in marriage; marital separations; divorce; single parenthood; mental and emotional disorders, addiction in all its many forms; same–sex attraction; child abuse and family violence in all of its forms, etc. These life challenges represent ways in which our ideals may be tested. It is a mistake to view these realities as failures representing final outcomes. Our telestial existence is not a final state, so we must think in terms of living by our gospel-centered ideals as we face life's adversities.

Many children and young people find it extremely difficult to hold to time-honored beliefs and values as taught by parents and Church leaders.

Peer pressure, along with the cunning and deceitful counterfeits of Satan, too often draw family members down paths that lead first to inappropriate behavior, then to a loss of testimony, and eventually to the potential forfeiture of God's richest blessings.

Examples abound where poor individual choices bring long days and nights filled with pain, sorrow, and suffering to parents, spouses, children, siblings, and extended families. The fervent prayers of family members over their loved ones ring out in a seemingly endless chorus of fear, sadness, and frustration. Feeling helpless, families too often watch their loved ones use the God-given gift of agency to create a bondage spoken of by the ancient American prophet Nephi when he wrote:

> And others will he pacify, and lull them away into carnal security . . . and thus the devil cheateth their souls, and leadeth them away carefully down to hell. And behold, others he flattereth away, and telleth them there is no hell . . . and thus he whispereth in their ears, until he grasps them with his awful chains, from whence there is no deliverance. (2 Ne. 28:21–22)

In ever-increasing numbers, families in the Church are experiencing these sadly familiar problems. The following example of a young woman named Andrea is only one of untold numbers of strikingly similar stories shared by LDS families around the world.

Andrea's Story

Andrea was born into a typical active LDS family. Always happy and blessed with endless energy, Andrea enriched the lives of others through acts of kindness and service even as a small child. At age twelve Andrea entered the Young Women's program of the Church where she flowered into an excited young woman. Enthusiastic about the goals most Latter-day Saint girls hold, Andrea dreamed and planned for the day she would enter the House of the Lord. She dreamed of a loving home where she would be honored as a mother and a wife of a faithful husband.

At home Andrea enthusiastically planned and participated in family home evenings, daily scripture reading and family prayers. She attended early morning seminary and to the age of fifteen Andrea was a model of LDS young womanhood.

During her fifteenth year she found new friends and spent more and more time away from home and family. She became increasingly defensive and argumentative with her parents and family. The slightest attempt to reach out and express love or concern was met with mistrust and anger. Much of her behavior, though of concern to her parents and family, was accepted as part of the adolescent struggle for independence and identity. Andrea's parents and siblings were among the last to learn that she was deeply involved in the use of illegal drugs and its associated lifestyle. By the time her family became aware of the extent of Andrea's serious problems, she had estranged herself from home and Church.

Her worried parents refused demands to stay out of Andrea's life and faced the realization that she needed medical and psychiatric help. At sixteen Andrea was involuntarily hospitalized. Her hospitalization led to her commitment to change the direction of her life. Family, Church leaders, and friends in the Young Women program all gathered around to provide love and support in Andrea's efforts to come back.

In a relatively short time Andrea turned to previous friends and to a life of lies and secrecy. Married civilly at 18 to a man of questionable character and dependability, Andrea believed she could find happiness outside of the Lord's appointed way.

During still another period of promised change, recommitment and repentance, Andrea's husband was taught the gospel and baptized. Her family's hearts were filled with joy and hope when Andrea and her husband became parents themselves. They worked with a loving bishop and eventually entered into the temple to receive their own endowments and to be sealed together as a family. Tremendous outpourings of love and affection for the return of the prodigal daughter were expressed. The fatted calf was figuratively prepared because the entire family was finally one.

Sadly, this is not the end of the story. Other children were eventually born under this union. Andrea's marriage was plagued with conflict, unhappiness, separation, and eventual divorce. Again, drug abuse was a prominent issue and neither parent lived a life worthy of the covenants previously made in the house of the Lord. Not only was Andrea's life seemingly out of control, but her family increasingly felt fear and anxiety for her children, whose lives were now being influenced by an environment over which they had no control.

Andrea and her small children moved back home with her parents. The lies and the drug use continued; however, for the sake of the children,

Andrea's parents and siblings attempted to hold the little broken family together. Andrea eventually moved in and out of her parents' home and from apartment to apartment. Drug use continued while the parents continued to try to do what they could to help their daughter and grandchildren. Prayers were offered constantly on her behalf, but when guidance or counsel was offered in any form, Andrea rejected it as an attempt to control her life.

Promises to change her life and go through drug rehabilitation were made and broken. Living with a known drug abuser and suspected drug dealer in a small home where drugs were reportedly used and sold, Andrea continued to rear her children. She continued to deny the drug abuse and the unsavory nature of her living environment to anyone she feared might be able to interfere in her life or take away her children.

Andrea eventually married the man she had been living with and divorced herself from contact with her parents and family. Taking the children, the couple moved to another state, ending all contact with Andrea's family. Her family continues fasting and praying, often pleading with the Lord simply to know where their daughter and sister are and if the children are safe.

Andrea's story, like many other examples, is an unfinished chapter in the book of life, in which gospel-based ideals of family life are yet to be lived fully by all family members. However, the extent of the pain and suffering for everyone involved can be fully appreciated only by those who have experienced such things. The terms *agency* or *going astray,* though accurate, truly do not capture the depth and severity of the damage that can come to families in such situations. Andrea's story, though disheartening, is not atypical of families in the Church where the life choices of individual members tear at the very fabric of the eternal nature of the family. Elder John K. Carmack explains that

> typical and normal parental reactions [to family problems with wayward children] include sorrow, despair, desperation, depression, feelings of guilt and unworthiness, and a sense of failure. In such circumstances, parents may also experience anger and withdrawal and may feel like simply giving up. These reactions usually make matters worse, deepening the problems they face.[8]

One great consolation is found in historical examples of people we revere and the knowledge that other parents (often perceived to be better than ourselves) have walked the same path: Consider Adam and Eve, Abraham and Sarah, Isaac and Rebekah, Lehi and Sariah, Alma the Elder, Mosiah, etc. In their time, all shared a common bond of sorrow with families of today who pray fervently for family members who currently lack the strength to withstand the ways of the world.[9]

And our Heavenly Father knows far better than any mortal the pain and sorrow associated with having children who exercise their moral agency to their condemnation rather than exaltation. Can there be any better parent than God himself? Children's decisions may bring us sorrow no matter how obedient in teaching them we have been. This consolation does not excuse families from their obligation to teach and model correct principles and try to lead their children to Christ. However, it does bring a clearer perspective of the divine work of parents and families.

Space does not permit a discussion of every way in which gospel ideals may not be fully experienced in family life. The many potential problems to be faced by families and individual family members were anticipated by the Creator, and He has provided a plan by which His children might return to Him triumphant. This plan involved entering into and living covenants made between a loving God and His faithful children. In His infinite love, God has prepared a way that faithful earthly families might reclaim their currently lost or floundering members from ill-fated choices. The path is certainly not easy, but is nevertheless a shining ray of hope wherein obedience to promises made between God and man on this earth can ultimately lead to the realization of family relationships beyond the grave.

THE POWER OF COVENANTS

When specific ideals are not realized in family life it is tempting to view the entire family in a negative way. Often we overlook the many positive things a family experiences only to view the perceived "failure" of not realizing specific, sought-after ideals. The assumption is easy to make that if we have not attained something in its most excellent form, no other alternative is acceptable.

In 1964, President David O. McKay declared that "no other success can compensate for failure in the home."[10] Many sincere and faithful members of the Church mistakenly believe that their life circumstances (e.g., divorce, separation, single status, single parenthood, wayward children, addictions, same-sex attraction) have rendered them a failure. These Saints and families often believe that all their offerings to the Lord are unacceptable. Fortunately, such thinking is incorrect.

In an unrelenting campaign to destroy the souls of men and women, Satan has created an impressive arsenal of counterfeits to deceive God's children on this earth. Any thought that a specific life circumstance is the sole measure of one's worth and value in the eyes of God is wrong. President McKay's prophetic statement was intended to inspire members of the Church toward the attainment of ideals in family living, not as a judgment against those who strive to live desired ideals but have not yet or may never perfect them in this life. A loving God has provided a plan in which the making and faithful observance of sacred covenants by couples, sealed for time and all eternity in the new and everlasting covenant of eternal marriage, can assure not only their own eternal destiny, but that of their offspring as well.

Speaking of families in which children are born under the new and everlasting covenant of marriage, President Joseph Fielding Smith said:

> Those born under the covenant, throughout all eternity, are the children of their parents. Nothing except the unpardonable sin, or sin unto death, can break this tie. If children do not sin as John says, "unto death" (1 John 5:16–17), the parents may still feel after them and eventually bring them back near to them again.[11]

President Brigham Young counseled:

> Let the father and mother, who are members of this Church and kingdom, take a righteous course, and strive with all their might never to do wrong, but to do good all their lives; if they have one child or one hundred children, if they conduct themselves towards them as they should, binding them to the Lord by their faith and prayers, I care not where those children go, they are bound up to their parents by an everlasting tie, and no power of earth or hell can separate them from their parents in eternity; they will return to the fountain from whence they sprang.[12]

Family histories throughout the Church abound with examples of personal stories in support of President Young's powerful promise to faithful parents. In the 1919 general conference of the Church, Elder Alonzo A. Hinckley presented the following example:

> How my heart did thrill this morning, in that Mutual Improvement meeting, when Brother B. F. Grant stated that he was the son of a prophet, a man who stood beside Brigham Young as a counselor, and his mother was one of the choice souls in the early days of the Church; that for thirty-nine years of his life he got off wrong, and he continued to go wrong, believing that there was nothing in this gospel which the Lord God has restored in these the last days, until, stricken with sorrow, he looked upon the lifeless form of his little girl, his own flesh and blood, and then he said, "O God, can it be possible that this is the end, and that I shall see her no more?" To which the Spirit made reply, "It cannot be, this is not the end!" And then came into his life the day of repentance, the day of cleansing himself, purifying himself, the hours and the days of prayer. The Lord brought him back, until he stands now and bears a testimony of the Lord's wonderful goodness unto him![13]

The potential for blessings realized by faithful observance to covenants made in the house of the Lord are nowhere more clearly described by the Lord's modern-day prophets than are those associated with eternal family bonds. In his April 1992 general conference talk entitled "Our Moral Environment," Elder Boyd K. Packer declared: "It is not uncommon for responsible parents to lose one of their children, for a time, to influences over which they have no control. They agonize over rebellious sons and daughters. They are puzzled over why they are so helpless when they have tried so hard to do what they should. It is my conviction that those wicked influences one day will be overruled."[14]

Orson F. Whitney, an early member of the Quorum of the Twelve Apostles, declared:

> You parents of the wilful and the wayward! Don't give them up. Don't cast them off. They are not utterly lost. The Shepherd will find his sheep. They were his before they were yours—long before he entrusted them to your care; and you cannot begin to love them as he loves them. They have but strayed in ignorance from the Path of Right, and God is merciful to ignorance. Only the fulness of knowledge brings the fulness of accountability. Our Heavenly Father is far more merciful, infinitely more charitable, than even the best of his servants, and the Everlasting Gospel is mightier in power to save than our narrow finite minds can comprehend.[15]

We are blessed on this earth through righteous participation and commitment to covenants between a loving God and His mortal children. These covenants, by their nature, are intended to bring the sweetest blessings God has to offer to those who exercise faith in the gospel plan and prove themselves worthy through obedience. God did not place His most precious spirit children here on earth without providing the means by which they could realize the effects of His love and desire for them to return to His presence.

Despite this merciful doctrine, individuals will be held strictly accountable for their sins. And no son or daughter of God will be forced back into His presence in violation of their own agency. In the same vein, Elder Whitney said:

> The Prophet Joseph Smith declared—and he never taught more comforting doctrine—that the eternal sealings of faithful parents and the divine promises made to them for valiant service in the Cause of Truth, would save not only themselves, but likewise their posterity. Though some of the sheep may wander, the eye of the Shepherd is upon them, and sooner or later they will feel the tentacles of Divine Providence reaching out after them and drawing them back to the fold. Either in this life or the life to come, they will return. They will have to pay their debt to justice; they will suffer for their sins; and may tread a thorny path; but if it leads them at last, like the penitent Prodigal, to a loving and forgiving father's heart and home, the painful experience will not have been in vain. Pray for your careless and disobedient children; hold on to them with your faith. Hope on, trust on, till you see the salvation of God.[16]

So, we see that the challenges in families like Derek's as well as disheartening examples such as those of Andrea and thousands of others need not be an end but rather can be a beginning. Our trials can be a challenge to live up to promises we make between ourselves as earthly parents and a loving God to accept His will and continue in faith to the end. Regardless of the nature of the trials faced in mortality, no greater comfort can be given than the knowledge that the Savior's Atonement is for all humankind who will accept Him. Satan's efforts have been intensified in these closing days of the last dispensation to turn the hearts of as many as possible.

However, through sacred covenants made in holy temples, God has provided a way that ideals might be realized. We often speak of the Lord's plan and of the path that He has shown us that leads to eternal happiness. We progress on this path through righteous participation in and commitment to covenants. These covenants are the Lord's way of giving to us far more than is asked in return. Through covenants we partake of the mercy of a loving God, willing to bring us back into His presence if we will but do our comparatively small part.

We will forever give praise to a loving God for the blessings of covenants associated with the eternal family entered into in the house of the Lord. It is through covenants made between God and His children that His purposes may be fulfilled in this telestial existence. "And this is life eternal, that they might know thee the only true God, and Jesus Christ, whom thou hast sent" (John 17:3). "For behold, this is my work and my glory—to bring to pass the immortality and eternal life of man" (Moses 1:39).

NOTES

1. Bruce R. McConkie (1996), *Mormon doctrine* (2nd ed.) (Salt Lake City: Bookcraft), 633.

2. Neal A. Maxwell (1988), *Not my will but thine* (Salt Lake City: Bookcraft), 77.

3. Robert D. Hales (1996, November), The eternal family, *Ensign*, 26(11), 64–65.

4. Sheri L. Dew (1999, May), Our only chance, *Ensign*, 29(5), 67.

5. Boyd K. Packer (1992, May), Our moral environment, *Ensign*, 22(5), 68.

6. R. C. Solomon (1976), *The passions* (Garden City, NY: Anchor Press/Doubleday), 287.

7. Solomon (1976), 287.

8. John K. Carmack (1997, February), When children go astray, *Ensign*, 27(2), 7.

9. Carmack (1997, February), 9.

10. David O. McKay (1964), *Home and family* (Salt Lake City: The Church of Jesus Christ of Latter-day Saints), 5.

11. Bruce R. McConkie (1955), *Doctrines of salvation: Sermons and writings of Joseph Fielding Smith* (Salt Lake City: Bookcraft), 90.

12. Brigham Young (1948), *Church News*, March 13, 1948, 8. Quoted by Joseph Fielding Smith, The blessing of being born under the Covenant.

13. Alonzo A. Hinkley (1919), in Conference report, 159.

14. Boyd K. Packer (1992, May), Our moral environment, *Ensign*, 22(5), 68.

15. Orson F. Whitney (1929, April), in Conference report, 110.

16. Whitney (1929), 110.

TEMPLE COVENANTS AND FAMILY RELATIONSHIPS

JACK D. BROTHERSON AND SEAN E. BROTHERSON

God has instructed us to go to the holy temple in order to receive the full blessings of the gospel—those covenants and ordinances that allow couples and families to be united forever. The temple is a place of light, truth, inspiration, blessing, and grace. It is meant to bless the lives of all who enter. Individuals and families can use the blessings of the temple to strengthen themselves and their family relationships in many ways.

LEARN AND TEACH ABOUT TEMPLE BLESSINGS

Important first steps in bringing the blessings of the temple into family relationships are to learn about the temple's significance and teach family members of its blessings. Suggestions for doing this include:

• Provide children and other family members with gospel lessons and instruction on the temple and its blessings through family home evening and scripture study.

• Display pictures of the temple in prominent places in the home and refer to them as a reminder of the Lord's desires for us as individuals and families. Assist children to draw, photograph, or write about the temple.

• Visit the temple grounds as a family, when possible, and set individual and family goals to participate in temple worship by receiving personal temple blessings, marrying in the temple, and performing temple work for ancestors. Also, visit Family History Centers, visitors' centers, temple open houses, and temple dedications when possible to learn more about the temple.

• Serve as a temple ordinance worker, if possible.

• Attend temple preparation class.

• Study the magazine about temples published by the Church.

• Mark temples on a map of the world.

RECEIVE TEMPLE ORDINANCES AND COVENANTS

Each individual and family in the Church can establish the goal of receiving the full blessings of the temple and performing temple ordinance work for ancestors. Parents and children who labor together to seal family members for eternity strengthen family bonds here and hereafter. Family participation in the saving ordinances of the temple can be accomplished as we:

• Prepare to enter the temple and receive its blessings by living worthily and keeping the commandments of the Lord.

• Find the records of ancestors through family history research and prepare their names so that temple work might be performed for them.

• Enter the temple individually and together as

family members to receive our own temple blessings and to marry in the temple for time and eternity.

• Perform ordinance work in the temple for ancestors. All worthy members twelve and older can participate in vicarious baptismal ordinances in the temple.

MODEL HOME LIFE AND FAMILY RELATIONSHIPS AFTER THE TEMPLE PATTERN

The temple teaches us a pattern for family life that can make our relationships stronger and give our homes a positive, loving atmosphere. We can model our home life and family relationships after this pattern as we:

• Commit ourselves to live a life of moral purity and genuine love for others through keeping the commandments and following the teachings of Christ. Being worthy to obtain a temple recommend helps us to do this.

• Strive to act with fairness, consideration, and love for each family member and to keep a contentious spirit out of our relationships.

• Keep the atmosphere of our homes clean and free of influences that would make it uninviting to the Spirit of the Lord. This might include being careful in the types of music or media influences we allow in the home, taking care with our language, and focusing on diligence and learning.

• Focus on practices and values modeled in the temple that will strengthen us as families, such as prayer, reverence, gospel instruction, hard work, and study.

INCREASE SPIRITUAL STRENGTH AND UNDERSTANDING

Ultimately, we are meant to draw personal and family spiritual strength from the temple as we receive its blessings and follow the Savior. The temple can provide individuals and families with greater spiritual understanding and power. We can experience these blessings as we:

• Participate in temple ordinances as often as possible in order to serve God and those who have died and also renew the sacred covenants that we have made with God.

• Receive the blessings of inspiration and the companionship of the Holy Ghost by seeking answers to life's challenges in the temple.

• Appreciate the gifts of God in making it possible for our marriage and family relationships to continue beyond this life because of the sealing ordinances of the temple.

• Enjoy the protection and blessings of heavenly beings as a result of our participation in the temple ordinances.

• Follow the example and teachings of the Lord Jesus Christ as instructed in the temple, where we grow spiritually as we increasingly understand and appreciate His grace and His atoning sacrifice.

Within the walls of the temple, worthy members of the Church can receive the inspiration of heaven and families can find the "pearl of great price" promised in the scriptures—the promise of eternal life.

CHAPTER 19

AWARENESS OF ABUSE IN THE FAMILY

JINI L. ROBY, MICHAEL S. BUXTON, B. KENT HARRISON, C. Y. ROBY,
DIANE L. SPANGLER, NANCY C. STALLINGS, AND ELAINE WALTON

We warn that individuals who violate covenants of chastity, who abuse spouse or offspring,
or who fail to fulfill family responsibilities will one day stand accountable before God.
(The Family: A Proclamation to the World, ¶ 8)

In this chapter we address problems of abuse within the family as they pertain to the Proclamation. We acknowledge the discomfort a person may feel when reading about abuse, especially a person who wonders if abuse has been part of his or her experience, or someone who is in initial phases of healing. Our intention is to inform and educate the reader in the gospel light regarding abuse. We will examine the common dynamics in all types of abuse, then focus on some that are unique in couple, parent–child, and elder–caregiver relationships. In the next chapter, we will discuss preventing and healing from abuse.

The family is ordained of God as the indispensable human community whose primary objective is to assist us in achieving our eternal destiny, which is to live again with our heavenly parents. To that end, each of us has a responsibility to nurture other family members and to foster their eternal growth. The prophetic warning contained in the Proclamation to those who disregard this responsibility is sobering. Latter-day prophets have spoken clearly and repeatedly regarding this matter. President Gordon B. Hinckley said:

> You cannot abuse your little ones without offending God. Any man involved in an incestuous relationship is unworthy to hold the priesthood. He is unworthy to hold membership in the Church and

should be dealt with accordingly. Any man who beats or in other ways abuses his children will be held accountable before the great judge of us all. If there be any within the sound of my voice who are guilty of such practices, let them repent forthwith.[1]

President Hinckley has said similar things regarding spouse abuse[2] and abuse of the elderly.[3]

As in all things, choices are inherent in family relationships. In order to bring forth righteousness through the use of our agency, we must also have the opportunity to do the opposite (see 2 Ne. 2:11). Nowhere is there more consistent opportunity to bring forth goodness and fulfillment than in the family. However, as noted family researchers have pointed out, "the group [family] to which most people look for love and gentleness is also the most violent civilian group in our society."[4] The very nature of family life is to be confronted continuously and intensively with opportunities to nurture or abuse, which can at times be frustrating.

Although we are children of God and are to experience great joy (see 2 Ne. 2:25), we are all subject to the conditions of a fallen state of existence, and the selfish tendencies of the "natural man" exist in us all (see Mosiah 3:19). At times, we must struggle to overcome our negative tendencies and repent of the unrighteous things we have done in relationships. It is important for all Latter-day Saints to recognize that we are not exempt from these difficulties by virtue of our membership or position in the Church. Abuse in families is, in fact, of grave concern to our leaders. President Hinckley recently said:

> Harsh language, one to another, indifference to the needs of one another—all seem to be increasing. There is so much of child abuse. There is so much of spouse abuse. There is growing abuse of the elderly. All of this will happen and get worse unless there is an underlying acknowledgment, yes, a strong and fervent conviction, concerning the fact that the family is an instrument of the Almighty. It is His creation.[5]

We must be on guard to keep our attitudes and actions from escalating into abuse. We must also be prepared to help ourselves, our families, and others take appropriate steps to end abuse when it occurs in our relationships. Understanding and acknowledging the effects of abuse, when it has occurred, is the beginning of restoring spiritual wholeness and healthy family relationships.

COMMON ELEMENTS AND DYNAMICS OF ABUSE

At the core of all types of abuse is the misuse of one's agency, which is the power to act upon a variety of choices. It is taking the power the Lord gave us to use to protect and nurture our families and doing the opposite. When such stewardship is misused, especially toward a vulnerable person with limited agency, such as a child or an elderly person, it can result in painful consequences for the perpetrator and the victim and brings penalties from God and society. In this chapter and the next, the terms *perpetrator* and *victim* are used. Neither of these terms describes the whole person but refers only to the abuse that occurred. The term *victim* sometimes carries the connotation of helplessness, which is not implied here.

What constitutes abuse? Abuse can be acts of commission or omission, but we will discuss mainly those acts constituting physical or verbal violation of divinely and socially established interpersonal boundaries, including physical, verbal, emotional, mental, and sexual abuse between family members. Abusive behaviors often develop into an observable cycle or pattern. They are detrimental to the well-being of the victims and, from a spiritual perspective, to the perpetrator. They are typically hidden from public view. The perpetrator usually has more power and resources, and the victim is dependent upon the

perpetrator for some forms of care. The victim does not always understand how or why the action is harmful and may even try to protect the abuser or join the perpetrator in being in a state of denial regarding the abuse, or both. In other cases, the perpetrator will go to great lengths to ensure the abuse is kept secret, often using implied or direct threats against disclosure. The perpetrator may ignore or discount the abuse and refuse to call it such. Other perpetrators may feel bad, apologize for the abuse, and want to make up, but return to abusive behavior when problems arise. Perpetrators who abuse with some frequency can be master manipulators, psychologically damaging the victim by attempting to place the burden of responsibility for the abuse on the victim.

All forms of abuse can happen at varying levels of frequency and intensity. The more extreme the abuse, the more people agree it is harmful. At the less severe end of the continuum, people tend to have less agreement as to what constitutes an abusive action or neglect. Spanking is a good example of this—some call any form of physical punishment abuse, while others do not. In this and the subsequent chapter, we refer more to the moderate and severe types of abuse. These tend to occur, more or less, across all kinds of abusive relationships. However, there are some characteristics that are unique to marital, parent–child, and elder–caregiver relationships, and these are described subsequently.

ABUSE BETWEEN SPOUSES

Definition and Prevalence of Spouse Abuse

The abuse of one's spouse is distinct from the other forms of abuse described in this chapter because it occurs, as we describe it, between two adults who have promised to nurture and cherish each other, and who have equal rights under the law. Spouse abuse is a definitive prelude to family breakups all over the world, including the Latter-day Saint community. Although it is hoped that the incidence of spouse abuse is less among the active Latter-day Saints than in the general population, no statistics are available to support or refute it. We have, however, heard the warning voice of our prophet.

Physical and sexual abuse. Spouse abuse can include pushing, slapping, hitting, burning, beating, strangling, and other forms of physical violence. Physical restraint of a spouse may be experienced as abusive or domineering because adults have rights to freedom of movement and expression. While either spouse can be the aggressor, most studies indicate that husbands are the usual perpetrators of physical abuse. Reasons include their larger size and their dominant position in most societies. Some sources report approximately equal numbers of physical aggressive acts by husbands and wives against their partners.[6] However, other studies show that women are much more likely than men to experience physical injury as a consequence of physical abuse. Women tend to resort to violence for self-defense or retaliation.[7] Violence often escalates and may be meant to intimidate, dominate, or terrorize the spouse.

Sexual abuse occurs when nonconsensual sexual intercourse or other types of sexual activity are forced upon a spouse. Approximately 14 percent of U.S. women have been subject to marital rape.[8] Most states have laws against it, although some states limit its definition, and few cases are prosecuted because of the difficulty of proof and embarrassment associated with disclosure.

Psychological abuse. At a minimum, psychological abuse between spouses is characterized as a lack of mutual respect and courtesy. A pattern of name-calling, ridiculing, discouraging, or intentional negative social comparison is extremely hurtful to spouses and to the relationship. This type of abuse contributes extensively to the psychological harm of the abused spouse and to marital breakup, although typically it is not litigated and thus the incidence is unknown. Rates of psychological abuse by husbands or wives may be similar, but the spouse with fewer alternative sources of strength and support—often the wife—may experience greater vulnerability and harm.

Spiritual abuse. When the powers and proper authority of the priesthood are either misunderstood or misused to gain personal advantage within a marriage, there is potential for what can be termed "spiritual abuse." This can occur when a husband withdraws the exercise of priesthood blessings in order to seek revenge from his wife, or to "teach her a lesson." It can occur when a wife, rather than using encouraging methods, repeatedly berates her husband on the grounds that he is not doing what in her mind is his "priesthood duty." Certainly any man who practices any form of "vain ambition, . . . control or dominion or compulsion . . . in any degree of unrighteousness" has the heavens withdraw, and he has no more priesthood authority (see D&C 121:37) and eventually loses the respect and confidence of his family. The scriptures imply that the heart of spiritual abuse is the unrighteous attempt to constrain a person's agency.

Roots of Spouse Abuse

Socio-environmental factors. Experts typically identify socio-environmental factors (such as family, peer groups, and culture and ethnic group influences) as well as individual factors, as primary contributors to spouse abuse. Nearly 90 percent of studies exploring risk factors for spouse abuse found witnessing parental abuse to be a significant predictor of abusing one's own spouse as an adult.[9] For example, Straus, Gelles, and Steinmetz found that males who witnessed severe marital abuses between their parents were nearly 10 times more likely to abuse their spouses than those who had not witnessed such abuse.[10] Children of abusive parents may imitate abusive modes of interaction that they witnessed in their homes if they are not taught to use more appropriate, non-abusive ways to express emotion or resolve disagreement.

Individual factors. The majority of children who are exposed to abuse do not go on to abuse their own spouses, and some individuals who did not grow up in abusive environments choose to abuse. Thus the individual has the ability to choose his or her own attitudes and behaviors. How else could a person be held accountable before men and God, unless he or she has choices and an ability to make correct ones? Lehi explained "Wherefore, the Lord God gave unto man that he should act for himself. Wherefore, man could not act for himself save it should be that he was enticed by the one or the other" (2 Ne. 2:16). We also know that Satan can entice with much power, "Now the cause of this iniquity of the people was this— Satan had great power, unto the stirring up of the people to do all manner of iniquity . . ." (3 Ne. 6:15).

The individual factors most strongly associated with perpetrating spouse abuse include:

- The degree to which the individual ascribes to egalitarian versus nonegalitarian attitudes. Persons who believe that spouses are unequal or that one spouse should have authority over or dominate another are more likely to abuse their spouses.[11]
- The degree to which an individual condones the use of violence and blames others for his or her choice to use violence. The more tolerant a person is of the use of force, the more likely he or she is to engage in spouse abuse.[12]
- Those who abuse their spouse are more likely to blame others or external factors for the abuse.[13]

- The degree to which an individual has not learned and practiced particular emotional management and social skills such as how to appropriately handle disagreements, rejection, or stress.[14] One often sees deficits in both communication and social skills in those who abuse spouses.[15]

- The degree to which a person has developed specific psychological characteristics. Those who are emotionally dependent on others, jealous, and exhibit low self-esteem and insecurity are more likely to abuse a spouse.[16]

- The degree to which a person is depressed or is abusing alcohol or drugs. Experiencing high levels of depression or abusing substances increases the risk of perpetrating spouse abuse.[17]

Consequences of Spouse Abuse

Spouse abuse results in deep and painful consequences. Studies of abused spouses have documented a typical set of responses to living in an abusive marriage, commonly known as *battered spouse syndrome*.[18] Battered spouse syndrome is a direct consequence of abuse and can occur as a result of any form of prolonged abuse, not only physical abuse. The effects of abuse on the recipient vary somewhat depending upon the nature and severity of the abuse and individual characteristics of the abused, but most victims of spouse abuse suffer from at least some degree of physical, psychological, economic, and spiritual injury. Spouse abuse also wreaks havoc with the abuser in similar dimensions, although from the outside the damage may be less apparent.

Physical consequences. The physical injuries from spouse abuse range from small bruises to severe wounds that result in death. Physical injuries can weaken the victim's ability to resist abuse and can reduce her or his capacity to function in educational or occupational endeavors, thus decreasing the ability to function independently. Furthermore, the abuser's threat of future injury (to either the victim, children, or property) can be used to manipulate the abused person into staying in the abusive situation.

Although the abuser does not frequently suffer physical consequences, in some cases the abuser, too, is seriously injured and in rare cases even death may result. Such severe consequences may be the result of the victim's attempt to escape the abusive environment or to protect her children from an abusive husband who may also be abusive or extremely threatening with their children.

Psychological consequences. There are several types of psychological consequences associated with being a victim of spouse abuse. First, in an attempt to prevent future abuse, the victim can become preoccupied with tracking her or his own behavior and that of the spouse. This can result in the victim's being distracted and having difficulty focusing on other activities. Second, being the recipient of continual criticism and blame lowers feelings of self-worth and of efficacy. Follingstad, Rutledge, Berg, Hause, and Polek found that almost 75 percent of the women in their sample believed that husband psychological abuse had a more severe negative impact on them than husband physical aggression.[19] Victims report feeling as though they are incompetent and worthless, and some mistakenly believe they are to blame for the abuse or deserve it. Victims of spouse abuse consistently report lower levels of self-esteem than nonabused persons.[20] Third, victims can develop psychological disorders such as depression or post-traumatic stress disorder (PTSD). Finally, spouse abuse alters the victim's view of others and the world. Relationships may be viewed as dangerous, making it difficult for victims to trust or seek assistance from others. The world, in general, can come to be viewed as primarily dangerous and hurtful, undermining self-efficacy and hope. Due to these psychological consequences of abuse, victims may believe that nothing they do will change or improve their situation or that they must accept their current situation to maintain custody of their children.

In addition to the above-described psychological impact, it is important to understand that there is a great deal of ambivalence on the part of many victims toward the abuser, sometimes even when the abuse has been long term. This is because the victim has developed an attachment to the abuser. It may not be a healthy attachment, but it is nevertheless a force the victim must struggle with. The marriage, although riddled with difficulty, may have offered a degree of intimacy and connectedness that is hard to let go. If the victim is helped to recognize her ambivalence, there follows a period of mourning for the relationship that was wished for, compared to what it actually is.

Despite the damage and ambivalence a victim experiences, a large percentage of victims of spouse abuse do eventually leave their spouses,[21] although it often takes more than one separation before the relationship is permanently terminated. However, expecting the victim to end the abuse by leaving reflects the inaccurate belief that ending the relationship is the only available option and that the victim is responsible for stopping the abuse.

Abusers typically suffer from feelings of inadequacy. Such feelings often lead to frustration and violent outbursts. Ironically, abusive episodes only reinforce the abuser's deeply held beliefs of worthlessness and inadequacy. Feelings of guilt, for those who are still sensitive to the whisperings of the Spirit, can be painful—but those who feel the pain are the lucky ones who may repent successfully and be forgiven. The shame and humiliation of being "caught" and the loss of social status can be devastating for most abusers.

It becomes increasingly difficult for individuals who persist in their abuse to stop. "But remember that he that persists in his own carnal nature, and goes on in the ways of sin and rebellion against God, remaineth in his fallen state and the devil hath all power over him . . ." (Mosiah 16:5). This is a powerful testimony of the potential limits of individual agency and the negative consequences of abuse.

Legal and economic consequences. Although victims have some legal recourse to obtain protection, such proceedings are humiliating for some and intimidating, especially if the abuser is present and is represented by powerful counsel. The abuser frequently has controlled or forbidden the spouse's access to resources such as money, education, transportation, and housing. The abused spouse may find it difficult to establish any financial or material independence and therefore remains economically dependent upon the abuser as a direct consequence of the abuser's acts. Additionally, when victims are able to work, the physical (e.g., injuries) and psychological (e.g., depression) consequences of abuse interfere with obtaining work and with job performance.

For the abuser, the potential legal and economic consequences are serious. In the past, the victim's willingness to press criminal charges controlled the legal consequences faced by the abuser. If the abuser persuaded the victim not to press charges, the victim had the option to withdraw the complaint, leaving no opportunity for the law to intervene. More recently, based on research findings that arrest was a more effective deterrent to continued violence than was separation of the couple and mediation,[22] many states now charge at least one participant in the domestic violence. Such actions may assist both the abused and the abuser in two ways: (1) in coming to the realization of the seriousness of the problem; and (2) the typical requirement by the court that one or both

members of the couple must be involved in treatment. Additionally, the children who witness domestic violence now receive counseling as well.[23]

The abuser may be arrested, charged, and convicted of a number of criminal offenses. The victim may also seek restraining orders and file a civil suit for money damages. In many states, engaging in spousal violence also constitutes child abuse and can be prosecuted separately. All of these legal processes take a great social and financial toll. If the abuser is incarcerated following conviction, most often the entire family will suffer financially due to loss of a job and related income. The abuser may lose a professional license or be fired, and the criminal record may follow him for many years or even indefinitely, making some jobs off limits forever. Abuse often leads to divorce, which is also costly. The abuser may be ordered to pay for long-term therapy for the victim and any children involved, as well as restitution and criminal fines.

Spiritual consequences. Although some victims draw strength from God and Church members to help them resolve abusive situations, others withdraw from God and church activity due to the abuse. For some, abuse is wrongly intertwined with the gospel, such as when an abuser justifies abuse in the name of priesthood authority. In these cases, victims can come to associate power or authority with abuse and domination, rather than believing that such powers are only to be used to bless and never to control. Consequently, victims may find it difficult to approach church leaders, such as bishops or Relief Society presidents, for help, believing that the leaders may misuse power or authority in a domineering, hurtful way. Beliefs that others are abusive can also be extended to views of God, where the victim may view God as controlling, unforgiving, and vengeful. Such views of God can result in a loss of faith and a decreased desire to pray or understand their true relationship with God. Distortions often also include viewing the self as defective, unworthy, and inconsequential to God. Since the abusive spouse often acts in unloving and belittling ways, the belief in the existence of love and God's love for each person can be undermined.

Misunderstandings of gospel or spiritual principles can also be used to perpetuate abusive situations. Spiritual commitments to spouse or to children may influence the abused spouse to mistakenly believe that she or he must endure the abuse. Principles such as charity and forgiveness can also be misunderstood either by the victim or the abuser, resulting in pressure on the victim to tolerate or accept the abuse.

The Lord has directed the husbands of the Church: "No power or influence can or ought to be maintained by virtue of the priesthood, only by persuasion, by long-suffering, by gentleness and meekness, and by love unfeigned" (D&C 121:41). He also gives us some of the most specific insights into the spiritual consequences for abusers. In Doctrine and Covenants 121:38 the Lord warns those who would misuse their authority: "Behold, ere he is aware, he is left unto himself, to kick against the pricks, to persecute the saints, and to fight against God." Thus, the support of the Lord is withdrawn from that person before he even knows it. He is then left to himself, often in some degree of denial about the actual effects he has had on others, and lacking in taking full, personal responsibility for the abuse. To "kick against pricks" means to damage oneself as one tries to manipulate or fight against the Church and God. This is extremely shaky ground for a priesthood holder who pretends that all is well, or deceives himself and others by repeatedly saying that the offense is minor, tries to get the family to hide the sin, or repeatedly apologizes but continues to abuse. The Lord simply will not tolerate this behavior for long, for of such He said "the heavens withdraw themselves; the Spirit of the Lord is grieved; and when it is withdrawn, Amen to the priesthood or the authority of that man" (D&C 121:37).

President Hinckley has reiterated this precept on many occasions. Speaking in general conference to the women of the Church he said:

> Unfortunately a few of you may be married to men who are abusive. Some of them put on a fine face before the world during the day and come home in the evening, set aside their self-discipline, and on the slightest provocation fly into outbursts of anger.
>
> No man who engages in such evil and unbecoming behavior is worthy of the priesthood of God. No man who so conducts himself is worthy of the privileges of the house of the Lord. There are children who fear their fathers, and wives who fear their husbands. If there be any such men within the hearing of my voice, as a servant of the Lord I rebuke you and call you to repentance.[24]

In addition to its effects on spouses, domestic violence often results in tragic consequences for the entire family. Families can disintegrate through divorce or death. Abuse between parents distresses children and inhibits their growth and functioning in varied ways such as contributing to the development of psychological disorders, limiting development of social skills, and interfering with concentration and school performance, all of which are costly not only for the individual but for society as well. In addition, witnessing parental abuse is detrimental to the future family relationships of the children.

ABUSE OF CHILDREN IN THE HOME

> Husband and wife have a solemn responsibility to love and care for . . . their children. . . . Children are an heritage of the Lord. . . . (Ps. 127:3). Parents have a sacred duty to rear their children in love and righteousness, to provide for their physical and spiritual needs . . . mothers and fathers will be held accountable before God for the discharge of these obligations (¶ 6).

During 1997, more than 3,000,000 children were reported for child abuse and neglect to Child Protective Service (CPS) agencies in the United States.[25] This figure represents an increase over the 1988 figures. Of the more than 3,000,000 reported cases, 1,054,000 were confirmed, or in other words, 15 out of every 1,000 U.S. children were confirmed to be the victims of actual child maltreatment in 1997.[26] These figures do not include the abused children whose abuse or neglect was never reported. In addition, because it is difficult to prosecute emotional abuse successfully, it is generally underreported.[27]

There are several types of child maltreatment. In the remainder of this section we will discuss the physical, sexual, and emotional abuse of children in the home—what each type of abuse comprises, what their roots may be, and what their effects are. Due to space limitations, the serious and widely prevalent problem of child neglect is regrettably not included in this chapter.

Definitions

The physical abuse of children refers to nonaccidental injury inflicted by a caregiver.[28] Physical abuse may include shoving, slapping, beating, burning, biting, strangling and scalding with resulting physical damage, including bruises, welts, broken bones, scars, or internal injuries. Child *sexual abuse* is any sexual behavior with a child or the use of a child for the sexual gratification of someone who is significantly older than the child.[29]

Activities constituting child sexual abuse include inappropriate exposure, sexual contact, sexual exploitation of a child, and even extremely violent forms of abuse. *Incest* is the sexual abuse of a child by a blood relative in the child's nuclear family, or by anyone in a legal relationship with the child in which a sexual relationship is prohibited (such as a stepfather). Incest accounts for about 45 to 60 percent of all child sexual abuse cases;[30] strangers make up 10 to 30 percent; and the rest are attributable to others, including male friends of the family and neighbors.[31] The most common type of incest is between a father-figure (including stepfathers) and a daughter.

Emotional or psychological abuse of children is a pattern of behavior that thwarts the positive growth of the child by means of verbal and emotional mistreatment. It is harmful by itself, but it also is at the foundation of other types of abuse and includes

- **Assault:** The adult verbally or emotionally assaults the child—includes name-calling, negative labeling, belittling the child, and treating the child with disrespect.
- **Rejection:** The adult refuses to acknowledge the child's worth and the legitimacy of the child's needs. The adult repeatedly trivializes the child's feelings, joys, and worries.
- **Isolation:** The adult cuts the child off from normal social experiences, prevents the child from forming friendships, and makes the child believe he or she is not deserving of such relationships.
- **Terrorizing:** The adult verbally assaults the child, creates a climate of fear (e.g., by destroying personal possessions and torturing pets), and bullies and frightens the child.
- **Ignoring:** The adult deprives the child of essential stimulation, affection, and responsiveness, stifling emotional growth and intellectual development.
- **Corruption:** The adult "mis-socializes" the child, stimulates the child to engage in destructive and antisocial behavior, reinforces deviance, and makes the child unfit for normal social experience.[32]

Roots of Child Abuse

The contributing factors to child abuse are similar to those of spouse abuse. They include (1) the individual characteristics of the abusive parent and the vulnerable child, (2) the interactional patterns between the parent and the child, and (3) problems within the broader social environmental factors that contribute to the abuse.

Individual factors. The physically and emotionally abusive parent may have difficulty bonding, lack the ability to trust, or possess low frustration tolerance, immaturity, or a history of substance abuse. She or he may have been a victim of abuse and is caught up unwittingly in repeating a cycle of abuse[33] or may be seeking care and comfort from the child, who does not or cannot provide it. Self-centeredness, poor impulse control, or severe depression or other mental illnesses have also been identified as plaguing the abusive parent.[34] Substance abuse by the parent often leads to maltreatment, subjecting the child to such things as social isolation, emotional deprivation, and alienation from the parents, resulting in the secondary consequences of emotional abuse—shame and humiliation.[35]

Of course no child intentionally invites or deserves abuse, but some characteristics of a child have been identified as increasing the risk of victimization. These risk factors include being born prematurely or out-of-wedlock, having congenital or post-birth developmental disabilities, having inadequate bonding with the parent, being colicky, manifesting feeding problems, resisting holding, being overly aggressive or active, having learning disabilities based on neurological or psychological causes, and being rebellious in adolescence.[36] These conditions certainly do not result in abuse for most parents and children—sometimes the vulnerable or "difficult" child engenders extra tenderness and concern on the part of the mature and giving parent, who is able to nurture the child.

Most experts agree that the sexual abuser is motivated by emotional rather than sexual needs. Abusers share common emotional characteristics—a deep-seated feeling of helplessness, a sense of vulnerability, and dependency.[37] They also have a difficult time controlling their impulses[38] and are likely to lack close adult relationships, including those with their spouses. These common characteristics in the sexual abuser can result in two potential responses. In the first, he may become passive and dependent, becoming emotionally isolated and separate from others. Lacking any consistent sense of intimate attachment, he may experience low self-confidence and social rejection, which can in turn lead to his replacing adults with children, who are less threatening and more accommodating.[39] With the second type, the abusing father may overcompensate for his sense of inadequacy by becoming a tyrant whose main method of guiding his family is through harsh use of power and control. His underlying sense of powerlessness may lead him to rule his family in destructive ways, including feeling entitled to perpetrate physical or sexual abuse on his children.[40]

In cases of sexual abuse, the average age at the onset of the incest is 8 to 10 years[41] while the highest percentage of girls are abused between 11 and 14.[42] Some children are at an increased risk of abuse due to their developmental and familial circumstances. Being socially isolated, having a mother who is absent or emotionally distant from the child, fathers who abuse substances, and parents who are experiencing marital difficulties are factors related to the elevation of the risk of abuse.[43] Children with disabilities are particularly vulnerable.[44] The risk of sexual abuse is also much greater for female children living with a single mother who depends on male childcare givers. Mother's cohabiting boyfriends pose an increased threat of sexual abuse.[45] While some erroneously believe that the "willingness" of the victims at times contributes to the abuse, it has been shown that behavior that may be construed as "willing" is in fact a result of abuse.[46] Children's natural awe of adults, their relative physical weakness, and their need for adult affection and approval all place them at risk.

Family Interaction and Power Patterns

The unrealistic expectations of parents are another contributor to all forms of child abuse. This may be due to lack of information about the child's capabilities at certain stages of development or because the child may not measure up to the parent's idea of a good or lovable child. The parent and child may develop a pattern of reinforcing the current pattern because that is the range of their knowledge in managing that relationship. While most parents can put the needs of the child above their own, some parents, especially during times of stress, fail to do so.[47]

Parental patterns of power constitute a major role in abuse. If the abusive parent wields absolute power over the family and the other parent is afraid to challenge the abuser, the abuser may feel entitled to impose his or her power in unrighteous ways. In cases of incest, this may include an abuser's treatment of his son or daughter as an object of his whims. If, on the other hand, the abuser feels inadequate in the marital relationship he may impose the role of his sexual partner on his child or stepchild. Where both of the parents are weak and needy they may both turn to the children for nurturance.[48] Finkelhor found that even if the abuser is able to rationalize the abuse

within himself, the awareness and resistance of the other parent could prevent the abuse.[49] Again, the importance of adequate supervision, especially in single-parent homes, must be emphasized, although sexual abuse can and does happen despite normal supervision because parents cannot supervise each child 24 hours a day.

In terms of emotional abuse, there is a strong emphasis in Latter-day Saint families to raise righteous children who follow the gospel and excel in school and other activities. LDS parents tend to invest significant material and emotional energy in their children; their reward, they hope, is outstanding children. This is an ideal of which we should not be ashamed. However, the problem arises if parents are so insecure in themselves that they expect their children to make them "look good" or to serve as a reflection of the parents' worth as individuals. Such a dynamic can set up a pattern in which the parent is more concerned about how he or she looks to others than in guiding and loving the child. Such expectations can place undue strain on the parent–child relationship, possibly resulting in abuse when the child does not conform.

Environmental-Sociological-Cultural Factors

Some parents may not have the necessary skills to cope with the challenges of parenting, especially during times of crisis such as unemployment, poverty, relocation, or family problems. The social acceptance of violence combined with parental lack of effective, nonharmful methods of discipline, lead to some parental loss of control. Some parents even feel that parenthood is an imposition on them.[50] Culture can also play a major role in what is perceived as child abuse. For example, in some cultures parental authority is considered absolute. Parental love may be viewed as having complete control over the child and varying degrees of physical discipline methods may be expected or accepted within that culture. What one culture may consider child physical abuse may be deemed acceptable in another.[51]

Covitz suggests that the roots of emotional maltreatment lie in the prevailing attitude that parenting is not rewarding.[52] Some of the abuse may stem from poor role modeling in the parent's family of origin. Unhealthy communication patterns, family disruption, difficult marital relationship, divorce, and outside stressors such as poverty, unemployment, mobility, and isolation have all been correlated with emotional abuse. Some cultural expectations and practices can be viewed as being abusive, such as the use of "shame" as a motivator for behavioral change,[53] or the rejection of a darker-complexioned child in some cultures.[54]

Sexual maltreatment is prevalent despite the strong social taboo against it. Some feel that there is a preoccupation in society with sexuality. It is used to sell things and ideas. Men and boys are taught that their worth is measured by their physical, financial, or sexual prowess, and this can lead them to seek out someone in whose eyes they will "measure up." Many other social and environmental factors such as our culture of immediate gratification and substance abuse have all been correlated with abuse. Even though Latter-day Saints are taught to be in the world but not of the world (see John 17:15), we are influenced by the degradation of sexuality all around us and are vulnerable to the misuse of our agency.

Understanding what triggers the abuse is helpful and can aid in the repentance and healing process. However, understanding the reason does not excuse the abuse. Sexually appropriate conduct is the individual responsibility of the abuser. Placing the blame on the child or adolescent victim or any other factors displaces the proper responsibility of the perpetrator. Displacing responsibility is a sign of unrepentance on the part of the perpetrator and collusion by others in the misdeeds. President Hinckley declared "the terrible, inexcusable, and evil phenomenon of physical and sexual abuse . . . is unnecessary. It is unjustified. It is indefensible."[55] The Proclamation is clear in its teachings that sexual powers are divinely appointed and to be used correctly. Sexual abuse of a child is *never* a right decision and everyone has the ability to shun it (see e.g., Mosiah 16:12).

Effects of Child Abuse

> But whoso shall offend one of these little ones which believe in me, it were better for him that a millstone were hanged about his neck, and that he were drowned in the depth of the sea. (Matthew 18:6)

We learn from Jesus' stern warning and from modern-day research that the effects of child abuse are painful both for the victim and the abuser. The pain is a natural consequence of breaking a sacred covenant—that of keeping trust in family relationships. In all cases of abuse, the victim and perpetrator suffer painful consequences unless the problems can be properly resolved. The victim does not "grow out of" the pain of being abused, nor can the abuse be forgotten at every level of consciousness. In fact, the negative consequences of abuse can be the greatest when the victim is unable or unwilling to deal with the pain of the abuse.

Although not every behavioral or emotional difficulty associated with childhood abuse can be directly linked to the abuse, there are common symptoms shared by victims of child abuse. Generally, the victim experiences the anger, confusion, and pain of the abuse either outwardly or inwardly. When dealt with outwardly, the victim may have temper tantrums, show aggression, and engage in assaultive or delinquent behavior. When the anger is taken inside of the victim, an entire array of symptoms are possible. The most striking manifestation of the inwardly turned pain may be the abused child's impaired capacity to enjoy life. The child may seem "old" for his or her age and lack the ability to play in a manner consistent with peers. He or she may also suffer from age-inappropriate enuresis (inability to control bladder functions), encopresis (fecal soiling), and nightmares. Low self-esteem and learning problems are common[56] as are social withdrawal, hyper-vigilance (a stance of being constantly on the look-out), and unusual fears of failure. Adolescents may engage in substance abuse, suffer from eating disorders, become involved in premature sexual activity, or run away from home.[57] They may become involved in gangs in an effort to build up a sense of control and power and to join another "family" where they may feel more valued.[58] Depression and even suicidal thoughts are common among women who have not dealt with childhood sexual abuse issues. In extreme cases, the victims can lose a sense of reality or slip into a dissociative state, where the victim experiences a sense of being separated from self or external reality.[59] Not surprisingly, the most enduring and painful consequence for some victims is an impaired ability to build and maintain trusting personal and family relationships in their adult lives, therefore robbing them of the greatest joy in life.

We have outlined many of the negative effects of child abuse on children. Within the past 25 years, much research has come forward describing common symptoms, nearly all of which has identified problems. In reality, many victims of childhood abuse are resilient and, in many ways, have or are overcoming their negative experiences. Most who have been abused as children go on to live as productive, nonabusive adults while addressing the hurt and scars of the past.

ABUSE OF THE ELDERLY

Some elderly persons are vulnerable to abuse, neglect, self-neglect, and exploitation due to their circumstances such as social isolation, dependence on others, diminished mental capacity, and a desire to keep peace. Though for many the latter years can be "golden," for some they are "tarnished" years.

Like other forms of abuse or violence, elder abuse occurs most commonly within the home and abusers are known to the victim. Most often, they are the adult children of the elderly victim. Experts estimate that as few as 1 in 14 elderly abuse victims ever receive help. Victims are often isolated from the community; perhaps they no longer attend church regularly or participate in activities, so no one notices their gradual decline or other warning signs. In some cases, the elderly are frail and dependent on caregivers; abusive caregivers may deny visitors and claim the person is too sick to be seen. Thus, elder abuse is often hidden from view.

Although some of the dynamics of elder abuse are similar to spouse or child abuse, there are notable differences. Mistreated children are protected by mandatory laws while competent adults have the legal right to choose their lifestyle even when they choose one that is not in their best interest. Adults have a lifelong history of independence and decision-making; they have resources and assets that are attractive to potential perpetrators; they have established family patterns and roles compounding the relationship; and they are in a pattern of increasing dependence while their children's dependence decreases over time.

Definitions

As with spouse and child abuse, there are several forms of elder abuse. *Physical abuse* is hitting, bruising or restraining the person against his or her will when such action is not necessary for the victim's safety. *Sexual abuse* includes nonconsensual sexual contact with the adult victim and also includes sexual exploitation of incapacitated adults who cannot give valid consent. *Neglect* occurs when a caregiver fails to provide adequate medical care, nutrition, habilitation, supervision, or safety. Caregivers may have good intentions but lack sufficient resources or training to provide appropriate care. An overburdened caregiver can experience "burnout" and fall behind in attending to the elder or disabled adult. Other caregivers may be mentally ill or resent the older person's need for care. *Emotional or psychological mistreatment* such as threatening, name-calling, or treating someone like a child often accompanies other forms of mistreatment. In addition, *financial exploitation* is the misuse of a person's money, credit, and assets; it may continue until there is no home or money left for medical care, nursing home, or even burial for the victim.

Roots of Elder Abuse

The roots of elder abuse are familial, societal/environmental, and developmental. Within some families, mistreatment or dysfunctional relationships are the norm. Many adult abusers experienced abuse or neglect as children and later may mistreat their elderly parents out of revenge. Other families live with mental illness and drug or alcohol abuse; lack of behavior control results in abuse of family members. The cycle of violence described in other forms of family violence is also applicable to elder abuse.[60] The family relationships, roles, authority, and intimate knowledge of each other's lives increases the potential for the cycle of an explosive event followed by reconciliation and then building tension. Another environmental risk is isolation. Many elderly or disabled adults live in rural communities or no longer drive. They are isolated physically. Other victims may be socially isolated: health problems, inactivity, immobility, and chronic illness may lead to depression and withdrawal.

Caregiver stress and burnout is a major environmental factor in elder abuse. Some families are unable to cope with extended years of care that will ultimately result in death of the loved one. Daily routines of work, household chores, children's activities, and church commitments must be continued. Perhaps there is a feeling of guilt for feeling the fatigue or even temporary anger at the overwhelming list of chores. Even the strongest of families have stumbled under such a load. "The sin is not in needing the help, but in needing it and not asking" (from the film *Breaking Point*).[61]

Life cycle factors play a part in some cases, as when, despite their own life-stage issues, some adults are also obligated to care for older family members. As reflective of the phenomenon of increased longevity, some senior citizens are now being called on to be caregivers for their frail parents and siblings who have become dependent. Retirement years may become caregiving years. Many abusing adult children are suffering from mental illness, substance abuse, or developmental and physical disabilities.

Another significant risk for abuse and neglect is the victim him- or herself. Contrary to popular advertising, some older people are not passive or cheerful or cooperative. Instead, they are mistrusting, angry at the world, and even abusive to those who offer assistance. This difficulty may be due to mental illness such as schizophrenia, depression, or dementia; in some cases, mistrust may be traced to alcohol or substance abuse. Such cases are difficult for would-be helpers; it's hard to watch someone choose to live at risk or in danger.

How and why does an older person tolerate abuse, neglect, exploitation, or even self-neglect? The major factors are fear, shame, denial, and a sense of being overwhelmed. Fear of an abuser's retaliation keeps many victims from telling their story. Perpetrators often use the threat of a nursing home placement or isolation from grandchildren and family to coerce an elder to transfer money or keep quiet about mistreatment. Few people are willing to be alone and estranged from family at the end of life and so they will tolerate a difficult situation. Some victims have had unfortunate experiences with social or governmental agencies and refuse to seek intervention because they fear complications and loss of control of their lives.

Shame is another powerful motivating factor in elder abuse. Concerns about the family's reputation in the community keep many victims quiet about family problems. Elderly parents fear that their parenting will be judged by the abusive behavior of adult children or grandchildren. Shame is also expressed by frail elders who are no longer able to care for themselves or who have been duped into signing over assets. Admission of incapacity or victimization can be humiliating for once self-reliant adults.

Denial is common in abusive families. A familiar rationale is that "it's not that bad" or "it doesn't happen every day." Mistreatment is tolerated on the belief that things will improve and the crisis will pass. Rarely do things turn out that way; in fact, abuse usually escalates over time because the abuser and victim are caught in a web of anger, shame, guilt and fear of discovery. Victims of elder abuse express a sense of being overwhelmed by the prospect of revealing their story to friends or police.

Maintaining dignity and independence in the later years of life poses challenges to individuals, families, and church communities. The most important issues are awareness of the risks and planning for services and support. While abuse and self-neglect are difficult, there are many things that can be done to minimize the risks; these are presented in the next chapter.

CONCLUSION

Understanding abuse and acknowledgment of the facts and pain associated it are the first steps to recovery for both the victim and the abuser. Denial and avoidance of the important issues involved are not the way of the gospel, and therefore do not serve to heal. In this chapter, we have only provided an introductory outline of abuse. In the next chapter, we discuss prevention and healing from abuse. Furthermore, the reader is encouraged to learn more about this important topic to help self and others. The Lord, through His ancient and modern prophets, has never avoided addressing this matter with His children, and neither should we. We are fortunate to live in an era in which more understanding and assistance are available than perhaps ever before, and we must have the courage to take advantage of that blessing "while the arms of mercy [are] extended toward [us] . . ." (Mosiah 16:12).

NOTES

1. Gordon B. Hinckley (1985, May), To please our Heavenly Father, in Conference report, 50.

2. Gordon B. Hinckley (1991, November), Our solemn responsibilities, in Conference report, 49–52.

3. Gordon B. Hinckley (1997, November), Look to the future, in Conference report, 67–69.

4. M. A. Straus, R. J. Gelles, and S. K. Steinmetz (1980), *Behind closed doors: Violence in the American family* (Garden City, NY: Anchor), 80.

5. Hinckley (1997), 69.

6. M. A. Straus and R. J. Gelles (1990), *Physical violence in American families: Risk factors and adaptations to violence in 8145 families* (New Brunswick, NJ: Transaction); J. E. Stets and M. A. Straus (1990), The marriage license as hitting license: A comparison of assaults in dating, cohabiting, and married couples, in M. A. Straus and R. J. Gelles (Eds.), *Physical violence in American families*, 227–244.

7. D. E. H. Russell (1990), *Rape in marriage* (Rev. ed.) (Bloomington: Indiana University).

8. Russell (1990).

9. G. Hotaling and D. Sugarman (1986), An analysis of risk markers in husband and wife violence: The current state of knowledge, *Violence and Victims, 1,* 101–124.

10. Straus et al. (1980).

11. J. Coan, J. M. Gottman, J. Babcock, and N. Jacobson (1997), Battering and the male rejection of influence from women, *Aggressive Behavior, 23,* 375–388; D. H. Coleman and M. A. Straus (1990), Marital power, conflict, and violence in a nationally representative sample of American couples, in M. A. Straus and R. J. Gelles (Eds.). *Physical violence in American families,* 287–304.

12. S. M. Stithe and S. C. Farley (1993), A predictive model of male spousal violence, *Journal of Family Violence, 8,* 183–201; D. B. Sugarman and S. L. Frankel (1996), Patriarchal ideology and wife-assault: A meta-analytic review, *Journal of Family Violence, 11,* 13–40.

13. A. Holtzworth-Munroe, N. Smutzler, L. Bates, and E. Sandin (1997), Husband violence: Basic facts and clinical implications, in W. K. Halford and H. J. Markman (Eds.), *Clinical handbook of marriage and couples interventions* (New York: Wiley), 129–156.

14. A. Holtzworth-Munroe (1992), Social skills deficits in maritally violent men: Interpreting the data using a social information processing model, *Clinical Psychology Review, 8,* 331–344.

15. G. K. Kantor and J. L. Jasinski (1998), Dynamics and risk factors in partner violence, in J. L. Jasinski and L. M. Williams (Eds.), *Partner violence: A comprehensive review of 20 years of research* (Thousand Oaks, CA: Sage), 1–43.

16. Kantor and Jasinski. (1998).

17. E. T. Gortner, J. K. Gollan, and N. S. Jacobson (1997), Psychological aspects of perpetrators of domestic violence and their relationships with the victims, *Anger, Aggression, and Violence, 20,* 337–352.

18. L. E. Walker (1983), The battered woman syndrome study, in D. Finkelhor, R. J. Gelles, G. T. Hotaling, and M. A. Straus (Eds.). *The dark side of families* (Beverly Hills: Sage), 31–48.

19. D. R. Follingstad, L. L. Rutledge, B. J. Berg, E. S. Hause, and D. S. Polek (1990), The role of emotional abuse in physically abusive relationships, *Journal of Family Violence, 5,* 107–120.

20. M. Cascardi and K. D. O'Leary (1992), Depressive symptomatology, self-esteem, and self-blame in battered women, *Journal of Family Violence, 7,* 249–259.

21. Holtzworth-Munroe et al. (1997).

22. L. W. Sherman and R. A. Berk (1984), The specific deterrent effects of arrest for domestic assault, *American Sociological Review,* 49(2), 261–272.

23. D. O Lewis, S. S. Shannock, J. H. Pincus, and G. H. Glaser (1979), Juvenile delinquents: Psychiatric, neurological, psychological, and abuse factors, *Journal of the American Academy of Child Psychiatry,* 18(2), 307–319.

24. Gordon B. Hinckley (1996, November), Women of the Church, in Conference report, 68.

25. National Committee to Prevent Child Abuse (NCPCA) (1998), *Child Abuse and Neglect Statistics* (available from the National Committee to Prevent Child Abuse, 200 S. Michigan Avenue, 17th floor, Chicago, IL 60604).

26. NCPCA (1998).

27. C. Crosson Tower (1989), *Understanding child abuse and neglect* (4th ed.) (Needham Heights, MA: Allyn and Bacon).

28. Tower (1989).

29. Tower (1989).

30. A. Mayer (1992), *Women sex offenders* (Holmes Beach, FL: Learning Publications).

31. D. Popenoe (1996), *Life without father* (New York: Martin Kessler Books), 66.

32. J. Garbarino, E. Guttmann, and J. W. Seeley (1986), *The psychologically battered child* (San Francisco, CA: Jossey-Bass), 8.

33. D. C. Factor and D. A. Wolfe (1990), Parental psychopathology and high-risk children, in R. T. Ammerman and M. Hersen (Eds.), *Children at risk* (New York: Plenum Press), 171–195.

34. M. Boisvert (1974), The battered child syndrome, in J. Leavitt (Ed.), *The battered child* (Fresno, CA: General Learning Corp), 141–146.

35. G. Morrow (1987), *The compassionate school: A practical guide to educating abused and traumatized children* (Englewood Cliffs, NJ: Prentice-Hall).

36. S. Gold (1986), *When children invite abuse* (Eugene, OR: Fern Ridge Press).

37. R. F. Hanson, J. A. Lipovsky, and B. E. Saunders (1994), Characteristics of fathers in incest families, *Journal of Interpersonal Violence,* 9(2), 155–169.

38. K. Meiselman (1978), *Incest: A psychological study of causes and effect with treatment recommendation* (San Francisco: Jossey-Bass).

39. A. N. Groth (1979), *Men who rape* (New York: Plenum Press).

40. M. de Young (1982), *The sexual victimization of children* (Jefferson, NC: McFarland); K. C. Faller (1988), *Child sexual abuse: An interdisciplinary manual for diagnosis, case management and treatment* (New York: Columbia University Press).

41. D. Finkelhor (1984), *Child sexual abuse* (New York: Free Press).

42. NCPCA (1998).

43. S. Sgroi (1981), *Handbook of clinical intervention in child sexual abuse* (Lexington, MA: Lexington Books); B. James and M. Nasjleti (1983), *Treating sexually abused children and their families* (Palo Alto: CA: Consulting Psychologists Press); D. Finkelhor (1984).

44. de Young (1982).

45. Popenoe (1996), 67.

46. H. Maisch (1972), *Incest* (New York: Stein & Day); Meiselman (1978).

47. H. P. Martin (Ed.) (1976), *The abused child* (Cambridge, MA: Ballinger).

48. M. Stern and L. Meyer (1980), Family and couple interactional pattens in cases of father-daughter incest, in B. Jones, L. Jenstrom, and K. MacFarlane (Eds.), *Sexual abuse of children: Selected readings* (Lexington, MA: Lexington Books), 83–86.

49. D. Finkelhor (1979), *Sexually victimized children* (New York: Free Press).

50. B. Justice and R. Justice (1976), *The abusing family* (New York: Human Services Press).

51. Tower (1999).

52. J. Covitz (1986), *Emotional child abuse: The family curse* (Boston: Sigo Press).

53. M. K. Ho (1989), Social work practice with Asian Americans, in A. Morales and B. W. Sheafor (Eds.), *Social work: A profession of many faces* (Boston: Allyn and Bacon), 521–541.

54. Tower (1999).

55. Gordon B. Hinckley (1994, November), Save the children, in Conference report, 53.

56. H. P. Martin and P. Beezley (1976), Personality of abused children, in H. P. Martin (Ed.), *The abused child,* 105–111.

57. A. H. Green (1981), Child abuse and the etiology of violent delinquent behavior, in R. J. Hunner and Y. E. Walker (Eds.), *Exploring the relationship between child abuse and delinquency* (Montclair, NJ: Allenheld and Schram), 152–160.

58. Tower (1999).

59. C. T. Wang and D. Daro (1997), *Current trends in child abuse reporting and fatalities: The results of the 1997 annual fifty state survey* (available from the National Committee to Prevent Child Abuse, 200 S. Michigan Avenue, 17th floor, Chicago, IL 60604).

60. L. E. Walker (1979), *The battered woman* (New York: Harper & Row).

61. *Breaking Point* [Film] (available from Tera Nova Films, Inc., Winchester Avenue, Chicago, IL 60643. Phone: 1–800–779–8491).

CHAPTER 20

PREVENTING AND HEALING FROM ABUSE

JINI L. ROBY, MICHAEL S. BUXTON, B. KENT HARRISON, C. Y. ROBY,
DIANE L. SPANGLER, NANCY C. STALLINGS, AND ELAINE WALTON

*We warn that individuals who violate covenants of chastity, who abuse spouse or offspring,
or who fail to fulfill family responsibilities will one day stand accountable before God.*
(The Family: A Proclamation to the World, ¶ 8)

In the previous chapter we described the painful topic of abuse in family relationships—between spouses, parent and child, and the elderly and the family member who serves as the caregiver. In this chapter we offer information and guidelines for preventing abuse in the first place and for healing from experiences of abuse, both as an abuser and as the victim. The Proclamation can be a wonderful guide to help us prevent or heal from abuse because it reveals the truth about our nature, destinies, and relationships. Through this chapter various Proclamation principles will be applied to prevention and healing from abuse.

We define prevention as conscientious planning and taking necessary precautions to avoid abuse—as much as we can—in the future. To do this, it is necessary for us to examine those aspects of ourselves, our history, our environment, and relationships that place us at any sort of risk to inflict or receive abuse. We define healing from abuse as taking steps to end any current or probable abuse, acknowledging the associated facts and pain, securing safe environments, and recovering any sense of damaged spirituality and self-worth, trust, and proper uses of agency.

We first acknowledge that Jesus Christ is the Savior of all and was and is the master healer. It is inspiring to consider the consuming effort Jesus devoted to physical and emotional healing during His mortal ministry. In the example of the woman who was healed by merely touching the hem of His garment (see Matt. 9:20–22) we learn how aware He is of the slightest act of faith, and how willing and eager He is to intervene for good in our lives. To His disciples He said, "He that believeth on me, the works that I do shall he do also; and greater works than these shall he do . . ." (John 14:12). This suggests that He gave power and authority to His servants to act in His stead, to be healers in His name, and to give accurate direction to the lost, wounded, and weary. Those that lead in the restored gospel have the same keys, the same power and purpose, which is to lead us to safety and healing. Our ability to prevent abuse and heal ultimately depends primarily on the faith and obedience we give the to Lord and His servants.

PREVENTION OF ABUSE

The most important concept related to prevention of abuse is the knowledge that each individual is a child of God. From this comes a respect for self and others that defines who we are in relation to others; all other teachings spring from this foundation of truth regarding human beings.

Understand and Teach Our Divine Destiny

The Proclamation reminds us that each person "is a beloved spirit son or daughter of heavenly parents, and as such each has a divine nature . . ." (¶ 2). As such, each is deserving of respect and love regardless of age or circumstance. From infancy children should consistently be reminded of their unique spirits, their eternal nature, and their special value as heirs to the glories of God. This process does not simply build the child's self-esteem in the conventional sense, but instills the core of a child's divine identity and its eternal implications. Parents should teach about the sanctity of the human body and the spirit—the body being the temple of the spirit (see 1 Cor. 3:16). These truths not only remind parents of the nature of their child, but a child whose self-identity is firmly rooted in this concept will not likely abuse others or tolerate abuse by others.

Understand Divine Roles in Family Relationships

An integral part of our divine destiny is to perpetuate family relationships beyond this life. In order to do so, we must learn to be obedient to the principles outlined for us. The Proclamation specifically instructs in the role of parents: "Parents have a sacred duty to rear their children in love and righteousness, to provide for their physical and spiritual needs, to teach them to love and serve one another . . . mothers and fathers—will be held accountable before God for the discharge of these obligations" (¶ 6). Latter-day Saints are further taught in a booklet published by the Church, *A Parent's Guide,* that the parents' "only purpose in dealing with a child is to bless the child with their efforts. If what they are doing is causing the child to be angry or to experience physical or emotional harm, then their efforts need to cease until they can determine a better course to follow."[1] We are further admonished to understand that the child is *only* a child and lacks experience and maturity, while the parent is an adult, albeit human and imperfect. Because of the great responsibility parents have, and the inexperience of children, parents are to exercise love unfeigned, which brings the ability to direct one's efforts toward God's purposes rather than toward the parent's own. Separating one's self from the child at a moment of anger and engaging in the company of other adults at such times is strongly recommended.[2]

Likewise, the Proclamation teaches that the divinely appointed duty of spouses is "to love and care for each other" (¶ 6), to "honor marital vows with complete fidelity" (¶ 7), and to fulfill their respective responsibilities as parents and equal partners (¶ 7). In some marriages these ideals are not realized because one or both spouses bring into the marriage beliefs and ideas that are inconsistent with the true nature of an eternal marriage. Chief among the harmful ideas held by those who abuse the marital relationship are (1) the belief that one spouse is superior to the other, (2) the belief that one spouse should or can dominate and control the other, (3) the belief that the use of force or demeaning acts (of any kind) are acceptable, and (4) the belief that one is entitled to have his or her way, or that his or her opinion is the only acceptable perspective. The scriptures (e.g., D&C 121:37; Mosiah 23:7) and Church leaders[3] have consistently warned against developing such prideful and selfish attitudes and have instructed us to forsake such false beliefs or traditions. The aforementioned ideas are counter to the Proclamation's ideals of "respect, love, [and] compassion" (¶ 7) as being some of the chief cornerstones of a successful marriage. Developing Christlike beliefs of equality between spouses, individual agency, charity, and humility are powerful means to prevent becoming abusive. Such an alternative would require forsaking of any beliefs identified above and a commitment to

- recognizing that there is never justification to abuse one's spouse in any way
- developing respect for the agency of one's spouse and her or his right to disagree
- encouraging and finding joy in the spouse's growth
- being open to feedback about ways one may be hurtful to one's spouse and being able to apologize and admit mistakes.

Another set of beliefs may put persons at risk for tolerating abuse from their spouse. These include (1) the belief that one's spouse can or should make personal decisions for the other spouse or has the right to control the other spouse, (2) the belief that one should always have the same opinions as one's spouse, (3) the belief that one must submit to all forms of suffering, and (4) the belief that one is deserving of abuse or is to blame for the occurrence of abuse. These beliefs are contrary to the divine nature and destiny of each individual and should be countered by a firm commitment to one's identity as a person who deserves respect and equality in a marriage partnership.

Mate-Selection

Thoughtful and timely mate selection can also be important to preventing later spouse abuse. Young persons approaching marriage should make a firm resolve not to engage in abusive behavior or to tolerate such behavior by their potential spouses. Although one cannot always predict who will later become abusive, particular characteristics observed during a courtship of adequate length can serve as a forewarning of future abusiveness. These characteristics include being controlling, jealous, and unwilling to compromise or to admit mistakes. Any form of abuse that occurs during courtship, such as slapping, grabbing, berating, or humiliating, is also highly suggestive of future problems. Pushing physical intimacies beyond appropriate limits is sign of gratifying one's own desires at the expense of the other's dignity. Sarcasm (which is not the same as a sense of humor) and belittling are also warning signs that the requisite respect is lacking and the relationship is not founded on true principles of respect and love. People are usually on their best behavior during courtship; thus, it is unlikely that significant problematic attitudes or behaviors will change after a couple is married. Courtship is an important time to think objectively of one's choice of a mate, since the attitudes and behaviors present in courtship will become the foundation upon which the family will be built. Feedback from trusted family and friends regarding their views of the potential mate can also be helpful, because outsiders can sometimes see characteristics of a relationship that the persons in the relationship may not see. Finally, and most important, one must seek divine confirmation of the prospective marriage for oneself through fasting and prayer, and not simply rely on the opinion of the potential mate.

Fostering Relationships with Love and by Example

Parents should model respect in their behavior toward each other and their children, recognizing that children are eternal spiritual beings with unlimited potential but limited knowledge of this world. No matter how special a child is told he or she is, the way he or she is treated will speak more loudly. Carefully selected and gentle discipline should be used only for the purpose of teaching. Physical violence and loud yelling may have some immediate impact, but are more likely to harm the relationship in the long run. Brigham Young taught: "Bring up your children in the love and fear of the Lord; study their dispositions and their temperaments, and deal with them accordingly, never allowing yourself to correct them in the heat of passion; teach them to love you rather than to fear you."[4]

Discipline should be based solely on the best interest of the child and not serve as a mere venting of anger for the parents. Although some parents feel that children learn best from punishment, it is contrary to teaching by example and love. Our Savior Himself paved the way for such teaching when He refused to condemn the adulterous woman, forgave her, and encouraged her to "sin no more" (John 8:3–11).

At times loving parents must allow their children to suffer the natural and logical consequences of the children's decisions and actions. When parents and a child have respectfully discussed the child's goal and desire and have agreed upon positive or negative consequences, parents may be the "deliverer" of the consequences. Coupled with respect and tenderness toward the child, the parent's carrying out of the consequences should reinforce all other aspects of the positive and loving relationship between the parent and child. Brigham Young emphasized the need to follow through with positive consequences and to be cautious in delivering negative consequences (including chastisement) of a child's behavior.[5] In other instances the consequences will be imposed on the child by others or simply by the circumstances. Parents can help their children learn from these consequences by taking the time to discuss them and helping their children to learn from those experiences.

Maintain Open Communication

When a child has confidence that the parent will listen with empathy and understanding, the child will turn to the parent with questions or concerns as he or she grows older. When this opportunity is not available to the child, he or she may withdraw from the parent and stop communicating and look elsewhere for the answers to the problems or mysteries of life—most likely his or her peers, some of whom may be struggling with the same issues. Likewise, a spouse who feels the support, encouragement, and respect of the other spouse will be more open to discuss his or her concerns and dreams with the other spouse, leading to more fulfillment in the marriage. In this kind of marriage, the normal and extraordinary challenges of family life will become less taxing and the joys of everyday life enhanced. When the trials and vicissitudes of life can be talked about and innermost feelings shared between spouses, they become one in heart as the Lord intended. They become a team facing difficulties together and, in this setting, trials can often become opportunities to become closer and stronger.

Learn and Teach Skills

Individuals with skills to handle a variety of life's problems will be better equipped to avoid abusing or being abused. These may include coping skills (handling disappointment, failure, anger, and stress), relationship skills (such as communication, negotiation, proper interpersonal boundaries, and assertiveness); work habits (through chores, lessons, etc.); and self-sufficiency skills. The scriptures, Church magazines and publications, and conference talks are all rich sources of helpful material. Priesthood and Relief Society leaders, or an LDS Family Services counselor or educator may be able to direct families to other books, seminars or courses, and local counselors or agencies if they feel additional information is necessary.

Respond Quickly to Any Warning Signs of the Preconditions of Abuse

The causes of abuse discussed in the previous chapter can apply to anyone—even faithful Latter-day Saints. Warning signs may not be obvious to some family members, but the contributors to abuse discussed in the previous chapter are the most common red flags to watch out for. When difficulties arise, take caution not to allow the stresses to be heaped up on other family members, especially those who are young, weak, or otherwise vulnerable. Families must not ignore possible problems. They should seek help outside the family if necessary, including turning to their bishop or branch president for both material and spiritual assistance with potential problems.

Trust in the Lord and Follow His Guidance

Above all else, couples and families must look to the Lord and His servants for guidance in their relationships. "Trust in the Lord with all thine heart; and lean not unto thine own understanding" (Prov. 3:5). There is a proliferation of secular knowledge about enhancement of marriage and family life. However, before attending marriage enrichment seminars and parenting skills workshops that are based on secular ideas, parents should first make sure that they are being obedient to the guidelines provided by living prophets. If the basic elements of scripture study, family prayers, family home evenings, and the blessings of the priesthood are missing in the home, the family is depriving itself of the most promising route to a happier family life. Certainly other resources and activities can be added to the basic foundation as long as they are in harmony with the Lord's teachings, but families should focus first on those of the revealed gospel. The Lord has given us much counsel on a broad range of topics concerning marriage and family through His servants. Parents should seek fervently to know the will and guidance of the Lord on matters pertaining to family relationships. The scriptures as well as latter-day leaders' guidance is available through the standard works, conference reports, ward libraries, LDS websites, and LDS bookstores, where these resources can be found.

Prevention of Elder Abuse

In addition to the general principles previously listed, elderly people and their families are offered the following advice:

- Be realistic about the difficulties and demands of caregiving as well as sources of help such as the local agency on aging or the ward.
- Develop a "buddy system" with friend(s) and meet outside the home at least once a week or more.
- Let church and community know you appreciate and need visits.
- Stay active and participate as long as you are able.
- Read your own mail, telephone bills, and bank statements; ask the bank for help when you do not understand something.
- Arrange to have Social Security or pension checks deposited directly to your accounts.
- Get legal advice and plan for disabilities, powers-of-attorney, and wills that specify your wishes; give control of your property when *you* are ready to do so; know where important documents are.
- Don't sign any document unless it has been reviewed by someone you trust; wait until you feel well enough to understand or have had your questions answered.
- Don't accept personal care in return for transfer of property or assets; hourly wages and contracts for care are customary and can be easily drawn up.
- Hold family conferences *before* a crisis. Plan ahead for care, housing, and finances. Tackle tough questions about who will be responsible when the time comes, the family's ability to pay for services, and long-term care arrangements.
- Be especially aware of the difficulties that may

arise when you have an older parent living in your home. Caregiver burnout is a major cause of elder abuse or neglect. Don't be afraid to call for respite care or other help (shopping, housekeeping, home-delivered meals, home health, transportation, etc.) if needed.[6]

HEALING FROM ABUSE

Help to all who have been affected by abuse is available through the infinite grace of our Savior if we will follow His plan. Our modern-day leaders have outlined the means by which those who have suffered the ravages of abuse can be healed, and the means by which perpetrators of abuse can repent of their grievous sins and receive healing from their self-inflicted wounds. The important means of healing from abuse are activating the Atonement by faith and hope in Christ, moving on to forgiveness and repentance, focusing on eternal goals, forsaking of unrighteous traditions, understanding and honoring sacred covenants, and receiving assistance.

Activating the Atonement: Faith and Hope in Christ

Elder Vaughan J. Featherstone, along with other leaders, has stated clearly that those who have been abused are *not* accountable for the abuse. He said: "For a person who has been involved in incest, who has been involved in abuse of any kind against his or her will (and that includes rape), there is no transgression—not as long as time shall last or the earth shall stand, or there shall be one man upon the face thereof."[7] This is often a first step toward healing for those who have been abused—to let go of any doubt as to their accountability. However, healing involves further steps of exercising faith in the Lord Jesus Christ (see Matt. 9:22) and activating the redemption offered by Him (see Alma 15:8). Furthermore, there must follow the difficult process of forgiving the abuser (see D&C 64:10).

The scriptures are filled with references and stories of the healing nature and powers of Christ. "Is not this the fast that I have chosen? to loose the bands of wickedness, to undo the heavy burdens, and to let the oppressed go free, and that ye break every yoke?" (Isa. 58:6). Following the years of terror at the hands of the wicked just prior to the coming of Christ to the Lamanites and Nephites, and after the terrible day of destruction and disorientation before His appearance,

Jesus extended His gracious and loving plea to come unto Him . . ."that I may heal you" (3 Ne. 9:13). Could there be a greater way to receive comfort and safety than in the arms of the Shepherd?

On the other hand, those who abuse *are* accountable to the Lord, as well as to the victim and others, and the failure to repent brings serious consequences. The amazing and deeply comforting part of the Lord's plan is that the Savior's Atonement applies to both the abuser and the abused. Justice and mercy work together to bring about healing for both the perpetrator and the victim. To the abuser, the Lord offers cleansing of the sin following repentance accompanied by a broken heart and contrite spirit. Surely the Lord, who suffered unfathomable pain for us, stands ready to cleanse and soothe our pain and suffering.

Repentance and Forgiveness

The processes of forgiving and repentance are closely related. For both, the essential ingredients are humility, empathy, and faith in Christ. Humility is the ability to be meek and teachable before the Lord. For one who has been abused, humility is not the first emotion normally felt. Usually anger, outrage, or even a sense of guilt may precede the ability to learn from the experience. For the abuser, humility is difficult—denial and blaming some external source other than him- or herself for the wrong choices is common. Humility requires that he or she accept full accountability for the abusive actions, which can be painful for the abuser. Empathy is the ability to understand how the other feels. It is often difficult for the abused to understand the motivation of the abuser, and the abuser often has little appreciation for the damage caused by the abuse. For forgiveness and full repentance to occur, empathy is an essential ingredient. Faith in Christ propels the abused to lay the question of justice before the Savior's feet. As Elder Featherstone said, "Justice 'according to the supreme goodness of God' means that we do turn [matters needing justice] over to him. It will not be left undone. We can have that absolute assurance."[8] Likewise, faith in Christ makes it possible for the abuser to repent of his or her sins, forsake old patterns of behavior, and become a "new" person.

For the abuser, spiritual healing requires full repentance. Elder Richard G. Scott has said, "Healing best begins with your sincere prayer asking your Father in Heaven for help. That use of your agency allows divine intervention."[9] The restriction and violation of agency are at the core of abuse. The Lord said, "when we undertake to . . . exercise control or dominion or compulsion upon the souls of the children of men, in any degree of unrighteousness, behold, the heavens withdraw themselves; the Spirit of the Lord is grieved; and when it is withdrawn, Amen to the priesthood or the authority of that man" (D&C 121:37).

In *The Miracle of Forgiveness,* President Spencer W. Kimball noted five major steps of repentance: (1) sorrow for sin; (2) abandonment of sin; (3) confession of sin; (4) restitution for sin; and (5) doing the will of the Father.

Sorrow for sin. The abuser must acknowledge the damage he or she has caused to the victims and those who care. He or she must not make excuses or try to justify or rationalize the abusive behavior. The abuser must not attempt to rush the repentance process or attempt to have others meet the abuser's time frame in obtaining forgiveness for abusive actions.

Abandonment of sin. The abuser must discontinue not only the abuse, but must learn to recognize the precursors to such abuse. All abusive behaviors and the behaviors and thoughts which are the precursors of abuse must be abandoned.

Confession of sin. The abuser must admit the full extent of the abuse to the victim(s) and to others involved in the healing process—i.e., one's bishop.

Restitution for sin. There may appear to be little an abuser can do to repay one for having acted abusively but the reality is that there may be a number of steps one can take to assist the abused in the healing process. For example, depositing money in an account which is controlled solely by the victim, assisting the victim in obtaining an education or in other ways attempting to reduce the dependence the victim often feels in an abusive situation may do much to give back the dignity, hope, and feelings of control the victim lost as a result of being abused.

Doing the will of the Father. Complete repentance requires not only that the abuser forsake the abusive behavior, but also that he or she attempts to obey all of God's commandments.[10]

Forgiveness is perhaps the most difficult when one has been violated by someone in a relationship of trust such as a spouse, parent, or adult child. Among the normal feelings experienced by victims of severe abuse and those who care for them are denial, fear, anger, rationalization, self-hatred and self-blaming, and deep sadness. These may be mixed with feelings of attachment and even love for the perpetrator, especially if that person was a family member and provided some degree of care. Some people feel more anger toward those who they feel should have protected them than toward the abuser. Each individual is different.

Healing from abuse usually involves the recovery of a sense of one's agency, which needs to be nurtured by caring and trusted people. Elder Scott said, "Know that the wicked choice of others cannot completely destroy your agency unless you permit it."[11] Elder Neal A. Maxwell put it this way, "Of course our genes, circumstances, and environments matter very much, and they shape us significantly. Yet there remains an inner zone in which we are sovereign, unless we abdicate. In this zone lies the essence of our individuality and our personal accountability."[12] The responsibility of the victim and those who are in positions to protect and care for the victim is to allow agency to be a powerful healing balm by trusting in the Lord. "You must understand," Elder Scott said, "that *you are free to determine to overcome the harmful results of abuse.* Your attitude can control the change for good in your life."[13] Furthermore, "I feel the pace is generally set by the individual and not by the Lord. He expects you to use other resources available, including competent professional help when indicated; then He provides the balance needed according to His will."[14] What a wonderful and respectful testament to the power of individual agency! Great patience and time may be needed by all involved, but in this we follow the example of God whose "hand *is* stretched out" to His children continually (see Isa. 9:21; 10:4; 14:27).

Along with the recovery of agency, a victim's healing is fostered by understanding the link between forgiving and faith. A common misperception held by victims encountered by bishops and professional counselors is that faith in the gospel of Jesus Christ should allow victims to bypass feelings they would typically suffer and that if those feelings are present, the victims believe they have insufficient faith. Two principles may dispel this false thinking. First, there is nothing that we can possibly feel that Christ Himself has not felt as He led a life being "despised and rejected of men" (Isa. 53:3) and as He faced the tortures of the Atonement, "which suffering caused myself, even God, the greatest of all, to tremble because of pain" (D&C 19:18). The greatest of all, who least deserved to suffer, suffered the most. He genuinely felt a variety of painful feelings, and so do we. Second, even though He suffered these pains for all of us that we may not have to suffer even as (see

D&C 19:17) He did, we—especially the righteous—must endure (at times innocently) the sins of the world.[15] Can we name even one righteous person who has lived a full life and not endured suffering, sometimes intensely? We are assured however, that, like Joseph Smith and Jacob, the son of Lehi, our "adversity and . . . afflictions shall be but a small moment" and if we endure them well (D&C 121:7–8) "he shall consecrate thine afflictions for thy gain" (2 Ne. 2:2).

Does forgiving the abuser mean that the victim should continue to subject him- or herself to the abuse? *Absolutely not!* Aileen Clyde of the General Relief Society presidency addressed the misbelief held by some regarding charity, especially in the context of spouse abuse: "It is not charity or kindness to endure any type of abuse or unrighteousness that may be inflicted on us by others. . . . It is not charity to let another repeatedly deny our divine nature and agency. It is not charity to bow down in despair and helplessness. That kind of suffering should be ended."[16]

Other Church leaders have also made it clear that there are circumstances, including abuse, which are intolerable violations of the marriage covenant and thus allow us to consider terminating the marriage state.[17] Counselor Wendy Ulrich notes that "to forgive is *not* (1) to condone or approve the sin, (2) to trivialize in any way our own suffering, (3) to continue being victimized, (4) to refrain from feeling angry about the injustice of the sin."[18] Such self-defeating behavior has never been recommended by our leaders. Furthermore, since forgiveness and love are such central components of the gospel—in fact signs of our discipleship—they have to be addressed in the context of an abusive relationship. Concerning these matters, Maxine Murdock, a therapist who works mainly with Latter-day Saints in Salt Lake City, has said "Forgiveness is a personal and often lengthy process. . . . No one can predict how long it should take to forgive."[19] Many abuse victims feel pressure to forgive quickly because of insensitive comments from others who do not understand the individual nature of the healing process. One may hear the counsel to "forgive and forget," but this is not part of our scriptural directive. Such comments are judgmental and should be avoided. Forgiveness is most often one of the later components of healing, brought about after one has experienced appropriate grief and sorrow and overcome feelings of rage and bitterness. However, striving for forgiveness is not a therapeutic goal for some counselors, who may encourage the victim not to forgive, fearing future vulnerability. Persons entering counseling should ask the counselor his or her opinions on this matter and then use their own judgment in following the Spirit.

For the victim, and others who have been hurt by the abuse, we have been promised that forgiveness can be most beneficial. "Forgiveness heals terrible, tragic wounds, for it allows the love of God to purge your heart and mind of the poison of hate. It cleanses your consciousness of the desire for revenge. It makes place for the purifying, healing, restoring love of the Lord."[20] Therefore, forgiveness is a self-strengthening tool and signals that the victim is truly recovering a sense of self-worth.

One should not confuse love and forgiveness with trust in the abuser. The Lord commands us to forgive, but not necessarily to trust in the abuser. Trustworthiness must be regained by the perpetrator of abuse. One victim related, "I think the most important thing I've learned is that forgiveness is not reconciliation."[21] Healing the individual requires the willingness of the individual; healing a relationship requires at least two. One goal of forgiveness is that it is "not forgetting but being able to remember with peace."[22] After justice is satisfied, then mercy encompasses the following principles: (1) while we do not condone the sin, we do not condemn the sinner; (2) we relinquish vengeance; (3) we offer compassion. One should eventually lay aside the status of being a victim, regain one's initiative and agency, and become empowered to act for oneself rather than be subject to another's dictates or poor choices—or, empowered to regain trust in people and in life. One can regain faith and trust, allowing oneself to heal, to become a fully functioning person and to take control of one's future.

Focus on Eternal Goals

As we address ways of healing and prevention, we remember that much abuse comes in the context of family. Two statements in the Proclamation are keys to consider as family members heal. The first, "the family is central to the Creator's plan for the eternal destiny of His children" (¶ 1) was reiterated by Elder Dallin H. Oaks: "All Latter-day Saints understand that having an eternal family is an eternal goal. Exaltation is a family matter, not possible outside the everlasting covenant of marriage."[23] The second Proclamation statement, which must be equally considered, is "We affirm the sanctity of life and of its importance in God's eternal plan" (¶ 5). To this end, Elder Oaks said:

> Not . . . everything related to mortal families is an eternal goal. There are many short-term objectives associated with families—such as family togetherness or family solidarity or love—that are methods, not the eternal goals we pursue in priority above all others. For example, family solidarity to conduct an evil enterprise is obviously no virtue. Neither is family solidarity to conceal and perpetuate some evil practice like abuse. . . . even the love of family members is subject to the overriding first commandment, which is the love of God (see Matthew 22:37–38) and "if ye love me, keep my commandments" (John 14:15).[24]

Forsake Unrighteous Traditions

Ultimately, healing from abuse in the Lord's way involves leaving behind false and destructive family beliefs, traditions, loyalties, or even ties when they serve to disregard the sanctity of life. As has been alluded to already, when one has the power—mentally and physically—to protect one's self or other vulnerable people (children, elderly, handicapped), one has the right and the responsibility to do so, even if it means the disruption of family relationships. In no instance has the Lord decreed that we should tolerate ongoing abuse or to resign ourselves to a lifetime of unrighteous demands from those who should care for us. In contrast to societal or institutional endorsement of notions of male privilege over females, Latter-day Saints have been consistently admonished not to adhere to such ideologies (see D&C 121).[25] Elder Richard G. Scott, who has spoken and written much on this topic, specifically instructed Church members to give up such incorrect cultural traditions:

> Is yours a culture where the husband exerts a domineering, authoritarian role? That pattern needs to be tempered so that both husband and wife are equal partners . . . No family can long endure under fear or force.[26]

Elder Scott also admonished:

> Talk to your bishop in confidence. His calling allows him to act as an instrument of the Lord in your behalf. . . . Your bishop can help you identify trustworthy friends to support you. He will help you regain self-confidence and self-esteem to begin the process of renewal. When abuse is extreme, he can help you identify appropriate protection and professional treatment consistent with the teachings of the Savior.[27]

Honoring Sacred Covenants

Those who have made sacred covenants and who abuse children, spouses, or the elderly are covenant-breakers. "Wo unto them; because they have offended my little ones they shall be severed from the ordinances of mine house" (D&C 121:19). Breaking of sacred covenants is subject to the judgments of God regardless of whether the sins are detected in mortality or not. On this topic, Elder Featherstone stated:

> And those who have perpetrated . . . abuse on others may get out of this life without ever having confessed. People may believe that they didn't do it, and so the perpetrator may escape punishment. . . . the innocent suffer and the guilty do not. No. Justice is "according to the supreme goodness of God," and by and by, all those who have been guilty will pay the cost. We will either repent or suffer; there isn't any way around that.[28]

When such abuse occurs, the question for the victim becomes one of: "How do I continue to honor my sacred covenants?" Under the condition of broken spousal or parental covenants and contracts, victims may be released from certain obligations toward the abuser, and this may be necessary to completely protect, heal, and follow the Lord "with full purpose of heart" (3 Ne. 18:32). Again, victims of abuse are not expected to continue to submit to the abuse. Many persons stay in abusive marriages for psychological, economic, or religious reasons. However, some do end the marriage with divorce, which is more acceptable in the LDS community than it used to be.[29] Whether the abuse and the potential for change are such that "honoring the sacred covenants" would mean staying in the relationship, leaving it, or obtaining help is a matter of grave importance and should be determined with much soul-searching and counsel with one's bishop and the Lord. When determined to be appropriate, professional counseling may be helpful to make such an important decision, provided that the counselor respects the values of the victim and the assistance is consistent with those values.

Obtaining Assistance

For healing to begin, an environment that can sustain healing must be created for all involved. Sanctity of life begins to be restored by ending the abuse and taking every legal means necessary to maintain protection. This will require disclosure and, depending on the severity of the abuse, the coordination of trustworthy people both in and outside the family and sometimes people within and without the Church. These provide necessary systems of accountability, support, and expertise. Families that find themselves in these circumstances often underestimate the degree to which a problem must be faced and "confessed" in order to be truly "forsaken" (see D&C 58:43). This is partially why family members are reluctant to disclose abuse; it usually requires being disloyal to unwritten family rules that maintain secrecy and regard "outsiders" as suspicious and harmful. In the case of severe abuse, the perpetrators often go to great lengths to keep victims from disclosing abuse. Some are expert, calculating manipulators, and they teach victims these methods through their example.

Child abuse, or even suspicion of child abuse, is required to be reported in all the United States. Elder abuse is required to be reported in most states, while spouse abuse is required to be reported in only a handful. When the police or social service agency in the community receive such reports, those responsible for receiving these reports will determine if an investigation into the allegations is necessary, depending on the nature and severity of the abuse. If it is determined that abuse or neglect is such that intervention is necessary, a range of services are available to benefit both the victim and perpetrator. Courts may need to intervene to provide appropriate protection and rehabilitation or punishment. Submitting to properly handled civic authority is part of our observance of the twelfth article of faith. Once the victim is safe and the risk of the abuse has been stemmed, the healing process can begin.

Professional treatment will most often be necessary in order to change firmly set thought and behavior patterns. This treatment process for abusers will be necessarily painful. For one, treatment will force the abusers to look deep within themselves and confront their most vulnerable and ugly issues. The abusers may find that they have deep feelings of inadequacy, misusing their relationships with their child or spouse. They may discover that they have caused untold damage to people they may care for deeply in their own way. They may come to realize that their own selfishness and unrighteous desires have caused an eternal family to break up. However, without changing their thoughts and behaviors, the burden of the abuse will never leave them, and they continue to be a risk to others, especially to those who stay or enter into intimate relationships with them.

Treatment for the abuser may be voluntary or court-ordered. In either case, it will likely involve various evaluations and individual and groups psychotherapy ("talk therapy"). Some of the work may be done in dyads in which the abuser and the victim work together in order to establish healthier interaction patterns and to prevent further abuse. This dyadic intervention should not occur until the victim is fully prepared for and will benefit from such an encounter. Family members may also be involved in educational courses if necessary. The following are some of the issues that should be addressed through treatment:

1. Acceptance of responsibility for behavior without minimization or externalizing blame;

2. Identification of patterns or the cycle of offense behavior;

3. Ability to interrupt the cycle before an offense occurs and to control behavior;

4. Victimization in the history of the offender such as sexual abuse, sexual trauma, physical abuse, emotional abuse, abandonment, rejection, loss, etc.;

5. Development of awareness or empathy to a point where potential victims are seen as people rather than as objects;

6. Power and control versus helplessness and lack of control;

7. The role of sexual arousal in offenses and reduction of deviant sexual arousal;

8. Development of a positive sexual identity for self;

9. Understanding the consequences of offending behavior to the offender, the victim, and the victim's family in addition to developing empathy for the victim;

10. Family issues or dysfunctions that support or trigger offending;

11. Cognitive distortions, irrational or erroneous thinking that support or trigger offending;

12. Identification and expression of feelings;

13. Appropriate social relationships with peers; and other relationships;

14. Addictive or compulsive qualities contributing to reinforcement of deviancy;

15. Role of substance abuse in functioning if any;

16. Skill deficits that interfere with successful functioning; and

17. Options for restitution or reparation to victims and community.[30]

Although treatment is typically a lengthy and often emotionally difficult process for the abuser, the victim(s), and other family members, the rewards for successfully leaving behind a life of abuse, dishonesty, and immorality are great.

ADVICE FOR INDIVIDUALS IN SPECIFIC CIRCUMSTANCES

Spouses Who Stay in an Abusive Marriage

Usually an abusive spouse will not improve on his or her own. Attempts by a wife to "fix" things, to cater to her husband's wishes, or to change herself almost always make no difference in her husband's behavior. Professional intervention is often necessary (if the abuser can be persuaded to seek it). The abuser, typically the husband, usually goes through what is called the "cycle of violence." This cycle includes (1) the abuse itself, followed by (2) remorse, apology, and attempts to make up (the "honeymoon" phase), but then (3) increasing tension over a period of time, culminating in another bout of abuse, and the cycle repeats.[31] The wife needs to recognize that the honeymoon phase is temporary and that abuse will recur.

An abused person should not blame himself or herself but should recognize that the other spouse has agency and has chosen his or her actions. It is usually fruitless to try to explain the spouse's abusive behavior in rational terms. The abused person may seek counseling. If possible, one should shield the children, although this usually is not possible. Detrimental effects on children are often seen as a reason to end the marriage. If the abuser is able to feel responsibility for his actions, marital counseling is likely in order. Also, the abused person may attend support groups where possible.

A wife may prepare for the possibility that the marriage may eventually break up. Such preparation could include saving money, gaining education for future employment (if possible), familiarizing oneself with local women's shelters, and even packing suitcases and gathering important items (birth certificates, medications, keys, emergency cash, etc.) in one easily accessible place in case of need for a hurried departure. If a wife is going to leave the marriage, she should plan a course of action in case the husband threatens harm to her after leaving, as sometimes happens.

A Spouse Who Has Left an Abusive Marriage

One must first find a place to live and a source of financial support. Sometimes a parent and children may live with other family members. Women's shelters provide temporary refuge and experienced advice, support, and child care. Almost always the woman will need to get a job. A vindictive former spouse can continue to cause trouble. The abused spouse can obtain a restraining order and take other legal steps if harm has been threatened or to gain access to family resources and support. One should seek counseling; its cost may be covered through one's local church leader.

Families Where Child Abuse Is Present

The most urgent issue is the safety of the victim. The child victim must also have at least one adult with whom the abuse can be openly and confidentially discussed, preferably the other parent if he or she is able to maintain composure and the ability to protect and reassure the child. This adult must convey that the victim is not guilty of sin and that God still loves that child.[32] Following disclosure and report, the question of whether or not immediate separation of the abuser or victim is necessary should be answered. There are a variety of services that can be provided in the home or outside the home, such as parenting skills training, individual and group therapy, and other services that may be provided with or without a court order. In addition to those services, it is advisable for the family to build up its network of support and accountability, including the extended family network.

Adults Who Were Abused as Children

When child abuse is not appropriately treated and families not healed, the emotional and social development of the abused child is stunted. Such abused children may become scarred adults,[33] although they may not be consciously aware that their problematic thoughts, feelings, or behavior are directly related to childhood abuse. They may have been in denial or repressed the memories of abuse, or they may not have been allowed (or allowed themselves) to label their childhood experience as abuse.

Consequently, even when these victims are adults they rarely seek help for the effects of childhood abuse. Instead, they present themselves in counselors' offices to get relief from low self-esteem, depression, self-destructive behavior (such as eating disorders, substance abuse, sexual promiscuity, and prostitution), being socially introverted, or a myriad of other difficulties in their relationships with others.[34] Many of these difficulties arise out of the victim's inability to set appropriate personal boundaries or confusion in differentiating between love and sex or between sex and punishment as a result of the abuse. Moreover, they may carry a deep sense of guilt stemming from years of secrecy in which they may erroneously view themselves as a "willing" partner.

Healing from abuse as an adult is more complex than healing as a child. In addition to the abuse itself, a variety of complicating disorders related to the abuse may now need to be addressed. It is important to acknowledge the trauma and suffering caused by the abuse and not to take the blame or expect quick recovery. The resolution of the abuse will most likely require professional intervention. If such intervention is to be used, the victim is advised to be a wise consumer of services to assure that the assistance he or she receives is consistent with revealed spiritual values. Bishops and stake presidents can usually start the process of exploration and provide guidance along the way. LDS Family Services and some Latter-day Saint psychotherapists have contributed to the professional resources of Church members, and it may be helpful to become aware of those resources.[35] Other professionals who are not members but are respectful of LDS values may also be helpful.

Ecclesiastical and Other Leaders

Leaders should listen and seek to discern the truth, calling upon the Lord's assistance to bring about His will. Accounts can vary between the victim and the perpetrator. Leaders should recognize that often the perpetrator is either in denial or attempting to minimize the abuse, or both. Leaders should not minimize or trivialize the effects of abuse as it has affected the victim and should recognize the need for support such as blessings, prayers, ecclesiastic counsel, and, in many cases, professional help. Provision of an abuse-free environment for victims is important, in their own homes if possible but elsewhere if needed. It must be recognized that there are circumstances in which dissolution of the marriage may be

necessary. Restoration of victims' self-esteem, spiritual sense of worth, and trust is essential. Understanding and love should come from the entire church community. Education of support persons is important; they should be nonjudgmental, not blaming the victim for the abuse or on the basis of where she or he is in the steps of healing. Forgiveness of perpetrators by victims is important if it can be achieved, but it *must not be rushed* and should be allowed to take what time is needed. Perpetrators will need education, counseling, and sometimes ecclesiastical action or civil penalties. This assistance, of course, should uphold the privacy of the family, but the involvement of the extended family may often be helpful if they are part of the solution and not the problem.

Conclusion

In this and the preceding chapter we have addressed the sensitive and difficult topics of abuse in the family. We have described the many facets of abuse and offered some suggestions for preventing and healing. We hope that these ideas help you to enjoy marriage and family relationships where love, respect, and harmony abound, and where individuals can acheive their earthly potential and reach their eternal goals. Healing from abuse is possible for both the abuser and the abused. To heal such wounds, the Lord died for each of us.

NOTES

1. *Parent's guide* (1985) (Salt Lake City: The Church of Jesus Christ of Latter-day Saints), 32.

2. *Parent's guide* (1985), 32.

3. Gordon B. Hinckley (1998, November), What are people asking about us? *Ensign, 28*(11), 70–72; Richard G. Scott (1998, May), Removing barriers to happiness, *Ensign, 28*(5), 85–86.

4. Brigham Young (1998), *Teachings of Presidents of the Church: Brigham Young* Reprint, ed. John A. Widtsoe (Salt Lake City: Bookcraft), 172.

5. Brigham Young (1998).

6. Many of these recommendations came from American Association of Retired Persons (1992), *Domestic mistreatment of the elderly: Towards prevention some dos and don'ts* [Brochure] (Washington, DC).

7. Vaughn J. Featherstone (1995, September), A man after God's own heart, in *1995–96 BYU Devotional and Fireside Speeches* (Provo, UT: Brigham Young University Press), 21–28, esp. 23.

8. Featherstone (1995, September), 23

9. Richard G. Scott (1992, May), Healing the tragic scars of abuse, *Ensign, 22*(5), 32.

10. Spencer W. Kimball (1969), *The miracle of forgiveness.* (Salt Lake City: Bookcraft).

11. Scott (1992, May), 31.

12. Neal A. Maxwell (1996, May), According to the desire of [our] hearts, *Ensign, 26(5)*, 21.

13. Scott (1992, May), 31.

14. Richard G. Scott (1994, May), To be healed, *Ensign, 24(5)*, 8.

15. See Dallin H. Oaks (1992, July), Sin and suffering, *Ensign, 22(7)* 70–74.

16. Aileen H. Clyde (1991, November), Charity suffereth long, *Ensign, 21(11)*, 77.

17. L. J. Hansen (1993), Abuse, covenants, and divorce, in A. L. Horton, B. K. Harrison, and B. L. Johnson (Eds.), *Confronting abuse* (Salt Lake City: Deseret Book), 215–227.

18. W. L. Ulrich (1993), When forgiveness flounders: For victims of serious sin, in A. L. Horton, B. K. Harrison, and B. L. Johnson (Eds.), *Confronting abuse* (Salt Lake City: Deseret Book), 347–361.

19. Maxine Murdock (1994, June), I have a question, *Ensign, 24(6)*, 60–61.

20. Scott (1992, May), 33.

21. Name witheld (1992, March), She is not alone, *Ensign, 22(3)* 80.

22. Anonymous (1993), The path to wholeness: A survivor's story and recovery, in A. L. Horton, B. K. Harrison, and B. L. Johnson (Eds.), *Confronting abuse* (Salt Lake City: Deseret Book), 362–373.

23. Dallin H. Oaks (1999), Weightier matters, 148 (available from Speeches, 218 University Press Building, Provo, UT 84602, (801) 378-4711).

24. Oaks (1999), 148.

25. Hinckley (1998).

26. Scott (1998, May), 86.

27. Scott (1992, May), 32.

28. Vaughn J. Featherstone (1995, September), A man after God's own heart, *1995–96 BYU Devotional and Fireside Speeches* (Provo, UT: Brigham Young University Press), 21–28.

29. Hansen (1993).

30. National Adolescent Task Force (1993), Revised report in the *Juvenile and Family Court Journal, 44(4)*, 43–44.

31. L. E. Walker (1988), Spouse abuse: A basic profile, in A. L. Horton and J. A. Williamson (Eds.), *Abuse and religion: When praying isn't enough* (Lexington, MA: D. C. Heath), 13–20; A. Jones and S. Schechter (1992), *When love goes wrong* (New York: HarperCollins).

32. For the strength of youth (1990) (Salt Lake City: The Church of Jesus of Christ of Latter-day Saints), 15.

33. E. Gil (1988), *Treatment of adult survivors of childhood abuse* (Walnut Creek, CA: Launch Press).

34. C. H. Cole and E. Barney (1987), Workers dealing with mother blame in sexual assault cases, *Journal of Child Sexual Abuse, 6*, 65–80; Gil (1988).

35. See for example A. L. Horton, B. K. Harrison, and B. L. Johnson (1993), *Confronting abuse: An LDS perspective on understanding and healing emotional, physical, sexual, psychological, and spiritual abuse* (Salt Lake City: Deseret Book).

CHAPTER 21

THE FAMILY CRUCIBLES OF ILLNESS, DISABILITY, DEATH, AND OTHER LOSSES

JASON S. CARROLL, W. DAVID ROBINSON, ELAINE SORENSEN MARSHALL,
LYNN CLARK CALLISTER, SUSANNE FROST OLSEN,
TINA TAYLOR DYCHES, AND BARBARA MANDLECO

Disability, death, or other circumstances may necessitate individual adaptation.
(The Family: A Proclamation to the World, ¶ 7)

THE CRUCIBLE OF HUMAN EXPERIENCE

The Proclamation says that it is essential to our Eternal Father's plan that His children "obtain a physical body and gain earthly experience" (¶ 3). Few of our earthly experiences are as universal and significant as those that occur as a result of the temporal nature of our bodies. Elder A. Theodore Tuttle noted, "Adversity, in one form or another, is the universal experience of man. It is the common lot of all men to experience misfortune, suffering, sickness, or other adversities."[1] This chapter presents a "family crucible perspective," a way to think about adversity and loss using ideas from both secular and prophetic sources. Some specific issues of illness, disability, infertility, and death are addressed. Finally, gospel-based principles for healing from and growing through family adversities are exemplified through personal narrative from family members who have experienced these challenges.

While illness, disability, infertility, and death are temporal occurrences, their influence extends beyond the physical portion of our lives. These experiences have the potential to become catalysts to change how we view ourselves and our relationships with others. In short, they are what President Marion G. Romney called "the crucible of adversity and affliction."[2] A crucible is a furnace-like vessel that endures intense heat and chemical reactions that result in the refinement and transfiguration of raw materials. Crucibles facilitate a catalytic process that purges away impurities and creates a qualitatively different final product. In industry, crucibles are used to create high-grade steel and alloys of unusual strength that actually differ in quality from the original ingredients themselves.

A metaphorical meaning of crucible is a severe test or trial that refines and purifies. This meaning is evident in prophetic writings referring to the "refiner's fire" (Isa. 48:10; 1 Ne. 20:10).[3] Speaking of this type of change through trial, President James E. Faust observed:

Into every life there come the painful, despairing days of adversity and buffeting. There seems to be a full measure of anguish, sorrow, and often heartbreak for everyone, including those who earnestly seek to do right and be faithful. The thorns that prick, that stick in the flesh, that hurt, often change lives which seem robbed of significance and hope. This change comes about through a refining process which often seems cruel and hard. In this way the soul can become like soft clay in the hands of the Master in building lives of faith, usefulness, beauty, and strength. For some, the refiner's fire causes a loss of belief and faith in God, but those with eternal perspective understand that such a refining is part of the perfection process.[4]

Adversities such as illness, disability, infertility,

and death are unavoidable parts of our earthly experience and are spiritual crucibles with the potential for positive or negative life change. For some families, these life-altering experiences tear at relationships and drown family members in feelings of heartache, injustice, and bitterness. For others, these unexpected challenges serve as a "call to consciousness"[5] that enhances relationships among family members, renews appreciation for significant aspects of life, and inspires faith in the wisdom and grace of God. These challenges and the complex relationship processes that surround them become defining experiences in family life and are essential components of a comprehensive study of families.

Illness, disability, infertility, and death are examples of profound human losses: loss of health, loss of function, loss of joy, loss of life. This chapter explores how shared experiences with such losses influence families. The primary goal is to help readers of this text appreciate the role of a gospel perspective in dealing with these issues in their own lives, as well as in the lives of others.

THE IMPORTANCE OF PERSPECTIVE

When illness, loss, or other physical trials touch families, the first question is often, "Why?" "Why is this happening to me?" "Why must Grandma suffer for so long?" "If God loves us, why did he allow my brother to die?" How families answer these questions has a profound influence on how adversity affects their lives. Our perspective often determines how we define and respond to such situations. The term *perspective* refers to one's way of thinking about and making meaning of life experiences and can be thought of as "our frame of reference, our beginning assumptions, our way of seeing, or our way of thinking."[6] Different perspectives involve "unique way[s] of thinking, asking questions, gathering information, applying ideas, and answering questions."[7] Perspectives can be held by single individuals or families, or they can be shared by larger groups of people in neighborhoods or communities. Some perspectives are so widely accepted that they become part of a society's way of thinking about and responding to life experiences.

Family Scholarship and a Crucible-Oriented Perspective of Life's Adversities

In modern society, personal and collective perspectives influence how family members and professionals deal with illness and loss in families.

Family scholars have recently begun to identify viewpoints for understanding family experiences with illness, disability, death, and other losses. In contrast to early theory and research that focused on how families become disrupted and incapacitated by stress, a crucible perspective highlights the potential for adversity to bring both detrimental and *beneficial* effects to family life. Rather than assuming that the stress brought on by life's most difficult adversities and losses are automatically harmful, crucible-oriented perspectives focus on how some ways of managing adversity may actually promote growth and adaptation. Latter-day Saint family scholars Wesley Burr and Shirley Klein asserted that "family stress often has a silver lining" in that some aspects of family life are often improved "as families are constrained to unite in their efforts to overcome the potential negative effects of the stress."[8] Pauline Boss, a prominent scholar in the field of family stress, has also noted that families have "the potential to grow and learn from a crisis"[9] and that while recovering from stressful experiences they often "reorganize above past levels of functioning."[10]

Difficulties associated with illness and death provide insights into ways families can alleviate distress. A crucible perspective expands upon these insights by recognizing that family members' interpretations and beliefs play a major role in how illness affects their lives.[11]

A Gospel-Based Family Crucible Perspective

Adversity and loss are essential components of our experience on earth and provide us with opportunities for eternal refinement and growth. Thus, a gospel-based, crucible-oriented perspective that appreciates the complex nature of stressful trials can shed meaningful light on how these life challenges influence family life. Recognizing that individuals and families generate personal and shared meanings and explanations for their life challenges is an important insight into understanding families. The gospel of Jesus Christ offers an eternal perspective that helps families understand that there are profound purposes to the adversities of this life. President Spencer W. Kimball noted, "If we look at mortality as a complete existence, then pain, sorrow, failure, and short life could be a calamity. But if we look upon life as an eternal thing stretching far into the pre-earth past and on into the eternal post-death future, then all happenings may be put in proper perspective."[12] Gospel principles offer spiritual comfort and a widening of perspective from one that is solely crisis- or coping-oriented, to one that includes the potential for growth and development.

Expanding Our Perspective

The Proclamation teaches that the cumulative purpose of all of our experiences in this life is to help us "progress toward perfection" (¶ 3) and realize our destiny as heirs of eternal life. Having faith in God's "divine plan of happiness" (¶ 3) is the core principle of a gospel-based, family-crucible perspective. Similar to a wide-angle lens on a camera, this perspective expands our frame of reference and helps us to appreciate certain aspects of our experiences with adversity and loss. This section presents several "perceptual expansions" that are fundamental to viewing adversities as family crucibles.

From Crisis to Crucible

It is natural to view adversity as a crisis, but by embracing a crucible perspective, we can recognize the sorrow and feelings of loss that accompany adversity while also acknowledging the potential for personal growth and enhanced family relationships. It is important to note that a gospel-based crucible perspective is not merely a positive outlook that glosses over the hurt and loss involved with death and serious illness; rather, it views the inescapable sorrow and suffering that come from adversity as pathways toward refining spiritual and relational development. Growth occurs in part because of the pain, not in spite of it. Elder Bruce C. Hafen wrote, "Our understanding of the Atonement is hardly a shield against sorrow; rather, it is a rich source of strength to deal productively with the disappointments and heartbreaks that form the deliberate fabric of mortal life. The gospel was given to us to heal our pain, not to prevent it."[13] Within a gospel-based, crucible perspective, the reality of sore trials is not avoided; rather, afflictions are viewed and experienced in a way that gives purpose to pain and developmental guidance to change.

From Individual to Family

The Proclamation teaches "that the family is central to the Creator's plan for the eternal destiny of His children" (¶ 1). We learn from this principle that our Father in Heaven intends for life experiences to be shared within families. Illness, disability, infertility, and death are best understood as experiences that are shared by all members of the family. Because an illness, disability, or other adversity "resides" with an individual, it is easy to assign "ownership" to that particular family member. For example, we may say "John has multiple sclerosis" or "Sarah is infertile." Too often, we do not think of these as family ailments or adversities. When a mother "has" cancer, all members of the family "have" cancer. They all experience the disease and the personal losses associated with it. Loss of one spouse's ability to function due to illness or disability affects both husband and wife. A husband experiences a loss when his wife has a miscarriage. By appreciating the relational component of these experiences, we can become sensitive to all who need care and concern.

From Event to Process

While we often think of adversities and losses merely as "events" in people's lives, it is useful to expand our perspective to see them as processes that affect family functioning over long periods of time, even perhaps for generations. In this sense, family crucibles are best understood across the life span with an appreciation for the developmental nature of the individual and the family.[14] This is most apparent with chronic conditions where family roles and relationships change during the extended process. Adversities such as illness and death take on a different meaning when they afflict family members at different stages of life. The death of a young child is almost always believed to be more untimely than that of an elderly parent who has lived a long and productive life. These developmental considerations are important in understanding how life challenges influence particular families.

From Temporal to Spiritual

Because physical illnesses and disabilities are often visible to others, it is common to view them primarily through a biological or temporal lens. This viewpoint is supported by the technical manner in which illness is diagnosed and treated in many modern societies. However, in recent years, there has been an increased focus on the spiritual and emotional aspects of illness. This expansion is significant because, while it is true that specific physical problems have common symptoms, individuals and families create their own personal and spiritual meanings from such experiences. In this way, illness and disability become defining factors in how families members view themselves and their relationships with others.

Opposition and the Family Crucible Perspective

In many ways, viewing adversity from a crucible perspective is dependent upon understanding and appreciating the oppositional or dialectical nature of life's experiences. In counseling his son Jacob, the Book of Mormon prophet Lehi taught: "For it must needs be, that there is an opposition in all things. If not so, my first born in the wilderness, righteousness could not be brought to pass, neither wickedness, neither holiness nor misery, neither good nor bad. Wherefore, all things must needs be a compound in one" (2 Ne. 2:11). Why is opposition needed? The Lord taught Adam that opposition is needed in life so that the children of God can "taste the bitter, that they may know to prize the good" (Moses 6:55). While imprisoned in Liberty Jail, the Prophet Joseph Smith was taught a similar principle when the Lord revealed, "Know thou, my son, that all these things shall give thee experience, and shall be for thy good" (D&C 122: 7). To appreciate the purpose of adversity in our lives, it is important to understand that profound lessons can often be gleaned from the process of comparing the contrasting elements of life experiences. Commenting on this learning process, Elder Bruce C. Hafen noted:

> Somehow, our joyful experiences mean more when we are fully conscious of the alternatives and the contrasts that surround us. We prize the sweet more when we have tasted the bitter. We appreciate our health when we see sickness. We truly love peace when we know the ugliness of war. These contrasts do not deter our idealism. Properly understood, they only make the moments of true joy worth waiting for.[15]

Family scholars have also noted the oppositional or paradoxical nature of illness experiences in people's lives.[16] In particular, they have noted that family crucibles may create an "emotional roller-coaster ride that is both draining and empowering."[17] There are at least four important opposites that are often part of the crucible experience for family members.

1. Isolation vs. Connection

One of the emotional polarities that families experience is isolation versus connection.[18] Because adversity befalls individuals, it can be a lonely and isolating experience. This isolation frequently occurs as family members struggle with their unique experiences. Likewise, families may feel isolated from others outside the family as they adapt to their situation. This is profoundly true for individuals dealing with the death of a spouse or other close family member. On the other hand, significant losses can have a profound bonding influence on families when an eternal perspective is part of that family. Many lingering contentions have been resolved through the process of pulling together in a family's time of need. The isolation associated with illness, death, and other losses often confirms the central priority of family relationships and motivates people to establish deeper levels of intimacy and understanding with their loved ones.

2. Essential vs. Non-essential

When confronting a crucible, families often learn to distinguish between the parts of their lives that are essential, such as their personal relationships with family members and the Savior, and those activities that are less important, such as doing spring cleaning, weeding the garden, or going to music lessons.[19] It is not that such things are not important and necessary, but at the time of a family member's illness or passing, these matters may need to be postponed or delegated. Such important, but non-essential activities provide opportunities for others to offer meaningful service to families dealing with such adversities.

3. Senselessness vs. Meaning

The search for meaning is a prevalent theme for individuals and families experiencing illness or death.[20] Some who face these adversities fall into despair, questioning the senselessness of such experiences in life. For others, this search for meaning "takes the form of a spiritual quest" that often leads to a "heightened awareness of life's gifts."[21] Such awareness often involves an increased appreciation for the common or prosaic things in life such as spending time with one's spouse or children, enjoying the beauties of nature, or doing simple acts of service.

4. Old World vs. New

The Proclamation states, "Disability, death, or other circumstances may necessitate individual adaptation" (¶ 7). This counsel has two important considerations for families. First, successful adaptation to adversity often requires flexibility and creativity, which have been identified as critical coping

	OTHER EMOTIONAL CRUCIBLE THEMES[23]	
EMOTIONAL THEME*	**DESCRIPTION**	
Fear vs. Courage	Fear is a common part of adjusting to crucibles. When families find courage in the face of adversity, they do not banish or even conquer fear. Rather, they find the strength to live with their uncertainties and fear and carry on.	
Guilt vs. Forgiveness	Questions of personal responsibility or failure can engender a sense of guilt for many people. The antidote is forgiving ourselves and others, a process that involves accepting our mistakes and understanding our limits.	
Loss vs. Renewal	The pain of loss is frequently associated with the joy of appreciation and the renewed commitment to life goals and values.	
Secrecy vs. Sharing	Illness is often thought of as a private experience. Such a need for secrecy may result from trying to be brave and not burden loved ones, or it may reflect a belief that disabilities are a personal failing of some sort. A healing task for families is to find ways to balance personal preferences for privacy with family member's needs to be helped and comforted by others.	

Table 21.1

resources in helping people manage stress.[22] Second, we should be careful not to judge others, as we are often not aware of the private crucibles in their lives that have necessitated changes in their family roles and responsibilities. Adversity and loss often create the need for changes in family roles, routines, and daily lifestyles. Like immigrants in an unfamiliar land, families confronting these changes often feel as if they have been pushed into a "new world" where many things that were previously taken for granted are now missing. The difficulties associated with adapting to the new world can be compounded when family members have differing views about how much they should continue old patterns of interacting versus how much routines need to change. Family members often take one of several "worldviews" as they navigate the transition to their new world.

One such view has been referred to as an "old worldview."[24] This perspective is one in which the family, or individuals within the family, try to continue life as if nothing has changed. Like new immigrants

holding to traditions and customs of their native land, family members may try to minimize the effects of an illness or disability or in extreme situations may even refuse to believe that the impairment exists. Some even refuse medical treatment. Another problem with an old worldview is that family members may suffer alone because the illness is either not accepted or the unspoken rule is that no one should talk about it.

An illness-saturated new worldview is the other extreme for families or individuals. In this view, family routines and activities become centered around the disability or illness. When this happens, relationships may become strained by guilt or resentment, as there is a sense that the illness or disability is constantly present in family interactions.

Though it may be adaptive and appropriate for individuals to temporarily adopt either one of these worldviews, problems usually arise when a family gets stuck at one of the extremes for a prolonged period of time. In a balanced new worldview, the family acknowledges that the illness or disability exists and

A PSYCHOSOCIAL TYPOLOGY OF ILLNESS AND DISABILITY[25]

DEFINING CHARACTERISTIC	DEFINITION	TYPES AND EXAMPLES
Onset	The way in which the symptoms of the illness or disability present themselves	Acute or Sudden Onset: heart attacks, strokes, birth defects Gradual Onset: rheumatoid arthritis, Parkinson's disease, chronic lung disease
Course	The extent to which the illness or disability is present in the person's and family's daily life	Progressive Course (increases in severity): incurable cancers, Alzheimer's disease Constant or Stable Course: spinal cord injury with paralysis, blindness, mental retardation Relapsing Course (fluctuating episodes): chronic back trouble, kidney stones, migraines
Outcome	The extent to which the illness or disability will affect the person's life span	Nonfatal Outcome: blindness, lumbosacral disc problems, spinal cord injuries Shortened Life Span (or possible sudden death): cystic fibrosis, hemophilia Fatal Outcome: metastatic cancer, AIDS, Huntington's disease
Incapacitation	The degree of limitation or impairment caused by the illness or disability	Ranges from None to Mild to Moderate to Severe: This characteristic of illnesses and disabilities is a cumulative one that encompasses several areas, including: limitations to physical functioning, impairment to mental or cognitive functioning, social stigma, family roles, expectations, emotional and financial resources, etc.

Table 21.2

requires some modification in family roles and routines, but they also honor their established traditions by striving to forge a new life that combines meaningful elements of both the old and new worlds. Table 21.1 shows some other polarities that are frequently involved in family crucible experiences.

PERSPECTIVES OF UNDERSTANDING

Building upon the family crucible perspective, the next section will use this conceptual perspective as a guiding lens through which to view the specific experiences of illness and disability, infertility and pregnancy loss, and death and mourning.

Illness and Disability

"In the narrative of every human life and every family, illness is a prominent character. Even if we have avoided serious illness ourselves, we cannot escape its reach into our family lives and our friendship circles."[26] Because of its wide-reaching effects on

THE TIME PHASES OF ILLNESS AND DISABILITY

PHASE	(1) ACUTE/CRISIS	(2) CHRONIC	(3) TERMINAL
Markers	Symptoms/Diagnosis/ Adjustment	"The Long Haul"	Preterminal/Death/ Mourning
Description	During the acute stage, anxiety is often high as the family is adjusting to the initial shock of the diagnosis. Gaining information about the condition is a common focus for many families at this time. Some conditions resolve themselves in the acute phase (e.g., broken leg, concussion) but others continue into the chronic stage.	The chronic stage begins when families have gained some understanding of the condition and have passed through the initial adjustment phase. Some disorders are chronic by definition while others result because the body is unable to fully repair itself. Issues of stamina and endurance are prevalent during this stage.	Here, the family is informed that the condition will end in death. This stage is difficult as family members are confronted with the imminent death of a loved one. Trying to balance care giving, while maintaining family patterns and routines can be extremely difficult.

Table 21.3

families, physical or mental illness or disability will affect all of us at one time or another. Therefore, it is important for each of us to develop an understanding of how these crucibles affect families, so that we can respond in meaningful ways. Issues addressed here include the types and phases of illness and disability, the family life cycle, caregiving, and the shared experience of illness and disability.

It should be noted that illness and disability are not the same. The term *illness* is typically used to denote any condition that is contrary to physical or mental health. It usually implies specific symptoms or diagnosis of disease. The term *disability* has been described as a condition resulting from a loss of physical, learning, or social functioning that limits an individual's major life activities.[27] While serious illnesses often involve some form of disability, not all disabilities are the result of illness. For example, Alzheimer's disease involves mental disabilities, and an individual who is disabled as a result of mental retardation is usually free of physical illness. Because of these distinctions, families often pursue different paths to adapt to disability than they do to illness and vice versa. The topics to be discussed here provide only a background or foundational understanding of some

of the issues families may experience with illness and disability.

We have not distinguished between mental and physical illness as is traditionally done in Western society. Such distinctions do not adequately recognize the intricate ways in which biological functioning and emotional, spiritual, and social processes are interconnected—especially in families.[28] Also, sometimes mental illnesses or disabilities are falsely linked to a lack of spirituality, or even sin (see John 9:3). Thus, individuals experiencing a condition such as diabetes or blindness may openly acknowledge their condition, while people suffering from illness such as depression often keep their condition hidden, as it may be viewed by themselves or others as a personal or spiritual weakness. By recognizing the reciprocal nature of physical and emotional health and legitimizing all types of illness and disability, we hope to encourage readers to extend their circles of empathy to all in need.

Types and Phases of Illness and Disability

Typically, illnesses and disabilities are classified according to biological criteria. While these distinctions are useful in medical treatment, they do not offer much insight into the distinct emotional and social demands these conditions place on families. John Rolland,[29] a prominent researcher in the area of families and health, has developed a "psychosocial" typology that provides meaningful and useful categories for distinguishing the similarities and differences of various types of illnesses and disabilities. Table 21.2 briefly details several of these distinguishing characteristics.

Many illnesses and disabilities last over long periods of time. Table 21.3 (also based on Rolland's work) provides a general overview of the time phases that are frequently a part of the challenges many families face when dealing with illness and disability. While these phases apply to a wide range of situations, not every condition will progress through all of the stages.

The Family Life Cycle

How a family experiences an illness or disability is strongly influenced by the life cycle stages of the individuals involved. There is no ideal time for illnesses to enter into a family system. However, issues that make the transition more difficult involve (1) timing of the illness or disability, (2) interference with normative family transitions, and (3) which family member is afflicted.

1. *Timing.* Illness may occur at an age when most people would not expect it, such as cancer in a child or a heart attack or stroke in a young adult. While almost all illness and disabilities take families by surprise, there seems to be a stronger argument that "this isn't fair" when illness seems to strike prematurely.

2. *Interference.* It is also difficult when illnesses or disabilities interfere or overlap with normative family transitions because these are times in life when family members are already experiencing the stress of adapting to new roles and responsibilities.[30] The obligations placed upon families during this "transition overlap" can disrupt, and at times even stop, normative progression through life stages. Examples include leaving college to care for a disabled parent or postponing one's marriage because of a life-threatening illness.

3. *Member afflicted.* Finally, the particular individual who is afflicted can create special issues for the family. If the afflicted member is the primary provider, there may be fear about the family's financial situation and guilt about not being able to provide. If the ill or disabled person performs the role of primary caregiver, family patterns surrounding child care and home can become disrupted. When a child or an elderly parent is ill, important considerations involve who will be available for caregiving.

Caregiving

Caregiving is a key issue for families confronted by some types of illness and disability. In most societies, the responsibility of direct caregiving usually falls upon women. Depending upon the condition, caregiving can range from minimal adaptation of daily routines to a complete lifestyle change. In some cases, the physical and emotional toll on the family caregiver can be enormous, including the fear of doing something wrong, lack of personal time, and losing energy for other roles such as work, child care, or involvement in other relationships. The degree of burden depends upon the stage and severity of the condition and the resources available to the family.

Guilt is often associated with caregiving for both the recipient of care and the caregiver. For the recipient, guilt can emerge from feeling responsible for placing demands on the caregiver. For the caregiver, guilt can arise because there may be times when caring for a loved one becomes overwhelming. However, recent research has shown that caregiving relationships can promote personal growth and closer family ties.[31] This is consistent with a family crucible perspective, wherein difficulty and growth can be a part of the same experience. In Essay L a mother of a child with a special need describes the joy and pain of this challenge.

Shared Experience of Illness

While it is true that illness and disability influence all family members, it should not be assumed that all family members have identical experiences. While there may be elements of the experience that are collectively shared among family members, it is common for each individual to have distinct ways of interpreting and experiencing the crucible. Because of personal beliefs, previous life events, or a myriad of other reasons, each family member will have parts of the experience that are unique. A woman recovering from breast cancer expressed: "I remember sitting there with the chemotherapy going in me and at that moment thinking, "you know, there is a very clear reality that we are alone in this world and even though we can feel comfort from other people, there are things that we do in our lives that are done *alone*. I don't think I ever admitted that before or ever saw it as clearly. It was a solitary piece to a journey."[32]

When confronted by adversity, each family member may experience a unique sense of loss. Parents and even grandparents have reported feelings of guilt or grief for the loss of the perceived ideal child.[33] Herein lies another paradoxical component of families' experiences with illness and disability. As families recognize and appreciate that their personal experiences may be different from one another, their collective experience as a family becomes more "shared." In other words, the validation of difference brings unity. In this sense, illness and disability can be "shared," even if family members maintain separate and even contradictory views of the experience. This is because individuals feel most supported when their personal experiences are not devalued or ignored. By disclosing feelings and concerns and appreciating each person's unique ways of thinking and doing things, family members are able to build connections with one another, develop empathy, and adapt to challenges in ways that benefit everyone involved.

INFERTILITY AND PERINATAL LOSS

The scriptural injunction to "be fruitful, and multiply, and replenish the earth" (Gen. 1:28; see Proclamation, ¶ 4) is a pervasive expectation in Judaism, Christianity, and Islam as well as most other faiths.[34] According to the Proclamation, "The family is central to the Creator's plan for the eternal destiny of His children" and "the first commandment that God gave to Adam and Eve pertained to their potential for parenthood" (¶¶ 1, 4). Consequently, the family crucibles of infertility and perinatal loss are painful, poignant, and often enduring struggles for couples who long for a child.

Infertility

Give me children, or else I die (Gen. 30:1).

Infertility is often a silent and solitary crucible, since it is not visible, life-threatening, or disfiguring.[35] Infertility diagnosis and treatment are often emotionally and physically exhausting experiences. Couples frequently report high levels of stress, a loss of hope, and feelings of frustration related to the use of complex reproductive technology, the medicalizing of intimacy, invasive procedures, surgeries, and potent drugs with problematic side effects. Painful losses often associated with infertility include loss of the childbearing experience; loss of relationships; loss of health; loss of status or prestige; loss of self-worth; and a loss of a potential child.[36]

At times, couples who are having trouble getting pregnant must also deal with well-meaning family and friends, who may perpetuate such myths as "infertility isn't a physical problem—it's all in your head; just relax and you'll get pregnant" or "infertility is a female problem." Other misguided and hurtful remarks include "go ahead and adopt a baby: then you'll conceive" or "if you would just exercise more faith in God, you'll get pregnant."[37] Likewise, some may assume that childlessness is by choice. Being nonjudgmental of couples who have not had children is crucial. The Church teaches that decisions about the number and timing of children are left to each couple and the Lord and encourages people not to judge their fellow Saints in this area.

Experiencing the intensity of the family crucible of infertility, spouses may feel anger toward themselves and others. There may be feelings of guilt or unworthiness as individuals falsely assume a connection between perceived unworthiness and impaired fertility. Because they may feel a lack of control, it is not uncommon for either spouse to feel depressed and powerless, no matter what efforts are made or what resources are accessed.[38] Infertile Latter-day Saint couples may feel isolated by constant reminders of their loss in not being parents.

Coping strategies used by couples struggling with infertility may include distancing themselves from reminders of infertility (such as avoidance of families with children), instituting measures for regaining control, acting to increase self-esteem by being the best (such as striving to achieve professional success), looking for hidden meaning in infertility, or sharing the burden with others. One woman said, "I built an emotional wall around myself, trying to shut out the pain. The wall provided a buffer that protected me for a time, from anyone or anything that reminded me that I had no children."[39]

In a period of life that may already be filled with relational and economic struggles, couples confronted by infertility are also challenged with sorting through a technically complex and potentially costly decision-making process surrounding possible treatment alternatives. The Church teaches that if parents are sealed then children conceived by artificial insemination or in vitro fertilization are born in the covenant. The Church strongly discourages using an egg from anyone except the wife or semen from anyone other than the husband, but teaches that the couple has ultimate judgment in these personal issues.

In Latter-day Saint literature, comforting counsel

and eternal perspectives are offered to ameliorate the pain and help families emerge from the crucible of infertility. Speaking to the women of the Church, Patricia Holland focused on the eternal role of motherhood:

> Eve was given the identity of the mother of all living years, decades, perhaps centuries before she had ever brought forth a child. It would appear that her motherhood preceded her maternity just as surely as the perfection of the Garden preceded the struggles of mortality. I believe "mother" is one of those very carefully chosen words, one of those rich words—with meaning, after meaning, after meaning . . . I believe with all my heart that it is first and foremost a statement about our nature, not a head count of our children. . . . Some women . . ."mother" all their lives but have never given birth.[40]

Perinatal Loss

Before I formed thee in the belly I knew thee; and before thou camest forth out of the womb I sanctified thee (Jer. 1:5).

The term *perinatal* loss refers to miscarriage (spontaneous abortion), ectopic pregnancy, having a stillborn child, and the experience of neonatal death. Other types of perinatal losses may include recurrent pregnancy loss; the loss of a perfect child; the death of a twin during pregnancy or labor; and the relinquishment of a child to adoption.

The study of grief and loss has a long history in family research, but there is a smaller body of research on perinatal loss. Family researchers conclude that "the emotional sequelae of perinatal losses are not well understood."[41] The major focus of the research to date has been on mother's experiences, but there is a growing investigation of the paternal experience of perinatal loss.[42]

Perinatal bereavement is a unique mourning situation, as "the parents' expectations and joy at the prospect of the new life change into despair and grief."[43] Perinatal losses include the loss of the creation of a new life; the loss of the anticipated child; the loss of the dream and hopes for parenthood; and the loss of an extension of both parents.[44] Societal acknowledgments of perinatal loss are also noticeably absent. One mother noted, "When I lost my baby at the beginning of the second trimester . . . there was no memorial service, no outpouring of sympathy, no evidence I gave birth and lost a baby."[45]

Parental responses to perinatal loss range from minimal heartache to intense and sustained grief.[46] The intensity of the loss, the range of emotions experienced, and the impact on health may depend on the gender of the parent, the perception of the loss, age, the life changes brought by the loss, cultural or spiritual beliefs, personal ability to cope with the loss, and support systems.[47] The term *incongruent grief* is sometimes used to refer to gender differences in how perinatal loss is expressed by each parent.[48] In these times, one spouse may distance or detach himself or herself from the experience or from the family as a protective mechanism to avoid the pain and grief. However, for other couples, the strain associated with the crucible of perinatal loss creates a context in which partners rely upon each other more and the marital bond is strengthened.

Other family members, both immediate and extended, experience perinatal loss as well. Siblings of the lost child experience grief and loss and have been termed "forgotten mourners."[49] Siblings may feel left out, neglected, guilty, or sad. Grandparents also experience pain, as one grandmother described her experience with her grieving daughter, "I sit with her and I cry with her. She cries for her daughter and I cry for mine."[50]

To be offered the choice of terminating a pregnancy in the case of anomalies that are incompatible with life may be a painful challenge for the childbearing couple. When facing this dilemma, Latter-day Saints should counsel together and with their bishop and prayerfully seek divine confirmation. Church doctrine is not explicit on the status of children who have been lost through miscarriage, ectopic pregnancy, abortion, or stillbirth, but emphasizes that faith in the Lord's love for all His children and urges support for all who suffer this experience.

The Prophet Joseph Smith provided an eternal perspective on the restoration of such losses when he taught, "All your losses will be made up to you in the resurrection."[51]

Having knowledge of an impending perinatal loss may give families an opportunity to plan, feel more in control of their situation, and say good-bye in a special way. According to the desires and needs of parents, seeing and holding the baby, bathing and dressing the child, naming the child, and being provided with tangible mementoes such as a lock of hair, handprints and footprints, or a photograph, and holding memorial services may be very comforting to grieving parents.[52]

The influence of infertility and perinatal loss on

family life cannot be underestimated. The development of a lifelong grief response filled with comfort and creativity, coupled with sorrow, may be more realistic and fulfilling than the myth that parents should just "get over it."[53] Those who discover a sense of meaning for such adversity are often able to find bittersweet resolution.

DEATH AND MOURNING

The Proclamation notes that as "spirit sons and daughters [we] knew and worshipped God as [our] Eternal Father and accepted His plan . . . [to] obtain a physical body" and that "the divine plan of happiness enables family relationships to be perpetuated beyond the grave." Sacred temple ordinances "make it possible for individuals to return to the presence of God and for families to be united eternally" (¶ 3). Elder Russell M. Nelson reminded us that "We need not look upon death as an enemy. With full understanding and preparation, faith supplants fear. Hope displaces despair. The Lord said, 'Fear not even unto death; for in this world your joy is not full, but in me your joy is full' (D&C 101:36). An eternal perspective eases the pangs of death."[54]

Even with the Gospel's marvelous comforting perspective, among the most difficult of life's crucibles is the loss of a loved one by death or facing one's own imminent passing. The bereavement and mourning associated with such losses nearly always provoke profound life changes. Although death is a universal part of life, the experience of grief is unique for each individual and each family. The death of an elderly or chronically ill family member may be expected and more easily accepted by some family members, but still very difficult for others. The death of a young parent or spouse causes not only the loss of a father or mother, wife or husband, but the loss of an entire way of living for surviving family members.[55] The death of a child is among the most intense and profound adversities for a family where parents and others wrestle with their loss of both the present and anticipated future earthly experiences with the child. Moments of mourning often resurface as "would have been" milestones are marked by other children of the same age.

Death by suicide is among the most difficult of tragedies. Family members may blame themselves for not preventing the loss[56] or wonder about the eternal salvation of the deceased. Elder M. Russell Ballard counseled, "Suicide is a sin—a very grievous one, yet the Lord will not judge the person who commits that sin strictly by the act itself. The Lord will look at that person's circumstances and the degree of his accountability at the time of the act."[57]

To Mourn with Those That Mourn

We may feel powerless to know what to say or how to help families who are grieving. However, we are admonished as a covenant people to "mourn with those that mourn" and "comfort those that stand in need of comfort" (Mosiah 18:9). Elder Bruce R. McConkie noted that "wholesome and proper mourning—mourning based on sound gospel knowledge—is a profitable and ennobling part of life. Men are commanded to fast, and pray, and mourn: all these are essential parts of true worship" (see Alma 30:2; Hel. 9:10).[58] Even with a firm knowledge of the life hereafter and the plan of salvation, the anguish of grief can be surprisingly intense. Pain can be eased by sharing with others. Researchers have found that bereaved individuals who share their feelings with family members experience fewer physical and emotional health problems.[59]

When attempting to comfort another, often the most helpful thing to do is just be present. The simple words, "I am sorry," accompanied by a willingness to listen are more helpful than possibly unwelcome statements such as, "It's God's will," "She's no longer suffering," or "He's in a better place." Such "non-anxious presence" allows the grieving person to feel supported without needing to respond. It is often helpful to talk about the positive memories of the person or give concrete help such as child care, house cleaning, or a car wash.[60] Offering living symbols, such as planting a tree in honor of the lost one, can be especially comforting.[61]

Comfort through grief comes according to individual and family needs and time. There is no typical time frame for recovery nor are there specific chronological stages of grief. Surges of pain, numbness, anger, guilt, and relief may come and go, and then return in unexpected ambushes. Tangible reminders of the person, such as photographs or belongings, may be comforting. Do not assume that because the survivor does not mention the deceased person that he or she is not constantly thinking of the loved one. It is often comforting to talk about the deceased person, rather than avoid his or her name in conversation, as if the person never existed or does not continue to exist. Anniversaries and holidays, such as birthdays, the date of the death, or Christmas, may be especially difficult. People who have lost beloved family members report that the ache is always present to some degree and that they eventually learn to live with the loss as a constant companion.

A Gospel Path to Healing from Affliction and Loss

As we view life's experiences with illness, disability, and death as crucibles intended to further our eternal development, we allow ourselves to benefit more fully from the principles of healing found within the gospel of Jesus Christ. A knowledge of our Eternal Father's plan can ease the losses associated with adversity and can provide needed guidance along the unpredictable journey toward healing. Speaking on the scriptural question the Savior posed to the grieving Mary Magdalene, "Woman, why weepest thou?" President James E. Faust suggested that the Savior was not just speaking to the sorrowing Mary, rather he was also speaking to all of us, "for the tears of sorrow, pain, or remorse are the common lot of mankind." He further explained that "all of us can benefit from the transcendent blessings of the Atonement and the Resurrection, through which the divine healing process can work in our lives."[62] While the specific steps in the process are unique to each person's situation, the gospel of Jesus Christ provides a firm directional course for families to follow as they move along their own personal pathways to healing.

There are a few principles upon which the Lord's "divine healing process" is predicated. The term *healing* may need clarification. The scriptures record numerous occasions where faithful individuals were physically healed from their illnesses and disabilities, even raised from the dead. While such miracles are a part of our Lord's plan and such signs "follow them that believe" (Mark 16:14–20), the use of the term *healing* here pertains to a more spiritually oriented interpretation of the word. Elder Richard G. Scott explained:

> It is important to understand that [the Lord's] healing can mean being cured, or having your burdens eased, or even coming to realize that it is worth it to endure to the end patiently, for God needs brave sons and daughters who are willing to be polished when in His wisdom that is His will.[63]

When viewed in these terms, the concept of healing is appropriately considered as a process of supported growth and refinement rather than a cure or removal of suffering. This support generally comes over time as we seek to understand the Lord's divine purposes in our lives.

Elder Scott further noted that the surest, most effective, path to healing comes through an application of the teachings of Jesus Christ in our lives. He noted that such a path "begins with an understanding and appreciation for the principles of . . . the atonement of Jesus Christ," which "leads to faith in Him and obedience to His commandments."[64]

Principles of the Atonement

The prophet Alma provided a crucial insight into the nature of the Atonement and Christ's healing power when he addressed the people of Gideon. Referring to the Savior, Alma taught: "And he shall go forth, suffering pains and afflictions and temptations of every kind; and this that the word might be fulfilled which saith he will take upon him the pains and the sicknesses of his people. . . . And he will take upon him their infirmities, that his bowels may be filled with mercy, . . . that he may know according to the flesh how to succor his people" (Alma 7:11–12).

From this scripture, we learn two important truths. First, the Savior's Atonement's healing power is not only for overcoming the effects of sin, but also extends to the entire range of mortal suffering and adversity.[65] Elder Neal A. Maxwell noted, "Since not all human sorrow and pain is connected to sin, the full intensiveness of the Atonement involved bearing our pains, infirmities, and sicknesses, as well as our sins."[66] The second truth we learn from Alma's words is that because the Savior has experienced the complete range of human suffering and loss, He is uniquely able to comprehend our pain and succor us in our times of personal suffering. Elder Merrill J. Bateman counseled: "The Savior's atonement in the garden and on the cross is intimate as well as infinite. Infinite in that it spans the eternities. Intimate in that the Savior felt each person's pains, sufferings, and sicknesses. Consequently, He knows how to carry our sorrows and relieve our burdens that we might be healed from within, made whole persons, and receive everlasting joy in his kingdom."[67]

As we realize that the blessings of the Atonement extend to all of life's suffering and that the Lord truly understands our personal situations, we can more fully turn to the Savior in times of illness or death and accept His invitation: "Come unto me, all ye that labour and are heavy laden, and I will give thee rest. Take my yoke upon you and learn of me; for I am meek and lowly in heart: and ye shall find rest unto your souls" (Matt. 11:28–30).

Healing is also found in the believer's hope for the promised gift of the resurrection. The Proclamation states that our Eternal Father's "divine plan of happiness enables family relationships to be perpetuated beyond the grave" (¶ 3). The comfort provided by a knowledge of the resurrection and the potential for families to be united eternally can be the balm of Gilead that eases the losses associated with death and provides hope to family members on both sides of the veil. As grieving family members have faith in the Savior and His atoning sacrifice, "death's sting is softened as Jesus bears the believers' grief and comforts them through the Holy Spirit."[68] President Spencer W. Kimball taught: "And, while disabilities are a part of the imperfect world in which we now live, in the resurrection there will be no blind eyes, no deaf ears, and no crippled legs. In eternity there will be no retarded minds and no diseased or injured bodies. In the eternal perspective such infirmities exist but for a moment."[69]

Faith and Obedience

While confronting life's crucibles, exercising faith in Jesus Christ involves trusting that the Lord knows what is best for us and can direct our lives in those ways that will allow us to reach our fullest potential. Our trust in the Lord must be more powerful and enduring than our confidence in our own feelings and experience.[70] Often this means being willing to obey, even when we do not know the end from the beginning. As the book of Proverbs counsels: "Trust in the Lord with all thine heart; and lean not unto thine own understanding. In all thy ways acknowledge him, and he shall direct they paths" (Prov. 3: 5–6). President Ezra Taft Benson taught, "Men and women who turn their lives over to God will discover that He can make a lot more out of their lives than they can."[71] Surrendering ourselves to God's will is not an easy process, but as we follow the Savior's example and sincerely pray unto the Lord, "Thy will be done" (Matt. 6:10; see also Matt. 26:39) we position ourselves to receive of the Lord's divine healing power.

Another principle of receiving the Lord's healing and support is that of keeping our sacred covenants with Him and continuing to be obedient to His commandments. Whether we are experiencing the

challenges of blindness, depression, cancer, or the death of a loved one, His requirements are the same—we are to keep ourselves clean before Him through obedience. President Kimball declared, "The way to perfection is through obedience. Therefore, to each person is given a pattern—obedience through suffering, and perfection through obedience."[72] Elder Jeffrey R. Holland also illustrated this idea: "Obedience and submission to the end, including whatever suffering physically or spiritually that may entail, are the key to our blessings and our salvation. In the suffering as well as in the serving, we must be willing to be like our Savior."[73]

Through willing obedience to the Lord's commandments, we are able to receive the full extent of our Lord's guidance and support. President Romney said, "In sympathy and love I say to you . . . being tried in the crucible of adversity and affliction: Take courage; revive your spirits and strengthen your faith. In these lessons so impressively taught in precept and example by our great exemplar, Jesus Christ, . . . we have ample inspiration for comfort and for hope."[74]

A gospel-based family crucible perspective provides a guiding lens through which we can more fully understand and appreciate how individuals and families are influenced by experiences with illness and disability, infertility and pregnancy loss, death and mourning, and other profound experiences with adversity and loss. Such expanded understanding helps us to realize more fully the two greatest resources of healing we have been given in this life: the gospel of Jesus Christ and our families. Through searching for the eternal purposes of adversity, we become more receptive to the divine influence of the Holy Spirit, who in turn will guide us as we progress through this life's experiences of refinement and growth.

NOTES

1. A. Theodore Tuttle (1967, December), Sweet are the uses of adversity, *Improvement Era,* 47.

2. Marion G. Romney (1969, December), The crucible of adversity and affliction, *Improvement Era,* 68.

3. James E. Faust (1979, May), The refiner's fire, *Ensign,* 9(5), 53–59.

4. Faust (1979, May), 53.

5. D. S. Williamson (1991), *The intimacy paradox* (New York: Guilford).

6. W. R. Burr, R. D. Day, and K. S. Bahr (1993), *Family science* (Pacific Grove, CA: Brooks/Cole), 8.

7. W. R. Burr et al. (1993), 31.

8. W. R. Burr and S. R. Klein (1994), *Re-examining family stress: New theory and research* (Thousand Oaks, CA: Sage), 198.

9. P. Boss (1988), *Family stress management* (Newbury Park, CA: Sage), 51.

10. Boss (1988), 50

11. L. M. Wright, W. L. Watson, and J. M. Bell (1996), *Beliefs: The heart of healing in families and illness* (New York: Basic Books).

12. Spencer W. Kimball (1982), *The teachings of Spencer W. Kimball*, ed. Edward L. Kimball (Salt Lake City: Bookcraft), 39–39.

13. Bruce C. Hafen (1989), *The broken heart: Applying the Atonement to life's experiences* (Salt Lake City: Deseret Book), 5.

14. J. S. Rolland (1989), Chronic illness and the family life cycle, in B. Carter and M. McGoldrick (Eds.), *The changing family life cycle: A framework for family therapy* (Needham Heights, MA: Allyn & Bacon), 433–456.

15. Hafen (1989), 79.

16. S. H. McDaniel, J. Hepworth, and W. J. Doherty (Eds.) (1997), *The shared experience of illness: Stories of patients, families, and their therapists* (New York: Basic Books); W. D. Robinson (1999), *Co-creating family therapy interventions with families experiencing the crucible of cancer through the use of action research,* unpublished doctoral dissertation, Brigham Young University, Provo, UT; W. D. Robinson, W. L. Watson, and J. S. Carroll (1998, October), *Co-evolving interventions for families with cancer,* poster session presented at the annual conference of the American Association for Marriage and Family, Dallas, TX.

17. S. H. McDaniel et al. (1997), 3.

18. McDaniel et al. (1997).

19. Robinson et al. (1998).

20. McDaniel et al. (1997); Robinson et al. (1998).

21. McDaniel et al. (1997), 8.

22. S. E. Hobfall and C. D. Speilberger (1992), Family stress: Integrating theory and measurement, *Journal of Family Psychology,* 6, 99–112.

23. Adapted from McDaniel et al. (1997), and W. D. Robinson (1999).

24. W. D. Robinson (1999).

25. Adapted from Rolland (1994).

26. McDaniel et al. (1997), 1.

27. M. L. Hardman, C. J. Drew, and M. W. Egan (1999), *Human exceptionality: Society, school, and family* (6th ed.) (Boston: Allyn & Bacon).

28. See S. H. McDaniel, J. Hepworth, and W. J. Doherty (1992), *Medical family therapy: A biopsychosocial approach to families with health problems* (New York: BasicBooks); J. S. Rolland (1994), *Families, illness, and disability* (New York: Basic Books), for a review of these issues.

29. J. S. Rolland (1989); J. S. Rolland (1994).

30. R. Shuman (1996), *The psychology of chronic illness* (New York: BasicBooks).

31. C. O. Conger and E. S. Marshall (1998), Re-creating life: Toward a theory of relationship development in acute home care, *Qualitative Health Research,* 8(4), 526–546.

32. Robinson (1999).

33. E. S. Marshall, S. F. Olsen, K. W. Allred, B. L. Mandleco, and T. T. Dyches (1998, November), Themes of religious support among Mormon families with a child with disabilities, paper presented at National Council on Family Relations, Milwaukee, WI.

34. L. C. Callister (1995), Cultural meanings of childbirth. *Journal of Obstetric Gynecologic and Neonatal Nursing,* 24(4), 327–331; L. C. Callister, S. Semenic, and J. C. Foster (1999), Cultural and spiritual meanings of childbirth: Orthodox Jewish and Mormon women, *Journal of Holistic Nursing,* 17(3), 280–295.

35. C. J. Schoener and L. W. Krysa (1996), The comfort and discomfort of infertility, *Journal of Obstetric, Gynecologic, and Neonatal Nursing,* 25(2), 167–172.

36. G. P. Johnston (1994), *The wish, the wait, the wonder* (New York: HarperCollins).

37. L. J. Boswell (1992), A fertile faith, in D. H. Anderson and M. Cornwall (Eds.) (1996, Spring), *Women steadfast in Christ* (Salt Lake City: Deseret Book), 195–203; M. Rutter (1996), Those other couples in the Church: Families without children, *This People,* 38–51.

38. A. S. Boxer (1996), Images of infertility, *Nurse Practitioner Forum,* 7(2), 60–63; C. L. Johnson (1996, spring), Regaining self-esteem: Strategies and interventions for the infertile woman, *Journal of Obstetric, Gynecologic, and Neonatal Nursing,* 25, 291–295.

39. J. N. Christensen (1996, August), I yearned for a baby, *Ensign,* 27(8), 52–53, in *LDS Women's Treasury* (Salt Lake City: Deseret Book), 152.

40. Patricia T. Holland (1987, June), With your face to the Son, *BYU Today,* 33–36, 48–54; also in Jeffrey R. Holland and Patrica T. Holland (Eds.) (1989), *On earth as it is in heaven* (Salt Lake City: Deseret Book), 94.

41. S. S. Bansen and H. A. Stevens (1992), Women's experiences of miscarriage in early pregnancy, *Journal of Nurse Midwifery,* 37, 85.

42. D. Duncan (1995), Fathers have feelings too, *Modern Midwifery,* 5(1), 30–31.

43. I. Radestad, C. Nordin, G. Steineck, and B. Sjogren (1996), Stillbirth is no longer managed as a nonevent: A nationwide study in Sweden, *Birth* 23(4), 209–217.

44. M. B. Gibbons (1993), Listening to the lived experience of loss, *Pediatric Nursing,* 19(6), 597–599.

45. S. D. Wittwer (1994), *Gone too soon: The life and loss of infants and unborn children* (American Fork, UT: Covenant Communications), 29.

46. A. Powell (1997), Grief and the concept of loss in midwifery practice, *Professional Care of Mother and Child,* 7(3), 76–78.

47. M. Jones (1997), Women with special needs—Mothers who need to grieve: The reality of mourning the loss of a baby, *British Journal of Midwifery,* 5(8), 478–481.

48. F. A. Murphy and S. C. Hunt (1997), Family issues, early pregnancy loss: Men have feelings too, *British Journal of Midwifery,* 5(2), 87–90.

49. K. M. Hanna (1996), Helping grieving parents explain perinatal death to children, *Journal of Perinatal Education,* 5(3), 45–50; J. Thomas (1998), The death of a baby: Siblings and memories. *Journal of Neonatal Nursing,* 4(5), 25–29.

50. Wittwer (1994), 57–58.

51. Joseph Smith (1976), *The teachings of the Prophet Joseph Smith,* ed. and comp. Joseph Fielding Smith (Salt Lake City: Deseret Book), 296.

52. C. A. Malacrida (1997), Perinatal death: Helping parents find their way, *Journal of Family Nursing,* 3(2), 130–148.

53. N. J. Moules (1998), Legitimizing grief: Challenging beliefs that constrain, *Journal of Family Nursing,* 4(2), 142–166.

54. Russell M. Nelson (1992), Eternal perspective eases pangs of death, *Church News,* April 11.

55. P. R. Silverman and J. W. Worden (1992), Children's reactions in the early months after the death of a parent, *American Journal of Orthopsychiatry, 62*(1), 93–104.

56. M. Séguin, A. Lesage, and M. C. Kiely (1995), Parental bereavement after suicide and accident: A comparative study, *Suicide and Life-Threatening Behavior, 25*(4), 489–498.

57. M. Russell Ballard (1987, October), Suicide: Some things we know, and some we do not, *Ensign, 17*(10), 8.

58. Bruce R. McConkie (1966), *Mormon doctrine* (2nd ed.) (Salt Lake City: Bookcraft), 518.

59. C. M. Sanders (1980), A comparison of adult bereavement in the death of a spouse, child, and parent, *Omega, 10*(4), 303–321.

60. E. B. Farnsworth, and K. R. Allen (1996, October), Mothers' bereavement: Experiences of marginalization, stories of change, *Family Relations,* 360–366.

61. Sorensen, E. S. (1990, July), Our tree of life, *Ensign, 20*(7), 66–67.

62. James E. Faust (1996, November), Woman, why weepest thou? *Ensign, 26*(11), 52.

63. Richard G. Scott (1994, May), To be healed, *Ensign, 24*(5), 7.

64. Scott (1994, May), 9.

65. Hafen (1989).

66. Neal A. Maxwell (1988), *Not my will, but thine* (Salt Lake City: Bookcraft), 51.

67. Merrill J. Bateman (1995, May), The power to heal from within, *Ensign, 25*(5), 14.

68. Bateman (1995, May), 13.

69. Spencer W. Kimball (1977), *Tragedy or Destiny?* (Salt Lake City: Deseret Book), 6.

70. Richard G. Scott (1995, November), Trust in the Lord, *Ensign, 25*(11), 16–18

71. Ezra Taft Benson (1988), *The teachings of Ezra Taft Benson* (Salt Lake City: Bookcraft), 361.

72. Kimball (1982), 168.

73. Jeffrey R. Holland (1997), *Christ and the new covenant: The messianic message of the Book of Mormon* (Salt Lake City: Deseret Book), 304.

74. Romney (1969, December), 68.

Raising a Child with a Mental Disability: A Personal Story

Marleen S. Williams

I remember holding my daughter, Nikki, in my arms for the first time. My husband and I had two sons, ages two and four, but now having a daughter fulfilled a longing I had kept in my heart for many years. I had grown up in a loving family, but we had limited financial resources. I looked forward to the ability to offer my daughter many of the opportunities I had wanted in my own life: a college education, training to develop talents and abilities to their full potential, travel opportunities, and the pretty dresses I had wanted but could never afford. My mind explored dreams of how I would nurture her talents. We would share together my love of music, art, and history. We would cook and sew together. I would read the scriptures to her, and she would have an understanding of gospel principles. I brought her home from the hospital feeling confident that if I mothered her well, she would fulfill the longings of my heart.

As she grew, I began to notice differences between her development and what I had experienced with her two older brothers. At first, I attributed the discrepancy to a different temperament. But when her first birthday arrived, and she had never attempted to stand on her feet nor even engage in normal verbal babbling, I began to worry. I asked her pediatrician if something was wrong. He questioned me about the ages of my two other children and then declared, "You have just had too many children too close

together. Go home and pay more attention to her and she will catch up."

I puzzled over where I might have failed, but vowed to work even harder to be a good mother. After five more years of frustrating mothering, medical and psychological evaluations, tears, and prayers, we were informed that Nikki was mentally retarded. We were told that she would probably never progress beyond the third- or fourth-grade level of cognitive functioning. I felt flooded by a confusing mixture of thoughts and feelings: relief (it wasn't my fault); inadequacy (I didn't know how to raise a child with retardation); anger (life had played a cruel trick on me); and guilt (I must have done something wrong to deserve this). I didn't realize at the time that I was embarking on one of the most instructive and spiritually enlightening experiences of my life.

I soon became aware that raising a child with mental retardation assured me a front row seat in the battle between the polarized forces of good and evil. As Nikki grew, she was often teased, ridiculed, and made the focus of cruel jokes. There were also more subtle ways that people ostracized her. Some parents would make excuses as to why Nikki was not allowed to play with their children. Because Nikki looked "normal," it was often difficult for people to believe that she could not "act her age," even when she truly tried. I marveled more, however, at the tender sensitivity that flowed from other children who seemed to sense Nikki's frustration and helplessness. Some children would rush to comfort and assist her.

Nikki became a source of instruction to teach others compassion. For example, one day she returned with tears and bleeding hands from a Sunday School class party. A ten-year-old boy in her class had called her a "retard" and pushed her down in a pile of rocks. My husband and I visited the boy's family, sat down with him and his parents and explained what retarded meant. We asked the boy to imagine what it would be like to not be able to do what others do so easily. How would he want to be treated? The boy eventually became one of Nikki's defenders and allies. He treated her kindly thereafter. I began to understand that much of the cruelty, prejudice, and unfair judgment that is directed against people who are different or disabled comes from psychological defenses. People want to protect themselves from a fear that they, too, could become disabled or ostracized. Those who could love and accept themselves in their own mortal humanness seemed more easily able to accept Nikki.

Having a member with a disability affects everyone in the family. Nikki could not keep up with the fast-paced lifestyle on which the rest of the family thrived. What our other children experienced as challenging and invigorating, she experienced as frustrating and demoralizing. Family outings were often punctuated with tantrums, tears, and holy terror. Mental retardation not only interferes with the process of academic learning, but also makes difficult any acquisition of social and emotional skills and maturity. Nikki, like many children with retardation, had a short attention span and was hyperactive. Everyone in the family had to slow down and simplify activities in order to accommodate Nikki's needs. As I look back on her childhood, I can now see the blessing she has been to our family. Her brothers learned that having a bright mind is a gift to be used to serve others, not an entitlement to have others serve them.

Adolescence was a particularly difficult time for Nikki. Her father died when she was thirteen years old. She missed him, and had difficulty understanding and expressing her own grief. She often acted out her feelings because of her inability to express them adequately. On several occasions, she disappeared from home and could not be found at any of the neighbors' homes. I always found her huddled in the bushes outside the window of the bishop's office at the church. Her father had been the bishop of the ward before he died. Nikki said she felt "close to him" there. The Young Women of the ward rallied around Nikki. They comforted her and included her in parties and activities. I began to understand the power and necessity of a Zion society. It is only when the strong sacrifice to serve the weak that both can become sanctified.

Nikki continues to struggle with challenges, but has grown to be a loving and contributing adult member of society. She works as a lunchroom aide at an elementary school and serves in the nursery in our ward. Several years ago, she received her patriarchal blessing, in which she was told that her mortal life is of great importance. Her disability was not an accident. She came forth in this life under special circumstances so that the Lord could give her the responsibility of affecting the lives of others. She has become a tool in the Lord's hands to brighten the lives of others. She was promised that she will eventually come forth to claim all of the joys of earth life. There is no limit to the blessings that are in store for her.

My story of raising a daughter has been different than I had expected. But the process has been richer in meaning for me than I would ever have dared to hope. Nikki and I share a bond of deep eternal love for each other. We look forward to a continued eternal relationship. I am grateful for all that she has had the courage to teach me. I have learned that love is not only for the swift and the strong, nor just for the accomplished and powerful, but also for the struggling and confused. I have learned that if I, in my weakness, can deeply love Nikki through all of her struggles, then surely God in His greatness loves each of us.

CHAPTER 22

PRACTICES FOR BUILDING MARRIAGE AND FAMILY STRENGTHS

STEPHEN F. DUNCAN

. . . to promote those measures designed to maintain and strengthen the family . . .
(The Family: A Proclamation to the World, ¶ 9)

This chapter focuses on practical ways to strengthen your marriage and family by presenting numerous activities developed by family life educators and family counselors that have been found helpful in strengthening relationships.[1] As you read, you may want to decide in what ways your family is already strong and identify one or two areas in which you want to be stronger.

CHARACTERISTICS OF STRONG, HEALTHY MARRIAGES AND FAMILIES

What makes marriages and families strong and healthy? For years researchers have worked to answer this question. There is now widespread agreement among professionals about the characteristics of strong, healthy families.[2] The research has identified the following nine characteristics: caring and appreciation, time together, encouragement, commitment, communication, adaptive ability, spirituality, community and family ties, and clear responsibilities. It is interesting to note that the principles given in *The Family: A Proclamation to the World* by prophets of God designed to strengthen marriage and family have been supported by years of excellent scholarly research on marriage and family strengths.[3] To illustrate this, in Box 22.1 the nine characteristics discovered through research are linked with corresponding principles found in the Proclamation.

Throughout the rest of the chapter, you'll find each strength listed, with ideas for developing the strength in your family.

Strength #1: Caring and Appreciation

Family members are strengthened by expressions of caring and appreciation. "Strong family members not only love each other; perhaps more important, they also genuinely like each other."[4] Even when a family member makes mistakes, members of strong families find ways to affirm and support each another. They make a conscious effort to develop emotional closeness and show love at home.[5]

Recent national studies revealed that expressions of affection toward children reduce the incidence of problem behaviors and contribute to positive development.[6] Another study shows that unkindness was the strongest predictor of lowered family life satisfaction.[7] Other studies document that a husband's expression of appreciation for his wife is, by far, the strongest predictor of the wife's sense of fairness and satisfaction with how housework and child care are divided in the home.[8] Little wonder that the Lord commanded families to "live together in love" (D&C 42:45). Here's an activity that will help you foster love at home:

Caring Days. Love in families needs constant feeding if it is expected to last. To nurture love, we would

LINKING THE STRONG, HEALTHY FAMILIES MODEL DISCUSSED IN RESEARCH
WITH THE PRINCIPLES IN THE PROCLAMATION ON THE FAMILY

STRONG, HEALTHY FAMILIES MODEL	THE FAMILY: A PROCLAMATION TO THE WORLD
Caring and Appreciation	Families show forgiveness, respect, compassion, loving and caring for each other.
Time Together	Wholesome recreational activities strengthen families.
Encouragement	Parents teach children to love and to serve one another; teach them to be law-abiding, good citizens.
Commitment	Spouses have a solemn responsibility to love and care for each other and their children; spouses should honor marital vows with complete fidelity.
Communication	The processes of parents teaching and rearing children in righteousness, family members loving and serving one another and sharing wholesome recreational activities are fostered by good communication.
Adaptive Ability	Circumstances of life may necessitate individual adaptation.
Spirituality	Family success is tied to living principles of the gospel such as faith, prayer, and repentance; marriage and family is ordained of God; families have a sacred duty to observe the commandments of God and to understand the divine and eternal nature and purpose of families.
Community and Family Ties	Extended family supports and helps nuclear family and vice versa; parents teach children to be law-abiding citizens.
Clear Responsibilities	Family responsibilities include work; fathers are to preside; mothers' primary responsibility is to nurture; there is equal partnership between spouses; gender is an essential eternal characteristic.

Box 22.1

be wise to get into the habit of sending messages of love several times a day. But we need to communicate these messages of love in a language the other understands. So, it's important to first find out from our loved ones what communicates love to them and then to send those messages often. Otherwise, the intended love-messages may not be received as such.

One way to learn to speak each other's love language is "Caring Days." This activity was first

introduced by therapist Richard Stuart and has been clinically shown to strengthen marriages.[9] Here's how to do it.

First, sit down with your spouse and select, discuss, and agree on 18 behaviors or actions (nine each) that you find loving and would like to receive from him or her. These actions must be

1. Specific (such as "Tell me you love me at least once a day")

2. Positive (not "Don't do this" or "Stop doing that")

3. Small enough to be done on a daily basis (such as "Call me at work during lunch, just to see how I'm doing") and

4. Not the subject of any recent conflict.

Second, agree to doing five of the actions on the Caring Days list each day, regardless of whether or not your spouse follows through. Even if your spouse doesn't follow through right away, be patient and persist in doing the actions.

Third, put the list of actions in a conspicuous place, such as on the refrigerator door. The actions will be listed in the middle column, with your name and your spouse's name listed at the top of the left and right columns. When you receive a requested action from your spouse, place the date next to the specific action. This visual reminder helps reinforce the actions. Some couples have listed actions like "Take me on a date each Friday night," "Hold my hand when we sit together," "Tell me you love me at least once each day," and "Give me at least three hugs each day."

Persist in doing five actions per day for two weeks, so that sending these messages of love begins to become a habit. At the end of two weeks, evaluate how your relationship has changed because of the activity.

You can adapt Caring Days so that the whole family can be involved. For a family home evening activity on love, each of you make a list of the many things that people do to make you feel loved. Share your lists with each other, then hang them up in a conspicuous place so all can see them. Then begin having Caring Days. Perhaps your preschooler told you that "building sandcastles in the sandbox with me" makes him or her feel loved. Before your child asks you, take him or her out to build sandcastles.

Most people are not good at reading the minds of their loved ones. Thus, having them tell us what makes them feel loved, and then doing it, can go a long way in fostering love at home.

Strength #2: Time Together

When 1,500 school children were asked what they thought made a happy family, they didn't list things like money, cars, or other material things. The answer they gave most often, according to family strengths researchers Nick Stinnett and John DeFrain, was doing things together.[10] In two national studies,

joint activities and family outings were associated with fewer problem behaviors in children and, subsequently, as young adults.[11] An influential researcher, John Gottman, found that couples who continued to improve their relationship following his marriage workshops were devoting an extra five hours a week to their relationship.[12] He calls this time "The Magic Five Hours." During this time, couples attended to four things: learning one thing about your spouse's life that day, having a stress-reducing conversation at the end of each workday, doing something every day to show genuine affection and appreciation, and having a weekly date.

True "quality" time needed for marriages and families emerges from spending adequate "quantities" of time with each other. Family members should be "anxiously engaged" (D&C 58:27) in the good cause of giving families their time, sharing together many wholesome recreational activities. Here are some ideas to foster this strength at home:

Mealtime. Today, families spend less time eating together than in previous generations. Many family experts recommend that families eat together at least one meal each day.[13] Turn off the television and put all other cares aside. Invite family members to share the day's experiences, their interests, plans, and ideas. Tell jokes and share funny stories. Avoid talking about disciplinary matters—addressing them at mealtime creates more indigestion than solutions. Instead, reserve these things for private interviews and family councils.

After the meal, instead of running off to other activities, try lingering awhile around the table for relaxed and pleasant conversation. Let family members know that mealtime is a family occasion.

During or after the meal, have each member "earn" their dessert by telling something interesting or funny about his or her day or by sharing a new joke, an experience from the past, or something nice about someone else in the family.

Just the Two of Us. Make a point to spend one-on-one time with each child at least once each month. Brainstorm the kinds of activities you'd like to do together and how much time and money (if any) each activity will take. At the beginning of the month, such as during family council, mark the date and activity on the calendar.

Continue Courtship. The best gift parents can give their children is to love each other. President Spencer W. Kimball taught that marital love is like a flower and needs regular feeding if it is to last. One way to foster this love is to follow the counsel of Church leaders and schedule a weekly date night with your spouse, or at least a bi-weekly date.[14] No Children are Allowed. Double dates usually don't count because they are primarily social occasions with friends. Reserve some time and do something fun. Nurture the feelings and friendship that first ignited your love for one another.

Strength #3: Encouragement

As the Proclamation states, each family member is a son or daughter of God, endowed with divine destiny and purpose (¶ 2). Couples and families that practice encouragement have this realization and do things to promote one another's growth and development toward their full potential. They structure family life so that members can develop intellectually, physically, spiritually, and socially.

You'll find encouragement-oriented couples and families developing skills, participating in extracurricular activities, and celebrating one another's successes and growth. They structure the home environment so that parents and children can pursue individual activities such as hobbies, homework, reading, and other activities. They structure family time to allow for relationships and growth activities outside the family. One national study found that encouragement of independence is associated with fewer behavior problems among youth.[15]

There are many ways to foster encouragement at home:

Discovering Talents. The Lord has declared that "to every man is given a gift" (D&C 46:11). You might hold a family home evening to help family members discover their gifts or talents. Help them understand the purpose for talents—"that all may be profited thereby" (D&C 46:12). On a sheet of paper, have family members list things they feel they are good at. In addition to obvious talents such as music or athletics, help them be aware that skills such as listening and being compassionate are also talents that should be celebrated and that can be developed. During this activity, parents can also point out talents or abilities they have seen in their children of which children may not be aware.

Encourage family members to develop their talents. Have them select a talent they would like to work on during a specified period of time. Provide opportunities for all to share their talents inside and outside the home, "that all may be profited thereby."

Strength Bombardment. At the dinner table or during a family home evening, take turns sharing with each other the positive traits that make each family member special. Focusing on assets and strengths helps build feelings of self and family worth.

Encouraging Words. Sometimes life gets rough and we need all the encouragement we can get. An encouraging word from a family member can really come in handy. Think of some things you might say to a family member, like these:

"Good luck on your exam!"

"Smile! You look great in braces!"

"You are great with your hands. You'll do well on that science project."

Put the words on sticky notes or on 3x5 cards. Tuck or stick them in places where they can be found, such as on bathroom mirrors, in briefcases, shirt pockets, or other places.

Strength #4: Commitment

Strong families are committed families. Committed couples and families have a sense of being a team and they work together to preserve couple and family well-being. Often, outside pressures (such as work) threaten to remove family from its proper priority. When such pressures occur, committed family members will take action and make those sacrifices that are necessary to preserve family well-being.[16] In national studies, higher levels of parental commitment to marriage and family were associated with lower incidence of behavior problems and parent–child conflict among children and adolescents.[17] Couples who are personally dedicated to the health of their marriage are far more likely to be happy with their relationship.[18] Commitments based on eternal covenants transcend feelings of love which may wax and wane, enabling and encouraging us to stay devoted to one another even during the hard times.

There are many ways to foster commitment at home:

Renewing Marriage Vows. Reviewing vows made at marriage can build commitment. If you have a temple marriage, participate in sealings of husbands and wives at a temple. Sit together in the celestial room or sealing room (with permission) and reverently review the marital covenants you have made and the blessings they have brought into your relationship. You might want to do this for your anniversary. If your marriage was performed outside a temple, take time together on a special occasion such as an anniversary and review the vows you made to one another. You might want to invite a few family members or friends over to witness the occasion and afterward hold an informal reception.

Discovering and Enhancing Family Traditions. A family tradition is an activity or event that occurs with regularity and holds special meaning to a family. Family traditions promote feelings of warmth and unity. A fun activity is to identify and evaluate traditions you now have and make plans to add new ones.

Have someone act as scribe and list your family's traditions. Some family members may disagree on which things are traditions. List as many as you can think of. You may have more than you realized. Some traditions are such a part of family life that you may not think of them right away, like pancakes on the weekend or family prayer morning and night.

Go over your list and discuss how much you enjoy these traditions. Are there some you'd like to do more? Are there some that are no longer enjoyable? If there are any you decide to drop, cross them off the list. Put a star by any you'd like to do more often.

Finally, list anything you'd like to add as a family tradition. It can be anything your family does that makes family time special. Let your imagination soar. One father suggested "Midnight Pancakes" so that he could stay better connected to his dating teens. Keep the list handy in a visible area for a few days to see if you think of anything else.

Strength #5: Communication

Strong families communicate. They take time to talk and listen to one another. They share their hopes and dreams, feelings and concerns. Good communication in families is vital. In one national study, strong parent–child communication was associated with fewer behavior problems, higher ratings on school behavior, and less delinquent behavior, depression, and drug use.[19] Communication problems, especially unresolved conflict, predict unhappiness in marriage better than complaints in other areas.[20] The scriptures admonish us toward good communication (see Matt. 5:37; 1 Cor. 15:33; Eph. 4:29; Col. 3:8, 4:6). There are many ways to foster good communication at home:

Take Talk Time. Sometimes we get so busy that we get out of touch. Make the time to talk. Turn off the TV and have a conversation about something. Talk about feelings and experiences while riding in the car, working in the yard, or doing the dishes. Encourage family members to share by saying things like "Tell me more" and "Wow! What a great (scary, etc.) experience."

Try playing a talking game at dinnertime or other times set aside for just conversing. On small pieces of paper, write fun questions you'd like family members to answer, like "What age would you like to be?" and "If I were an animal, I would like to be . . ." or more serious ones, such as "What are you most deeply afraid of? Why?"

Listening with the Head and Heart. This involves listening beyond words to the meanings and feelings attached to them. Practice head-and-heart listening when family members speak with you about their day:

1. Give full attention. Put aside lectures, reactions, feelings, perceptions, and judgments, eliminate distractions, and try to see the world through his or her eyes.

2. Acknowledge feelings by saying things like "You must have been embarrassed" or "This is really important to you."

3. Invite more discussion. Often, acknowledging a person with a simple "Oh . . . Mmm . . . I see" is enough.

4. Show understanding by paraphrasing. This is the process of restating or reflecting (not parroting) the essence of or feelings embedded in what the other person has said. It can be especially useful when trying to help a person get to the heart of a problem. For instance, "It sounds as though you felt really discouraged when your teacher didn't take your opinions seriously. Is that right?"

Strength #6: Adaptive Ability

Strong families develop predictable routines, roles, and rules that govern everyday life and provide for continuity and stability. However, they make sure that these patterns remain flexible enough to cope with everyday and unexpected stressors and strains that may require changes in the way a family normally operates.[21] In one national study, family adaptability was associated with fewer behavior problems among children aged 10 to 17.[22]

The following activities may help you foster adaptive ability at home:

Accentuate the Positive. Because of their transgression, Adam and Eve were commanded to change residences permanently (see Moses 4:31). Notice, however, their insights as they adapted to these stresses. Adam said: "*Because of my transgression* my eyes are opened, and in this life I shall have joy" (Moses 5:10, emphasis added). Then Eve added: "*Were it not for our transgression* we never should have had seed, and never should have known good and evil, and the joy of our redemption, and the eternal life which God giveth unto all the obedient" (Moses 5:11, emphasis added). Adam's and Eve's sorrow at departing the Garden apparently became part of their rejoicing later on. The Lord encourages us to "Be of good cheer" regardless of our life circumstances and challenges.

Families are more adaptive when they see the positive in stressful situations. Begin a family home evening discussion by stating that we are told by Lehi that there is opposition in all things (see 2 Ne. 2:11) yet are admonished by the Lord to "be of good cheer" (John 16:33). Make a list of daily (doing routine chores, dealing with traffic, etc.) and unexpected (natural disasters, death) events that can be stressful. Then complete the phrase with a positive statement about what could be gained from the experience: "Because of (insert the event), (positive statement). For instance, "because of Dad's heart surgery, I had to learn to chop wood, which was fun."

What Would We Do If . . . During a family home evening or another time, discuss severe stresses and crises faced by individuals and families in scripture, such as Job's catastrophic personal and family experiences, Lehi's family leaving Jerusalem, or Adam's and Eve's expulsion from the Garden. Then discuss hypothetical situations relating to your own family, prefaced by the statement "What would we do if. . . ." For example, What would we do if: the house burned down; Dad were seriously ill; Mom were seriously ill; Grandma needed to come live with us; we had to move to another town? Choose one of these events and write down the changes that would take place and the adjustments each family member would need to make for the family to adapt well.

In addition to stories from scripture, television and movies can be a catalyst for discussions about crises. Consider crises portrayed in dramas and ask, "What can a person (family) do in this situation? Who could help? What did this person (family) do that helped or hindered?"

Strength #7: Spirituality

Research has shown that strong families have a strong spiritual/religious orientation. They believe in something greater than themselves and agree about what is right and wrong. Religious commitment and religious practices such as prayer help protect youth from a variety of negative behaviors, such as substance use and premature sexual involvement.[23] Top and Chadwick surveyed Latter-day Saint youth and found that religiosity, independent of peer influences, has a significant effect on youth behavior. Of the measures of religiosity, "private religiosity," consisting of private religious behavior (e.g., personal prayer and personal scripture study), religious beliefs (e.g., a belief that God lives and Jesus is the Christ), and spiritual experiences (e.g., feelings from the Holy Ghost) were the strongest deterrent to delinquent behavior, defined as fighting, smoking, drinking, petting, sex, vandalism, stealing, and truancy.[24] Religious couples report being happier in their marriages and have a lower rate of divorce.[25] The Lord and His prophets have long admonished us to engage in practices that can bring spirituality into family life, such as family prayer, family scripture study, and family home evening. Activities that foster spirituality at home include the following:

Spiritual Practices at Home. During a family council, make a list of things you want to do in your family on a regular basis to build spiritual strength. This list might include things like family home evening, family prayer, family scripture study and other uplifting reading, attending church, caring for the needy, or using a mild voice when speaking to each other. Choose one or two practices and begin working on them until they become a habit. Then move on to other practices.

Bridling Anger. Anger experts say that anger develops more often in the family—in marriage and with children—than in any other human relationship. While anger may be viewed as a normal emotion, in fact contention is of the devil and should be done away with (see 3 Ne. 11:29–30). The prophet Alma counseled his son to "bridle all your passions, that ye may be filled with love" (Alma 38:12).

During a family home evening or other discussion, read the Lord's admonition about anger and contention, and Alma's counsel to bridle all our passions (which includes anger). Then talk about bridles, whether you are a horseman or not. All bridles serve to lead a horse to where you want it to go. As much as we like horses, few of us would be willing to ride one (especially a wild one) without a bridle. Mention that anger is like an unbridled wild horse. Unless we harness it, we are at its mercy. Next, list and discuss ways to effectively bridle anger, such as counting slowly to 10, breathing deeply, praying, splashing cold water on the face, taking a walk, chopping wood, listening to music, increasing humility, and other approaches that have a calming influence. Challenge family members to use one or more of these practices the next time they become angry.

Strength #8: Community and Family Ties

Strong families don't cloister themselves; they are closely involved with extended families and friends, schools, churches, and local organizations that promote the well-being of individuals and communities. That is, they are in the world, but not of the world (see John 17:15–16). Three national studies found that social connectedness is associated with less problem behavior among the young.[26] Gospel teachings encourage strong relationships with extended family, friendship, neighborliness, and community involvement. There are a number of ways to foster community and family ties:

Note Night. Choose from a list of relatives and friends one who is "note-able" and write that person or family a brief note. Make it fun. Tell about funny happenings as well as more serious stuff.

Community Involvement. Often, issues affecting entire communities are decided with little input from citizens. Church leaders periodically encourage the Saints to be involved in strengthening communities. As a family, attend a community meeting such as a school board meeting or community planning board meeting. Get the agenda beforehand and prepare verbal and written comments to share. This will reinforce participatory democracy, beginning with your family!

School Connections. Recent research has found a strong connection between parents' tendency to be less involved after kids get to high school and lower high school student achievement.[27] Find ways to stay involved in your child's education until the end of their education. Share a talent in the classroom, attend parent–teacher conferences, support school events, and participate in school policy-making. Make your home a learning place. Show your children you love to learn. Have children write down their academic goals. Discuss and agree on rules about homework.

Strength #9: Clear Responsibilities

Members of strong families have a clear idea about their day-to-day responsibilities in and to the family.[28] However, responsibilities are flexible, so that they can be adapted in times of need. For instance, it's okay for someone who usually cooks to take over fixing the car and vice versa because of a need or even boredom.

Many responsibilities are shared. For example, strong families make decisions, solve family problems, and do family work together. Everyone participates. Marriage relationships are based on equality, although the husband may take the major leadership responsibility in some areas and the wife in others.

Connected to clear responsibilities is the issue of power, specifically the manner in which parents carry out their leadership responsibilities in the home. In strong families, there is a clear recognition that the parents are in charge. However, they share power through seeking input from their children—they are rarely viewed as coercive.[29] They adopt an "authoritative" approach to parenting, characterized by love, warmth, having clear and consistent expectations, and avoiding severe or harsh discipline. Numerous studies show that authoritative parenting is associated with a variety of positive child outcomes.[30]

The Proclamation teaches that fathers are to preside over, provide for, and protect the family; and mothers' primary responsibility is to nurture the children. The Lord charges parents to bring up their children in righteousness (see D&C 68:25–28), using means that are in harmony with gospel principles (see D&C 121:41–44). Here are some ideas for fostering the clear responsibilities strength at home:

Family Councils. Long recommended by Church leaders and family experts alike, family councils provide a choice opportunity for clarifying family responsibilities and expectations. Family councils can be used to set goals, distribute household work, resolve family problems, and celebrate one another's successes. When councils are conducted properly, they allow each person to voice his or her opinions and feelings and be involved in solving problems and making decisions.

Schedule a regular time for family councils, say each Sunday. Councils shouldn't always be used to air concerns and solve problems. Try to talk about fun things, too—like planning family activities. Set and follow an agenda. Rotate conducting responsibilities between parents and older children. Prior to the council, encourage family members to write down things they want on the agenda for discussion. You might post a large piece of paper on the refrigerator or a bulletin board for this.

Set ground rules for the council such as (1) everyone is free to express his or her opinions and feelings without fear of being blamed or insulted, and (2) everyone is expected to listen to what is being said. Interruptions are not allowed. Limit the council to an hour, and end on a cheerful note—with a joke or with refreshments.

Panic Pick-Up. To help family members share the responsibility for keeping the home tidy, announce a "Panic Pickup." Assign family members to their work stations or tasks. Set a timer for 10 minutes and shout "go!" The goal is to get as much done as quickly and as efficiently as possible before the buzzer goes off.

Job Jar. Use a job jar to distribute household chores fairly among family members. Make a list of chores that family members can help to do. Mark a "W" next to weekly chores and a "D" next to daily chores. Cut construction paper into "chore" strips. Write one chore per slip—daily chores on red strips and weekly chores on blue strips. Put the chores into a screw top jar or cookie jar. Decide how long each chore duty should be: one week, two weeks, etc. Decide how many strips of each color family members should draw for each chore period. Tasks should reflect the varying ages and abilities of family members.

CELEBRATE YOUR MARRIAGE AND FAMILY STRENGTHS

Spend some time together identifying your marriage and family strengths. Then celebrate them. From the foundation of existing strengths, chose one or two additional strengths to work on as a family. Become involved in activities that will help your family build those strengths. Latter-day Saints believe in eternal progression. Eternally progressing in building couple and family strengths is one of the most important ways to serve God and each other.

NOTES

1. S. F. Duncan (1997), *The activity book: Activities for building family strengths* (Bozeman: Montana State University Extension Service); S. F. Duncan (1998), *Building family strengths* (Bozeman: Montana State University Extension Service); T. R. Lee (1988), *Family connections: Keys to strengthen family life* (Logan: Utah Cooperative Extension Service); H. W. Goddard and M. Morgan (1995), *The great self mystery* (Auburn: Alabama Cooperative Extension Service); N. Stinnett and J. DeFrain (1985), *Secrets of strong families* (Boston: Little, Brown, and Co.); T. Day, S. Small,

and E. Fitzsimmons (1987), *Family times* (Madison: Wisconsin Clearinghouse); R. B. Stuart (1980), *Helping couples change: A social learning approach to marital therapy* (New York: Guilford Press).

2. M. Krysan, K. A. Moore, and N. Zill (1990), *Identifying successful families: An overview of constructs and selected measures* (Washington, D.C.: Child Trends); J. DeFrain and N. Stinnett (1992), Building on the inherent strengths of families: A positive approach for family psychologists and counselors, *Topics in Family Psychology and Counseling, 1*(1), 15–26.

3. See Krysan et al. (1990).

4. DeFrain and Stinnett (1992), 20.

5. H. A. Otto (1975), *The use of family strength concepts and methods in family life education: A handbook* (Beverly Hills, CA: Holistic Press); D. H. Olson, H. McCubbin, H. Barnes, M. Muxen, and M. Wilson (1983), *Families: What makes them work?* (Beverly Hills, CA: Sage); D. Curran (1983), *Traits of a healthy family* (Minneapolis: Winston Press).

6. K. A. Moore (1993), *Family strengths and youth behavior problems: Analyses of three national survey data bases* (Washington, D.C.: Child Trends).

7. T. R. Lee, W. R. Burr, I. F. Beutler, F. Yorgason, H. B. Harker, and J. A. Olsen (1997), The family profile II: A self-scored, brief family assessment tool, *Psychological Reports, 81,* 467–477.

8. A. J. Hawkins, C. M. Marshall, and S. M. Allen (1998), The orientation toward domestic labor questionnaire: Exploring dual-earner wives' sense of fairness about family work, *Journal of Family Psychology, 12*(2), 244–258.

9. Stuart (1980); C. W. LeCroy, P. Carrol, H. Nelson-Becker, and P. Sturlaugson (1989), An experimental evaluation of the caring days technique for marital enrichment, *Family Relations, 38,* 15–18.

10. Stinnett and DeFrain (1985).

11. Moore (1993).

12. J. M. Gottman (1999), *The seven principles for making marriage work* (New York: Crown Publishers).

13. W. J. Doherty (1997), *The intentional family: How to build family ties in our modern world* (Reading, MA: Addison-Wesley).

14. Spencer W. Kimball (1978), *Marriage* (Salt Lake City: Deseret Book).

15. B. V. Brown (1993), *Family functioning and adolescent behavior problems: An analysis of the national survey of families and households* (Washington, D.C.: Child Trends).

16. N. Stinnett (1986), Prepared statement before House Select Committee on Children, Youth, and Families, in *The diversity and strength of American families* (Washington, D.C.: U.S. Government Printing Office); cited in Krysan et al. (1990).

17. Brown (1993).

18. S. M. Stanley and H. J. Markman (1997), *Marriage in the 90s: A nationwide random phone survey* (Denver, CO: PREP).

19. B. W. Sugland (1993), *The effect of family strengths on youth behavior: An analysis of the national survey of children* (Washington, D.C.: Child Trends).

20. P. Noller and M. A. Fitzpatrick (1990), Marital communication in the eighties, *Journal of Marriage and the Family, 52,* 832–843; H. J. Markman, S. M. Stanley, and S. L. Blumberg (1994), *Fighting for your marriage* (San Francisco: Jossey-Bass).

21. D. H. Olson, C. S. Russell, and D. H. Sprenkle (Eds.)

(1989), *Circumplex model: Systematic assessment and treatment of families* (New York: Haworth Press).

22. Sugland (1993).

23. M. D. Resnick et al. (1997), Protecting adolescents from harm: Findings from the national longitudinal study on adolescent health, *Journal of the American Medical Association, 278,* 823–832.

24. B. L. Top and B. A. Chadwick (1998), *Rearing righteous youth of Zion* (Salt Lake City: Deseret Book).

25. Markman et al. (1994).

26. Brown (1993); Sugland (1993); D. R. Morrison and D. Glei (1993), *Assessing family strengths in the national longitudi-nal survey of youth–child supplement* (Washington, D.C.: Child Trends).

27. L. Steinberg, B. B. Brown, and S. M. Dornbusch (1996), *Beyond the classroom: Why school reform has failed and what parents need to do* (New York: Simon & Schuster).

28. Krysan et al. (1990); N. B. Epstein, L. M. Baldwin, and D. S. Bishop (1983), The McMaster family assessment device, *Journal of Marital and Family Therapy, 9*(2), 171–180.

29. J. M. Lewis (1979), *How's your family? A guide to identifying your family's strengths and weaknesses* (New York: Brunner/Mazel).

30. See C. A. Smith, D. Cudaback, H. W. Goddard, and

IDEAS FOR KEEPING THE SABBATH HOLY AS A FAMILY

E. JEFFREY HILL

While most Latter-day Saints can easily think of the ways to keep the Sabbath holy as an individual, it takes creativity, flexibility, and joint commitment to keep the Sabbath holy together as a couple or family. What follows is a broad spectrum of ideas for parents to consider as they plan family time together on the Sabbath. It is hoped that readers may find some of these ideas helpful as they plan to keep the Sabbath holy as a family.

A. *Make the Family Sabbath Different from All Other Days*

1. Wear Sabbath clothes all day. Exactly what is worn is less important than that the clothes are somehow different from everyday clothes.

2. To distinguish the Sabbath from other days, many families do not watch TV, except for certain religious programs (like general conference). If you choose to watch television, do not watch everyday television programs. Six days provide more than enough time to watch all the sports, action, drama, variety, and comedy that one could want.

3. Spend the Sabbath together with family members. Many families believe Sunday is a day for children to play with their siblings and parents, not with friends.

4. For young children, set aside a number of quiet Sabbath toys that are not played with on any other day.

5. Play special Sabbath music which is not played on other days. Refrain from playing everyday music.

B. *Worship the Lord Together as a Family*

1. Pray together. On the Sabbath, some families have special family prayers where each person in the family may be the voice.

2. Give father's blessings. Turn the hearts of fathers and children toward each other through the power of the holy priesthood.

3. Read the scriptures with family members. One family has a tradition that each child read the Book of Mormon before they are baptized at age eight. On many Sabbaths this family reads with this child to reach this goal.

4. Study the scriptures together as a family. Pause on one verse and liken it to your family. Think of all of its potential applications to the family.

5. Parents can read patriarchal blessings with their children and talk about the guidance they contain.

6. Write a sacrament meeting talk and give the talk to family members.

7. Purchase copies of the Book of Mormon and have each family member write his or her

testimony on a paper to be affixed inside the front cover, perhaps with a photograph of the writer or the family. Ask each family member to share their written testimony. Give the books to the full-time missionaries (perhaps with cookies made by the family).

C. Bring the Power of Fasting into Your Home

1. Begin your fast by eating a meal together as a family on Saturday afternoon/evening, discussing common purposes for the upcoming fast, and then beginning the fast with a kneeling family prayer.
2. Remind each other throughout the fast day of your family fasting purposes.
3. On fast Sunday, have a family testimony meeting. As children observe their own parents bear testimony, and have the opportunity to do so themselves, their testimony of the gospel will grow and family bonds will be strengthened.
4. In the spirit of fasting, the patriarch of the family may want to give a father's blessing to each child on the fast Sunday after his or her birthday.
5. Break the fast by kneeling in a family prayer and praying sincerely about the purposes of the fast. Ask children what they feel prompted to do as a result of their fasting.

D. Build Your Eternal Marriage Relationship

1. Read and discuss the scriptures together with your spouse, relating them to your marriage.
2. Read and discuss conference talks and *Ensign* articles, especially those about marriage.
3. Set couple goals for the next week/month/year/decade/century/eternity.
4. Envision your marriage 15 years from now. Write a detailed journal entry taken from your journal in that year (e.g., if it is now 2001, then the entry would be from 2016).
5. Take a walk and let your spouse talk about anything he or she wants. Focus on being a listener and not a speaker.
6. Read old love letters together, written during your courtship and the first years of marriage.
7. Write love letters to your spouse, to be opened on certain days of the coming week.
8. Look through journals, photo albums, and videotapes of your courtship and marriage.
9. Take a nap with your spouse.

E. Create One-on-One Time, Parents with Children

1. Go for a walk together with a child and talk about whatever the child wants to talk about. Be a good listener.
2. Knock on the child's bedroom door and go in and sit down and just listen.
3. Sit down alone with a child and help him or her set goals for the coming week/month/year.
4. Have a formal monthly stewardship interview with each child.
5. For a sensitive matter, give a private father's blessing to a concerned child.

F. Connecting with the Family's Forebears

1. Read or tell stories to the children about their ancestors.
2. Create a four-generation pedigree chart with each child.
3. On a map, place tacks and labels to indicate where ancestors were born and died.
4. Make a dinner with food from the country of a particular ancestor.
5. Gather conversion stories of ancestors encountering the gospel and accepting it as the truth restored.
6. Research which ancestors have served Church missions and when. Gather missionary stories from their experiences.

G. Connect with Living Family Members Who Are Not at Home

1. Gather the family around a speaker phone and call grandparents, parents, spouse, siblings, uncles, aunts, cousins, children, grandchildren, etc.
2. Write a family letter to family members who are missionaries or for other reasons away from home.
3. Put together a "care package" to mail to family members who are away.

H. Serve Others as a Family on the Sabbath

1. Go to a retirement home and present a family fireside, musical program, or just talk to the residents.
2. Make a treat together and deliver it as a family to those in the neighborhood.
3. Go to the hospital together to visit friends, relatives, or ward members who are there.

4. Make a family quilt together for the Church's humanitarian aid projects.

5. Invite a less active, part-member, non-member, or new family over for Sunday dinner or dessert.

6. Contact a local soup kitchen or homeless shelter to inquire about activities (such as serving a meal or helping with laundry) that would give your family an opportunity to serve.

7. Call ward members and offer to give them a ride with your family to church meetings, stake conference, or a fireside.

8. Invite recent converts to join your family for a televised conference and dinner, or dessert.

9. Invite the full-time missionaries to join the family for dinner and ask the junior companion to teach a missionary discussion to the family, if their schedule permits.

I. Create a Shared Family History

1. Write a family history, writing about key family highlights from the parents' courtship to the present day.

2. Together bring family scrapbooks and photo albums up-to-date.

3. Have each family member bring his or her journal and share one personally meaningful entry.

4. Renew family memories by going through photo albums or watching family videos.

5. Near birthdays, share your journal entries from when the birthday child was born.

6. Ask each family member to answer this question: "What is one moment when our family was very close?"

J. Plan for the Future

1. Hold a weekly couple/family planning meeting where each individual can address his or her needs and wants.

2. Make a list of one hundred things the couple and family wants to do in the next 50 years.

3. Set family goals related to temple work, missionary work, and perfecting the Saints.

K. Relate the Gospel to Young Children in Age-Appropriate Ways

1. Act out scripture stories (e.g., finger puppets, charades).

2. Play scripture trivia games.

3. Leisurely read the scriptures, letting young readers speak the words they recognize.

4. Put together "Sunday" jigsaw puzzles (e.g., temples, prophets, gospel prints).

5. Help children choose to fast to the degree appropriate for their age (a five-year-old might choose to fast one meal; an eight year-old might choose to fast two meals; a 12-year-old might choose to fast 24 hours).

6. Read and talk about *Friend* articles with small children.

7. Read and talk about *New Era* and *Ensign* articles with adolescents.

8. Cut out pictures out of old Church magazines and create a Sabbath collage.

L. Make Sunday Dinner a Family Sabbath Dinner

1. Play peaceful Sabbath music in the background during preparation, eating, and cleanup.

2. Encourage everyone in the family to help prepare the family Sabbath dinner so it is not a burden to anyone.

3. Eat a leisurely family Sabbath dinner and feed the soul with conversation and thanksgiving, not just the belly with food.

4. Ask what each person learned in Sunday School, Primary, Relief Society, priesthood, Young Women, Young Men, and sacrament meeting.

5. Ask family members about their best experience of the day.

6. Linger at the table and talk about anything that is important to family members

7. Encourage everyone in the family to help with clean up, so that everyone can keep the spirit of the Sabbath.

M. Worship the Lord As a Family with Music

1. As a family, sing along with recorded hymns and primary songs (even if one or more family members have difficulty staying in tune).

2. Select a hymn to be learned by the family during the course of the week. Offer a family reward for learning all of the verses. Sing the hymn of the week as family members gather for morning and evening prayers.

3. Gather around the piano and sing hymns and other sacred music.

4. If family members play musical instruments, gather everyone together and perform

arrangements of the hymns or other sacred music.

5. Make a list of fun family songs and sing them.
6. Play and sing along with a recording of Handel's *Messiah* vocally and instrumentally.
7. Compose and sing your own family hymn.

You may wish to sing this hymn weekly and write a new verse each year.

N. Read Good Books Together as a Family

1. Read an inspirational classic book out loud, as a family.
2. Read inspirational biographies.

Six Characteristics of a Family-Friendly Ward

E. Jeffrey Hill

Introduction

In recent years Church leaders have emphasized the importance and eternal destiny of families and the need for special care to be given to family responsibilities. Though Church doctrine and policy are decidedly pro-family, it is sometimes difficult to balance one's personal and family involvement in the Church with the need to preside, provide, protect, rear, teach and nurture one's family. President Boyd K. Packer explained, "Many members face conflicts as they struggle to balance their responsibility as parents together with faithful activity in the Church."[1] The ward calendar may be so full of activities and meetings that many families may consider the time- demands too much.

This essay offers a few practical thoughts that have been tried in wards and that a ward leadership may consider in an effort to harmonize faithful activity in the Church with essential family needs. Since wards of The Church of Jesus Christ of Latter-day Saints have a rotating lay leadership, many members will have the opportunity to serve in priesthood and auxiliary callings. It is hoped this essay will promote an active and creative response to Church leaders's counsel to preserve and foster family time while planning ward activities. This smorgasbord of suggestions for supporting a balance of Church and family time and activity is grouped into six characteristics of what could be called a family-friendly ward.

Characteristic 1: A Family-Friendly Ward Reserves Time Exclusively for the Family

Keep family home evening sacred. Recently the First Presidency, in a letter to Church members throughout the world, stressed the importance of family time together: "Monday nights are reserved throughout the Church for family home evenings. We encourage members to set aside this time to strengthen family ties and teach the gospel in their homes."[2] Thus, family-friendly wards reserves Monday evenings *exclusively* for families to hold home evenings. Some units have justified gathering families together at the church for an occasional "ward home evening" of fun family activities and refreshments. However, in the same letter, the First Presidency clearly stated, "Church buildings and facilities should be closed on Monday evenings. No ward or stake activities should be planned, and other interruptions to family home evenings should be avoided."[3] In addition to a "zero Monday activity" policy, wards leaders could use their influence with ward members to eliminate church-related phone calls, visits, or other interruptions on Monday night. It is intrusive to be in the middle of a spiritual moment with family and then to receive a phone call to follow up on a church assignment. Of course, an appropriate option is simply not to answer the phone. Family home evening is so essential that perhaps Church members could coordinate efforts to follow the First Presidency's suggestion "to encourage community and school leaders to avoid scheduling activities on Monday evenings that require children or parents to be away from their homes."[4]

Schedule Leadership Meetings at Times of Less Family Impact

A recent First Presidency directive stated, "Wherever possible, Sunday meetings, other than those under the three-hour schedule and perhaps council meetings on early Sunday mornings or firesides later in the evening, should be avoided so that parents may be with their children."[5] For many families, while early Sunday morning may not be a high-quality family time, Sunday afternoon could be. The bishop could consider scheduling ward leadership meetings for the early morning, rather than during prime Sunday afternoon family time. The bishop could also consider not scheduling ward meetings during the hour or so before the three-hour block of meetings. Both parents could then help their children get ready for Sunday meetings. Also, families who live at a distance from church meetings could more easily arrange transportation together, rather than traveling to church in more than one vehicle.

Create Ward "Family Time" Each Sunday

Many large families have had the experience of this father of 10: "We were disheartened to realize that except for Sacrament meeting there was not a single waking hour of the Sabbath when we were all together. The rest of the day there were quorum and class presidency meetings, choir, planning meetings, firesides, home teaching, priesthood interviews, priesthood leadership meeting, etc. One or another of the family was always gone."[6] One solution to this is the creation of "Sunday family time." Sunday family time is similar in purpose to family home evening, except it is during Sunday afternoon or evening instead of Monday evening. During a certain two- or three-hour block, possibly Sunday evenings, there would be no church activity of any kind sponsored by the ward: no meetings, no interviews, no choir, no telephone calls, no home or visiting teaching, no interruptions. This gives every family, including the bishop's family, some regular quality Sabbath time they can count on.

Implement a Monthly Family Sabbath

This is akin to Sunday family time except it potentially creates a 10-hour block of family Sabbath time once a month. During the monthly family Sabbath there would be no church activities at all, except for the Sunday block. All priesthood leadership meetings are canceled. One busy priesthood leader, whose ward practices a family Sabbath, related, "It is so wonderful to be able to count on a whole day of Sabbath activities with my family." During this time, families may wish to study the gospel together, take a family walk, visit the sick together, put together a family scrapbook, call extended family on the speaker phone, write a family letter to missionaries, read Church magazines out loud, take a nap together, or do anything else appropriate to the Sabbath that brings the family together. (See Essay M for further suggestions on Sabbath activities.)

Cut Back on Activities That Separate Families.

President Packer warned, "We must be careful lest programs and activities in the Church become too heavy for some families to carry."[7] To create more family time, a family-friendly ward might initiate a Ward Activity Night each week in which all youth and adult activities and meetings would be held. There could be Mutual, Relief Society Home, Family, and Personal Enrichment Meeting, a nursery, Ward Council meeting, and presidency meetings, all in one weeknight, and then reserve the rest of the nights to be scheduled by families. Meetings with overlapping attendees that do not meet every week could be scheduled to avoid conflicts, where possible. This is often done in far-flung wards where extensive travel requirements necessitates consolidating the number of trips, but could also be adopted in other wards. One ward opted to limit youth activities to once a week. When there is a campout or youth fireside, the weekday activity is canceled.

CHARACTERISTIC 2: A FAMILY-FRIENDLY WARD HAS A FAMILY-FRIENDLY WARD COUNCIL

Put Families First and Calendars Last on the Ward Council Agenda

Speaking of the ward council, President Packer emphasized, "Here Church leaders of the priesthood, themselves fathers, and sisters of the auxiliaries, themselves mothers, can, with inspired insight, coordinate the work of the organizations, each of which serves different members of the family."[8] While serving as bishop, I asked our ward council to take an hour to answer the question, "What can our ward do to strengthen our families?" I told them to think "outside the box" and to generate as many creative ideas as they could. We brainstormed and our executive secretary filled several blackboards with the ideas that came. One exciting suggestion was to use the extensive number of retired couples in our ward to strengthen young struggling families. Several mature couples, who no longer had children of their own at home, could be called as mentors to college-age couples, far from home and often struggling under the weight of several small children and heavy church responsibilities. These mentors could sit with the family at church, care for their children at times, and provide a wholesome example and a calm perspective. Each ward council could produce its own list of possible suggestions.

Plan Ward Activities That Strengthen Marriages and Families

In ward council, leaders could proactively plan activities that provide the opportunity to strengthen marital unions and parent–child relationships. It may plan a ward family talent night, where couples or whole families can perform together. Ward family campouts are especially popular with children. Some wards have established the tradition of a harvest square dance and invite the whole family to the event. The weekend around Valentine's Day might be the perfect time for a couples-only ward activity. Even youth conference can be used to strengthen families. On one occasion our ward included interactive activities for parents and their teenagers in our youth conference. Each day we had the youth and parents read the same *New Era* or *Ensign* article that dealt with parent–teenager interaction. Then we had the parents and teenagers write each other a letter likening the articles to their family. They read their letters individually and then parents and teenagers came together on a daily basis to discuss how to make their families better. There was great dialogue, even in some families where communication had been caustic. It was one of our most successful youth conferences.

CHARACTERISTIC 3: IN A FAMILY-FRIENDLY WARD, CALLINGS ARE IN HARMONY WITH FAMILY LIFE

Take into Consideration the Family When Considering and Extending Callings

President Boyd K. Packer stated, "I *do* want to encourage leaders to carefully consider the home lest they issue calls or schedule activities which place an unnecessary burden on parents and families."[9] For example, it may be burdensome to call both the father and mother of a financially struggling family with young children to serve in Young Men and Young Women. Calling a mother with three preschool children to serve in a large nursery might not be a spiritually renewing experience for her. President Packer also said, "Would our perspective be more clear if we could, for a moment, look upon parenthood as a calling in the Church. Actually, it is so much more than that; but if we could look at it that way for a moment, we could reach a better balance in the way we schedule families."[10]

Provide Opportunity to Serve One's Own Family Members in One's Calling

In a family-friendly ward, members could be given the opportunity for Church stewardship with their own family members. Sons are often called to home teach with their fathers. Mothers are often called to be Achievement Day leaders of their school-age daughters. It might be a good idea to consider calling a scoutmaster who has Scout-age sons. Grandparents with preschool grandchildren could be considered for callings in the Primary. When parents "double-dip" their time, fulfilling both a church calling as well as time with their children, they may do better in their calling and better in nurturing their offspring.

Seek Counsel from One's Family Members in One's Calling

In a family-friend ward husbands and wives appropriately consult with each other and their children about their church callings. As a bishop I found the counsel of my wife to be indispensable. Many times she suggested things that, with the confirmation of the Spirit, we implemented to move the ward forward. Likewise, one's children can have valuable insights for callings in the Primary, Young Men, Young Women, and Sunday School.

Counsel with Parents before Extending Calls to Family Members

A leader should respect the family stewardship in the home. Before calling a son or daughter to be in a quorum or class presidency, leaders should counsel with the parents. My wife and I have greatly appreciated those wards where we were called in together when callings to either of us were extended. All family members should be invited to be present for all ordinances and setting apart for callings (including Aaronic Priesthood quorums and Young Women class presidencies). In addition, it might be a meaningful experience to involve the father the first time a new deacon passes the sacrament, a new teacher prepares the sacrament, or a new priest administers the sacrament.

Implement Flexible Service Arrangements in Church Callings

In the workplace, job sharing has been shown to increase harmony between work and home. The same thing can hold true in the ward. When I was bishop, our ward had many young couples with small children, so we had a large nursery. We had little choice but to call women who had been with their babies all week to come to church and care for other babies in the nursery. To make church more renewing for these couples we implemented "calling sharing." Two couples were called together to fill one position. Now they could attend Sunday School, priesthood, and Relief Society every other week, and on the weeks they were serving they could spend time together as a couple caring for children, something good to learn.

CHARACTERISTIC 4: IN A FAMILY-FRIENDLY WARD THE CHURCH IS INTERWOVEN WITH FAMILIES

Make the Temple a Source of Family Strength

Ward members should be encouraged not only to qualify themselves for temple recommends, but also to participate with family members in sacred temple ordinances. As a bishop, I invited husbands and wives to come together to temple recommend interviews. After interviewing each individually, I would invite them both into my office to kneel together with me in prayer. I would ask the Lord to bless them individually, bless their marriage union, and bless their children. When I knew of particular family challenges (e.g., marital difficulties, a wayward teenager, employment challenges, health concerns), I prayed specifically for the Lord's support in the resolution of these family challenges. Another idea is to invite teenage children to come with their parents to be interviewed for yearly recommends to do baptisms for the dead. This would be a good time to encourage family members to do

family history work so they could go to the temple together to do the work for their ancestors.

Make "Family" the Topic of Regular Church Meetings

Many sacrament meetings, joint priesthood–Relief Society meetings, Young Women and Young Men meetings, and other lessons could be centered on gospel topics related to the family. When planning sacrament meetings, the bishop might call on the children and parents to provide the talks and music together, as a family. The topic of a sacrament meeting talk might be, "What we can learn about parenting from the life and teachings of Jesus." One ward assigned the young men and young women to handle Primary one Sunday so that all the adults of the ward could join together on a fifth Sunday to share a beautiful message about marriage during Sunday School and priesthood–Relief Society time.

Use Various Ward Communication Channels to Strengthen the Family

Put quotes from Church leaders about family life into the weekly ward bulletin and the ward newsletter. Create a family photo ward directory so that ward members can think of each other as families. Instruct the home teachers to deliver a message about families from the most recent general conference. These are just a few examples of messages that could be deliberately circulated to ward members.

Use Tithing Settlement as a Time to Strengthen Families

The bishop may invite the family to attend tithing settlement together and express to the children how blessed they are to have parents who care enough about the commandments to pay a full tithing. He may share with them why the blessings of tithing are important to families and conclude with prayer, in which he calls down the blessings of heaven upon this family.

Support the Bishop in Taking Time for His Own Family.

A bishop must be an example that, even though he is very busy doing important church work, his most important work is with his own family within the walls of his own home. He makes the time to support his own children. He makes the time to have a date with his wife each week. He is as involved as he can be in his own family life. He lets the members of the ward know they are important but that it is even more important for him to foster the eternal relationships in his own home. Ward members work to support the bishop in having time for his family responsibilities.

CHARACTERISTIC 5: A FAMILY-FRIENDLY WARD IS ALSO FRIENDLY TO SINGLE ADULTS AND THOSE WITH FAMILY CHALLENGES

Because of death, disability, divorce, or other circumstances, many families no longer have a father, or in some cases a mother, in the home. Some have never had the opportunity or have chosen not to marry. Others have parents who are not active or struggle with wayward children. In a family-friendly ward, all are embraced in the love of the gospel of Jesus Christ.

A family-friendly ward provides fathers for the fatherless and mothers for the motherless through both formal and informal means. Caring home teachers in such homes make more than monthly courtesy calls. They actually support the family by playing with the kids out in the yard, encouraging their talents, and attending activities such as music recitals and ball games. Other families, without a formal assignment, look to fill needs in areas like home maintenance, sharing physical resources, and being an emotional support. For the growing number of Saints who have not had the opportunity to have children, opportunities are provided to serve in callings where "parental" skills are employed (e.g., Primary, Young Men, Young Women, Sunday School, etc.). As we make the Church more "family friendly," we must make sure we do not make it unfriendly to others.

CHARACTERISTIC 6: A FAMILY-FRIENDLY WARD REACHES OUT TO THE COMMUNITY.

Finally, a family-friendly ward creates a caring community of Saints who foster initiatives to strengthen their communities. They reach out to other families. They "keep an eye" on things in the neighborhood. When they observe teenagers involved in unlawful or immoral behavior, they care enough to call the parents in a loving way to let them know

what's going on. They may provide a "neighborhood watch" to protect the community from the insidious clutches of drugs and crime. They join with families of other faiths to work for common causes that support the safety and morality of the community.

PARTING WORDS

President Packer explained that the only time the Lord used the word *rebuke* to chasten the Prophet Joseph Smith was when he failed to teach his children (see D&C 93:47–48).[11] Had I been Joseph Smith at that time I might have justified putting my family on hold for awhile because I was extremely busy doing important church work. After all, I could have said I was busy prophesying the American Civil War (see D&C 87), receiving the Olive Leaf (see D&C 88), revealing the Word of Wisdom (see D&C 89), and taking steps toward organizing the First Presidency (see D&C 90 and 92), all while preparing an inspired translation of the Old Testament (see D&C 91). Yet, apparently, Joseph was also expected to be teaching his children. If the head of the dispensation of the fulness of times was expected to make time to teach his children, then we ought to do the same. Whatever else our stewardship in the kingdom may be, it should not get in the way of our family responsibilities. Creating a family-friendly ward can help us all move along the right path toward perpetuating family relationships beyond the grave. And as the First Presidency emphasized, "As we strengthen families, we will strengthen the entire Church."[12]

NOTES

1. Boyd K. Packer (1998, November), Parents in Zion, *Ensign, 28*(11), 22.

2. The First Presidency (1999, October 4), Letter to members of the Church throughout the world, 1.

3. The First Presidency (1999, October 4), 1.

4. The First Presidency (1999, October 4), 1.

5. The First Presidency (1999, February 11), Letter to members of the Church throughout the world, 1.

6. D. Flake (1989, October), Campaign for Sunday family time, *DAD/S Newsletter* (3), available from author.

7. Packer (1998).

8. Packer (1998).

9. Packer (1998).

10. Packer (1998).

11. Packer (1998).

12. First Presidency (1999, February 11).

CHAPTER 23

VALUING, PRESERVING, AND TRANSMITTING FAMILY TRADITIONS

JILL TERRY RUDY, ERIC A. ELIASON, AND KRISTI A. BELL

I shall endeavor to write some of these things upon this record,
for the benefit of my posterity that shall come after me
(Abr. 1:31).

Church leaders have spoken regarding the power and importance of family traditions:

Let us then continue on in this important work of recording the things we do, the things we say, the things we think, to be in accordance with the instructions of the Lord. For those of you who may not have already started your books of remembrance and your records, we would suggest that this very day you begin to write your records quite fully and completely.
—President Spencer W. Kimball[1]

If we will build righteous traditions in our families, the light of the gospel can grow ever brighter in the lives of our children from generation to generation. . . . Our family activities and traditions can be a beacon to the rest of the world as an example of how we should live to merit His choice blessings and live in peace and harmony until the day that He returns to rule and reign over us.
—Elder L. Tom Perry[2]

Where family or national traditions or customs conflict with the teachings of God, set them aside. Where traditions and customs are in harmony with His teachings, they should be cherished and followed to preserve your culture and heritage.
—Elder Richard G. Scott[3]

That which I do not in some way record will be lost at my death, and that which I do not pass on to my posterity, they will never have. The work of gathering and sharing eternal family keepsakes is a personal responsibility. It cannot be passed off or given to another.
—Elder Dennis B. Neuenschwander[4]

The authors of this chapter are folklorists—we study what people make, say, and do and what their creations, words, and actions mean to them. In this chapter we present ideas that we have learned from interviews with hundreds of people over many decades about the importance of family traditions, ways to preserve traditions (through record-keeping), and how to transmit traditions to the next generation. We also provide dozens of examples of traditions that have been collected by students at Brigham Young University or Utah State University over the past 30 years.

FASHIONING CUSTOMS AND TRADITIONS THAT STRENGTHEN FAMILIES

When conceived in principles of righteousness, and when performed in a spirit of noncoercive participation, a heritage of family customs can serve as the social glue that holds families together, ushers family members through difficult life passages, and weaves loving ties of eternal duration. Extensive scholarship has demonstrated the power of traditions to strengthen family bonds. *Traditions* are defined as beliefs and practices enacted repeatedly from generation to generation and taught by face-to-face contact within small groups. Healthy traditions support the values of the Proclamation, which states, "Successful marriages and families are established and maintained on principles of faith, prayer, repentance, forgiveness, respect, love, compassion, work, and wholesome recreational activities" (¶ 7). The family unit becomes one of the initial and most crucial groups a person can belong to, and strong traditions support the unity, love, and growth of family members. Attention to Proclamation principles can foster the maintenance of family traditions and heritage. Consider the following seven issues related to the creation and perpetuation of family traditions:

1. *Distinguish between good and bad traditions:* Families should distinguish between traditions that reinforce gospel ideals and those that are not in harmony with gospel principles. Recognizing that some time-honored customs are inconsistent with Proclamation principles can help family members avoid perpetuating these actions and help find appropriate alternatives that will avoid negative consequences and enrich family life.

2. *Encourage a unique family style:* Variations in worship practices can help solidify family identity and encourage children to honor the gospel heritage passed on to them. For example, some families hold family prayer in the kitchen, some in the family room, some wherever they happen to be. Some families play specific games or have a particular treat after the family home evening lesson. Children enjoy and remember these particular customs as part of their family and gospel heritage.

3. *Be selective and creative in fashioning new traditions:* When new families are formed by marriage, couples or parents should adapt old family traditions from both spouses. Selecting, changing, or abandoning some practices of the extended families will encourage the development of a healthy new family unit, rather than favoring the traditions of one in-law group over the other.

4. *Be inclusive:* Parents fashioning the most useful family traditions take care to consider the variety of interests and abilities of all family members and choose inclusive activities that foster family relationships. Rules for games or the celebration of special days can be adapted to include all members of the family according to their age and ability to contribute.

5. *Be service-oriented:* Families should consider traditions that involve all members in service toward each other, as well as toward neighbors or strangers. Serving Thanksgiving dinners at a shelter, providing Secret Santas or Twelve Days of Christmas, or acting as Halloween phantoms all teach the values of sharing and caring for others. Small acts of service lead to habits that creative and energetic individuals will perfect as they mature. Performing service as a family is one of the best ways to perform service within the family.

6. *Foster storytelling:* Knowing family history and stories is central to building healthy families with a strong sense of identity and values. Connecting family history with Church and world history unites family members with their ancestors and with significant events of the past. For recent converts or families new to the gospel, telling conversion stories and sharing stories about the struggles and triumphs of living gospel principles will establish a heritage of faith. Sharing the stories of daily experiences, both humorous and difficult, encourages a sense of common experience that also unites families—sometimes over generations. These stories should be remembered through oral retellings and by written journal entries or life story accounts.

7. *Nurture natural traditions:* Successful family traditions often grow out of things that the family already does such as game playing, celebrating holidays, eating, working, traveling, singing together, and holding family prayer, scripture study, and home evenings. Parents can gauge the popularity of a tradition by requests to repeat the activity and by resistance to changing the custom. Traditions that are unrelated to actual family life often feel forced and uncomfortable; with good reason, these are the least likely customs to be continued.

PRESERVING BENEFICIAL FAMILY TRADITIONS

When beneficial family traditions have been created, they can be preserved through continuing performance and record-keeping. One of the greatest gifts people can give to future generations is a written record of their most cherished family traditions. This allows traditions to be transmitted for generations to come. Although some traditions change or are lost over time, many can be revived and altered for current situations if enough details have been pre-served in the memories or records of family members. Even families that feel they have no strong traditions may be surprised to recognize how many of their practices bring the family unity and enjoyment. The following suggestions will help family members identify and record the details of ongoing family traditions:

1. *Recognize the times your family keeps traditions:* A daily journal, a calendar, and an awareness of important life-cycle events can help identify ongoing traditions. Daily traditions may include meal and bedtime rituals, family prayer, nicknames, family mottoes, family greetings or leave-takings, inside jokes and sayings, favorite scriptures and hymns, and songs. Home and yard decorations such as gardens, yard ornaments, family picture walls, temple pictures, or handmade items also provide a daily sense of identity and can reinforce gospel principles. Weekly traditions may include specific home evening prac-tices, household chores, Sunday dinners, extended family gatherings, or participation in hobbies such as camping, raising and showing animals, shopping, and playing sports or games. Celebrating holidays, birth-days, blessings, baptisms, reunions, missions, and weddings fills out a monthly or yearly calendar.

2. *Record the details of performing the tradition:* Describing daily or recurring traditions in detail may not seem an obvious element to include in journal entries but will preserve traditions and make the journal more lively and valuable to family members. Including the activities required for celebrating the family Fourth of July, Thanksgiving, or Christmas—with details about food ingredients and preparation, customs or games, and a brief sketch about who is responsible for or knowledgeable about performing each part of the tradition—will enrich a family history or life story. Compiling a specific collection of daily, weekly, monthly, yearly traditions, and special family events also assures the level of detail and background information to help preserve the tradition.

DOCUMENTING FAMILY TRADITIONS

Family traditions can benefit from arrangement into an informal or formal Family Tradition Archive. Traditions may be recorded randomly in journals, life stories, and several places around the home including in photo albums and scrapbooks. Taking inventory of where these items are located, noting and filling in omissions in recorded traditions, and maintaining a list

or index of family traditions will augment other family history records and encourage the continued perform-ance of valued traditions. Strong and beneficial tradi-tions enrich family life, and documenting traditions helps preserve and pass on meaningful sayings, cus-toms, and material items. Items may be documented using several forms of communication and technology:

1. *Face-to-face communication:* Most traditions initially are learned in action or performance through face-to-face communication. Assuring that younger family members learn traditions well enough to per-form them is one key to preserving and documenting family traditions. Listening, observing, and imitating the performance of family customs helps perpetuate them. For example, one might help a child learn all the words to favorite family songs or poetry.

2. *Journals, life stories, and written communication:* The details of performing traditions may appear in written journals and life stories. Traditions may also be mentioned on calendar entries and described in more detail in letters, newsletters, Christmas cards, or in specific collections of customs. Because traditions may be embedded with other details, reading through written family communication and noting the tradi-tional stories, sayings, and actions is a productive way to document these items. Listing out page numbers in journals and histories or arranging letters and newsletters by number will help make items more accessible. Keeping similar items together in a folder or box and designating a specific location in the house for storage also is useful.

3. *Tape-recorded and transcribed interviews:* Because many traditions may not be recorded in writ-ten sources, conducting tape-recorded interviews becomes a valuable way to document family memo-ries and customs. You can tape family bedtime stories, songs, holiday customs, vacation memories, travel games, and stories about traditional items such as handmade quilts. Having the information on tape and in writing increases its accessibility and usefulness.

4. *Photo albums, scrapbooks, and visual media:* Many families naturally use photographs, scrapbooks, slides, movies, and videos to record traditions and important events and customs. While the visual images document an event, details such as names, dates, and places should also be included on or with the item to extend the usefulness of the image to later generations. Scrapbook magazines, photography companies, and specialty stores encourage the com-bination of photography and writing and provide information about using archival-quality materials.

Visual items also can be used to spark added detail in taped interviews, as family members tell the stories behind the photos or videos.

5. *Computer software and technology:* Some technologically advanced students and family historians are using computer software, CD-ROMs, and the Internet to document family traditions. Life stories and family histories can be prepared with word processing software, allowing easier manipulation of written texts; some software even allows a combination of written, spoken, and visual images. One student prepared his grandmother's life story on a CD-ROM disk; the story could then be viewed on computer or on a large projection screen. Voice-activated software automatically prints spoken comments on the computer screen, although several steps must be followed to allow the computer to record specific voices. Software and scanning equipment exists to transfer photos to the computer and to manipulate and enhance visual images. Families also are using email and family websites to share information, maintain communication, and create new traditions.

A Sample of Family Traditions

The list of traditions at the end of this chapter is intended to illustrate some of the various types of traditions that families have found meaningful. The list was collected mainly by BYU students in folklore classes and some were provided by students in the Family Proclamation class. The list is organized into general categories including holiday traditions, daily traditions, secular and religious life event traditions, and "words to live by" (fun or meaningful sayings that became part of a family's tradition). We hope couples and families draw inspiration and motivation from this short list to strengthen the use of uplifting, enjoyable, and sacred traditions in their marriages and families.

Examples of Family Traditions

This sample of family traditions was gathered mainly by BYU students in folklore classes and also by students in Family Proclamation classes. It is divided into five topics and includes two kinds of information: (1) quotes from interviews with descriptions of family traditions, (2) ideas for family traditions. The numbers in the parentheses after quotes indicate where the entry is located in the BYU Folklore Archives. There are five categories examined. They are: holidays, everyday traditions, life cycle events, words to live by, and family games. Readers can add their own ideas in the spaces provided.

QUOTES	IDEAS

I. Holidays

New Year's

1. "On New Year's Eve, each person in the family sets a plate out on the hearth for the new Little New Year to leave them a gift and note. The Little New Year gives each person 10 cents for each year of his or her life, a candy bar, and usually a small game, toy, or trinket. The biggest treat, however, is the note each of us receives. It is always written in sloppy handwriting, as if a baby has written it, and it tells us how nice we have been the past year and how the Little New Year hopes we will be just as nice in the year to come. One year I had wrecked my car in December and the Little New Year gave me a new car—a Mattel matchbox car. Whatever the Little New Year says to us and gives us is always pertinent to what is going on in our lives." Collected by Alison Miner Van Orden (8.1.2.10.1).

New Year's

1. Go winter camping. Sit in front of campfire and exchange stories about the last year.
2. Bang pans at the stroke of midnight.
3. Write down resolutions, save and read them at the end of the year.
4. Hang up Christmas stockings for a refill.
5. Leave shoes outside the door for baby New Year to fill with candy.
6. Make large pot of black-eyed peas and ham hocks to share with visitors for good luck during coming year.
7. Have a shrimp fry.

<table>
<tr><td>

QUOTES

</td><td>

IDEAS

</td></tr>
</table>

Valentine's Day	*Valentine's Day*

Valentine's Day

1. "The week before Valentine's Day . . . we would all pull names out of a hat. The person then became our secret pal. During the week we were supposed to do nice things for that person. It was nothing big, just little things like writing notes . . . , loading the dishwasher, cleaning their room. . . . On Valentine's Day we had a party and everyone revealed their secret pals. It really helped everyone feel good about doing things." Collected by Laurel Batchelor (8.2.1.1.1).

2. "The most important item concerning Valentine's Day and our family is love. We express this family love through sentimental cards and small gifts. When the family is together for this occasion, we participate in a 'Red' dinner. The dinner usually consists of red Jell-O, cherry cake, red punch, and beets. After dinner, telephone calls are made to other relatives wishing them a Happy Valentine's Day." Collected by Ronda Zander (Project 138).

Valentine's Day

1. Make and decorate special Valentine cookies.
2. Make handmade Valentines for the widows in the ward.
3. Have a family candlelight dinner with special, elegant foods.
4. Write a letter to each member of the family telling why they are special to you.
5. Have a cookie decorating contest.
6. Have a lollipop tree.
7. Make it a day of love, not just romance.

April Fool's Day

1. "Everyone in the family tries to do as many services as possible for the other members of the family during the day. That night the family gets together and writes down all the service performed for them and who they think did it." Told by Heather Maxwell.

April Fool's Day

1. Parents play harmless jokes like putting green food coloring in eggs, ham, and milk.
2. Serve dinner at breakfast.

Easter

1. "Every Easter my family goes up the canyon and rolls our decorated Easter eggs down the hill. This represents the stone rolling away from Christ's tomb." Collected by Floris Olsen (Project 1091).

Easter

1. For Easter dinner eat foods similar to what Jesus would have eaten at the Last Supper.
2. Have Easter egg hunt and picnic the day before Easter.
3. The Easter bunny leaves large floury footprints.
4. Color eggs by boiling them with onion skins.
5. Go to grave of family member early Easter morning and talk about the resurrection.
6. Read the scriptural accounts of the Atonement, Crucifixion, and Resurrection of Christ.

Memorial Day

1. "Talk and learn about past wars that have been fought for freedom." Told by Melissa Judson.

Memorial Day

1. Clean gravestones, decorate grave with flowers, and tell stories about the people buried there.
2. Decorate graves of veterans with small flags.

QUOTES

Independence Day

1. "Read stories about the many heroes that fought for our freedom." Collected by Melissa Judson.

2. "Every Independence Day, my family has a big barbeque with our extended family. We decorate everything in red, white, and blue. Sometimes we play outdoor games, and the kids have water fights. In the evening, we go as a family to one of the local fireworks displays. Then we go home and light sparklers, eat dessert, or watch a rented movie together." Told by Laura Gilpin.

Pioneer Day

Halloween

1. "Every year on the Monday before Halloween, my family gets together and has a special family home evening. The reason it's so special is because we carve pumpkins and tell 'scary' stories." (8.10.2.1.1)

2. Family makes ghost cookies: "I think the importance of this recipe to our family lies in the fact that my Dad made the cookie cutter for my Mom. It shows the love that he has for her. She wanted a ghost cookie cutter. So he made one for her, and to her specifications. It also shows Mom's commitment to establishing family traditions and to keeping them going, even after her children leave the nest. . . . When I got married, I wanted to continue the tradition of the cookies in my family, so I begged my father to make me a cutter like my mother's. He did it as a wedding gift for me." Collected by Paige M. Albrecht (Project 1683).

Thanksgiving Day

1. "Every Thanksgiving, my family and all my dad's brothers and sisters would get together at my aunt's in Clarkston. We would have a big, delicious dinner, then afterward my aunt would bring out her 'Jack Horner Pie.' This was a round laundry basket filled with gifts. Each gift had a string attached to it, leading to the outside. It would be covered with paper to make it look like a pie. My sisters and my cousins and I would gather around, find a string, and when everyone was ready, we would tug on our strings and pull out our gift. This was the most exciting part of Thanksgiving and I looked forward to it every year." Collected by Diana Romney (8.11.2.7.1).

2. "Every year on Thanksgiving morning we go for a walk and talk about how beautiful the world is and how grateful we are to Heavenly Father for creating it."

IDEAS

Independence Day

1. Read stories about great patriots.
2. Parent reads the Declaration of Independence.
3. Decorate kids' bikes and wagons with red, white, and blue crepe paper and streamers and hold a parade.

Pioneer Day

1. Attend a parade.
2. Attend a rodeo.
3. Talk about pioneer heritage and use heritage items.

Halloween

1. Have a Halloween dinner with items like bat wings and ghost breath.

Thanksgiving Day

1. Participate in a multi-generational sports event like bowling, basketball, football.
2. Place kernels of corn on each plate and ask the individual to name one blessing for each kernel.
3. Eat unique family foods.
4. Take a group nap after dinner.
5. Have a storytelling session after Thanksgiving dinner.
6. Play games like how many words can you make from the word "Thanksgiving" and have small prizes for the winner.

QUOTES

Christmas Season

1. "Each person is assigned a certain family member, and then they are to make a gift for that person that is given on Christmas Eve after their program. The gift must be handmade by that person." Collected by Robyn Larsen (8.12.1.5.1.3.1).

2. "Every Christmas morning the children would find their presents wrapped all around with knotted strings. They had to undo all the knots on every present before they were permitted to open any of them." Collected by Alice D. Eck (8.12.1.5.1.10.1).

3. "A jigsaw puzzle would sit in our dining room on a card table throughout the Christmas season." Collected by Janice Cherry (8.12.1.5.1.19).

4. "Each year around Christmas my wife and I go out shopping for a Christmas tree ornament to symbolize the year in some way." Collected by Richard Lance (8.12.1.6.6.1).

5. "My family has a tradition of stockings that's kind of unusual. Every Christmas Eve we write a letter to Santa—put it in our stockings and hang our stockings up. And, then on Christmas morning we find them with a letter in it from Santa. It's usually a rhyming poem-type letter that tells the things that Santa thinks about us, or about our life that year." Collected by Ron Hampton (8.12.1.7.2.1).

6. "The first thing Santa does at my house, before he fills even one stocking, is leave a small flashlight by the bed of each child so that they can see their way around during the night without waking up mom and dad or turning on all the lights." Collected by Michelle K. Fosse (8.12.1.8.1.1).

7. "The special treat left for Santa Claus is a large bowl of oyster stew, which happens to be . . . Dad's favorite treat." Collected by Augusta Robinson (8.12.1.8.2.2).

8. "Every year a month or two before Christmas, Aunt Nadine would put out little elves all around the house. She then would warn her children that Santa's little Elves were keeping a watch on them at all times so they had better be nice or when Santa came on Christmas Eve the elves would tell him just what each child deserved to have that year. (It seemed to keep the children in line in spite of the holiday excitement!)" Collected by Beverly Dunford (8.12.1.9.1.1).

IDEAS

Christmas Season

1. Spend December 23 with family baking and delivering baked goods to neighbors. In the evening gather for hot chocolate and discuss the birth and life of Joseph Smith.

2. Have special family home evening activities leading up to Christmas like making gingerbread houses, decorating the trees, making ornaments, etc.

3. On Christmas Eve eat foods like those Christ would have eaten.

4. Father reads the Christmas story from Luke.

5. Read the Christmas story in the Book of Mormon.

6. Children all sleep in the same room on Christmas Eve.

7. Children open up Christmas gift of pajamas on Christmas Eve.

8. Invite widows and missionaries to home for special Christmas Eve dinner and program.

9. Go caroling and deliver homemade bread.

10. Eat foods that reflect family's ethnic heritage on Christmas Eve.

11. Family members take turns telling about their best Christmas.

12. Everyone dress in pajamas and drive around town looking at Christmas lights.

13. Extended family has a progressive dinner on Christmas Eve.

14. Family acts out the Christmas story.

15. Father and one of the children are responsible for preparing Christmas Eve dinner.

16. After eating Christmas dinner, run around the outside of the house three times to help burn off the dinner.

17. Each day in December burn a candle while participating in a family activity; by Christmas Day the candle should be gone.

18. Children wake up parents on Christmas morning by singing Christmas carols.

19. Children make breakfast before waking up parents.

20. Make gingerbread house for Christmas decoration and eat it on New Year's Eve.

21. Give Baby Jesus a gift of a goal for the coming year. Write it on a piece of paper and put it in the nativity. Next Christmas each person evaluates their progress on their goal.

QUOTES

9. In one extended family "each year someone takes pictures (slides) of the young children in different nativity scenes. Then on Christmas Eve they meet at one home and show the slides, telling about the nativity and reading the story out of the Bible." Collected by Margene Stringham (8.12.1.10.3.1).

10. "Our family has this set of china that has the 12 days of Christmas designed on it. Each plate has a different day of Christmas. Before eating our Christmas dinner we have to sing the Twelve Days of Christmas. Each person has to sing the part that is on their plate. For instance if I have the five gold rings, that is the part I sing." Collected by Lars A. Morgan (8.12.1.11.4.1).

11. "Each year for about the last 10 years, after the children have gone to bed, we put an envelope for each child on the tree with just a 3x5 card inside on which we give each child a special place to take the family or a special treat for the family. It is from Dad and Mom (us, that is) but when we do each of these things it is as though that child is treating the family. Here are some of the things we have done (all are for the whole family): treat the family to dinner at a special Mexican restaurant, trip to the zoo, ice cream cone at Thrifty Drug, tour of a ship, harbor cruise, steak dinner with all the trimmings at home, bus trip to the beach, water slide in summer, roller skating party, donuts at Winchells, etc." Collected by Margene Stringham (Project 115).

12. "Every Christmas Eve it seemed like we'd be sitting around in the living room playing with toys or what not and it always seemed very late at night, but it was probably only five or six o'clock, but to me it always seemed very late, and there would be a knock on the door and she would say, 'Boys who's that? Go answer the door.' And one of us would scamper to the door and open the door and a Christmas Tree would be outside the door and Mom would say, 'It must have been an elf.' She told us it must have been an elf, you know, that left the Christmas Tree at the door. And then, 5 or 10 minutes later, Dad would come in the door and share in the mystery of the elf, asking where the tree had come from." Collected by Gregor Makechnie (Project 1261).

IDEAS

22. Every child receives a new wind-up toy for Christmas as a reward for being good during the year.
23. When the Christmas tree is thrown out, leave one ornament as a gift to Christmas so Christmas will return.
24. Each child receives a small jar of pickles in their stocking.
25. Each child receives a can of olives in their stocking.
26. Each child receives mandarin oranges in their stocking.
27. Leave Christmas cookies and milk for Santa and carrots for the reindeer.
28. Begin the story of Christ's birth with Zacharias's angelic visitor.
29. Take lunch or dinner to a homeless shelter or go help prepare and serve meals there.
30. Eat a five-course breakfast before opening presents.
31. Stick presents in pillowcases rather than under the tree.

QUOTES	IDEAS

13. "Each year I purchase several new Christmas books to add to our Christmas story collection. We have enough books that I am able to read a Christmas story each night before Christmas to my two little children. They love this and I love reading about different aspects of Christmas to them and having fun with books." Collected by Lance Eli Black (Project 967).

14. "One of our Christmas traditions is that we put an emblem on our Christmas stockings each year symbolizing a major highlight of the past year. For example: When we moved out to Utah from Canada we cut out a felt shape of Utah and glued a sequin where Orem would be. Then I sew them on to our stockings. We do the same thing for our children so when they leave home they will have a stocking to take with them with special remembrances on." Collected by Lance Eli Black (Project 967).

15. "The one tradition that became special—that grew out of the Christmas Eve tradition [of visiting grandparents on Christmas Eve] is that we would not only decorate graves of Grandpa and Grandma Solomon on Memorial Day, but that we would take holly and other kinds of greens and decorate their graves on Christmas Eve." Collected by Heather S. Cromar (Project 965).

16. "Our family thinks it's important that gifts and a big dinner not be the 'climax' of Christmas. On Christmas afternoon we play games, begin a jigsaw puzzle, or perhaps go to a movie if there's one everyone would enjoy. The idea is to do something together and enjoy each other's company as a family."

II.   EVERYDAY TRADITIONS

1. Make special memories—"Every fall Melanie's parents would bundle all of the kids in blankets and put them in the back of their pickup. They would head for the hills, all the while singing songs. After they found a good berry patch they would all pick and eat until the kids and the buckets were full. They would then head home and make homemade ice cream with the picked berries." Collected by Mikel Rowley (2.2.0.3.1).

2. "On Sundays the plates are always stacked by my father's place at the dinner table. He would dish out everyone's food. This only happened at Sunday dinner never any other night of the week." Collected by Lars A. Morgan (2.2.1.5.1).

1. "Earn your dessert" with a joke, story, song, etc.
2. Say "I love you" whenever you say "goodbye" or "goodnight."
3. Parent wakes up children with morning song. Examples could include "Little Bunny Fufu," "The BYU Fight Song," "Little Mary Sunshine," or a made-up song.
4. Family court used for discipline. Arguments must be sung.
5. Sing hymns such as "There Is Beauty All Around" to break up dissension.
6. Parent makes special foods (such as Swedish pancakes) unique to your family or heritage.
7. Establish traditional foods for Sunday that reflect the tastes of the family.

QUOTES

3. Create family songs: "'We are beavers one, we are beavers all, we all get together and give our beaver call.' After these words are sung everyone puts their top front teeth over their lower lip and makes a smacking beaver-like noise three or four times." Collected by Gwen Ostergar (2.2.4.4.1).

4. "Family members write short notes of love and support and hide them in the luggage of another family member who is about to leave home for a time." Collected by Carol Lee Stott (2.2.6.2.1).

5. "Everyone gathers around the table and sits after all of the food and place settings have been set on the table. One person slaps their hands together directly overhead and keeps them there. The others around the table do the same as quickly as possible. The last one to assume this position says the blessing on the food." Collected by Allyson Wride (2.4.2.3.1).

6. "Dad loved to buy 'rock fields.' I don't know if it was because the land was cheaper or if he wanted to build character in his kids. Regardless of his purpose, he made an unmistakable impression on us. We would have to pick up rocks in the oldest truck that had 50,000 colors on it. This was a really old truck. It was maybe 50 years old. My dad probably still has it parked somewhere. I can't remember who got to drive it, but it wasn't me. They would drive it down the row while everyone else would pile rocks in the bed of the pickup. Karla, who was the youngest, would sit on the roof on the truck and sing. That was her contribution." Collected by Mark Weisenburger (Project 1002).

7. "It was a big deal to my Dad that we all have family prayer twice a day. Now I can see that the principle he was trying to instill in us was that it was so important that it was worth getting up for. And I didn't really see it then, but I see it now." Collected by Tim Mitchell (Project 74).

8. "Once my father had, I think he'd lost his job. And they had just enough to pay their tithing but they didn't have enough to buy food. They had the rent, but they didn't have food money. They went ahead and paid their tithing and they got a check in the mail and they didn't know who it was from but it was for exactly the amount they spent every month on food, to the penny. And they always claimed that that was the benefit of paying their tithing. That was really emphasized in our family, probably more than any other commandment, was tithing." Collected by Tim Mitchell (Project 74).

IDEAS

8. Have family members take turns planning and preparing meals.

9. Sing parts of Handel's *Messiah* on family car trips.

10. Create a repertoire of family songs.

11. Prepare and print family newsletters.

12. Have family testimony meetings.

13. Parents sing goodnight songs rather than tell stories.

14. Grandma has gift drawer with inexpensive gifts for her visiting grandchildren.

15. Send grandchildren book with a tape of grandparent reading the book.

16. Grandma wears apron with big pockets filled with treats for grandchildren.

17. Say dinner prayers in languages learned on missions.

18. Family members give each other nicknames that are used within the family.

19. Family works together to can apple butter.

20. Have a pancake breakfast once a week. Parent makes pancakes in shapes of person's initials.

21. Go on family vacations as an extended family.

22. Phrase "just around the bend" used to tell children how much further the family needs to travel to get to their destination.

23. Traditional 5K run as part of family reunion.

24. Have family council on Sunday and plan menus for the week.

25. Dinner conversation on Sunday revolves around church and family; weeknights, school is generally the topic.

26. Samoan custom of removing shoes when entering a house shows respect for the homeowners.

27. Once a week go out to eat and then to the library. Check out books, which you try to finish reading by the next week's trip.

28. Have a "family hymn" you sing at children's baptisms and mission farewells.

QUOTES

IDEAS

9. "When we were all small we would gather together in our parents' room on the bed to talk. This usually happened on Saturday morning when Mom and Dad slept in." Collected by Sara Ann Smith (Project 391).

10. "Everyone helps work in the garden but afterwards everyone gets to take part in the treat. They go get an ice cream cone." Collected by Sara Ann Smith (Project 391).

11. "Men and boys in family go to grandparents' house for sardines after priesthood meeting." Collected by Jana McNaughton (Project 1337).

12. "I believe that the culture of a family, or any other organization for that fact, is passed on through stories. People will forget the things that we sometimes spend so much of our lives pursuing, but the stories will be told for years to come. As long as we get together as a family, this culture will continue and grow as the family grows." Collected by Jana McNaughton (Project 1337).

13. "Sometimes my mother would treat me to a shopping trip to Salt Lake City. On these occasions I could always look forward to lunch at Hotel Utah's Coffee Shop. Our favorite lunch was this cold Borscht soup served with chopped chicken livers and pumpernickel bread. This became a tradition with my mother and me, our own private one." Collected by Colleen Carlisle (Project 17).

14. "When we were young, Mom would get us to eat our leftovers by 'playing restaurant.' She made menus for everyone and set the table with all the forks, nice plates, and napkins. She was the waitress and she took our orders and wrote them in a notebook. Then, she would warm up our food in the microwave. We did this every Friday night. She got us to eat leftovers (which we wouldn't eat any other way) and taught us etiquette at the same time because we had to pretend we were in a very nice restaurant and had to use our best manners." Collected by Heidi Quist (Project 1643).

15. "Remember when Dad was working for food service at Boston University. We would always beg him to take us to the kitchen with him so that we could help roll the rolls. It was hard to keep up with him though because he could roll two rolls at once, one in each hand. I thought of those days often this summer when we were working at the bakery, rolling rolls and molding bread. The experience with Dad helped out a lot." Collected by Gregor Makechnie (Project 1261).

QUOTES	IDEAS

III. LIFE CYCLE TRADITIONS

1. "My trousseau consisted of $1,500 in the bank. . . . To this my father added a college education, which he said was the best trousseau a girl could have." Collected by Ronda Walker Knudsen (Project 1557).

2. "Every year our . . . family has a reunion. . . . Each year a different one prepares and arranges the reunion. Last year it was at the Sweetwater Resort at Bear Lake. Things we do—we have a meeting with the family heads and we take pictures and take count of new members and we make genealogy assignments for names to be worked on the coming year. We socialize and have fun with everybody." Collected by Dan Vilho Johnson (Project 281).

3. "At the dinner table, not all the time but many times, Dad would announce his love for Mother and kiss her and say she was the sweetest mother in the world. We all then pointed to Mother and clapped. Then he would go around the table with each of us and say, 'Who's the sweetest Jane in the world?' and everyone would point to me and clap and hurrah. I would be so happy at this that I would shout, 'Daddy-O, I praise you.' He really liked that. I was just a little kid." Collected by Dan Vilho Johnson (Project 281).

4. "Dad confirmed all of us members of the Church and ordained us to offices in the Aaronic Priesthood. We all served at one time as his ward teaching companion. He'd always reward us with a Bristol's ice cream cone. There was a tradition of the priesthood at home. It was the comfort blessing Mom would get before the birth of each child. When one of the kids was sick, Dad called the bishop and they would administer to us with the consecrated oil he always kept. Whatever happened, it was the will of God." Collected by Dan Vilho Johnson (Project 281).

5. "Go out to breakfast at 1:00 A.M. with entire family." Told by Heather Tanner.

6. "Before my father leaves for work each day, he gives all of us children a kiss on the cheek and my mother a kiss on the lips. It has been a bonding experience for us children to our father, and lets us know he loves us." Told by Jennifer M. Flinders.

1. The night before someone in the family gets married, the family concocts an enormous sundae and everyone eats it together.
2. Have special foods on birthday.
3. Tell the birthday child the story surrounding his or her birth.
4. Parents serve birthday child breakfast in bed and visit with child while he or she eats.
5. Hide birthday presents and play "you're getting warmer" game to help birthday person find presents.
6. Have special, traditional presents to mark certain birthdays.
7. Birthday person kisses gift giver before opening present.
8. After [family] prayer has been said, with everyone kneeling around in a circle, each person extends his right arm to the center, cups his hand and grasps hands with the others in a circular formation. The group moves their hands together up and down while saying in unison, "Sure love ya."
9. Father's blessings are given to each child at the beginning of the school year.
10. Father's blessings given on birthdays to the birthday child.
11. To celebrate wedding anniversary, go to the temple for an endowment session or sealings.
12. Send rose to mother when it is your birthday.
13. Birthday child picks the menu and is excused from chores.
14. Birthday child eats off special plate.

QUOTES	IDEAS

IV. Words to Live By

QUOTES

1. "Grandpa always called his grandsons 'Top Hand' because they were a helper, and that's what you always called your helper on the ranch or the farm; and he always called his sons that. And he always called his granddaughters 'Doll Girls'—they were always Doll Girls. I know he always said 'Top Hand' and 'Doll Girl' for his grandkids." Collected by Steven J Stewart (Project 1271).

2. "I remember working out in the field. And it was in November, I'm sure, and it was cold and sleet was coming down. And it was just a bitter, nasty cold day. And we were loading beet tops or piling beet tops. And I was complaining because I was so cold and my nose was running and my feet were cold and I was just having a miserable time. And I was complaining to Daddy and he says, 'Well, Laynie, you're just built wrong. Your nose runs and your feet smell!'" Collected by Heidi Tobler (Project 729).

3. "We were sitting around in the kitchen of Mom's and Pop's house and Ross said he wanted to go to Tautphous Park and ride the Ferris wheel and the other rides. Mom said we couldn't go until after he [Ross] had taken a nap. Ross became indignant. He didn't want to take a nap and he didn't like Mom telling him he had to take one. So he turned away from Mom and said to my mother, 'She thinks she's the big boss. She thinks she's the big boss of the *whole world. She* thinks *she's President Kimball!*'" Collected by Heidi Tobler (Project 729).

4. "Generally the best escape mechanism is a fast and adequate solution." Collected by Charles William Ryan (Project 377).

5. "I get pretty involved in people's lives. Then I realize how lucky I am and how minor my problems really are." Collected by Charles William Ryan (Project 377).

6. "My father always told us 'Be where you're supposed to be, when you're supposed to be there.' He tried to always do this and was a great example for us." Told by Jennifer M. Flinders.

7. "Whenever we left the house our mother would say, 'Remember who you are and what you stand for!' This helped us get out of tricky situations, because we didn't want to disappoint Mom." Told by Amanda M. Sorenson.

8. "My father use to come in to my room every night and sit at the foot of my bed. He would ask me, 'What was your happiest thing today?' This was a special time I had with my dad and when things got hard in life it helped me focus on the positive aspects of life." Told by Robin Heath.

IDEAS

1. Family folk phrases help photographs come to life. Words convey an attitude about life and evoke memories of specific experiences.
2. Act like somebody—God didn't take time to make a nobody.
3. Although the tongue is boneless, it has the power to crush bones.
4. Busy hands are happy hands.
5. The better the day, the better the deed.
6. By the yard it's hard; by the inch it's a cinch.
7. A chain is no stronger than its weakest link.
8. Do not worry about tomorrow, because you do not even know what may happen today.
9. Eat it up, wear it out, make it do, or do without.
10. From postponement always comes a cancellation.
11. The greatest leaders are always the greatest servers first.
12. A good laugh is better than a three-mile jog.
13. He who does a good turn should never remember it; he who receives a good turn should never forget it.
14. It is a silly dog that bites itself.
15. If you want to kill time, work it to death.
16. It is better to wear out than rust out.
17. Marriage is not just finding the right person—it is being the right person.
18. Many hands makes light work.
19. The only way for evil to win is for good men to do nothing.
20. Talking is silver; silence is golden.
21. Willing hands make light work.
22. You cannot kindle a fire in any heart until it is burning in your own.
23. You must learn to crawl before you walk, and walk before you run.
24. Love is like a potato salad, share it and you have a picnic.
25. Worrying is like rocking in a chair: it gives you something to do, but it doesn't get you anywhere.
26. A closed mouth gathers no foot.
27. Christ is the head of every home, the unseen guest at every meal, the silent listener at every conversation.
28. Indecision becomes decision with the passing of time.
29. Make a daisy chain with a friend, and you'll have a friend for life.

QUOTES	IDEAS

V.   FAMILY GAMES

1. "The object of the game was for siblings to remain quiet for a certain amount of time or to see who could be quiet the longest. Mom and Dad brought cheap toys that they had bought as prizes. Collected by Dan Vilho Johnson (Project 281).

2. "We played the ABC game different, it was a communal effort. We just had to go through the alphabet. It was just, like, find the 'a' then we'd move on and find the 'b.' Well, whoever found the 'z' won. So we went through the alphabet together but you wanted to stay alert so that when 'z' came up, cause if someone said 'y' and you didn't know it you might not be looking for 'z.'" Collected by Tierza Rose Draper (Project 1286).

3. "One game we played was 'my grandfather owns a grocery store.' What you do is you say 'My grandfather owns a grocery store and in his store he has, and then you give a clue about some item in a grocery store and then you give a clue about it like it's round or what fruit group it's in or whatever and everyone else asks questions until they get it right." Collected by Tierza Rose Draper (Project 1286).

4. "Sardines is the opposite of Hide and Go Seek. Everyone stands in the kitchen and one person goes and hides. And the point of the game is to find that one person and hide with them. At the end whoever is the last one to find everyone, they're the one who's it next time." Collected by Tierza Rose Draper (Project 1286).

5. "You have to have a lot of people to play this game, that's why it's good to play it at a family reunion. You count off in threes. All of the ones are poodles. All of the twos are Dobermans. All of the threes are weenie dogs. Three people are chosen to be dog catchers, and everyone else lines up on one side of the field. When the dog catchers yell out one of the names, all those kinds of dogs have to run to the other side without being tagged by the dog catchers. If they get caught then they have to go to the dog pound (jail). The last three to remain free get to be the next dog catchers." Collected by John Sorenson (Project 724).

1. Try to find a license plate from each of the 50 states.
2. Hide an object while someone is out of the room. When they return yell 'Hot' or 'Cold' to guide them towards the object.
3. Play "I Spy," adapted to age and interest of kids.
4. List states and their capitols from memory.
5. Pick raindrops on the window and see whose raindrop makes it to the bottom of the window first.
6. Play "Pooh Sticks." (See A. A. Milne (1965), *The House at Pooh Corner* (New York: E. P. Dutton), ch. 6, pp. 92–108.

QUOTES

6. Crab Soccer—"Everyone gets down on their hands and feet with their back arched and their stomach pointing to the ceiling in crab position. You have two teams and each team tries to kick the largest ball you can find into the opposing team's goal. The first team to five wins." Collected by John Sorenson (Project 724).

7. "There is one especially long tunnel that we have to go through on our way to Utah. Usually Daddy is driving. If he is then he will start honking the horn and we will open the windows and listen for the echoes. If Mom is driving then she won't honk the horn so instead we open the windows and scream. Then we'll listen for that noise to echo." Collected by Rebecca L. Smith (Project 697).

NOTES

1. Spencer W. Kimball (1982), Keep journals and family records, in *The teachings of Spencer W. Kimball,* ed. Edward L. Kimball (Salt Lake City: Bookcraft), 349.

2. L. Tom Perry (1990, May), Family traditions, *Ensign, 20*(5), 19–20.

3. Richard G. Scott (1998, May), Removing barriers to happiness, *Ensign, 28*(5), 85–87.

4. Dennis B. Neuenschwander (1999, May), Bridges and eternal keepsakes, *Ensign, 29*(5), 83–85.

IDEAS

RESEARCH ON THE BENEFITS OF FAMILY TRADITIONS

LLOYD D. NEWELL

Traditions are at the center of family life; they are what make a house a home, a kin-group a family. Family science researchers have described traditions (or rituals) as the "heart" of a family,[1] an "anchor" in the family,[2] and the "core" of family life.[3] In this essay I briefly review the research—including my own—on the role and value of family traditions.

Traditions provide a source of strength to families

Family members often think of traditions in terms of the cohesiveness that they engender. To describe what traditions do for them and their families, family members often use words like *cement, glue, anchor, bond,* and *foundation.*[4] Research has shown that traditions strengthen families by maintaining family contact; by promoting sharing, closeness, bonding, and communication; by providing memories; and by creating a family framework that can engender feelings of safety and security and help families deal with change.[5] Mize has noted that rituals and traditions help stabilize family life as well as organize daily life in the home.[6]

Children, in particular, benefit from the security and safety that comes from repeated family traditions and rituals,[7] and traditions have been found to provide stability and continuity—especially during periods of stress.[8] Traditions also promote the solidarity of the family.[9] For example, researchers studying Nebraska and North Dakota families found that the strongest families had the highest frequency of family rituals, or traditions.[10] Families that are intentional about eating, playing, and praying together, observing holiday and family celebrations and traditions, as well as participating in regular, repeated, and meaningful activities, feel more cohesive, unified, and secure.[11] As a mother said so well, "Traditions are the cement that keeps the family together . . . and help you withstand the storms that come."

Traditions create a sense of personal and family identity

Traditions are powerful organizers of family life and give a family a sense of who they are, what they believe and value, and where they are headed.[12] Families use traditions to transmit the family's values, attitudes, and goals to all family members;[13] to help in the construction of a family "code" or a system of beliefs and definitions that are used to guide the family's behavior inside and outside the home;[14] and to convey and maintain the family's identity.[15] As a mother of seven said, "Traditions help you understand your life, and your space in the world, and also help you interpret yourself. . . . I know who I am because of our traditions."[16]

Traditions also help to preserve the family's "story." When family members share their memories and experiences—often associated with traditions and rituals—they are brought closer together, family unity is reinforced, and family identity is strengthened. Children and other family members can become acquainted with the lives of deceased family members and ancestors through family traditions and repeated celebrations. One family regularly visits the burial place of a grandfather the children never knew. They read from his history, and their father tells stories and shares memories of their grandfather. Visiting the grave site on his birthday and other consistent occasions has become a treasured tradition that has helped the children understand their family origin and identity.

Traditions are a source of connection between generations

Family traditions create and strengthen generational continuity as they link practices and beliefs across generations.[17] "By inculcating ritual in the next generation, families assure themselves of one kind of immortality. . . . ritual has the power to link past, present, and future."[18] Schvaneveldt and Lee noted that rituals and traditions can provide intergenerational continuity and cohesiveness, solidarity, and meaning to all family members and, across generations, show children how their family circle is "the living link in a chain of generations."[19] Like cherished family heirlooms, family traditions help beliefs, values, and practices span generations and transcend space and time.

Traditions are much more than repeated interactions—they are richly meaningful to the relational and generational life of the family. Generations of families can become connected through simple traditions and rituals. For example, a mother who sings her toddlers to sleep with a lullaby her father used to sing to her as a baby; a father who builds rockets with his son just as his father did with him in his youth; a young girl who helps her mother bake cranberry bread just as her mother did with her grandmother—all do more than participate in a favorite activity. In these examples, lullabies, rockets, and bread enact meaningful and generative traditions that connect them with their forebears.

Traditions allow families to examine themselves

Traditions give families a window into the interior of the family and thereby become sources of evaluation and adjustment for family members. One father explained, "Our traditions help us get a sense of where our family is right now and to make course corrections when needed." Another father concurred, "Traditions help us find out and know what's going on in their [children's] lives. You can talk about it. It's a constant evaluation, reevaluating what is going on in your family, also what's going on outside your family."[20] Traditions provide a window to see into the quality of relationships inside the home, the goals and aspirations of each member, as well as the values and priorities of the family.

Traditions are a means to the heart or "inside" of family relationships. They can provide a mirror for each family member to see himself or herself, reflected in the image of each other. Rituals and traditions create a compressed, structured means for truly seeing the family and oneself in a vivid, meaningful way. As a mother said, "I see myself in my children. . . . And so often it's through our traditions that I can really see my children and myself up close."

Traditions are laden with meaning

Rituals and traditions are full of meaning. For many families, the meaning of various traditions is lodged in their faith or at least related to some kind of religious faith.[21] The transcendent power of tradition in terms of grounding faith, although difficult to describe, is nonetheless real. One mother relates that the most important part of sharing a tradition is "the peace and the transcendence that it brings to the household."[22] Traditions have the power to lift the family out of the everyday and into a realm of meaning and purpose.

Traditions give meaning to families and individuals by linking the past with the present and thereby allowing for continuity or change. Traditions have meaning not only because of what they represent now, but also because of what they represent of the past or presage for the future. Because of the significance of traditions and rituals in family life, clinicians have found them to be effective means of intervention.[23] Researchers concur that not only can traditions significantly strengthen a family, they also have the power to change and mold a family into a more functional unit.

NOTES

1. M. Cox (1998), *The heart of a family* (New York: Random House).

2. S. J. Wolin and L. A. Bennett (1984), Family rituals, *Family Process, 23,* 401–420.

3. J. H. Bossard and E. S. Boll (1950), *Ritual in family living* (Philadelphia: University of Pennsylvania Press).

4. L. D. Newell (1999, December), Traditions: A foundation for strong families, *Marriage and Families,* 2–7; L. D. Newell (1999), *A qualitative analysis of family rituals and traditions,* doctoral dissertation, Brigham Young University.

5. Newell (1999); W. H. Meredith (1985), The importance of family traditions, *Wellness Perspectives, 2*(2), 17–19; R. R. Kobak and D. B. Waters (1984), Family therapy as a rite of passage: Play's the thing, *Family Process, 23,* 89–100; J. D. Schvaneveldt and T. R. Lee (1983), The emergence and practice of ritual in the American family, *Family Perspective, 17*(3), 137–143.

6. L. K. Mize (1995), Ritual experience and its emergence with story: An experience in meaning, *Contemporary Family Therapy, 17*(1), 109–125.

7. S. Albert, T. Amgott, M. Krakow, and H. Marcus (1979), Children's bedtime rituals as a prototype rite of safe passage, *The Journal of Psychological Anthropology, 2*(1), 85–105.

8. B. H. Fiese (1992), Dimensions of family rituals across two generations: Relation to adolescent identity, *Family Process, 31,* 151–162; S. J. Wolin, L. A. Bennett, and J. S. Jacobs (1988), Assessing family rituals in alcoholic families, in E. Imber-Black, J. Roberts, and R. Whiting (Eds.), *Rituals in families and family therapy* (New York: Norton), 230–256.

9. E. W. Jensen, S. A. James, T. Boyce, and S. A. Hartnett (1983), The family routines inventory: Development and validation, *Social Science Medicine, 17*(4), 201–211.

10. W. H. Meredith, D. A. Abbott, M. A. Lamanna, and G. Sanders (1989), Rituals and family strengths: A three-generation study, *Family Perspectives, 23*(2), 75–83.

11. Newell (1999); W. J. Doherty (1997), *The international family: How to build family ties in our modern world* (New York: Addison-Wesley).

12. Newell (1999); B. H. Fiese and A. J. Sameroff (1989), Family context in pediatric psychology: A transactional perspective, *Journal of Pediatric Psychology, 14*(2), 293–314.

13. Meredith et al. (1989).

14. D. Reiss (1989), The represented and practicing family: Contrasting visions of family continuity, in A. J. Sameroff and R. N. Emde (Eds.), *Relationship disturbances in early childhood* (New York: Basic Books), 191–200.

15. Wolin and Bennett (1984).

16. Newell (1999), 90.

17. Fiese (1992); D. Reiss (1981), *The family's construction of reality* (Cambridge, MA: Harvard University Press); L. E. Troll (1988), Rituals and reunions, *American Behavioral Scientist, 31*(6), 621–631.

18. Wolin and Bennett (1984), 412.

19. Schvaneveldt and Lee (1983), 138.

20. Newell (1999), 6, 109.

21. Newell (1999).

22. Newell (1999), 117.

23. J. Roberts, (1988), Setting the frame: Definition, functions, and typology of rituals, in E. Imber-Black, J. Roberts, and R. A. Whiting (Eds.), *Rituals in families and family therapy,* (New York: Norton), 3–46.

Government Resources and Policies to Maintain and Strengthen Families

Shirley E. Cox and Jini L. Roby

We call upon responsible citizens and officers of government everywhere to promote those measures
designed to maintain and strengthen the family as the fundamental unit of society.
(The Family: A Proclamation to the World, ¶ 9)

Many governments enact legislation and establish programs intended to strengthen families. Latter-day Saints must make choices, informed by gospel principles, about participation in these programs. In addition, the Church has repeatedly counseled its members to be responsible citizens—especially when matters of morality are involved. As a result, Latter-day Saints should be informed about and involved in matters of family policy.

Accordingly, the first part of the chapter discusses the principles of the Church Welfare Program and then addresses various public and private resources designed to assist families. This part of the chapter is designed to help families understand and determine if, when, and how they might need to reach out for and use outside resources to strengthen and preserve the family.

The second part of the chapter addresses U.S. and international family policy by discussing laws and policies intended to strengthen families and relating these policy efforts to principles from the Proclamation. This section will assist readers to better understand the complex issues that surround legislation on marriage and the family and become better informed in their ability to articulate and defend the Proclamation.

The Family Is the First Line of Defense

The Church teaches families to be self-reliant and to do everything possible to sustain themselves. Home industry, gardening, food storage, emergency preparedness, and avoidance of debt reflect the applications of self-sufficiency.[1] Elder Neal A. Maxwell, in warning against premature reaching out to state and national resources, indicated that "Looking beyond the family to other institutions, programs, or activities—which may be good and helpful in their spheres—can be disastrous. The family is still the most efficient means for producing human happiness and human goodness, as well as for preparing us for the world of immortality that is to follow."[2]

The *Encyclopedia of Mormonism* elaborates under the entry on "Self-Sufficiency (Self Reliance)" that teachings pertaining to Welfare Services place considerable importance on family independence or self-reliance. However, it goes on to note that when the resources simply do not exist within the immediate family, the Church also encourages families to seek help from their extended family systems.[3] This advice is consistent with the Proclamation statement that "extended family should lend support when needed" (¶ 7). One example of how that may be applied is when extended family members rally together to avoid placing an elderly member in a long-term care.

Often they divide the responsibility to provide the required supervision and daily care among members of the extended family organization. Or, when that is not possible, they pool financial assets to hire someone to come and provide the required services for the elderly individual at home.

CHURCH WELFARE SERVICE IS NECESSARY FOR US ALL

When the family or extended family cannot meet its own needs for basic survival, it is essential that the community or greater society step up to provide those basic services. There have been, there are now, and there will be families that despite their best efforts cannot meet their own needs for food, clothing, shelter, or medical care. In his address during April conference 1999, Elder Joseph B. Wirthlin reminded us, "If the Savior were among us in mortality today, He would be found ministering to the needy, the suffering, the sick."[4] Elder Wirthlin also mentioned that "miraculous acts of mercy and kindness, some widely known, others quiet and gentle, define for me one of the salient characteristics of the Savior: His love and compassion for the downtrodden, the weary, the weak, the suffering. Indeed, these acts of compassion are synonymous with His name."[5]

The Church Welfare and Humanitarian systems provide thousands of carloads of small and large goods and unnumbered service hours throughout the world, in aid of our fellow beings and their families. Though these offerings are far too numerous for us to conceive, each of us is aware of a few examples like the following: a visiting teacher who offers a loaf of bread and a listening ear to a new mother who fears she can't go on, a home teacher who augers out the shower drain of a member who can't use it without help, a man who offers to plant the garden of a sick neighbor, a teenager who reads to a blind senior down the street, a bishop who reaches out to offer food to a nonmember family within his ward boundary, a dentist who offers his surplus equipment and goes to demonstrate its use in a small community in a developing nation, missionaries who serve as volunteers each week in addition to their other duties, and an industrialist that donates a cement factory and the experts to teach its management to a country devastated by earthquakes. In addition to the food, clothing, and other supplies, the Church has sent missionaries and other personnel to aid victims of natural disasters. And church buildings are often used as temporary emergency shelters. All are important services in keeping with the example of our Savior.

The Church emphasizes the dual focus of the welfare system: the aid to the recipient and the aid to the provider. President Marion G. Romney in his 1982 October conference address stated that "there is an interdependence between those who have and those who have not. The process of giving exalts the poor and humbles the rich. In the process, both are sanctified. The poor, released from the bondage and limitations of poverty, are enabled as free men to rise to their full potential, both temporally and spiritually. The rich, by imparting of their surplus, participate in the eternal principle of giving."[6]

Not only do the families served benefit from welfare services, the families of those who can give would not go forward toward eternal life without the principles of charitable service. Latter-day Saint adults and children need the benefits of giving freely to neighbors, working on the stake farm, feeding the homeless, visiting the prisoners, and bringing light to those in darkness. The Apostle Paul asserted, "Though I speak with the tongues of men and of angels, and have not charity, I am as sounding brass, or a tinkling cymbal" (1 Cor. 13:1).

And Alma commented upon the reason for great happiness among his people during a time just after the initiation of the reign of the judges:

> And thus they were all equal, and they did all labor, every man according to his strength. And they did impart of their substance, every man according to that which he had, to the poor, and the needy, and the sick, and the afflicted: And thus, in their prosperous circumstances, they did not send away any who were naked, or that were hungry, or that were athirst, or that were sick, or that had not been nourished; and they did not set their hearts upon riches; therefore they were liberal to all, both old and young, both bond and free, both male and female, whether out of the church or in the church, having no respect to persons as to those who stood in need. (Alma 1:26–27, 30)

COMMUNITY RESOURCES MAY BE NECESSARY FOR FAMILY SURVIVAL

There are times when needed services are simply beyond the reach of the family, the neighborhood, or the Church. A family may need services that only state and national legal entities can provide. These services that exceed local individual, family, and neighborhood capacities are often those required to address such community-wide exigencies as adequate food, water, shelter, education and training, or medical, social, or mental health needs. Still other services are legal in nature and address such concerns as marriage, adoption, and protection of individual and family rights.

In our various cultures and societies we need the assistance of government to provide us a method or system for realizing these benefits. However, at the same time, we need to be skilled participants in or recipients of these services. We need to be able to determine if the value gained by our families is worth the price paid for the benefits.

One way to determine this is by examining the public welfare program according to the so-called "product" approach: What is the program offering? Who is eligible to receive the service or commodity? How it is delivered? Who pays the cost? What values, theories, and assumptions support the delivery of the service or commodity? For example, if your family needs to use governmental services for a physically or mentally challenged child, it would be important to explore the product (investigate and answer the above five questions) before agreeing to participate in the program and receive the benefits offered. The same is true (you need to answer all five questions) if you are seeking services for an elderly parent who requires, but cannot afford, bypass surgery, or if you need money to support specialized training to follow a career in medicine. The following section will apply this "product" (five question) system to a welfare service program many people need to use to appropriately and adequately provide for their families.

Marty Jenkins and his four siblings were concerned about the best plan for medical care and supervision of their aging mother. He used the five-question product analysis to assemble information on the Medicare program. Following is the brief report that he shared with his mother, his siblings, and their spouses at a family meeting set up to consider the alternatives.

What does the program provide? Everything provided by Medicare is an in-kind, reimbursable medical service. There is no money awarded to provide for living expenses. Program benefits include services by medical personnel for home health care, hospice care, skilled nursing facility care, in-patient hospital care, and medical equipment and supplies.

Who is eligible to receive the service? Recipients must be sixty-five years of age or older to be eligible or they must be younger people with specific

permanently disabling conditions. Also, to be eligible for Medicare, the recipient, her spouse, or other family members must have made previous payments into the FICA fund.

How are the services delivered? Individuals can receive specified services from any medical institution or professional provider who has been certified and issued a medical provider number. There is little recipient input and decisions about services are primarily made by expert authorities. Panels of professional medical practitioners determine the recommended services and length of time services may be received.

How are the services financed? Medicare is funded by combined sources. Participants in the U.S. Medicare Part A program for hospital payment must pay an up-front deductible charge of approximately $760 before the plan covers any of the medical costs incurred. Also, an approximate $200 per day copayment is required for hospital costs from day 61 through day 90. Another source of revenue is individual participation in Part B, Supplementary Medical Insurance coverage, for which individuals pay a monthly fee of approximately $45.00. Money is provided from general federal tax revenues, as needed.

What values, theories, and assumptions support the delivery of this service? Equality is an important value—services are standardized for all individuals who qualify. However, there is little respect for individual or family capabilities to influence their own situations. Family members are not encouraged to assist with the standard medical costs or services until the medical coverage has run out or expired.

Marty, his family members, and their mother made a decision that she would participate in the Medicare program, but also that they would stay involved. They would accompany their mother to medical visits, help her to ask appropriate questions of the medical providers, and monitor the quality of care received. They also made long-term plans to be of assistance to her should an emergency arise that would not be paid for by the program.

All families need to choose wisely from the community services available to help them meet their needs and the needs of their individual family members. Asking possible service agencies and programs specific questions and listening carefully to the answers helps.

The following outline built from the model proposed by Neil Gilbert and Paul Terrell of the University of California is the "product" or five-question

PRODUCT (FIVE-QUESTION) OUTLINE
FOR EVALUATING PUBLIC ASSISTANCE
PROGRAMS AND SERVICES[7]

What does the program provide?
 Cash
 Goods
 Services
  Limited or Diversified
Who is eligible to receive the goods or services?
 All applicants or only
 Certain individuals, who are eligible because they
 Fit the program category or
 Diagnostic criteria, or have
  Limited assets, and/or
  Limited income, or have
 Paid the required Insurance premiums
How are the services delivered?
 Openness of access to information about the
  program or agency
 Agency administrative policy-making control and
  authority structure
 Amount of recipient and/or family participation
  allowed
 Amount and type of expert or professional
  participation in service delivery, and
 Amount and type of untrained or paraprofessional
  participation
 Primacy of interest in the client's welfare vs.
  interest in supporting the bureaucracy
 Program premises and building condition
 Accessability
 Extended service network and availability
How are the services financed?
 Client fees-for-service
  Family Capacity
 General tax revenues (Federal, State, Local)
 Social Insurance
 Voluntary contributions
What values, theories, and assumptions support the
delivery of this service?
 Adequacy of services and facilities
 Professionalism of staff and of care
 View of identity and value of recipients, clients,
  or patients
 Respect for individual and group capabilities to
  influence their own situation
 Freedom of choice vs. social control
 Freedom of dissent vs. efficiency of service delivery
 Cost effectiveness vs. social effectiveness
 Degree of local/family control and input to service
  delivery

Box 24.1

system used by Marty and his family. It could be of assistance to families considering government resources of various types.

Remember that, while the product outline in Box 24.1 may be of help to you in this process, your inspiration from our Heavenly Father is the most important part of the process.

GOVERNMENTAL LEGAL EFFORTS TO STRENGTHEN THE FAMILY

After exploring the role of individuals and groups in providing and selecting community welfare services to support or strengthen families, it is important to examine another important aspect of public welfare services: how national and international governmental agencies are defining and directing the policies under which we must live as families. The family has been the subject of increasing intervention by state and federal governments. Many individuals and leaders of federal units believe that because the traditional family is in peril, it has become necessary for them to intervene, especially in legislation addressing child, spouse, and elder abuse. This section will explore the variety of efforts being exerted by governments and international bodies to define, strengthen, and propel the family in the direction they believe most desirable.

Much has been done in the United States, by both federal and state governments, toward strengthening families. Due to the pluralistic nature of the American culture, such effort is confronted initially with the definition of a family or its subunits, such as "what constitutes a legally valid marriage?"

The Defense of Marriage Act

The Defense of Marriage Act (DOMA) is an example of the federal government's effort to define marriage as being legal only between a man and a woman. The government's intent is made clear on the face of the House Bill text, which declares that the legislation is targeted to "define and protect the institution of marriage" and this intent was repeated in identical manner on the face of the Senate Bill.[8] In the end, the legislation was amended by adding the following major provisions:

> Section 1738C. Certain acts, records, and proceedings and the effect thereof:
> No State . . . shall be required to give effect to any public act, record, or judicial proceeding of any other

State . . . respecting a relationship between persons of the same sex that is treated as a marriage under the laws of such other State . . . or a right or claim arising from such a relationship.[9]

Section 7. Definition of "marriage" and "spouse"

In determining the meaning of any Act of Congress, or of any ruling, regulation, or interpretation of the various administrative bureaus and agencies of the United States, the word "marriage" means only a legal union between one man and one woman as husband and wife, and the word "spouse" refers only to a person of the opposite sex who is a husband or a wife.[10]

DOMA was passed during the pendency of an appeal to the Hawaii Supreme Court of a case by three same–sex couples appealing the trial court's decision not to order the issuance of marriage licenses to them on the grounds that they were members of the same sex. In effect, the DOMA invalidates any marriages between members of the same sex for any federal purposes (such as spousal social security benefits). It also gives states the option to circumvent, at least partially, the Full Faith and Credit clause of the Constitution which, in the family law arena, requires recognition by states of a marriage considered valid in another state.[11] Members of the gay and lesbian community argued that the DOMA was unconstitutional. However, the Hawaii Supreme Court affirmed the decision of the trial court and a legislative referendum failed; same–sex marriages failed to become legal in Hawaii. Many states have also passed their own laws refusing to recognize same–sex marriages, either by express prohibition or by refusing to validate such marriages.

Family and Medical Leave Act

Another example of the federal government's efforts to strengthen families can be seen in the *Family and Medical Leave Act (FMLA)* (Pub. L. No. 103–3).[12] Under FMLA, an employee is legally entitled to take up to 12 weeks of unpaid leave per year for any of the following family-related medical reasons: "(1) the birth of a [child] of the employee, (2) 'the placement of a son or daughter with the employee for adoption or foster care,' (3) to provide care for the employee's son, daughter, spouse, or parent who has a serious health condition or (4) the serious health condition of the employee which prevents the employee from working."[13] "Employers are required to provide health insurance coverage during the leave,"[14] and "restore an employee to his or her position or to an equivalent position with equivalent benefits, pay and other terms and conditions of employment."[15] While it is not a general grant of leave protection covering all family crises nor a panacea for minor family illnesses, the FMLA represents a landmark legislation in favor of the employee's need to tend to family medical needs. Its intent was "to balance the demands of the workplace with the needs of the families, to promote the stability and economic security of families, and to promote national interests in preserving family integrity."[16]

LAWS RELATED TO THE PROTECTION OF VULNERABLE FAMILY MEMBERS

The Adoption Assistance and Child Welfare Act of 1980 has been haled as the "most important child welfare legislation"[17] because it provides a comprehensive scheme of protection and service to abused and neglected children and their families, including extensive requirements for services to keep the family together. There are reporting laws for actual or suspected abuse of the elderly or disabled adults in most states. While not every state requires the report of elder abuse or neglect, the Older Americans Act of 1965 mandated the creation of services in each state to protect and serve the needs of the elderly.[18] Similarly, although one is not legally required to report spouse abuse in every state, much attention has "trickled down" from the federal level on the issue of domestic violence. All of these federal initiatives are tied to funding of services at the state and local levels and encourage the protection of family members from abuse and neglect.

The Personal Responsibility and Work Opportunity Reconciliation Act of 1996 is the single most important social welfare reform legislation since the Social Security Act of 1935.[19] The Act abolished the Aid to Families with Dependent Children (AFDC) program and established the Temporary Assistance to Needy Families (TANF) program. While AFDC was a federal entitlement program, the TANF is a temporary cash assistance program based on block grants to the states. The major thrust of the PRWORA is to reduce welfare dependency. One provision requires that a teenage parent who is single and under the age of 18 must reside with his or her parents or legal guardian and either have a high school diploma or be enrolled in school full time in order to receive financial assistance. This policy is based on research that suggests that children of women who give birth before age 18 tend to have lower cognitive abilities and are more likely to drop out of school and become teenage parents themselves than children of older mothers.[20] The PRWORA identified teenage parents as a population requiring special encouragement to finish school while providing a relatively stable environment for themselves and their children.

States traditionally have had the authority to regulate family life, from marriage and divorce to death and birth-related laws. This has included the authority to protect vulnerable family members. While family privacy has long been considered the foundation of American family law, the concept of *parens patriae,* or the state's authority to act as an intervening authority in matters of family life, has also been accepted as a necessary evil, even by proponents of family autonomy. This has been especially true since the beginning of the twentieth century and culminating in the decades following the 1960s in the arenas of child abuse and neglect. Spouse abuse received much attention in the 1980s and 1990s, and in recent years, state legislatures have turned their attention to the needs of the elderly.

Beyond the protection of individual family members, states have also been grappling with issues of preserving and protecting the family as an entire unit. The following is a representative sampling of some of these laws designed to strengthen the couple or family as a whole.

COVENANT MARRIAGE LEGISLATION

A recent policy development in some states is the passage of "covenant marriage" legislation. The covenant marriage movement has developed in response to the no-fault divorce system currently in operation in all 50 of the United States. Under the no-fault system, a married couple can obtain a divorce simply by requesting it and alleging "irreconcilable differences." The couple need not list their private problems in court documents or prove them in a court of law. The courts respect the individuals' wishes to dissolve their marriage regardless of who "caused" the divorce. However, one problem with no-fault divorce is that either spouse can end a marriage unilaterally for no serious reason. In contrast, under a covenant marriage the couple chooses to enter into marriage with an additional legal "contract" that, should the marriage founder, the couple will seek counseling, and should one spouse wish to end the marriage, he or she will be required to prove that there are "grounds" (i.e., legally valid reasons) for the

divorce. These grounds may be based on the commitment of adultery, abandonment, commission of a felony crime, physical or sexual abuse, or a few other reasons constituting serious "fault" on the part of the other spouse.[21] In addition, couples who choose a covenant marriage are required to have premarital counseling and to promise that they have disclosed to their partner all information about themselves that reasonably could adversely affect the decision to marry (e.g., having children by a previous relationship).

Not surprisingly, covenant marriage has received mixed reviews from legal and social science scholars as well as policy-makers and practitioners.[22] Proponents of covenant marriage hope that those who choose this form of marriage will enter into marriage better prepared for the realities of married life and more committed to making it work and that they will be more motivated to work through difficult problems to keep a marriage strong. Moreover, they value the additional legal remedies under covenant marriage provided to "innocent" parties whose spouses violate their marital promises and cause the break-up of a family. On the other hand, opponents of covenant marriage believe that it will bring back all the elements of the old divorce laws where a family's "dirty laundry" will necessarily be aired in public, increase the financial and emotional costs of divorce, and create greater difficulties for wives who are generally the less powerful partner in the marriage. Opponents are especially worried that covenant marriage will trap women in abusive relationships, despite the provision in covenant marriage laws for the immediate termination of the marriage upon proof of abuse.

The ambivalence about covenant marriage is seen in the fact that as of December 1999, only two states—Louisiana and Arizona—have adopted covenant marriage statutes. About two dozen other states have proposed covenant marriage statutes so far. In most cases, that legislation has been stalled in the legislative bureaucracy; in a few cases, the legislation has been voted down. Moreover, the early data in Louisiana and Arizona suggests that less than 5 percent of couples are choosing the covenant marriage option, although most couples don't even know there is a choice. Clearly, unless more states adopt covenant marriage statutes and more couples in those states choose covenant marriages, proponents' hopes of decreasing the number of divorces with this legal movement will be dashed.

FAMILY PRESERVATION AND COMMUNITY-BASED SERVICES LEGISLATION

Family preservation services is an integrated effort to strengthen families before more intrusive services are required. The main goal of such services is to prevent family dissolution, reduce inappropriate and lengthy placement of children in out-of-home settings, and to bolster the family's ability to meet its own needs.[23] This legislation is based on the finding that even where abuse or neglect exists, most children and parents are strongly attached to each other and that the trauma of separation can be harmful for children.

Similarly, states are increasingly providing for community-based educational and treatment programs that can be used by parents either voluntarily or under court order to avoid the break-up of families. These programs often address maternal and child health, parenting and developmental education, social support, and programs for children at high risk of delinquency.[24] Other community and neighborhood-based programs are also being provided by legislation, such as suicide prevention services, family conflict resolution services (including psychological and mediation services), support and resources for disabled or developmentally delayed family members, and mentoring programs for the youth.[25]

GRANDPARENT VISITATION AND KINSHIP LEGISLATION

Many state policy-makers are becoming aware that the support and strength received from the extended family is especially important to children when the nuclear family undergoes times of crisis such as divorce, abuse, or neglect. Not infrequently parents object to visitation of their children by either set of grandparents for a variety of reasons, including the motivation to use children as pawns in a divorce, family loyalty issues, or concern over parental control. In the past, grandparents were at the "mercy" of parents to gain access to their grandchildren, but this is changing. Most states have adopted the policy through legislation of allowing grandparent visitation by giving them the right to visit their grandchildren balanced against the parental authority, if the court determines that such visitation is in the best interest of the child(ren) involved.[26] Grandparent visitation is available in some states even when the child has been adopted, if the adoption occurs within the extended family network on either side of the child's family.[27]

Most states now mandate that preference be given to kin for visitation and placement in cases where children may be removed from their parents because of abuse or neglect.[28] Even when the child may not be able to live with kin, the courts are increasingly involving the extended family in making decisions that influence the placement of abused or neglected children. In Oregon, for example, the law mandates that a Family Group Conference be held before placement of an abused child is made outside the family. At this conference, members of the extended family are invited to make a binding decision regarding placement of and services for the child. Often, the subject child is placed with a relative, avoiding the trauma of being separated from loved ones and familiar surroundings.[29]

INTERNATIONAL FAMILY POLICY

Family policies are a product of each nation based on its own traditions, culture, and political composition. The nations of the world are moving more toward a consensus on issues such as "gender equality and the role of the family"[30] and there is an increasing amount of discussion on family well-being at the international level.[31] While there is no international body authorized to generate laws or policies superseding the domestic laws of the nations regarding such issues, the domestic laws and policies of each nation can be influenced by international conventions and agreements even when a nation has not ratified them and is therefore not bound by them, as nations look to international standards when considering their own policies.[32] It is therefore important to understand the current trends in the international arena regarding the family.

An enormous tension exists in the international community between "liberals" and "traditionalists" regarding the role of family and the nature of relationships between subunits within the family. The conceptual tension rests mainly on the balancing of the rights of the individual versus the family unit and also between the family and the government. Generally the liberal camp tends to broaden the definition of family, and to push for the rights of the individual; while the traditional camp would empower the nuclear family of one man and woman with children. The main differences in the two camps are graphically displayed in their interpretation of, and reaction to, two major conventions: The Convention on the Rights of the Child (CRC) and the Convention on the Elimination of All Forms of Discrimination Against Women (CEDAW). Both have been adopted by the United Nations and ratified by a large majority of the world's nations. The United States has ratified neither.

Convention on the Rights of the Child

The CRC is based on the 1959 United Nations Declaration of the Rights of the Child. Initiated as part of the celebration of the 1979 International Year of the Child, the CRC was adopted by the United Nations in 1989. It has been heralded by some as a "Magna Carta for children" and has been accepted quickly and with much apparent enthusiasm by 187 of the member nations, excluding a handful of nations that include the United States.[33] An examination of why the United States has resisted ratification illustrates the pull between the philosophical, cultural, and political tensions embedded in a sweeping international agreement.

Among other provisions, the CRC calls for member nations to safeguard children's survival, nurture their development, protect children from various forms of abuse and oppression, and allow children to participate in activities of importance to them. While the provisions are intended to free children growing up in oppressive cultures from parental and societal tyranny, the traditionalists fear that these provisions will interfere with parental authority over their children and in fact relegate inexperienced children into the role of raising themselves "free" from parental guidance. Granting children such premature autonomy has been characterized by Elder Bruce C. Hafen as the "abandoning [of] children to their autonomy,"[34] by removing them from the protection of families, churches, and other institutions that have traditionally cared for and nurtured them. Among some of the controversial issues involved in child "autonomy" vs. parental guidance are abortion, education, discipline, and personal freedoms such as freedom of thought, conscience, and religion.

Although the CRC does not address abortion directly, there are provisions that support family planning (Article 24(4)(f)) and the right to privacy (Article 16), which, taken together, can be interpreted as being pro-abortion. Proponents of the provisions counter with the language in the Preamble to the CRC, which in effect provides protection to all children, both before and after birth. In addition, Article 6 contains the phrase "every child has the inherent right to life." Proponents of the CRC argue that under these provisions each member state should be able to draft its own legislation concerning abortion.

On the issue of education, some argue that Article 29 of the CRC could restrict parental rights to educate their children "in accordance with their religious beliefs." Additionally, traditionalists fear that the CRC would make discipline methods such as spanking illegal, thus restricting parental rights to mold their children's limits of behavior.[35] Carried further, it may also interfere with parental ability to "chastise" their children based on the parents' moral values.[36] In short, conservatives are suspicious of the CRC as an "anti-parent" and "anti-family" instrument. This suspicion was expressed by Senator Jesse Helms: "The [UN's CRC] is incompatible with the God-given right and responsibility of parents to raise their children."[37] Another concern is that parents could be found in violation of the CRC when they allow their young children to be christened or baptized into the parents' religion or take them to their religious services before the child is ready to make such determination for him- or herself.

Proponents of the CRC believe that Article 5 shows a respect for family autonomy and is laudable for including a broader definition of family than the "nuclear" family. Article 5 states:

> Parties shall respect the responsibilities, rights and duties of parents or, where applicable, the members of the extended family or community as provided for by local custom, legal guardians or other persons legally responsible for the child, to provide, *in a manner consistent with the evolving capacities of the child*, appropriate direction and guidance in the exercise by the child of the rights recognized in the present convention.[38]

Furthermore, Article 14(3) addresses parental rights to control the religious upbringing of their children; however, CRC proponents acknowledge that the drafters of the provision did not wish to grant parental rights at the expense of children's rights, therefore including the qualification which is italicized above.[39]

It should be noted that the CRC attempts to provide a guideline to all people of the world and is therefore not acceptable in its totality to all people. In its attempt to discourage the abuse of children, its language may in effect undermine the integrity and autonomy of well-functioning families in which children are loved and cared for.

The Proclamation firmly states that those who abuse children will stand accountable before God and that the disintegration of the family will bring calamities to individuals, communities, and nations (¶ 8). It is therefore important for Latter-day Saints to abhor the abuse and neglect of the children worldwide and simultaneously work to ensure that the foundation of the family is built upon love, respect, and gospel truths.

Convention on the Elimination of All Forms of Discrimination Against Women

The Western ideal of equality between men and women and husband and wife is quite unfamiliar in some cultures of the world. Violence against women is reported to be the most pervasive violation of human rights in the world today.[40] Deeply embedded in many cultures, violence against women can be subtle yet powerfully debilitating. Women experience such abuse and discrimination at all levels of society, including within the context of marriage and family. Some forms of the maltreatment women receive within the family include genital mutilation of girls and women; the practice of "honor killing," wherein girls and women are killed at the will of the husband, father, or brother in order to restore "honor" to the family; dowry deaths; sexual and physical abuse of girls and women; and economic powerlessness within marriage and society in general. Unfortunately, many of these practices are allowed to occur in many parts of the world and are condoned informally by government officials even when laws exist prohibiting them. For example, in 12 Latin American countries, a rapist can be exonerated if his victim agrees to marry him.[41] Equal rights and respect for women is sorely needed and in some societies more than others.[42]

The Convention of the Elimination of All Forms of Discrimination Against Women (CEDAW) is an effort by the international community through the United Nations to stop these atrocities and other forms of discrimination against women. It was adopted by the United Nations General Assembly in 1979 and entered into force as an international treaty in 1981. While more than one hundred countries have signed, the United States has not. The CEDAW is well intended and is geared to counterbalance the most horrific forms of abuse and discrimination against women.

However, opponents worry that some of the language may make some traditional customs illegal, and the result does not necessarily make the lives of women better. Some of the provisions that are worrisome to traditionalists include those that require "the maximum participation of women on equal terms with men in all fields"; the recognition that the "upbringing of children requires a sharing of responsibility between men and women and society as a whole"; the provision stating that "a change in the traditional role of men as well as the role of women in society and in the family is needed to achieve full equality between men and women"; terms defining as discrimination "any distinction . . . on the basis of sex which has the effect or purpose of impairing or nullifying the . . . exercise by women . . . of human rights and fundamental freedoms in the political, economic, social, cultural, civil or any other field"; and those requiring all nations "to modify the social and cultural patterns of conduct of men and women, with a view to . . . elimination of . . . customary and all other practices which are based on . . . stereotyped roles for men and women."[43]

The previously presented provisions of the CEDAW and many others could be interpreted to be contrary to the Proclamation which reinforces the "traditional" concept that fathers are to be providers and that mothers are primarily responsible for the nurture of the children. Religious traditions that form the guiding principles of many groups of people, including Latter-day Saints, could be construed as "customary practices" to be eliminated. Hence, the CEDAW's major incompatibility with the Proclamation is its overreach into the private individual and religious traditions of many peoples of the world, who may actually be fostering the values of overall equality and respect toward women. As Latter-day Saints, we must find a way to respond to the shameful practices of violence and discrimination against women, while at the same time preserving the practices that are in harmony with the Proclamation.

SUMMARY AND CONCLUSION

Throughout the world, government leaders are struggling to pass laws and policy agreements and to create social welfare programs that both strengthen families and protect vulnerable family members. We, as involved citizens, however, must remain vigilant to monitor these policies and public programs and select carefully those programs and services that will receive our support or participation. Some will serve us and others well and some will wear away at the foundations of our families.

NOTES

1. *Welfare Services Resource Handbook* (1980) (Salt Lake City: The Church of Jesus Christ of Latter-day Saints), 21.

2. Neal A. Maxwell (1974), *That my family should partake* (Salt Lake City: Deseret Book), 7.

3. Daniel H. Ludlow (Ed.) (1992), *Encyclopedia of Mormonism*, 4 vols. (New York: Macmillan).

4. Joseph B. Wirthlin (1999, May), Inspired Church welfare, *Ensign, 29*(5), 78.

5. Wirthlin (1999, May), 76.

6. Marion G. Romney (1982, November), Celestial nature of self-reliance, *Ensign, 12*(11), 93.

7. N. Gilbert and P. Terrell (1998), *The dimensions of social welfare policy* (4th ed.) (Needham Heights, MA: Allyn & Bacon).

8. Defense of Marriage Act of 1996, 28 U.S.C.S. § 1738C (1999) (West 1996).

9. Defense of Marriage Act (1996).

10. Defense of Marriage Act (1996).

11. S. Ruskay-Kidd (1997), The Defense of Marriage Act and the overextension of congressional authority, *Columbia Law Review, 97*, 1435.

12. Family and Medical Leave Act of 1993, 29 U.S.C. § 2612 *et seq.* (West 1993).

13. 29 U.S.C. 2612 (a)(1)–(1)(D).

14. 29 U.S.C. 2614 (c)(1).

15. See 29 U.S.C. 2614 (a)(1)(A-B).

16. 29 U.S.C. 2612 (a)(1).

17. D. S. Liederman (1995), Child welfare overview, in *Encyclopedia of Social Work* (Washington, D.C.: NASW Press), 426.

18. Older Americans Act of 1965, 42 U.S.C.A. § 3001 (West 1965).

19. Personal Responsibility and Work Opportunities Reconciliation Act of 1996, 42 U.S.C.S. § 602 (1999) (West 1996).

20. Moore et al. and Havemen et al. (1997). In R. G. Wood and J. Burghardt, *Implementing welfare reform requirements for teenage parents: Lessons from experience in four states, for the office of the assistant secretary for planning and evaluation,* online, available at http://aspe.os.dhhs.gov/hsp/isp/teepareq/xsteen.htm

21. See, e.g., Louisiana Revised Statutes 9:307; in Marriage: General Principles, La. Rev. Stat. 9:224–307 (1998); Marital and Domestic Relations, Ariz. Rev. Stat. § 25–901–903 (1998).

22. For reviews of the arguments for and against covenant marriage, see S. L. Nock, J. D. Wright, and L. Sanchez (1999), America's divorce problem, *Society, 36*(4), 43–52.

23. See Fla. Stat., 409.152, 1998; in Dissolution of Marriage; Support; Custody; Fla. Stat. § 61.13 (1998).

24. See, e.g., Fla. Stat. 402.45; in Family Preservation Services, Fla. Stat. § 409.152 (1998).

25. See, e.g., Children's Code, Colo. Rev. Stat., 26–5.7–103; 26–18–104; in Children's Code, Colo. Rev. Stat. § 19–1–103 (1998).

26. See, e.g., Family Code, 3104; in Cal. Fam. Code § 3104 (1999).

27. See, e.g., Code of Alabama, 26–10A-30; in Infants and Incompetents, Code of Alabama § 26–10A-30 (1998).

28. See, e.g., Child and Family Services, Utah Code Ann., 62A-4a-202.3(4)(b); in Child and Family Services, Utah Code Ann. § 62A-4a-202.3 (1998).

29. See, e.g., Children and Family Services, Oregon Rev. Stat., 417.365 to 417.375; in Children and Family Services, Ore. Rev. Stat. § 417.365–417.375 (1997).

30. R. G. Wilkins (1996), International agreements and domestic law: They don't displace, but they may define, in S. Roylance (Ed.), *The traditional family in peril* (3rd ed.) (South Jordan, UT: United Families International), 150–153.

31. R. G. Wilkins and B. N. Roylance (1996), The impact of UN conference declarations on international and domestic law, unpublished manuscript in the possession of author.

32. Wilkins (1996).

33. Convention on the Rights of the Child (1989).

34. Bruce C. Hafen (1996), Abandoning children to their autonomy, *Harvard International Law Journal, 37*, 449.

35. A. D. Renteln (1997), United States ratification of human rights treaties: Who's afraid of the CRC, *Journal of International and Comparative Law, 3*, 629.

36. CDC as quoted in Renteln (1997).

37. CDC as quoted in Helms (1995), in Renteln (1997).

38. CDC as quoted in Renteln (1997).

39. See also S. Roylance (1996), Appendix I: Excerpts from Convention on Rights of the Child, in Roylance (Ed.), *The traditional family in peril,* 182.

40. C. Bunch (1997), The intolerable status quo: Violence against women and girls, in *The progress of nations* (New York: United Nations Children's Fund), 41–49.

41. Bunch (1997).

42. Bunch (1997); Roylance (Ed.) (1996), *The traditional family in peril.*

43. Roylance (1996), Appendix II: Excerpts from Convention on the Elimination of All Forms of Discrimination Against Women (CEDAW), in S. Roylance (Ed.), *The traditional family in peril,* 184–185.

Family Life Education

Tamara Talbot and Natalie C. Goddard

We call upon responsible citizens and officers of government everywhere to promote those measures
designed to maintain and strengthen the family as the fundamental unit of society.
(The Family: A Proclamation to the World, ¶ 9)

I f the universal truths about family life declared in the Proclamation stir something deep inside you, it is because family life is what life is all about. As Dr. Carl Whitaker noted, "there are no individuals in the world; we are only fragments of families."[1] The Proclamation's powerful descriptions of the family and the nature of family life are concluded with an equally powerful call to action: "We call upon responsible citizens and officers of government everywhere to promote those measures designed to maintain and strengthen the family as the fundamental unit of society" (¶ 9).

It is not enough to believe that the family is important. In a world where the family is being attacked and family life destroyed, we must be active not only in strengthening our own families, but in reaching out into our communities to fight for the family's place in all cultures of the world. But first we must discern which measures will effectively strengthen family life and the family's status in society.

In the past few years an exciting new field has emerged that directly serves to maintain and strengthen families. It's called *family life education*. It involves the proverbial fence-on-the-cliff approach—teaching families the foundational principles of healthy, happy family life to keep them from falling off the destructive cliffs of abuse, neglect, divorce, and other dangers. Traditionally, family life education has taken the form of formal workshops or seminars on parenting, marriage enrichment, or family relations, but it is growing into dynamically diverse means of promoting families that anyone can do.

As a career, the field of family life education has developed in conjunction with other professions—therapists incorporating education as part of their practice, clergy offering classes in their ministries, etc. To make a living as a full-time family life educator is still a challenging, even pioneering effort, but more and more opportunities are opening all the time. The National Council on Family Relations now offers a professional accreditation as a Certified Family Life Educator (CFLE) and many organizations are opening positions for educators. There are CFLEs moving into military family centers, corporate human resource centers, social service agencies, state extension programs and public education arenas.

Working in these areas doesn't have to be part of your career, though. People who are dedicated to promoting family principles will find many sectors of their communities open to family life education on a volunteer or part-time basis. With a little work, many individuals have successfully set up family classes or workshops at local libraries, hospitals, community centers, fire departments, or for private groups (e.g., wards or stakes, ministries, men/women's clubs, employee gatherings) as a one-time or even monthly service.

Beyond the class-style instruction, there are

endless alternative means to spread understanding of family life and relationships. Several effective mentoring programs have been developed that use families to teach families through joint family activities. Research has shown that these "lay educators" are every bit as helpful in influencing family life as professional educators.[2] Other innovative programs have developed media delivery options—video or audio presentations, interactive CD-ROM programs, Internet sites. Books or newspaper or magazine articles written about principles and skills for happy families are a great means of teaching many families. Making simple statements of family life principles in family places, such as on grocery store carts or receipt backs, movie theater preview screens, doctor's office reception rooms, or on restaurant tables can be a small but influential means of teaching, too. Sometimes the more creative the delivery, the more effective it is in capturing and influencing peoples minds. Whatever your hobby— singing, painting, quilt making—you can use it as a means of teaching principles of family life.

We have found that many people who would be wonderful in the practice of family life education are not contributing simply because they do not know how to get started. With our education in family science and as Certified Family Life Educators, we established a nonprofit organization for the purpose of helping people to help people—or, more specifically, to help family life educators help families. We began by getting down in the trenches of the field to learn and gain a perspective of reality. We created a few basic workshops using principles from the Proclamation combined with good research and our own experiences. The county health department asked to list our family workshops for local businesses and organizations. The family classes were requested more than any of the traditionally offered nutrition and disease-awareness types of workshops. The community continuing education organization also contacted us, though they didn't have a section for family classes in the catalog. They had the usual offering of pottery, computer, and sports classes. They first listed our parenting and marriage classes under personal development and business, but after some encouragement, by the second season they added a family subsection. We were excited about such favorable responses because they represent the real possibility for family life education to make a difference in communities. Also, we began working at a young mother's high school in a pilot effort to incorporate marriage and family curriculum into the public

education system. We met with community councils, the local legal system, and professional conventions in an effort to promote awareness of family life education and family advocacy.

As a result of these experiences, we felt strongly that the successes we began to see suggested that others could do as well in their communities, if they just had some help getting started and support in their endeavors. Now we are preparing to offer that support and the resources that can make contributing to the field easier—both for full-time professionals and for anyone who wants to be involved. We offer training, a resource list, basic curricula, a guide to creating your own programs, family advocacy and promotional materials, a directory to list workshops, networking opportunities, and creative alternative delivery ideas. Those interested may contact the Family Life Education Institute at 1–800–452–5662 or go to *www.familylifeeducation.org* for information.

Though the Proclamation clearly states that "Happiness in family life is most likely to be achieved when founded upon the teachings of the Lord Jesus Christ," its call to strengthen families in society urges us to move beyond the LDS community. We need to educate people with fundamental principles of family life that will ring true to all people regardless of their religious or nonreligious beliefs. True principles will always be founded in Jesus Christ, but not everyone is ready to accept them from Him. Developing workshops and material based on universal truths with application for families of diverse cultures is challenging, but essential to effective family life education.

Working with families and family research daily sometimes only emphasizes the dichotomy between the ideals described in the Proclamation and the discouraging problems so many families experience. Still, we need to respond to the call of modern prophets. We have found motivation and hope in the experience of the ancient prophet Jacob. He described the wicked state of the Lamanite nation of his day but then prophesied of their salvation, declaring that because of their observance of just one thing (see Jacob 3:6) they would become a "blessed people": "Behold, their husbands love their wives, and their wives love their husbands; and their husbands and their wives love their children" (Jacob 3:7).

Even if we just teach husbands and wives, parents and children the principles of family love, the effect can be more powerful and eternal than we may now know. As you do what you can to answer the prophets' call to strengthen families through whatever measures you find, you will be working at the center of our Creator's plan for the eternal destiny of all His children.

NOTES

1. Quoted in N. Stinnett and J. DeFrain (1985), *Secrets of Strong Families* (New York: Berkeley Publishing Group), vii.

2. S. M. Stanley, H. J. Markman, L. M. Prado, P. A. Olmos Gallo, L. Tonelli, M. St. Peters, B. D. Leber, M. Bobulinski, A. Cordova, and S. Whitton, unpublished paper, Community based premarital prevention: Clergy and lay leaders on the front lines, available from author.

Strengthening Families through the Entertainment Industry

Alan R. Osmond

In this essay I briefly describe some of the work that my wife, Suzanne, and I, along with many others, have been involved with in strengthening families through media and entertainment.

I am the oldest member of the Osmond Brothers and The Osmonds performing family and had been an entertainer with 42 wonderful years of experience. I say "had" because a few years ago I was physically slowed by the crippling disease called Multiple Sclerosis (MS). Although I may have MS, MS does *not* have me! I now spend my time for families and for charity—thinking, creating, and focusing my efforts on what I can do to strengthen families.

A few years ago, Suzanne and I felt impressed to start a nonprofit organization, nonpolitical, and nondenominational foundation for the purpose of strengthening families. We did so, naming it the One Heart Foundation (www.oneheart.org) and locating its headquarters in the "heart" of America: Kansas City, Missouri.

We knew that hundreds of excellent family organizations already existed and were trying to share their messages and programs. We learned that some family organizations were stronger, with better written materials than others, and that some focused on research and data about the family while others focused on practical skills training. However, all seemed to share the same overall goal of strengthening families—they were of "one heart" for the family

cause. Given that there was already much good written content available, we wondered what unique contribution the One Heart Foundation should make to help strengthen families.

We considered whether we should pattern One Heart after a successful approach we had employed in the charity arena. Much good had been done through the Osmond Foundation and its creation of the Children's Miracle Network, (CMN) which, to date, is the largest telethon in the world, having donated more than two billion dollars to children's hospitals with 100 percent of the money staying in the local market where it was raised. The CMN created a vehicle for the many wonderful children's hospitals around the country to raise funds and spread their message in a united fashion via a telethon rather than independently promoting their cause. Under the Children's Miracle Network banner, all these hospitals received maximum donations and message awareness with exposure to millions of viewers.

We thought it might be helpful to mirror somewhat the design of the Children's Miracle Network by having the One Heart Foundation provide a similar type of service for the many existing family organizations, thus creating opportunities to work together and maximize efforts for strengthening families. We felt that if we could somehow get family groups working together and still maintain their autonomy, we could become a force for good. We decided to provide opportunities for family-oriented charities to receive both revenue and publicity to help further their causes.

In addition, since we live in a society where many people get most of their information from media rather than from reading, we knew the tremendous power of the media to influence people for good or ill. There were good reasons to build on our strengths and use my contacts and experience in media and entertainment so we could create ways for good family organizations to get their messages out. With my love of creating live events, producing TV and music, publishing via the Internet and media, networking, committing celebrity friends to the work, and bringing sponsors who also share the same "heart" for family causes, we believed that One Heart could help make a difference. Since I really believe that families are especially strengthened when they do things together, live events and fun activities have become a focus of One Heart.

One Heart Foundation produced an event in Branson, Missouri, where 30–40,000 people showed up for a family gathering called "Branson Blast!" There were thrill acts, fireworks, and many big-name entertainers involved in this family evening on the lake. It was free to the public, but in order to get tickets, with some exceptions, they needed to come and participate as a family. The entertainers who performed all agreed to take a moment and share one of their favorite family experiences. An organization called the American Family Society was our guest charity and throughout the evening they gave several 30-second thoughts for families to think about. The local press noted this as one of the most successful family events the city has had.

We turned a large veterans celebration into one of family recognition of veteran parents and grandparents, called "Kids for Vets." Bob Hope was invited and dedicated a gazebo-covered statue of an eagle to the veterans as original music honored kids of today as "The Hope of America." The kids honored their family heroes with song and dance and the neighboring mall presented music, pageantry, stars, and fireworks to wrap up the family/veteran tribute.

In November 1999, we participated in the World Congress on Families II in Geneva, Switzerland, where the One Heart staff was asked to produce the entertainment, produce an opening film, and create a closing production on Lake Geneva with music and fireworks. Music is a medium that crosses the language barriers, and we arranged for and produced wholesome, family-centered musical entertainment each evening. In the closing production, images of families from many nations were projected on two large screens, a song about the family was sung in five languages, and a large choir of families with children waving the flags of the world performed. The 1,575 people from more than 45 nations and from many cultures and religions left the Congress with positive feelings about the traditional family being the basic unit of civilization. David Brewer, of One Heart, filmed, taped, and broadcast the messages of the Congress on our web site (www.thefamily.com) and on the Congress's web site (www.worldcongress.org).

We have developed a national State Fair promotion to take the family message across the country with music and special effects that will help various family organizations get their publications and programs out to people throughout America. We also have several artists donating their music on special family-oriented CD's and videos that are made available on our web site (www.thefamily.com), which also publishes a monthly e-magazine.

One Heart's goal is to lead out and gain the confidence and support of families, family organizations, and become the hub of a big wheel that brings together the best of family content and activities using every medium, stage, dollar, and good idea to strengthen families. We invite all individuals and organizations that share the desire to be of one heart in strengthening families to join with us.

DEFENDING MARRIAGE AND THE FAMILY THROUGH LAW AND POLICY

LYNN D. WARDLE, RICHARD N. WILLIAMS, AND RICHARD G. WILKINS

We call upon responsible citizens and officers of government everywhere to promote those measures designed to maintain and strengthen the family as the fundamental unit of society.
(The Family: A Proclamation to the World, ¶ 9)

Editor's Note: The Proclamation concludes with a clarion call for individuals everywhere to promote measures to strengthen the family as a "the fundamental unit of society" (¶ 9). Consistent with this statement, The Church of Jesus Christ of Latter-day Saints has itself become involved in several widely publicized defenses of the institutions of marriage and the family and has asked its members to do so as individual citizens.

This chapter consists of three essays dealing with defending marriage and the family through law and policy. The essays are written by two BYU professors of law, Lynn Wardle and Richard Wilkins, and by BYU professor of psychology, Richard Williams. Each of these professors has been on the front lines in the challenging effort to defend the institutions of marriage and family as defined in the Proclamation.

Essay R overviews the recent attempts to legalize same–sex marriage and provides strong legal and moral reasons to strenuously oppose these attempts. Essay S reviews and critiques the research on same–sex parenting and refutes the argument that research shows no differences in parenting by same–sex parents and heterosexual parents. Essay T summarizes the startling attacks on the institutions of marriage and the family coming from some international groups lobbying the United Nations, and also describes an opposing effort designed to strengthen the institutions of marriage and the family called the World Congress of Families. Together, the essays in this chapter articulate the need for citizens and officers of all governments to work to strengthen the *institutions* of marriage and family in all societies.

LEGAL AND MORAL ISSUES OF SAME-SEX MARRIAGE

LYNN D. WARDLE

The Church of Jesus Christ of Latter-day Saints, like several other churches, has been significantly involved and has encouraged its members to be active in opposing the legalization of same–sex marriage. The work of the Church and its members in Hawaii, Alaska, California, Vermont, and other states in grassroots coalition efforts to prevent the legalization of same–sex marriage has produced some highly publicized hostility against the Church. Some have asked why the Church has been so actively and persistently involved in a "political" issue, especially when they encounter such bitter opposition. For several years, I have been involved professionally and personally in legal battles to protect the family, including the institution of marriage. My answer to the question of why the Church should be involved in this issue has many dimensions.

Why the Church Should Defend the Institution of Marriage

The threat to radically redefine marriage is not an idle threat. The movement to legalize same–sex marriage is a serious effort with powerful support in many jurisdictions. Internationally, for example, between 1989 and 1999, legislatures in Denmark, Norway, Sweden, Iceland, the Netherlands, and France enacted laws creating "registered domestic partnerships," authorizing the formal registration of same–sex unions and extending to them all of the economic and many of the noneconomic legal attributes of marriage. Likewise, the legislature in Hungary, following a decision of the national supreme court, legalized common law same–sex live-in companionships for purposes of recognizing their mutually owned purchases and acquisitions. The governments of many other countries are considering similar domestic partnership registration bills. And in 1999, the government of the Netherlands (which already allows same–sex domestic partnership) announced that it would introduce a bill to allow same–sex couples to marry. In many cities of the world, same–sex couples already can obtain official registration "certificates," which have no legal effect but symbolize official recognition of same–sex marriages.

Because marriage laws in the United States do not allow same–sex marriage, advocates of same–sex marriage must change the laws in order to legalize same–sex marriage. Since the marriage laws are enacted by state legislatures, one might expect that the effort to legalize same–sex marriage to focus on the legislatures. However, because legislatures generally reflects public opinion on highly controversial issues, and because opposition to same–sex marriage in the general public is very strong in the United States (usually ranging from two- to three-to-one against it), advocates of same–sex marriage have made few efforts to change the marriage law by legislation.

Instead, proponents of same–sex marriage have made many efforts to legalize same–sex marriage through the back door, by judicial decree. They have had some notable successes.

In the United States, between 1993 and 1998, three state courts entered rulings favorable to same–sex marriage; in one of those cases a court ordered a state to issue marriage licenses to same–sex couples (the order was stayed pending appeal). Each of those judicial rulings was later neutralized, but it took massive grassroots political efforts, involving LDS and other churches, to protect the institution of marriage.

In March 1993, the Hawaii Supreme Court ruled in *Baehr v. Lewin*, that the state's marriage license law allowing only male–female couples to obtain marriage licenses "discriminates based on sex against [same–sex] couples," in apparent violation of the Equal Protection Clause and Equal Rights Amendment of the Hawaii Constitution. In that decision, the Hawaii Supreme Court reinstated a suit by gay and lesbian couples seeking marriage licenses that had been dismissed and sent the case back to a lower court for a trial to determine whether Hawaii had a compelling state interest for not permitting same–sex marriage. After many delays and a short trial, a state trial court ruled in December 1996 that the state had no compelling interest to deny marriage licenses to same–sex couples and ordered the state to issue marriage licenses to same–sex couples who apply for them. That ruling was appealed to the Hawaii Supreme Court, and the order was held in abeyance pending appeal. A few months later, the Hawaii Legislature proposed a constitutional amendment to guarantee that marriage could be limited to traditional (male–female) marriages. The Church and many members joined with several other churches and many other individuals in a coalition to secure passage of the amendment. In November 1998, the people of Hawaii ratified the amendment by a ratio of 69 percent to 29 percent, overwhelmingly voting to preserve marriage as an exclusively male–female institution.

Similarly, in Alaska same–sex couples denied marriage licenses sued under state law asking the state court to order the state to issue marriage licenses to gay and lesbian couples. In February 1997, a state trial court denied the state's motion for summary judgment (judgment on the law and undisputed facts), ruling instead that Alaska Constitution protected the right of same–sex couples to marry as a matter of "privacy" and that denial of same–sex marriage appeared to violate the Equal Protection guarantees of the state constitution. The Alaska legislature responded immediately by proposing an amendment to the Alaska Constitution that would define marriage as the union of one man and one woman. Again, The Church of Jesus Christ of Latter-day Saints and many members joined with the other churches and persons in an interfaith coalition to support passage of the marriage amendment. In November 1998, the people of Alaska overwhelmingly ratified the marriage amendment by a vote of 68 percent to 32 percent.

In both Alaska and Hawaii, it took tremendous effort and contributions of many individuals and organizations, including the Church and other churches and many of their members, to protect the institution of marriage. Without those efforts, same–sex marriage would likely have been legalized as a result of the judicial rulings. Thus, the threat of legalization of same–sex marriage is serious and urgent.

A second reason why the Church has been actively involved in opposing legalization of same–sex marriage is that it would have far-reaching consequences, opening a Pandora's box of tremendously detrimental effects. In every state, hundreds of laws tailored for and intended to protect the institution of marriage would be transformed into "gay rights" laws. For example, homosexual couples could claim the right as married couples to adopt children and to become foster parents; public school curricula designed to prepare students for marriage would have to promote and teach about homosexual unions along with traditional marriage. Public benefits designed to strengthen marriages and defray the costs of contributions that marriages make to society would subsidize gay and lesbian couples. Same-sex couples could insist on "equal" enjoyment of all marriage benefits provided by law, including tax exemptions, welfare benefits, retirement benefits, eligibility for housing, etc. Various "civil rights" laws would more easily be used to penalize citizens who have personal moral and religious beliefs opposed to homosexual behavior. Organizations such as the Boy Scouts, day-care centers, nurseries, elementary and junior high schools, and churches could risk being punished if they refused to hire homosexuals.

Third, legalizing same–sex marriage would severely undermine the status and meaning of marriage in ways that would mislead and confuse individuals, weaken society, and demean the institution of marriage. The historic message of the law that marriage is a unique and uniquely valuable relationship would be replaced with a message that any committed union of adults, including same–sex liaisons, are considered by society to be equally valuable, safe, fulfilling, and socially beneficial. The law would send a message that gender is not a relevant factor in marriage; that the conjugal union of a man and a woman is no different than the sexual partnership of two men or two women. The historically proven reality that the marital union of a man and a woman creates a unique relationship, potentially stronger, potentially more beneficial, potentially more valuable for the individuals and for society, would be rejected. By equalizing marriage and same–sex partnership, the law would convey a false message that same–sex partnerships are just as safe, just as secure, and contribute just as much to society as traditional marriages between a man and a woman.

Fourth, the consequences for individuals on the "fringes" of society would be particularly devastating. Same-sex unions are fraught with risks to the individuals involved, as well as to society. Increased numbers of vulnerable persons would become victims of the same–sex lifestyle and all its physical and spiritual risks if same–sex marriage or marriage-like domestic partnership were legalized. The economic and social costs to society of the consequences of the increased number of persons experimenting with same–sex lifestyles would be tremendous.

In short, the Church has boldly spoken out on this issue, despite criticisms and harassment, and has encouraged its members and other "responsible citizens and officers of government everywhere to promote those measures designed to maintain and strengthen the family as the fundamental unit of society" (Proclamation, ¶ 9) in order to sound a warning to individuals and to society. *The Family: A Proclamation to the World* expresses an explicit warning "that the disintegration of the family will bring upon individuals, communities, and nations the calamities foretold by ancient and modern prophets" (¶ 8).

Arguments for Legalizing Same–Sex Unions and Responses

One argument for same–sex marriage is that marriage is a fundamental constitutional and human right. That is true, but the union of a man and a woman is the only kind of relationship that has been so preferred and protected. Marriage is, by long-standing definition, the union of a man and woman. Same-sex unions have never been deemed to be

within the definition of the "marriage" relationship that is rightly considered to be a fundamental human and constitutional right. That exclusive definition of "marriage" continues to receive overwhelming support. For example, a worldwide survey taken by Wirthlin Worldwide, reported before the World Congress of Families II in 1999, found that 84 percent of adults around the world agree that the definition of marriage is "one man and one woman." (For more information, see http://www.worldcongress.org)

Another argument for same–sex marriage invokes the right of privacy. However, "marriage" is not merely a "private" status; it is a public, legal status. While many kinds of illicit private cohabitation may be tolerated, only the union of a man and woman has been given the special, preferred, formal, public legal status of "marriage."

Another argument made for same–sex marriage asserts that the law should treat all adult consensual relationships equally. However, the law distinguishes among relationships, preferring those that promote the interests of society, tolerating some other relationships that are not harmful, and even prohibiting some adult consensual relationships that are potentially dangerous (such as incestuous relationships, bigamous relationships, adulterous relationships, etc.). Same-sex unions are not given equal legal status as traditional marriages because they are not in fact equal with heterosexual marriages in terms of the contributions they make to society and to the public interest.

Contributions made to Society by Male–Female Legal Unions

Traditional (male–female) marriages and same–sex unions differ markedly in the contributions they make to society in terms of social purposes for legalizing marriage. While data continues to accumulate, it appears that the marriage union of a man and woman provides, among other things: (1) the best setting for the safest and most beneficial expression of sexual intimacy (the only safe sex); (2) the best environment into which children can be born and reared (the profound benefits of dual-gender parenting to model intergender relations and show children how to relate to persons of their own and the opposite gender are lost in same–sex unions); (3) the best security for the status of women (who take the greatest risks and invest the greatest personal effort in maintaining families); (4) the strongest and most stable companionate unit of society (and thus the most secure setting for intergenerational transmission of social knowledge and skills); (5) a functional and historic social stability that same–sex marriage would undermine (marriage between man and woman is the basic unit of society and the historic foundation of civilization); (6) the seed-ground for democracy and the most important schoolroom for self-government (the best training ground for civic virtue, the ability to forego personal gratification or immediate profit for the greater welfare of society); and (7) the basis for intercultural understanding (male–female marriage is one of the few constants across cultures and across time).

From the perspective of these critical social interests underlying marriage, the evidence of the tremendous contributions made by male–female marriages is well established and continues to grow, while evidence of potentially equivalent valuable contributions made by same–sex unions is tenuous at best. Since same–sex unions do not make comparable contributions to society, their claim for equivalent legal status fails.

Beyond empirical and consequential reasons for opposing same–sex marriage are profound moral and religious reasons relating to concerns that transcend short-term consequences and statistical measures. The Proclamation makes clear "that marriage between a man and a woman is ordained of God . . ." (¶ 1). It also declares that "[g]ender is an essential characteristic of individual premortal, mortal, and eternal identity and purpose" (¶ 2). During the October 1999 general conference, President Gordon B. Hinckley explained "Why We Do Some of the Things We Do," including why the Church had been so heavily involved in the effort to prevent legalization of same–sex marriage. He emphasized: (1) the sacred nature of marriage—that it "lies at the heart of the Lord's eternal plan for His children"; (2) that it is "a matter of morality"; (3) the importance of the issue for the "moral fiber of society"; (4) that male–female marriage has provided the "the basis of civilization for thousands of years"; (5) that preserving marriage for male–female union is "of critical importance to the future of the family"; and (6) that "we are compelled by our doctrine to speak out." He said:

> We regard it as not only our right but our duty to oppose those forces which we feel undermine the moral fiber of society. Much of our effort, a very great deal of it, is in association with others whose interests are similar. We have worked with Jewish groups,

Catholics, Muslims, Protestants, and those of no particular religious affiliation, in coalitions formed to advocate positions on vital moral issues. Such is currently the case in California, where Latter-day Saints are working as part of a coalition to safeguard traditional marriage from forces in our society which are attempting to redefine that sacred institution. God-sanctioned marriage between a man and a woman has been the basis of civilization for thousands of years. There is no justification to redefine what marriage is. Such is not our right, and those who try will find themselves answerable to God.

> Some portray legalization of so-called same–sex marriage as a civil right. This is not a matter of civil rights; it is a matter of morality. Others question our constitutional right as a church to raise our voice on an issue that is of critical importance to the future of the family. We believe that defending this sacred institution by working to preserve traditional marriage lies clearly within our religious and constitutional prerogatives. Indeed, we are compelled by our doctrine to speak out.

> Nevertheless, and I emphasize this, I wish to say that our opposition to attempts to legalize same–sex marriage should never be interpreted as justification for hatred, intolerance, or abuse of those who profess homosexual tendencies, either individually or as a group. As I said from this pulpit one year ago, our hearts reach out to those who refer to themselves as gays and lesbians. We love and honor them as sons and daughters of God. They are welcome in the Church. It is expected, however, that they follow the same God–given rules of conduct that apply to everyone else, whether single or married.

> I commend those of our membership who have voluntarily joined with other like-minded people to defend the sanctity of traditional marriage. As part of a coalition that embraces those of other faiths, you are giving substantially of your means. The money being raised in California has been donated to the coalition by individual members of the Church. You are contributing your time and talents in a cause that in some quarters may not be politically correct but which nevertheless lies at the heart of the Lord's eternal plan for His children, just as those of many other churches are doing. This is a united effort.[1]

The Need for Individuals to Work to Make a Difference for the Sake of Families

I am convinced that men and women who are willing to become involved in professional and civil affairs can make a difference in the laws and government policies that are adopted regarding families. For example, one reason the effort to legalize same–sex marriage has had some notable success in courts is that law review literature for many years has been overwhelmingly one-sided, favoring same–sex marriage. Similarly, professional literature in several other disciplines reflects the popularity of same–sex marriage among publishing academics and social scientists. In many academic circles, it is "taboo" to express criticism of homosexual lifestyle or opposition to legalization of same–sex marriage or other homosexual family relationship proposals.

It seems that what is needed most is a careful, reasonable defense of the "obvious," when the obvious has been taken for granted so long that it has become considered "outmoded" and new alternatives have become the "in" fad. Some Latter-day Saint scholars have made significant contributions to the professional literature in their disciplines to explain the unique values and benefits of marriage. By their example, they have influenced other scholars and professionals to speak out in defense of the marriage-based family.

For example, when I wrote a law review article critiquing proposals to legalize same–sex marriage, published in the *B.Y.U. Law Review* in 1996, only one other previous law review study (out of 73 published pieces) had opposed legalizing same–sex marriage. As a result of writing that article, I was invited to help draft and to testify before Congress in support of a law designed to protect the right of states to not recognize same–sex marriages (called the Defense of Marriage Act), which passed Congress by overwhelming margins and was signed by President Clinton in 1996. Perhaps more important, my writing, speaking, and organization of professional conferences has helped motivate and support other scholars to publish their own criticisms of proposals to legalize same–sex marriage, providing much more published material for lawyers to use in defending the institution of marriage. Today, William Duncan, a young graduate of the J. Reuben Clark Law School with whom I worked in law school, is working full time for the Marriage Law Project at the Catholic University of America, providing professional responses to arguments for same–sex marriage, supporting lawyers defending marriage laws, and assisting legislators to draft laws to protect marriage.

The Family Studies Center in the School of Family Life at Brigham Young University is an important leader in promoting efforts among social scientists to strengthen and defend the family. By sponsoring professional conferences and encouraging faculty at BYU and at other universities to publish significant scholarly and professional articles designed to help people understand the importance of families and marriage, and to strengthen marriage and family relations, the Center is a valuable resource clearinghouse for academics addressing family policy issues and for professionals working with families.

But one need not be a lawyer, other professional, or university scholar to make a valuable contribution to the cause of promoting government policies that recognize and protect the family. For example, in Hawaii, many Latter-day Saints, Catholics, and Protestants from all walks of life contributed greatly to the effort to protect marriage by contacting their elected representatives, writing letters to the newspapers responding to arguments to legalize same–sex marriage, participating in public rallies, helping to pay for advertising to get the message out to the public, and so on. Their grassroots effort was what made the difference, what persuaded the legislature that it needed to propose a constitutional amendment to protect traditional marriage. Similarly, in Alaska a grassroots coalition consisting of members of several churches (including our church, The Roman Catholic Church, and Protestant churches) provided critical support for the successful effort to enact a state constitutional amendment defining marriage as the union of a man and a woman. Such grassroots effort (such as letters, telephone calls, personal contact, participation in civil meetings, donations, etc.) was critical in providing support to elected officials who were willing to propose and support the measure and in educating and persuading "uncommitted" voters about why the measure was needed.

The effort to defend the family is not without opposition. I have experienced some hostility and harassment for speaking in defense of marriage, including "shunning" at some professional meetings, having gay students interrupt my presentations and verbally attack me, enduring snide "putdowns" by other speakers or panelists, having an angry lesbian law professor literally scream at me at a major professional meeting, receiving "hate" mail, and other forms of opposition. Because opposition must be expected, it is especially important for those defending the family to be respectful of all others and to give no just cause for the negative attacks that are sure to come. Nonetheless, you must expect opposition.

You will be opposed because you can and will make a difference. I have witnessed the positive rallying effect that often results when one person is willing to speak up—others, knowing that they will not stand alone, are motivated to speak up also. Since most open-minded and fair-minded people are appalled when they see activists behave inappropriately, or rudely, or to harass someone simply because he or she disagrees with them, even the opposition you encounter sheds important light on the nature of the issues. Finally, there are many people who will be influenced for the good by the efforts you make to explain why families are important and why particular policies or proposals should or should not be

supported because of their harmful effects upon families. There is a famine in the land, a dearth of information, good reasons, responsible arguments, and clear conviction regarding the value of marriage, marriage-based families, the importance of both mothers and fathers to children, and the benefits and advantages of moral and stable family relationships. If we do not neglect the opportunities and responsibilities we have to share our understanding of the importance of the family and of the principles family life articulated in the Proclamation, we can make a difference.

E S S A Y   S

A CRITIQUE OF THE RESEARCH ON SAME-SEX PARENTING

RICHARD N. WILLIAMS

Among the most controversial issues surrounding homosexuality are those of the effects on children of being reared by gay or lesbian parents. This issue is frequently debated in the public forum because it is relevant for many decisions that are made within the legal system, such as whether same–sex marriages will be recognized, whether gay or lesbian couples may adopt children or serve as foster parents, or whether the sexual orientation of parents should be considered in making custody decisions following divorce. Perhaps because the welfare of children is at stake, it is an issue debated with some passion.

In a 1996 case before the Circuit Court of Hawaii,[2] which dealt with the question of same–sex marriage, both the state, in its defense of the state law restricting marriage to heterosexual couples, and the plaintiffs—homosexual couples who had been denied marriage licenses—decided to argue the case almost entirely around the issue of the possible effects on

children of allowing same–sex marriages. All of the witnesses called for both sides of the case either were social scientists or commented on social scientific research in order to persuade the court which family structure would ultimately be in the best interest of the child.[3]

The essence of the argument was that there is no direct social scientific evidence that the sexual orientation of parents has any negative effects on children. While this may not be precisely true, given the body of research presented in this volume regarding the beneficial influences of heterosexual parents and stable families on children's lives and development, it is true that there are few direct empirical tests of the hypothesis that parents' sexual orientation negatively affects children's cognitive or emotional health and development. The research studies that have been conducted specifically on the topic of same–sex parenting have generally not reported adverse effects on children nor notable negative differences in parenting.

The argument, then, is that since the research has failed to show an effect, the conclusion that the sexual orientation of parents is irrelevant is warranted. Whether it is indeed warranted based on the evidence depends on the logic involved in drawing conclusions from a lack of findings and on the quality of the extant research. The rest of this essay is devoted to an evaluative review of the research findings in this area.

RESEARCH ON THE EFFECTS OF PARENTS' SEXUAL ORIENTATION ON CHILDREN

In discussions of the effects of parents' sexual orientation on children, the same rather sizeable body of literature is almost always cited. There have been a hundred or more published (in one form or another) studies on homosexuality and variables related to parenting. However, a close examination of the literature and the way it is used reveals two basic problems. First, the research is interpreted as support for the thesis that sexual orientation has no effect on children; however, it is used in a way that violates the logic of rigorous empirical science. Second, the research itself has little scientific merit because of errors in design, subject selection, and measurement.[4]

Based on these two problems, it is my professional opinion that there is no empirical support for the conclusion that parents' sexual orientation has no effect on children. Because of this, the issue must be decided on other grounds—such as evidence about the relative quality of life in intact families, the role of fathers and the effects of fathering versus father absence, and moral and legal principles. We will first turn attention to the logical problems entailed in the research literature on sexual orientation and parenting.

Predicting and Proving "No Effect"

The conclusion wrongly but most often drawn from the literature on the effects of parents' sexual orientation on children is that there is "no effect" on children growing up in a home headed by homosexual parents. When an empirical study fails to find a statistically significant difference between groups, researchers conclude that there is no difference, and that this lack of evidence is a positive finding in favor of a hypothesis of "no effect." This, however, violates one of the fundamental tenets of scientific logic. It is illegitimate to predict that no effect will be found and

then claim, on the basis of not finding one, that there really is no effect in the real world. The reason for this is that the failure to find an effect is exactly what would be predicted if a study were poorly designed or if the measuring instruments were inappropriate and insensitive. In other words it is impossible in principle to separate "no effect" because there is none from "no effect" because the study is fatally flawed by design errors. A research strategy that predicts, finds, and touts "no effect" has little scientific merit. This problem is usually phrased in more philosophical language as a maxim: It is impossible for science to prove a negative.

Some who would acknowledge this problem and grant that existing studies are not of good quality would propose that even though scientific logic has been violated it is still better to base a decision on poor data rather than no data at all. This argument not only dismisses the scientific requirement of logical consistency, but is refuted by the study of history. In the nineteenth century, women had a high mortality rate following childbirth due to "childbed fever." The best medical research and practice of the day revealed no evidence that the disease was spread by the germs on doctors' hands. However, subsequent theory and research produced strong evidence otherwise. The price of acting on "no effect" was tragically high. It is, in principle, inadvisable to base important decisions on a body of noneffects. Absent findings do not aggregate.

Statistical Significance

The body of research that is purported to show "no effect" for parental sexual orientation all relies on traditional statistical significance testing. When an empirical study finds a statistically significant effect or difference, it simply means that a pattern of numerical relationship was found in the data (often a correlation or a difference between groups) that was so large that there is a small probability of its coming about by chance alone. Statistical significance is usually claimed only when the chances are fewer than five in 100 that the numerical effect could have occurred by chance alone. This, however, is a conservative criterion; it was devised chiefly to prevent social scientists from being too liberal with themselves, claiming to have found something that is not really "there." There may be many findings that are highly significant morally, socially, clinically, or legally that would not show up as statistically significant, but the experimental results would be used to support a finding of "no effect." For example, a study could conceivably find that abused women are not significantly different from nonabused women on a measure of parenting skill. One would hardly want to conclude on the basis of such evidence that spouse abuse has no effect on parenting. The traditional logic of hypothesis testing may not be the best criterion to apply to the question of the effects of parents' sexual orientation.

We turn attention now to a more particular evaluation of the literature on the sexual orientation of parents. I conducted a review of the research literature in this area in 1996 as part of my preparation as a witness in the Hawaii court case mentioned above. In a subsequent review of the literature I have found no studies that change the findings. In an attempt to deal with the large volume of research literature, I decided to apply two simple but fundamental criteria of scientific rigor. I excluded any study from the review that did not meet two minimal standards. First, I excluded any study that did not include two groups of children, one reared by heterosexual parents and one by homosexual parents. Without these two groups, there could really be no information about comparative effects on children of parents' sexual orientation. Second, I included only studies that actually gathered data from children, rather than just from parents' ratings of themselves or their children. When these criteria were applied, the body of a hundred or so research studies shrank to nine studies.[5] This process of elimination is strong testimony of the lack of scientific rigor of the body of research and the inadvisability of drawing conclusions from it. In addition to this global lack of rigor, there were more particular problems with the studies.

Sample Size and Sample Selection

Sample sizes in all of these studies were small, never exceeding 30 parents or 50 children per group. The majority of the studies were much smaller than these figures. Sample size is a problem for two reasons. First, small size works in favor of finding "no effect," since sample size is directly related to the power of a statistical test to detect effects in the data. Second, the samples were too small to permit generalization to the entire population of homosexual or heterosexual parents. Thus scientific merit is compromised on two counts.

None of the homosexual parents who participated

in the studies were randomly selected from a known population. They were recruited through homosexual newspapers and other publications, or from personal acquaintances. Often similar nonrandom procedures were used to select heterosexual participants as well. It is not clear whether participants were informed as to the purpose of the studies. If they knew the study's purpose, that could have a significant biasing effect. Here again the generalizability of the findings is, in my judgment, fatally compromised.

Intervening Variables

One of the vital aspects of good research design is the control of extraneous or potentially intervening variables. That is, a good study that provides valid findings about the effects of some variable must be designed in such a way that other variables could not possibly be found to be responsible for the effect. Thus, if a study were to effectively study two groups of children (reared by heterosexual versus homosexual parents) to see the effects of parents' sexual orientation, the study must be designed to insure that no other variable other than parents' sexual orientation would be differentially manifested in the two groups. None of the studies solved this problem. In all but one of the studies the children had lived for a period of time with parents of both genders in the home (generally before a divorce). In one study[6] where children were never reared by parents of both sexes, there was no real control group of children of heterosexual households; comparisons were made to test norms. Other potentially intervening variables in the study were educational level, socio-economic status, age of children, parents' living arrangements, and contact with biological fathers, among other things. It is important to note also that none of the studies involved gay men as parents; all homosexual parents were lesbian.

Inappropriate Measures

One of the primary difficulties in studies of parents' sexual orientation is the selection of measures on which to evaluate the effects on children. Often in the literature on this question there is no theoretically derived reason to use any particular measure. Sometimes the measures are not appropriate. The Flaks et al.[7] study found no difference between children reared in lesbian versus heterosexual households on "cognitive development." The measure employed was the traditional Wechsler IQ test. This test has been specifically designed to be insensitive to as many social, cultural, and family variables as possible. It is therefore not surprising that no differences were detected in the study. This seems an odd choice of a measure of cognitive development because cognitive development is usually distinguished from IQ. Also, a study designed to assess potential group differences on some variable ought to use an instrument that has not been designed specifically to be immune to group differences. Especially where "no effect" is found, it is crucial that we are absolutely convinced that we have measured what is most relevant to our concerns, and that we have measured it validly. The research on this topic cannot satisfy either concern.

CONCLUSION

This brief review can do no more than introduce the problems in the literature on same–sex parenting. Of greater importance, perhaps, is that there are indications in the literature that parents' sexual orientation does make a difference in the lives of children. These findings are often not reported or elaborated. Perhaps the best designed research available was that done by Golombok et al.[8] and Golombok and Tasker.[9] Those were the only studies that followed the children of lesbian and heterosexual parents into adulthood to look for differences that might be expected to appear only in adulthood. The follow-up study in 1996 showed children of homosexual parents were significantly more likely to have (a) considered engaging in a homosexual relationship and (b) actually engaged in a homosexual relationship. In the report of the research, little is made of this finding, and it does not dissuade the authors from concluding that there is no evidence of an effect of parents' sexual orientation. This oversight is difficult to explain, but is found in other studies as well. Huggins,[10] for example, found a difference in the variability of self-esteem (i.e., how spread out the children were along the self-esteem scale) between children of homosexual versus children of heterosexual parents. However, she

did not bother to test it for significance—although my analysis found the difference to be significant. She chose not to comment on it further. Patterson[11] found, but left unreported, a similar difference; and Lewis,[12] in a qualitative study, found evidence of emotional and social difficulties in the lives of children of homosexual parents, but the findings did not affect her conclusion that there were no effects.

The much publicized conclusion that there is no research evidence of an effect on children of parents' sexual orientation is conceptually problematic, violates the logic of scientific rigor, and is empirically untrue. At the same time, we should not be surprised at the lack of a large body of research finding effects on children. Given the ethical constraints on social scientific research, such research likely could not be carried out. It would not only be potentially politically charged, but gaining access to good samples would be difficult, especially if potential participants understood the potential effects of findings of significant effects on children. The most reasonable conclusion to be reached in this matter at this point in time is that the body of research on the topic of effects of parents' sexual orientation on their children is of little scientific merit. The current body of research certainly does not justify a conclusion that there is no effect on children of parents' sexual orientation. On the contrary, there is some evidence of such effects.

Social scientific research can provide useful information and evidence in support of important public policies, but it must be of the highest quality in its design, instrumentation, and conceptual rigor. At the same time, such empirical research can never provide ultimate justification for decisions and policies that are essentially moral and reflect our deepest values. In the final analysis, the justification must derive from our vision of the highest and most noble things of which we as cultures and individuals are capable. If this vision is worthy, we ought not be timid about confronting the issues and seeking support for the vision in the research arena.

Defending the Family through International Policy

Richard G. Wilkins

I first became involved with issues of family policy and society in June 1996 when, almost by accident, I attended a UN Conference in Istanbul, Turkey. The conference, known as Habitat II, was the culmination of a decade-long series of conferences designed to develop a "blueprint" for international (and ultimately national) legal relations during the coming century. These conferences have been accurately perceived as significant international law-making events.[13] They have also followed a predictable (and extreme) ideological course primarily championed by a powerful lobby that, according to one scholar, "ha[s] marginalized parents, ignored the family, denigrated cultural and religious values," and enshrined "reproductive rights" and "sexual health"[14] (which are interpreted to include universal access to abortion).

The Istanbul Conference was remarkable because it departed from this course. As a result of an unusual series of events, I was selected to give a four-minute speech before one of the drafting committees at the Habitat Conference. The speakers who took the podium before me urged the conferees to recognize same–sex partnerships, increase funding for adolescent sexual reproductive services, provide 18 to 20 hours a day of government-sponsored childcare, and take all "necessary steps" to insure that every woman was "fully employed" outside the home. Marriage and family, if noted at all by these speakers, were referenced primarily as institutions that reinforce odious cultural stereotypes and that subjugate and demean women.

My message was rather different. I began my remarks by informing the conference that the family—as recognized in the Universal Declaration of Human Rights and other important UN documents—is the fundamental unit of society. It *is* the fundamental unit, moreover, precisely because it is the place where women and men learn cooperation, sacrifice, love, and mutual support and is the training ground where children learn the public virtues of responsibility, work, fair play, and social interdependence. I reminded the delegates that if we don't learn these skills within the home, there is little chance we will learn them elsewhere. Accordingly, I urged the delegates to do what they could to strengthen the family, rather than expend the vast majority of their energies creating substitute social structures.

At the conclusion of my short remarks, I emphasized the essential message of the First Presidency's *The Family: A Proclamation to the World*: that there is a fundamental connection between a decent society and the reinforcement of strong, stable families. The basic structure of society, I asserted, is built upon the fundamental values fostered by strong families. I concluded by urging the conference to consider seriously the need to protect traditional values in drafting and implementing the Habitat Agenda.

The reaction to the speech was remarkable. Many of the speakers who had preceded me at the podium hissed as I returned to my seat. But most of the delegates in the audience gave me a standing ovation. Indeed, after the speech, I was approached by the ambassador from Saudi Arabia, who embraced me warmly. "Where have you been?" he asked. Next, he asked an important question: "What can we do?"

I gave the ambassador a short list of items that could be changed in the draft Habitat Agenda that would strengthen, rather than weaken, the family's central role. Thirty-six hours later, the heads of the Arab delegations in Istanbul issued a joint statement, announcing to the entire Habitat Conference that its members would not sign the Habitat Agenda unless (and until) certain important changes were made.

As a result, and at the insistence of the heads of the Arab delegations, several very important changes were made in the Habitat Agenda. Instead of defining *marriage* and/or *family* in a manner that explicitly legitimated same–sex marriages and families (as did the original draft), the final Habitat Agenda defined the marital relationship as one between "husband and wife."[15] Instead of numerous explicit paragraphs mandating worldwide abortion on demand, only one (somewhat hedged) reference to "reproductive health" remained. The Habitat Agenda, finally, formally recognized the family as "the basic unit of society" that "should be strengthened."[16]

These developments, viewed from the perspective of current American and European legal trends, are significant. The Habitat Conference sent a strong message that strengthening the family—not the simple recognition of more "rights" or the creation of additional substitute social units—is the answer to many of our modern problems.

The World Family Policy Center

Because of this experience and my commitment to become involved in defending marriage and the family in the international arena, I founded the World Family Policy Center at Brigham Young University. Beginning in Istanbul in 1996, and continuing at various United Nations Commission meetings since then, BYU representatives acting through the World Family Policy Center have attempted, with varying degrees of success, to remove anti-family language from negotiated documents and to reaffirm fundamental human rights guaranteeing family privacy, freedom of religion and conscience, and the rights of parents to guide the upbringing of their children.

Anti–traditional-family NGOs (non-governmental organizations), supported by numerous academic centers, have been consolidating power on the international scene and successfully lobbying the United Nations for at least the past 30 years. Until recently, there were virtually no pro–traditional-family NGOs (and no pro–traditional-family academic centers) to oppose them. The World Family Policy Center has been working with a small, but growing, coalition of NGOs sponsored by Catholics, Evangelicals, and Muslims who are working to save traditional religious values as they relate to the family. The BYU personnel are the only ones in the coalition who have any expertise in law or the family sciences. The World Family Policy Center, moreover, is the only academic institution involved in an ongoing basis with the Proclamation's side of the family policy debate. As a result, the pro-family NGO coalition increasingly looks to us for leadership. Furthermore, we are making many friends among the delegates of conservative countries (usually predominantly Catholic or Muslim). They, too, are looking to us for leadership and expertise.

The World Congress of Families

The World Congress of Families II, held in Geneva, Switzerland, in November 1999 is the most recent major effort of the World Family Policy Center. The Center was one of the two cosponsoring organizations of the World Congress of Families II (along with The Howard Center for Family, Religion and Society).

The process resulting in the World Congress of Families II began in Rome, in May 1998. During the course of a remarkable one-week meeting held in a building predating the Christian Era, 27 members of the Planning Committee (composed of prestigious academic, political, and lay leaders representing all of the world's great monotheistic religions) drafted "A Call from the Families of the World." The Call, subsequently translated into 45 languages and signed by more than four hundred thousand individuals worldwide prior to November 1999, provided the foundation for the congress.

The Call states that "we come together from diverse national, cultural, social and faith communities to affirm the natural human family," which the Call defines as "the fundamental social unit, inscribed in human nature, and centered around the voluntary union of a man and a woman in a lifelong covenant of marriage." The most important goal of the Congress was to demonstrate—in a concrete fashion—that this language from the Call is not mere rhetoric. The congress achieved this objective.

During the course of three and one-half days, 88 speakers addressed more than 1,575 delegates—drawn from 45 countries and representing more than 256 non-governmental organizations—on issues related to marriage, parenthood, children's rights, gender rights, population growth, and religious liberty. The messages delivered by these 88 speakers were backed by the findings of an international survey of family attitudes conducted by Wirthlin Worldwide, which found (among other things) that 84 percent of persons around the globe agree that "the definition of marriage is one man and one woman."[17]

Many presentations were made by prominent members of various religious communities and included Alfonso Cardinal Lopez Trujillo, president for the last nine years of the Pontifical Council on the Family; Sister Mary Ellen Smoot, general president of the Relief Society of The Church of Jesus Christ of Latter-day Saints; Sister Margaret Nadauld, general president of the LDS Young Women; Rabbi Daniel Lapin, president of Toward Tradition; Madame Jehan Sadat, widow of the late Egyptian President Anwar Sadat; and Fatemah Hashemi Rafsanjani, secretary general of the Women's Solidarity Association of Iran. A speech prepared by the Grand Imam Mohammed Ali Taskhiri (titular head of the Shiite Branch of Islam) was also read at the congress. One of the most significant presentations at the congress was given by Elder Bruce C. Hafen on the dangers presented by the UN Convention on the Rights of the Child (many of the congress addresses are available on-line at *www.worldcongress.org*).

The congress demonstrated, in an undeniable fashion, that there is a widespread consensus, transcending both religion and culture, regarding the definition and centrality of the natural family. This demonstration of such worldwide agreement on important questions relating to motherhood, fatherhood, gender, the duties and prerogatives of parenthood, and the relevance of faith to social life is perhaps the most important achievement of the congress.

Congress delegates adopted (with near unanimity) two important documents: The Geneva Declaration and the Geneva Youth Declaration (available online at *www.worldcongress.org*). These documents could have significant impact on the future formulation and implementation of family-centered policies at the local, national, and international levels.

The Geneva Declaration addresses such issues as society, marriage, children, sexuality, life, population, education, government, and religion. The declaration "affirm[s] that the natural human family is established by the Creator and essential to good society." It also provides a strong statement of principles that has been endorsed by a 1,500-member interdenominational assembly and supported by more than 400,000 signatures on "A Call from the Families of the World." These principles are generally consistent with those stated in *The Family: A Proclamation to the World.* The declaration is not prescriptive. Rather, it sets out principles that can be used by people of faith throughout the world to guide policy discussions on local and international levels. As such, it stands as a strong counterpoint to other declarations of principles that have been used by various groups to undermine family, marriage, and faith at the United Nations and in other meetings.[18]

The congress provided some important opportunities for future cooperative efforts between Brigham Young University and various actors on the international scene. Among other things, the BYU World Family Policy Center was invited to participate in a conference on the challenges facing Palestinian youth and was invited to present a "family agenda" for adoption at the meeting of the International Conference of Ministers of Foreign Affairs of the Organization of Islamic Conferences in Malaysia in May 2000.

The ultimate impact of the congress will not be known for some time.

But as the World Congress of Families has demonstrated, BYU's presence on the international family policy scene has made a difference. The World Family Policy Center—and the World Congress—have succeeded in slowing down those forces that would diminish the importance of the natural family.

NOTES

1. Gordon B. Hinckley (1999, November), Why we do some of the things we do, *Ensign, 29*(11), 54.

2. Baehr v. Miike, Hawaii Circuit Court, Civil No. 91–394–05.

3. The fact that the legal system would put such faith in the social sciences and in their scientific knowledge base is of deep import and problematic for at least two reasons. First, there is a strong argument that a legal system, as well as the culture on which it is based, and whose values that system ought to reflect, should be based on principles and, in the words of our Declaration of Independence, "self-evident truths," which can

achieve some degree of transcendence of time and circumstance. The rule of law requires adherence to principles of moral value that can be applied with some degree of independence of transient circumstances and accidents of nature, in order to assure that such laws are applied equally to all. Scientific findings are notoriously, and in the most mature, sophisticated of sciences, self-consciously transient. Scientific knowledge in our contemporary age has a short life span. Therefore, for the legal system to rely on what appears at any point in time to be scientifically valid for making legal judgments is short sighted and revolutionary in the history of democratic societies. Important legal precedents are to be set on the basis of constitutional and moral principles, not on the basis of whatever scientific theories and findings happen to enjoy some currency at a particular point in history.

The second reason why it is problematic to decide important legal and social issues based on social scientific data has to do with the scientific status of the social sciences and the empirical data that support it. An abundance of scholarly literature persuasively argues that the social sciences, along with their methods and data, do not rise to the status of scientific credibility enjoyed by the more mature natural sciences (cf. R. J. Bernstein [1983], *Beyond objectivism and relativism: Science, hermeneutics, and praxis* [Philadelphia: University of Pennsylvania Press]; J. Bohman [1993], *New philosophy of social science: Problems of indeterminacy* [Cambridge, MA: MIT Press]; J. Dupre [1993], *The disorder of things: Metaphysical foundations of the disunity of science* [Cambridge, MA: Harvard University Press]; D. Polkinghorne [1983], *Methodology for the human sciences: Systems of inquiry* [Albany, NY: SUNY Press]; B. D. Slife and R. N. Williams [1995], *What's behind the research? Discovering hidden assumptions in the behavioral sciences* [Thousand Oaks, CA: Sage]; and R. N. Williams [in press], Epistemology, in A. E. Kazdin [Ed.]. *Encyclopedia of psychology* [New York: Oxford University Press]). Thus, it can be persuasively argued that social scientists do not have the intellectual and epistemological grounding sufficient to offer *conclusive opinions* on questions of decisive cultural and legal impact. This issue, however, is beyond the present discussion.

4. P. A. Belcastro, T. Gramlich, T. Nicholson, J. Price, and R. Wilson (1993), A review of data based studies addressing the affects [*sic*] of homosexual parenting on children's sexual and social functioning, *Journal of Divorce and Remarriage, 20,* 105–122.

5. Those studies are D. K. Flaks, I. Ficher, F. Masterpasqua, and G. Joseph (1995), Lesbians choosing motherhood: A comparative study of lesbian and heterosexual parents and their children, *Developmental Psychology, 15,* 105–114; S. Golombok, A. Spencer, and M. Rutter (1983), Children in lesbian and single-parent households: Psychosexual and psychiatric appraisal, *Journal of Child Psychology and Psychiatry, 24,* 551–572; S. Golombok and F. Tasker (1996), Do parents influence the sexual orientation of their children? Findings from a longitudinal study of lesbian families, *Developmental Psychology, 32,* 3–11;

J. S. Gottman (1990), Children of gay and lesbian parents, *Marriage & Family Review, 14,* 177–195; R. Green, J. B. Mandel, M. E. Hotvedt, J. Gray, and L. Smith (1986), Lesbian mothers and their children: A comparison with solo parent heterosexual mothers and their children, *Archives of Sexual Behavior, 15,* 167–184; S. L. Huggins (1989), A comparative study of self-esteem of adolescent children of divorced lesbian mothers and divorced heterosexual mothers, *Journal of Homosexuality, 18,* 123–135; G. A. Javaid (1993), The children of homosexual and heterosexual single mothers, *Child Psychiatry and Human Development, 23,* 235–248; M. Kirkpatrick, C. Smith, and R. Roy (1981), Lesbian mothers and their children: A comparative study, *American Journal of Orthopsychiatry, 51,* 545–551; and C. J. Patterson (1995), Families of the lesbian baby boom: Parents' division of labor and children's adjustment, *Developmental Psychology, 31,* 115–123.

6. Patterson (1995).

7. Flaks et al. (1995).

8. Golombok, Spencer, and Rutter (1983).

9. Golombok and Tasker (1996).

10. Huggins (1989).

11. Patterson (1995).

12. K. G. Lewis (1992), Children of lesbians: Their point of view, in D. J. Maggiore (Ed.). *Lesbians and child custody: A casebook* (New York: Garland), 85–98.

13. E.g., Nafis Sadik (1995), *Reflections on the International Conference on Population and Development and the Efficacy of UN Conferences,* 6 Colo. J. Int'l L.&Pol, 249, 252–253.

14. Mary Meaney (1996, July 15), Radical rout, *National Review, 48(13),* 25–26.

15. In the original draft, the Habitat Agenda stated that "[i]n different cultural, political and social systems, various forms of the family exist." This broad sentence, in the same paragraph that provided that all family forms are "entitled to receive comprehensive protection and support," would almost certainly have extended legal protection to same–sex marriages (Draft Habitat Agenda, par. 18). The final version of paragraph 18 now adds that, while "various forms of the family exist," "marriage" arises out of the "free consent of the intending spouses, and husband and wife should be equal partners" (Habitat Agenda, Chapter II, Goals and Principles, par. 18). Thus, "marriage" involves "spouses" who are "husband and wife."

16. Habitat Agenda, Chapter II, Goals and Principles, par. 5.

17. The detailed findings of the Wirthlin study are available on request from The World Family Policy Center. http://www.ngofamilyvoice.org.

18. Compare, e.g., Round Table of Human Rights Treaty Bodies on Human Rights Approaches to Women's Health, with a Focus on Sexual and Reproductive Health and Rights (report of a Roundtable Discussion sponsored by the UN Population Fund, calling for "a gender perspective on health and human rights").

CHAPTER 26

THE PROCLAMATION AND THE PHILOSOPHIES OF THE WORLD

M. GAWAIN WELLS AND WESLEY R. BURR

Happiness in family life is most likely to be achieved when founded
upon the teachings of the Lord Jesus Christ.
(The Family: A Proclamation to the World, ¶ 7)

We live in a world where many beliefs about family life are based upon the traditions of men and not the teachings of the Lord Jesus Christ. The Apostle Paul warned us to "beware lest any man spoil you through philosophy and vain deceit, after the traditions of men, after the rudiments of the world, and not after Christ" (Col. 2:8). Elder Merrill J. Bateman stated, "It is particularly revealing to compare the teachings of the proclamation with contrasting philosophies and practices of the world"[1] This chapter analyzes how fundamental truths from the Proclamation relate to underlying philosophical ideas in the broader culture. Comparing and contrasting "the philosophies of the world" with the revealed truths in the Proclamation may help readers better understand the doctrine of Christ on marriage and family life. The first section discusses various ways that human beings obtain knowledge and confirm truth. The second section discusses how underlying value assumptions or worldviews prominent in Western culture compare and contrast with Proclamation principles.

SOURCES OF KNOWLEDGE AND THE PROCLAMATION

"Epistemology" is the branch of philosophy that deals with how we obtain knowledge. It considers the methods, sources, and limitations of our knowledge, and how we establish its validity.[2] There are four ways of obtaining knowledge that are particularly relevant to this chapter—empiricism, rationalism, the scientific method, and revelation. We make some assumptions about these ways of getting knowledge, and if we understand them and use them in concert with the Proclamation it can help us know which beliefs about family life we should accept and which we should reject.

Empiricism

Empiricism is founded on the proposition that all knowledge comes through experience. This is the method we use when we rely on our five senses to give us knowledge. Scientists conduct empirical experiments to test theories that involve being able to observe with the senses. Empirical methods of gathering and testing knowledge have many advantages from which society has benefitted, and people tend to have great confidence in our ideas when they are able to validate them with the five senses.

Rationalism

A second way of obtaining knowledge is rationalism or reasoning. Techniques of rationalism include induction, deduction, analysis, hypothesizing, theorizing, pondering, and concluding. Almost the opposite of empiricism, a rational approach assumes that there are some ideas that are clear and dependable upon which we can build other knowledge. The ideas believed to be certain then become premises to reach other conclusions.

Careful use of analytical principles has produced both some important methods as well as conclusions that are valued in society. Many of the rules of law, for instance, have been constructed through a rational process of argument, debate, and consideration of what is just.

Scientific Method

The scientific method is born of the union of rationalism and empiricism. One tests rational ideas (hypotheses) by arranging experiments that show whether the ideas work or not in ways that can be measured physically. Knowledge is constructed gradually by testing ideas to determine how they hold across situations. Scientists then use rationalism to build a theory of how things work more generally.

Scientific findings, of course, have created major advances and opportunities in society, from the knowledge of physics that permits rapid transportation to the diagnosis and treatment of disease. From science we have learned valuable concepts for family life as well, such as healthy dimensions of parenting or the long-term effects of divorce. Latter-day Saints believe that God has inspired men and women of science to make some of the important discoveries by which we enjoy our lives and by which the gospel is spread throughout the world. However, we must be aware when scientists step from being scientists to presuming to be authorities on matters beyond what their data demonstrates. In addition, recent philosophers known as postmodernists, such as Michel Foucalt or Jacques Derrida[3] suggest that because scientists' biases are an ingredient in any work, their interpretations of data are unavoidably influenced by their perspective.[4] This is especially true of social scientists studying matters like marriage and family.

Revelation

Revelation from God is knowledge that God makes known to human beings. Such knowledge may occur through inspiration, visitations from heavenly individuals, and answers to prayer. Spiritual insights also come from dreams, promptings, and from moments of meditation and worship. As a source of knowledge, revelation can provide information by means other than scientific method or rational deduction, relying on spiritual, apparently intangible methods. Elder Bruce R. McConkie powerfully taught the importance of revelation, declaring:

> True religion comes from God by revelation. It is manifest to and understood by those with a talent for spirituality. It is hidden, unknown, and mysterious to all others. To comprehend the things of the world, one must be intellectually enlightened; . . . to know and understand the things of God, one must be spiritually enlightened. One of the great fallacies of modern Christendom is turning for religious guidance to those who are highly endowed intellectually, rather than to those who comprehend the things of the Spirit, to those who receive personal revelation for the Holy Ghost.[5]

Parenthetically, it is important to note that Satan attempts to masquerade as a source of revelation. Having been struck dumb by God for his evil insistence upon a sign, Korihor admitted that the "devil hath deceived me; for he appeared unto me in the form of an angel, and said unto me: Go and reclaim this people, for they have all gone astray after an unknown God" (Alma 30:53).

Authority

An additional epistemological source is authority. With this method we rely on a person or organization that has demonstrated expertise, such as a church, a government, cultural traditions, an individual, or group. When we are children, we rely on our parents for much of our knowledge. Later in life, we turn to others, such as teachers, coaches, mentors, and consultants.

When people hear the voice of authority, they should consider whether the person is an expert and whether they can trust the authority to teach the truth. Throughout life, people learn by watching, talking and listening to other people, then choosing and responding to those whom they consider authorities. Indeed, many important truths and skills can be learned only by apprenticeship to an expert who teaches the apprentice what to do and how to do it.

Acquiring knowledge through an authority also has advantages and disadvantages. It is efficient because it would be impossible to test empirically every idea we encounter or to find the rational basis for every idea or to get our own revelation about every spiritual idea. There are also important limitations to authority. Some may not have accurate information, and there are so many different people and organizations that disagree with each other that it is difficult to know which authorities have true and which have false information. Obtaining revelation about which authorities can be relied upon for different types of knowledge is crucial.

THE "SO WHAT?" QUESTION

Having examined several different means of gathering knowledge, one might ask, "So what?"

How can understanding epistemology help one recognize the difference between truth and error, between the philosophies that are 'after Christ' and those that are the 'vain deceits after the traditions of men' (Col. 2:8), and how does it pertain to the Proclamation?" Current controversies in family life provide examples. It is a widely accepted conclusion from scientific population research is that the earth is in danger of being overpopulated by human beings. Widespread birth control and abortion are therefore seen as necessary methods for protecting the quality of life for future generations on a crowded planet. By contrast, the Proclamation declares "God's commandments for His children to multiply and replenish the earth remain in force " (¶ 4). And, "We affirm the sanctity of life and of its importance in God's eternal plan" (¶ 5).

It is helpful to look at the epistemological sources of these two beliefs. First, let us examine the epistemological sources of the Proclamation. The Proclamation was written by prophets and apostles and given to the world by President Gordon B. Hinckley. If one accepts the *authority* of prophets of God, then the Proclamation is accepted as true because it is prophetic. And if one has received *revelation*—a personal witness from the Spirit—then one accepts that the ideas or knowledge in it are true. The other two methods of knowing are not particularly relevant for us. We have not empirically tested the ideas in the Proclamation to see if they are true. Frankly, we wouldn't know how to go about such an experiment or test, even though there is nothing in the Proclamation that is inconsistent with anything that we have observed with our five senses. Also, we have not arrived at the conclusion that it is true through reasoning, other than to recognize that there is nothing in the Proclamation that is inconsistent with our reasoning in the context of acceptance of LDS doctrine and prophetic authority.

Now, let us examine the epistemological sources of the idea that the world is in danger of being overpopulated and the belief that more birth control (and even abortion) are desirable. The observations about the rapid population growth in the last several centuries are based on *scientific method* data. However, the predictions about a future of world famine are based on statistical projections about the future, and they use a number of assumptions that may or may not be true. The conclusion that more birth control and abortion are desirable is not based on empirical evidence, but is based on *rationalism:* If the world is in danger of using up its food resources, then limiting population growth even by means of abortion seems like good reasoning.

Thus, one side of this debate is based on spiritual sources of knowledge, and it is not based on scientific evidence or a rationale. The other side is based on ideas that have some empirical evidence and a great deal of reasoning. As we look at the epistemological roots of the ideas they help expose their foundations. When we do not look at the epistemological roots, the ideas that are based on "scientific evidence" may appear to have more credibility than warranted.

Interestingly, in many of the current controversies about how to strengthen families, the issue is not whether the experts consider themselves pro-family. Many individuals are trying hard to strengthen families and they advocate what they believe are "family values." Yet, they differ about what should be done to strengthen families. If we look only at whether someone says he or she is "pro-family" or has "family values" we won't know which ideas to accept or reject. It is often much more helpful to look at the epistemological sources of the ideas. Thus, one of the insights one can gain from an analysis of the sources of knowledge is to realize how valuable it is to use revelation and the spiritual aspects of authority whenever we are trying to use empiricism and reasoning to gain knowledge. Using the Proclamation as our anchor point, we can compare finding other methods of acquiring knowledge for their value in promoting family values consistent with Father in Heaven's plan of happiness.

Another advantage of knowing about different epistemological sources is that it helps us realize that we get different types of knowledge from the different sources. Revelation and authority provide us with knowledge about more universal, fundamental aspects of life. It is through revelation and authority that we learn where we come from, why we are here, and where we are going spiritually as humans. We learn basic values and principles, how to feel, love, revere, worship, relate, and grow. We learn the higher and more noble aspects of what it means to be human and to be children of a loving Heavenly Father and that we are part of an eternal perspective.

On the other hand, the Proclamation does not provide specific knowledge about ways of disciplining and teaching children or organizing daily routines to create effective families. Because the methods of empiricism and reasoning seldom address more comprehensive, fundamental parts of life, but may be useful in developing knowledge about the means of achieving temporal, specific goals, such as strengthening marriage and family life, different ways of knowing may be more or less helpful at different times.

In summary, each method by which we acquire knowledge is a useful tool. We can be grateful for the discoveries that have come through empiricism and science, for the power of reasoning, and for the voices of authority who have taught us so much that is valuable. However, the knowledge that we can receive from God is much more important. Elder Dallin H. Oaks put it this way:

> We are commanded to seek learning by study, the way of reason, and by faith, the way that relies on revelation. Both are pleasing to God. He uses both ways to reveal light and knowledge to his children. But when it comes to a knowledge of God and the principles of his gospel, we must give primacy to revelation because that is the Lord's way.[6]

VALUE ASSUMPTIONS AND THE PROCLAMATION

Next we consider fundamental assumptions or core philosophies that are sometimes called values. They are crucial to understand because we may often overlook how they translate into everyday life. Understanding these assumptions in light of the Proclamation can indicate which of the many controversial ideas about family life advocated in society are wise and which are unwise.

Values are abstract or general beliefs about what is important and unimportant in life. It is helpful to understand what values are and how they influence us because there is such a large number of different and conflicting ideas being taught in our culture about how to be successful in family life. When we mentally step back to examine ideas in terms of their underlying values it helps us tell worthwhile suggestions from those less fruitful.

Five values seem particularly relevant to discerning between false philosophies and Proclamation truths. They are secularism, individualism, hedonism, altruism, and materialism.

Secularism

Secularism is the belief that the answers to life are found through rational means—through the concrete, observable, and practical world of people and things. A secular approach denies or devalues sacred or spiritual meanings. Most secularists believe that the religious, spiritual, or sacred parts of life are merely the inventions or delusions of people who haven't yet been appropriately educated. This belief is thus in contrast to the belief that the sacred, spiritual, or religious part of life is important and real. One example of secularist thinking is Dietrich Bonhoeffer's argument that scientific knowledge has led humanity beyond a dependence upon a supernatural God and that there is no need to create a myth of a God to explain or reach to in moments of personal crisis.[7]

It is difficult for many Latter-day Saints to understand and appreciate this belief because they rely so much on the truthfulness of the spiritual and sacred parts of life. However, this philosophy is a widespread assumption among the intellectual leaders in our society, who do not believe in anything divine.

Secularism can become a means of distracting people from righteousness, leading them to endure difficulty and grief. For example, when a loved one dies, a Christian may be comforted by Christ's assurance: "I am the resurrection, and the life: he that believeth in me, though he were dead, yet shall he live" (John 11:25). A person who did not believe in the resurrection but had confidence only in the secular and observable might feel that the loved one is gone forever. The secular provides no hope beyond this life. The loss of hope is a clue: sadly, those who believe in secularism in our modern society do not recognize that this philosophy is inspired by the devil, who seeks to lead everyone to despair (see Moro. 10:22).

These differences in the sacred and secular philosophies are illustrated with the following contrasting beliefs.

The positions people subscribe to in their value assumptions lead to dramatic differences in their specific beliefs about how to have effective families. For

COMPARISON OF SACRED TRUTHS TAUGHT IN PROCLAMATION AND SECULAR PHILOSOPHIES

PROCLAMATION IDEAS ILLUSTRATING A *SACRED* PERSPECTIVE	IDEAS ILLUSTRATING *SECULARISM*
1a. Marriage is ordained of God.	1b. Marriage is created by societies or cultures.
2a. Marriage and family are central to the Creator's plan for the eternal destiny of His children.	2b. Marriage is an optional social arrangement.
3a. All human beings—male and female—are created in the image of God.	3b. Gods are "created" by humans to explain unexplainable phenomena.
4a. Each person is a beloved spirit son or daughter of heavenly parents.	4b. The idea of heavenly parents is a comforting myth.
5a. Each person has a divine nature and destiny.	5b. Humans evolved from lower forms of life and genetics are the determinants of destiny.
6a. Family relationships may continue forever.	6b. Family relationships end at death.

Box 26.1

example, some people who have a secular perspective have argued that marriage is an outdated way of relating and it ought to be eliminated. Others have suggested that people ought to have a series of marriages, or have suggested that society would be better off if sexual interaction were separated from marriage, leaving people free to have sexual behavior with anyone they choose. Some have suggested that children would be more successful if reared by trained child-rearing professionals rather than their parents.

One of the issues that is currently being debated in society is whether people of the same gender should be able to marry each other. Many of those who are leading advocates of "gay rights" have arrived at their beliefs by starting with a secular perspective. Many of those who oppose this idea do so because they believe that marriage involving a man and woman has divine origins.

Thus, one of the ways to help us understand which specific ideas about family life are wise and which are unwise is to try to identify the underlying assumptions about the sacred and secular that provide the philosophical underpinnings for the specific ideas.

Individualism

A second belief that is abstract and a central part of people's values has to do with what they assume about individualism. Individualism is the belief or assumption that the rights, freedoms, and privileges of individuals should be given higher priority than the rights of society or groups (such as families). The belief began to develop in Europe when kings and other rulers had great control over the lives of individuals and individuals had little control over their own lives.

Individualism is a perspective that has gradually grown and expanded over the centuries. It became an intensely debated issue in the first decades of the seventeenth century, and it was a central issue in the English revolution of the 1640s and the American and French revolutions in the late eighteenth century. As the belief in the importance of individual rights grew, it led to the addition of the Bill of Rights to the U.S. Constitution in 1787. The Bill of Rights dramatically limited the power of the government and gave a number of important rights to individuals. Thus, the belief in individualism has become a dominating value or assumption in Western society, and it has improved the quality of human life in many ways. People who valued individualism helped eliminate the domination governments and churches had over people in medieval society, provided the impetus for the abolition of slavery, and established the rationale for the women's suffrage movement in the late nineteenth and early twentieth centuries. They also have helped create extensive educational opportunities and helped in many other ways to give individuals the freedom to make decisions about their own lives.

In the last half of the twentieth century, however, some important differences have appeared in the assumptions people make about individualism. Some scholars have pushed the ideal of individual rights so far that they have broken with the traditional beliefs about individualism and have advocated radical individualism or extreme individualism. For instance, Ruddick[8] suggests that the self-sacrifices of traditional mothering are defects rather than virtues. Those who believe in moderate levels of individualism argue that even though considerable emphasis should be given to the rights and privileges of individuals, there should be a limit; many individual rights and privileges should be sacrificed for the good of others. Those who believe in high levels of individualism give more emphasis to individual's rights and less emphasis to the rights of others.

COMPARISON OF THE DEGREE OF INDIVIDUALISM TAUGHT IN THE PROCLAMATION VERSUS EXTREME INDIVIDUALISM

PROCLAMATION IDEAS ILLUSTRATING *MODERATE INDIVIDUALISM*	**IDEAS ILLUSTRATING** *EXTREME INDIVIDUALISM*
1a. Fathers are responsible to provide the necessities of life and protection for their families.	1b. Women should be freed from the oppression of motherhood and realize their full potential through careers.
2a. Husband and wife have a solemn responsibility to love and care for each other and for their children.	2b. Government should share in the responsibility of child rearing in order to free parents of onerous responsibility.
3a. Parents are accountable before God for how they treat their children.	3b. Parents are accountable only to themselves and government authorities.
4a. Life is sacred and should be protected even when personally inconvenient.	4b. When pregnancy is not convenient, people should have the right to take the life of the child through abortion.
5a. Children are entitled to birth within the bonds of matrimony and to be reared by a father and a mother.	5b. Unwed single parents and same–sex couples are as good as married heterosexual parents.
6a. Husbands and wives are to honor their marital vows with complete fidelity.	6b. Individual sexual expression is paramount and sexual indiscretions are normal and understandable.
7a. Fathers are to preside over their families in love and righteousness.	7b. When men lead, it necessarily oppresses women and children.
8a. Mothers are primarily responsible for the nurture of their children.	8b. If a mother spends "quality time" with her children, she can arrange for other caregivers as often as needed in order to pursue her individual interests.

Box 26.2

The Proclamation clearly teaches that individuals are important, but that family or collective responsibilities and obligations are also central to healthy homes. The list in Box 26.2 contrasts ideas in the Proclamation that illustrate what might be called a moderate level of individualism and ideas that emphasize high levels of individualism. Notice the subtle difference between one's accepting responsibility for others versus the assumption that people should be free to seek their goals without interference from others' claims upon their time and energy.

Even though individualism has accomplished much good, when it becomes extreme it becomes dangerous to the welfare of family life as described in the Proclamation. Today, in the name of individualism, some people demand the right to live as couples without the obligations of marriage, the right to easy divorce, and the right to abdicate the responsibilities of parenthood. On the other hand, the principles of the Proclamation imply much more moderate individualism. Indeed, speaking about the importance of the Proclamation, Elder Robert D. Hales suggested, "It is not enough to save ourselves. It is equally important that parents, brothers, and sisters are saved in our families. If we return home alone to our Heavenly Father, we will be asked, 'Where is the rest of the family?' This is why we teach that families are forever. The eternal nature of an individual becomes the eternal nature of the family."[9]

It is also helpful to look at the different epistemological sources as we try to understand these debates. The ideas in the Proclamation come from revelation and religious authorities, and the beliefs in extreme individualism tend to come from reasoning and secular authorities. In addition, there is a growing body of scientific evidence that supports the conclusion that too much individualism is harmful in family life. One example is the following observation by John Bowlby, an eminent child psychiatrist, who had been studying the needs of children for more than 30 years.

> Before I go into detail, however, I want to make a few more general remarks. To be a successful parent means a lot of very hard work. Looking after a baby or toddler is a twenty-four hour-a-day job seven days a week, and often a very worrying one at that. For many people today these are unpalatable truths. Giving time and attention to children means sacrificing other interests and other activities. Yet I believe the evidence for what I am saying is unimpeachable. Study after study . . . attest[s] that healthy, happy, and self-reliant

adolescents and young adults are the products of stable homes in which both parents give a great deal of time and attention to the children.[10]

Hedonism and Altruism

A third set of values that affect family life is how much a person values hedonism versus altruism. Hedonism is the belief that it is the accepted nature of people to seek pleasure and avoid pain as the highest good. In fact, good is identical with pleasant and evil is identical with unpleasant. The good life is the life that finds as much delight and satisfaction as possible with the smallest amount of sacrifice and discomfort. This perspective is compatible with a secular and individualistic perspective; often the values go together.

Hedonism is a philosophy that dates at least back to the Greek culture in the fifth century B.C. Aristippus was the Greek philosopher who first emphasized this philosophy.[11] Although it is seldom called by the name, hedonism is a widely accepted value assumption in the world today. For many decision makers, hedonism is the basis of morality and legislation, because it is widely believed that humans will do the most good when it leads to their own pleasure and happiness.

Altruism is almost the opposite of hedonism. It is the belief that the greatest good and happiness occurs when people are devoted to the welfare of others, building a society and community of mutual care for one another. From the altruist's point of view, the Good Samaritan would not only accept responsibility for the welfare of his neighbor, but also would be the happier person for it than the priest or the Levite.

The Savior's teaching that "he that loseth his life for my sake shall find it" (Matt. 10:39) clearly recommends the altruistic approach as the value productive of greatest meaning and happiness. Whether it is called service, love, or charity, a belief in altruism is pervasive throughout the scriptures. King Benjamin's pronouncement "ye may learn that when ye are in the service of your fellow beings ye are only in the service of your God" (Mosiah 2:17) is an excellent example of the value that God places on altruism. Even God's description of His purpose exemplifies altruism: "For behold, this is my work and my glory—to bring to pass the immortality and eternal life of man" (Moses 1:39).

The Proclamation is fundamentally oriented to altruism, emphasizing charity, love, and devotion to

COMPARISON OF THE PROCLAMATION'S ORIENTATION TOWARDS ALTRUISM VERSUS HEDONISTIC PHILOSOPHIES

PROCLAMATION IDEAS ILLUSTRATING *ALTRUISM*	IDEAS ILLUSTRATING *HEDONISM*
1a. The sacred powers of procreation are to be employed only between man and woman, lawfully wedded as husband and wife.	1b. Casual sex is a harmless, intensely pleasurable (and therefore desirable) activity.
2a. Happiness in family life is most likely to be achieved when founded upon the teachings of the Lord Jesus Christ.	2b. Happiness comes through seeking pleasure and avoiding pain.
3a. Sacred temple ordinances and covenants make it possible for families to be united eternally.	3b. People should not be tied to their families when they will find personal fulfillment elsewhere.
4a. God's commandment for His children to multiply and replenish the earth remains in force.	4b. Children interfere with advancement in careers and are mainly for the personal enjoyment of parents.
5a. Successful marriages and families are established and maintained on principles of . . . forgiveness, respect, love, compassion.	5b. Successful marriage comes when each spouse allows the other to seek pleasure and self-fulfillment at will.

Box 26.3

others rather than oneself. The good life, a life of joy and fulfillment, it declares, is a life of service, charity, benevolence, compassion, and kindness. It is essential to recognize the difference between the Proclamation's focus on "happiness in family life" and "wholesome recreational activities" (¶ 8) and people insisting upon pleasure even at the sacrifice of the welfare of others.

Contrasting ideas that come from these two values can help us understand their differences. (Note that we will not repeat concepts from the Proclamation already described in earlier tables.)

The evils in the hedonistic approach are sometimes so subtle that it is easy to be deceived by it. President Gordon B. Hinckley counseled:

> Sisters, guard your children. They live in a world of evil. The forces are all about them. I am proud of so many of your sons and daughters who are living good lives. But I am deeply concerned about many others who are gradually taking on the ways of the world. Nothing is more precious to you as mothers, absolutely nothing. Your children are the most valuable things you will have in time or all eternity. . . .
>
> I think the nurture and upbringing of children is more than a part-time responsibility. I recognize that some women must work, but I fear that there are far too many who do so only to get the means for a little more luxury and a few fancier toys.[12]

There are certain combinations of values that are particularly dangerous. For example, the combination of secularism, excessive individualism, and hedonism is particularly dangerous, and it has led to some ideas about family life that are destructive. One example of this is the emphasis on enhancing self-esteem that has become so popular in recent years. The idea that enhancing self-esteem helps strengthen individuals and families gradually emerged after William James suggested in the 1890s that we should pay more attention to the self as a psychological concept. Gradually more social scientists focused on the psychological self and upon efforts to enhance self-esteem. However, an increasing number of scholars have recognized that many of the goals of enhancing self-esteem are derived from a set of values that are secular, excessively individualistic, and too hedonistic. The result may be that when therapists and educators try to help people enhance their self-esteem the results may worsen the original problems they are trying to solve. Attempts to improve self-esteem focus the attention on the self rather than on self and others in a combined way or on the welfare of others. People who focus on the self become more selfish, and selfish people rarely make wonderful spouses and parents.

Notice, for example, the differences in the value assumptions when we talk about enhancing self-esteem and enhancing individual worth. The idea of self-esteem focuses on the self isolated from others, whereas an emphasis on individual worth focuses on respect for the dignity and worth and importance of all people, and the self is a minor part of this totality. The difference has a profound effect on what we are trying to change, and the therapeutic or educational change is quite different. When we think that the self is the key, we believe the popular idea that "you can't love others until you love yourself," and we try to change the individual's view of self as a vehicle to improve his or her life situation. When we take the other perspective, we realize that all individuals are intricately intertwined in social networks. And, if we add a value for the sacred to this, we believe that part of this network includes God and other things that are sacred. The therapeutic or educational change we then try to make is to help people learn how to heal relationships with others, and to cultivate love and harmony and forgiveness in their relationships. A growing number of scholars believe this approach is much more likely to be helpful and less likely to create new problems. It is likely that the twentieth century will go down in history as the century of the "self" and that the dominant views in the twenty-first century will be much more concerned about the networks in which people live.

Materialism

Materialism is the belief that material objects, needs, and considerations are most important and should be given much emphasis. This value assumes that happiness comes from accumulating tangible possessions, and those who have a materialist orientation often devalue spiritual ideas and values.

The Western world has become increasingly materialistic in recent centuries. Most people highly value new technologies, inventions, and objects that make life comfortable and raise the standard of living. Wonderful inventions and technological discoveries like microwave ovens, computers, increasingly sophisticated cars, airplanes, and cell phones have transformed the way people and families live. However, this materialistic emphasis wrongly suggests that happiness can be found only in the possession of objects.

Although at first glance it may appear that materialism is another form of hedonism, we have chosen to focus on this value assumption because there is a difference in the philosophy of life between those for whom materialism is a central and primary value—a defining aspect of their beliefs—and those who view material possessions as merely tools that are helpful for other goals, ends, or values. There are many who are so caught up in their materialism that this one value overrides and overshadows many or more of their other ideals or values. When this occurs, people often give little emphasis to such things as family relationships, and responsibilities, and the spiritual aspects of life.

The Proclamation places the emphasis on non-materialistic goals—family life being part of an eternal plan, responsibilities, duties, and obligations. It teaches that happiness does not come from possessions but from the "teachings of the Lord Jesus Christ" (¶ 8). Elder Joe J. Christensen said it beautifully in a general conference talk at Easter of 1999:

> Giving really is at the heart of our faith. At this Easter time, we again commemorate that "God [our Heavenly Father] so loved the world, that he gave his only begotten Son," who came to the earth and could have possessed any material thing but rather chose to give to all of us an example of a simple life free from any shade of greed, selfishness, or overindulgence. May we strive daily to live more like He lived, the ultimate example of a life of depth and meaning.[13]

CONCLUSION

In deciding about the many things people suggest are needed to have happiness and create successful families, it is helpful to consider the basic values that support the suggestions. Identifying how much the specific suggestions emphasize the sacred versus the secular, individualism, hedonism versus altruism, and materialism may indicate difference between righteous and unrighteous ideas in contemporary society.

Values are the underlying beliefs about what people should do to be happy and are presented in many ways and through many sources, from science to advertising, from cultural traditions to neighbors down the street. Knowing the epistemological sources of the ideas we encounter, and knowing what kind of values underlie them, are valuable tools. These tools are also useful in reading other chapters of this book.

The philosophies or values we have examined are more important when we think about them and examine them as a set rather than when we look at them individually. A philosophy of life in which our most salient lenses are individualism, secularism, hedonism, and materialism stands in sharp contrast to the ideas taught by the Proclamation of responsibility and duty, service and sacrifice, the sacred being important, altruism and spiritual values. Crudely characterized, the worldly philosophy might be summarized as, "You are essentially alone in this life, so take all you can and enjoy it while you can, because there is nothing that comes after."

Pondering the role of these abstract ideas, it is instructive to think about how easy it is to unwittingly have the worldly ways become our ways, to have the "vain deceits of men" be incorporated into our lives. Advertising is ubiquitous, enticing us to give more emphasis to materialism than the Savior would like. Having wholesome recreation can gradually shift to pursuing an encompassing goal, wherein seeking pleasure becomes addictive because it can never satisfy. Individual rights have provided rich blessings, but the tide of the movement has carried many away from appropriate concern for the good of the family and the community. Secular answers that negate sacred principles may have the gradual effect of focusing one's attention only upon this world.

We believe the Proclamation is part of the light that God has sent to show us the way in our family relationships. We suggest that, as a sacred document, it must be studied and pondered while seeking to be in harmony with the Spirit. Remember Paul's counsel: "For what man knoweth the things of a man, save the spirit of man which is in him? Even so the things of God knoweth no man, but the Spirit of God" (1 Cor. 2:11). Like the scriptures, the Proclamation contains layer upon layer of truth and wisdom, but the understanding of those truths depends on our receptivity to the source of knowledge of the things of God. In its light we can see sacred and eternal truths that help us define who we are and what we need to do to find our way to our eternal home with our family members at our sides.

NOTES

1. Merrill J. Bateman (1998), The eternal family, *Brigham Young Magazine, 52*(4), 26.

2. S. M. Honer, T. C. Hunt, and D. L. Okholm, (1996), *Invitation to philosophy: Issues and options* (7th ed.) (Belmont, CA: Wadsworth Publishing Company).

3. Steven Conner (1989), *Postmodernist culture: An introduction to the theories of the contemporary* (Oxford: Basil Blackwell).

4. Y. S. Lincoln, and E. G. Guba (1985), *Naturalistic inquiry* (Newbury Park, CA: Sage Publications).

5. Bruce R. McConkie (1973), *Doctrinal New Testament commentary* (Salt Lake City: Bookcraft), 83–84.

6. Dallin H. Oaks (1991), *The Lord's way* (Salt Lake City: Deseret Book), 72.

7. Honer, et al. (1996).

8. S. Ruddick (1987), Remarks on the sexual politics of reason, in E. Feder Kittay and D. T. Meyers (Eds.), Women and moral theory (Totowa, NJ: Rowan & Littlefield), 237–260.

9. Robert D. Hales (1996, November), The eternal family, *Ensign, 26*(11), 65.

10. J. Bowlby (1988), *A secure base: Clinical applications of attachment theory* (London: Routledge Publications), 1–2.

11. W. P. Montague (1925), *The ways of knowing, or, the methods of philosophy* (New York: Macmillan).

12. Gordon B. Hinckley (1998, November), Walking in the light of the Lord, *Ensign, 28*(11), 99.

13. Joe J. Christensen (1999, May), Greed, selfishness, and overindulgence, *Ensign, 29*(5), 11.

CHAPTER 27

THE CENTRALITY OF FAMILY ACROSS WORLD FAITHS

TRUMAN G. MADSEN, KEITH LAWRENCE, AND SHAWN L. CHRISTIANSEN

The family is central to the Creator's plan for the eternal destiny of His children.
(The Family: A Proclamation to the World, ¶ 1)

INTRODUCTION

The major religions of the world agree in fundamental ways about the nature and the importance of the family. Such harmony reflects the promise that through the seed of Abraham the Lord would disperse truth and understanding among "all the nations of the earth" (Gen. 18:18). As Orson F. Whitney proclaimed, God has sent "good and great men" to His children in all nations "to give them, not the fulness of the Gospel, but that portion of truth that they were able to receive and wisely use."[1] In February 1978, the First Presidency of the Church affirmed:

> The great religious leaders of the world such as Mohammed, Confucius, and the Reformers, as well as philosophers including Socrates, Plato, and others, received a portion of God's light. Moral truths were given to them by God to enlighten whole nations and to bring a higher level of understanding to individuals. . . . [A]ll men and women, regardless of religious belief, race, or nationality, . . . are truly [our] brothers and sisters because we are sons and daughters of the same Eternal Father.[2]

This chapter rests on the premise that the principles enunciated in the Proclamation are God-given and that the timeless nature of these principles is supported by the teachings of other world religions about the nature and purposes of the family. Our intent in this chapter is to affirm and emphasize the divine heritage we share with our brothers and sisters around the world.

The first part of the chapter compares selected teachings of the Proclamation with the doctrines of religions within the biblical tradition: Judaism, New Testament Christianity, Roman Catholicism and other orthodox traditions, Protestantism, and Islam. The second part of this chapter considers connections between five fundamental principles of the Proclamation and doctrines on the family espoused by representative world religions, including the written traditions of ancient Babylonia, Mesopotamia, and Greece; selected oral traditions of Africa and the Americas; and the major nonbiblical religions of the contemporary world—Confucianism, Taoism, Hinduism, Buddhism, and Shinto.

PART I: THE FAMILY IN JUDAISM, CHRISTIANITY, AND ISLAM

In this section, we outline dominant views in Jewish, Catholic, Protestant, and Islamic thought on marriage and family and trace some of their philosophical roots.

Judaism and the Family

Novelist Herman Wouk, an orthodox Jew, sums up the heart of Jewish marriage and family life in these words: "One of the three questions asked in the world to come will be, 'Did you raise a family?' The single life is in our faith a misfortune; childless marriage, a disaster; and a good wife, the chief delight a man can hope for." Again, "Judaism takes the verse in Genesis, 'Be fruitful and multiply,' as part of its statutory law. Because it is the first law in the Torah [Old Testament], it holds a special eminence."[3]

One root of this long-standing view is the Creation narrative of Genesis. There, the name *Adam* is plural: "Male and female he created them, and called their name Adam." Some rabbis conclude from this that Adam is fully man only when he is linked to woman, and Samuel Hirsch, the main voice of nineteenth-century Jewish orthodoxy, concludes, "The Jewish Sages know nothing holier or nearer to God than marriage."[4] The oral law of Moses later formulated in the Talmud goes so far as to say that an unmarried man is "without good, without help, without joy, without blessing, and without forgiveness" (Kohelet Rabbah, 9, 7). In the same spirit, Jewish traditions say a groom is like a king and the bride like a queen. The hour of marriage is the hour of coronation. The Talmudic minimum of children per marriage is two, preferably both a son and a daughter. Furthermore, a man who has no children is said to be incomplete and as if he were dead (Nedarim, 64; Rala Mehemna, III, 34a). The Abrahamic heritage of Judaism both commends and promises a numerous posterity, a posterity like the stars in number and radiance. Because the family is so precious, the crucial test of Abraham and Sarah is the *akedah* or binding of Isaac. Abraham's demonstrated willingness, after Sarah's lifetime of barrenness, to give up their only son represents the ultimate sacrifice.

Jewish high holy days, especially the feasts of Dedication, of Tabernacles, and, preeminently, of Passover, were and remain to this day family gatherings around the home "altar." After the destruction of the Temple, in about A.D. 70, the home became at least as central to Jewish worship as the synagogue. Whatever else of Jewish observance was diluted in the Diaspora (dispersion) of the Jews in later centuries, family cohesion usually was perpetuated. The Jewish Sabbath is the celebration of family life par excellence. Its observance over the centuries has led to the saying that not only did the Jews keep the Sabbath, but the Sabbath kept the Jews.

The Family in New Testament Christianity

Jesus' attitudes toward family seem characteristically Jewish. He speaks throughout His ministry of the "Father," *Abba,* in supreme reverence. His first miracle at Cana is performed at a wedding celebration in which He and his mother participate. He goes up to Jerusalem with His family to celebrate Passover. He likens the kingdom of heaven to a wedding feast, where the wise virgins attend an all-night celebration (see Matt. 25). Eventually, He teaches, the Church is to be adorned as a bride and He, the Bridegroom, will come to the Church in triumphal reunion (see Rev. 19:7).

Aside from these affirmations are sayings that have led to differing interpretations and conflicts in Christian tradition. For example:

Christ apparently remains unmarried and seems to commend celibacy (see Matt. 19:10–12). Yet He is so insistent on the perpetuation of the marriage state that He ascribes divorce to hardness of heart (see Mark 10:5) and likens divorce to adultery (see Matt. 5:32; Luke 16:18). And He answers the Pharisees that marriage is an institution ordained of God (see Matt. 5:32).

He speaks of a resurrection in which "they neither marry, nor are given in marriage" (Matt. 22:30; Luke 20:35) and thus seems to deny that family relationships continue beyond the grave.[5] Yet He says of husband and wife that "they twain shall be one flesh" (see Matt. 19:5; Mark 10:8) and admonishes, "What therefore God hath joined together, let not man put asunder" (Matt. 19:6), thereby leaving this question hanging: Why should God put marriage asunder in the life to come?

When His mother and relatives approach a gathering of His disciples and are announced, He asks, "Who is my mother? and who are my brethren?" Then He gestures to all His disciples and says, as if signifying that His gospel community is intended to replace the family, "Behold my mother and my brethren!" (Matt. 12:48–49). Yet His tenderness for His mother in Cana (see John 2) and on Calvary (see John 19:26–27) suggests that He might have meant the reverse—namely, that the Church itself should become *most like* the family.

He says, "Whoso loveth husband or wife more than me is not worthy of me" (Matt 10:37). Yet He heals Peter's mother-in-law and exhorts those men and women who have come away with Him to Jerusalem to return and meet Him in Galilee, after the Resurrection, as if for a family reunion.

The book of Acts shows that the dynamics of the Church in the first generation were family centered and home based. Homes became the focus for preaching the gospel (see Acts 5:42), for administering baptism (see Acts 16:15), and apparently for the observance of the Lord's Supper (see Acts 2:46). Also in the home were systematic teaching (see Acts 20:20), regular scripture reading, gospel discussion, and hymns.[6]

The Family in Roman and Orthodox Traditions

The impact of Greek philosophy on Christian thought in the third and fourth centuries may have contributed to somewhat negative views of marriage. Plato had taught a radical dualism of body and immaterial soul, thereby contrasting this world and the realm of beatific vision. Augustine, a neo-Platonist, embraced and intensified these dualities in his view of original sin—the belief that a taint attaches to everyone born in the world. Much of Augustine's writing suggests that marriage, at best, is a compromise with flesh and the world and, at worst, is sin.

Both the Latin and Greek churches came to affirm original sin. And it was not until the twelfth century that marriage was included as one of the seven sacraments in the Roman tradition. In Eastern Orthodoxy there was no marriage ritual until the seventeenth century. By then several Roman dogmas detached the conception, birth, and life of Jesus from any association with worldly marriage that had been introduced. In conjunction with the biblical doctrine of the virgin birth emerged the dogmas of the immaculate conception of Mary, the perpetual virginity of Mary, and the bodily assumption of Mary into heaven.

Roman and Greek Christianity also borrowed from Aristotle a theory of natural law, reinforced by the great Catholic philosopher and theologian Thomas Aquinas in the twelfth century. Aquinas taught that man has an essence or core-nature and that his good consists, without exception or qualification, in honoring the unfolding of that nature. Marriage then came to be defined as natural. So did the birth process and proper parenting. Celibate priests and nuns are, in this view, living above nature.

Protestantism and the Family

Reformationist Martin Luther, in contrast to the Augustinian or Roman Catholic traditions and to Eastern Orthodoxy, commended marriage for priests and nuns as for others. Anxious to avoid the abuses arising from the Roman sacramental system, he taught that every man was his own priest and that marriage was not a sacrament, like baptism, but a vocation, like the priesthood.

Nevertheless, almost all Christians agree that marriage is in some sense ordained of God. They likewise maintain that the oneness between husband and wife is a mystery that reflects the oneness of the Godhead.

Quaker leader Elton Trueblood wrote what may be a family manifesto for all biblical religions:

> A family in which each does what he can and each receives what he needs, wholly without calculations of earning or merit, represents the highest known ideal, our only true approximation to the Kingdom of God, yet countless humble families, made up of fallible persons, demonstrate this ideal in great measure every day of their lives. This is a foretaste of what the world ought to become. The categorical imperative for every family is this: So act that the fellowship of the family becomes an advance demonstration of the heavenly kingdom.[7]

The Family in Islamic Tradition

Islam is the religion of the descendants of Ishmael, Abraham's son. Islam is built squarely upon the Judaic and Christian traditions, accepting Adam, Abraham, Isaac, Jacob, Joseph, Moses, Jesus, and others as genuine prophets who taught the word of God—but rejecting the Christian conviction that Jesus, in addition to being a prophet, was literally God's son. Islam has its origins with Muhammad, who was born in Mecca, Arabia, about A.D. 570. Believed by his followers to be the most important prophet ever to have lived, Muhammad was, from a young age, given to spiritual meditation and to social and political reflection. When he was between 30 and 40 years old, he had the first of many visions said to have been delivered personally to him by the angel Gabriel, visions that were eventually compiled by Muhammad's disciples as the Qur'an (or Koran), literally meaning "recitation."

The Qur'an teaches truths about the origins of humankind similar to those of the Old Testament, proclaiming that Adam and Eve were created by God and that all the human family comes from them (see suras 7, 35, 40, 42, 75), that God is intimately involved in human affairs so that nothing occurs without His knowledge (see suras 22, 46, 49), and that there will be a literal resurrection of the body (see sura 22).

It also retells or alludes to many other narratives of the Old Testament. And it contains many references to the life and teachings of Jesus. Although marriage, children, and family are not so central as in the Old Testament, the sanctity of marital and familial relationships is an important theme of the Qur'an, which insists upon marital fidelity and sexual purity, family loyalty, respect for and obedience to parents, reverence for all life, and the compassionate and responsible rearing of children.

The Islamic doctrine of marriage is expansive and precise. The Qur'an declares that "God is the Creator of the heavens and the earth: He has made for you pairs from among yourselves . . . by this means does he multiply you" (42:11). The Qur'an stresses that a righteous marriage sanctioned by God brings together a believing man and believing woman, and that marriage and family relationships survive beyond the grave: "those who fulfil the Covenant of God and fail not in their plighted word" will enjoy "the final attainment of the [Eternal] Home," living there as families (13:20).

Parental duty to children and a child's responsibility to parents are core doctrines of Islam. In the Qur'an, parents are instructed in clear terms to care for their children:

> The mothers shall give suck to their offspring for two whole years, if the father desires to complete the term. But he shall bear the cost of their food and clothing on equitable terms. But fear God and know that God sees well what you do. (2:233)

Children are given complementary guidance about their duties to parents:

> And we have enjoined on man to be good to his parents: in travail upon travail did his mother bear him, and in years twain was his weaning: Hear the command, "Show gratitude to Me and to thy parents." (31:14; see also 46:15)

According to the Islamic Society of North America, "Parents are greatly respected in the Islamic tradition"; mothers, who deserve "special consideration and kindness," are "particularly honored." And as "the foundation of Islamic society," a "stable family

unit" is "essential for the spiritual growth of its members."[8] In the traditional Muslim family, "children are treasured and rarely leave home until the time they marry." Finally, for Muslims, "serving one's parents is a duty second only to worshipping."[9]

The Qur'an assumes both the importance and necessity of lawful sexual relationships, but denounces adultery, fornication, homosexuality, and all lustful behavior. Sura 70:29–31 is a forceful and concise doctrinal statement on sexual virtue: "And those who guard their chastity, / . . . are not to be blamed, / But those who pass beyond this are transgressors." According to the Qur'an, God oversees and ordains all the processes of life, especially the procreative processes (41:47; see also 22:5–6; 35:11; 40:67–68; 75:36–40). Perhaps the supreme example of chaste behavior in the Qur'an is that of Joseph, who, when tempted by the wife of the Egyptian 'Aziz, declares, "Truly no good comes to those who do wrong!" Joseph proved himself, says Muhammad, to be "one of [God's] servants, sincere and purified"— one "indeed of those who are ever true and virtuous" (12:23, 24, 51). Sexual sin and infidelity, the Qur'an implies, are taught by "the evil ones" as "the means to sow discord between husband and wife," destroying happiness and all that the family rests upon (see 2:102 ff.).

PART II. THE FAMILY IN OTHER WORLD RELIGIONS

We will now discuss selected doctrines on the family espoused by the representative world religions listed in our introduction, including selected written and oral traditions of the ancient world and the major contemporary religions of Asia. We will provide a brief historical introduction to each of these religions, emphasizing general attitudes toward the family. Then we will compare views of the family held by these representative religions with the principles established by the Proclamation.

HISTORICAL INTRODUCTIONS TO REPRESENTATIVE WORLD RELIGIONS

The Written Religious Traditions of the Ancient Western World

By the time of Isaiah, Jeremiah, and other major Hebrew prophets of the seventh and eighth centuries before Christ, the religions of Babylonia and

Mesopotamia had deteriorated into hedonistic cults largely focused on fertility rituals and other practices contrary to family order and stability. But ancient texts show that, initially, the peoples of these ancient cultures had inherited a fundamental understanding of the importance of the family. For example, the *Enuma Elish,* the Babylonian creation epic, implies that, following the order established by the gods, a man and woman joined in marriage are responsible to replace chaos and confusion with order and stability—and to preserve the righteous elements of society through strong family associations. The *Epic of Gilgamesh,* the core religious text of ancient Mesopotamia, describes the world as a divinely created sphere for human habitation, asserts the beauty of life and the importance of morally responsible behavior, and emphasizes marriage above all other human relationships. It even suggests that immortality is reserved for couples joined in marriage.[10]

The religious traditions of ancient Greece are perhaps best represented by Hesiod's *Theogeny,* compiled sometime during the eighth century before Christ. Christians generally are troubled by the pantheon of gods in the *Theogeny,* gods who frequently seem all-too-human in their rivalries, passions, and conceits. Yet in its idealization of human virtues—individual agency, personal integrity, marital fidelity, family loyalty, and social responsibility—the religious tradition of ancient Greece was enormously creative and gave rise to some of the most sublime works of philosophy, art, literature, and architecture in the world. Many Greek writings remind us of the blessings of familial stability and the profoundly tragic consequences of familial disruption or disintegration.

The Native Religions of China: Confucianism and Taoism

Although every major world religion is concerned with family relationships, including those between husband and wife, parent and child, and living family members and ancestors, perhaps no religions address these issues more directly or insistently than do those of Asia, especially Confucianism, Taoism, and Buddhism. (In Asia, and particularly in China and Japan, most people embrace syncretism, or the synthesizing of disparate religious beliefs, in fashioning their religious or spiritual identities. Thus, most Chinese may claim to be Confucian, Taoist, and Buddhist; in Japan, the majority of people are simultaneously Buddhist, Confucian, and Shinto.)

Confucianism is a quasi-religious philosophical tradition deriving from the teachings of Confucius (K'ung Ch'iu), who was born about 550 B.C. Confucius insisted that one's destiny was dependent not upon pleasing the gods through the performance of religious ritual, but upon adhering to a worldview and way of life centered in the individual's "own good words and good deeds."[11] The religious devotion of Confucian followers may be described as a familial devotion, demonstrated through regular visits to temples and shrines, praying to or for ancestors at the family shrine within the home, and making sacrifices to worthy deceased family members.[12] One overriding metaphor in Confucian thought is the metaphor of filial piety, of a child's genuine respect for and devotion to parents. The same deference a child shows to parents is to be extended by the child to all older members of society. By the same token, older members of society are obliged to instruct, train, and patiently nurture younger members of society as parents would.

Taoism, or "The Way," emerged over several centuries from the teachings of a long line of philosophers beginning with Lao Tzu, a disciple and contemporary of Confucius. Taoism seeks to explain the natural order of things and insists that humankind should live in harmony with the universe. Such harmony is cultivated by sensitivity to others and to nature; by living simply, responsibly, and peaceably; and by valuing community more than individuality, harmony more than personal desire. Unlike the Westerner, who sees the temporal world as a world of opposites—light and dark, hot and cold, male and female, pleasure and pain—the Taoist, looking to the ideal marital relationship for understanding, sees instead a world of complements, where each complementary pair forms a whole. While the Westerner is inclined to see a world characterized by tension and conflict, the Taoist—again idealizing honorable male/female relationships—is more likely to see balance and harmony.

The Native Religions of India: Hinduism and Buddhism

Hinduism, one of the world's oldest religions, has no single founder or belief system. Instead, it emerged slowly over a period of about three thousand years, beginning around 2000 B.C., as a complex amalgamation of primitive rituals and hymns, elaborate religious doctrines, folk traditions, and codes of social and political behavior. For Hindus, the ideal life follows four stages: apprenticeship, which extends from Hindu initiation rites performed when the subject is about 8 years old until the subject marries; householdership, which extends from marriage until the time one's children reach adulthood, a time focused on the rearing of children and the worthy fulfillment of social duties; retirement, the period of "grandparenting" when one refines one's own social and spiritual maturity and passes wisdom to youth; and renunciation, as one renounces all worldly things and achieves spiritual liberation.[13] Primary Hindu texts include the Vedas, Aryan hymns dating from about 2000 B.C. and focused on the hope of an afterlife in heaven; the Dharmasastras, or codes of the ideal life; and the Mahabharata and Ramayama, epic narratives replete with didactic episodes and instructive, inspiring poetry.

Buddhism emerged in India at roughly the same time Confucianism and Taoism were developing in China. According to tradition, the man we know as Buddha was a prince born about 600 B.C. Renouncing the asceticism of Hindu priests on one hand and the licentiousness of the culture in which he was reared on the other, Buddha preached a life of moderation and rightness in thought, speech, and action, sometimes referred to as the Middle Path.[14] While Buddhism is more "self-concerned" than Confucianism or Taoism, it nevertheless demands respect for and compassionate service to family members and others, especially the poor, the abandoned, and the infirm. Like the religions of China, it establishes honorable family relationships as the hallmark of a sound, harmonious society.

Shinto, the Native Religion of Japan

Shinto (meaning "the way of the gods")—the native religion of ancient Japan—is a loosely organized collection of beliefs, customs, rituals, and superstitions; it has no founder, no fixed doctrines, and no official scriptures. Its two most important texts—which incorporate elements of Shinto ritual and belief—are the Kojiki (or Records of Ancient Matters) and the Nippongi (or Chronicles of Japan), compiled in A.D. 712 and A.D. 720, respectively. Because Shinto has, over the centuries, attempted to integrate teachings from Buddhism and Confucianism,[15] it is difficult to identify core Shinto beliefs. One unique Shinto belief, however, is that the spirits of *kami* or the gods inhabit all things—rocks, animals, plants, streams, clouds, rain, mountains, valleys.[16] The essence of Shinto devotion is to be found in the agricultural rituals and customs of rural Japan.

Of most relevance here is the belief that all Japanese are connected by blood and consciousness as an immense family. The gods and the Japanese people are believed to be allied in a struggle to supplant evil and sorrow with goodness, happiness, and prosperity. This struggle, in practical terms, is often portrayed as an alliance among the gods, deceased ancestors, and the family against the forces of unhappiness and evil. Thus, Shinto religious practice is in one sense centered in establishing and maintaining a close-knit and harmonious family.

The Oral Traditions of Africa and the Americas

The peoples of Africa traditionally perform or chant socio-religious epic narratives with a common narrative structure centered around a heroic male—often divine—that we in the West might be tempted to call a Christ-figure. In most African epics, the hero comes into the world through a virgin or other unusual birth and matures in a precocious way, sometimes intellectually, sometimes physically. He embodies stunning moral and physical strength; he possesses endless courage. His supreme accomplishment is to slay an enormous monster—embodying evil—that has swallowed entire communities. Following the destruction of the monster, the hero establishes his people, who look to him as their father.[17] Often, the epic ends in the hero's marriage, thereby ennobling the family as the supreme social body and dictating the principles whereby the king and queen—and, by extension, all fathers and mothers—are to exercise their parental authority: love, wisdom, justice, generosity, and compassion.

The peoples of the Americas and Polynesia share many oral traditions. Here, we select only two peoples who represent such traditions: the Quiché-Maya of Guatemala and the Navajo of the southwestern United States. The central religious text of the Quiché-Maya is the *Popol Vuh,* or Council Book, a sacred text of narrative, counsel, and prophecy. In oral form, the *Popol Vuh* probably dates from sometime between A.D. 1000 and 1200; a hieroglyphic version survives from the late fifteenth century. The *Popol Vuh* is first and foremost a family narrative. It traces the history of primary gods and their mortal descendants, shows how both gods and mortals are rewarded for family loyalty and chaste behavior, and emphasizes the negative and endless repercussions of immorality and familial disloyalty or disrespect.

The religion of the Navajo people is intimately tied to the landscape of the southwestern United States. In this landscape, the Navajo see reflected the shapes of the evil monsters slain by the half-divine, half-mortal twin brothers who established and first taught the ancestors of the Navajo. For the Navajo, the landscape is also witness to their own quiet hardiness and endurance.[18] Perhaps their most important religious narrative is the *Diné Bahanè,* or the Navajo Creation Story, likely dating from sometime after A.D. 1300. Like the *Popol Vuh,* it is a family history, telling how the ancestors of the Navajo ascended, level by level, from a world deep within the earth to their final home on the surface. There, First Man and First Woman gave birth to Changing Woman, who, in turn, bore the twin sons mentioned earlier, the sons who, following their own marriages, established the Navajo people. In the *Diné Bahanè,* the family represents the highest social order; the Navajo people themselves comprise a large family body with familial obligations and ties. The *Diné Bahanè* demands of the Navajo marital fidelity and sexual purity, generosity, compassion, clarity of spiritual purpose, and self-sacrifice.

PART III. PRINCIPLES ESTABLISHED BY THE PROCLAMATION

We now will outline how certain fundamental principles taught in the Proclamation are affirmed or supported by doctrines on the family espoused by selected world religions.

The Human Family Is Literally or Metaphorically the Offspring of Deity (¶ 2)

An intriguing element of world history is that virtually every world civilization is fundamentally religious. Each, through its ancient written or oral narratives, traces its origins to a divine source. In explaining the nature of the divine, such narratives emphasize the relationship of humanity to and our dependence on the creator or creators who gave us life. Like the Old Testament, most religious texts from ancient world civilizations—including the Enuma Elish and the Epic of Gilgamesh—teach that men and women are created in the divine image. Hesiod's *Theogeny* and his *Works and Days* teach the ancient Greek belief that Pandora, the first mortal, was

fashioned by the gods in their image and given wonderful gifts by each of them. Once on earth, she wed the god Epimetheus and together they began the human family. Of all ancient religions, the polytheism of the Greeks was perhaps most insistent in perceiving human emotions, needs, and behavior as reflective of the divine origins of humankind, and in seeing in the human body itself the clearest and most profound reflection of the divine realm.

In the pre-Confucian Shang era of ancient China, most people believed in a "supreme anthropomorphic deity who sent blessings or calamities, gave protection in battles, [and] sanctioned undertakings"[19]—a being whose human offspring were the original members of China's royal family. Shinto, the native religion of Japan, espouses similar beliefs, insisting that Jimmu, the mythical first emperor of the Japanese archipelago, was the son of Amaterasu, the goddess of the sun.

The Popol Vuh, the Mayan account of creation, delineates the generation of the gods, beginning with the Makers and continuing through the miraculously conceived twin gods, Hunahpu and Xbalanque, to the first four mortal leaders of the Quiché people. As in Hesiod's *Theogeny,* the gods and the first humans form a single and continuous family in which humans are created in the physical and emotional likeness of the gods.

Marriage Joins Together a Man and a Woman in a Divinely Instituted Covenant (¶¶ 1, 6, 7)

Joseph Campbell, renowned scholar of world cultures and religious mythology, suggests that, in all cultures, the marriage union of man and woman is so important that the religious and folk narratives recounting "the hero-deeds of all time and all the world" tend to be focused on it.[20] In an important section of the *Epic of Gilgamesh,* the title character rejects the marriage proposal of Ishtar, goddess of the harvest. Anthropologist and literary scholar Paul Davis suggests that Gilgamesh's rejection is an act of independence and self-creation.[21] But it is also an act of selfishness, of shrinking from the responsibility to sacrifice self for others—especially one's own family. At the conclusion of the narrative, the opportunity to receive immortality is taken from Gilgamesh, at least partially because he hasn't understood the importance of marriage and self-sacrifice.

An early Hindu creation narrative from the Brihadaranyaka Upanishad presents marriage as having been established by deity and asserts that neither a man nor a woman is whole until they are made one through marriage—that they "are not happy when they are alone," but are "like one of the halves of a split pea."[22] The *Bhagavad-Gita* teaches that "Marriage on principles of religious life is . . . current in all civilized human society" because it is the only avenue for "procreation . . . for [the] begetting [of] good children."[23]

As previously stated, most African oral narratives end in a marriage celebration (as do many epic narratives from around the world). An especially striking example is the epic *Ibonia* told by the Merina people of Madagascar. Although the epic is overtly concerned with Ibonia's redemption of the land that the Merina people eventually will occupy, it is centered in Ibonia's spiritual quest to redeem the woman to whom he is betrothed. Indeed, without his marriage, without his establishing the family that becomes the Merina nation, the epic would be meaningless. It teaches, first of all, that marriage between a man and a woman is the will of the gods, but also that from a single honorable marriage can come a righteous nation.

In the *Diné Bahanè,* the Navajo Creation Story, the ancestors of the Navajo have been created as males and females. They live together in couples as husbands and wives. When the four Holy People eventually create the first human beings, they create a man and a woman who are instructed to be loyal to each other, to have children, and to teach them well.

Children Are a Precious Inheritance from Deity; Parents and Children Have Deep and Lasting Obligations to One Another (¶¶ 4,5,7,8)

In the culture of ancient Greece filial duty is prominent as a theme in art and literature. Sophocles, in particular, returns to this theme repeatedly, showing the horrific consequences of neglecting or abusing one's filial obligations (as in *Oedipus Rex* and *Medea*) and exploring the psychological turmoil caused by conflicts between filial responsibility and unrighteous law (as in *Antigone*).

According to Confucian doctrine, one's most important role is found within the immediate family; one's most important obligations are to immediate and extended family members, especially parents. A similar, albeit metaphorical, respect is extended to ancestors through ancestor worship.[24] Fulfilling the Confucian ethical imperatives associated with filial piety helps create a principled and ordered society. A

child's respect for parents and obedience to them are forms of repayment for the care, nurture, and training that parents have provided the child. In the Confucian tradition, one of the primary responsibilities of parents is to instill within their children the ideological and moral perspectives that will allow the children to mature appropriately and to fulfill social responsibilities effectively.[25] Confucius taught in the *Analects* that "young men should be filial when at home and respectful to their elders when away from home" (1:6).

When Confucius was asked which single word could be used as a meaningful life principle, he said, "Perhaps the word, 'reciprocity': Do not do to others what you would not want others to do to you" (*Analects* 15:23).[26] The Japanese term for this reciprocity is *on*. In a familial context, *on* or filial piety emphasizes a reverential repayment to parents for the nurture, care, and training that the child has received from them.[27] While this filial debt can never be repaid, the process of trying to repay it leads a child to moral reflection and necessary social development.[28] From a Western perspective, Confucian ethics relative to filial duty seem extraordinarily demanding. Comparative religion scholar G. A. De Vos has observed that, for many Westerners, "The idea of voluntarily taking on the burden of a senile in-law, but more than that, finding a sense of self-realization in such a dedication, is incomprehensible."[29]

Buddhist texts avoid extensive discussion of filial piety, in part because Buddhism is primarily a religion of self-salvation. Indeed, in ascetic Buddhism, the disciple finds salvation only in giving up family, taking vows of celibacy, and withdrawing from the world. Such an intense focus on the individual runs counter to Confucian teachings on filial piety. Thus, in order for Buddhism to survive in Confucian societies, a dualistic philosophy of family emerged. Only Buddhist monks and nuns were required to leave family behind, while lay Buddhists retained all filial obligations. In Japan, this duality was partially circumvented by allowing monks to marry and by requiring that priestly duties be passed down through family lineage.[30]

Buddhist doctrinal texts dictate that, for lay members, a son is to revere parents by (1) increasing their wealth, (2) caring for their affairs, (3) providing for their needs, (4) giving up personal desires, and (5) offering all possessions to them. Conversely, parents are to provide a son (1) nurture and care, (2) sufficient food, (3) sufficient money, (4) a beneficial marriage, and (5) a full inheritance. Those keeping these obligations were promised success in life and a place in heaven after death. That lay Buddhists respect their mothers was especially important. An eighth-century text highlights the sacrifice mothers make in carrying a child and giving it life, emphasizing the incapacity of the child ever to repay this sacrifice.[31]

One also finds deeply ingrained codes of filial responsibility in the cultures of northwestern Africa, especially those influenced by Islam. *The Oral Epic of Askia Mohammed,* for example, a religious folk narrative of the Songhays of West Africa, contains a long account of how a son who is divinely appointed to spread Islam among his people is protected and nurtured by his royal parents and how, in turn, his life is blessed as he carefully follows the directives he receives from them.[32]

Sexuality Is a Precious Divine Gift That Must Be Exercised within Divinely Instituted Parameters (¶¶ 4, 5, 7, 8).

Sexuality is, in the majority of world religions, emphatically portrayed as the most important and most sublime of all divine gifts to humankind. The *Epic of Gilgamesh,* for example, suggests that divinely sanctioned physical love can spiritually transform the individual, establishing wisdom and humanity in place of a formerly wild and ungoverned nature.[33] In contrast, inappropriate sexual relations are viewed by the gods with sorrow and displeasure; erring humans eventually suffer the consequences of their sinful behavior.

Most world religions teach that only within the marriage covenant can a man and woman legitimately express their sexual love for one another. Indeed, as one of the most fundamental of divine laws, chastity invites divine approval and blessings while unchastity insures divine anger and divine retribution. Of *The Book of Odes,* an ancient Chinese anthology of religious poetry, Confucius taught in the *Analects* that "all three hundred odes can be covered by one of their sentences, and that is, 'Have no depraved thoughts'" (2:2). Step four of the Eightfold Path espoused by Buddhists is "right behavior"; this is broken down into five directives: "Do not kill," "Do not steal," "Do not lie," "Do not be unchaste," and "Do not take drugs or intoxicants."

The *Bhagavad-Gita* enjoins the chastity of both women and men and asserts that the act of a husband and wife appropriately engaging in sexual relations "is a representation of [Krishna]" (172). Campbell has observed that in some depictions of Hindu deities and of Buddha and bodhisattvas, the hands are horizontal, one positioned with the palm up and the other with the palm down. The upturned palm, says Campbell, signifies the grateful reception of all divine gifts, including sexuality, while the down-turned palm represents the necessity of governing the use of such gifts with wisdom, sensitivity, and restraint.[34] In Hindu mythology, the sacred marriage between the god Shiva and the goddess Shakti is the union that "sustains the life of the universe."[35] In its sacred dimension, say Hindus, appropriate physical relations collapse the opposites personified by the two genders—eternity and time, life and death, strength and weakness, mind and heart—and help penetrate all the worldly concerns that obscure the *atman,* the eternal soul of man. Accordingly, sexuality allows the righteous mortal couple to intuit the loving and eternal nature of God.[36]

In the *Diné Bahané,* the ancestors of the Navajo originally occupied a world several levels beneath the surface of the earth. For a time they lived together in peace, but eventually they began quarreling and fighting. "And this is how it happened," the narrative states: "They committed adultery, one with another. Many of the men were to blame, but so were many of the women."[37] As punishment, they were driven from the first world to a second, where they lived until they committed the same sins again. This cycle was repeated several times until they eventually came to the surface of the earth, a world that they loved. They held a council meeting and made a covenant of chastity.[38] The Navajo ancestors were then visited by the gods, the four Holy People, who cleansed them, purified them, and taught them.

The Family Is the Most Important Potential Source of Mortal Joy and Fulfillment as the Fundamental Social Entity (¶¶ 1–3, 6–9).

People worldwide, religious or otherwise, tend naturally to center their lives in the family. Identity is inextricably linked to the nuclear and extended family. Life's milestones—birth, adolescence, matriculation, marriage, life achievements, death—are family-centered. Children almost universally desire to be attached to a secure and happy home life. Most adults desire to marry and to begin families of their own. Most aging adults desire the perpetuation of meaningful relationships with children, grandchildren, or other extended family members. When incapacitated, they want to be cared for or supported by family. Thus, world religions quite naturally perceive the family as the greatest potential source of temporal joy and fulfillment, underscoring the principle that, if families are healthy, vibrant, and strong, the larger society flourishes.

Asian religions appear to have the most extensive doctrines on the close and profound connections between families and society. Given the Confucian focus on everyday life, its teachings are predictably concerned with finding harmony in family and society.[39] And because the Confucian seeks self-improvement not for selfish reasons but so that he or she may more effectively serve others,[40] a direct link between the stability of the family and the stability of the nation is emphasized.[41] In *The Great Learning* Confucius declares, "If there is righteousness in the heart, there will be beauty in the character; if there is beauty in the character, there will be harmony in the home; if there is harmony in the home, there will be order in society; and when there is order in society, there will be peace in the world."[42] A related Confucian teaching is that one can change the larger systems of community and government through fulfilling one's duties to family. Confucius cites a teaching from the *Book of Documents* to make this point: "Simply by being a good son and friendly to his brothers a man can exert an influence upon government."[43]

Connections among individuals, families, and society are suggested as well by Shinto. While many Shinto rituals are centered in the worship of the *kami,* many others are devoted to human ends. Indeed, on one level, the purpose of Shinto is to establish connections and loyalties among all things. Of human-centered rituals in Shinto, perhaps the most important are linked to the observance of family milestones.[44] One family ritual, for example, provides for the naming of children. Through a highly stylized ritual, the name is given to the child and subsequently recorded at the family's Shinto shrine.[45] Other Shinto rituals are enacted when a family member dies; sometimes these are combined with Buddhist rituals. Buddhist and Shinto funerary rites are meant to help deceased family members on their way in the afterworld. They also provide opportunities for family members to grieve, support one another, and remember their ancestors. Confucian family rituals teach children their connection and responsibility to parents and ancestors, strengthening emotional ties among immediate and extended family members and creating bridges to "family lands" and the surrounding community.[46]

In Shinto, Confucian, and Buddhist ritual performance, the family household plays a primary role. Most worship occurs within the family home, where a shrine or altar honoring deceased ancestors is located in a place of honor. At this shrine, prayers for or to dead ancestors are offered. Around the shrine are placed other items of worship or deference, such as ancestral tablets, genealogies, or artistically scripted names of deities and guardian spirits. Marriages and funerals may also take place inside the home, and memorial days for ancestors are often observed there.[47] Thus, the Asian home becomes a sacred place, a place of worship.

Shintoists, Confucians, and Buddhists also visit family and public temples to worship or pray for ancestors, request divine assistance for living family members and friends, or seek personal aid. Many extended families have an ancestral temple where ancestors are venerated and in some cases deified.[48] Worship at home shrines and at temples cements family members to one another and connects them to the surrounding community, perpetuating the continuation of families and society.

Two Native American narratives point to the connection between family health and social stability. In the Popol Vuh, the two older brothers of the divinely appointed twins, Hunahpu and Xbalanque, reject their younger brothers out of jealousy and spite. The actions of the older brothers are not a petty matter, but constitute a willful wrenching of family relationships that is destructive to all family members and to the surrounding society. Eventually, the older brothers are punished by decree of the gods, losing their human form and their place in the family and becoming animals forever. The *Diné Bahané* echoes this theme, emphasizing that when individuals trespass sacred family boundaries and commitments, all of society suffers the consequences.

CONCLUSION

The beautiful, eternal truths of the Proclamation are affirmed by the central teachings of world religions about the nature and character of the family. Indeed, there is a striking consistency across disparate faiths in the perspective that the human family derives from deity, that marriage and family life is divinely appointed, that parents and children have deep and lasting commitments to each other, that sexuality is a gift to be exercised within divinely established limits, and that the family is the central institution of society and the most important source of mortal joy and fulfillment. These shared convictions, properly understood, help bring all peoples of the earth together and help us join in defending families against the forces that would weaken and destroy them.

NOTES

1. Orson F. Whitney (1921, April), in Conference report, 30.

2. The First Presidency, Statement of February 15, 1978, cited in S. J. Palmer (1978), *The expanding Church* (frontispiece), (Salt Lake City: Deseret Book).

3. Herman Wouk (1988), *This is my God: The Jewish way of life* (Boston: Little, Brown), 124.

4. Samuel Hirsch (1956), *Judaism eternal: Selected essays from the writings of Rabbi Samson Raphael Hirsch,* ed. and trans. I. Grunfeld (New York: Soncino Press), 2:90.

5. This verse in Matthew is absent from the earliest Greek manuscripts. But if authentic, it, with the parallel version in Luke, does not say that no marriage performed before the resurrection will endure; but rather that "no marriage or giving in marriage" will occur after the resurrection.

6. D. N. Freedman (Ed.) (1991), *Anchor bible dictionary* (New York: Doubleday), 769.

7. E. Trueblood (1953), *The recovery of family life* (New York: Harper & Brothers), 53.

8. Transcom International (1999), Discover Islam 20: Why is the family so important to Muslims? Online, available: www.discoverislam.com/20.html, 15 March 1999.

9. Transcom International (1999), Discover Islam 22: How do Muslims view the elderly, death, and the afterlife? Online, available: www.discoverislam.com/22.html, 15 March 1999.

10. *The Epic of Gilgamesh* (1994), trans. M. G. Koracs, in M. A. Caws and C. Predergast (Eds.), *The HarperCollins world reader: Antiquity to the early modern world* (New York: HarperCollins).

11. W. T. Chan (Ed. and Trans.) (1963), *A source book in Chinese philosophy* (Princeton: Princeton University Press), 3; W. Tu (1998), Confucius and Confucianism, cited in W. H. Slote and G. A. DeVos (Eds.) (1998), *Confucianism and the family* (Albany: State University of New York Press), 3.

12. D. S. Choi (1997), *Confucianism,* cited in S. J. Palmer, R. R. Keller, D. S. Choi, and J. A. Toronto (Eds.) (1997), *Religions of the world: A latter-day Saint view* (Provo: Brigham Young University); L. M. Hopfe (1987), *Religions of the world* (4th ed.) (New York: Macmillan).

13. See H. Smith (1994), *The illustrated world's religions* (San Francisco: Harper), 18–41.

14. Smith, 60–72; S. J. Palmer (1978), World religions and Mormonism, in Daniel H. Ludlow (Ed.), *The encyclopedia of Mormonism* (New York: Macmillan), 4:1588–1595.

15. L. M. Hopfe (1987), *Religions of the world* (4th ed.) (New York: Macmillan); T. Kuroda (1993), Shinto in the history of Japanese religion, in M. R. Mullins, S Shimazono, and P. L. Swanson (Eds). *Religion in modern society: Selected readings* (Nagoya, Japan: Nanzan Institute for Religion and Culture).

16. Hopfe (1987).

17. M. A. Caws and C. Prendergast (Eds.) (1994), *The HarperCollins world reader: Antiquity to the early modern world,* (New York: HarperCollins), 1047–1048.

18. M. A. Caws and C. Prendergast (Eds.) (1994), 1282–1285, 1324–1325.

19. W. T. Chan. (Ed. and Trans.) (1963), *A source book in Chinese philosophy* (Princeton, NJ: Princeton University Press), 4.

20. J. Campbell (1968), *The hero with a thousand faces* (Princeton: Princeton University Press), 344.

21. P. Davis, et al. (1995), *Western literature in a world context, volume 1: The ancient world through the Renaissance* (New York: St. Martin's), 797.

22. Quoted in Campbell (1968), 278.

23. A. C. Bhaktiedanta Swami Prabhupada (Ed.) (1975), *Bhagavad-Gita: As it is,* (New York: Bhaktivedanta Book Trust), 81, 172.

24. E. C. Y. Kuo (1998), Confucianism and the Chinese family in Singapore: Continuities and changes, in Slote and DeVos (Eds.) (1998), *Confucianism and the family.*

25. D. S. Choi (1997), Confucianism, in S. J. Palmer, R. R. Kaller, D. S. Choi, and J. A. Toronto (Eds.) (1997), *Religions of the world: A latter-day Saint view* (Provo, Utah: Brigham Young University Press); K. K. Lee (1998), Confucian tradition in the contemporary Korean family, in Slote and DeVos (Eds.) (1998), *Confucianism and the family.*

26. Cited in L. M. Hopfe (1987), *Religions of the world* (4th ed.) (New York: Macmillan).

27. G. A. DeVos (1998), Confucian family socialization: The religion, morality, and aesthetics of propriety; see K. K. Lee (1998), Confucian tradition in the contemporary Korean family, in Slote and DeVos (Eds.) (1998), *Confucianism and the family.*

28. W. Tu (1998), Probing the "three bonds" and "five relationships" in Confucian humanism, in Slote and DeVos (Eds.) (1998), *Confucianism and the family.*

29. G. A. DeVos (1998), Confucian family socialization, 365, in Slote and DeVos (Eds.) (1998), *Confucianism and the family.*

30. L. R. Lancaster (1984), Buddhism and family in East Asia, in G. A. DeVos and T. Sofue (Eds.), *Religion and the family in East Asia* (Osaka, Japan: National Museum of Ethnology), 139–151.

31. Lancaster (1984).

32. The oral *Epic of Askia Mohammed* (1994), in M. A. Caws and C. Prendergast (Eds.) (1994), *The HarperCollins world reader: Antiquity to the early modern world* (New York: HarperCollins), 1057–1063.

33. The *Epic of Gilgamesh* (1994).

34. J. Campbell (1979, March 7), *Mask of Oriental gods: Symbolism of Kundalini Yoga,* unpublished transcript of lecture presented at the Literature of Belief Symposium, Brigham Young University.

35. H. Zimmer (1946), *Myths and symbols in Indian art and civilization* (New York: Pantheon Books), 127.

36. H. Smith (1994), *The illustrated world's religions* (San Francisco: Harper), 22.

37. Diné Bahanè: The Navajo creation story (1994), in M. A. Caws and C. Prendergast (Eds.), *The HarperCollins world reader:*

Antiquity to the early modern world (New York: HarperCollins), 1327.

38. Diné Bahanè (1994), 1334.

39. G. A. DeVos (1998), Confucian family socialization in Slote and DeVos (Eds.) (1998), *Confucianism and the family.*

40. G. A. DeVos (1998), Confucian family socialization, 355.

41. See J. M. Kitagawa (1968), *Religions of the East* (Philadelphia: Westminister Press), 86, 52.

42. Quoted in Kitagawa (1968), 86.

43. W. Tu (1998), Confucius and Confucianism, in Stole and DeVos (Eds.) (1998), *Confucianism and the family,* 12.

44. Lancaster (1984).

45. Lancaster (1984).

46. Lee (1998).

47. Kitagawa (1968).

48. F. L. K. Hsu (1998), Confucianism in comparative context, in Slote and DeVos (Eds.) (1998), *Confucianism and the family.*

ADDITIONAL ACTIVITIES TO ASSIST IN THE APPLICATION OF PROCLAMATION PRINCIPLES

LAURA E. GILPIN

INTRODUCTION

As mentioned in this volume, families that are "intentional"—that take the time to set family goals, plan activities, do things together, and talk together about family life—are more likely to be successful and happy families. This section is a resource to help families be more intentional in applying Proclamation principles to strengthen their family relationships.

While many chapter and essay authors have included application ideas within their chapters and essays, this section is a collection of additional application ideas specific to each chapter subject. It is not absolutely necessary to have read the corresponding chapters in the book beforehand, although it would be helpful to read and incorporate ideas from the chapters into these application activities.

The goal of this section is to help you progress in your family life and gain greater family happiness and togetherness as you strengthen your understanding and testimony of family life, move forward with faith in your relationships, and share and defend Proclamation principles.

USING THESE ACTIVITIES

These activities are designed to give families ideas on what they could do during family home evenings (FHE), family councils (FC), family prayer, at meal times, or other times when families are gathered together. Many of the activities below are designed for specific groups and are labeled "For Individuals," "For Single Adults," "For Couples," "For Parents," or "For Families" accordingly. Those labeled "For Everyone" can easily be used by any group of two or more.

Due to variations in chapter content, few chapters have an activity for every category. However, many activities can be adapted for use by any group and *readers are encouraged to modify activities to fit their current situations and needs.* For example, single adults could adjust those labeled "for families" for use with roommates or as lesson ideas for single adult activities. Single parents may wish to call upon extended family, home or visiting teachers, or friends to help them with some of the activities. Young women could consider some of the ideas as Personal Progress goals. Most of the activities will require some modification to best suit each reader's specific situation.

Fathers and mothers are encouraged to work together as *equal partners* (¶ 7) in a united effort to decide how the activities can best be carried out. Each can prayerfully decide what they will personally do to encourage family progress in a specific area before presenting the activities and ideas to their children. Of course, no family should do all of these activities since individuals, couples, and families need to grow in different ways. Because the purpose of this section is to help you strengthen family relationships, you are encouraged to counsel with your family and prayerfully consider which activities best suit your needs and could most benefit your family.

This book (including this set of activities) is meant to be a resource for you in your quest to strengthen your family. It offers ideas and suggestions to help you apply principles from the Proclamation in your home and family life. However, it is not an exhaustive composition, nor is it a individualized handbook specifically for your family. You are encouraged to read Essay A, "Drawing Specific Inspiration from the Proclamation," and the ideas in the box below, and seek divine guidance from the Spirit on how the Lord wants you specifically to be blessed by the inspired document *The Family: A Proclamation to the World.*

CHAPTER-BASED ACTIVITIES

Chapter 1: Families and the Great Plan of Happiness

1a. *For Parents:* Draw the elements of the plan of salvation (i.e., premortal life, veil, earth life, etc.) to help children visually see who they are, where they came from, where they are, and where they want to go in the future. Discuss with them how gospel and Proclamation principles fit into the plan. You could use small pictures of your children and move them along as you discuss each phase to help children apply the plan to themselves.

1b. *For Everyone:* List a few families of patriarchs in the scriptures or Church history. Discuss how they lived the gospel and followed the plan of happiness *in their family lives.* Discuss how they put God and family above all else in their lives. What experiences of spiritual growth were they able to have as members of earthly families? How did they, and *how can we,* help family members return to Heavenly Father? Talk about why it is important to keep an eternal perspective in our interactions with family members.

1c. *For Everyone:* Invite extended family members or friends over to watch the video "Together Forever" (Church Distribution Item # 53411). Afterward, discuss how families fit into the great plan of happiness and what a blessing it is that we are able to share our lives together as families.

Chapter 2: The Enduring, Happy Marriage: Findings and Implications from Research

2a. *For Couples:* List the ways your lives have been blessed since you were married and share them with each other. Each write a letter of gratitude to your spouse for the ways he or she has blessed your life and give it to him or her.

2b. *For Everyone:* Spend an evening with a couple who appears to have a happy, enduring marriage. Ask them to share what makes them successful, how they work on their marriage, and how their individual lives have improved since they were married. If you are married, counsel with your spouse as to what you learned from this experience and if you would like to emulate any of the things discussed.

Chapter 3: Preparing for an Eternal Marriage

3a. *For Single Adults:* For a single adult activity, have each person list at least 10 qualities they are looking for in a future spouse and rank them in order of their relative importance. Allow them time to compare their lists and discuss the reasons behind their choices. Then, discuss with them the importance of not only finding the right person to marry, but concentrating on "being the right person." Instruct them to write a second list of at least 10 qualities they will cultivate in themselves as they prepare for marriage, holding themselves to the same high standards they

---

GUIDELINES FOR ADAPTING APPLICATIONS OF PROCLAMATION PRINCIPLES TO YOUR FAMILY LIFE

1. Seek the inspiration of the Lord and follow the promptings of the Holy Ghost.
2. Parents, work together as equal partners and counsel together regularly.
3. Focus on building relationships more than on completing tasks.
   a. Honor the moral agency of family members by not forcing participation in activities.
4. Counsel together as a family to set goals and make plans for family "togetherness time."
   a. Select and adapt activities that will support family goals.
5. Respect and consider the individual needs, abilities, ages, and interests of all family members.
   a. Find ways to include all family members in as many activities as possible.
   b. Simplify the more complex activities to make them understandable for young children.
   c. Involve older children in the planning/preparing for activities.
6. As a family, evaluate the effectiveness and enjoyment of completed activities to help plan future activities.

used to make their first list. Discuss as a group how individuals could go about developing some of these qualities.

3b. *For Single Adults:* Divide into two groups, males and females. Each individual should first list the five main concerns he or she has about his or her future marriage, then, in your two groups, incorporate those ideas into an integrated list of 10 for each group. Then each group should list what they think the other group's 10 main concerns are. Compare your group lists. Which concerns are similar, and which are different? Did each group have an accurate idea of what the other's concerns would be? Which concerns were a surprise? What can you learn from this experience about members of the other sex?

3c. *For Parents:* Discuss the importance of temple marriage with your children. Allow each child to choose a picture of a temple they like and place it in his or her room. Discuss with them the things they will need to do to have a successful temple marriage. Help or encourage them to write down the goals they will work on now to prepare for their temple marriage. During a FHE or meal, discuss as a family the importance of temples in family life.

3d. *For Everyone:* Read the Apostle Paul's description of charity in I Corinthians 13 or Moroni's description in Moroni 7:44–47, substituting the phrase "marital love" for charity. Think of opposites for each of the attributes Paul or Moroni describes. Discuss how marriages can be improved when people act toward each other as Paul and Moroni counseled.

Chapter 4: Chastity and Fidelity in Marriage and Family Relationships

4a. *For Families:* Have an adult (or older child) and a young child both attempt a difficult physical challenge, such as threading a needle. Most likely, the task will be easier for the older person. Explain to your children that just as we gain greater control of our bodies as we mature, we can gain greater control of our emotions. Explain to them how achieving this control is vital to our eternal salvation. Discuss what can happen when we don't control our bodies and emotions.

4b. *For Everyone:* During a mealtime, brainstorm a list of songs, movies, Internet sites, etc., that cultivate a positive view of chastity and fidelity (i.e., intimacy is reserved for marriage, husband and wife are faithful to each other, etc.). Make an appointment to enjoy at least one of them together.

Chapter 5: Equal Partnership and the Sacred Responsibilities of Mothers and Fathers

5a. *For Couples:* Counsel together on how you can help each other with your sacred responsibilities as they are described in the Proclamation and/or how you can become more "equal partners" (see Boxes 5.3 and 5.5). Concentrate for a week on doing everything you can to support your spouse's ability to fulfill his or her sacred responsibilities. After the week, come together to discuss how you will continue to support each other as equal partners.

5b. *For Parents:* Discuss with your children the responsibilities they have as males and females (see Proclamation, ¶ 7) and how they are different. Brainstorm with them ways they could begin to practice these responsibilities in certain contexts (such as playing with other children or siblings, dating, babysitting, courtship, etc.) and apply them in your current family situation.

5c. *For Parents:* Encourage teens to think seriously about the skills, talents, and habits they will need to develop as they mature that will help them to fulfill their responsibilities as eternal companions and parents. Sit down with your teens one-on-one and help them compile a list of things they could work on now. Do they need to learn more independent living skills like cooking and cleaning? Do they need to learn more about how to care for young children? Help them develop a "plan of action" specific to their needs.

Chapter 6: Home as a Sacred Center for Family Life

6a. *For Families:* If your family has not been able to have meals together as often as you would like, hold a family council to discuss ways you could increase the quantity and quality of time spent together at family meals. Discuss ways mealtimes can be made more enjoyable for all family members. Brainstorm meaningful topics you could discuss during meals.

6b. *For Everyone:* Consider the home in which you dwell. Decide together how you can create an atmosphere more conducive to the Spirit. Set specific goals together to do things that will bring about a more sacred atmosphere. Work on at least one of your goals for a week, and at the end of the week, discuss together how this change has affected your home. Discuss ways you could modify your goal to make it even more successful.

6c. *For Everyone:* During a family home evening, compare your home to the temple. How are they the same? How are they different? Counsel together on how to appropriately incorporate the principles that make the temple a sacred place into your home and family life. You could place pictures of your family together at the temple in your home to remind family members of the sacred nature of their family and home. Have each person commit to doing at least one thing to make your home a more sacred center for your family life (see "Home and Temple: In These Holy Places" section in chapter 6).

Chapter 7: Proclamation-based Principles of Parenting and Supportive Scholarship

7a. *For Parents:* Go on a "date" with each of your children separately and invite them to talk about how they feel about your home and family life. What things would they like to do more or less often? What new things would they like to start doing? Is there anything that bothers them that they would like to change? Counsel together during a FHE, FC, or meal time on how to incorporate some of your children's ideas into your family life to strengthen your family.

7b. *For Everyone:* Brainstorm three or more different scenarios in which children are misbehaving. Use the principles from the chapter to hypothetically resolve each of the situations in a way that would be positive for both the parent and the child.

7c. *For Everyone:* Reflect with a sibling or your spouse on your parents' ways of parenting. What was particularly effective, and what was less effective? Discuss what you plan to continue and what you want to change in your own parenting.

Chapter 8: Understanding and Applying Proclamation Principles of Parenting

8a. *For Single Adults or Couples:* Decide on some things you will want to do when you have children and implement them now with your roommates or spouse, such as FHE, FC, family prayer, family scripture study, family meals, or wholesome family recreation.

8b. *For Everyone:* Talk with preschool or school-aged children regarding what they like about or wish for in their relationship with their parents. (e.g., What things do their parents do or say that makes them feel good? What would they like to spend more time doing with them?) Compare what the children say with parenting research and the teachings of the General Authorities in chapters 7 and 8. Apply what you have learned from this experience into your plans as a future parent or your current parenting.

Chapter 9: Intergenerational Ties, Grandparenting, and Extended Family Support

9a. *For Individuals:* Prayerfully choose attributes of the family in which you were raised that you feel are important to continue, as well as attributes that you would like to leave behind or change. Choose specific goals to work on, and write down several ways you can accomplish them. Set dates to evaluate your progress, and keep track of how you are doing in your journal.

9b. *For Families:* Choose a grandparent or other extended family member that you would like to know more about. What do you already know about him/her and his/her life, such as his/her childhood, schooling, dating, spirituality, marriage, parenting, occupation, hobbies, etc.? What would you like to learn about him/her? Write down several questions and interview the person (or his/her close family members if he/she is no longer living) to find out the answers to your questions. Record what you learned by writing it down or using audiotape or videotape for future generations to enjoy. Share what you learned about this person during a FHE or family meal.

9c. *For Families:* Discuss aspects of your family history together. You could ask an extended family member to give a lesson on your family history during your next FHE. Discuss what your family history means to you. Are there ancestors that you know of whose actions have blessed the lives of generations of their posterity? Discuss as a family how each individual's actions affect future generations for good or ill. Have each person choose something he or she will do in hopes that it will bless his or her posterity.

9d. *For Families:* Spotlight a different extended family member for a few minutes at the beginning of a mealtime once a week, once a month, or on his or her birthday, noting what special things they bring to the family. Show their pictures to children who may not be very familiar with them yet, or if possible, invite them to join you for the meal at which they will be spotlighted.

9e. *For Families:* At family gatherings to celebrate major life events (missions, marriages, new babies, etc.) have the members of your family who have already experienced that event create a circle with the member(s) going on a mission, getting married, etc., in the middle. Go around the outside circle allowing each of the "veteran" family members to give advice to the member(s) on the inside of the circle. You could invite each person to write down advice and give all of the notes to the member(s) inside the circle.

Chapter 10: Faith and Prayer in a Christ-centered Family

10a. *For Individuals:* Think of a time when your actions or motivations were influenced by hedonism, moralism, or relativism (as discussed in chapter 10). What was it about the circumstances surrounding this event that influenced you to act the way you did? What could you have done in the same circumstance to change your heart, mind, and actions to be receptive to holier influences and center yourself on Christ and His teachings?

10b. *For Families:* Talk to your children about how Heavenly Father blesses our daily lives, how He is deeply concerned for each of His children, and how prayer is our way of regularly communing with Him. To help children recognize God's hand in their lives, before daily family prayer for one week, discuss briefly as a family some of the struggles or joys the family experienced that day. Ask the person who will be giving the prayer to remember to specifically thank Heavenly Father for the joys and challenges that were experienced and seek help for the struggles.

10c. *For Everyone:* During a meal or FHE, have everyone in your home explain an important goal in his or her life. Discuss how these goals fit into the gospel and how important it is to set goals that are centered on Christ's life, teachings, and desires for His children. Discuss how faith in the Lord Jesus Christ and prayer can help individuals and families attain their eternal goals.

10d. *For Everyone:* Evaluate the media used in your home. Discuss what videos you own, TV shows you watch, video games you play, Internet sites you visit, etc. Are there aspects of the media you use that do not support a Christ-centered home? What messages do they promote? Are they edifying and good, or debasing, crude, and hedonistic? Discuss how individuals and families can combat the negative images and messages found in the media. Set goals that will help you to work toward viewing or using only wholesome entertainment.

Chapter 11: Repentance, Forgiveness, and Progression in Marriages and Families

11a. *For Individuals:* Think of a family member you need to forgive. Prayerfully study the process outlined in chapter 11 (see Box 11.4) for forgiving others. Without "re-telling the offense," discuss with a family member or church leader the process you went through, or record the process in your journal.

11b. *For Everyone:* Prayerfully and carefully study the parable of the prodigal son (Luke 15) and discuss the lessons Christ taught in this parable. Apply these lessons to your family life.

Chapter 12: Love, Respect, and Compassion in Families

12a. *For Everyone:* Create a list of different actions and attitudes that accompany pride, disrespect for others, and contention in the home. Use this list as a periodic self-check of your personal progress toward avoiding these actions and attitudes and incorporating more love, respect, and compassion in your family life. You could do this activity as a family and monitor your progress together. Decide what attitudes and behaviors need to change to avoid pride, disrespect, and contention in your home. Counsel together to formulate a plan of action to help you make these changes.

12b. *For Everyone:* Teach a lesson about the example of the Savior. Make a list of some of His qualities together. Discuss how He showed love, respect, and compassion for all people (forgiving the Roman soldiers who crucified Him, inviting the children to come unto Him, etc.). Place the list you made in a prominent place in your home and encourage everyone to emulate the Savior by developing these qualities in themselves by working on a different positive attribute each week.

Chapter 13: The Meaning and Blessings of Family Work

13a. *For Families:* Hold a special FHE to acknowledge the work each member of your family does. Take time to thank each family member personally for their contribution. Then, have each family member agree to do a job or chore normally done by another family member during the coming week. At the next FHE, discuss as a family what each member learned from the experience. Did they gain a greater appreciation for other family members and the work they do? Did they enjoy serving the family in a new way?

13b. *For Families:* Give a FHE lesson on the importance of not only work itself, but working together. Discuss how working togther can strengthen family relationships. Decide on a meaningful work project you can all do together as a family and make plans to do it.

13c. *For Families:* Counsel as a family to decide how mealtime work could be more effectively shared to facilitate a better mealtime experience for every family member. Is someone doing a lot of work alone who could use some help? Is someone being left out of meal preparation or clean-up? Are children given opportunities to learn and develop planning, cooking, and cleaning skills?

Chapter 14: Wholesome Family Recreation

14a. *For Families:* Counsel together as a family about your typical recreational or leisure activities. Categorize activities as either "wholesome family recreation" or "aimless leisure" and estimate your family's participation in each. Discuss together how you will increase your wholesome family recreation and decrease your aimless leisure. After one month, counsel together on how you are improving and discuss ways you can continue to progress in this area.

14b. *For Families:* As a family, plan wholesome recreational activities that appeal to each person or age group in the family. Make plans to carry out some of these activities over a reasonable period of time. Discuss as a family how sometimes sacrifices need to be made by some family members to help others enjoy recreation suited to their age or interests. After you have done some of the activities you planned, come together as a family to evaluate the activities and set new goals.

Chapter 15: The Sanctity and Importance of Human Life

15a. *For Parents:* Learn about current controversies concerning sanctity of life issues (e.g., abortion, assisted suicide, etc.) that are in the news and discuss them with your children during a meal or FHE. Familiarize yourself with various arguments, facts, laws, opinions, policies, or statistics surrounding these issues by looking for information in the media or the library or by visiting websites that present material on sanctity of life issues. Invite your children to ask you questions about these issues and explain to them how a knowledge of the sanctity of life helps us to see them in the appropriate light.

15b. *For Parents:* Discuss with your children (together or one-on-one) the important relationship between the law of chastity and the sanctity of life. Explain to them why their bodies and the bodies of the children they will one day bring into this world are sacred, and how the law of chastity helps them to protect and preserve both their bodies and the bodies of their future children. (See chapter 16 for further information on the sacredness of the human body.) You may choose to use this as an opportunity to discuss modesty as well.

Chapter 16: The Divine Nature of Each Individual

16a. *For Individuals:* Make a list of some things that help you to remember that God loves you. Place this paper in a prominent place in your home that you will see daily to remind you of your eternal worth.

16b. *For Individuals:* For a certain period of time, consciously treat each member of your family as a "beloved son or daughter of heavenly parents" (¶ 1). This should help you to cultivate more loving feelings toward them and improve your interactions with them. Record your experiences and feelings in your journal.

16c. *For Everyone:* Discuss how it is possible to both love sinners (as we all are) and despise sin, and the difference between worth and worthiness. Talk about how we can judge a sin as wrong, but still not judge others unrighteously. Discuss the difference between acceptance of individuals and acceptance of sin. Make sure everyone understands that he or she has a divine and unchangeable worth as a spirit child of our Heavenly Father, independent of his or her current or previous personal worthiness.

16d. *For Everyone:* Teach a FHE lesson on the divine nature of each individual using the principles included in the chapter and encourage everyone to treat others (especially family members) with the appropriate kindness and respect.

Chapter 17: Single Adults and Family Life

17a. *For Single Adults:* Find ways to live and develop the principles of the Proclamation right now to enhance your personal life and strengthen marriages and families in your community. For example, get involved in community groups that strengthen families, or lobby to enact family friendly legislation in your town, state, or country.

17b. *For Families:* Invite single friends or family members to join you for a family activity. Discuss as a family beforehand the points outlined in Boxes 17.5 and 17.6 to assure that your friends or family members feel welcome while they are there. Apply the points in Boxes 17.5 and 17.6 to the specific situations of your friends or family members.

Chapter 18: Gospel Ideals and Adversity in Family Life

18a. *For Individuals:* Live, for one week, with a spirit of "no defense/no accusations" (as described in the story about "Derek" in the chapter). Write in your journal about the experience, then share it with a friend or family member.

18b. *For Families:* Split into pairs and give each pair a small section of a puzzle to complete. Then bring all of the sections together to complete the puzzle. Discuss how each member of the family is important and all must work together to achieve family goals. Counsel together about what some of your family goals are or should be and invite each member to say what they will do personally to help the family achieve these goals.

Chapter 19: Awareness of Abuse in the Family

19a. *For Couples or Parents:* Counsel with your spouse regarding what you each feel are appropriate and inappropriate ways to interact with and discipline children. Prayerfully decide together on clear verbal and behavioral boundaries for your family (consistent with modern revelation and the principles discussed in chapters 19 and 20), for interactions between parents, between parents and children, and between siblings. Agree to continue counseling together as children grow and challenges occur.

19b. *For Families:* Counsel together about whether or not members of your family ever act in ways that may be hurtful (or even abusive) to other family members. Do members use criticism and sarcasm? Do siblings treat each other with kindness, or are they sometimes hurtful verbally or physically? If there are some negative interactions in your home, discuss as a family what each individual and the family as a whole will do to prevent such behavior in the future.

Chapter 20: Preventing and Healing from Abuse

20a. *For Individuals:* Use your time or talents to help people who have been abused. You could offer to help at a shelter that cares for abuse victims or volunteer as a "big brother" or "big sister" to a child who had been in an abusive environment.

20b. *For Everyone:* Discuss the "red flags" that indicate the potential for future abuse discussed in the section labeled "Mate Selection" in chapter 20 with a group of young people. Discuss how to understand and recognize "red flags" in different situations. Discuss the importance of choosing righteous people to date and ultimately to marry.

Chapter 21: The Family Crucibles of Illness, Disability, Infertility, Death, and Other Losses

21a. *For Parents:* Using examples from your family history or personal experiences, explain to your children during a FHE the role agency plays in our responses to "crucible type" experiences. Explain that although we may not always be able to control or prevent difficult events in our lives, we can control how we respond to what happens to us.

21b. *For Everyone:* Christ learned "obedience by the things which he suffered" (Heb. 5:8). Discuss the trials that Christ had to overcome during His mortal life. How did He react to them? How did He endure them? What was gained from them? How can what the Savior experienced and accomplished help us with our personal, marital, or family crucibles?

21c. *For Everyone:* Ask a few older adults about the trials they have experienced in their lives. Ask them to share what effects these trials have had on their lives, and what effect their attitudes had on how they experienced the trials. Do they consider these trials to be "crucibles" in that they feel they have grown or gained something as a result of the trial?

Chapter 22: Practices for Building Marriage and Family Strengths

22a. *For Couples:* Counsel with your spouse regarding the quantity and quality of time you spend alone together. Are you both happy with this aspect of your married life? Are there things you would like to do together that you haven't done (or haven't done in a long time)? When you have determined what it is you would like to do together, schedule a time to do it, make all of the necessary arrangements well ahead of time, and place a reminder of the event and its scheduled time in a prominent place in your home to assure that it is not forgotten or preempted by other things.

22b. *For Families:* Plan a FHE activity designed to help each family member understand that they play a positive role in your family. For example, go around the room once for every person and have each family member think of something that person does to meaningfully contribute to the family. Perhaps they make people laugh, keep things organized, or help keep the peace. Stress that everyone is important in making your family life unique and happy. Families could also do this during regular family prayer times or meal times. The person who offers the prayer on a certain day of the week, for example, could be the one whose contributions are recognized.

22c. *For Families:* Counsel together to create a family checklist including such things as family prayer, family scripture study, FHE, family recreation, etc., that you feel are important for you to do as a family. Evaluate the list and decide which areas need the most work, and why and how you can improve in those areas by working together. Later, counsel again as a family about your development in the areas you chose to work on and decide what you will do together to progress further.

22d. *For Families:* Create a family calendar where all of the important events in your family will be posted. The first Sunday of every month, sit down together and plan out family events and write them on the calendar. Write in family time first, and make sure everyone knows that if it is on the calendar, you can count on it happening. Compare the amount of "togetherness time" you have as a family during the months when you committed to set plans to the amount you had in months when nothing was planned.

Chapter 23: *Valuing, Preserving, and Transmitting Family Traditions*

23a. *For Families:* Ask your grandparents and parents about the traditions they remember in their families when they were young, and make a list of all of the activities they mentioned. With your spouse and children, choose from among the items on the list those traditions you would like to carry on in your family. During the next month, try practicing at least one of these traditions in your family. During the next year, integrate those traditions you chose into your

family life until they become established traditions for your family.

23b. *For Families:* With your spouse and children, be an "intentional family" by choosing a unique new tradition that you will establish as a family and scheduling a time to do it.

Chapter 24: *Government Resources and Policies to Maintain and Strengthen Families*

24a. *For Families:* Contact or visit a government agency or charitable organization in your area and learn about its policies, practices, and goals in relation to the principles in the Proclamation. As a family, volunteer time with an agency to help strengthen families in your community.

24b. *For Parents:* For a FHE, teach a lesson on self-reliance. Discuss with your children the importance of being self-reliant as individuals and as families. Give them examples of some of the ways you try to be self-reliant (e.g., working hard, planting a garden, maintaining food storage, sewing, etc.), and discuss the benefits to your family and society that come when people are being self-reliant. Discuss with your children ways they can become more self-reliant (in age-appropriate ways).

Chapter 25: *Defending Marriage and the Family through Law and Policy*

25a. *For Individuals:* Learn about the bills that will be debated in your state or federal legislatures and look for those that may have implications for families—for good or ill. Read them carefully and decide whether you think they will be a strengthening force for families or further the break-down of the family. Then write to your representative(s) to express your family-centered opinions regarding the legislation and encourage them to vote in a way that would most benefit families in your state or country.

25b. *For Parents:* Take your children with you when you vote. Explain the process of voting to them and (if allowed) show them how to do it. If you are voting on an issue that will affect families in your area, explain to your children how your vote may help to strengthen families.

Chapter 26: *The Proclamation on the Family and the Philosophies of the World*

26a. *For Families:* During FHE, have each family member look through a variety of lenses, such as binoculars, a magnifying glass, prescription glasses, sunglasses, colored glass, etc. Discuss how our perspectives influence our perception of the world and how the philosophies we accept as truth influence these perspectives. When we change our perspective, we change how we perceive the world, just as the world looks differently to us through different lenses. Explain that we should look at the world through "gospel lenses," which will help us to have an eternal perspective and see the world and our experiences in the clearest, truest, purest light.

26b. *For Everyone:* Find examples in the media of secularism, extreme individualism, hedonism, and relativism (as discussed in the chapter). Talk about why the media might use these perspectives. Discuss how the LDS perspective differs and provides a better way of understanding other people, ourselves, our lifestyles, and our belongings.

Chapter 27: The Centrality of Family across World Faiths

27a. *For Individuals:* Talk with someone of another faith regarding their beliefs about marriage and family. Share with them the LDS perspective on family life *using the Proclamation,* and perhaps give your friend his or her own copy. Discuss together the similarities you find.

27b. *For Families:* On your next family vacation, make an effort to learn about the religious beliefs of the people in the area you are visiting. You could visit religious sites, talk with members of the local churches, etc. Discuss with your children the similarities and differences between the LDS perspective on families and the perspective of members of that faith.

Author Note:

My thanks to Shirley K. Klein, David and Mary Dollahite, Jeffrey and Juanita Hill, Suzanne Frost Olsen, Lili D. Anderson, Jo Scofield, Rachel Brammer, Rachel D. J. Syphus, Natalie Peterson, Erin Allen, and to the students in MFHD 395R Fall 1999 Semester for their helpful input on these activities.

ABOUT THE EDITOR

David C. Dollahite, Ph.D., is an associate professor of marriage, family, and human development (MFHD) in the School of Family Life at Brigham Young University where he teaches courses on marriage and family life, including a class on the Proclamation. He has also taught Book of Mormon and New Testament as an adjunct professor of ancient scripture at BYU. Dr. Dollahite has published extensively on families, fathering, and faith. He has served as president of the Utah Council on Family Relations and is a member of the planning committee for the World Congress of Families III. He and his wife, Mary, are the parents of seven children. Brother Dollahite, a convert to the Church, served a mission in New England and has served in numerous Church callings, including bishop, bishop's counselor, stake mission president, high councilor, ward mission leader, gospel doctrine teacher, and stake institute instructor.

ABOUT THE CONTRIBUTORS

Linda Hunter Adams is Director of the Humanities Publications Center at BYU, where she teaches editing. She served on a general churchwide single adults committee under Elder Russell M. Nelson.

Howard M. Bahr, Ph.D., is a professor of sociology at BYU. He and his wife, Kathleen, have two children.

Kathleen Slaugh Bahr, Ph.D., is a professor of MFHD at BYU. She is the wife of Howard M. Bahr and the mother of two sons, Alden and Jonathan.

Brent A. Barlow, Ph.D., is a professor of MFHD at BYU. He is married to the former Susan Day and they have seven children and seven grandchildren.

Kristi A. Bell, M.A., is the archivist for the BYU Folklore Archives and teaches composition at BYU. She and her husband, James, are the parents of six daughters.

Ivan F. Beutler, Ph.D., is a professor of MFHD at BYU. He cherishes life with his wife, Lucy, and their six children.

Mae Blanch, retired professor of English literature at BYU, focused her teaching and research in literature dealing with family life and created a class titled, "The Family in Fiction," taught as an honors course.

Douglas E. Brinley, Ph.D., is a professor of church history and doctrine at BYU. He and his wife, Geri, have six children.

Jack D. Brotherson, Ph.D., is a professor of botany and range science at BYU. He is married to Karen Earl Brotherson and is the father of six children and has six grandchildren.

Sean E. Brotherson, Ph.D., is assistant professor and extension family science specialist at North Dakota State University. He is married to Kristen Walch Brotherson and is the father of four children.

Lora Beth Brown, Ed.D, RD, is an associate professor in BYU's Department of Food Science and Nutrition. She is the proud grandmother of 10.

Wesley R. Burr, Ph.D., is professor emeritus of family life at BYU. He and his wife, Ruth, have four children and 15 grandchildren.

Mark H. Butler, Ph.D., teaches in BYU's School of Family Life and is a marriage and family therapist. He and his wife, Shelly, are the parents of five children.

Michael S. Buxton, Ph.D., is an assistant clinical professor in the BYU Counseling and Career Center. He and wife, Debbie, are parents of four boys.

Lynn Clark Callister, R.N., Ph.D., is an associate professor in the College of Nursing at BYU. She and her husband, Reed, are the parents of six sons and five daughters and have 24 grandchildren.

Jason S. Carroll, M.S., is pursuing a Ph.D. in family social science at the University of Minnesota. Jason and his wife, Stafani, have two sons.

David J. Cherrington, D.B.A., S.P.H.R., is professor of organizational behavior at BYU. He and Marilyn Daines Cherrington are the parents of four children, all married, and five grandchildren.

Shawn L. Christiansen, Ph.D., is an assistant professor of human development and family studies at Penn State Worthington Scranton. He and his wife, Tiffiney, are parents of Christopher, Camilla, and Emma.

Maribeth C. Clarke, Ph.D., CFCS, is an associate professor of home economics, School of Family Life, at BYU. She and her husband, Michael, are the parents of four children.

Chad P. Conrad teaches Jr. Seminary in Orem, Utah. He and his wife, Stacy, have a six-month-old child.

Shirley E. Cox, Ph.D., is an associate professor and director of the School of Social Work Field Internship Program at BYU. She is the mother of four children and the grandmother of seven.

Mary Kimball Dollahite, J.D., is a wife, a

mother, and a homemaker. She and her husband, David, are parents of seven children. She occasionally teaches a class on family law and policy in the BYU MFHD department.

Guy L. Dorius, Ph.D., is an assistant professor of Church history and doctrine at BYU. He received a Ph.D. in family studies. He and his wife, Vicki, have six children.

Cynthia Doxey, Ph.D., is an assistant professor of Church history and doctrine at BYU. Her research and teaching focuses on family history and premarital and marital relationships. She enjoys the title "Favorite Aunt."

Richard D. Draper, Ph.D., is an associate professor in the Department of Ancient Scripture at BYU and studies Jewish family life during the first century A.D. He and his wife, Barbara, have six children and five grandchildren.

Stephen F. Duncan, Ph.D., is a professor in the School of Family Life at BYU. Steve and his wife, Barbara, have five children.

Tina Taylor Dyches, Ed.D., is an assistant professor in the Department of Counseling Psychology and Special Education at BYU. Her research focuses on the education and treatment of individuals with significant disabilities and autism.

Eric A. Eliason, Ph.D., is an assistant professor of English at BYU. He and his wife, Stephanie, have three children.

Camille A. Fronk, Ph.D., assistant professor of ancient scriptures at BYU, received her Ph.D. in family studies. Her research interests include Palestinian families, the early Christian Church, and women in scripture.

Carolyn Garrison, Ph.D., is an assistant professor of home economics at BYU and teaches in the area of household equipment.

Laura E. Gilpin, CFLE, received her B.S. in MFHD from BYU with a minor in communications. She is married to Warren Gilpin and is the daughter of Richard and Donna Finter.

Jon D. Green, Ph.D., is an associate professor of humanities at BYU. He and his wife, the former Karen Broadbent, have 10 children and seven grandchildren.

H. Wallace Goddard, Ph.D., is an associate professor of family and human development at Utah State University. He and his wife, Nancy, have three children and are busily collecting toys for their grandchildren.

Natalie C. Goddard, CFLE, delights in being wife of Andy and mother of Miracle Maxwell. She graduated from BYU's School of Family Life and founded the Family Life Education Institute.

Cynthia L. Hallen, Ph.D., is an associate professor of linguistics at BYU. She has two nieces, one nephew, and a great-niece.

James M. Harper, Ph.D., is the director of the School of Family Life at BYU. He and his wife, Colleen, are the parents of five children.

B. Kent Harrison, Ph.D., professor of physics and astronomy at BYU, is on the board of trustees at the Center for Women and Children in Crisis in Utah County. He is married with three sons, one daughter, and 11 grandchildren.

Craig H. Hart, Ph.D., is a professor and chair of the MFHD Program in the School of Family Life at BYU. He and his wife, Kerstine, have four children.

Alan J. Hawkins, Ph.D., is a professor of MFHD and director of the Family Studies Center at BYU. He and his wife, Lisa, have two children.

Brian J. Hill, Ph.D., is an associate professor of recreation management and youth leadership at BYU. He is married to Karen Dalton Hill, and they are the parents of four children.

E. Jeffrey Hill, Ph.D., has worked for IBM for 22 years as a work and family expert and at BYU for two years as an associate professor in the School of Family Life. He and his wife, Juanita, have nine children.

Thomas B. Holman, Ph.D., is a MFHD professor at BYU and a CFLE. He and his wife, Linda, have been married for 27 years and have five children and two granddaughters.

Peggy Honey, M.S., is an assistant professor of interior design at BYU. She and her husband have three children.

Valerie Hudson, Ph.D., is a professor of political science at BYU. She and her husband, David E. Cassler, have five children.

Jerry L. Jaccard, Ed.D., is an associate professor of music at BYU. He and his wife, Alta, have five children, a foster daughter, and 10 grandchildren.

Larry C. Jensen, Ph.D., is a professor of psychology at BYU. He and his wife, Janet, have 10 children and 20 grandchildren and are still in the process of learning how to be parents.

Daniel K Judd, Ph.D., is an associate professor of ancient scripture at BYU. He holds a Ph.D. in counseling psychology. He and his wife have four children.

Shirley R. Klein, Ph.D., is an associate professor of MFHD at BYU. She and her husband, Mike, raised eight children and are grandparents of six.

Jeffrey H. Larson, Ph.D., is a professor and program chair of marriage and family therapy at BYU. He and his wife, Jeannie, have four children.

Keith Lawrence, Ph.D., is an associate professor of English at BYU. He is married to Dr. Tracy Todd Lawrence, a licensed marriage and family therapist. They are the parents of five children.

Barbara Day Lockhart, Ed.D., works in the BYU Physical Education Department and is the BYU Faculty Athletics Representative to the NCAA and MWC. She was also a member of the USA Olympic speed skating team.

A. Scott Loveless, J.D., is an attorney for the U.S. Department of the Interior and a doctoral candidate in family studies at BYU. He is the husband of Cheri A. Loveless and the father of eight.

Cheri A. Loveless, mother of eight children, has served as associate editor of *This People* and *Meridian* magazines. She is a founder of the national support organization Mothers at Home and a mother of eight.

Catherine Lundell, M.S., worked as a family therapist for LDS Social Services for four years, is now starting a private practice, and is a full-time mom. She and her husband, Randy, have one daughter.

Truman G. Madsen, Ph.D., is an emeritus professor of philosophy at BYU and formerly Richard L. Evans Professor of Christian Understanding. He and his wife, Ann, are presently parenting four children and grandparenting 16 grandchildren.

Barbara Mandleco, R.N., Ph.D., is an associate professor of nursing at BYU. She has clinical expertise in pediatrics and researches sibling relationships. She is a mother of two children.

Kristine Manwaring is a graduate of BYU. A wife of 15 years, she and her husband, Todd, are parents of four children.

Elaine Sorensen Marshall, R.N., Ph.D., is dean and professor of the College of Nursing at BYU. She is married to Dr. John Marshall and is the mother of four children.

Richard K. Meeves, Ph.D., received his Ph.D. in marriage and family therapy, and works as a therapist in a wilderness program for at-risk teens as well as maintains a private marriage and family therapy practice.

Lloyd D. Newell, Ph.D., is an assistant professor of Church history and doctrine and an associated faculty member in the School of Family Life at BYU. He and his wife, Karmel, are the parents of four children: Hayley, McKay, Abigail, and Jacob.

Nora Nyland, Ph.D., R.D., is an associate professor and the dietetics program director in BYU's Department of Food Science and Nutrition. She appreciates delicious food as one of the Lord's gifts to his children.

Susanne Frost Olsen, Ph.D., is an associate professor of MFHD in the School of Family Life at BYU. Her research interests include parenting, intergenerational relationships, and families of children with disabilities.

Terrance D. Olson, Ph.D., is a professor of MFHD in the School of Family Life at BYU. He is married to Karen Miller, of Stockton, California, and they are parents of six children.

Alan R. Osmond and his wife, Suzanne Pinegar Osmond, are the parents of eight sons. As an entertainer, Alan has acquired over 33 gold and platinum records, People's Choice Awards, and he has been involved in hit television series, production studios, and theaters. He is the creator of an Internet site on families.

Kyle Lynn Pehrson, Ph.D., serves as the director of the School of Social Work at BYU. He and his wife, Edyth, have seven children and six grandchildren.

Melinda J. Petersen attended BYU, studying both philosophy and psychology. She is currently pursuing a Ph.D. in theoretical and philosophical psychology there, where she met and recently married Dayne Petersen.

Pearl Raynes Philipps, M.S., is a teacher educator for home economics education at BYU. She and her husband, Robert A. Philipps, have five children.

Bernard E. Poduska, Ph.D., is an associate professor of MFHD at BYU. He has been married for 28 years and helped raise five children to adulthood.

Caroline Prohosky is an associate professor of modern dance at BYU.

Maureen Rice, Ph.D., is a counselor and assistant clinical professor at the Counseling and Career Center at BYU and teaches courses dealing with career exploration and career transitioning.

W. David Robinson, Ph.D., is a family therapist currently working as a faculty member of the Department of Family Medicine at the University of Nebraska Medical Center. He and his wife are parents of three children.

C. Y. Roby, Ph.D., is a clinical psychologist, specializing in the assessment and treatment of sexual abuse perpetrators and sexually reactive adolescents. He and his wife, Jini, have three daughters.

Jini L. Roby, J.D., M.S.W., M.S., is a licensed attorney and a social worker and teaches social work welfare law and policy at BYU. She and her husband are the parents of three daughters.

Maxine Lewis Rowley, Ph.D., CFCS, is the program chair for Home Economics/Family Life Education in the School of Family Life at BYU. She and her husband, Arthur, have two daughters and two foster sons.

Jill Terry Rudy, Ph.D., is an assistant professor of English and BYU Folklore Archive director. She and her husband, Bill, have three children: Katelyn, Matthew, and Spencer.

Susan Sessions Rugh, Ph.D., is a professor of history at BYU. She and her husband, Thomas F. Rugh, are the parents of three sons.

Lisa Sine teaches family and human development at Virginia Tech and is a marriage and family therapist in Washington, D.C.

Brent D. Slife, Ph.D., is a professor of psychology at BYU and maintains a private practice in family therapy. He has been happily married to his wife, Karen, for almost 25 years, and they have three sons: Conor, Nathan, and Jacob.

A. Don Sorensen, Ph.D., is an emeritus professor of political science at BYU after teaching for 28 years. He and his wife, Necia, have six children and 11 grandchildren.

Diane L. Spangler, Ph.D., is on the faculty in the psychology department at BYU. Her research and clinical work focus on cognitive theory, depression, eating disorders, treatment evaluation, and gender issues. She is married to Scott Temby.

Robert F. Stahmann, Ph.D., MFT, CFLE, is a professor of marriage and family therapy at BYU. He and his wife, Kathy, have five children and two grandchildren.

Nancy C. Stallings, M.A.M., is training specialist for the State of Utah. She has taught in elementary schools and worked in human resources.

Joseph B. Stanford, M.D., MSPH, is assistant professor of family and preventative medicine at the University of Utah. He and his wife, Kathleen, have six sons.

Tamara Talbot, CFLE, completed her bachelor's degree in psychology at BYU. She is the director of Family Life Education Institute, teaches part time at BYU, and loves being an aunt.

Alan Taylor, Ph.D, CFLE, is an assistant professor at Syracuse University in the Department of Child and Family Studies. Alan and his wife, Kelly, have three children.

Kelly DiSpirito Taylor, M.S., uses the knowledge gained from her psychology and family sciences degrees as a full-time homemaker. Kelly and her husband, Alan, are the parents of Bronson, Holden, and Camryn.

Mary J. Thompson, Ph.D., is an assistant professor of home economics at BYU. She is married and has two sons and two daughters.

Jacqueline S. Thursby, Ph.D., teaches English methods, folklore, and mythology in the English Department at BYU. She is the mother of four grown children and grandmother of nine.

Elizabeth VanDenBerghe, M.A., is a full-time homemaker, occasional writer/editor, and erstwhile college instructor. She is the wife of Jed VanDenBerghe and the mother of John, Will, Christian, Grace, Anika, and Ben.

Elaine Walton, Ph.D., is an associate professor in the School of Social Work at BYU, where she also develops and evaluates family-strengthening programs in the child welfare system.

Lynn D. Wardle, J.D., is a professor of law at the J. Reuben Clark Law School at BYU. He is married to Marian Eastwood, and they have two sons.

Wendy L. Watson, Ph.D., is a professor in the Marriage and Family Therapy Graduate Program within the School of Family Life at BYU. She chaired BYU's Women's Conferences in 1999 and 2000.

M. Gawain Wells, Ph.D., is a professor of psychology and director of the BYU Comprehensive Clinic. He and his wife, Gayle, have six children and four grandchildren.

Mark A. Widmer, Ph.D., is graduate coordinator of the Youth and Family Recreation Program (RMYL Department) at BYU. He and his wife, Suzy, have four children.

Richard G. Wilkins, J.D., is a professor of law at BYU and is currently director of The World Family Policy Center at BYU. He is married to Melany Moore Wilkins and is the father of four children.

Marleen S. Williams, Ph.D., is an associate clinical professor of counseling psychology at BYU. She and her husband, Dr. Robert F. Williams, have a blended family of 10 children.

Richard N. Williams, Ph.D., is a professor of psychology and assistant to the associate academic vice president at BYU. He and his wife, Camille, are the parents of five children.

Mary Jane Woodger, Ed.D., is an assistant professor of Church history and doctrine at BYU. Her research includes Latter-day Saint women's history.

She looks forward to using the Family Proclamation in her future roles as a wife and mother.

Vaughn E. Worthen, Ph.D., is a counselor in the Counseling and Career Center at BYU. He is married to the former Anita Bidstrup, and they are parents of four boys.

Rita R. Wright is a part-time instructor at BYU and currently working on her Ph.D. at the University of Utah in history. She is married to artist Wesley Wright. They have five children and one grandchild.

Index

ISBN 1-57345-824-4

53995

9 781573 458245

SKU 4024444 U.S. $39.95